MACROMEDIA FLASH MX 2004 DEMYSTIFIED

SHAWN PUCKNELL,
BRIAN HOGG,
AND CRAIG SWANN

WITH CONTRIBUTIONS BY GLEN RHODES, GRANT SKINNER,

GLYN THOMAS, AND JOHN COWIE

macromedia®
PRESS

Macromedia® Flash® MX 2004 Demystified
Shawn Pucknell, Brian Hogg, and Craig Swann
Published by Peachpit Press, a division of Pearson Education, in association with Macromedia Press.

Peachpit Press
1249 Eighth Street
Berkeley, CA 94710
510/524-7178 • 800-283-9444
510/524-2221 (fax)

Find us on the World Wide Web at:
http://www.peachpit.com
http//www.macromedia.com

Copyright © 2004 by Peachpit Press

Publisher: Nancy Ruenzel
Associate Publisher: Stephanie Wall
Production Manager: Gina Kanouse
Senior Acquisitions Editor: Linda Bump Harrison
Development Editor: Lisa M. Lord
Project Editor: Michael Thurston
Macromedia Technical Reviewers: Angela Drury, Alex Hearnz
Indexer: Cheryl Lemmens
Interior Design: Mimi Heft
Compositor: Ron Wise
Cover Design/Layout: Aren Howell
Marketing: Scott Cowlin, Tammy Detrich, Hannah Onstad Latham
Publicity: Kim Lombardi, Susan Nixon

Notice of Rights

Trademark Notice

Notice of Liability

International Standard Book Number: 0-7357-1397-9

06 05 04   7 6 5 4 3 2

Printed and bound in the United States of America

Acknowledgments

Shawn Pucknell:

A book of this size is not put together by one person; it takes a great deal of people. First and foremost, I'd like to thank my co-authors, Brian Hogg and Craig Swann, both of whom I've known for years and who were as excited as I was when invited to get involved with this book. Both are well known in the community and have been working with Flash for a long time. Their skills and personality brought a great deal to this book, and I'm very honored to have had them involved. I could not have done it without them.

I'd also like to thank the contributors, each one selected for his specific area of expertise. Over the years Flash has been around, we've seen the breadth of skills in it grow immensely. Some topics, such as OOP, have entire books dedicated to them. We needed to find contributors who could cover their topics in one chapter, in an easily understood format. I'm confident we chose the right people for the job: Grant Skinner (www.gskinner.com), Glen Rhodes (www.glenrhodes.com), Thomas Glyn (www.thomasglyn.com), and John Cowie (www.nisolutions.ca).

I also want to thank Mike Roberts for his expert help. A traditionally trained animator, Mike was incredibly helpful in finishing the chapter on animation. As well, I'd like to thank Luca Bogdan for his illustrations in the animation chapter.

I'd like to thank our lead editor, Lisa Lord, for her infinite patience and expertise in helping us focus and polish this book. Her help along this road, new for many of us, made it a much smoother trip.

And last, but not least, I'd like to thank Linda Bump-Harrison, our acquisitions editor, for her patience, trust, and faith in all of us and in this book.

Brian Hogg:

It's hard to decide who to thank first; on the one hand, there's Peachpit, who chose us to write the first Demystified book for Flash, and on the other, there's Macromedia, without whom there'd be nothing to write about.

I'd like to thank Shawn for inviting me to write the book with him and Craig. Thanks also to the contributors for their great contributions.

Thanks to Linda Bump-Harrison for being such a great help to us, and to Lisa Lord, our editor, and the rest of the *Flash MX 2004 Demystified* team.

Thanks to Macromedia for putting out such great software.

Thanks to David Bastedo and the rest of the crew at Ten Plus One Communications for their understanding and assistance during the writing of this book. It was very much appreciated.

Thanks to family and friends, too numerous to mention, who pried me away from the monitor, time and again, after I'd spent too many hours using the computer.

And, as with everything, thanks to Deborah.

ABOUT THE AUTHORS

Shawn Pucknell (shawn@pucknell.com), active in the interactive community, is the founder and president of the Toronto Flash users group, FlashinTO (www.FlashinTO.com), and is also responsible for starting Canada's annual FlashintheCan Festival (www.flashinthecan.com). Other experience includes co-founder of Ten Plus One Communications (www.10plus1.com), working as a Senior Flash Technologist at Blastradius (www.blastradius.com), and working at Maclaren McCann Interactive (www.maclaren.com) as a Senior Technical Developer.

Shawn has been recognized by the interactive community and selected to sit on several Interactive panels, including the inaugural FlashForward 2000 conference in San Francisco. He has won 12 Interactive and Advertising Industry Awards for his Flash work, including two Gold Canadian Marketing Awards as well as an entry in the *1999 British Design & Art Direction* annual. Shawn is currently a freelance consultant who works from home, and is always looking for interesting projects or community events to get involved with. For more information on Shawn, visit www.pucknell.com.

Brian Hogg Brian Hogg (brian@mrhogg.com) is a freelance Macromedia Flash developer and writer working in Oakville, Ontario. Previously he worked at Ten Plus One (www.10plus1.com) in Toronto, where he was involved with creating and developing Flash applications. Before coming to Ten Plus One, Brian spent three years as a Flash developer for Medium One Productions. In addition to his professional duties, Brian maintains mrhogg.com (www.mrhogg.com), a Flash resource site, and inelegant.net (www.inelegant.net), a pseudo-literary blog that allows him to rant about anything that isn't Flash.

Craig Swann (craig@crashmedia.com) is the founder of CRASH!MEDIA Corp. (www.crashmedia.com), an award-winning, Toronto-based interactive design agency that has produced Flash work for such notable brands as Intel, Coca-Cola, Miller Brewing, Calvin Klein/Maverick Records, Bacardi, Alliance Atlantis, CBC, and YTV. He has been an active member of the Flash community since its beginning and has contributed to six Flash books, including *FlashMX Audio Magic* and *XML in Flash*. Swann has spoken in Canada, America, and the UK about the power of web audio and is particularly interested in the role audio plays in interactive experiences, which led to the development of the award-winning www.looplabs.com.

ABOUT THE CONTRIBUTORS

Glen Rhodes (glen@glenrhodes.com) started out making computer games in his basement when he was about 12 years old and began developing professional games for the original Sony Playstation when he was 19. Six years later, he discovered Flash and found he could channel all his previous experience into Flash and make it do things that other people just weren't doing, including professional-level games. This year he was a judge in the games category for FlashForward 2003 NYC. Today he's the lead Flash developer at Dot Com Entertainment Group, where he makes games full-time. In his spare time, he has written and contributed to six books, including *Flash Games Studio*, *Flash Math Creativity*, and *Flash MX ActionScript Designer's Reference*. Glen has spoken on "Flash Games" and the "Flash MX Communication Server" at several conferences including Flashkit and Flashinthecan. In 2003, at FlashintheCan, he won the "Iron Flash" competition along with teammate Craig Swann. Glen keeps a website with his Flash experiments, developments, projects, and a blog at www.glenrhodes.com.

Grant Skinner's (grant@gskinner.com) varied education and experience enables him to fuse his coding prowess with interface design, marketing, and business logic. For the past four years, he has been developing applications and games in Flash, while trying to apply practices and approaches from established technologies, such as Java, to ActionScript. He has been internationally recognized for his work on gskinner.com, FlashOS2, and gModeler. He has won awards in the Technical Merit and Application categories of the Flash Film Festival at FlashForward 2003 San Francisco and for Technical Excellence in the 2003 FlashintheCan awards, where he presented "Object Oriented Concepts for Flash Applications." He has also spoken at FlashForward New York on RIA interface design and Siggraph 2003 on a similar topic. Grant presently operates on a freelance basis, focusing on cutting-edge RIA conceptualization, development, and deployment, and his work can be seen at www.gskinner.com.

Glyn Thomas (thomasglyn@hotmail.com) is a freelance Flash developer with a focus on programming and creating games and 3D effects with Flash. He was the lead programmer on joint projects with SayDesign.com, Papermotion.com, and IWantMyFlashTV.com. Thomas has also spoken at several conferences, including Flashkit and Flash Forward. He likes to keep up with the Flash community with his flashblog on his site at www.thomasglyn.com, especially with news related to 3D and gaming in Flash.

John Cowie (john@johncowie.ca) is the creative director at NI Solutions Group Inc. (http://www.nisgroup.com) in Toronto, Canada. John's vision and expertise in website development comes from his vast amount of experience in the new media industry. His experience in film, video, sound, and photography combined with his experience in graphic design and web programming have been instrumental in success for his clients. Over the past two years, John has spent much of his time working with the integration of ColdFusion and Flash to create rich experiences for his clients. John is an active speaker and teacher on ColdFusion and Flash, having spoken at MX on the Rocks, MX North, and FlashintheCan, and is the manager of the Toronto ColdFusion User Group (http://www.cfugtoronto.org).

ABOUT THE TECHNICAL REVIEWERS

Angela Drury started her career as a freelance photographer, moving into the tech industry in 1996. She has worked with Macromedia for four years serving many roles, including Dreamweaver, Contribute, and Flash web content editor and international trainer of Dreamweaver MX. Over the past two years, Angela has provided numerous technical reviews of books, course materials, and technical articles for Dreamweaver and Flash. Before joining Macromedia, she worked for Industrial Light + Magic as a technical project manager. During her free time, Angela is taking pictures, working with Photoshop, and cruising around the San Francisco Bay area with her dogs, Lola and Ginger.

Alex Hearnz is an independent agent performing training, development, and consulting on various development platforms, including Macromedia, Microsoft, and Sun. He is a systems architect, designer, developer, and trainer with more than 20 years of leading-edge information technology experience. Alex is a Microsoft Certified Systems Designer and Trainer, a Macromedia Flash MX certified developer and instructor, a certified Advanced Macromedia ColdFusion trainer and developer, and a Sun JAVA2 Certified Developer. He specializes in helping organizations optimize their web development efforts by using various tools, including Macromedia's Dreamweaver MX, Flash MX, ColdFusion MX, and JRun, and he provides hands-on training, consulting, and development assistance. In his off time, Alex enjoys family time, sports, and motorcycling.

Laura McCabe is a freelance multimedia designer and developer currently living in Baltimore, Maryland. Her eclectic interests have led to an undergraduate degree in psychology, graduate studies in art, design and multimedia, and work as a writer, trainer and editor. She has honed her skills in web design, development, and information architecture while working with clients such as AARP, Hershey, and the FDA. In her spare time she is a photographer and inveterate book junkie.

Larry Drolet is a developer and dreamer, one of those people who, when "well caffeinated," has about an idea a minute. While in graduate school, he wrote a paper on Internet law, and wouldn't you know it this developed into a hobby and a passion that ultimately led him to starting a dot-com. Sounds all too familiar! Currently he is working at Arizona State University with the Business Information Technology group, developing applications for the online MBA program. When not working or in class for another degree, Larry can be found speaking at user groups in southern California and Arizona, or surfing near San Diego.

Contents at a Glance

TABLE OF CONTENTS

Chapter 4: Exploring Views and Panels 97

Chapter 5: Importing   125

Chapter 6: Animation, Effects, and Masking   141

Chapter 7: Behaviors   183

Part II: ActionScript

Chapter 10: ActionScript: Functions, Events, and Objects   265

PART III: ELEMENTS

Chapter 14: Images   433

Chapter 15: Audio   453

PART IV: EXTENDING FLASH

Chapter 18: Advanced Communication 553

PART V: NEXT STEPS

Chapter 19: Writing Code That Rocks:
ActionScript Best Practices 601

Chapter 20: OOP for Flashers   625

Chapter 21: Math for Flashers   657

Chapter 22: 3D in Flash   683

PART VI: FINISHING

Chapter 23: Publishing   715

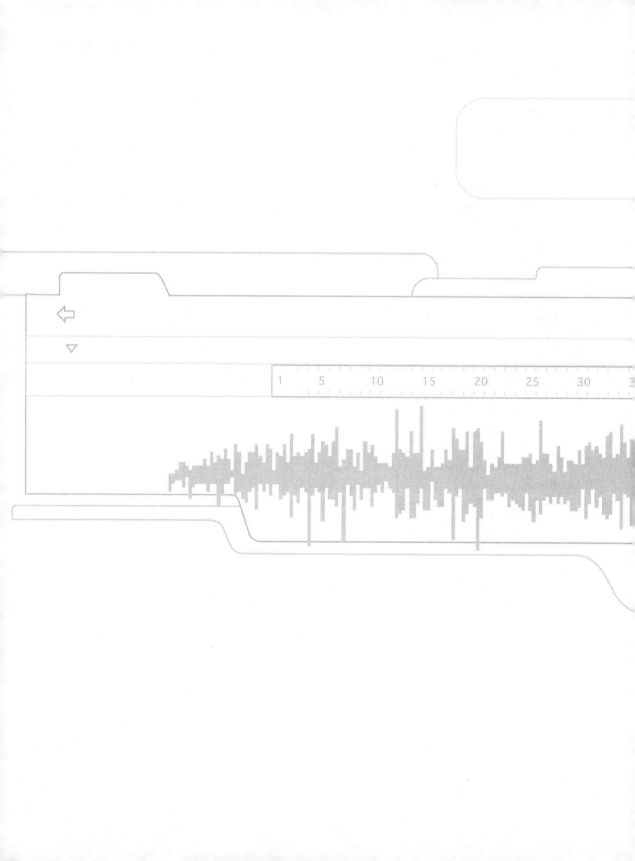

INTRODUCTION

MACROMEDIA FLASH MX 2004 IS A POWERFUL TOOL FOR QUICKLY AND EASILY creating high-quality animated effects (even entire cartoon shows) and engaging interactive experiences. With these two latest versions of Flash (Flash MX 2004 and Flash MX Professional 2004), the tools are much more robust and feature-rich.

Because there's so much to learn in this new version of Flash, this book is written to help you get a handle on it. This book goes through Flash's interface and tools in a logical manner, explaining what you can do with them and giving you many opportunities to practice on your own.

We hope you find this book useful. Scratch that—we hope you find it indispensable. A great deal of effort has gone into making this book the best we could write *and* the best value for you. We hope we've succeeded.

It's been, for all of us, a wonderful opportunity to work on this book and to get a chance to give back to the Flash community what has been given to us. We hope you like it; we had a great time writing it.

Enjoy *Macromedia Flash MX 2004 Demystified!*

WHO THIS BOOK IS FOR

This book is intended as a technical reference for users of previous Flash versions. Although this book attempts to dissect Flash's features, it's not intended strictly for an advanced audience. Our target is the designer/ developer audience, although people with no previous experience with Flash will be able to get a lot out of the book. Also, this book should be useful to those currently programming in other languages who want to migrate to Flash.

HOW THIS BOOK IS ORGANIZED

Macromedia Flash MX 2004 Demystified is divided into seven sections that categorize the content thematically and match the learning curve of most readers. The book begins by with an overview of Flash features, moves to the basics of using Flash MX 2004, and then builds in complexity and scope with each successive chapter. By the time you get to Part VII, you'll have gained enough skill and knowledge to feel comfortable using Flash.

Part I: The Basics

- **Chapter 1, "Welcome to Flash MX 2004,"** presents a brief overview of Flash, compares it with other media formats, and offers a look at the history of Flash. You also get a look at the key features of Flash's new versions.

- **Chapter 2, "Overview of the Interface and Tools,"** gives you an overview of the interface, showing you where everything is and how it works, and introduces you to the most commonly used tools.

- **Chapter 3, "The Library, Symbols, and the Timeline,"** introduces and explains the Timeline, layers, frames, and symbols, all of which make up the heart and soul of Flash. You'll also learn about the Library, where all your symbols are stored.

- **Chapter 4, "Exploring Views and Panels,"** explores some of the other windows and panels in Flash and covers the available views, which includes working with rulers, grids, and guides and snapping.

- **Chapter 5, "Importing,"** shows you what types of information can be brought into Flash and how to import those files.

- **Chapter 6, "Animation, Effects, and Masking,"** covers principles of animation and how to make the best use of them in the Flash authoring environment.

- **Chapter 7, "Behaviors,"** introduces you to Behaviors, a new tool that enables designers to quickly add interactivity to their movies.

Part II: ActionScript

- **Chapter 8, "Introduction to ActionScript,"** begins your education in programming, laying out some fundamental programming concepts and illustrating how they are applied to Flash.

- **Chapter 9, "ActionScript Basics: Data and Statements,"** continues your programming education with information on a variety of data types. You also learn how to use ActionScript to manipulate a movie's visual elements.

- **Chapter 10, "ActionScript: Functions, Events, and Objects,"** delves into programming concepts, introducing functions, arrays, event handlers, and classes, including many of Flash's built-in classes.

- **Chapter 11, "Animation and Drawing with ActionScript: The Drawing API,"** covers the Drawing API, used to draw elements on the stage during runtime. You also learn a number of tips and tricks to help you make exciting scripted animations.

- **Chapter 12, "Components,"** introduces you to Flash components and explains how to use them. You also see how to make your own components.

Part III: Elements

- **Chapter 13, "Text,"** takes a look at text elements in a Flash movie, focusing on controlling text with ActionScript. You also learn about some of the new Flash 2004 text features, such as support for small fonts and cascading style sheets.

- **Chapter 14, "Images,"** explains how to use images in Flash, including tips on when to use bitmap or vector images. You learn how to optimize images in Flash and transform photos into vector art.

- **Chapter 15, "Audio,"** explores using audio in Flash and explains how to load and manipulate sounds.

- **Chapter 16, "Video,"** shows you the finer points of using video in Flash, including new ways of handling video within Flash and tips and tricks on making your video look better.

Part IV: Extending Flash

- **Chapter 17, "Accessing External Data,"** introduces you to a myriad of ways to access external data sources via Flash. Everything from passing URLs to your movie with your browser to loading XML and database information is explained.

- **Chapter 18, "Advanced Communications,"** introduces you to two important features of Flash: Remoting, which lets you connect directly to various data sources, and Flash Communication Server, which enables you to create multiuser applications.

Part V: Next Steps

- **Chapter 19, "Writing Code That Rocks: ActionScript Best Practices,"** shows you how to streamline and optimize your code and highlights several best practices designed to help you write effective, efficient code.

- **Chapter 20, "OOP for Flashers,"** introduces you to object-oriented programming (OOP) and explains how to take advantage of it in Flash.

- **Chapter 21, "Math for Flashers,"** shows you how to use high-level mathematics in your Flash movie. This concept is extremely useful for bringing a sense of physical realism to your Flash-based games and visual effects.

- **Chapter 22, "3D in Flash,"** highlights the use of Flash in creating and manipulating 3D effects. You learn how to import 3D files into Flash and how to use ActionScript to create a 3D space within your movies.

Part VI: Finishing

- **Chapter 23, "Publishing,"** takes you on a tour of Flash's publishing functionality. Learn the ins and outs of exporting your movies and how to optimize them for their destination.

- **Chapter 24, "Developing for Pocket Devices,"** introduces you to the many portable devices that currently support Flash and offers insight and tips on developing content for those devices.

- **Chapter 25, "Troubleshooting,"** explains the finer points of troubleshooting your code, including a tour of the Debugger and ActionScript classes, such as the `Error` class.

- **Chapter 26, "Accessibility,"** shows you how to make your Flash movies accessible to viewers who have disabilities, which is essential for reaching the widest possible audience.

- **Chapter 27, "The Flash Player,"** welcomes you to the new version of the Flash Player. Learn the differences between Flash Player 7 and previous versions, and explore the host of new features available in this release.

Conventions and Features Used in This Book

At the end of most of the chapters, you'll find chapter projects that give you a way to apply the knowledge you have gained from the chapter. These chapter projects are presented in a straightforward, point-by-point manner and should be easy to complete. If you find you're having difficulties, you can download the completed FLAs from the *Flash MX 2004 Demystified* web site and see how the examples are produced.

You can visit the *Flash MX 2004 Demystified* web site at www.flashdemystified. com. The official companion to this book, it gives you access to all the examples described in the book as well as a variety of other helpful content.

As you're reading through the chapters, pay attention to the following features for extra information:

Interesting background information or general comments are often high-lighted as notes.

Tips offer helpful information on techniques to save you time and effort and help you avoid errors.

Pointers on potential trouble spots are highlighted as cautions.

Check here for cross-references to other chapters where pertinent concepts are explained in more detail. This icon is used to point out features that are new to Flash MX 2004.

This icon is used to point out features that are new to Flash MX 2004.

Resources

At the end of some chapters, you'll find a list of resources you can inves-tigate for more information.

The following typographic conventions have been used in this book:

- A `monospace` font is used for code and for text the reader types in, such as values changed in a dialog box or filenames used to save projects.

- A **bold** font is used for keyboard shortcuts.

- *Italics* are used for new terms that are introduced and sometimes for emphasis.

PART I:
THE BASICS

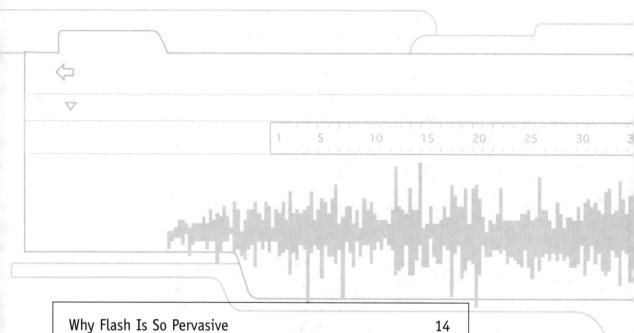

CHAPTER 1

WELCOME TO FLASH MX 2004

Welcome to *Macromedia Flash MX 2004 Demystified*! It's a great opportunity for all those involved in this book to be able to write one of the first Flash books for this new iteration of the software, and we hope that our enthusiasm—and knowledge—come across on every page.

Macromedia Flash MX 2004 is the ideal tool for developers and designers who are developing multimedia content. Manipulating audio, video, bitmaps, vectors, text, and data are all possible with this new version of Flash. And what a version of the software it is! In the past few years, Flash has matured from an animation-and-light-scripting package to a robust application development environment for both designers and developers. Flash now enables you to connect easily to a myriad of web services and data sources, and, with companion products such as Flash Communication Server, create engaging multiuser applications with unparalleled ease.

Not to forget the designers out there, Macromedia has piled on usability enhancements to its software, making this product even better if your goal is to create visually stunning web experiences. So many new features have been added to Flash MX 2004, in fact, that Macromedia split the software into two versions—Flash MX 2004 and Flash MX Professional 2004—for developers interested in creating sophisticated web applications. This book primarily covers the features of Flash MX 2004, although it should provide a good base for Flash MX Professional 2004 users.

We hope you find this book useful and that it helps you make a quick transition from developing in Flash MX or even Flash 5. Or, if you're new to the Flash community, we hope this book serves as a pleasant, easy-to-understand entry point into this stellar piece of software. Enjoy!

Why Flash Is So Pervasive

What makes Flash so pervasive? Why is it the format of choice for so many developers? Since its inception in 1997 as a browser plug-in, it's evolved into one of the most common browser add-ins for many people. Beginning as a simple animation tool, Flash has grown to be a robust and powerful application development tool, and the Flash Player plug-in is the most downloaded file in the history of the web! How did Macromedia accomplish that?

Bringing Designers and Programmers Together

One of the greatest strengths of Flash is that it's traditionally been an easily accessible program and an application development tool that's suitable for people in different roles and disciplines. With Flash, designers can create beautiful works of art, and hard-core programmers can code to their hearts' content. Because of Flash's diversity, developers and designers of all kinds can work together to create artistic and functional content. This diversity has helped Flash grow within the industry. Its ability to appeal to and be accessible to both sides of the community has been the cornerstone of its success.

True Multimedia and Integration of Digital Media

Within the digital world, there are many different types of content. Whether the content is audio files, video files, bitmap and vector artwork, or text, Flash brings them all together into one format. This capability alone is incredibly powerful, true multimedia—the integration of all the different digital media.

Not only does Flash enable you to integrate all these different digital media, but it also gives you complete control over them so that whether you're an artist, developer, or programmer, you can fully realize your vision. Doing this with most other tools is difficult, if not impossible.

File Size

One of the major concerns when creating web content is file size. Although tremendous strides in broadband penetration and availability have been made, file size remains a concern with any project destined for the web. Flash, with its capability to stream content and its small file size (for both the plug-in and the content), has made it much easier for developers to create persuasive content that can be effectively delivered over the web.

Market Penetration

The latest statistics, according to Macromedia, put the percentage of users who can view Flash content over the web at 97.4%.* This means that of the estimated 448 million web users, 436 million have the Flash Player installed on their systems. As stated earlier, the Flash Player is the *most downloaded file* in the history of the web. To achieve this, Macromedia has made some smart choices. First, it has kept the Player's file size manageable. Second, it's managed to ensure that the Flash Player comes bundled with many of the most popular browsers. Third, it's developed a powerful and easy-to-use authoring program that many developers and designers have embraced, and it has continued to develop Flash to meet users' needs.

Why is this heavy market penetration important to you? Those who were using Flash in the Flash 1, 2, and 3 days know the answer to this question. Try telling clients that you'll create their websites, but site visitors will have to download a special plug-in to access the site. Not an easy sell. However, now that most users have the Flash Player, convincing clients to use Flash isn't an issue any longer. Now clients are telling developers and designers "We want it in Flash!" Of course, you should do your homework and determine what version of the Flash Player is at a penetration level that's acceptable for your specific project.

Control

Most of the development for web-based projects involves teams. More often than not, the team consists of a designer and a developer. The

---

*Source: http://www.macromedia.com/software/player_census/flashplayer/
penetration.html

designer creates the graphics and hands them to the developer to build. Because Flash allows complete control over fonts, colors, and layouts, developers can build applications that express the designer's creative concept. This control isn't always possible in other formats, such as HTML, which have limitations on how much control you have over content.

Dynamic Content

Flash's capability to support dynamic content makes it incredibly powerful. Being able to pull data into Flash from an external source, such as a database, means you can deliver Rich Internet Applications that can be integrated with any application server. This feature allows for a truly dynamic application that offers the user up-to-the minute content, a giant advance over static applications.

Write Once, Publish Anywhere

After you've created a project in Flash, you can deliver it to your audience in a number of different ways quite easily, something that's fairly difficult, if not impossible, with other formats. You can publish to the web, to handheld devices, to broadcast video, to a CD or DVD, or to a kiosk.

CHOOSING BETWEEN FLASH MX 2004 AND FLASH MX PROFESSIONAL 2004

With this latest release of Flash, you now have two versions to choose from: Flash MX 2004 and Flash MX 2004 Professional. Flash MX Professional 2004 is designed for advanced developers and includes all the features of Flash MX 2004, along with several new tools and features. It provides project-management tools, external scripting capabilities, a new forms-based visual programming environment, advanced components, data binding, and prebuilt data connectors for accessing Web Services and XML.

Not only can you use Flash MX 2004 to open content created in previous versions of Flash, you can also save files created in Flash MX 2004 as Flash MX files, allowing you to continue sharing Flash documents with those who haven't yet upgraded. As far as functionality of movies developed in Flash MX (or earlier), all your existing content should work fine in Flash MX 2004.

Unsure which version of Flash is right for you? If you use Flash for the following tasks, Flash MX 2004 is probably right for you:

- Creating animation

- Building basic web sites

- Writing light scripts

On the other hand, if you use Flash for the following tasks, Flash MX Professional 2004 is most likely the version for you:

- Building Rich Internet Applications

- Accessing Web Services

- Authoring advanced components

- Working on large Flash projects with teams that share the same Flash files

NEW FEATURES IN FLASH 2004

The features described in the following sections are available in *both* Flash MX 2004 and Flash MX Professional 2004.

Productivity Features

The following new features available in Flash MX 2004 help you create content faster and easier. These features improve productivity and further streamline publishing your content:

- **Timeline effects**   This series of effects has been built into Flash, allowing you to quickly and easily create some of the more common effects, such as fade-ins, blurs, and shadows, that were done manually in earlier versions of Flash. See Chapter 6, "Animation, Effects, and Masking."

- **Behaviors**   Behaviors are designed to be a drag-and-drop solution to some of the more basic commands available in Flash. You can now add interactivity to Flash without writing a line of code. This feature makes it quick and easy to add some basic commands to your Flash movie. See Chapter 7, "Behaviors."

- **Accessibility support in the authoring environment** Extended accessibility support has been added to the Flash 2004 authoring environment, making it faster and easier to add improved accessibility features to your Flash content. See Chapter 26, "Accessibility."

- **Updated templates** All new and improved templates have made creating Flash content even easier. Templates include presentations, e-learning, advertisements, and mobile devices. See Chapter 2, "Overview of the Interface and Tools."

- **Integrated Help system** In Flash 2004, all the different help files are grouped into one place: the Help panel. The new Help panel includes an in-context reference, an ActionScript reference, Flash lessons, and a feature for updating your help files with the most recent files from the Macromedia servers. See Chapter 4, "Exploring Views and Panels."

- **Spell checker** You can now search your text for spelling errors. See Chapter 13, "Text."

- **Document tabs** The new and improved interface now includes document tabs to quickly and easily locate and switch between open documents. See Chapter 2.

- **Start page** A new central Start page includes commonly used tasks, such as creating a new document, lists available templates, and enables you to quickly open your most recent files. See Chapter 2.

Rich Media Support Features

The following list describes the new rich media features that Flash MX 2004 supports:

- **New import formats** You can now import Adobe PDFs and Adobe Illustrator 10 files directly into Flash. See Chapter 5, "Importing."

- **Video Import Wizard** You can use this new wizard to simplify video encoding and importing videos into your Flash projects. See Chapter 5 and Chapter 16, "Video."

- **Small font size rendering** This feature gives you crisper rendering of small font sizes. See Chapter 13.

Publishing Features

The publishing options available in Flash have been streamlined and improved:

- **Flash Player detection**   Now it's easier than ever to detect what version of the Flash Player your users have and to direct them to the correct pages. See Chapter 23, "Publishing."

- **Publish profiles**   When determining your publish settings, you can now create and save a profile of those settings. This feature is great for reusing publish settings or sharing Flash documents and their publish settings in a team project environment. See Chapter 23.

- **Accessibility and components**   New features and new components offer tab ordering, tab focus management, and improved support for screen readers and closed-caption programs. See Chapter 12, "Components," and Chapter 27, "The Flash Player."

- **Globalization and Unicode**   Multilanguage authoring is now even easier with enhanced globalization and Unicode support. See Chapter 13.

- **Strings panel**   This new panel makes it even easier to publish in multiple languages by creating XML files for each specified language. See Chapter 13.

- **Security**   The new Flash Player now enforces a stricter security model than ever before. See Chapter 27.

Other Improvements

Flash also offers the following improvements in this new version:

- **Flash Player runtime performance**   Runtime performance has been dramatically improved, with a playback speed that's two to five times faster for video, scripting, and display. See Chapter 27.

- **ActionScript 2.0**   The all-new ActionScript 2.0 is an object-oriented language that follows the ECMAScript language and specifications and supports inheritance, strict typing, and the event model. See Chapters 8 through 10, as well as Chapter 20, "OOP for Flashers."

- **History panel**   This new panel enables you to track each action, so it's easy to replay, go back, and create reusable commands. See Chapter 4.

Other enhancements you'll find in Flash include the following:

- The all-new ActionScript editor has been updated in a number of ways, including word wrapping, pinning multiple scripts, and the new Script Navigator. See Chapter 8, "Introduction to ActionScript."

- The Output window is now a panel that supports docking, allowing you to customize your authoring environment.

- Improved error reporting at runtime makes troubleshooting your project faster and easier. See Chapter 25, "Troubleshooting."

- Existing components have been rebuilt using an all-new component architecture, including tab ordering and tab focus management. See Chapter 12.

- Mouse wheel support enables you to not only scroll text content with the mouse wheel, but also assign any number of actions to the scrolling of the mouse wheel.

NEW FEATURES IN FLASH MX PROFESSIONAL 2004

The following features are available *only* in Flash MX Professional 2004:

- **Screens**   Screens gives users an authoring interface with structural building blocks, making it easy to create complex Flash documents, such as slide presentations or form-based applications. There are two different types of screens:

  - **Flash form applications** are a forms-based visual programming environment for developing applications. These simple containers allow you to create form-based applications, such as online registration or e-commerce forms, quickly and easily.

- **Flash slide presentations** enable you to quickly and easily create Flash documents that have sequential content, such as slide shows. Default navigation is built in so that users can use arrow keys to navigate.

- **Advanced component support** New prewritten components included in Flash support focus management, allowing you to control tab navigation. Components based on the new Flash 2004 v2 component architecture share core functionality, such as styles, event handing, skinning, focus management, and depth management.

- **Data binding** Connect any prewritten components to various data sources through components or directly by writing ActionScript.

- **Prebuilt data connectors for Web Services and XML** New components allow you to easily connect to Web Services and XML data sources.

- **Project management** The new Project panel allows centralized project file management, version control, and workflow optimization for teams of Flash developers working together on the same project.

- **Source code control** For project teams with multiple Flash developers, new features in Flash MX 2004 allow source code control integration with plug-ins to industry-leading source control systems, such as Microsoft Visual Source Safe.

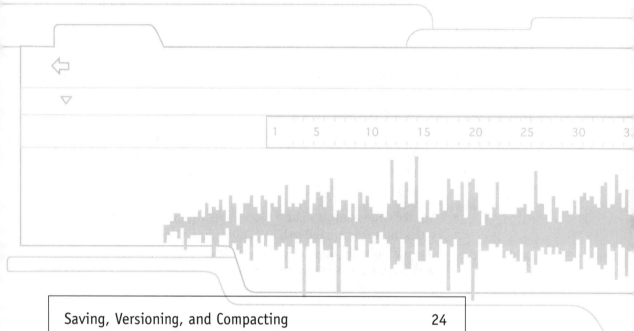

CHAPTER 2

OVERVIEW OF THE INTERFACE AND TOOLS

IN THIS CHAPTER, YOU'LL LEARN ABOUT THE DRAWING TOOLS IN MACROMEDIA Flash MX 2004 through hands-on-interaction. You're encouraged to participate and do the quick exercises throughout the chapter. The chapter is set up in a linear fashion, as each tool builds on previous tools as you progress.

Feel free to experiment with the tools as you learn them. Remember, you can't break anything, so have some fun. Anything you do can always be undone with the trusty Undo command (Windows: **Ctrl+Z**; Macintosh: **Command+Z**).

SAVING, VERSIONING, AND COMPACTING

Before you jump in, you need to understand the importance of saving your work, which can help you avoid untold hours of frustration and rework in the long run. Get into the habit early of saving often. Learn the keyboard shortcut **Ctrl+S** (Macintosh: **Command+S**), and use it frequently. Getting into this habit will save you much frustration. There's nothing worse than having your system crash, only to realize you haven't saved your work for the past few hours or even days.

You should also get in the habit of *versioning* your files. Some people recommend doing it every couple of hours; others do it only when they make substantive changes. To version a file, simply choose File, Save As from the menu, and give your file a new name. A good guideline to follow is using *incremental naming*. In other words, if you start with a file named `filename_01.fla`, each time you save and version it, increase the ending number by one: `filename_02.fla`, `filename_03.fla`, and so forth. A system crash can corrupt the file you're working on at the time, and you could lose days, even weeks, of work if you can't open the file. With versioning, however, you can go back to the most recent version of the file, which might not be ideal, but it's better than losing days or weeks of work. You might also want go back to earlier versions if you need to check your work at an earlier stage in your project, for example.

Users and developers of previous Flash versions discovered that Flash wasn't *compacting* FLA files when they were saved. That meant if you imported large images or videos and then deleted them from your project later because you didn't need them or substituted other images or videos, the file size of your FLA didn't decrease. In other words, Flash wasn't clearing those previous multimedia files from your FLA, which meant file size could increase pretty quickly. The only way to have Flash compact the file was to use the Save As command. However, Flash MX 2004 has introduced the Save and Compact command, which essentially does just that—clears previously deleted multimedia files from your FLA file. You don't need to use this command every five minutes, but using it occasionally is a good idea. How often you use it depends on the type of work you're doing. If you're importing and deleting lots of multimedia assets, you should use Save and Compact more often than if your Flash movie is mostly ActionScript code.

THE START PAGE

The first thing you see when you open Flash is the new Start page (see Figure 2.1). This portal page gives you access to the three most common items you use when starting Flash and includes some other useful links.

If you don't see the Start page when you run Flash, it's possible that you or someone else has changed the settings. To set the Start page to appear when you first run Flash, choose Edit, Preferences from the menu, and select Show Start Page under the On Launch option, which is on the General tab.

FIGURE 2.1
The Start page.

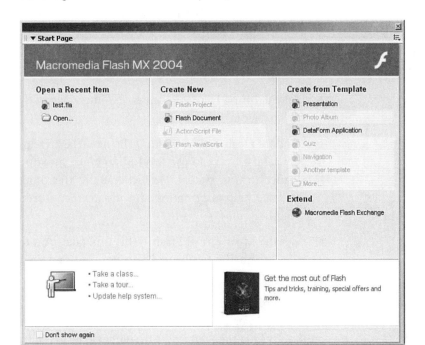

- **Open a Recent Item**   Use this list of recent Flash documents you've worked on as a quick way to get to the document. There's also an Open icon you can click to open any Flash file on your system.

- **Create New**   This is a quick link to creating a new Flash document, Flash project, ActionScript file, or Flash JavaScript.

- **Create from Template** These are quick links to templates included with Flash to start projects. Under each category, you'll find a few templates (FLA files) to work from. So if you're making a banner ad but can't remember the size these ads are usually created at, Flash has a template that's the correct size, which saves you some trouble. The more-advanced templates include instructions and more-complex functionality. After you've learned some basics of Flash, returning to this section to explore some of these templates is highly recommended.

- **Macromedia Flash Exchange** This is a quick link to the Macromedia Flash Exchange, a website where you can download components, extensions, custom tags, scripts, content, and other items for extending the functionality of Flash.

- **Take a Lesson** Here you'll find links to some interactive Flash lessons.

- **Take a Tour** Here you can access interactive tours of Flash from the Macromedia website.

- **Update Flash Help System** The new Flash Help system is incredibly robust. You can use this link to make sure updates are downloaded to your system. Flash checks the Macromedia servers for any updated help information, downloads the information, and updates your help files.

- **Get the Most out of Flash** This link takes you to the Flash section of Macromedia's website, where you can find tips, tricks, and special offers.

If you'd prefer not to see the Start page when you open Flash, click the Don't Show Again check box in the bottom-left corner. You can turn it back on (or off) from the Preferences dialog box (choose Edit, Preferences from the menu).

GETTING STARTED WITH BASIC TOOLS

Upon opening Flash, the first window you see is the Start page. Under the Create New section, click Flash Document and take a look inside. You'll see the toolbar on the left side of the screen and the document window in the center, currently called Untitled-1 (see Figure 2.2). The document window contains the stage, which is the large white area in the middle, and above that, the Timeline.

FIGURE 2.2
Opening Flash.

STAGE

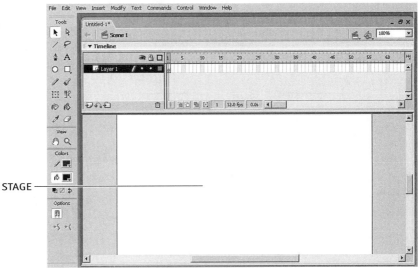

 If you've already opened and played with Flash, your screen might have other windows open as well. If any other windows are open, click the menu icon in the top right of that window's title bar and close them for now.

The Toolbar

Take a look at the toolbar, shown in Figure 2.3. You'll be using all these tools in this chapter and the next two chapters. The icons usually make it easy to remember what the tools are used for, such as the magnifying glass icon for zooming in for a closer look. If you're ever unsure, however, simply place your mouse over the tool icon. A small tooltip pops up, telling you the name of that tool.

 The choices available in the Options section of the toolbar change depending on what tool you have selected. With the Line tool selected, for example, the Snap to Objects option is available; with the Lasso tool selected, different Magic Wand options are available.

 By default, the toolbar is docked on the left side of your screen. Most people find this placement the most comfortable, but you can change it by clicking the edges of the toolbar and dragging it to a new location.

FIGURE 2.3
The Flash toolbar.

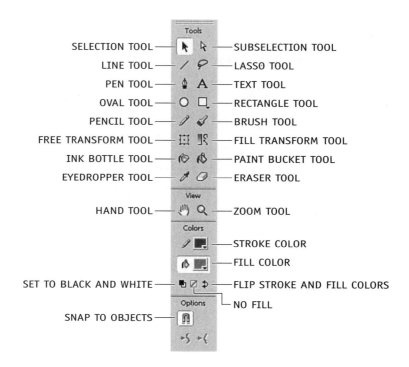

The Oval Tool

Begin by drawing on the stage, the large white rectangle in the middle of the screen. From the toolbar, select the Oval tool (keyboard shortcut: **O**). When you select this tool, the pointer changes to a small black cross. To draw an oval, click and hold near the top-left corner of the stage, drag your mouse down toward the bottom-right corner, and then release the mouse button.

If you like, you can select the color of the oval's fill and outline (called the *stroke*) before drawing the oval. To do this, use the tools in the Colors section of the toolbar. The top one sets the stroke color. The one underneath it sets the fill color. Clicking either tool opens a quick color palette where you can select a color that's applied to any oval you create. Later in this chapter, you'll see how to change the fill color as well as the stroke color and height after it's actually drawn on the stage.

You'll learn more about color later in this chapter and in Chapter 4, "Exploring Views and Panels."

To draw a perfect circle, you can hold down the Shift key while you're dragging. The Shift key forces the oval's height and width to be equal, thus creating a circle. The Shift key can be used with other tools, too.

If you don't like the oval's size, shape, or color, simply press **Ctrl+Z** (Macintosh: **Command+Z**) to undo your action. Flash, by default, remembers your last 100 moves, so it's easy to undo the last few actions you've performed. If you want to increase the number of moves Flash remembers, you can change this setting in the Preferences dialog box (choose Edit, Preferences from the menu).

The Selection Tool

You need an object on the stage to use the Selection tool, so use the oval you just drew. From the toolbar, click the Selection tool (keyboard shortcut: **V**). The pointer changes to a black arrow. Next, select the inside of the oval (the fill) by clicking anywhere inside it. A pattern on top of the color indicates that the fill is selected. After you select the fill, you can move it by clicking and dragging it or pressing the arrow keys on your keyboard. You can also delete it by pressing the Delete key. You'll learn more about coloring and modifying fills later in this chapter and in Chapter 4.

When working with more-complex artwork, it can be difficult to see what's selected and what's not selected. As a result, when you have an item selected and want to select another item, it's a good practice to deselect the current item before selecting another one. To deselect, simply click an empty white part of the stage. In this case, anywhere *but* the oval you drew will do. After deselecting, you'll notice that the oval's fill is no longer selected. The keyboard shortcut for deselecting is **Ctrl+Shift+A** (Macintosh: **Command+Shift+A**).

Now select the oval's outline (stroke). When the mouse is over the edge of the circle, the pointer changes to an arrow with a small curved line to indicate that it's positioned over a stroke (see Figure 2.4). If you click there, the stroke will be selected. Click on the oval's outline to select it.

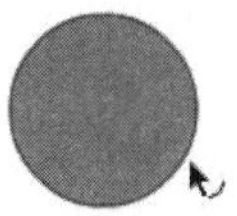

FIGURE 2.4
The mouse pointer changes when it's over a stroke.

How do you select both the fill and stroke? If the fill and outline are still together, double-click the fill. You can also select the fill or stroke with one click, hold down the Shift key, and select the other item (the fill or stroke).

Another method is clicking and dragging a selection box around the entire oval to select both the stroke and fill. To do this, visualize a rectangle large enough to encompass the entire oval. Click a corner of that rectangle, and then drag your mouse to the opposite corner. While you're dragging the mouse, you'll see the selection box form. When you release the mouse button, any items inside the selection box are selected. You can use this method to select only part of the oval, too. Try selecting only half of the oval and then moving it around.

The Fill Color Tool

Next, you'll select the oval's fill and change its color to red. To do this, click the Fill Color tool on the toolbar to open the quick color palette (see Figure 2.5). Next, click the red square in the palette. The quick color palette should close, and the oval's fill should change to red.

FIGURE 2.5
Using the quick color palette to change the fill color.

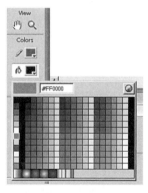

Experiment, and try changing the oval's fill to another color. You'll learn other ways of changing fill colors; this method is just one of many.

Remember that the last fill color selected becomes the default color. Any drawings you create later will have that fill color.

The Stroke Color Tool

Using the same oval, click the Selection tool and select the oval's stroke. Next, click the Stroke Color tool in the Colors section of the toolbar, and change the stroke to any color you'd like, using the quick color palette. As with the fill color, there are many ways to change the stroke color.

Remember that the last stroke color selected becomes the default stroke color. Any strokes created later will have that fill color until that color is changed.

THE PROPERTY INSPECTOR

Now that you've learned about a few basic tools, it's time to see what you can do with the Property inspector. Most developers keep this useful panel open at all times. To open it, choose Windows, Properties from the menu (keyboard shortcut: Windows **Ctrl+F3**; Macintosh **Command+F3**). The Property inspector, which is usually docked at the bottom of your screen, displays information about whatever is currently selected. Depending on what you've selected, the information in the Property inspector changes. Different types of objects (fills, lines, movie clips, text fields) have different properties that you can easily view and change in the Property inspector. The following sections explain how the Property inspector changes, depending on whether you've selected a document, a shape, or a stroke.

Document Properties

Click an empty area of the stage to deselect the oval you've been working with, and the Property inspector should look like Figure 2.6, displaying a few properties of the current document.

FIGURE 2.6
The Property inspector showing the current document information.

You can find the following information in the Property inspector when a document's selected:

- **Name** At the left of the Property inspector, you'll see the name of the current movie. The default name for a brand-new movie is Untitled-1. You can change it simply by saving the movie and giving it a name (choose File, Save or File, Save As from the main menu).

- **Size** The default is 550×400 pixels. Click this button to open the Document Properties dialog box and change the dimensions of your movie.

For more information on publish settings, see Chapter 23, "Publishing."

- **Publish Settings button** Click this button to open the Publish Settings dialog box, where you can adjust the settings for publishing your movie. To the right of this button are three settings from the Publish Settings dialog box: the Flash Player version (set to 7 by default), the ActionScript version (2 by default), and the publishing profile (set to Default).

See Chapter 4 for more information on document settings and the frame rate.

- **Background color** This square acts exactly like the Fill Color and Stroke Color tools. You use it to select the background color of your Flash movie.

- **Frame Rate** This setting indicates the rate at which the movie's frames will play, measured in frames per second. The default setting is 12fps (frames per second).

Shape Properties

Again, using the oval you have on the stage, select its fill and stroke by double-clicking the oval or using one of the other methods explained previously. Notice that the information in the Property inspector changes to what's shown in Figure 2.7.

FIGURE 2.7
The Property inspector showing information on a selected shape.

Again, the left side of the Property inspector shows what's selected—in this case, the oval shape. It also shows the width, height, and x- and y-coordinates, all of which can be edited. If you want to constrain the ratio of the width and height (so that changes to one setting update the other setting to maintain the same ratio aspect), click the padlock icon to the left of the width and height text boxes.

On the right side, you'll find more information about the shape, such as stroke and fill colors and the stroke height (that is, the thickness of the stroke line) and style. You can change any of these settings here in the

Property inspector. For example, clicking the fill or stroke color icon opens the same quick color palette you used in the toolbar. The following section covers more stroke options.

The Property inspector, by default, is docked at the bottom of the screen. You'll learn more about docking later, but for now, notice the small white arrow on the bar between the document window and the Property inspector (see Figure 2.8). You can click it to expand the document window, thereby hiding the Property inspector whenever you like.

FIGURE 2.8
Click this arrow to hide or display the Property inspector.

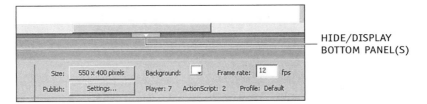

HIDE/DISPLAY
BOTTOM PANEL(S)

Stroke Properties

When a stroke is selected, notice the drop-down list of stroke styles in the Property inspector (see Figure 2.9). The default style is Solid, but you can choose other stroke styles, such as dashed or dotted lines. Anything other than a solid or hairline stroke is usually very processor-intensive, however. If you must use these types of lines, use them sparingly.

FIGURE 2.9
The Stroke Style drop-down list.

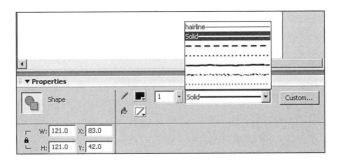

You can also customize the stroke style by clicking the Custom button, but again, use customized stroke styles sparingly. Clicking the Custom button opens the Stroke Style dialog box, shown in Figure 2.10.

FIGURE 2.10
The Stroke Style dialog box.

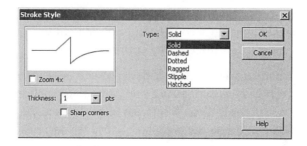

You can also adjust the stroke height anywhere between .25 and 10 in the Property inspector. To adjust the height, click in the stroke height field and enter a number, or use the slider to the right, as shown in Figure 2.11.

FIGURE 2.11
Adjusting the stroke height with the slider.

MOVING ON TO MORE TOOLS

Now that you've learned how to use the Property inspector, continue reading to see how to work with more tools and adjust them in the Property inspector.

The Line Tool

Next you'll learn how to draw a line on the stage. Click the Line tool in the toolbar. Then click the stage where you want the first point, hold and drag to where you want the line to end, and release the mouse button. You can choose the line's color and height in the Property inspector before you start drawing it. For this example, use a solid blue line set to a stroke height of 6 (see Figure 2.12).

Flash has an automatic Snap To feature, which makes it easy to create perfectly horizontal or vertical lines. To toggle this feature off and on, click the Snap to Objects icon (the magnet in the Options section) in the toolbar. You can further control how the line is drawn by holding down the Shift key, which constrains the lines to 45 degrees.

FIGURE 2.12
The Property inspector while using the Line tool.

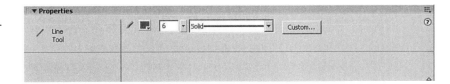

Click the Selection tool in the toolbar, and take a closer look at this line. If you roll over the line with your mouse, the mouse pointer shows a small curve icon; if you roll over the end of a line, the mouse pointer shows a corner icon (see Figure 2.13).

FIGURE 2.13
Selecting different parts of a line.

If you click and drag an end point of the line, you can drag that end point around and move it, while the opposite end point remains stationary. However, if you click and drag the middle of the line, you can curve the line (the two end points remain stationary). To move the entire line, you need to select it by clicking anywhere on it, and *then* click and drag it where you'd like it moved.

The Zoom Tool

To make it easier to work with the shapes you're drawing, you need to learn how to zoom in and out on the stage. Click the Zoom tool in the toolbar (the magnifying glass in the View section). Your mouse pointer changes to a small magnifying glass icon, and when you click the stage, you zoom into that area at twice the magnification level. So if you were at 100%, you're now at 200%. Clicking again doubles the magnification level again to 400%. You can continue zooming in to a maximum of 2000%.

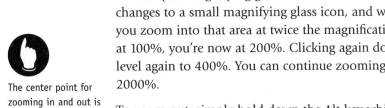

The center point for zooming in and out is set by your mouse. Wherever you click is the center point.

To zoom out, simply hold down the Alt key while clicking the stage. Each time you click, your magnification level is cut in half, up to a minimum of 8%.

Temporary Keyboard Shortcuts for Zooming

An easier way to zoom in and out is with temporary keyboard shortcuts because you don't have to change tools in the toolbar. (These keyboard shortcuts are called "temporary" because they change the tool only while the keys are pressed.) Click the Selection tool again in the toolbar, press **Ctrl+spacebar** (Macintosh: **Command+spacebar**), and then click on the stage to zoom in. Notice that your pointer changed when you held down those two keys. After you release the keys, your original tool is still selected. To zoom out, press **Ctrl+Shift+spacebar** (Macintosh: **Command+Shift+spacebar**) and click the stage. Again, when you release the keys used for the shortcut, you're back to your original tool. You can use this temporary keyboard shortcut with most tools, except the Text tool.

You can double-click the Zoom tool in the toolbar at any time, which returns your magnification level to 100%.

Another set of keyboard shortcuts is very handy: **Ctr1+1**, **Ctrl+2**, and **Ctrl+3** (Macintosh: **Command+1**, **Command+2**, and **Command+3**). This is a quick way to set the magnification and center your content on the stage. Try them out now. **Ctrl+1** sets the magnification to 100%, and **Ctrl+2** sets the zoom to Show Frame, which resizes the stage so that it fills the available screen area in that window. **Ctrl+3** sets the zoom to Show All, which resizes the content, not the stage, so that the content fills the screen.

The Zoom Drop-Down List

Another quick way to control zooming is to use the drop-down list at the top-right corner of the Timeline window (see Figure 2.14).

FIGURE 2.14
Setting the magnification with the zoom drop-down list.

Simply drop down this list box and select a magnification level. You can also type in a number and press Enter.

The Hand Tool

You use the Hand tool (keyboard shortcut: **H**) to move the stage left, right, up, or down to help you see your content. This tool is especially useful if you've zoomed in very close. It works the same way as using the scrollbars at the right and bottom of the document window, but it gives you quicker and more precise control when moving around. To try this tool, create a very small circle using the Oval tool and zoom in to 800%. Click the Hand tool in the toolbar, and then click and drag on the stage. It looks like you're moving the oval around the stage, but you're actually doing the opposite—moving the stage around.

Temporary Keyboard Shortcut for the Hand Tool

There's an easy-to-use (and remember) temporary keyboard shortcut for the Hand tool: the spacebar. To try it, click the Selection tool (or press V), and then, with your mouse pointer on the stage, hold down the spacebar. Now you can click and move the stage around. Notice that the mouse pointer changes to a hand to indicate that you're in Hand tool mode while the spacebar is pressed. After you're finished moving the stage around, simply release the spacebar, and you're back to the Selection tool.

The Subselection Tool

The Subselection tool is used for moving and editing anchor points and lines. All vector shapes in Flash are made up of points, lines, and fills. An *anchor point* is just a point on a line: Think connect-the-dots.

To use this tool, you need an object to select. To use something a little more interesting than the oval you've been working with, you'll try drawing an eye made up of two overlapping ovals: a larger light one and a smaller dark one. Click the Oval tool in the toolbar and set the stroke and fill colors. You don't need an outline on these two ovals, so click the No Color icon in the quick color palette, shown in Figure 2.15.

When you create objects such as shapes in Flash, they're automatically stacked in the order they are created on a layer. You'll learn more about this stacking order in Chapter 3, "The Library, Symbols, and the Timeline," but for now, just make sure you draw the larger oval first, and then the smaller oval.

FIGURE 2.15
Selecting the No
Color icon creates
a shape with no
outline.

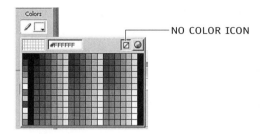

NO COLOR ICON

For the fill color, choose a light gray for the eye background color, and draw an oval on the stage. Then change the fill color in the toolbar to black, and draw a second oval, a bit smaller, underneath the first one, as shown in Figure 2.16. Press Shift while you're drawing this second oval to create a perfect circle.

FIGURE 2.16
The beginning of
drawing an eye.

Now click the Subselection tool in the toolbar (keyboard shortcut: **A**). Roll your mouse over the edge of the larger oval, and notice that the mouse pointer changes to show a solid or hollow square next to the pointer.

A hollow square signifies that the mouse is over an anchor point, and a solid square indicates that the mouse is over a line. Click a line (make sure the pointer shows a solid square) to highlight and show all the lines and anchor points this oval is made of. Next, still using the Subselection tool, select the anchor point at the far left and drag it to the left to try to make this shape look more like an eye (see Figure 2.17).

FIGURE 2.17
Selecting anchor
points and lines with
the Subselection tool.

Remember to use the Hand and Zoom shortcuts you've learned. Zoom in as close as you like using **Ctrl+spacebar** (Macintosh: **Command+spacebar**). You can also move the stage around (using the spacebar) so that the shape is in a comfortable area and size for you to work with.

Using Tangent Handles

Notice two small lines with dots extending from the anchor point you selected (see Figure 2.18). They're called *tangent handles,* and they control the curve or angles of the lines attached to that point. If you click a tangent handle and move it around, you'll see that it changes the curves of the line, and the handle on the other side of the point changes with it. If you want to move only one tangent handle, simply hold down the Alt key (Macintosh: Option key). Use these tangent handles to create an eye shape you're happy with. Remember to experiment and have some fun with it. You can always undo your last move with **Ctrl+Z** (Macintosh: **Command+Z**).

FIGURE 2.18
Using tangent handles.

Next, you need to move the small oval shape (the pupil of the eye). Click the Selection tool, select the pupil, and drag it on top of the larger oval, as shown in Figure 2.19.

FIGURE 2.19
Adding a pupil to the eye shape.

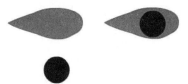

After you place the pupil and then deselect it, it's combined with the other oval shape. If you select the pupil again and move it away, you'll notice an empty space where the pupil was (see Figure 2.20). That's not a white fill; that's a blank area. Keep this in mind when you're moving shapes around. To avoid having a blank area when you move shapes, you can put shapes on different layers or convert them to symbols, but you'll learn more about that in Chapter 3.

FIGURE 2.20
The blank area that's left when you move a shape.

Now you have one eye, but you want two. To do this, first select both parts of the eye by double-clicking the shape. There are a few ways to duplicate shapes. You could select the entire eye, copy it with **Ctrl+C** (Macintosh: **Command+C**), and then paste it into another area on the stage with **Ctrl+V** (Macintosh: **Command+V**). Or, with the entire eye selected, click it and move it next to the original, but before you let go, press the Ctrl key (Macintosh: Option key). The mouse pointer shows a plus sign next to the pointer. When you let go of the mouse button (still holding down the Ctrl or Option key), the shape will be duplicated. Make sure the eyes aren't overlapping.

So now you have two eyes, but one is facing the wrong direction, so you need to flip it around. Deselect the eye. With the Selection tool, click and drag a rectangular selection box that covers the item you're selecting (see Figure 2.21).

FIGURE 2.21
Selecting one eye.

Next, you want to flip the eye on its horizontal axis. To do this, choose Modify, Transform, Flip Horizontal from the main menu. While the one eye is still selected, use the arrow keys to position it. Make sure it's relatively even with the left eye and not too close to the left eye.

The Free Transform Tool

To see how this tool works, use the eyes you drew in the previous section. Select the eyes on the stage, and then click the Free Transform tool in the toolbar (keyboard shortcut: **Q**), shown in Figure 2.22.

FIGURE 2.22

Selecting the Free Transform tool.

 FREE TRANSFORM TOOL

After you click the Free Transform tool, the eyes you selected display a black outline, with small black squares at the corners and in the middle of each side (see Figure 2.23). These squares are control points, which allow you to transform the shape of whatever you've selected.

FIGURE 2.23

Using the Free Transform tool.

If you roll directly over a corner, the mouse pointer shows double arrows, which lets you know you're rolling over a corner control point (see Figure 2.24). (If you're a little farther away from the corner, the mouse pointer changes to the rotate arrow, which is discussed next.) Click a corner control point, and move it around a little to resize the eye shapes. If you hold down the Shift key while doing this, the vertical and horizontal resizing are constrained to be exactly equal.

FIGURE 2.24

Selecting a corner control point.

 CORNER CONTROL POINT

The top and bottom control points (the ones in the center of the top and bottom borders of the selection box) change the height of the selection, and the control points at the sides (center of the left and right borders of the selection box) change the width of the selected shape.

If you move your mouse near a corner point, but not actually on the corner point, the mouse pointer changes to the rotate arrow, shown in Figure 2.25. Clicking and moving your mouse would rotate the shape. The default is to rotate from the transform center point, which is the white circle in the center of your selection. You can have it rotate from the opposite of the selected corner by holding down the Alt (Macintosh: Option) key while you drag the mouse. As well, you can move the transform center point by selecting it with your mouse and moving it to wherever you'd like. This changes the point from which transformations are applied, such as a rotation.

FIGURE 2.25
The rotate arrow.

If you roll over the lines between control points, the mouse pointer changes to the skew arrows shown in Figure 2.26. If you click a horizontal line, the shape is skewed horizontally. Clicking a vertical line of the selection box skews the shape vertically, as indicated by the direction of the skew arrows. If you hold down the Alt key, the transformation is applied from the transformation center point.

FIGURE 2.26
Skewing horizontally.

You can modify the shape in another way, by holding down the Ctrl key (Macintosh: Command key) as you roll over a corner control point. Your mouse pointer changes to a hollow arrowhead (see Figure 2.27). Click and move a few corner points around using this Free Transform method, which gives you even more freedom.

FIGURE 2.27
Using the Free
Transform method to
move control points.

If you hold down the Shift key in addition to the Ctrl (Macintosh: Command) key, the transformation is constrained by the corresponding horizontal or vertical corner, depending on the direction you move your mouse. This results in a transformation of two corners instead of one, similar to a bowtie effect. Notice that the mouse changes icons yet again, showing a bowtie icon under the hollow arrow when you have the Ctrl and Shift keys held down and are positioned over a corner point, as shown in Figure 2.28.

FIGURE 2.28
Using the Free
Transform method
with the Ctrl and
Shift keys held down.

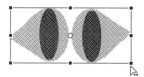

Of all the keyboard shortcuts, you'll probably find yourself using V (Selection tool), A (Subselection tool), and Q (Free Transform tool) the most, so get comfortable flipping between these tools with keyboard shortcuts. The spacebar (Hand tool) and **Ctrl+spacebar** (Macintosh: **Option+spacebar**) for zooming are also used often. While you're doing the exercises in this chapter, practice zooming in and out and moving around with the Hand tool shortcut.

Free Transform Tool Options

In the toolbar under the Options section, you'll see several icons that represent options for using the Free Transform tool (see Figure 2.29).

FIGURE 2.29
Free Transform tool options.

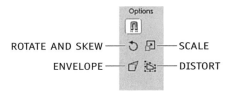

To use any of these options, simply click the icon. The following list describes what you can do with these options:

- **Rotate and Skew**   Turns your corner points into rotate points and your lines into skew points.

- **Distort**   Allows you to select any corner or midline point and move it around freely to distort the shape. Try it out—the results are interesting.

- **Scale**   Allows you to scale your object, in the same way as holding down the Shift key and selecting a corner point.

- **Envelope**   Gives you control of the Subselection tool. It's similar to the Distort option but gives you more points to choose from (see Figure 2.30). You can bend and stretch your shape a number of different ways.

FIGURE 2.30
Additional points are available with the Envelope option.

Try using these Free Transform options to play around with the eye shape. Try them with and without the Shift key so that you can see the difference on the corner points. Remember, you can always undo any actions and keep trying until you get the effect you want.

The Transform Panel

Now that you've learned about the Free Transform tool, open the Transform panel and take a look at the additional options available there (see Figure 2.31). To open the Transform panel, choose Window, Design Panels, Transform from the menu (keyboard shortcut: Windows **Ctrl+T**; Macintosh **Command+T**).

FIGURE 2.31
The Transform panel.

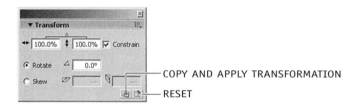

This panel serves two purposes: It allows you to see transformations numerically while you're applying them, and you can enter numbers directly in the fields to modify your shape. Press Tab or Enter to apply the settings after entering the numbers. There are also two buttons in the lower-right corner of the Transform panel:

- **Copy and Apply Transformation**   Use this button to apply a transformation and keep a copy of the original untransformed object. To use it, make your selection on the stage, perform your transformations using the fields in the Transform panel, and then click this button. The selected object on stage is the transformed one, with the original untransformed object underneath and not selected.

- **Reset**   The Reset button resets your shape to 100% with no rotation or skew. Keep in mind that after you've deselected your object, you can't reset it using this button. It works only if you've performed a transformation and haven't deselected the shape.

When you're transforming symbols, which you'll learn about in Chapter 3, keep in mind that you can deselect symbols, and then select them again, and the Transform panel shows you any transformations that have occurred, allowing you to alter or reset them.

When you're finished exploring the Transform panel, close or minimize it.

The Brush Tool

Click the Brush tool in the toolbar (keyboard shortcut: **B**). Notice that the options in your toolbar change. You now have two drop-down lists (see Figure 2.32). The one at the top is for selecting a brush size, and the one at the bottom is for selecting a brush shape. Chose a size and shape, and select a color using the toolbar or the Property inspector. To go with the eyes you've already created, paint a line to represent a nose on the stage.

FIGURE 2.32
Options for the Brush tool.

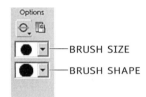

In the Property inspector, you have two options: Fill Color and Smoothing. The default for Smoothing is 50, but you can adjust it from 0 to 100. Setting it to 0 produces a very pixelated edge to your brush stroke; setting it to 100 smoothes out the line edges so that the brush stroke looks more fluid. Experiment with these options by painting several different lines, adjusting the brush size, brush shape, color, and smoothing level. Figure 2.33 shows some examples.

FIGURE 2.33
Lines created with the Brush tool.

The Pen Tool

If you have used Macromedia Freehand or Adobe Illustrator, you'll be familiar with the Pen tool, which allows you to draw using points and curves. It's similar to the Subselection tool in that you're drawing points that are connected with lines. If you're not experienced with this tool, it might take some getting used to.

First, click the Pen tool in the toolbar (keyboard shortcut: **P**), and then select fill and stroke colors from the toolbar or the Property inspector. For this example, select red for the stroke color and white for the fill color so that you can draw a mouth. In the Property inspector, set the stroke height to 3.

Click the stage, hold down the mouse button, and drag a bit before releasing the mouse button. Click another spot on the stage, and drag your mouse a bit before you release the mouse button. When you click and drag, you're actually controlling the angle of the curve that's between the two points. As you'll recall from working with the Subselection tool, this angle or curve is controlled by tangent handles. Dragging the mouse controls the tangent handles.

Use **Ctrl+Z** to undo any practice lines you've made with the Pen tool. With the Pen tool selected, you'll draw a mouth by clicking and dragging three points. Beginning with the left side of the mouth, click and drag your mouse straight down about a centimeter and release. The next point is the right side of the mouth, horizontally even with the first point; click and drag up about a centimeter before releasing. See Figure 2.34 for a reference.

FIGURE 2.34
Using the Pen tool to draw a mouth shape.

The final point is placed back at the original point you started with. Click this point and drag down about a centimeter before releasing, as shown in Figure 2.35. Notice that your pointer changes to show a small circle, called a *closing point* or an *endpoint*.

FIGURE 2.35
Completing the mouth shape with the Pen tool.

When you're using the Pen tool, you'll notice that your mouse pointer changes to several different icons. Here are the ones you'll see most often:

x cursor: Adding a point to a blank space on the stage

o shape: The closing point (endpoint) of a shape

Hollow arrow: Adjusting a tangent handle

In addition, if you hold your mouse cursor over the strokes and control points after you've drawn them, you'll see a few more icons:

+ cursor: Adding a control point to a stroke

- cursor: Removing a control point from a stroke

^ cursor: Removing tangent handles from a control point, making it a corner

You now have the basics of a mouth, and you can use the Subselection tool (keyboard shortcut: **A**) to modify it. Try adding a little curve in the top lip. You might also try the Free Transform tool with the Envelope option to modify the mouth shape.

Keep in mind that a transformation or resizing does not resize the stroke thickness or height. To change stroke height, you have to select the stroke and modify it in the Property inspector.

The Lasso Tool

The Lasso tool is a freehand selection tool, so it requires a steady hand. To try it, click the Lasso tool in the toolbar, and then click and drag the mouse on the stage to outline an area you want to select (see Figure 2.36). When you select an area, if you don't close the selection off, Flash connects your endpoint and start point with a straight line, so completing your selection area by connecting the start and endpoints is always safer, because you can be confident that the selection area is the shape you want.

FIGURE 2.36
Using the Lasso tool.

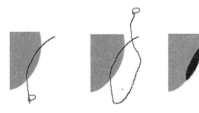

After you create a selection area, you can delete, transform, or change the color of that selection. You have two options for the Lasso tool: Magic Wand and Magic Wand Properties (see Figure 2.37). Use the Magic Wand to select a range of similarly colored adjacent pixels by clicking an image. The Magic Wand Properties option allows you to set the range of colors. If you set it to 0, you get only the pixels that are the same color as the one you selected. If you increase that number, you increase the range of the adjacent colors you can select.

MAGIC WAND ——— MAGIC WAND PROPERTIES

POLYGON MODE ———

Polygon Mode

When the Lasso tool is selected, you can select Polygon mode from the options in the toolbar (refer to Figure 2.37), which allows you to make a selection by using straight lines. Click, move your mouse, and then click again to draw the area you want to select. This method is useful if your selection area needs to be composed of straight lines. To finish selecting an area, simply double-click anywhere onscreen. When Polygon mode is not selected, if you make a selection and press **Alt** (Macintosh: **Option**) before you release the mouse button, you'll be in Polygon mode and can finish your selection with straight lines.

The Rectangle Tool

Click the Rectangle tool in the toolbar (keyboard shortcut: **R**). The Rectangle tool is similar to the Oval tool: You draw a shape by clicking and dragging from one corner to the other. If you hold the Shift key down, you constrain the vertical and horizontal lines so that it's a perfect square.

The Rectangle tool has one option in the toolbar: the Round Rectangle Radius, which is used to create a rectangle with rounded corners. Click the Round Rectangle Radius option in the toolbar, enter 10 for the Corner Radius setting, and click OK. This sets the radius of a rectangle's rounded corners to 10 points (see Figure 2.38).

FIGURE 2.38
A rectangle with a
corner radius of 10.

The PolyStar Tool

On the Rectangle tool icon in the toolbar is a small black arrow that indicates other options. If you click and hold the arrow, a small menu drops down (see Figure 2.39), showing the PolyStar tool. Click to select it.

FIGURE 2.39
The PolyStar tool menu.

In the Property inspector, click the Options button to access settings for controlling the PolyStar tool. You can select the style (Star or Polygon) as well as the number of sides and the star point size. Select a star with five points, leave the star point size at .5, and click OK. Figure 2.40 shows the results.

FIGURE 2.40
Creating a star with the PolyStar tool.

The Paint Bucket Tool

The Paint Bucket tool, which is very easy to use, allows you to change fill colors. After selecting this tool, select a fill color from the toolbar or the Property inspector, and click the fill you'd like to change. You can also use the Selection tool to select a fill and change it in the Property inspector.

The Ink Bottle Tool

Very similar to the Paint Bucket tool, the Ink Bottle tool is used for strokes instead of fills. If you'd like to change the color or height of any strokes you've drawn, you can use this tool. Simply select the tool, select a stroke color in the toolbar or the Property inspector, and then click the stroke you want to change. Using the Property inspector enables you to change the stroke height and style. You can also select a stroke with the Selection tool and change it in the Property inspector.

The Eyedropper Tool

Sometimes you need to find out exactly what color you've used in your work, and the Eyedropper tool comes in handy for this task. Select the Eyedropper tool (keyboard shortcut: I), and click any fill or stroke. The color is displayed in the toolbar and the Property inspector, allowing you to use it for other shapes, if you like. For a stroke, the stroke height, color, and style also show up in the Property inspector.

You can also use the Eyedropper tool to copy fill and stroke properties. Use the Selection tool to select a stroke, click the Eyedropper tool (making sure you leave the stroke selected), and then click another stroke. The properties of the originally selected stroke change to match the second one you selected with the Eyedropper tool. This method works the same way with fills.

The Eraser Tool

The Eraser tool is used to erase lines and fills freehand. One option for this tool, called the *faucet*, erases the entire shape when you click it (see Figure 2.41). It behaves similarly to the Paint Bucket tool, except it erases instead of fills. To use the faucet, simply select the Eraser tool, click the faucet icon in the Options section of the toolbar, and then click a fill. Poof! It's gone.

FIGURE 2.41

The Eraser tool.

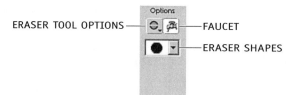

The drop-down list at the bottom, shown in Figure 2.41, allows you to select a shape for the Eraser tool. It's similar to selecting a brush shape for the Brush tool.

In Figure 2.41, notice the small drop-down list for selecting Eraser tool options. As shown in Figure 2.42, you can erase only fills, only lines (strokes), only selected fills, and inside an object. This last option, erasing from inside an object, works from where you start to erase and treats that fill as selected. Any erasing is confined to inside the fill you started erasing; it doesn't erase any other fills.

FIGURE 2.42
Options for the Eraser tool.

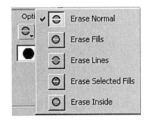

The Pencil Tool

The Pencil tool has one option in the toolbar, where you can choose from Straighten, Smooth, and Ink; these options affect how your lines are drawn. Click the Pencil tool in the toolbar, and try writing your signature a few times, using these three settings. To simulate handwriting, the Ink setting is usually the best. Select a dark blue stroke color and a stroke height of 1, and write your signature below the face you've drawn. Figure 2.43 shows a signature created with the Pencil tool; as you can see, unless you have a tablet, it's hard to write with a mouse.

FIGURE 2.43
Writing a signature with the Pencil tool.

There are a number of ways to straighten and smooth out lines in Flash. There are two reasons for doing this. The first reason is optimization. The more curves, tangent handles, and points you have, the larger the file size and the more processor-intensive, which means your content might play choppily on older computers. The second reason is visual. Sometimes you need to smooth out a line or a curve because that's the way you want it to look. One method is using the options available with the Selection tool. Underneath the magnet icon are two options: Straighten and Smooth.

You'll learn other ways to optimize shapes and lines in Chapter 14, "Images."

Select your signature with the Selection tool, and try both options. They are actual actions, so you can use them more than once. Each time you click with one of these options, it has a small effect on your lines. Try it on your signature. Remember, you can always undo any action.

The Text Tool

Select the Text tool from the toolbar (keyboard shortcut: **T**) and add some text to the stage. There are two basic types of text in Flash:

In this chapter, you learn about static text, and in Chapter 13, "Text," you'll learn about editable text.

- **Static text** This text is a graphic element, so you can color it, change the font, rotate it, skew it, turn it upside down, and even animate it. (Even though it's called static text, you can still edit it in the authoring environment, but not in a published movie.)

- **Editable text** Editable text can be input or dynamic text. Input text is used for user input, such as a username or a password; dynamic text can be controlled and changed with ActionScript.

With the Text tool selected, click anywhere on the stage to add an expanding text box, which simply means that the text box expands as you type in it. The only way to end a line in this type of text box is with a hard return. If you click and drag before releasing the mouse button, however, you can create a fixed-width text box that auto-wraps your text to fit the width of the box. For the purposes of this chapter, click just once to create an expanding text box.

Notice the text options available in the Property inspector (see Figure 2.44). Before you type anything in the text box you created, make some changes to the properties. Select Arial for the font, 36 for the font size, and black for the font color in the Property inspector. Among other options, you can select bold or italic formatting and adjust the alignment (left-justified is the default).

FIGURE 2.44
The Property inspector: Text.

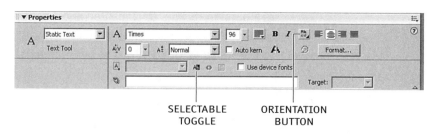

SELECTABLE
TOGGLE

ORIENTATION
BUTTON

Now type your first and last name in the text box, and notice that the box expands to fit your name. The small white circle in the top-right corner is the *handle icon* (see Figure 2.45). When it's a circle, that indicates you're working with an expanding text box.

FIGURE 2.45
An expanding
text box.

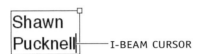
HANDLE ICON

Fixed-Width Text Box

If you click the handle icon shown in Figure 2.45 and move it left or right, you can set the width for this text box, thus changing it to a fixed-width text box. Click the handle icon and move it to the left so that the text box is wide enough to fit your name on two lines (see Figure 2.46).

FIGURE 2.46
Creating a fixed-width
text box.

Shawn
Pucknell I-BEAM CURSOR

Notice that the handle icon changes to a square to indicate it's a fixed-width text box. Any text you enter in this text box will now word-wrap to fit the width you've specified. You can also use basic text-editing commands in these text boxes, such as cut, copy, and paste. (Use the keyboard shortcuts or the commands in the Edit menu.) You can use these commands with text documents open in other applications; for example, you could copy text from your fixed-width text box and paste it into a Word document, or vice versa.

Notice the blinking cursor (the I-beam) in the text box at the end of your name. If you make any more changes to the properties, such as changing the font size, they aren't applied to your typed name because that text isn't currently selected. In Edit Text mode, selecting and editing text work in much the same way as other text editing programs: Use your mouse to highlight text, press the Delete key to remove text, press the arrow keys to move around within the text, and so on.

Select the entire text box by using the Selection tool. The text box changes to display a blue outline, meaning the text box is selected, but you're no longer in Edit Text mode (see Figure 2.47).

Whenever you see the I-beam cursor, you can't use any keyboard shortcuts while selecting a text box. If you type a letter, it appears in the text box because you are in Edit Text mode.

FIGURE 2.47
A selected text box.

Shawn
Pucknell

Text Properties

For more information
on working with text
properties, see
Chapter 13.

Now that the text box is selected, you can change text properties and
have them applied to the entire text box. You can change the color,
change the font, use bold or italic formatting, and so forth. If you do
change a setting that affects the text size, you might find that your name
no longer fits on two lines. Try setting the font at a slightly larger size;
you'll see that your name now takes up more than two lines, but you can
fix that. Double-click inside the text box to change to the Text tool and
enter Edit Text mode again. Now you can simply click the handle icon
and move it left or right until your name fits on two lines again. You can
also adjust the following text properties:

- **Alignment**   You can also adjust the alignment (justification) of your
  text box. The default is left, which is best for most uses. Click the center alignment button in the Property inspector to center the text.

- **Orientation**   If you click the Orientation button (shown in Figure
  2.44), you see three choices: Horizontal (the default); Vertical, Left
  to Right; and Vertical, Right to Left. Select Vertical, Left to Right. The
  text box is sized to hold your text horizontally, so the text looks a bit
  jumbled. To fix it, you need to make the font slightly smaller, but
  you can't do this in the Property inspector because text in the text
  box isn't selected. Remember, you can choose the Selection tool to
  get out of Edit Text mode, but you can also press Escape. When you
  do, you'll see that the text box is selected, you're out of Edit Text
  mode, and the Text tool is still your selected tool. Now any changes
  you make in the Property inspector will affect text in the selected
  text box. Decrease the font size until you can see your name on two
  lines. Try selecting the other two orientation options to see what
  happens. In the process of changing the orientation, you change the
  text box's width, so double-click inside the text box to enter Edit text
  mode, and adjust the width until your name fits on two lines again.

- **Kerning**   You can adjust kerning (character spacing) using the
  Property inspector, or deselect the Auto Kern check box if the font
  has built-in kerning information.

- **Selectable**   The Selectable toggle icon (shown in Figure 2.44) allows you to specify whether this text box can be selected in your SWF file. If it's selectable, viewers can select, copy, and paste the text in it. This option is useful for large text boxes of information that others might want to copy. You shouldn't use it for small text boxes, such as titles, or for text you don't want users to copy. The default is off, or non-selectable.

- **Paragraph Format**   If you click the Format button in the Property inspector, the Format Options dialog box opens (see Figure 2.48), where you can set indenting, line spacing, and margins for your text box.

FIGURE 2.48
The Format Options dialog box.

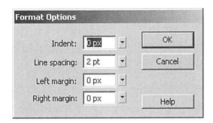

Note that you can also use the Text menu on the main menu bar to adjust a text box's font, size, style, alignment, and tracking, but you don't have a preview as you do in the Property inspector.

CUSTOMIZING YOUR TOOLBAR

This release of Flash allows you to customize your toolbar. Choosing Edit, Customize Tools Panel opens the Customize Toolbar dialog box (see Figure 2.49). Here you can map any tools available in Flash to different locations on the toolbar. Clicking a tool in the mini toolbar at the left selects the corresponding tool. You can then delete or add the selected tool, move toolbar items around, delete the ones you don't use often, or even bury tools in submenus of other tools, much like the PolyStar tool being found in a submenu of the Rectangle tool.

FIGURE 2.49
The Customize
Toolbar dialog box.

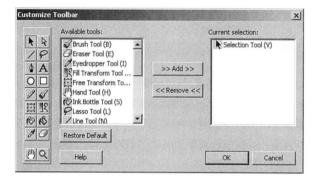

POINTS TO REMEMBER

- The templates available from the Start page are great starting points for projects of all kinds.

- You can always undo anything you've done in Flash (up to the last 100 moves), so don't be afraid to try out all the tools and experiment with them.

- It's a good habit to deselect objects before selecting any new objects, especially when you're working with many objects.

- Keyboard shortcuts save you time. Start by using the common ones, such as V for the Selection tool, A for the Subselection tool, Q for the free transform tool, and T for the Text tool.

- Temporary keyboard shortcuts are very useful, and make it practically unnecessary to use certain tools. For example, you can use **Ctrl+spacebar** to zoom in and **Ctrl+Shift+spacebar** to zoom out, and use the spacebar for the Hand tool.

- The Shift key often works to constrain height and width. When drawing an oval or rectangle, hold down the Shift key to create a perfect circle or square. When you're transforming objects, holding down the Shift key ensures that a transformation is applied to height and width evenly.

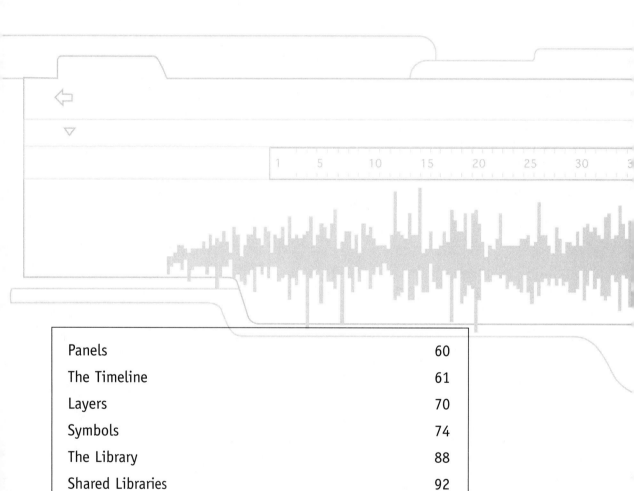

CHAPTER 3

THE LIBRARY, SYMBOLS, AND THE TIMELINE

THIS CHAPTER INTRODUCES YOU TO THE TIMELINE, LAYERS, AND THE ALL-powerful symbol. These components are the heart and soul of Flash, and understanding them is a huge step toward mastering Flash. You'll also learn how to use the Library, where all your symbols and multimedia assets are stored.

PANELS

Flash MX 2004 has 21 *panels* (windows) that you can open, close, and move around. Don't be intimidated by the number of panels, as most are self-explanatory. (For example, the Color Swatches panel is where you pick colors from swatches.) As well, you'll never need to have all panels open at once. In fact, after you know your way around and are creating your own Flash movies, you usually have only three to five open at any given time, as shown in Figure 3.1.

FIGURE 3.1
Flash MX 2004 with the Property inspector, the Library, and the Info panel open.

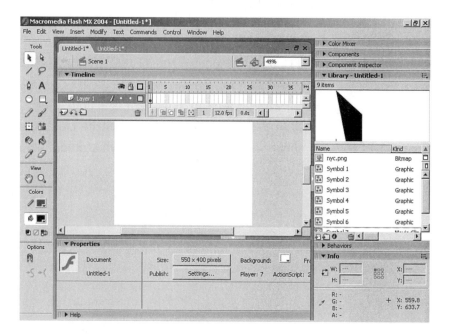

Panel States

Most panels can be in one of three states:

- **Maximized**   Open with content visible.

- **Minimized**   Open but minimized (visible only as a title bar).

- **Closed**   Not visible or open. To open, choose Window from the main menu or the corresponding keyboard shortcut, which can be found next to the panel name in the main menu.

A handy keyboard shortcut is the F4 key, which toggles between showing and hiding all panels. When you set panels to be hidden, the only windows you can see are the timeline and the stage.

Docking Panels

You can move a panel simply by clicking the icon at the top-left corner, called the *gripper*, and dragging the panel around the screen (see Figure 3.2). When you position your mouse over the gripper, the cursor changes to a four-way arrow.

FIGURE 3.2
Use the gripper to drag a panel to another location.

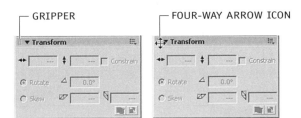

When a panel is moved close to a dockable area, such as the border at the right, top, or bottom of your screen, a black rectangle appears. If you release the panel while this black rectangle is showing, the panel snaps into place and is *docked*. To undock a panel, simply drag it away from the docked area using the gripper, and it becomes a floating panel again. You can dock many panels; the majority of them can be docked on the right side, but a few are situated better when docked at the bottom, such as the Property inspector and the Help and Action panels.

THE TIMELINE

The Timeline, which has traditionally been the heart of Flash, is usually docked directly to the document window. It allows you to see content while you're working, showing it to you along a series of time slices. The Timeline is one of the key concepts in Flash. For people with experience in Macromedia Director or any digital audio or video work, this concept should be fairly straightforward. Those coming from a traditional programming background might find it a little more difficult to grasp. Try using the Timeline features throughout the following section to make sure you understand how it works.

The Timeline is made up of two areas: layers and frames. The layer area is on the left side, and the frames area is on the right (see Figure 3.3). When starting a new project, you see a layer labeled Layer 1, which you can rename simply by double-clicking on the name.

Naming layers appropriately is a good practice, especially when you get into larger projects with dozens or even hundreds of layers, or if you share files with other people. You should also create layer folders to further organize layers in large projects.

FIGURE 3.3
The Timeline, showing the frames area and the layers area.

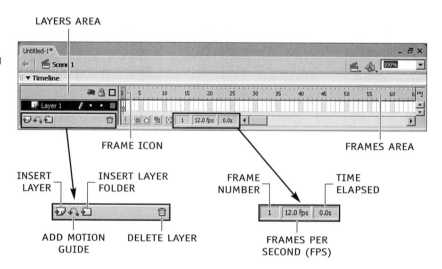

Frames Area

On the bottom bar of the Timeline, under the frames area, you see three numbers. The number on the left tells you what frame the playhead is currently on. The number in the middle is the frame rate, measured in frames per second (fps). The number on the right indicates how much time has elapsed, based on where the playhead is. As shown in Figure 3.3, no time has elapsed, because you're currently positioned on frame 1.

Layers Area

You can add, move, and delete layers as needed. Layers are useful for organizing your objects so that they can act independently of each other, especially when animating (covered in Chapter 6, "Animation, Effects, and Masking"). The order of these layers is important because they're exported in that order in your final movie. Anything on a top layer overlaps anything on a layer below it.

At the bottom of the layers area you'll see four icons (shown previously in Figure 3.3). These icons, covered in more detail later in this chapter, allow you to insert a layer, add a motion guide (explained in Chapter 6), add a layer folder, and delete a layer.

Working with Timeline Areas and Frame Views

Because you're starting out with an empty document, the first frame in the frames area on Layer 1 is shown as an empty rectangle with a small hollow circle inside (shown previously in Figure 3.3). Using the Oval tool, draw a fairly large circle on the stage. The Timeline doesn't indicate what's on the stage, but you can tell that this frame contains content now because the frame icon changes to a rectangle with a solid circle (instead of a hollow circle).

You can adjust the size and view of frames on the Timeline by using the drop-down list at the top-right corner of the Timeline (see Figure 3.4).

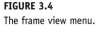

FIGURE 3.4
The frame view menu.

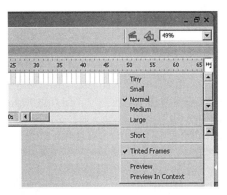

The default setting is Normal, which is how the frames presently look. You can adjust the size to Tiny, Small, Medium, or Large, which changes the width of the frames. Also, when you're working with a lot of layers, selecting the Short option shortens the height of the displayed frames. Try the different settings now to see the changes in your frames.

To see a preview in the timeline of what's on the stage, you can select Preview or Preview in Context. The Preview in Context option shows you the contents of the entire stage in the timeline frames, as shown in Figure 3.5.

FIGURE 3.5
Viewing frames with the Preview in Context option.

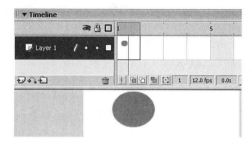

The Preview option also displays the contents of the stage in the frames, but it fills the frame with the content, as shown in Figure 3.6, instead of showing the entire stage as Preview in Context does.

FIGURE 3.6
Viewing frames with the Preview option.

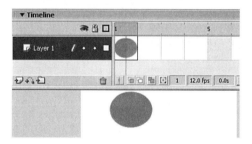

Selecting Frames

To select a frame, click it directly in the Timeline. Notice on the left side of the Property inspector that the icon and name indicate that a frame is selected, as shown in Figure 3.7.

FIGURE 3.7
The Property inspector with a frame selected.

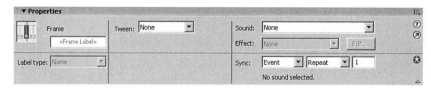

When a frame is selected, you can move it to another location on the timeline by clicking and dragging it.

With a frame selected, you can use any of the commands under the Modify, Timeline menu or use the Frames context menu (see "Using the Frames Context Menu" later in this chapter). You can also delete a selected frame with the Delete key. To select multiple frames, even on multiple layers, click and drag the frames you want. To select nonconsecutive frames, press Ctrl and click.

Using Keyframes

Change the view back to Normal. Click frame 1 in the Timeline, and add a frame by pressing F5, the keyboard shortcut for inserting a frame. You can also choose Insert, Timeline, Frame, but keyboard shortcuts are quicker. You now have two frames of content. Press F5 a few more times and add some more frames, until you have 15 frames total (see Figure 3.8). Notice the small white rectangle at the end of your frames. This is the endframe symbol, signifying the end of the frames.

FIGURE 3.8

Adding 15 frames on the Timeline.

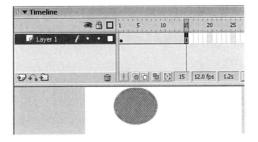

You can see that not all the frames have a solid dot—just the first frame. This indicates that you added frames, not keyframes. Every time content changes, it's indicated by displaying a dot to represent a new keyframe; keyframes define a change in Flash animation sequences. To see how this works, click frame 5 and press F6 to convert frame 5 to a keyframe. (You can also convert a frame to a keyframe by choosing Insert, Timeline, Keyframe from the main menu.) The content in frame 5 is technically the same, but Flash treats it as different content because you've converted the frame to a keyframe. With keyframes, you can easily tell Flash that you want content to change when you have content across many frames. You now have two dots, representing two keyframes, on your Timeline (see Figure 3.9).

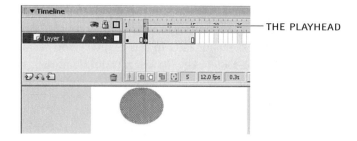

The small red rectangle shown in Figure 3.9 indicates the position of the playhead. You can move it by simply clicking and dragging. Move the playhead to frame 1, and change the color of the circle on frame 1. When you move the playhead across frames (moving across frames is called *scrubbing*), notice that you have different content. You have a circle on the stage from frames 1 to 4 and a different colored circle from frames 5 to 10.

Using Empty Keyframes

Click frame 10, and create an empty keyframe by choosing Modify, Timeline, Convert to Blank Keyframe (keyboard shortcut: **F7**). A blank keyframe is simply a keyframe without content (see Figure 3.10); regular keyframes include the previous frame's content, but blank keyframes do not. All the frames after a blank keyframe are also empty, but they aren't keyframes; they're just blank frames. Sometimes blank keyframes are used to indicate when layers have areas that don't require any content.

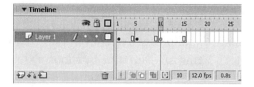

Take a look at Figure 3.11 and see what the frames look like in Preview mode.

FIGURE 3.11
Viewing your frames
in Preview mode.

As you can see, there's a circle from frames 1 to 4, a different colored circle from frames 5 to 9, and nothing from frames 10 to 15. Change back to Normal mode. Remember, you can change to any view you're comfortable with at any time.

A Quick Test of the Movie

Test the movie to see what it looks like. The simple way is to press Enter, which is the keyboard shortcut, or you can choose Control, Play from the menu. Flash plays your movie and stops at the end. Your first Flash movie! Press Enter a few more times to see it again. This method is a simple test, used to check graphics and placement more than anything else. You won't be able to test the movie's true speed, for example, because Flash plays a bit slower during this test method. You can't test most ActionScript and Behaviors with this method, either, but you can test them by using the Test Movie command (discussed next).

The next way to test your movie, which you'll use more often, is the Test Movie command. The keyboard shortcut is **Ctrl+Enter** (Macintosh: **Command+Enter**), or you can choose Control, Test Movie from the menu. With this method, you can see what your movie looks like rendered as an actual SWF file in the built-in Flash Player. You can also check settings such as the bandwidth profile, but you'll get to that in Chapter 23, "Publishing." Close the Test Movie window for now.

Clearing Keyframes

To see how to clear or remove keyframes, click the keyframe on frame 5 in the timeline, and press **Shift+F6**, the keyboard shortcut. You can also choose Modify, Timeline, Clear Keyframe from the menu. Remember that F6 adds a keyframe, so **Shift+F6** is the reverse—clearing a keyframe. Next, remove the keyframe at frame 10. You should end up with one keyframe at frame 1 and frames going up to frame 15.

Using Frame Labels

For more information on ActionScript and Behaviors, see Chapters 7, "Behaviors," and 8, "Introduction to ActionScript."

With a frame selected, you can enter a label in the Property inspector in the Frame text box. You can also specify one of the three types of labels (see Figure 3.12):

- **Name** This type of label allows you to use ActionScript and Behaviors to move the playhead of your movie. You can use frame names to tell the playhead where to go, as in "Go to the label called home." Name labels are also great for helping you keep your timeline organized because everything is clearly labeled in the authoring environment.

- **Comment** Comment labels are useful for adding comments in your Timeline for internal use. They are especially useful when working with teams, when more than one person is accessing the same FLA file. Comments don't have to be just a few words; you can make them as descriptive and as long as you like (even a few hundred characters).

- **Anchor** These labels are used to simplify navigation in Flash. Viewers can use them with the forward and back buttons in their browsers to move from anchor frame to anchor frame or scene to scene. To use anchor frame labels, you need to select the Flash with Named Anchors option in the HTML tab of the Publish Settings dialog box (see Chapter 23 for more information).

FIGURE 3.12
The three different types of frame labels.

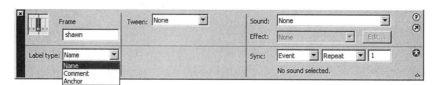

Using the Frames Context Menu

You can access many of the menu commands discussed previously by using the Frames context menu, shown in Figure 3.13. To access this menu, right-click (Macintosh: Control-click) any frame in your timeline. The commands in this menu are applied to the frames you've selected.

FIGURE 3.13
The Frames context menu.

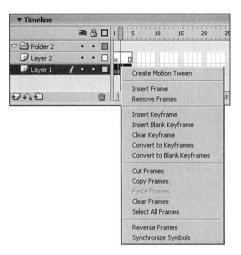

Any commands that are grayed out are not available because of the selected frame (or because no frame is selected). So you can't use the command to remove a frame if you don't have one selected, for example. The following commands are available from the Frames context menu:

- **Create Motion Tween**   Used when creating animation frames, this command is explained in Chapter 6.

- **Insert Frame**   Inserts a frame in the selected frame or empty area.

- **Remove Frames**   Deletes the selected frames.

- **Insert Keyframe**   Inserts a frame and makes it a keyframe using the content that's selected.

- **Insert Blank Keyframe**   Inserts a frame and makes it an empty keyframe.

- **Clear Keyframe**   If a keyframe is selected, this command changes it to a normal frame.

- **Convert to Keyframes**   Changes the selected frame to a keyframe.

- **Convert to Blank Keyframes**   Converts the selected frame to a blank keyframe.

- **Cut Frames**   Cuts the selected frames and moves them to your computer's clipboard, allowing you to paste them elsewhere.

- **Copy Frames**   Copies the selected frames to your computer's clipboard, allowing you to paste them elsewhere.

- **Clear Frames**   Removes any content in the selected frames.

- **Select All Frames**   Selects all frames in the timeline.

- **Reverse Frames**   Reverses the order of the selected frames.

- **Synchronize Symbols**   This command is used to synchronize symbols in animation tweens, which are discussed in Chapter 6.

LAYERS

In addition to creating frames, you can create layers. Simply click the Insert Layer icon at the bottom left of the Timeline (see Figure 3.14).

FIGURE 3.14
Adding a layer.

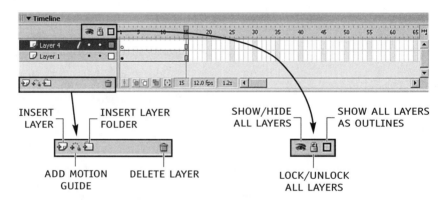

You can move any layer up or down to change its stacking order by clicking the layer's icon or the layer name and dragging it up or down. Remember that the top layer in the Timeline is the top layer in your rendered movie. Keep in mind, too, that the content on layers can overlap; sometimes this is an important aspect of your design. You can also delete a layer by selecting it and clicking the Delete Layer icon. Here are other actions you can perform on layers in the Timeline:

- **Layer Folders**   You can create layer folders by clicking the Add Folder icon, which is a smart way to keep your layers organized when you have several of them. Like most folders, you can open and close a layer folder to show its contents (see Figure 3.15). To name a layer folder, double-click the folder name and enter a name.

FIGURE 3.15

Two layer folders: one open showing two layers and one closed.

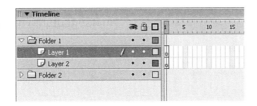

- **Show/Hide All Layers** If you want to hide a layer, click the dot under the Show/Hide All Layers icon (the eye) on that layer. To show that layer again, just click the dot again. To show or hide all layers, click the icon itself, which affects all layers. Note that this setting doesn't affect the published movie; it's just a different view in author mode. Hidden layers *are* published in your movie. This feature is handy when you have lots of objects and want to hide some layers to reduce clutter in your document.

- **Lock/Unlock All Layers** To lock a layer so that the content can't be changed, simply click the dot under the Lock/Unlock All Layers icon (the padlock) on the layer you want to lock. To unlock it, simply click again. Clicking the icon itself locks or unlocks all layers. You'll want to use this feature often so that you don't inadvertently change a layer's contents when changing other content.

- **Show All Layers as Outlines** You can have any layer displayed as outlines only. To do this, click the dot under the Show All Layers as Outlines icon (the small square) for that layer. To view the layer in normal mode, click it again. To view *all* layers as outlines, click the icon itself. Note that this setting doesn't affect the published movie; it's just a different view for authoring mode. It's useful if you have complex artwork on the stage that's causing Flash to slow down. It's also useful for aligning objects and seeing objects that are behind other items.

Using the Layer Context Menu

Most of the previous actions are also accessible through the context menu (see Figure 3.16). To open it, right-click a layer.

FIGURE 3.16
The Layer context
menu.

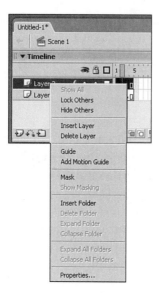

The commands in this menu change slightly depending on what state layers are in. If a command is grayed out, it's not available. These are the commands you can access:

- Show All (layers)

- Lock Others

- Hide Others

- Insert Layer

- Delete Layer

These next commands, used for animation layers, are explored in Chapter 6:

- Guide

- Add Motion Guide

- Mask

- Show Masking

The following commands are used with layer folders:

- Insert Folder

- Delete Folder

- Expand Folder

- Collapse Folder

- Expand All Folders

- Collapse All Folders

The last command, Properties, is explained in the next section.

Working with Layer Properties

You can open the Layer Properties dialog box with the context menu mentioned previously, or you can double-click the layer's layer icon. (Note that you must click directly on the layer icon. Too far left, and nothing happens; too far right, and you enter Edit Name mode for the layer.) You can also open the Layer Properties dialog box by choosing Modify, Timeline, Layer Properties from the main menu. Even though this dialog box is called Layer Properties, it actually shows the properties for a layer *and* a layer folder (see Figure 3.17).

FIGURE 3.17
The Layer Properties
dialog box.

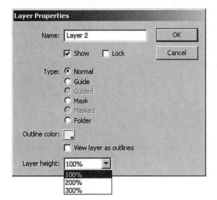

In this dialog box, you can adjust the following settings:

- **Name**   View and edit the layer name here.

- **Type**   View and change the layer type to one of the following options:

    - Normal

    - Guide

    - Guided

- Mask

- Masked

- Folder

- **Outline Color**   Double-click to change the layer outline color.

- **View Layer as Outlines**   Select this check box to view the layer as outlines, or clear it to view the layer in Normal mode.

Mask and guide layers are explained in Chapter 6.

- **Layer Height**   Select a layer height from this drop-down list: 100%, 200%, or 300%.

SYMBOLS

One of the most powerful features of Flash is the symbol. Symbols play a key role in Flash's capability to deliver low-bandwidth content and allow Flash to flex its interactive powers. *Symbols* are reusable elements that can contain graphics, images, buttons, sound, video, and text.

To see how symbols work, first draw a circle on the stage of a new Flash document. To convert this circle shape to a symbol, select the circle, including the stroke, and then choose Modify, Convert to Symbol (keyboard shortcut: **F8**). The dialog box shown in Figure 3.18 opens.

FIGURE 3.18
The Convert to Symbol dialog box.

Enter the name `circle`, and choose Movie Clip as the Behavior. Next to the label Registration are nine dots. The top-left dot is the default registration point and the most commonly used, but you can select any dot to change your movie's registration point (in other words, the movie clip's *origin*). When you're using ActionScript to move a symbol to the coordinates 0,0 on the stage, for example, the registration point you selected for your symbol is the point that aligns to 0,0 on the stage. Click OK to finish creating your circle symbol. Notice that there's now a blue keyline around your circle and a small black cross at the top-left corner, which is the registration point you picked.

Symbols and the Library

When you create a symbol, it's automatically added to the library. Open the Library panel, shown in Figure 3.19, by choosing Window, Library from the menu (keyboard shortcut: Windows **Ctrl+L**; Macintosh **Command+L**).

FIGURE 3.19
The Library panel.

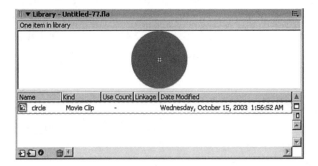

There's only one object in the library: a movie clip symbol called `circle`. You can see the name and type of the symbol (the symbol type is listed under the Kind column), how many times it's used in your movie, and data for linkage and the date modified. Clicking any of these headings re-sorts the items by that heading. Generally, the panel isn't open this wide, as you don't normally need all this information; usually the information in the Name and Kind columns is enough. The top part of the Library panel is the Preview window, which gives you a preview of the symbol you've selected in the Library. You can resize the Library panel if needed (see "The Library," later in this chapter).

If the Library panel is blocking the stage, use the gripper to move it to the right and dock it so that it's out of the way, but still open so you can see it. Make sure the circle on stage is selected, and delete it by pressing Delete. Notice that even though there's nothing on the stage now, the Library panel still shows your circle symbol. Flash stores all symbols in the library, whether they're used on the stage or not. A symbol on the stage is actually an instance of the original symbol, a copy that references the one in the Library. To illustrate, drag the circle symbol from the Library onto the stage. You can click the name and drag, but it's easier to drag the image from the Preview window at the top; this method also gives you a visual cue that you're selecting the right symbol. Next, drag two more symbols onto the stage, so you have three total instances, side by side.

Working with Symbol Properties

Select the instance of the circle symbol on the far left of the stage, and take a look at the Property inspector (see Figure 3.20). You can see and change the Behavior that's been assigned (currently set to Movie Clip), the height and width, and the x and y coordinates (the symbol's distance from the top-left corner—the registration point you set earlier). The Property inspector also indicates that this symbol is an instance of the circle symbol. You can use the Color drop-down list at the right to adjust the brightness, tint, and alpha. The Advanced option is a combination of the Tint and Alpha options.

FIGURE 3.20
Viewing a symbol in the Property inspector.

You can change the behavior or color of an instance of a symbol, but this change does *not* affect the original symbol in the Library. It changes only the instance of the currently selected symbol.

Choose the Tint option (see Figure 3.21) to change the circle's color. You can adjust the RGB values for your color using the three text boxes, or you can use the color picker. You can also set the color's saturation from 0 to 100%. Pick a blue color and set the saturation to 100%.

FIGURE 3.21
Tint options.

Select the middle instance of the circle symbol and change its color to yellow with 100% saturation. Then select the rightmost symbol and adjust its alpha (transparency) setting to 30%. Notice that the left and middle instances don't show any outlines or strokes because you set their saturation to 100%.

Using instances (copies) of symbols in the library helps reduce file size because Flash has to load that image only once. Every time an instance appears on stage, Flash needs to load very little information—usually just an x,y coordinate. If this symbol is a complex 100KB drawing, a large bitmap image, or even a video, thanks to the beauty of symbols, your end user needs to load it only once.

Editing Symbols

There are a few ways to edit a symbol, and you'll learn some more techniques later in this chapter. One way is through the Library panel. You can select a symbol in the Library and then double-click the image in the Preview window, or you can double-click the icon next to the symbol name in the Library. Choose one method and edit the symbol—perhaps by changing its size or color. The stage now shows the contents of the circle symbol. Notice that the information bar just above the Timeline now displays Scene 1 circle, which means you're editing the circle symbol and are no longer on the main Timeline, as shown in Figure 3.22.

FIGURE 3.22
The information bar.

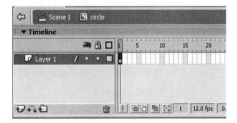

Draw a square about the same size as the circle, and position it so that it overlaps the circle's bottom-right corner. Make it a gray square with a black stroke, and remember to set the corner radius to 0. It should look similar to Figure 3.23.

FIGURE 3.23
Adding to a square to the circle symbol.

When you're done, return to the main Timeline. There are a few ways to do this. You can click Scene 1 in the information bar, or you can click the arrow at the far left of the information bar. The keyboard shortcut is **Ctrl+E** (Macintosh: **Command+E**). Because all the symbols on the stage are instances, the changes you made to this one instance have been applied to all the other instances.

Arranging Symbols

If your instances aren't overlapping, move them by using the Selection tool so that they are, as shown in Figure 3.24. Notice that you can see some of the middle instance through the instance on the right because it's transparent.

FIGURE 3.24
Three colored instances.

When you place items on a layer, they are layered or stacked in the order you place them, with the most recent on top. You can change that order if you want. Select the right circle instance, and choose Modify, Arrange, Send to Back from the menu. Now the middle instance no longer shows through the third instance; the middle instance is on top of the third instance, which is no longer transparent. In that same menu, you can toggle the Lock option off or on. Toggling it on locks the stacking order of any selected items and effectively prevents changes from being made to them.

Editing Symbols in Place

You can also edit a symbol in a slightly different way. Double-click the far-left circle on the stage. You'll be in Edit mode as you were before, but you can still see the content on the stage. This is Edit in Place mode. If you make any changes to this symbol, you can actually see them change on the stage as well. Use the Free Transform tool to modify the square by moving the top-left corner up a bit. When you do, you'll see your change reflected in the other two symbols on the stage. Remember, you're modifying the actual symbol, so all instances are affected. Even though you can see the other items on the stage, you can't move or select them, which is indicated by their grayed-out appearance. To return, click Scene 1 in the information bar, or press **Ctrl+E** (Macintosh: **Command+E**).

Duplicating Symbols

Right-click the circle symbol name in the Library, and select Duplicate to open the Duplicate Symbol dialog box. Change this instance name to Circle 2. You now have two movie clip symbols in the library. Even though they are identical in content right now, Flash treats them as completely different symbols. Edit the Circle 2 symbol by double-clicking the icon beside its name in the Library. Check the information bar to make sure you're editing Circle 2. Delete what's left of the circle, including any stroke. You should be left with the square you modified. Return to the main stage (keyboard shortcut: Windows **Ctrl+E**; Macintosh **Command+E**).

The stage still has the same three objects on it, indicating that nothing's changed. Select the middle instance on the stage, and in the Property inspector, click Swap. Select Circle 2 and click OK. You're returned to the stage, and the middle instance has been swapped with an instance of the Circle 2 symbol.

Using the Symbols Context Menu

Right-click the instance at the far left to see the context menu for a movie clip (see Figure 3.25). This menu has simple actions such as Cut, Copy, Paste, Select All, and Deselect All. (You can find these options in the Edit menu as well, but using context menus or keyboard shortcuts is faster.) This context menu also contains the following options:

- **Free Transform**   This option is the same as clicking the Free Transform tool.

- **Arrange**   The options in this submenu are shown in Figure 3.25. You can rearrange symbol instances by selecting Bring to Front or Send to Back, for example.

- **Edit, Edit in Place, and Edit in New Window**   Select these options to determine how you'll edit your symbol. Edit in New Window simply opens a new window (also available in the Edit menu), for example.

- **Swap Symbol and Duplicate Symbol**   You've already learned how to access these options using different methods.

- **Convert to Symbol**   This option might seem strange because you're already working with a symbol, but you could be right-clicking a shape, or, as you'll learn later, you can have a symbol within a symbol.

- **Timeline Effects**   You can use this option to easily and quickly create animation effects, such as Blur, Drop Shadow, and Explode. You'll learn more about these effects in Chapter 6.

- **Break Apart**   This option is for breaking apart symbols, groups, or bitmaps. Breaking apart a symbol on the stage effectively breaks apart that instance of the symbol, leaving you with whatever content was inside the symbol on your stage. The unaffected original symbol still exists in the Library, however. Breaking apart bitmaps and groups (breaking apart a group is equivalent to ungrouping) is explained in Chapter 14, "Images."

- **Distribute to Layers**   This option allows you to select multiple objects (bitmaps, shapes, symbols, and so forth) on one layer, and distribute each item onto different layers. Selecting three items on one layer and applying this command would result in three layers, each containing an object. As you'll learn in Chapter 6, tweens can have only one object on each layer; this Distribute to Layers command can help organize your assets for tweening.

FIGURE 3.25
The Symbols context menu.

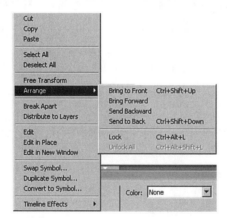

Symbol Behaviors

Now that you've looked at the basics of symbols, it's time to learn what types of behaviors they can have. Keep in mind that all symbol types—movie clips, graphics, and buttons—have their own timelines and appear in the Library. You can select the following symbol types (which are discussed in more detail in the following sections):

- **Movie clip**   A movie clip is like a mini Flash document. It can have actions, a timeline with as many frames as you need, and many layers, and can contain other movie clips, graphics, buttons, sounds—almost anything you can put in a Flash movie. Also, a movie clip's timeline is separate from any other timeline. All these features make movie clips powerful and useful in Flash.

- **Graphic**   A graphic symbol is a bit more limited in what it can do. It can't contain actions or audio, but it can contain content. A graphic symbol is mostly used to hold graphics that you use on the main timeline or in a movie clip. Graphic symbol timelines depend on the main timeline or the timeline of the movie clip symbol they're attached to.

- **Button**   Button symbols are prebuilt with a timeline made up of four standard frames: Up, Over, Down, and Hit. These frames enable you to quickly make interactive buttons that have different visual states.

 All three types of symbols—graphic, movie clip, and button—are sometimes referred to as *movie clips*, which can be confusing. This book refers to all three types as symbols and instances (of symbols), and individually, they're referred to as graphic symbols, movie clips (symbols), and button symbols.

The Movie Clip Symbol

Delete all the items from the stage and make another movie clip. Start with a text box with the number 1 in it. Select a font, and choose 54 for the font size and black for the font color. Select the text box, and convert it to a symbol by pressing F8. Give it a movie clip behavior, and name it demo. To edit the symbol, double-click its instance on the stage (Edit in Place mode), which is usually the easiest method. Next, draw a small green square under the number and over to the far left, as shown in Figure 3.26.

FIGURE 3.26
Starting the demo
movie clip.

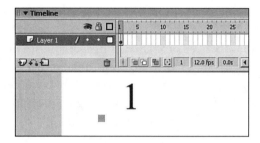

The default behavior
is the last one cho-
sen, so next time you
create a symbol, the
default behavior will
be Graphic.

Next, add 10 keyframes, and move the square a bit to the right each
keyframe. You might need to zoom in and out to do this. The most precise way to move the square is to press Shift and use the arrow keys,
which enables you to move the square one pixel at a time. Then delete
the square's stroke. (Remember from Chapter 2 that strokes are more
processor-intensive than fills, so when they're not needed, delete them.)
To make this square a graphic symbol, select it and press F8. Change the
Behavior type to Graphic, and name it `square`.

Next, click frame 2 and press the F6 key to create a keyframe. Make sure
you're on frame 2, and change the 1 in the text box to a 2. Select the
square, and move it to the right 10 pixels by pressing Shift and the right
arrow key. Repeat these two steps so that you end up with nine
keyframes; the number in the text box should change from 1 to 9 as you
go from the first keyframe to the last one, and the small square should
move 10 pixels to the right each keyframe. The final keyframe should
look like Figure 3.27.

You can use the keyboard to move left and right through the frames. Press
the comma key (,) to go left and the period key (.) to go right to check your
progress.

FIGURE 3.27
The demo movie clip
with nine keyframes.

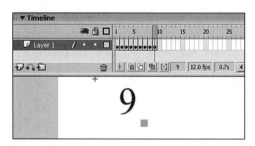

Return to the main timeline (keyboard shortcut: Windows **Ctrl+E**; Macintosh **Command+E**). You can see your demo movie clip now, but of course all you can see is the contents of the first frame: a large 1 and the small square to the left. The frames, and all the changes you just made, are inside the movie clip you created. This is a key concept to understanding Flash: Each movie clip has its own timeline.

Test the movie (keyboard shortcut: **Ctrl+Enter**) and take a look. After you've seen your movie play, close the Test Movie window by clicking the × in the top-right corner.

Next, make a duplicate of the demo instance on the stage (see Figure 3.28). A quick way to do this is to click and drag the instance to the right while holding the Ctrl (Command) key down.

FIGURE 3.28
Duplicating the demo instance.

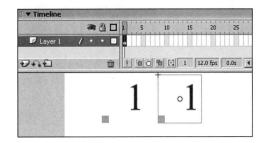

Next, use the Property inspector to change the new instance's tint to red with a saturation of 100%. Then rotate the instance 90 degrees clockwise using the Free Transform tool (keyboard shortcut: **Q**). Next, move the instance down so that it's about equal with the first instance. Test your movie again and see what it looks like.

It's a good general practice to make everything you can into a symbol of some kind. Generally, if the object will contain animation or interaction, make it a movie clip. If it will be static, make it a graphic.

You should be getting an idea of some interesting things you can do with movie clips. They are reusable movies within Flash, and even though each instance is based on the original movie clip symbol, you can alter these instances so that each one has unique characteristics.

You might be wondering why you converted the small green square into a symbol. The reason for doing that is so you can edit it and have those edits reflected in each instance. For example, if you double-click its icon in the Library and change it to a small circle instead of a square, this change takes place everywhere you've used the symbol. If you hadn't made your changes to the symbol, you'd have to change it in all nine keyframes, which would take much longer.

Now go back to your main timeline and delete the second instance of demo on the stage. Add five frames to the main Timeline (keyboard short-cut: **F5**). If you scrub through the Timeline, you'll notice that it still shows the first frame of that movie clip. It doesn't preview the other frames. If you're animating a character's mouth or eyes, for example, not being able to preview the other keyframes could be difficult, as you'd have to enter that movie clip to see the animation. Remove those keyframes you just added by using **Shift+F5**, or undo with **Ctrl+Z** (Macintosh: **Command+Z**). In the next section, you learn a way to preview a symbol's frames on the Timeline.

The Graphic Symbol

Select the remaining demo instance, and change the Behavior type to Graphic in the Symbol Properties dialog box. If you test your movie now, you'll see it's no longer animated and you see only the first keyframe. That's because graphic symbols don't automatically play through their frames, as movie clip symbols do. However, there's a way to see and show all the frames. With the instance selected, take a look at the Property inspector (see Figure 3.29). In the drop-down list next to the Swap button, you'll see these options: Loop, Play Once, and Single Frame. Select Play Once.

FIGURE 3.29
Graphic symbol
properties.

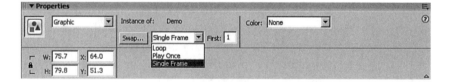

Now add 19 frames (use the F5 key) to the main Timeline. You can click frame 1 and press F5 14 times, or you can click frame 15 and press F5 once. Notice these are frames, not keyframes. To slow things down a bit, change the frame rate to 5 in the Document Properties dialog box (choose Modify, Document from the menu). You can also click an empty area of the stage and change the frame rate in the Property inspector.

When you test your movie, you'll see that the symbol plays once and seems to pause on the last frame. What's actually happening is that the playhead is playing from frame 1 to 15 on the Timeline. For each frame where you have a graphic instance on the Timeline, the playhead advances a frame. Because you used the Play Once setting, the graphic symbol stops on the last frame instead of looping. Note that when the main Timeline hits the end frame, it automatically goes back to the beginning, and the graphic symbol plays again from the beginning. Flash movies, by default, loop indefinitely unless told otherwise, as with a Behavior or some ActionScript (covered in Chapters 7 and 8).

If you scrub through the Timeline, you can actually see each frame of the symbol. This technique is incredibly useful for certain types of Flash animation, especially character animations, because you can preview the animation in the Timeline. You can't preview the animation with movie clips, but you can with graphic symbols. To see how this works, make a duplicate of your graphic movie clip by holding down the Ctrl key and dragging it to the right. In the Property inspector, change its type to a movie clip. Scrub through the movie, and test the movie again. Notice the differences? Now delete the movie clip instance.

If you change the graphic symbol's setting to Loop and then test the movie, you'll see the symbol play once completely (showing keyframes 1 to 9) and then play halfway (from keyframes 1 to 6). This happens because you have 15 frames on the Timeline and a symbol that's 9 frames long, so there are enough frames to play the symbol 1.5 times.

You can also set the symbol to Single Frame using the Property inspector, which locks that instance to one frame of the symbol. The default is frame 1, but you can change it to any frame of the symbol.

The Button Symbol

Delete any symbol instances on the stage, and delete any frames you have (use **Shift+F5**) until only one empty frame is left. To create a button symbol using a new method, choose Insert, New Symbol from the main menu (keyboard shortcut: Windows **Ctrl+F8**; Macintosh **Command+F8**). Name this symbol ButtonTest and make sure you give it a Button Behavior. This method not only creates a new symbol; it places you directly into Edit mode for that symbol. Notice that four frames have been added to the Timeline with the default names Up, Over, Down, and Hit (see Figure 3.30).

FIGURE 3.30
The timeline of a
button symbol.

These four labels are the four basic states needed to quickly and easily create a button:

• **Up**   The frame displayed when the mouse pointer is not over the button. It's the button's rest state.

• **Over**   The frame displayed when the mouse pointer is over the button.

• **Down**   The frame displayed when the button is clicked.

• **Hit**   The active area for the mouse to click. It allows you to define the button's clickable area. This frame is invisible in your finished rendered movie.

The Up Button State

Create another layer, and name the top layer Text and the bottom layer Shape. In the Text layer, on the first frame, create a static text box, choose black for the font color and 24 for the font size, and enter Home for the name. In the first frame of the Shape layer, draw a rectangle big enough to cover the text in the first frame. Choose a light color for the rectangle so that you can read the text (see Figure 3.31). Also, you don't need the stroke, so you can delete that part of the rectangle.

FIGURE 3.31
The beginnings of a
button.

Because you created this new button using the Insert, New Symbol command, it hasn't been added to the stage yet. Go back to the stage, drag an instance of the ButtonTest button from the Library onto the stage, and test your movie. Notice that when you roll over the button, the mouse cursor changes to a hand icon, signifying that the button is clickable. This action is built into all button instances. If you click now, however, there's no visual change yet. Close the Test Movie window, and double-click the button to enter Edit in Place mode so that you can continue editing it.

That first frame, named Up, is where you've placed what you want to display when the button is in the Up (normal) state. If the other three frames have no content, Flash uses whatever's in the first frame for those other frames.

The Over Button State

Now add a keyframe (keyboard shortcut: **F6**) to the Shape layer and the Text layer, under the Over state. (You can also select both frames and add a keyframe to both at the same time.) In the Shape layer, modify the Over frame so that the rectangle is dark gray. In the Text layer, change the text in the Over frame to white, as shown in Figure 3.32.

FIGURE 3.32
The button in the Over state.

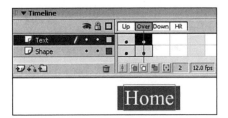

Test your movie. When you roll over the button now, you can see that it changes to the content in frame 2 (the Over frame) of your symbol. Notice that there's still no change when you click.

The Down Button State

Close the Test Movie window, and add a keyframe to the Down frame for both layers. Select the rectangle in the Down frame and open the Transform panel by choosing Windows, Design Panels, Transform from the menu (keyboard shortcut: Windows **Ctrl+T**; Macintosh **Command+T**). Set the rectangle to 80% in both the horizontal and vertical directions. Again, test your movie. You'll see a change now when you roll over and click the button. Close the Test Movie window.

The Hit Button State

Now back to editing the button. Add a keyframe to the fourth frame (the Hit frame) in both layers. The Hit frame is where Flash sets the active area for this button. For your button, set the active area to be a bit larger than the rectangle. You can delete the text from this frame, as shown in Figure 3.33, because the Hit state is never seen in your exported Flash movie. Select the rectangle, and in the Transform panel, change it to 150% of its current size.

FIGURE 3.33
The Hit state of a button.

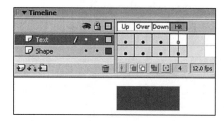

Now when you test your movie, you'll notice that when you move the mouse close to the button, the button is activated before the mouse actually rolls over the rectangle. This is because you've set the Hit state to be a bit larger than the button. You can customize these four frames to make more advanced buttons. You could add more symbols or maybe a movie clip in the rollover state that plays a little animation when you roll over the button. The creative possibilities are endless.

THE LIBRARY

As you've discovered, the Library for your movie contains all the elements you've created or imported for your movie. Take a closer look at Figure 3.34.

The labeled columns in the middle of the Library panel indicate the following information:

- **Name** Shows the element's name along with an icon showing what kind of element it is—a bitmap, a graphic, an MP3 file, a movie clip, and so on. Double-click the name to rename it.

- **Kind** Displays what type of element it is. You've learned about Graphic, Button, and Movie Clip symbols so far. Later in the book, you'll learn about other types, such as Sound, Bitmap, and Video.

- **Use Count** Keeps track of how many times this element is used in the current Flash document. See the next section, "The Library Menu," for more information on use counts.

- **Linkage**   This option is for exporting or importing for sharing, and is explained later in this chapter in "Using Runtime Shared Libraries."

- **Date Modified**   The date and time the item was last altered.

FIGURE 3.34
The Library panel.

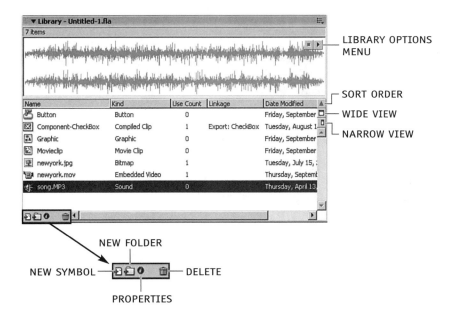

You can sort the order of the listed elements by clicking the column headings, or you can click the arrow at the right side of the panel (see Figure 3.34) to reverse the listed order.

Figure 3.34 also shows icons for toggling the view of the Library panel: narrow view and wide view. You can also use the icons at the lower-left corner (labeled in Figure 3.34) to create a new symbol, create a new folder, change a symbol's properties, or delete a symbol.

Creating folders is quite helpful for organizing your elements and is highly recommended, as is using clear, easy-to-understand names for your symbols.

The Library Menu

Select an item in the Library and access the Library options menu at the top-right corner (see Figure 3.35). Like all menus, if a menu item is grayed out, it's not available at that time or for that item.

The items in the options menu are as follows:

- **New Symbol** Creates a new symbol.

- **New Folder** Creates a new folder.

- **New Font** Embeds a font into your Library and movie (explained in more detail in Chapter 13, "Text").

- **New Video** Creates a new video symbol. You need to open the properties of this symbol after it's created and define the source of the FLV video file. For more information, see Chapter 16, "Video."

- **Rename** Renames the selected item.

- **Move to New Folder** Creates a new folder and moves the selected symbol item into it.

- **Duplicate** Duplicates the selected item.

- **Delete** Deletes the selected item.

- **Edit with/Edit with QuickTimePlayer** Depending on the type of symbol, allows you to open another application, such as Macromedia Freehand, Apple QuickTime, or Adobe Photoshop, to edit the symbol.

- **Properties** Opens the Symbol Properties dialog box. Different types of symbols have different dialog boxes. For more information, see Chapters 14, 15, and 16.

- **Linkage** Opens the Linkage Properties dialog box. For more information, see "Using Runtime Shared Libraries" later in this chapter.

- **Component Definition** Opens the Component Definition dialog box. See Chapter 12, "Components," for more information.

- **Select Unused Items** Selects all the elements that aren't currently being used in your Flash movie. This option is useful for cleaning up unused objects to lower your FLA file size. Be careful, however, if you're using elements through code. If they're not on the stage, Flash highlights them as unused, even if you're accessing them with ActionScript and linkage properties.

- **Update** Available only for certain external elements, such as bitmaps. This option makes Flash access the external file and update the symbol in Flash with it—effectively the same as importing a newer version of a file and then deleting the older one.

- **Play** If the element is a movie clip with more than one frame, a video clip, or an audio clip, you can check it in the Preview window of the Library panel.

- **Expand Folder** Expands the selected folder.

- **Collapse Folder** Collapses or closes the selected folder.

- **Expand All Folders** Expands all folders in the Library.

- **Collapse All Folders** Collapses all folders in the Library.

- **Shared Library Properties** This option is explained in the next section, "Shared Libraries."

- **Keep Use Counts Updated** Select whether you want Flash to keep the use count information in the Library panel current. If you're working with complex files, this constant updating can slow down your computer.

- **Update Use Counts Now** An alternative to having Flash keep the use count constantly up to date. Turn off Keep Use Counts Updated, and select this option whenever you need to see the current use count.

You can also access Flash Help from this menu and minimize and close this panel.

SHARED LIBRARIES

With the Shared Libraries feature of Flash MX 2004, you can access content from a library of another Flash file. This can help you optimize the process of using assets across multiple scenes and files and make the process of updating frequently used content more efficient. Using shared libraries, you can create resources that function as central libraries, allowing you to make changes to graphical, audio, or textual elements in one location and have those changes reflected automatically in any file that references those elements. You can access shared libraries in two ways: during author time (while editing an FLA file) and during runtime (when running an SWF file in a browser window, for example).

Using Author Time Shared Libraries

To import an external library for author-time sharing, you simply open another FLA as an external library by following these steps:

1. Open an external library by choosing File, Import, Open External Library (keyboard shortcut: Windows **Ctrl+Shift+O**; Macintosh: **Command+Shift+O**).

2. The Open as Library dialog box opens (which looks and behaves exactly like the Open File dialog box), where you select the FLA file containing the library you want to access. Click Open to import the external library.

You can interact with items in external libraries as you would with items from the library attached to the current document.

Using Runtime Shared Libraries

Using runtime shared libraries allows an exported SWF movie to access and use assets (such as a symbol) from a completely different SWF movie. Because more than one SWF file can be set up to access these assets, it's a great way to define a master library of assets that are used by a few different SWF files that then load the assets. To use shared libraries during runtime, you need to define assets in an FLA as being available for runtime access and define which assets will load the runtime assets.

Defining Runtime Assets

Open the FLA containing the items you want to share, and follow these steps:

1. Make sure your Library panel is open. If it isn't, open it by pressing **Ctrl+L** (Macintosh: **Command+L**) or choosing Window, Library from the main menu.

2. Next, do one of the following:

   Select a symbol (movie clip, graphic, or button) from the Library panel. Choose Properties from the Library options menu or from the context menu (right-click). If the advanced settings aren't visible, click the Advanced button in the Symbol Properties dialog box.

   For fonts, bitmaps, and audio, select a symbol and choose Linkage from the Library options menu.

3. Select Export for Runtime Sharing in the Linkage section of the Symbol Properties dialog box to make this item available for linking to a destination document (the FLA accessing your shared asset).

4. In the Identifier text box, enter a name without spaces. This is the name you'll use to refer to this item in your destination document.

4. In the URL text box, enter the address where the SWF file, when published, will be located (such as `http://www.mydomain.com/myFlashMovie.swf`), and click OK.

5. Export and upload the SWF to the location specified in the URL text box. If you don't, your shared asset won't load properly.

6. Repeat for all items you want to share.

That's all you need to do to set up an asset to be accessible to other files at runtime. The next step is to connect your shared assets to other FLAs.

Linking to Runtime Shared Assets

You use the Symbol Properties dialog box or the Linkage Properties dialog box to define sharing properties for an asset in your file. This is done to connect your document to the *source document*, which contains the element to be used in your movie. The following sections explain two methods for linking to an asset in another FLA.

Specifying the URL and Identifier

First, follow these steps to link to an asset in a source document by specifying the linked item's URL and identifier:

1. Open the destination document (the FLA file containing the items you want to share).

2. Open the Library panel.

3. Do one of the following:

   For movie clips, buttons, and graphic symbols, select a movie clip, button, or graphic symbol in the Library panel and then choose Properties from the Library options menu.

   For fonts, bitmaps, and audio, select a symbol and choose Linkage from the Library options menu.

4. Click the Advanced button to expand the Properties dialog box if the advanced options aren't displayed.

5. In the Linkage section, select Import for Runtime Sharing to link to the asset in the source document.

6. Enter a name for the symbol in the Identifier text box that's identical to the identifier used for the symbol in the source document. Do not use spaces in the name.

7. Enter the URL where the SWF source file containing the shared asset is posted, and click OK.

Dragging to Specify an Asset

If your source document has already been posted to a URL, you can specify a linked asset by dragging it to the stage from the source document's library. Just use these simple steps:

1. In the destination document, do one of the following:

   Choose File, Open from the main menu.

   Choose File, Import, Open External Library from the main menu.

2. Select the source FLA document containing the library asset you want, and click Open.

3. Drag the shared asset from the source document's Library panel into the destination document's Library panel or onto the stage.

If you want to embed your linked symbol in the destination document— which would break your connection to the source document and convert your symbol to a regular, internal one—you can turn off sharing for a shared asset in the destination document.

Turning Off Linkages in the Destination Document

To turn off the linkage for a symbol in the destination document, follow these steps:

1. In the destination document, select the linked symbol in the Library panel and do one of the following:

    For movie clip, button, or graphic symbols, select Properties from the Library options menu.

    For font symbols, bitmaps, or audio, select Linkage from the Library options menu.

2. In the Symbol Properties dialog box or the Linkage Properties dialog box, clear the Import for Runtime Sharing radio button, and click OK.

POINTS TO REMEMBER

-   All panels can be moved, docked, and minimized. Customize your workspace so that it's comfortable for you.

-   The Timeline contains the layers area and the frames area. Use the folders in the layers area to organize your layers.

-   Use keyboard shortcuts to add a frame (**F5**), add a keyframe (**F6**), delete a frame (**Shift+F5**), and clear a keyframe (**Shift+F6**).

-   The Test Movie command is used often to test your movie as you're working. The keyboard shortcut is **Ctrl+Enter** (Macintosh: **Command+Enter**).

-   Use the comment field in the Property inspector to add notes or descriptions for your movie frames.

-   There are three types of symbols: movie clip, graphic, and button.

-   A symbol on the stage is called an instance and is a duplicate of the symbol in the Library. You can have many instances of the same symbol on your stage.

-   Editing a symbol affects all instances of that symbol in your movie.

-   Create folders in the Library to organize your work.

CHAPTER 4

EXPLORING VIEWS AND PANELS

THIS CHAPTER COVERS THE DIFFERENT VIEWS AVAILABLE IN THE AUTHORING environment and explains how to use rulers, grids, guides, and snapping to make positioning objects quick and easy. You'll learn more about working with color and discover some helpful panels available in Macromedia Flash MX 2004, such as the Info, Align, History, and Help panels.

VIEWS

When you learned about the Zoom tool, you also learned a few short-cuts for changing the view in Flash. **Ctrl+1**, **Ctrl+2**, and **Ctrl+3** (Macintosh: **Command+1**, **+2**, and **+3**) change the view to 100%, Show Frame, and Show All Frames, respectively. You can also find these options under View, Magnification on the menu. Also under the View menu, you'll find Zoom In and Zoom Out. In this section, you'll learn about some other types of views. You'll need something to work with to see what effect these views have, so create a new document, draw a circle on the stage, add a text box, and type your name underneath it.

Preview Mode Views

When working in Flash, you are in authoring mode, also known as Preview mode. Under View, Preview Mode on the menu, you'll see other view options, shown in Figure 4.1. These different views adjust how information on the stage is displayed in your authoring environment, but they do *not* affect your published movie in any way.

FIGURE 4.1
Options on the
View menu.

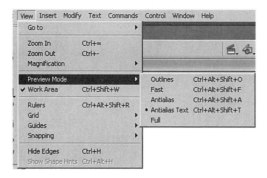

Select Outlines from the Preview Mode options, and notice that you can see only outlines of your objects on the stage. This view is often useful if you can't find an object because another object is overlapping it.

Next, select the Fast option. Moving between frames can slow down dramatically if you're working with a lot of vector elements (especially text) on the stage. This view is an efficient way to alleviate this problem, even though things look a bit rough around the edges on stage. This is because the quality setting is too low for objects on the stage, which turns antialiasing off. Again, this option doesn't affect your published work.

The next two view options—Antialias and Antialias Text—are used to preview content on stage. *Antialiasing* is an option for reducing jaggies, which is a stairstep-like effect along the outlines of an object or text. Antialiasing surrounds the pixels in the stairsteps with shades of gray or color to make the jagged lines look smoother. Compare the images in Figure 4.2 to see the difference. Keep in mind that antialiasing uses more processor power and can slow down playback.

FIGURE 4.2
An example of artwork with antialiasing off and on.

ANTIALIASING
OFF

ANTIALIASING
ON

For most projects, you can use the Full view option, which previews the work antialiased and as it would be displayed in your exported SWF file. If you're on a slower machine or are working with many objects and notice things moving slowly on the stage when you move from frame to frame, try switching to another view option.

 In authoring mode, you can switch between any of these views. Your exported movie is rendered in Full mode, so viewing it in that mode is a good idea to see what the finished movie will look like.

Using the Work Area

The next option following Preview Mode on the View menu is Work Area. When you're working in Flash, the stage's white area is the active space. The gray area around it is known as the *work area*. When the Work Area option is selected (the default setting), you can move around this work area and place objects on it. The work area is just that—an area to work in that allows you extra space to work with objects. It's a good place to manipulate and work on objects if your active area (the white area) is filled by objects you're using. You shouldn't leave objects in the work area, however, because they would be rendered in your final movie and affect file size, even though they aren't visible in the active area. When the Work Area option is not selected, you can move and see only the white area of the stage.

Using Rulers and Guides

Under the View menu, you can turn the Rulers option on and off. Rulers are set in pixel units by default, but you can change this setting in the Document Properties dialog box (explained later in this chapter). Figure 4.3 shows horizontal and vertical rulers displayed around the stage.

FIGURE 4.3
Using rulers and guides.

When the Rulers option is selected in the View menu, you can drag guides horizontally or vertically from the rulers by clicking anywhere on the ruler area and dragging toward the stage. In Figure 4.3, two guides have been dragged out: one horizontal guide at the 50-pixel mark, and one vertical guide at 100 pixels. Under View, Guides on the menu, you can select to show or hide guides, lock or unlock them, and clear all guides. You can also move a guide by selecting it with the Selection tool and delete it by dragging back into the ruler. Guides remain on the stage area if you create them and then turn the Rulers option off. Guides are not displayed or rendered in your final movie. Also, you can edit the color of guides by selecting View, Guides, Edit Guides from the menu (see Figure 4.4).

FIGURE 4.4
The Guides dialog box.

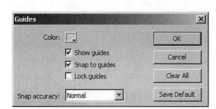

Using Grids

Under the View menu, you can turn grids on and off as well as edit the settings for a grid. The grid is displayed on your stage and used for positioning objects. It's not displayed in your finished SWF files, however. To configure the grid's color and size and specify whether you want objects to snap to the grid, choose View, Grid, Edit Grid from the menu, which opens the Grid dialog box (see Figure 4.5).

FIGURE 4.5
The Grid dialog box.

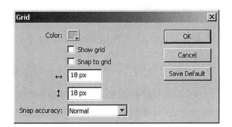

Snapping Objects

Snapping allows objects that you're moving to "snap" to a specific location, such as a grid or an edge, or be aligned with other objects. You can turn snapping on under View, Snapping on the menu, which has the following additional options:

- **Edit Snap Align**   Opens the Snap Align dialog box (see Figure 4.6), where you can set the snap align movie border, which refers to horizontal and vertical invisible guides placed a set number of pixels (in this case, 18 px) inside your movie border.

  You can also set the snap tolerance in this dialog box. Tolerance, also called *stickiness*, is the number of pixels an object needs to be within a target to snap to it. For example, if snap tolerance is set to 10 pixels, when a selected object is within 10 pixels of a guide (if Snap to Guides was selected) and you release that object, it snaps to the guide. You can also turn center alignment guides off and on in this dialog box.

FIGURE 4.6
The Snap Align
dialog box.

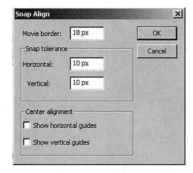

• **Snap Align**   Snaps selected objects into alignment with other objects on the stage. As you move an object around the stage near other objects, dotted lines appear and disappear as you move, showing you possible vertical and horizontal alignments with object edges in its proximity, as shown in Figure 4.7. Releasing the mouse button when one of these dotted lines is visible causes the object to snap into the alignment shown.

FIGURE 4.7
Snap alignment lines.

• **Snap to Grid**   This option works whether the grid is visible or not.

• **Snap to Guides**   This option allows selected objects to snap to guides on the stage as you move them.

• **Snap to Pixels**   This option ensures that objects snap to the 1-pixel grid, which is visible only at 400% or higher magnification.

• **Snap to Objects**   This option causes selected objects to snap to other objects on the stage.

Objects need to be selected by an edge or center point for snapping to work. You will know you've selected an edge or the center point because the mouse pointer displays a small white circle.

THE DOCUMENT PROPERTIES DIALOG BOX

To open the Document Properties dialog box, shown in Figure 4.8, choose Modify, Document from the menu (keyboard shortcut: Windows **Ctrl+J**; Macintosh **Command+J**). You can also click the Size or Publish Settings buttons in the Property inspector if the stage is selected. Note that even though you can adjust certain document properties directly in the Property inspector when the stage is selected, additional settings are available in the Document Properties dialog box.

FIGURE 4.8
The Document Properties dialog box.

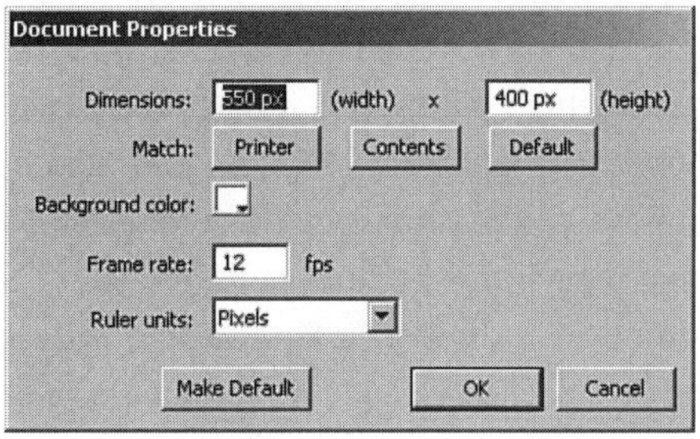

In this dialog box you can change various settings for your document, including the following:

- **Dimensions** Sets the height and width of your document. The default is 550×400, the minimum size is 1×1, and the maximum size is 2880×2880. Underneath are three buttons:

  - **Printer** Sets the size to the maximum available print area, as determined by the paper size minus the current margin selected in the Page Setup dialog box (Windows) or the Print Margins dialog box (Macintosh).

  - **Contents** Sets equal space on all sides around the current content on the stage.

  - **Default** Sets the document to 550×400 pixels, unless you have specified another setting by using the Make Default button (see later in this list).

- **Background Color** Sets the background color of your document using the color palette. The default is white.

- **Frame Rate**   Sets your document's frame rate in frames per second (fps).

- **Ruler Units**   Sets the ruler units for your Flash movie. Choose between Inches, Inches (decimal), Points, Centimeters, Millimeters, and Pixels.

- **Make Default**   Click this button to specify the settings you've entered as the default settings for any future Flash movies you create.

In the video world, 29.9fps is the standard frame rate. In Flash, 12, 21, and 31 are all commonly used. You can set it higher, but computers (depending on processor speed, the video card, amount of RAM, and other factors) do not always play back at these higher frame rates. You'll end up with a Flash movie that plays smoothly on a high-end machine, but playback can be choppy on older or slower machines. This is where testing comes in. Test your Flash movie often and on different machines—PCs and Macs, old and new—with different frame rates, and check the results. Send it to friends, post it online, and post in a forum, asking people to test it. Also, Flash movies with processor-intensive elements (gradients, alpha channels, masks, lots of elements, and so forth) affect playback. These factors are discussed throughout this book, but the bottom line is that setting your frame rate to 120fps doesn't necessarily mean your Flash movie will play back at that rate.

THE INFO PANEL

The Info panel shows specific information about any currently selected object (see Figure 4.9). It's helpful when you need to know the width, height, or x,y-coordinates of any object, including symbols, shapes, or text fields. To open it, choose Window, Design Panels, Info from the menu (keyboard shortcut: Windows **Ctrl+I**; Macintosh **Command+I**).

FIGURE 4.9
The Info panel.

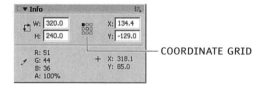

COORDINATE GRID

The top half of the Info panel shows you the following information about the currently selected item. To change information in these fields, just click a field (or press the Tab key to move between fields), change the information, and press Enter.

- **Width and height**   Shows the width and height in pixels of the currently selected item.

- **Coordinate grid**   The coordinate grid shows nine squares that represent a bounding box around your selected object, which all objects in Flash have. The black square signifies the registration point of the selected symbol (or the top-left corner of that object if it's not a symbol), and the x and y coordinates displayed to the right are taken from this point on the object. If you click the center square, the x and y coordinates are calculated in relation to the center of the selected object.

- **X and Y coordinates**   Shows the object's x and y coordinates in relation to the black square in the coordinate grid.

The bottom half of the panel shows you specific mouse information:

- **Current Mouse Position RGB and Alpha Values**   Displays the RGB and alpha values of the pixel directly under your current mouse position for bitmap images or vector artwork. Does not show colors if your mouse is over a symbol or grouped objects.

- **Current Mouse X and Y Position**   Displays the current x,y coordinates of your mouse position, as measured from the top-left corner of the stage.

THE ALIGN PANEL

The Align panel allows you to select objects and align, distribute, and match their size and spacing. This tool is incredibly useful when you have a number of objects on stage and you want them vertically or horizontally aligned quickly, easily, and exactly. To open it, use the keyboard shortcut **Ctrl+K** (Macintosh: **Command+K**). To use this tool, select your objects and then click one of the icons shown in Figure 4.10.

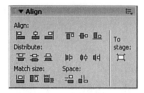

The following list explains what you can do with the icons in the Align panel:

- **Align** This section, used for aligning objects on the stage, contains six alignment buttons: three for horizontal (left edge, center, and right edge) and three for vertical (top edge, center, and bottom edge). Select two or more objects, and click one of these buttons. Flash then aligns those objects according to your selection. For example, the Align Left button moves all selected objects so that their left edges are perfectly aligned.

- **Distribute** This section, used to evenly distribute objects on the stage, contains six distribution buttons: three for vertical (top edge, center, and bottom edge) and three for horizontal (left, middle, and right). Select three or more objects, click one of the buttons, and Flash evenly distributes these items across the stage. Flash calculates the new distance between objects by adding the current distances and dividing by the number of objects. For example, say you have three objects on the stage and select the left edge option. The distance between the left edge of objects 1 and 2 is 50 pixels, and the distance between the left edge of objects 2 and 3 is 250 pixels. The new distributed space between the left edges of these objects would be 100 (50 + 250 = 300, divided by 3). The options specify where Flash takes those calculations from (that is, the left edge, the vertical center, and so forth).

- **Match Size** Use the buttons in this section after selecting two or more objects to quickly set their height, width, or both to be equal to the largest object in the group.

- **Space** Used with three or more objects, this option allows you to evenly space items vertically or horizontally on the stage. This command uses the space between objects to calculate and apply this option, as opposed to the distance between set points, which the distribute options use. The space options are most useful for objects of varying heights or widths.

- **To Stage**   When you click the To Stage icon, any action in this panel is applied in relation to the stage—for example, if you selected aligning to the horizontal center, clicking To Stage would align the selected object to the stage's horizontal center.

These commands are also available by choosing Modify, Align from the menu (see Figure 4.11).

FIGURE 4.11
The alignment commands available under the Modify menu.

Left	Ctrl+Alt+1
Horizontal Center	Ctrl+Alt+2
Right	Ctrl+Alt+3
Top	Ctrl+Alt+4
Vertical Center	Ctrl+Alt+5
Bottom	Ctrl+Alt+6
Distribute Widths	Ctrl+Alt+7
Distribute Heights	Ctrl+Alt+9
Make Same Width	Ctrl+Alt+Shift+7
Make Same Height	Ctrl+Alt+Shift+9
To Stage	Ctrl+Alt+8

WORKING WITH COLOR IN FLASH

There are a few different ways to control the color of shapes in Flash. The following sections describe the Color Swatches panel and the Color Mixer panel.

The Color Swatches Panel

You can open the Color Swatches panel, shown in Figure 4.12, by choosing Window, Design Panels, Color Swatches from the menu (keyboard shortcut: **Windows Ctrl+F9**; Macintosh **Command+F9**).

FIGURE 4.12
The Color Swatches panel and menu.

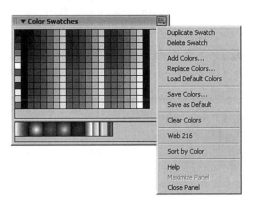

In Chapter 2, "Overview of the Interface and Tools," you learned how to change an object's stroke or fill color by using the toolbar. You can also change these colors in the Color Swatches panel, which offers you a few more options and allows you to see all the colors at once instead of constantly opening and closing the quick color palette in the toolbar. After you have a stroke or fill selected, click a color in the Color Swatches panel to automatically change the stroke or fill color. You can also customize a color by using the Color Mixer panel (discussed in the following section) and add that customized color to the Color Swatches panel.

The following menu options available in the Color Swatches panel are shown in Figure 4.12:

- **Duplicate Swatch**   Select the colored square (called a *swatch*) you want to duplicate, and then choose this option. As a shortcut, you can simply select the swatch you'd like duplicated, and then click under the swatches on an empty area. A paintbucket icon appears when you roll over this area. Click this icon to duplicate the selected swatch.

- **Add Colors**   You can import *color sets* (a collection of swatches) in the following formats: Flash color sets (`.clr`), color tables (`.act`), and GIF files (`.gif`). Adding colors this way adds them to the current set; it doesn't replace them.

- **Replace Colors**   You can use this option to import a color set, too, but unlike the Add Colors option, this option replaces the colors in your current set with the loaded set. If you don't save them, they are deleted and no longer available in your current color set.

If you're working with an image and want a color palette that matches it, you can open that image in Photoshop or Fireworks and save the color table as an `.act` file. You can then open the file in Flash by using Add Colors or Replace Colors from the Color Swatches panel menu.

- **Load Default Colors**   Loads the default swatch set, which is the Web 216 set unless you save another color set as the default (see the Save as Default option later in this list).

- **Save Colors**   Saves the current color set in Flash color sets (`.clr`) or color tables (`.act`) format, which can be accessed by Fireworks and Photoshop. Gradients are saved only in the `.clr` format.

- **Save as Default**   By default, the Web 216 set is the default in Flash MX 2004. To change it, load the set you want to use as the default, and then select the Save as Default menu option.

- **Clear Colors**   Clears all colors from the set, leaving only black and white.

- **Web 216**   Loads the Web 216 color set, which is the Flash default and contains the standard 216 web-safe colors. Even though most computers now support a higher number of colors, this palette is considered web-safe because it contains a selection of 216 colors that are displayed the same way in both Macintosh and PC platforms as well as in Internet Explorer, Netscape, and Mosaic web browsers.

- **Sort by Color**   This option changes the order of colors in your set. Normally, colors are displayed by using their mathematical values, but this option displays them by luminosity value, which some people find an easier and more logical way to view the swatches. Keep in mind that there is no undo for this move; you would have to reload another palette to change the order.

As in most panel menus, you can also choose options for help and close or minimize the panel.

The Color Mixer Panel

You use the Color Mixer panel to mix colors (see Figure 4.13). To open it, choose Window, Design Panels, Color Mixer from the menu (keyboard shortcut: **Shift+F9**). This panel shows RGB settings (red, green, and blue in values from 0–255) and hexadecimal values (#000000 format) for each color. In the panel menu, you can change the RGB settings to HSB (hue, saturation, brightness) if you prefer.

If you select a fill or stroke, you can change its color in this panel. To add new colors to this panel, use the Color Mixer menu (click the down arrow at the top-right corner), and choose Add Swatch. You can also adjust a color's alpha setting, with 100 being solid and 0 being completely transparent. Keep in mind that even though alpha settings create some cool effects, they are processor-intensive in Flash and should be used sparingly.

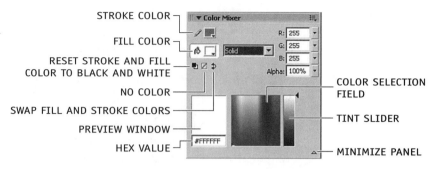

STROKE COLOR

FILL COLOR

RESET STROKE AND FILL
COLOR TO BLACK AND WHITE

NO COLOR

SWAP FILL AND STROKE COLORS

PREVIEW WINDOW

HEX VALUE

COLOR SELECTION
FIELD

TINT SLIDER

MINIMIZE PANEL

You can also create and modify gradients in this panel. A gradient contains two or more colors that fade or blend into one another. There are two types of gradients: Linear and Radial. The drop-down menu next to the Fill Color icon has options for Solid, Linear, Radial, and Bitmap. The Solid option is for a solid color, Linear and Radial are for gradients, and Bitmap allows you to use a bitmap object as a fill. Select the Linear gradient to see how this option works (see Figure 4.14).

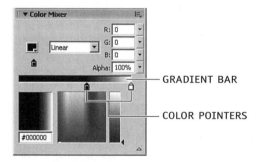

GRADIENT BAR

COLOR POINTERS

The preview window shows a linear gradient made up of black and white. Above that, the gradient bar shows two color pointers for this gradient: black on the left and white on the right. To change the colors in this gradient, select one of the color pointers and then change the color by using the RGB settings or clicking in the color selection field and adjusting the tint slider.

You can also select either pointer and drag it left or right to change the gradient. Sliding these pointers adjusts the level and position of that color in the gradient. To add another color to this gradient, simply click an empty spot directly under the gradient bar (if you roll over this area, your mouse pointer displays a + sign), and then choose your color using the RBG settings or the color selection field. See Figure 4.15 for an example of a linear gradient with seven colors. To remove a color pointer, click and drag it down away from the gradient bar. The minimum number of colors in a linear gradient is two. The preview window on the left updates any change to show the current gradient.

FIGURE 4.15
A linear gradient with seven colors.

If you select Radial from the gradient drop-down menu, you'll see the interface is the same, but a radial gradient is circular instead of linear. A radial gradient is handled in exactly the same way as a linear gradient in terms of adjusting, adding, and subtracting colors.

You can create some interesting effects with gradients, such as metal or chrome looks. However, like alpha settings, gradients are more processor-intensive than solid colors, so keep that in mind when you're testing your movie for smooth playback.

To see how radial gradients work, draw a circle on the stage, select its fill, and change the color in the Color Mixer panel. Select a radial gradient with three colors to simulate a 3D look, as shown in Figure 4.16.

FIGURE 4.16
A radial gradient.

To achieve a better 3D effect, you need to change the gradient's center point when you apply it to the circle. Select the circle's fill, and click the Paint Bucket tool. Under the Options section, make sure the Lock Fill option is disabled (it's enabled by default). Next, click the circle to fill it with your radial gradient. Where you click is where the gradient's center point will be. Try clicking in different parts of the circle to see how your results vary (see Figure 4.17). You can also determine the direction of a gradient fill by clicking and dragging before you release. The direction you drag sets the direction of the gradient, and the distance you drag sets the size. In the next section, you'll learn more about adjusting a gradient's size and direction and changing its center point, after the gradient has been applied to a fill.

FIGURE 4.17
Radial gradient
circles.

THE FILL TRANSFORM TOOL

The Fill Transform tool is used to transform a gradient or bitmap fill. You can adjust the size, direction, or center of a gradient on a shape or a bitmap image. (You'll learn more about bitmaps in Chapter 14, "Images.")

Use the circle with the radial gradient you just created. Next, select the Fill Transform tool from the toolbar, and then select the gradient fill you have on stage (see Figure 4.18).

FIGURE 4.18
Selecting a radial
gradient with the
Fill Transform tool.

A round bounding box with four editing handles (shown in Figure 4.19) appears around the radial gradient circle:

- **Center Point**   Click and move the center circle handle to change the center point of the gradient. The rollover icon for this handle is a four-way arrow.

- **Size** Click and move the middle handle icon on the edge of the bounding box to change the size of the gradient. The rollover icon for this handle is a circle with a small arrow inside it.

- **Rotation** Click and move the bottom handle on the edge of the bounding box to change the rotation of the gradient. The rollover icon for this handle is four arrows pointing in a circle.

- **Width** Click and move the square handle to adjust the width of the gradient. The rollover icon for this handle is a left-right arrow.

FIGURE 4.19
The Fill Transform tool rollover icons.

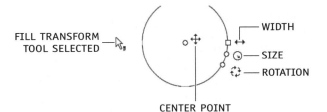

Adjusting these four options—width, size, rotation, and center point—gives you a great deal of control over the applied radial gradient. Notice that the radial gradient shown in Figure 4.18 had only three handles because you don't have or need a size handle; the figure shows handles for controlling width, rotation, and center point.

THE MOVIE EXPLORER

As you learned in Chapter 3, "The Library, Symbols, and the Timeline," the Library contains all the symbol elements created for your movie—buttons, movie clips, graphics, and so forth. Another panel called the Movie Explorer is similar to the Library, in that it lists items in your movie. However, the Movie Explorer gives you an overview of your movie by displaying the movie's assets in a hierarchical list that shows the relationship between objects and to the movie. It allows you to track, find, and modify any elements used in your movie. Although the Library lists all objects you've created or imported, regardless of whether they're used in your final movie, the Movie Explorer lists only the assets used in your movie and displays additional information about your project, such as scripts, frames, and text boxes. You can also easily perform searches and modify these elements. To open the Movie Explorer panel, choose

Window, Other Panels from the menu (keyboard shortcut: Windows **Alt+F3**; Macintosh **Option+F3**).

All items in your current open project are listed in the Movie Explorer panel. Each item has an icon showing what kind of asset it is, such as a symbol, a text box, a component, or imported files—bitmap images, audio, and video, for example. It also contains actions or scripts in your movie. Figure 4.20 shows the icons for the different types of elements. (For more information on actions and scripts, see Chapter 8, "Introduction to ActionScript.")

FIGURE 4.20
The Movie Explorer panel.

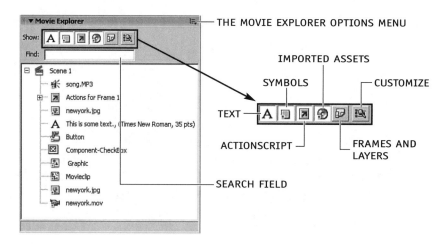

Movie Explorer Filters

At the top of the Movie Explorer, you'll see six icons in the Show section (labeled in Figure 4.20). The first five icons allow you to filter what assets are shown in the bottom area of the Movie Explorer, which is called the display list. Use the Customize icon to open the Movie Explorer Settings dialog box, where you can further configure what's shown in the display list (see Figure 4.21).

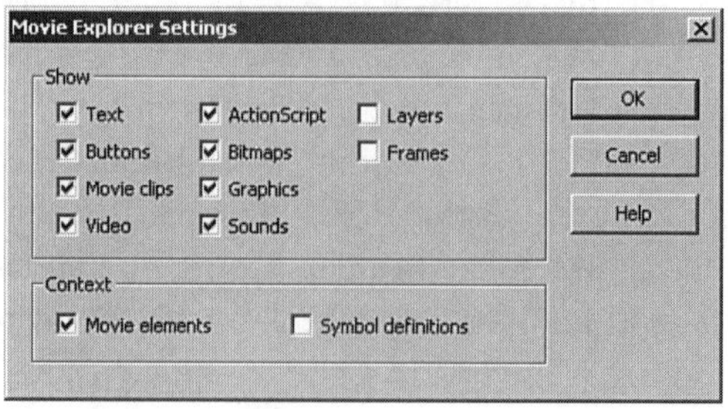

FIGURE 4.21
The Movie Explorer Settings dialog box.

The Movie Explorer Display List

When you select the first four filter icons shown previously in Figure 4.20, you see all your assets listed in the display list. When you select the Frames and Layers icon, you'll also see the layers and frames within your movie, with the content displayed in relation to what frame and layer it is on. For example, in Figure 4.22, you can see that song.MP3 is on Layer 1, Frame 1. You can also see that other assets are on that frame, such as Actions for Frame 1, newyork.jpg, some text, a button, and so forth.

FIGURE 4.22
The Movie Explorer panel with frames and layers shown.

Movie Explorer Context

Two types of lists can be shown in the display list: movie elements and symbol definitions. You can have one or both lists displayed and can make that choice in the Movie Explorer Settings dialog box under the Context section. Figure 4.23 shows both of these lists.

- Movie elements are all the elements that are in your current Flash document, including frames, layers, text, and ActionScript. When you select Frames and Labels in the Show section, movie elements are listed by scene, layer, and frame.

- The symbol definitions list displays all the symbols used in the movie.

FIGURE 4.23
The Movie Explorer window showing the movie elements list and the symbol definitions list.

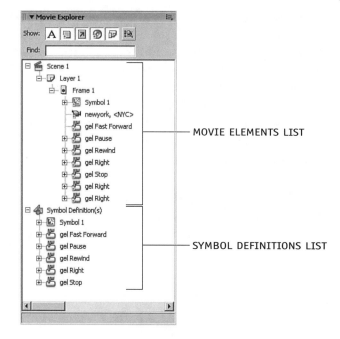

MOVIE ELEMENTS LIST

SYMBOL DEFINITIONS LIST

The Movie Explorer Options Menu

To open the Movie Explorer options menu (see Figure 4.24), click the menu button at the top-right corner. The following commands are available in this menu:

- **Go to Location**   This option takes you to the location of a selected item in your Flash movie.

- **Go to Symbol Definition**   This option is available if you have an item selected in the movie elements list and also have the symbol definition list open. It highlights the selected symbol in the symbol definitions list.

- **Select Symbol Instances**   When you have a symbol selected in the symbol definitions list, choosing this option takes you to the item in the Movie Elements list, if you have the movie elements list open.

- **Find in Library**   Highlights the selected element in the movie's library.

- **Rename**   Renames the selected item.

- **Edit in Place**   Edits the selected symbol. This option is the same as double-clicking the item on the stage to edit it.

- **Edit in New Window**   Opens the symbol in a new window to edit it.

- **Show Movie Elements**   Toggles on/off the filter to display movie elements.

- **Show Symbol Definitions**   Toggles on/off the filter to display symbol definitions.

- **Show All Scenes**   Shows all scenes in the display list.

- **Copy All Text to Clipboard**   Copies all text in the selected symbols to the Clipboard.

- **Cut, Copy, Paste, Clear**   Editing commands for any text in selected symbols.

- **Expand Branch**   Expands the selected branch. This is the same as clicking any of the + signs in the display list.

- **Collapse Branch**   Collapses the selected branch. This is the same as clicking any – sign in the display list.

- **Collapse Others**   Collapses all branches but the selected one.

- **Print**   Prints the selected element.

FIGURE 4.24
The Movie Explorer
options menu.

Go to Location
Go to Symbol Definition
Select Symbol Instances
Find in Library

Rename
Edit in Place
Edit in New Window

✔ Show Movie Elements
Show Symbol Definitions
Show All Scenes

Copy All Text to Clipboard
Cut
Copy
Paste
Clear

Expand Branch
Collapse Branch
Collapse Others

Print...

Help
Maximize Panel
Close Panel

THE SCENE PANEL

In Flash, a scene is similar to a chapter in a book. Scenes were used more frequently in earlier Flash versions; it's usually more efficient to load external SWF files than to use scenes, but some people still find scenes an easy way to organize their Flash movies.

The main Timeline, by default, is Scene 1. If you create a new scene, it's separate, yet it shares many of the same elements as Scene 1, such as frame rate, screen size, library, and so forth. When a Flash movie is rendered, the scenes are put together in the order they appear in the Scene panel. So if you don't have any actions stopping the playhead, the movie plays the scenes back to back. You can create actions or behaviors to control which scene the playhead is in, as explained in Chapter 7, "Behaviors," and Chapter 8.

To open the Scene panel, choose Window, Design Panels from the menu (keyboard shortcut: **Shift+F2**). The three options in this panel are the three icons at the bottom right: Duplicate, Add, and Delete (see Figure 4.25). Clicking a scene name takes you to that scene. To rename a scene, double-click its name in this panel.

FIGURE 4.25
The Scene panel.

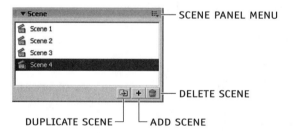

You can move between scenes in the authoring environment by using the Edit Scene menu on the document window (see Figure 4.26). You can also move between scenes using the Movie Explorer.

FIGURE 4.26
The Edit Scene menu.

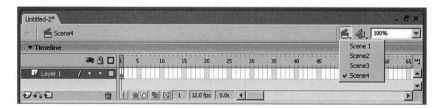

THE HISTORY PANEL

The History panel is a welcome addition to Flash. It allows you to see each action you've performed and go back to that action at any time. As well, you can select any action and save it as a command. Every selection and deselection, every cut and paste, and every action you perform in the authoring environment are captured here in the order they were performed, with the most recent action at the bottom. To open the History panel, choose Window, Other Panels from the menu (keyboard shortcut: Windows **Ctrl+F10**; Macintosh **Command+F10**).

Click and move the history slider in the bottom-left corner (see Figure 4.27) to move through the past actions you have performed. You can scrub backward and forward through your actions by moving this slider up and down. If you move the history slider up, this is similar to using the undo command, allowing you to go back through the history of your actions. You can stop and continue from any point, simply by dragging the history slider to a past action. Any actions below the history slider are grayed out and will be erased if you perform any action in the authoring environment. As long as you move the slider back to the bottom when you're done, no permanent changes are made to your movie.

FIGURE 4.27
The History panel and options menu.

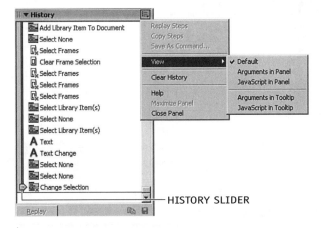

HISTORY SLIDER

History Panel Options Menu

Clicking the top-right corner of the History panel opens the options menu, which has options for replaying selected steps, copying them to your Clipboard, or saving them as a command, as explained in the next section. You can also select options under the View command on this menu to display different types and amounts of information. The Default setting shows you brief information for each action, such as Select Frames or Text Change. You can change this view to show arguments or JavaScript and have this information displayed in the panel or as a ToolTip. Figure 4.28 shows JavaScript in Panel view, and Figure 4.29 shows the arguments in Panel view.

FIGURE 4.28
The History panel with JavaScript in Panel view.

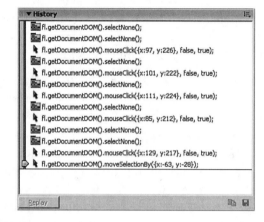

FIGURE 4.29
The History panel with arguments in Panel view.

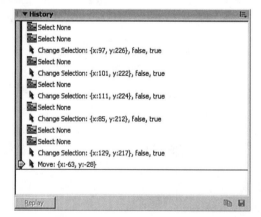

Creating Commands

You can select one or more actions in the History panel and replay them, or you can save them and create your own commands. After selecting an action, you can use the History panel options menu and select Replay Steps or Save as Command, which allows you to enter a name for the command. These saved commands are then available to you under the

Commands menu, as shown in Figure 4.30. This can be useful if you find yourself performing the same sets of commands over and over. Simply perform the action once, then select it, and create a command, which you can reuse in any Flash movie.

FIGURE 4.30
The Commands menu showing two custom commands.

To select actions, simply click on them. To select a block of commands, click and drag, or select the topmost item and then Shift+click the bottommost item. To select nonsequential items, Ctrl+click each item.

THE HELP PANEL

In previous versions of Flash, the help files were in a number of different places. In Flash MX 2004, all the help files are gathered in one place: the Help panel (see Figure 4.31). This panel is divided into three parts: the tabs with links on the left, the menu buttons at the top, and the content window.

Upon opening the Help window, the content window will contain a number of useful common task help files.

Click the Update button to check the Macromedia server for updated help files. If these files are newer than the files on your system, they're automatically downloaded.

At the top left are two tabs: Help and How Do I. The Help tab contains a number of reference sources:

ActionScript Dictionary

ActionScript Reference Guide

Getting Started

Using Components

Using Flash

In the How Do I tab, you'll find how-to files on many different topics within Flash.

FIGURE 4.31
The Help panel.

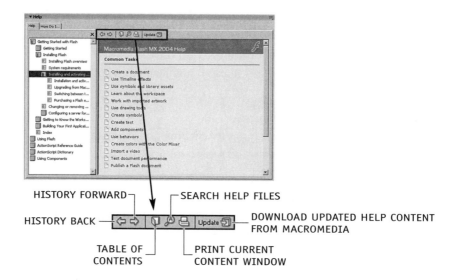

HISTORY FORWARD ─┐   ┌─ SEARCH HELP FILES

HISTORY BACK ────   DOWNLOAD UPDATED HELP CONTENT
                              FROM MACROMEDIA

        TABLE OF ─┘   └─ PRINT CURRENT
        CONTENTS   CONTENT WINDOW

PANEL SETS

By now, you've probably developed a preference for where you want certain panels positioned and which ones you keep open most of the time. In Flash you can save your current panel layout as a *panel set*. Flash includes a few panel sets, such as Default Layout and Training Layout, you can try. To use panel sets, do the following:

Loading or saving panel sets does *not* affect any content in your Flash movie.

- **Saving**   After you've arranged your panels the way you like, choose Window, Save Panel Layout from the menu. You're prompted to name the panel set and then save it. You can save as many different panel sets as you like.

- **Loading**   To open any panel set (built-in panel sets or ones you've created), choose Window, Panel Sets from the menu (see Figure 4.32).

FIGURE 4.32
Loading a panel set.

POINTS TO REMEMBER

- Changing the Preview mode while you're working can be helpful. Select from Outlines, Fast, Antialias, Antialias Text, and Full to change how your movie is displayed on the stage.

- Create guides by clicking and dragging from anywhere on the rulers. Rulers can be turned on and off under the View menu or with the keyboard shortcut **Ctrl+Alt+Shift+R** (Macintosh: **Command+ Option+Shift-R**).

- When snapping is turned on (under the View menu), you need to select objects from their edges or center point for snapping to work.

- Use the Document Properties dialog box to change your current document's dimensions, background color, frame rate, and ruler units. The keyboard shortcut is **Ctrl+J** (Macintosh: **Command+J**).

- The Info panel displays the height, width, and x,y-coordinates of any selected object, as well as the current mouse position and RGB and alpha values. The keyboard shortcut is **Ctrl+I** (Macintosh: **Command+I**).

- Use the Align panel to quickly align and distribute selected objects. The keyboard shortcut is **Ctrl+K** (Macintosh: **Command+K**).

- You can easily select and work with colors and color sets in the Color Swatches panel. The keyboard shortcut is **Ctrl+F9** (Macintosh: **Command+F9**).

- Mix your own colors and gradients with the Color Mixer panel. The keyboard shortcut is **Shift+F9**.

- The Movie Explorer panel displays a hierarchical list of all the objects used in your movie, allowing you to easily perform searches and modify these elements. The keyboard shortcut is **Alt+F3** (Macintosh: **Option+F3**).

- The new History panel allows you to see each action you've performed, so you can quickly review your actions and create your own custom commands to use in any Flash movie. The keyboard shortcut is **Ctrl+F10** (Macintosh: **Command+F10**).

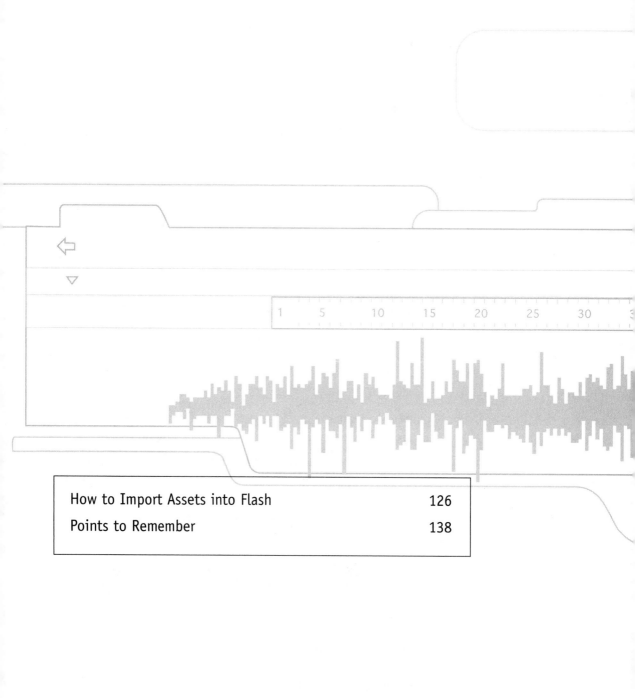

CHAPTER 5

IMPORTING

THE WORD *MULTIMEDIA* HAS MANY DIFFERENT MEANINGS. FOR THE PURPOSES of this book, it means the combination of any digital assets—audio, video, images, and text. And Macromedia Flash MX 2004 does just that, making it possible for you to import almost any digital file type. This capability makes Flash an incredibly powerful authoring tool.

This chapter discusses how to import the many different types of formats that Flash can handle. These formats are divided into three areas: images, audio, and video.

HOW TO IMPORT ASSETS INTO FLASH

As you can see in Figure 5.1, there's a long list of different formats you can import into Flash.

FIGURE 5.1
File types available for importing into Flash.

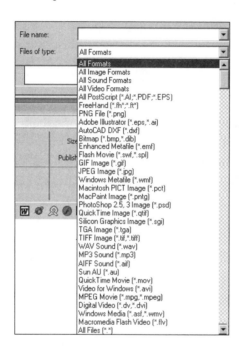

You can now import Adobe PDF documents and Adobe Illustrator 10 files into Flash.

In addition, a new import option related to PDF content is Macromedia FlashPaper. This printer driver technology for Windows 2000 and XP enables Contribute 2 customers to convert any printable document into a compact Flash format and then embed the document into a web page. For more information, visit www.macromedia.com/software/contribute/productinfo/flashpaper/.

For more details on working with these formats, please see Chapter 14, "Images," Chapter 15, "Audio," and Chapter 16, "Video."

To import digital assets, you can cut and paste a number of formats, such as bitmap images, vector artwork, and text blocks, directly into Flash. You can also use the Import command in Flash, which is often a safer method. Sometimes you get unexpected results from cutting and pasting more complicated assets into Flash, such as losing the alpha (transparency) channels in an image or losing gradients from vector artwork.

Choosing File, Import from the menu displays these three import options (see Figure 5.2):

- **Import to Stage**   This option imports the selected asset directly onto the stage, which is the most common method. You can also use the shortcut **Ctrl+R** (Macintosh: **Command+R**).

- **Import to Library**   This option imports the selected asset directly to the Library; any imported assets must then be placed on the stage. This option can be useful, especially when you're importing a series of images.

- **Open External Library**   Use this option to open an external Library from another Flash file, which enables you to access to all the assets for use in your project. After opening the external Library, you can then drag items onto your stage to use them.

FIGURE 5.2
Options available under the Import command.

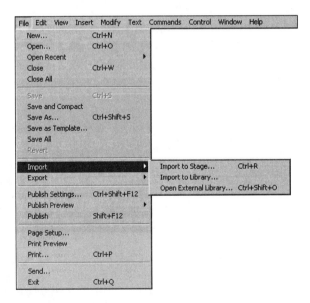

Importing Images into Flash

There are two types of images: vector and bitmap. *Bitmap images* (also known as "raster images"), such as JPGs, GIFs, and PSDs, are made up of a grid of tiny dots called *pixels*. Each pixel of an image is assigned a color. Bitmap images are generally larger in file size than vector artwork and often don't scale well; if you magnify a bitmap image, its quality

In Chapter 14, you'll see how to convert bitmap images to vector and learn other ways of modifying bitmap and vector images to help optimize them for file size and performance.

starts to deteriorate. Bitmap images are great for color-rich images, such as landscapes or people.

Vector images, such as EPS and Illustrator files, are images made up of points, lines, and fills and, therefore, are usually smaller in file size than bitmap images. Also, vector images can be scaled up or down without any loss in quality. Any drawing in Flash, for example, is vector. Vector images are great for line art, such as logos.

Importing Bitmap Images

You can easily import bitmap images into Flash. Table 5.1 lists common image formats that are recommended for importing into Flash.

TABLE 5.1 ## Recommended Bitmap Formats for Importing into Flash

Format	File Extension	Description
JPEG	.jpg	JPEG is probably the most commonly used format and is quite good for most bitmap images. You can set the compression level on JPGs when you create them, which gives you more control over image quality and file size. You can also adjust the quality of JPG images after they're imported into Flash.
GIF	.gif	GIF files are usually smaller than JPG files when the image is primarily solid colors. This format uses lossless compression (meaning no image data is lost or discarded during compression), but it is limited to 256 or fewer colors.
PNG	.png	The PNG format is useful because it can contain an alpha channel if you want to have transparent areas in your image. Unflattened PNGs created in Macromedia Fireworks also retain any vector artwork that has been created in Fireworks. This format is recommended for high-quality images.
Bitmap	.bmp, .dib	These Microsoft Windows formats support compression and alpha channels. On a Macintosh, you need QuickTime 4.0 or later to import these file types. (Don't be confused by the word bitmap. It's used generically to describe all bitmap file formats, but it's also a specific Windows format [.bmp].)

Format	File Extension	Description
PICT	.pct, .pict	This popular format supports lossless compression and alpha channels, but it is not as commonly used as some other formats. Good image quality, but file size is slightly larger.

All bitmap image formats use some form of compression, generally to reduce the file size yet keep the image quality acceptable. With some formats, such as JPG, you can set a compression rate between 1% and 100%, with 100% being the highest quality. Others, such as GIF, enable you to set the number of colors, with a lower number of colors creating a smaller file size.

Keep in mind that any compression applied to an image *before* it comes into Flash cannot be reversed. Therefore, if you import a JPG with compression of 75% into Flash, you can't improve the image quality to 80% from within Flash; you can only further compress it.

For more details on working with images and compression, see Chapter 13, "Images."

Importing a high-quality (that is, not heavily compressed) bitmap image allows you to export a higher-quality finished project but still gives you the flexibility to adjust its compression settings in Flash.

Table 5.2 lists less common image formats that aren't recommended.

Certain bitmap formats are not recommended because they aren't popular formats, so they aren't as well supported or documented. You will have fewer problems and more consistent results by using the more popular—and, therefore, recommended—bitmap formats.

TABLE 5.2 ## Less Common Bitmap Formats That Can Be Imported into Flash

Format	File Extension	Description
MacPaint	.pntg	An older Macintosh Paint program file type; not very popular these days.
Photoshop	.psd	Adobe Photoshop's proprietary file format. PNG or JPG file sizes are less bloated.
Targa	.tga	Used in some computer graphics and video industries; supports alpha channels. Not very common.
TIFF	.tif, .tiff	Common in the print world, this high-resolution image format usually produces quite large files. Generally, PNG or JPG formats are recommended over TIFF.
QuickTime	.qtif	Apple QuickTime's proprietary image format. Not very common.

Importing Vector Artwork

Vector artwork (such as Adobe Illustrator, PDF, EPS, and Macromedia Freehand files) is composed of points, lines, and fills. When you draw shapes in Flash, you're creating vector artwork. Adobe Illustrator and Macromedia Freehand are the most popular programs for creating vector artwork.

Table 5.3 lists the different vector file types you can import into Flash.

As with some bitmap formats, certain vector formats are not recommended because they're not popular formats, so they aren't as well supported or documented. You'll have more consistent results using the more popular, recommended file formats.

TABLE 5.3 **Vector Formats for Importing into Flash**

Format	File Extension	Description
Macromedia Freehand	.fh7, .fh8, .fh9, .fh10	Freehand is Macromedia's vector application. Freehand and Illustrator are similar in how they work, but because both Freehand and Flash are Macromedia products, you'll find they work together slightly better than Illustrator and Flash.
Adobe Illustrator	.ai, .eps	Adobe Illustrator (.ai files) is probably the most common application for vector artwork. You can also use .eps files, which are a bit more generic, but some of Illustrator's advanced features can't be stored in this format. If you have problems importing an .ai file, open it in Illustrator and save it as a lower version (such as Illustrator 6 or 7), or save it as an .eps file. Sometimes Flash doesn't work well with Illustrator's more advanced settings and options. However, now that Illustrator 10 files can be imported into Flash 2004, it's likely these issues have been resolved.
Adobe Acrobat	.pdf	New to Flash 2004 is the capability to import PDF (Portable Document Format) files. PDF files are becoming more popular as a digital format for exchanging information. When you import PDF files, you have the same options you have for vector artwork.

Format	File Extension	Description
Flash movie	`.swf`, `.spl`	Because Flash exports SWF files, it makes sense that you can import SWF files. Keep in mind, however, that Flash doesn't import any ActionScript, motion paths, or tweens. The file is imported frame by frame, symbols only. Importing SWF files can be useful if an SWF contains a symbol or bitmap and you don't have access to the FLA file or the original assets.
Sun AU	`.au`	The Sun Microsystems format isn't very popular, so it's not recommended.
AutoCAD DXF	`.dxf`	This image format is primarily used for drafting. It does not support fills.
Metafile (Enhanced and Windows)	`.emf`, `.wmf`	This proprietary Windows file format supports bitmap and vector, but it isn't recommended, as it's not a popular format.
Silicon Graphics Image (SGI)	`.sgi`	This proprietary image format from SGI isn't a recommended format.

Postscript is a language used by Adobe, not an actual file format. PDF files are written in Postscript, and EPS files are written in a subset of Postscript. Postscript is sometimes used to refer to vector artwork in general, such as Illustrator, PDF, or EPS files.

Here are some points to keep in mind when importing vector artwork:

- To ensure that you're importing the correct colors, make sure your file is set to RGB color mode, not CMYK. Generally speaking, the printing world uses CMYK, and the new media world works in RGB.

- The more points and elements vector artwork contains, the more processor-intensive it is. If you plan to animate your artwork, keep the number of elements and points down, if possible.

- Use—and name—the layers in your vector artwork. If you choose not to flatten vector images when you import them, Flash preserves the layers in imported images, which can help you keep your artwork organized.

- If your image has editable text, you'll need that font on your system. If you attempt to import fonts that aren't installed on your system, you get the warning message shown in Figure 5.3.

In Chapter 13, you'll
learn more about text
and how to work with
it in Flash.

When you import vector artwork, the Import Options dialog box (see
Figure 5.4) offers the following options:

- **Convert Pages To** If you have more than one page of information
  in your artwork, you can choose whether to convert these pages into
  scenes or keyframes.

- **Convert Layers To** You can select the Layers radio button to maintain the layers in your image. You can also convert the layers to
  keyframes or flatten the layers.

- **Which Pages to Import** Select which pages of your vector file
  you'd like to import. You can choose to import all pages or specify a
  range of pages.

- **Include Invisible Layers** Select this check box to import any invisible layers in your vector artwork.

- **Maintain Text Blocks** Select this check box to maintain text blocks
  as fonts so that you can edit the text, if needed.

- **Rasterize Everything** Select this check box to convert your vector
  artwork into a bitmap image, complete with transparencies. You can
  also set the resolution (in dpi). If you do want to convert vector artwork to a bitmap, you should use a program designed to do this job,
  such as Macromedia Freehand, Adobe Illustrator, Macromedia
  Fireworks, or Adobe Photoshop. These programs give you much
  more control over your file.

- **Rasterization Resolution** If you selected the Reasterize Everything
  check box, you can enter the resolution you want here. Normally, 72
  is sufficient for most web applications.

FIGURE 5.4
The Import Options
dialog box for vector
artwork.

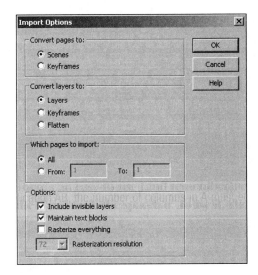

Importing Video

This section is meant
to help you dive in
and start playing
with videos in Flash
quickly. For a more
detailed look at video
in Flash, please see
Chapter 16.

Flash supports importing the following video formats:

Format	File Extension
Flash Video	.flv
QuickTime	.mov
Video for Windows	.avi
MPEG Movie	.mpg, .mpeg
Digital Video	.dv, .dvi
Windows Media	.asf, .wmv

As with bitmap images, compressing video is not reversible. Importing a good-quality video, and then compressing it in Flash, gives you better results.

When you import video files through the File, Import menu command, Flash's built-in Video Import Wizard starts (see Figure 5.5).

FIGURE 5.5
The welcome window
of the Video Import
Wizard.

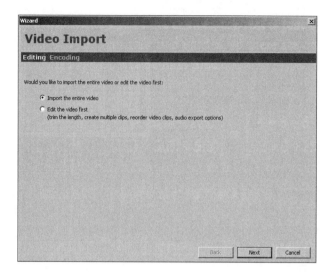

In the welcome window, you have the choice of importing the entire
video or editing the video first. For QuickTime files, you'll see another
option at the beginning of the wizard, asking if you'd like the file
imported or linked externally (see Figure 5.6).

FIGURE 5.6
QuickTime video
options.

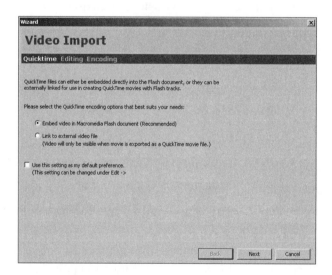

If you choose to edit your video first, you'll see the editing window
shown in Figure 5.7.

FIGURE 5.7
The editing window in the Video Import Wizard.

DELETE BUTTON

In this editing window, you can preview the movie and easily select the segments you want by clicking and moving the sliders on the small timeline underneath the preview of the video. After you've selected a clip, click the Create Clip button to add the clip to the window on the left. You can then name the clip and click Next to continue, or create other clips.

You can also delete any clip you've created by using the Delete button (refer back to Figure 5.7). To change a clip, click on it, make your changes, and click the Update Clip button. If you want to have all the clips made into a single Library item after you've finished editing, select the check box at the bottom of the window.

If you chose to import the entire video, or after you finish editing your video, you see the encoding window next, shown in Figure 5.8.

Click the Compression Profile list box to see the default options for compression settings, shown in Figure 5.9. You can read more about these options in Chapter 16.

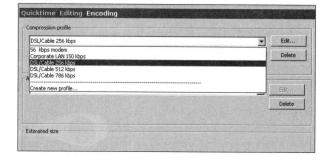

If you're importing a video to the stage, after you click Finish, you'll
likely see the message box shown in Figure 5.10. Flash determines how
many frames you need to display the entire movie in the Timeline. If the
frames aren't already present, it asks if you'd like Flash to insert the correct number of frames.

You can display and control video in Flash in a few different ways. One way is by placing your video on the Timeline, and then controlling the playhead with ActionScript (see Chapters 8 and 16 for more information) or Behaviors (see Chapter 7). In this way, you can stop or move the playhead to different parts of your movie (fast-forwarding or rewinding). You can also control your movie and playback without using frames by using the Video object, which is discussed in Chapter 16.

Importing Audio

This section is meant to help you get started with importing audio files in Flash. For a more detailed look at audio in Flash, please see Chapter 15.

Flash supports importing the following audio formats:

WAV (PC only)

AIFF

MP3

To import one of these formats, choose File, Import from the menu. Select Import to Stage (keyboard shortcut: **Ctrl+R** [Windows] or **Command+R** [Macintosh]) or Import to Library, and then choose your audio file. (With audio files, either option is the same: The audio file is stored in the Library, *not* placed on the stage.)

After you've imported an audio file, it's stored in the Library. You can see it by opening the Library panel under the Window menu (keyboard shortcut: **Ctrl+L** [Windows] or **Command+L** [Macintosh]). To adjust the sound file's compression, open its Properties dialog box by right-clicking on it in the Library and selecting Properties (see Figure 5.11.)

If your imported audio has been compressed, the Use Imported Quality check box is selected. If you clear this check box, you can choose another compression method from the Compression drop-down list (see Figure 5.12).

The text at the bottom of the Sound Properties dialog box updates to reflect changes to the file size as you adjust the compression settings. Click the Test button to hear the sound with the newly selected compression.

FIGURE 5.11
The Sound Properties
dialog box.

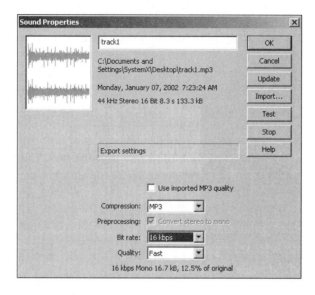

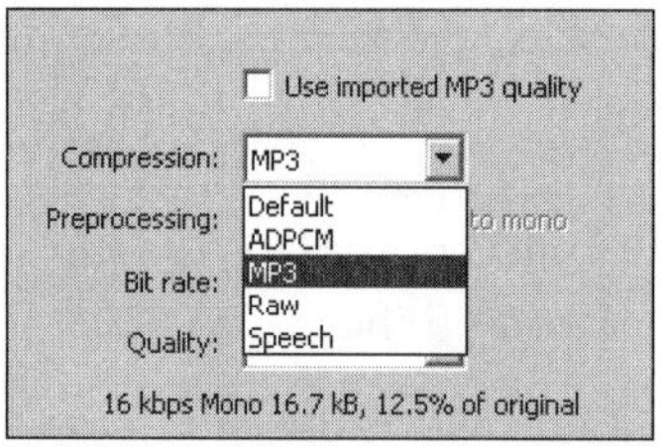

FIGURE 5.12
Selecting another
compression method.

Points to Remember

- Importing with the File, Import menu command is preferable to cutting and pasting.

- With audio, video, and image files, importing a high-quality, uncompressed file is usually a good practice. Your end result will be of better quality, and you'll have more options in Flash to work with the file.

- Make sure that image files use RGB color mode, not CMYK.

- Recommended bitmap image formats are PNG, JPG, and GIF.

- Recommended vector image formats are Illustrator, Freehand, and EPS.

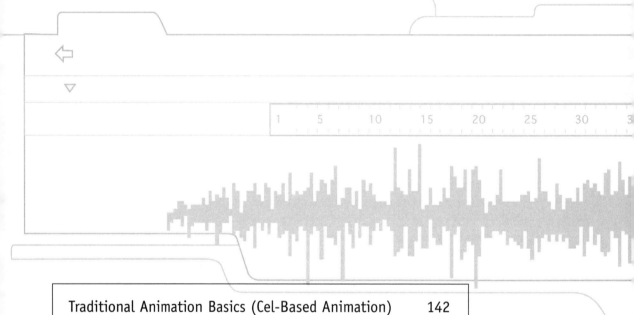

CHAPTER 6

ANIMATION, EFFECTS, AND MASKING

WHEN FLASH FIRST CAME OUT, IT WAS AN ANIMATION PROGRAM DESIGNED TO offer high-impact vector animation for the web and deliver it all in a small file size. Over the years, this simple idea is what has made Flash as popular as it is today. In the versions that came after Flash 1, many capabilities and options were added, making Flash projects even more rich and diverse in what they have to offer. At its core, however, Flash is still an animation program and still does that quite well, in much the same way it was originally designed to do animation.

This chapter explores some concepts of traditional cel-based animation, looks at the animation capabilities and methods available in Macromedia Flash MX 2004, explains masking, and explores the all-new timeline effects.

Traditional Animation Basics (Cel-Based Animation)

Animation is an optical illusion, tricking the eye into believing that an object is moving or changing. Films, videos, and animation are all composed of a series of still images shown rapidly in succession. Your eye registers a significant change in the images roughly 12 times a second. To give the audience a lifelike illusion, an animation's frame rate (the number of frames shown per second, abbreviated as *fps*) must stay in this range, depending on the motion's speed or complexity. High-quality classic animation can range from 12 to 30 drawings per second, although 12 is usually enough. North American video (the NTSC standard) plays at 29.97fps, European video (the PAL standard) at 25fps, and film is projected at 24fps. For a minute of video animation (at the NTSC standard), you would need about 1,800 frames. For 10 minutes, you'd need 18,000. That's a lot of frames.

When watching cartoons, you'll notice huge differences in style. Some, such as Disney films, have a full range of complex motions, backgrounds, and characters. In others, such as *South Park*, the movements are simpler, many elements (such as backgrounds) are reused, and characters are often simpler and more stylized. Although style differences are often a choice made by the director or animator, more often budget and time end up being the deciding factors. When you understand the basics of how animation works, you'll have a sharper eye for seeing how different animations are created.

Principles of Animation

It's important to understand the main principle of classic animation, no matter how simple your animation will be. There is far more to learn about animation, but if you apply these simple rules to almost everything you animate, you'll be fine for the majority of Flash animation tasks you undertake.

Timing

The most important principle of animation is timing! Timing is everything. It's what makes something seem real or "right." It's what gives animation the illusion of reality. Animate too quickly or too slowly, and you lose the audience because it's not believable anymore.

©Bogdan Luca, 2003 (www.portfolios.com/luca). Used with permission.

In actions, timing can be summed up simply. It's when the action happens, how long it takes for the action to happen, and the repercussions of that action. Most actions have a set timing. Jumping up and down? Grab a stopwatch. It probably takes you a second to jump and recover. If you were to animate yourself jumping and had the animation take place over 10 seconds, the animation wouldn't be believable. The only way to make sure the audience believes what it's seeing is by nailing the timing.

That's the easy part of timing, however. Figuring out the why and how is the difficult part of timing. You can get a good idea of when something should happen, but what is it about the timing that makes a slapstick joke funny, for example? This aspect of timing changes in every situation, and it's more of a subjective choice that you learn through trial and error. Until you've had more practice, it's going to feel like the hardest part of animating.

Anticipation and Recovery

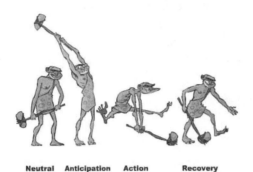

Neutral   Anticipation   Action   Recovery

©Bogdan Luca, 2003 (www.portfolios.com/luca). Used with permission.

Animation that conveys anticipation and recovery is much more realistic and believable. When an object starts to move, there's usually a small movement before it actually moves, usually in the opposite direction. Think of a sprinter at the starting line. He crouches down before he begins—this is a simple form of *anticipation*. In an animation, you might be animating a character's hand moving to pick up an object. Having it move slightly in the opposite direction before it actually begins its animation toward that object would be a simple form of anticipation. One of the purposes of anticipation is to alert the viewer that something is about to happen in that area of the artwork; as a result, the viewer's eye is drawn to that area before the animation begins.

Now try a real-world example to see how recovery works. Hold your hand in front of your face. Move it quickly from side to side, and stop abruptly after a few times. Try this action a couple more times. Notice how your hand doesn't stop exactly where you want it to? See how it has to go a little past its intended stopping point, and then come back to it? This is called *recovery*. Basically, your hand goes past its final resting point before it comes to a stop.

You'll notice a robot in a factory has almost no anticipation or recovery. You could say that robots have poor animation, so unless you're animating a robot, you should include anticipation and recovery in almost everything you animate. Even a piece of text looks better if it moves the opposite way for a few frames before it heads in the intended direction.

Depth

Because a computer screen is two-dimensional (height and width), you cannot create any real depth, as that would involve a third dimension. However, you can give the illusion of depth with some simple tricks. Objects appear larger as they get closer. If they are moving, say, left to right, the closer the objects are, the faster they seem to move.

For example, if you imagine an animation of a man walking through a forest, you can break this picture into different depths. As the camera follows the man, each element of the forest moves, too. However, there might be hundreds of trees in the forest at many different distances from the camera. Instead of animating every tree moving at a different rate, you can separate the animation's layers into foreground, middle ground, and background. The background—in this case, faraway trees and maybe the sky—would move very slowly and look smaller. The middle-ground trees would move a little more quickly and look a bit larger, and the man in front of those trees would move a little faster still and look proportionately larger. Because the foreground is so close to the camera, you might see only parts of tree trunks or some leaves, but they seem to move the fastest past the camera.

Lip Synching

Flash is a great tool for *lip synching*—creating lip animation that moves in sync with sound. To make lip synching convincing, you need to know the basic positions a mouth has while talking. Learning these positions is a matter of sitting down with a mirror and watching yourself talk. Your mouth moves in hundreds of subtly different ways, but for animation purposes, you can cut that number down to around 5 to 25, depending on the complexity. From there, you can reuse those positions every time the corresponding sound comes up in your animation.

The act of mapping out where mouth shapes should go on your lip synch is called *doping*. Doing the doping first is important so that actions line up with sounds. An advantage of Flash is that if you have your mouth positions drawn beforehand, you can just plug them into place in a movie clip within the head animation—basically, doping your animation as you do it.

Try to boil down your mouth positions to one for each vowel sound and a few for the unique consonants, such as *L* or *F*. Remember to look for places where you can use the same shape for a different sound. For example, look in the mirror while saying *fat* and *vat*, and you'll see that the *F* shape is similar to the *V* shape. Figure 6.1 shows some examples of mouth positions.

FIGURE 6.1
Examples of mouth positions for certain sounds.

M   A   E   O/U   L   F/V   S/T

©Bogdan Luca, 2003 (www.portfolios.com/luca). Used with permission.

ANIMATION: MOTION CAPABILITIES AND METHODS IN FLASH

Flash is great for creating high-quality animations quickly. Don't expect to create Disney-style animations right from the start; that takes years of training and a team of people working on the animation. You can still create interesting animations in Flash, however, if you're willing to put in a little time.

One way to cut down on the difficulty of creating complex animation (*and* reduce your workload) is to reuse objects. Making a flying bird? Put the bird's body on one layer, the wings on another, the beak on another, and so on. After the bird is finished, you can turn the wings into a movie clip, create a four- to five-frame animation of the wings flapping, and voilà! Your movie has a flapping bird that you can fly around the screen. There are three basic ways to animate in Flash:

- **Frame-by-frame animation (cel-based animation)** This method, also referred to as *classic animation*, involves drawing each frame of animation in Flash. You can see the frame-by-frame method in anything from Disney's *Beauty and the Beast* to an episode of *South Park*. Those examples illustrate the two ends of the spectrum of complexity—the Disney feature is complex animation, and *South Park* is simple animation.

- **Tweening (shape and motion)**   Tweening involves creating two different frames of content and having Flash create the animation between them. This method is usually used for animating an object that doesn't change its entire appearance, just its position, size, or color. For example, tweening could be used for a ball bouncing or text moving across the screen.

- **Scripted animation**   Using ActionScript, you can move and manipulate an object on the stage. You can control the x and y coordinates, the size, the color, and the alpha channel (transparency). You could use this method in, for example, a game with a spaceship that uses mouse position to determine where the spaceship moves.

What method you choose for your animation depends on what you are animating. Keep in mind that you can combine techniques throughout your project, if needed. This chapter explains the first two techniques, and in Chapter 11, "Animation and Drawing with ActionScript: The Drawing API," you'll learn about the scripted method. After you're familiar with all three methods, you'll have a better understanding of their strengths and limitations and will be able to select the method that best suits the work you're doing. Don't be afraid to experiment and have some fun. Some of the best examples of Flash animation have come from users pushing the limits, doing things differently, and experimenting.

Onion Skinning

Onion skinning is Flash's way of simulating the classic animator's light table and multiple pieces of semitransparent paper. Using onion skinning in Flash, you can see the content of the frames directly before or after your current frame on the stage, all at the same time, so you can easily line items up and track your progress in an animation. The content of these onion-skinned frames appears as semitransparent content. You can control onion skinning with the four buttons identified in Figure 6.2.

I have created a short animation of a ball morphing into a square to show how onion skinning works. When you click the Onion Skinning button to turn this feature on, you can see the frame you're currently on and the frames directly before and after your current frame, but they are semitransparent. The farther these frames are from your current frame and from the animation's end frame, the lighter, or more transparent, they appear.

FIGURE 6.2
Using onion skinning.

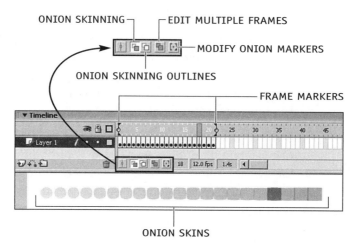

You also have Start Onion Skin and End Onion Skin frame markers (see Figure 6.2), which you can select and move left or right. This allows you to set the number of frames that can be viewed as onion skins. If you use the Modify Onion Markers button and set the start and end frame markers to two frames, for example, whenever you move your current frame, you'll see the two frames preceding it and the two frames following it.

Even though you can see other frames when onion skinning is on, you can edit only the current frame. The ability to edit multiple frames is discussed later in this section.

Onion skinning outlines (enabled by clicking the Onion Skinning Outlines button shown in Figure 6.2) work exactly like regular onion skinning, except that the onion-skinned frames are shown as outlines instead of transparencies (see Figure 6.3). You still have the Start and End Onion Skin frame markers that you can select and move.

FIGURE 6.3
Using onion skinning outlines.

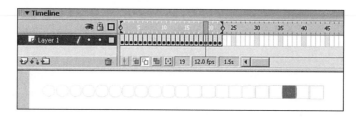

Click the Edit Multiple Frames button to view and edit multiple frames at the same time (see Figure 6.4). You can control how many frames by selecting and moving the start and end frame markers.

FIGURE 6.4
Editing multiple
frames.

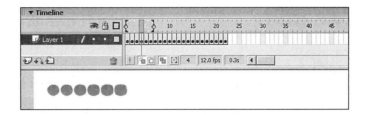

Clicking the Modify Onion Markers button gives you a small menu of options, shown in Figure 6.5.

FIGURE 6.5
Options for modifying
onion markers.

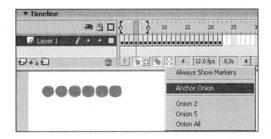

Here's a description of the available menu options:

- **Always Show Markers**   When this option is selected, you can see and move the start and end markers, even if the Onion Skinning, Onion Skinning Outlines, and Edit Multiple Frames options are disabled. When it's not selected, you can see the start and end markers only if the other onion skinning options are enabled.

- **Anchor Onion**   Normally, when you move the playhead, the start and end markers move, too. With Anchor Onion selected, the start and end markers remain stationary even if you move the playhead.

- **Onion 2**   This option sets the start and end markers to be two frames before your current frame and two frames after your current frame.

- **Onion 5**   This option sets the start and end markers to be five frames before your current frame and five frames after your current frame.

- **Onion All**   This option sets the start marker to the beginning of your animation and the end marker to the end of your animation, showing all frames in the animation.

Tweening

Tween is a word used in the animation world to mean "in between." In Flash, tweening enables you to create two keyframes and have Flash create the animation "in between" them. There are two types of tweens:

- **Shape**   Create an animation of a shape between two keyframes.

- **Motion**   Create an animation of a symbol between two keyframes.

Motion Tweening

To see how motion tweening works, start a new Flash document. Next, you need a symbol. Create a small red square fill on the stage with no stroke, and make it a graphic symbol called `square`. (You can also use a movie clip or a button symbol, if you like.) Make sure the square is near the left side of the stage. Next, name the layer `animation` and create a keyframe on frame 20. You should now have two keyframes, one on frame 1 and one on frame 20, with frames between them. The square instance is on both keyframes and is exactly the same.

Now go to frame 20 and move the square to the right side of the stage. To use tweening, select any frame between your two keyframes. In the Property inspector, select Motion from the Tween drop-down list (see Figure 6.6).

FIGURE 6.6
Options available in the Tween drop-down list.

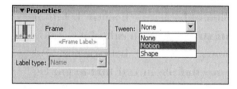

Notice the visual change to your frames: The color change along with the arrow indicates a tween between keyframe 1 and keyframe 20 (see Figure 6.7).

FIGURE 6.7
Tweened frames.

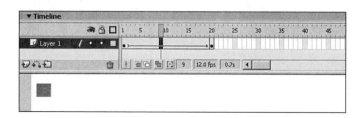

After you've selected a motion tween, the Property inspector displays the available tween options, shown in Figure 6.8.

FIGURE 6.8
Tween options in the
Property Inspector.

Test your movie (keyboard shortcut: **Ctrl+Enter**) and check your tweened animation. Very simple, and very easy. Close the test window, and continue to the next section to see what else you can do.

 You could animate an object from frame 1 to 20 by using keyframes as well. Put your object on frame 1, place it where you'd like it, create a new keyframe on frame 2, move the object a bit, and then create another keyframe, continuing this process all the way to frame 20. However, this method is time-consuming and requires a bit of effort to get it moving smoothly. Also, if you want to move the location of the first or last object, you would have to edit every frame. Tweening enables you to create an animation quickly and edit it easily.

 You can have only one *symbol* tweened per layer.

 You can use motion tweening to animate bitmapped images, too. Placing them inside a movie clip is recommended. In previous versions of Flash, applying a motion tween with a bitmap often caused a shift or jump in the image's appearance, usually on the last frame of the tween. To fix this, you had to set the bitmap's alpha channel to 99%, set its size to 99%, or make sure it was placed on a whole pixel (for example, using x=24.0 instead of x=24.3). In Flash MX 2004, however, this shift in the image's appearance is no longer a problem, so no workaround is needed.

Transform

On frame 20, enlarge the square's size. Make sure the Scale check box is selected in the Property inspector (shown previously in Figure 6.8). Test your movie again. As you can see, tweening also works on a symbol's size. You can also make transformations such as skew and scale to your symbols—the first symbol or the last one—by using the Free Transform tool or the Transform panel. You can also set rotation this way, or you can use the method described in the next section.

Rotate

To have your object rotate, you can select CW (clockwise) or CCW (counterclockwise) from the Rotate drop-down list in the Property inspector and enter the number of times you want it to rotate.

If you'd like to have your object rotate a smaller amount (such as 90 degrees), you can select Auto and then rotate your object by using the Free Transform tool or the Transform panel.

Color

As you've seen, tweening works on an object's location, size, and transformations. Tweening also works if a symbol's color or transparency has been adjusted, as discussed in earlier chapters. A fairly common use of this aspect of tweening is to set a symbol's alpha (transparency) at the beginning of a tween to 0%, and then set it to 100% on the last frame of the animation. When animated, these settings create the effect of your symbol fading in from nothing.

Ease

To see how easing works, try these steps:

1. Create an empty keyframe on frame 40 of your existing animation (keyboard shortcut: **F7**).

2. To copy a keyframe from frame 1, select frame 1, and then press **Ctrl+Alt+C** (Macintosh: **Command+Option+C**).

3. Paste the copied frame into frame 40 by pressing **Ctrl+Alt+V** (Macintosh: **Command+Option+V**).

4. Create a motion tween between frame 20 and 40 using the Property inspector.

5. Test your movie again. Your square should animate to the right and then back to the left, and repeat.

In the tweening you've done so far, notice that distance and speed for the symbol's movement between all the tweened keyframes have been consistent and even. If you change the frame rate, that would affect the entire movie and speed up or slow down the entire animation. You could also add or delete frames between the keyframes to control the animation's speed.

What if you wanted the animation to accelerate near the end of the animation only? Or slow down and ease into its final position? Well, you can by using easing. Notice the Ease field in the Property inspector (shown previously in Figure 6.8). You can enter a number between –100 and +100, or click the down arrow to the right of the Ease field and select a number. Keep in mind that 0 equals no easing, which is the default.

Select the first tween by selecting any frame between 1 and 20 and setting the Ease slider to –100. Test your movie, and notice that this setting causes that tween to ease *in*. Try it again, but set the Ease slider to +100, and notice the tween easing *out*. Feel free to set it at any number you like and try it out. Whatever you set the first tween to, try setting the next tween (frames 20 to 40) to the exact opposite and see the results (for example, –80 and +80).

Tweening Notes and Cautions

Here are guidelines and notes to keep in mind when using tweening:

* In the example you used a graphic symbol. You can also use a movie clip instance, which could contain animation as well.

* Don't overuse the alpha setting. Doing so could affect playback because it's relatively processor-intensive.

* Button symbols can be used but aren't recommended for tween animations because generally you don't want to move something you want people to click. If you need to do this, nest the button symbol inside a movie clip symbol.

If you see a caution icon in the Property inspector (see Figure 6.9), it means there's a problem with your tween.

FIGURE 6.9
The caution icon in the Property inspector.

The most common reason for seeing this caution icon is setting the tween type incorrectly. (You should select the Motion option for symbols and the Shape option for shapes.) Another common reason is not having keyframes at both ends of the tween. Check your work and make any necessary adjustments to remove this icon, or your tween won't function properly.

Shape Tweening

Shape tweening works much like motion tweening. You can create two instances and have Flash create the animation between them. Shape tweening also allows a degree of morphing between shapes. To see how it works, start a new Flash document, and create a small red square, with no stroke, on the left side of the screen (see Figure 6.10).

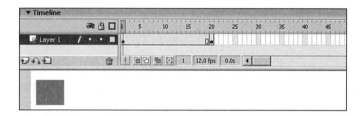

Next, create a new keyframe (keyboard shortcut: **F6**) on frame 20. Change the color of the fill on frame 20 to blue. Use the Free Transform tool and alter the shape of the square on frame 20 to look similar to Figure 6.11. In this figure, the object was deselected, and then the Free Transform tool was used to click and drag the corners of the square.

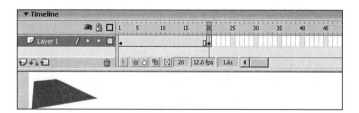

Next, select a frame anywhere between 1 and 20, and using the Property inspector, select Shape from the Tween drop-down list. Notice that the frames between frame 1 and 20 change color and display an arrow, which signifies a shape tween (see Figure 6.12).

Test your movie and see the results. Flash tweens between the two shapes you created, affecting the color, shape, size, and location.

FIGURE 6.12
Shape tween frames.

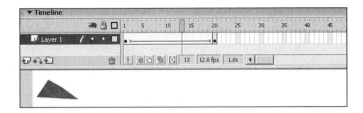

The results of shape tweening might seem random sometimes, but the tween is based on Flash interpolating points and lines. Try it with two shapes, one having an empty space in the middle (like a donut) and the other one solid, and see the results. Experiment with it; sometimes the results might not be what you intended, yet they still make interesting animations.

Blend

If you select a frame between your two keyframes, notice that you have two options in the Blend drop-down list in the Property inspector (see Figure 6.13). Distributive creates smoother and more irregular animation; Angular preserves apparent corners and straight lines in animated tween frames.

FIGURE 6.13
Options available in the Blend drop-down list.

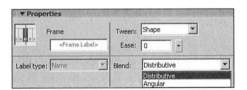

Shape Hints

When you check an animation (by testing your movie or scrubbing through the frames with the playhead), you might notice that even though Flash has the capability to tween two shapes together, the in-between frames that Flash creates aren't always exactly what you require. Flash uses its own methods for determining what points on the first shape match up with points on the second shape and selects the simplest path. The more complex the images, the crazier the results become. Even when working with simple shapes, Flash's choice for matching points isn't always the best result. This is where *shape hints* come into play, as they enable you to pick specific points or lines on the initial shape and then pick what points or lines on the ending shape they should correspond with.

On frame 1, change the color of your square to yellow. Delete the shape on frame 20, as you're going to create a new shape. Notice that your frames now show a dotted line (see Figure 6.14), which indicates an incomplete tween because there's no shape on frame 20 yet.

FIGURE 6.14
An incomplete shape tween.

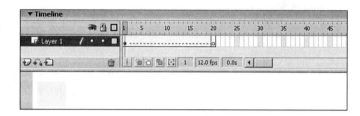

Next, draw a blue triangle shape on frame 20. I used the Square tool, with no stroke, and then altered the square with the Selection tool by deselecting the square and clicking and dragging the top-right corner point onto the top-left corner point (see Figure 6.15).

FIGURE 6.15
Making a triangle from a square.

To see how shape hints work, go to frame 1. Add a shape hint by choosing Modify, Shape, Add Shape Hint from the main menu, or use the keyboard shortcut **Ctrl+Shift+H** (Macintosh: **Command+Shift+H**). The small red circle with an *a* inside it is a shape hint (see Figure 6.16). You can click and move it around with the Selection tool. It automatically snaps to edges and corner points on your shape.

FIGURE 6.16
Using shape hints.

In this example, you'll move the *a* shape hint to the square's bottom-left corner. Notice that the shape hint turns green to indicate it's snapped onto a point or line of a shape. Create a total of four shape hints, all on frame 1, and move them all to points on each corner of the square (see Figure 6.17). Next, move your playhead to frame 20. The shape hints here match the ones you created in the first frame of your shape tween, *a* to *d*. Select them one by one, and place them as shown in Figure 6.17.

FIGURE 6.17
Shape hints on frame
1 and frame 20.

Flash normally piles all shape hints on top of each other in the ending frame of a shape tween, so you have to move the one on top to see the ones underneath. With more complicated shapes, you should create one shape hint, place it where you like in the tween's beginning and ending frames, go back to the beginning and create the next shape hint, and so on.

Test your movie, and you'll see that with all the shape hints in place, the tween now does what you want.

The number of shape hints required depends on the shape's complexity and the level of control you want. The more shape hints, the more control you have.

If you move your shape, the shape hints remain attached. In Figure 6.18, I've used the same animation and simply moved the ending shape over to the right side of the stage and turned on onion skinning to show the different frames of animation.

FIGURE 6.18
A shape tween using
shape hints.

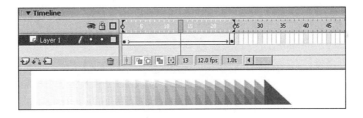

Depending on the complexity of your shapes, sometimes you can't create the effect you want with shape hints alone. In this case, you can add more keyframes, or separate your artwork into different layers of content.

Here are some tips on using shape hints:

- **Clearing shape hints**   You can clear all shape hints by choosing Modify, Shape, Remove All Hints from the menu. To clear just one, select it and drag it off the stage.

- **Viewing shape hints**   You can toggle between hiding and showing all shape hints by choosing View, Show Shape Hints from the menu.

- **Shape hints context menu**   Right-clicking (Macintosh: Control-clicking) a shape hint open the context menu shown in Figure 6.19, which allows you to add, remove, remove all, and show/hide all hints.

FIGURE 6.19
Shape hint options
on the context menu.

Motion Guides

When tweening between two objects in different locations on the stage, Flash tweens the locations by using a straight line between them. If you want to create an animation of a bouncing ball, for example, complete with a curved animation path, creating the motion by hand would be very time-consuming. However, Flash has *motion guides* to assist with this task.

To see how motion guides work, start a new Flash document and create a ball object on stage. Make it a graphic symbol and call it `ball`. Make sure you select the middle point for registration, as shown in Figure 6.20.

FIGURE 6.20
Selecting the center
registration point for
the ball graphic
symbol.

Name the layer the ball symbol is on `animation` (see Figure 6.21).

FIGURE 6.21
The ball symbol on
the animation layer.

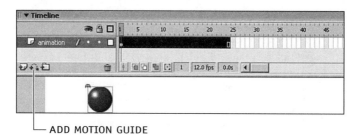

L— ADD MOTION GUIDE

With the animation layer selected, now add a motion guide layer by clicking the Add Motion Guide button shown in Figure 6.21. This adds a new motion guide layer on top of the animation layer.

Notice that the icon for the motion guide layer is different: It displays the motion guide icon, and the animation layer is indented under that new layer. Also, the motion guide layer is automatically named Guide: plus the name of the guided layer. In this example, the motion guide layer is automatically given the name Guide: animation, as shown in Figure 6.22.

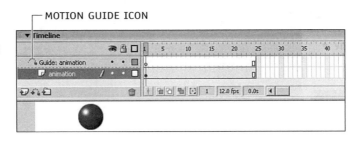

FIGURE 6.22
The motion guide and animation layers.

Any content on a motion guide is *not* displayed in your final movie. This layer is for internal use only, so it doesn't affect the file size of your finished exported movie.

Select the motion guide layer, and draw the motion path you would like the ball to travel. Use the Pencil tool, and set it to Smooth in the Toolbar. Then draw a bouncing ball motion path with four bounces, similar to the one shown in Figure 6.23.

FIGURE 6.23
Drawing a motion path for the ball.

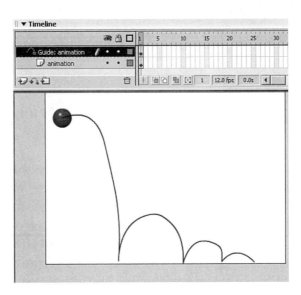

Next, lock that layer so that you don't accidentally select or change it. Click the dot under the padlock icon on the motion guide layer.

Next, you need to add some keyframes. Because you drew four bounces, you need four keyframes on the animation layer (keyboard shortcut: **F6**). You do not need keyframes on the motion guide layer because its content isn't changing. The first bounce is longer than the last bounce, so make the keyframes closer together as you go, as shown in Figure 6.24.

FIGURE 6.24
Adding keyframes to the animation layer.

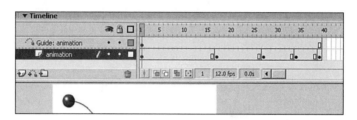

Even though you don't need any additional keyframes on the motion guide layer, you do need frames because you need that path available on all frames of the animation. Add enough frames on the motion guide layer (keyboard shortcut: **F5**) so that the number of frames match on your two layers.

Select between each keyframe on the animation layer, and add a motion tween to each one (see Figure 6.25) using the Property inspector. A shortcut method is right-clicking (Macintosh: Control-clicking) and choosing Create Motion Tween.

FIGURE 6.25
Adding motion tweens on the animation layer.

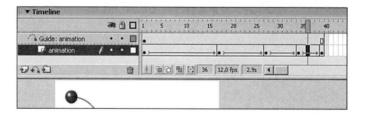

Next, move your playhead to frame 1 because you need to make sure the ball is snapped to the motion path line for the motion guide layer to work. You might have drawn the line right on the ball's center point, but to check, use the Selection tool. Select the ball on its center, move it away from the beginning of the motion path line and release it, and then select the ball again at its center and drag it back. It should snap to the line and display a hollow white circle icon in the center, as shown in Figure 6.26.

FIGURE 6.26
Snapping to a motion guide.

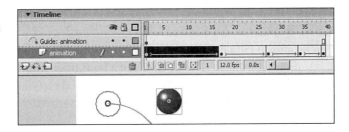

Move to the next keyframe, and then move the ball to the first bounce point, as shown in Figure 6.27.

FIGURE 6.27
Moving the ball to the second keyframe.

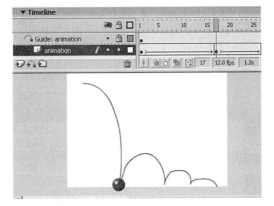

Move to the next keyframe, and move the ball to the next bounce point. Repeat this step for the next two keyframes. On the last keyframe, your ball should be at the end of the motion path line you drew. Test your movie, and check your bouncing ball animation. Figure 6.28 shows my final results.

FIGURE 6.28
The finished bouncing ball animation.

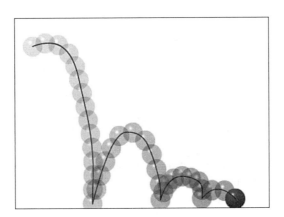

If you had any problems with this example, try checking the following points:

- Make sure your symbol's registration point is at the center, not the top-right corner.

- Make sure the symbol on each keyframe is snapped to the motion guide.

- Make sure you've selected the Motion option, not the Shape option, for your tween type.

- Make sure your ball is a graphic or movie clip symbol.

- Check the bounce points on the motion path line in your guide layer. Extra line pieces or overlapping lines, as shown in Figure 6.29, could prevent the ball from following the path. You can check for extra line pieces by zooming in and selecting the very end of the line. If it doesn't highlight one of the curves, just a small piece, delete the small highlighted piece. Your object will have difficulty following the path if there are too many endpoints in your curve, as in Figure 6.29. To fix this problem, you can edit or redraw your guide layer. To avoid similar difficulties with the guide layer, you could draw each curve separately and then join the points by selecting and dragging the endpoint of one of the curves.

FIGURE 6.29
Some common guide layer problems.

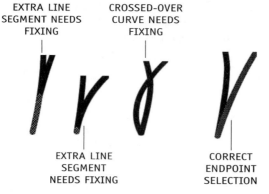

EXTRA LINE SEGMENT NEEDS FIXING

CROSSED-OVER CURVE NEEDS FIXING

EXTRA LINE SEGMENT NEEDS FIXING

CORRECT ENDPOINT SELECTION

You could have done this animation using only two keyframes—one at the beginning and the other at the end. However, you would have had less control over the timing between each bounce. If you like, delete all the keyframes (keyboard shortcut: **Shift+F6**) except the first and last, and see what the animation looks like.

Next Steps

To make your animation even more interesting, you can try some of the following modifications for an even more realistic look:

- Add or remove frames to tweak the timing.

- Have the ball roll at the end instead of ending on the last bounce. You could also add a stop command at the end of the movie so that the movie doesn't loop.

- Change the ball's graphic (maybe use a striped ball) so that it shows any rotations more clearly, and then have it rotate between bounces.

- Play with easing in and out of each bounce. To do this, you need to add more keyframes where the ball hits the top of the bounce curve.

- A real ball squishes slightly when it hits the ground. To create this effect, you need to add more keyframes.

- Add a shadow on another layer.

- Add graphics behind the ball, such as a sky and a ground.

- Have the ball bounce toward you or away from you by adjusting its size as it bounces.

- Have the movie stop on the first frame, and create a button with the play() command on it to start the animation.

- Add a bounce sound to each bounce.

Orient to Path

With an object animated along a motion guide, you can control the orientation of that object to a certain degree. To do this, with one of the tweened frames selected, enable the Orient to Path check box in the Property inspector. In Figure 6.30, Orient to Path hasn't been selected, so the arrow symbol points consistently to the right, instead of changing its direction to match the motion path.

In Figure 6.31, the Orient to Path check box *has* been selected, so the
arrow symbol changes its direction as it moves along the motion path.

Swap, Sync, and Snap

The ability to swap symbols in Flash is a useful feature. It allows you
to select a symbol on the stage and swap it for another symbol in the
Library, retaining any transformations you've applied to that symbol. A
good example of using this feature is the ball bounce animation used in
the symbol tween example. If you want to change the ball to a square
symbol, you could just swap the symbols instead of completely re-creating
the animation.

By simply right-clicking (Macintosh: Control-clicking) a symbol and
choosing Swap Symbol, you can swap it with any other symbol in the
Library. You can also use the Swap button in the Property inspector
when a symbol is selected, or choose Modify, Symbol from the menu.

If you need to swap a symbol that's in a tween, you want to make sure
that other symbols in that particular tween are swapped as well. When
you have a tweened frame selected, enabling the Sync check box in the
Property inspector (see Figure 6.32) ensures that any other symbols in
that tween are also swapped.

FIGURE 6.32
The Sync and Snap check boxes in the Property inspector.

Notice the Snap check box in Figure 6.32. When you have a tweened frame selected, by default this option is also enabled. The Snap option snaps your animated item to the motion guide.

Guide Layers

Guide layers enable you to snap objects to content in motion guides. Because guide layers aren't exported with your movie, they're also an easy way to test your movie as you're working. You can change a normal layer into a guide layer (for example, a large, heavy background layer) and quickly test your movie. Guide layers are also great for reference. You can use the guide layer to hold images or video files you've imported, and use it as a reference for drawing on another layer. Guide layers are basically motion guide layers without guided layers nested below them.

You can switch any layer to a guide layer. Simply right-click (Macintosh: Control-click) a layer and choose Guide (see Figure 6.33). The only exception to this is layers that are already under a guide layer. They can't be switched to guide layers unless they are dragged out from under the guide layer.

FIGURE 6.33
Changing a layer type to a guide layer.

You can also create a guide layer by double-clicking the layer icon, which opens the Layer Properties dialog box, shown in Figure 6.34.

FIGURE 6.34
Use the Layer Properties dialog box to insert and delete folders and layers and to change layer types.

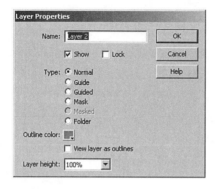

When you change a layer to a guide layer, its icon changes, as shown in Figure 6.35. You can switch a layer from one type to another and back again as needed.

FIGURE 6.35
The guide layer icon.

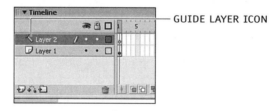

GUIDE LAYER ICON

A quick way to convert a guide layer to a motion guide layer is by simply dragging a layer underneath the guide layer. It automatically becomes a motion guide layer. Dragging a layer out from underneath a motion guide changes it back to a regular guide layer.

MASKING

Masking enables you to control what part of a layer can be viewed. To do this, you create another layer called a *mask layer*. The content on this layer will be the mask for the layer below it.

To see how to use mask layers, first import an image into a new Flash document and place it on frame 1. Name that layer Image. Next, you need to create a new layer. Call this layer Mask-Image, and make sure it's above the Image layer, as shown in Figure 6.36.

FIGURE 6.36
Adding the Mask-Image layer.

Right now, the Mask-Image layer is a normal layer. To make it a mask layer, right-click (Macintosh: Control-click) the layer and choose Mask (see Figure 6.37).

FIGURE 6.37
Creating a mask layer by using the layer context menu.

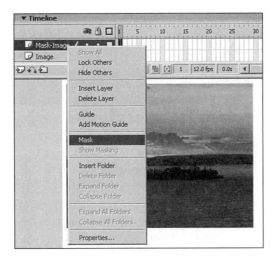

Notice that the Mask-Image layer icon changes, and that the Image layer is automatically indented and displays a different icon (see Figure 6.38). This action also changes the Image layer's type—it's now a *masked* layer—and locks both layers.

As mentioned in the previous section, you can also change the layer type by double-clicking the layer icon to open the Layer Properties dialog box.

MASK LAYER ICON

FIGURE 6.38
Different icons
indicate the type
of layer.

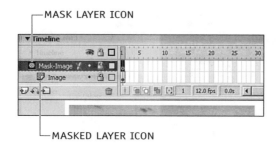

MASKED LAYER ICON

As mentioned, when Flash creates a masked layer, it automatically locks the mask and masked layers. Unlock the mask layer (by clicking the padlock icon in the Mask-Image layer), and draw a circle on top of the image. Make sure it's smaller than the image, as shown in Figure 6.39. It doesn't matter what color the mask is, but the general practice is to make masks red. You don't need outlines for this shape.

FIGURE 6.39
Adding a mask to the
Mask-Image layer.

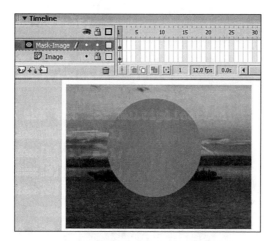

By drawing a circle, you have just created a mask. Any content on the mask layer is treated as a mask, which defines the viewable area on the masked layer.

Next, lock the mask and masked layer, and you'll see a preview of what it looks like on the stage. This is a good way to see the mask in action before testing your movie.

Test your movie, and notice that you see only part of the image from the Image layer. This viewable area matches the circle you drew (see Figure 6.40).

FIGURE 6.40
Testing the masked image.

When working with masks, keep in mind that Flash ignores bitmaps, gradients, transparency, colors, and line styles in a mask layer. In other words, use fills.

Animated Masks

Now try animating the mask. Using the previous example, add 19 frames to both layers (so you have 20 total on each layer), and then make your circle a bit smaller and move it over to the left side of the image, as shown in Figure 6.41. Now add a keyframe to frame 20 of the Mask-Image layer (keyboard shortcut: **F6**).

FIGURE 6.41
Setting up an animated mask.

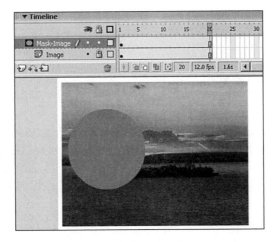

Next, move the circle on frame 20 to the far right side of the image (see Figure 6.42), and then select a frame between 1 and 20 on the Mask-Image layer. In the Property inspector, select Shape from the Tween drop-down list.

FIGURE 6.42
The end frame of the
animated mask.

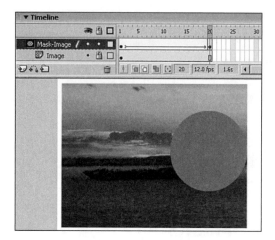

Test your movie, or lock the layers and test it right on the stage by scrubbing through your frames. Now the mask actually moves across the image, creating a spotlight effect—an animated revealing of the image. As you can see, animated masks can create nice effects.

 You can also create dynamic masks by using ActionScript. For more information, see Chapter 10, "ActionScript: Functions, Events, and Objects."

TIMELINE EFFECTS

 Animation and effects in Flash have always been a manual process: You create the frames, you create the tween, and you make any adjustments to the items you want, whether it's resizing them, changing the color or transparency, and so on. With timeline effects, new to Flash 2004, you can now quickly and easily create some of the more common effects.

Adding a Timeline Effect

When you choose Insert, Timeline Effects from the menu, the following options are available under the submenu items shown in Figure 6.43:

- **Assistants:**

  Copy to Grid

  Distributed Duplicate

- **Effects:**

  Blur

  Drop Shadow

  Expand

  Explode

- **Transform/Transition:**

  Transform

  Transition

You can also access this menu by right-clicking (Macintosh: Control-clicking) an object on the stage.

FIGURE 6.43
Options for timeline effects.

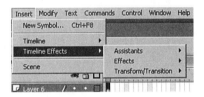

To use timeline effects, select the symbol or shape you want to apply the effect to, and chose an effect from the menu. A dialog box for that effect opens, where you can choose options and see a preview of what the effect will look like. Note that any shape you select is converted into a symbol after the effect is added.

Any change you make to these settings isn't displayed in the preview window until you click the Update Preview button at the top-right corner. When you're happy with the effect, click OK, and it's created on the stage.

When you add an effect to an item, Flash automatically creates a graphic symbol and a folder for that effect in the Library. The symbol has the effect's name (such as Blur) followed by a number, as shown with "Blur 1" in Figure 6.44. The folder is named "Effects Folder" and contains any elements used or created for that effect.

If you try to edit the symbol the effect has created, you see the warning message box shown in Figure 6.45, informing you that if you edit this symbol, you won't be able to edit its effect settings.

FIGURE 6.44
Effect symbols in
the Library.

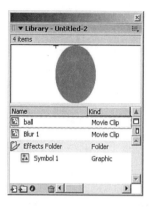

FIGURE 6.45
Effect Settings
Warning message box.

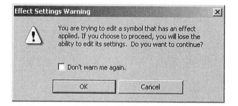

Editing Timeline Effects

After you've created an effect on a symbol, you can edit those settings.
Select the item that has the effect, and in the Property inspector, you can
see what effect has been applied to that item. Click the Edit button in
the Property inspector (see Figure 6.46) to open an effect settings dialog
box, where you can alter any of the settings.

FIGURE 6.46
Click Edit to modify
an effect.

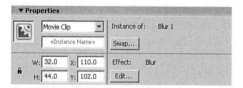

Using Options in the Assistants Submenu

Figure 6.47 shows the timeline effects options available under the
Assistants submenu. These options are explained in the following
sections.

FIGURE 6.47
Timeline effects: The
Assistants submenu.

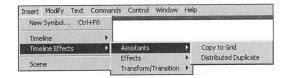

The Copy to Grid Effect

Use the Copy to Grid effect to create a grid from any symbol, as shown
in Figure 6.48.

FIGURE 6.48
The Copy to Grid
dialog box.

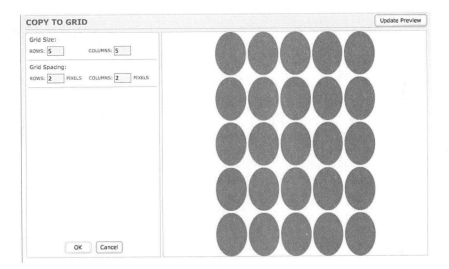

Use the settings in this dialog box to specify the number of rows and
columns in your grid and the vertical and horizontal space between
the items.

The Distributed Duplicate Effect

With the Distributed Duplicate effect, you can duplicate an item in a
line, as shown in Figure 6.49. Make your changes, and click Update
Preview to view the results before clicking OK.

Use the settings in this dialog box to specify the number of copies, the
offset distance (the distance between each copy), the rotation, and the
start frame. You can also change the scaling, color, and alpha transparency of the duplicated items. Make your changes, and click Update Preview
to view the results before clicking OK.

FIGURE 6.49
The Distributed
Duplicate dialog box.

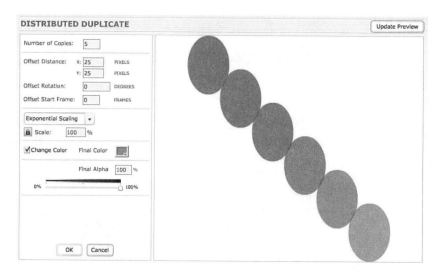

FIGURE 6.49
The Distributed
Duplicate dialog box.

Using Options in the Effects Submenu

Figure 6.50 shows the timeline effects available under the Effects submenu.

FIGURE 6.50
Timeline effects: The
Effects submenu.

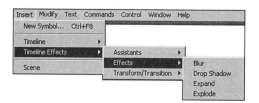

The Blur Effect

This effect creates an animated blurring of your symbol. Take a look at the Blur dialog box (see Figure 6.51), where you can set the following properties for this effect:

- **Effect Duration**   You can set the number of frames that the effect will last.

- **Resolution**   You can set the effect's resolution. The higher the resolution, the crisper the effect, but the more processor-intensive it is.

- **Scale**   Set the scale for the end result of your animation. Any number under 1 results in a smaller image for the end result. Any number higher than 1 produces a larger image for the end result.

- **Allow Horizontal Blur and Allow Vertical Blur** These options enable you to choose whether the effect is both horizontal and vertical or only one direction.

- **Direction of Movement** Click the arrows to adjust the direction of the effect.

FIGURE 6.51
The Blur dialog box.

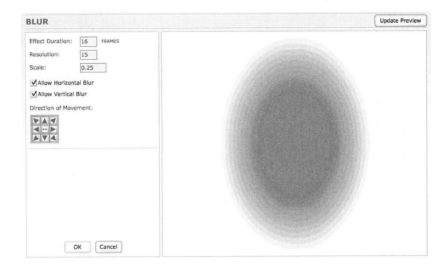

Any change you make to these settings is not displayed in the preview window until you click the Update Preview button at the top-right corner. When you're happy with the effect, click OK, and it's created on the stage.

The Drop Shadow Effect

With the Drop Shadow effect, you can quickly add a drop shadow to an object, as shown in Figure 6.52.

Use the settings in this dialog box to adjust the drop shadow's color, transparency, and offset location (the distance from the original). Change any of the settings, and then click Update Preview to view the results before clicking OK.

The Expand Effect

This effect creates an animation of a symbol being expanded over a set number of frames, as shown in Figure 6.53.

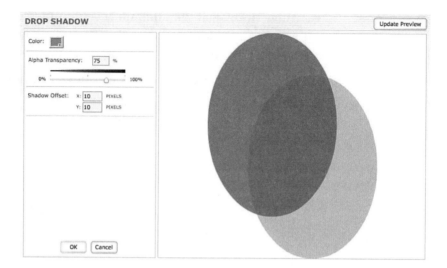

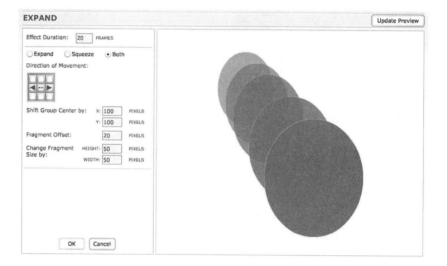

Use the settings in this dialog box to control the duration of the effect, to specify whether the effect is expanding or contracting (or both), to indicate the direction of the movement, and to specify by what amount to shift the group center. You can also control the fragments' (duplicated symbols) offset amount and size. Make your changes, and click Update Preview to view the results before clicking OK.

The Explode Effect

With the Explode effect, you can animate an explosion of your selected object, as shown in Figure 6.54.

FIGURE 6.54
The Explode dialog box.

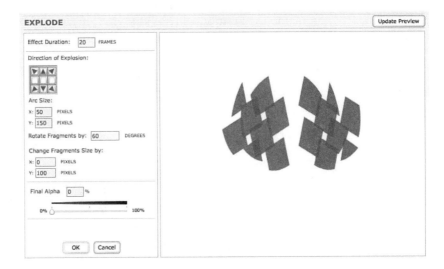

Use these settings to adjust the number of frames for the effect and the direction of the explosion. You can also specify the arc size, which controls the angle and distance at which the exploded fragments travel from the original symbol. You can also change the fragment size and its final alpha transparency.

Using Options in the Transform/Transition Submenu

Figure 6.55 shows the available options for timeline effects in the Transform/Transition submenu.

FIGURE 6.55
Timeline effects: The Transform/Transition submenu.

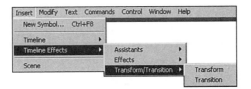

The Transform Effect

The Transform effect enables you to create a tween animation automatically, in which you set the size, color, location, rotation, and alpha transparency for the animation's ending frame (see Figure 6.56). This effect is similar to the Distributed Duplicate effect in some respects, but Transform creates an entire animation, and Distributed Duplicate creates only one frame.

FIGURE 6.56
The Transform dialog box.

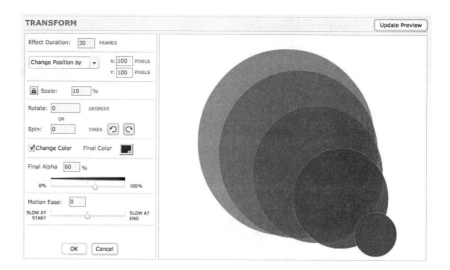

Use these settings to control the animation's end result. The settings include specifying the number of frames for the effect; configuring the end result's position, scale, rotation, color, and alpha transparency; and adjusting the ease for the animation's motion.

The Transition Effect

The Transition effect lets you quickly create a transition animation (fading or wiping in or out) of a selected object. Figure 6.57 shows the available settings.

You can control the transition's duration (number of frames) and the direction of the wipe. You can set it to transition in or out, and select a fade and/or a wipe for your transition. A fade transitions your object in by gradually adjusting the object's alpha transparency; a wipe wipes your object in (or out) from the top, bottom, left, or right side by gradually revealing the object. You can also change the easing of the animation for this transition, making it slower at the start and, therefore, faster at the end, or vice versa.

FIGURE 6.57
The Transition dialog box.

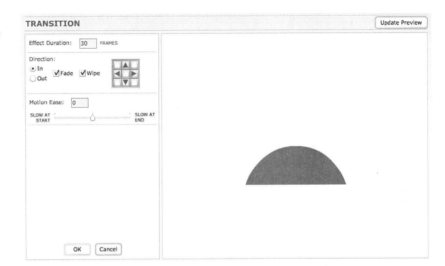

POINTS TO REMEMBER

- Timing is everything. Try to make your animation as realistic in its timing as possible.

- Incorporating anticipation and recovery makes your animation much richer. To achieve depth in your animation, divide your artwork and animation into a foreground, middleground, and background, and move them at different speeds.

- Motion in Flash can be achieved in three different ways: frame-by-frame animation, tweened animation (including effects), and scripted animation. You can use these methods separately or together, depending on the project.

- Onion skinning enables you to see the content of the frames before and after your current frames, and acts as a simulated animator's table, complete with semitransparent paper.

- Tweening allows you to create animations in Flash quickly and easily. Shape tweening is for shapes, and motion tweening is for symbols.

- Only one symbol or shape should be used per tween. Create a new layer for any additional items you want to tween.

- When tweening symbols, use a graphic or movie clip symbol. You can tween bitmap images, preferably in a symbol.

- Don't overuse the alpha setting, as it's processor-intensive and affects playback.

- Use motion guides to tween an object along a path.

- Use shapes for your masks, because Flash doesn't recognize bitmaps, fonts, or gradients in masks.

- Edit your timeline effects with the Edit Effect button in the Property inspector.

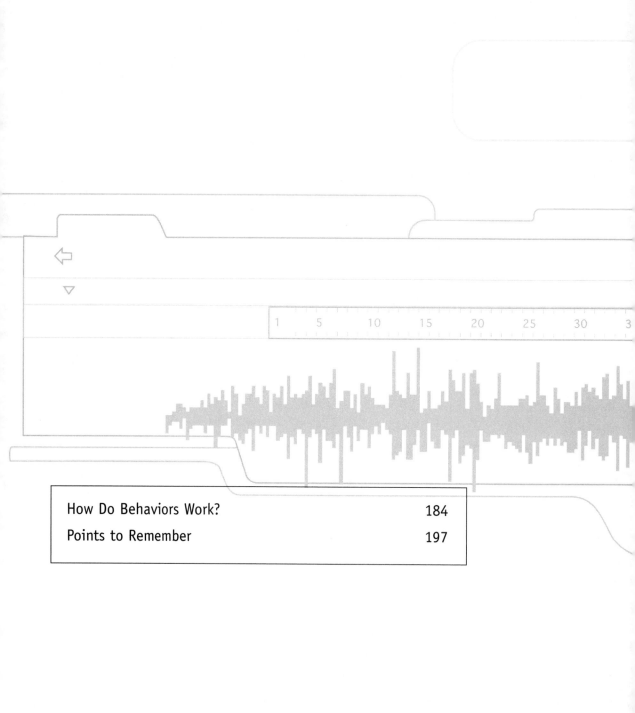

CHAPTER 7

BEHAVIORS

As you can tell by the table of contents, quite a few chapters are dedicated to ActionScript. Maybe you don't have the time or inclination to learn ActionScript. Maybe you *do* know a little but have trouble with the syntax, or you just want a quicker way to use some basic commands. This is where Behaviors come in.

New to Macromedia Flash MX 2004, Behaviors are designed to be a drag-and-drop solution to some basic Flash commands. They require no knowledge of ActionScript; you simply select the command you want, enter any information that's needed (such as a frame number or a URL), and it's done.

If you *are* interested in learning ActionScript, however, Behaviors can help you with that as well. When you create a Behavior in your document, Flash actually creates the correct ActionScript for you. In this way, you can see the actual code in the Actions panel.

HOW DO BEHAVIORS WORK?

Before Behaviors were introduced with Flash MX 2004, if you needed to add ActionScript to your Flash file, you opened the Actions panel and typed your script. With Behaviors, however, you can quickly add predefined scripts to your movie by using a pop-up menu. With this menu, you can easily add simple commands to your Flash movie, such as Goto and Play or Go to Web Page.

Even though you don't need to know ActionScript to use Behaviors, you do need to have an idea of where to place ActionScript code. To add a Behavior, you need an event—called a *trigger*—to tell Flash when to perform the Behavior.

You can place ActionScript (and, therefore, Behaviors) in two places:

- **On a frame**   The Behavior is performed when the playhead hits that frame.

- **On a movie clip**   The ActionScript is placed on an instance of a button or a movie clip. Depending on the Behavior you select, the ActionScript is performed when the playhead hits the frame containing the movie clip or when a user interacts with the button, such as clicking on it.

To open the Behaviors panel, shown in Figure 7.1, choose Window, Development Panels, Behaviors from the main menu, or use the keyboard shortcut **Shift+F3**.

FIGURE 7.1
The Behaviors panel.

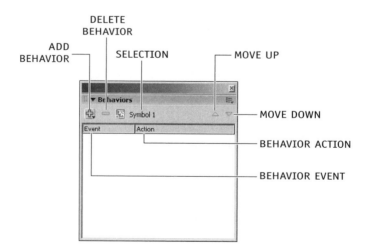

To use a Behavior, just follow these steps:

1. Click on a frame or an instance of a movie clip or button.

2. Click the Add Behavior button (the plus sign) in the Behaviors panel.

3. Select the Behavior you'd like to use from the pop-up menu shown in Figure 7.2.

FIGURE 7.2
The pop-up menu for the Add Behavior button.

4. Enter the information (called *parameters*) needed for that Behavior, such as a frame number or a URL.

To remove a Behavior, select the frame or movie clip where the Behavior is, select the Behavior in the Behaviors panel, and then click the Delete Behavior button (the minus sign) in the Behaviors panel (refer back to Figure 7.2).

 While you're working with Behaviors, check what's displayed in the Actions panel to help you become familiar with what ActionScript code looks like.

Behavior Types

Figure 7.2 showed the following categories of Behaviors you can add:

Data

Embedded Video

Movieclip

Projector

Sound

Web

Each category has different types of Behaviors you can add, as described in the following sections.

Behaviors in the Data Category

There's only one Behavior in the Data category: Trigger Data Source. It's a Behavior of the WebServiceConnector component, which is available only in Flash MX 2004 Professional, and it works with the XML connector. It writes some basic ActionScript, calling a function that triggers interaction with the data source.

Behaviors in the Embedded Video Category

To use the Behaviors in the Embedded Video category (shown in Figure 7.3), you must have a video in your project first. You also need to give your video an instance name, which you can do by using the Property inspector.

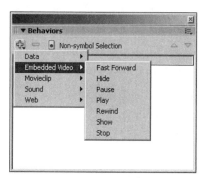

FIGURE 7.3
Behavior types in the Video category.

The Pause, Play, Stop, Fast Forward, and Rewind Behaviors control the playback or state of your video. These Behaviors are not added to a video but are added to the buttons that control a video.

The Behaviors in the Embedded Video category are fairly straightforward:

- **Play**   Plays the video.

- **Stop**   Stops the video. If you added a Play Behavior next, the video would start from the beginning again.

- **Pause**   Pauses the video at its current frame. Playing the video again restarts the movie from the paused frame, not from the beginning.

- **Fast Forward and Rewind**   Quickly advances or steps back through the video's frames. For these two Behaviors, you can set the number of frames to fast-forward or rewind (see Figure 7.4).

FIGURE 7.4
Specifying the number of frames to advance for the Fast Forward Behavior.

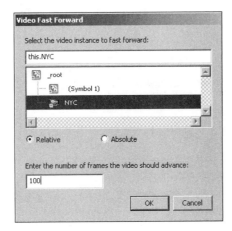

- **Hide and Show**   Use the Hide Behavior to make the video invisible and the Show Behavior to make it visible again.

While a video is invisible, keep in mind that you can still control it with the Play, Pause, and Stop commands, but the video becomes visible again if you use the Rewind or Stop Behavior.

To illustrate how these Behaviors work, I've put a few buttons from the Buttons library onto the stage underneath a video clip I've imported (see Figure 7.5). You can access the Buttons library by choosing Window, Other Panel, Common Libraries, Buttons from the main menu.

FIGURE 7.5
An imported video clip.

To add Behaviors, simply select the button where you want to add the Behavior, such as the Stop button. Click the Add Behavior button, and then select the Stop Behavior from the Embedded Video category, which opens the Stop Video dialog box, shown in Figure 7.6.

FIGURE 7.6
The Stop Video dialog box.

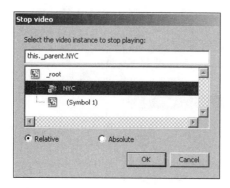

Select the target video you want to apply this Behavior to. Note that the target path (this.NYC, in this example) is automatically filled in after selecting the target video.

You can learn more about relative and absolute paths in Chapter 8, "Introduction to ActionScript."

You can also choose between relative and absolute paths. *Relative* means that the path, or location, of the selected video is *relative* to the movie clip containing the buttons you've selected. *Absolute* means that the path to the video is based on the video's path in relation to the movie's root, or main timeline. For this example, a relative path is used.

After clicking OK in the Stop Video dialog box, notice that the Behaviors panel shows the selected item—the Behavior for the currently selected frame or movie clip (see Figure 7.7). If you deselect the movie clip or frame, the Behavior is no longer listed in the Behaviors panel.

FIGURE 7.7
The current Behavior listed in the Behaviors panel.

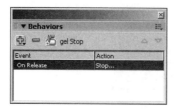

You can learn more about the different event types for buttons in Chapter 8.

The Behaviors panel has columns displaying events and actions for the currently selected Behavior. When you're placing Behaviors on buttons, the default event is On Release. To change it, you simply click the event to display a drop-down list with all the options for that event (see Figure 7.8).

FIGURE 7.8
The available events for a button.

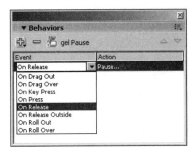

Behaviors in the Movieclip Category

In the Movieclip category, you'll see two different lists of available Behaviors, depending on whether you have a frame or a movie clip selected.

Behaviors for Frames and Movie Clips

Figure 7.9 shows your options for Behaviors added to a frame. These Behaviors are also available for movie clips.

FIGURE 7.9
Frame Behaviors in the Movieclip category.

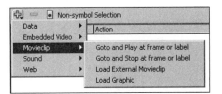

The following list explains what these frame Behaviors do:

- **Goto and Play at Frame or Label**   Use this Behavior to select a movie clip and send it a Play command. You can also choose the frame or label you want to start playing at (see Figure 7.10). To send this command to the main timeline, enter _root as the target.

- **Goto and Stop at Frame or Label**   This Behavior simply moves to the selected frame and stops on it. To send this command to the main timeline, enter _root as the target.

- **Load External Movieclip**   See the description of this Behavior in the following section.

- **Load Graphic**   See the description of this Behavior in the following section.

FIGURE 7.10
Selecting a frame at
which to start playing
the movie clip.

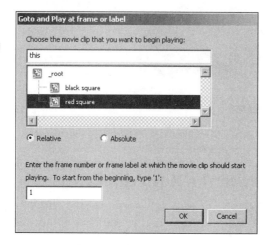

Behaviors for Movie Clips Only

Figure 7.11 shows your options for Behaviors added to a movie clip.

FIGURE 7.11
Movie clip Behaviors
in the Movieclip
category.

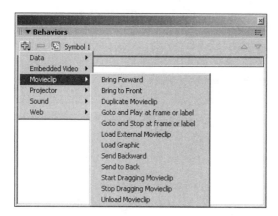

The following list explains what these movie clip Behaviors do:

• **Bring Forward, Send Backward, Bring to Front, and Send to Back**
  You learned earlier in this book that within a layer, Flash stacks objects
  based on the order in which they're created. These commands control
  how movie clips are stacked within a layer. Note that they don't move
  movie clips between actual timeline layers, however.

  Bring Forward and Send Backward move the selected item up or
  down one position in the stacking order. Bring to Front and Send to
  Back bring the selected item to the very top or bottom of that stacking order. To use these Behaviors, select the movie clip you want to
  move in the dialog box that opens (see Figure 7.12).

FIGURE 7.12
The Bring Forward
dialog box.

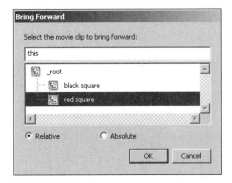

• **Duplicate Movieclip** This Behavior duplicates a movie clip onto the stage. When using this Behavior, you need to specify the movie clip you want to duplicate. You also need to fill in the X-offset and Y-offset fields, which set the position in pixels where the duplicated movie clip will be created in relation to the original (see Figure 7.13).

FIGURE 7.13
Specifying the posi-
tion for the duplicated
movie clip.

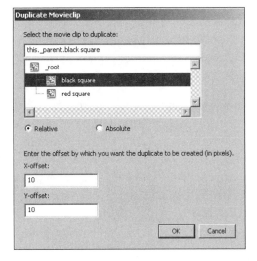

For a reminder on
registration points,
refer to Chapter 3,
"The Library, Symbols,
and the Timeline."

• **Load External Movieclip and Unload Movieclip** Similar to loading JPGs dynamically, this Behavior loads another SWF file into your movie dynamically. As with JPG loading, you need a movie clip to load the SWF into. In the Load External Movieclip dialog box (see Figure 7.14), enter the SWF you'd like to load and the movie clip you'd like it loaded into. Note that the upper-left corner of the loaded SWF is placed at the movie clip's registration point, and any existing content in the movie clip is replaced. The Unload Movieclip Behavior removes an external movie clip you've loaded previously.

FIGURE 7.14
The Load External
Movieclip dialog box.

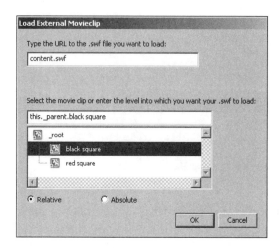

- **Start Dragging Movieclip and Stop Dragging Movieclip** Use these Behaviors to start and stop the dragging feature—having an object move with your mouse. These Behaviors are commonly used with the On Press-Start Drag and On Release-Stop Drag events.

The Load Graphic Behavior is also available for loading graphics files into movie clips. In Flash 2004, you can load JPG files dynamically. This means you can load a JPG that isn't in your Flash movie.

You can put the Load Graphic Behavior on a movie clip or a frame. After selecting this Behavior, you need to fill in two parameters in the Load Graphic dialog box: the name of the image you want to load and the movie clip where the image should be loaded (see Figure 7.15).

FIGURE 7.15
Indicating the target
movie clip for the
Load Graphic
Behavior.

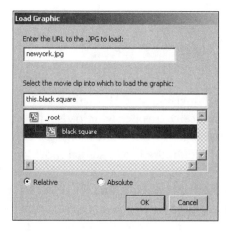

You must have a movie clip to load the image into. You can't load it onto the stage. Also, the movie clip must have an instance name. To give it an instance name, select the movie clip, access the Property inspector, and add the name there. For the Load Graphic Behavior to work, you also need to have the exported SWF file (the movie) and the image file in the same folder.

For the image name, you can use relative paths, such as a folder name. Use basic HTML path syntax, such as .. and /. An example is shown in Figure 7.16.

FIGURE 7.16
Specifying a relative path for the image name.

After you load the image into the movie clip you selected, it's placed with its upper-left corner positioned in the movie clip's registration point. Note that the loaded image replaces any existing content in the selected movie clip.

Behaviors in the Projector Category

The Projector category has one Behavior (see Figure 7.17), which is available only on a movie clip. When you're playing back your document as a standalone projector file, you can toggle in and out of Full Screen mode (see Figure 7.18).

For more information on creating projectors, see Chapter 23, "Publishing."

FIGURE 7.17
The Behavior type in the Projector category.

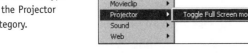

FIGURE 7.18
The message box that appears after adding the Toggle Full Screen Mode Behavior.

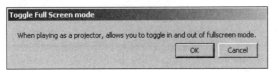

Behaviors in the Sound Category

All Behaviors in the Sound category (see Figure 7.19) can be added to movie clips or frames.

FIGURE 7.19
Behavior types in the Sound category.

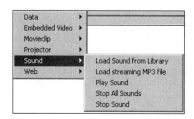

The following list explains these Behavior types:

You can learn more about adding linkage IDs in Chapter 15, "Audio."

- **Load Sound from Library**   To load a sound from the library, first you must give the sound a linkage ID. To do this, select the sound in the Library, right-click (Macintosh: Control-click), and choose Linkage. In the Linkage Properties dialog box (see Figure 7.20), enter a name in the Identifier text box and select the Export for ActionScript check box. Note: Leave the Export in First Frame check box enabled to preload the sound.

FIGURE 7.20
The Linkage Properties dialog box.

After giving your sound a linkage ID, you can use the Load Sound from Library Behavior (see Figure 7.21). Enter the linkage ID and add an instance name so that you can reference the sound later in your movie. Selecting the Play This Sound When Loaded check box does exactly that—plays the sound as soon as it's loaded.

- **Load Streaming MP3 File**   In Flash, you can also load an external MP3 file (see Figure 7.22). Enter the path and filename of the MP3 and give it a unique identifier so that you can reference it later in the movie. Remember to enter the full filename, including the `.mp3` extension. The MP3 file starts playing almost immediately, so you don't have to wait for it to load.

FIGURE 7.21
The Load Sound from
Library dialog box.

FIGURE 7.22
The Load Streaming
MP3 File dialog box.

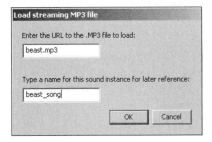

- **Play Sound**   To play a sound, you must give it an identifier name first. You can do this by loading a streaming MP3 file or loading a sound from the Library and then adding the identifier name, as explained earlier. Next, enter the identifier name in the Play Sound dialog box that opens when you choose this Behavior (see Figure 7.23).

FIGURE 7.23
The Play Sound
dialog box.

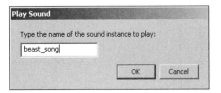

- **Stop All Sounds**   This Behavior does exactly that—stops all sounds that are currently playing (see Figure 7.24).

FIGURE 7.24
The Stop All Sounds
message box.

- **Stop Sound**   Use this Behavior to stop an individual sound. You simply enter the sound's identifier name (see Figure 7.25).

FIGURE 7.25
The Stop Sound
dialog box.

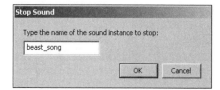

Behaviors in the Web Category

The Go to Web Page Behavior (see Figure 7.26) is perfect for adding to buttons used to open web pages and for inserting email links. These capabilities are important in Flash, and this Behavior makes them quick and easy to add.

FIGURE 7.26
The Behavior type in
the Web category.

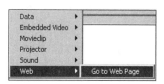

To use this Behavior, simply choose your target from the Open In drop-down list, and enter the URL (see Figure 7.27). Targets are explained in more depth in Chapter 8, but for now, "_blank" opens a new browser window to load the URL into, and "_self" loads the URL into the same browser window as the current SWF.

FIGURE 7.27
The Go to URL
dialog box.

To insert an email link instead of a URL, simply enter `mailto:` and then type the email address in the URL text box (see Figure 7.28). It should look something like this: `mailto:pucknell@flashinto.com`. The target shouldn't have any effect, so leave "_blank" selected in the Open In field.

FIGURE 7.28
Adding an email link.

POINTS TO REMEMBER

- Behaviors are designed to be a drag-and-drop solution to basic Flash ActionScript commands.

- Behaviors can be added to frames or movie clips.

- Behaviors write simple ActionScripts that you can view in the Actions panel, thereby helping you get familiar with what ActionScript looks like.

- Video Behaviors are added to buttons, not to video clips.

PART II
ACTIONSCRIPT

CHAPTER 8

INTRODUCTION TO ACTIONSCRIPT

THIS CHAPTER INTRODUCES YOU TO ACTIONSCRIPT AND HIGHLIGHTS SOME basic concepts of the language and principles for its use. Over the course of the next few chapters, you'll learn the fundamentals of ActionScript to give you a base for writing your own scripts. This chapter covers the following topics:

- Background information on ActionScript
- How to use the Actions panel
- Common ActionScript commands and functions
- Writing your first piece of ActionScript
- Basic handler concepts
- Using frame labels with ActionScript

What Is ActionScript?

ActionScript is a programming language, similar in structure to JavaScript, that you can use to create complex interactive effects in Macromedia Flash MX 2004. It adheres to the ECMAscript language specification and comes in two versions—ActionScript 1.0 and ActionScript 2.0—and both are real programming languages. ActionScript 2.0 in particular is a robust, evolving language capable of high levels of interactivity. In addition to all the features of ActionScript 1.0, ActionScript 2.0 supports

- A fully implemented class model, similar to those found in other languages, such as C++ and Java

- Strict data typing, which enables you to control the type of information your variables can contain (such as strings, arrays, or objects)

- An enhanced event model, with built-in support for a wide variety of event handlers and listeners

The ActionScript compiler has been almost completely rewritten for Flash MX 2004 and Flash MX 2004 Professional. That means when you write code in Flash 2004, it run two to ten times faster than in previous versions of Flash. Also, the new version of the Flash Player, Flash Player 7, runs from two to ten times faster than Flash Player 6. As a result, you'll see that video playback is better, components initialize faster, XML parsing is improved, and the authoring environment and new player handle memory much better.

Although it's nice to know that ActionScript can do more and do it faster, that still doesn't explain what ActionScript can *do*. ActionScript is what you use to control the playback of your movie and to create interactive applications. Using Flash and ActionScript, you can build applications such as a chat room, a message board, a video game such as Asteroids or Donkey Kong, an online storefront, or a data-driven application. The only limit to what you can build with ActionScript is what you choose for it to be.

THE ACTIONS PANEL

To add script to your Flash movie, start with opening the Actions panel by choosing Window, Development Panels, Actions from the main menu (keyboard shortcut: **F9**). After you have the Actions panel open (see Figure 8.1), you can start adding code.

FIGURE 8.1
The Actions panel.

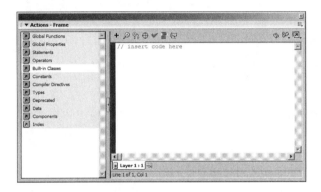

Along with just about every other aspect of the application, the Actions panel has changed in Flash 2004. If you're familiar with Flash MX, you might wonder where Normal mode is. In previous versions of Flash, you could operate the Actions panel in Normal and Expert modes. In Normal mode, you simply selected from a list of ActionScript keywords to build your code; in Expert mode, you could type code in manually. In Flash 2004, Normal mode has been replaced by Behaviors, and Expert mode remains as the only way to use the Actions panel.

For more information on Behaviors, see Chapter 7, "Behaviors."

The Actions Panel Interface

Figure 8.2 shows the menu buttons on the Actions panel.

Here's a quick overview of what you can use these buttons for:

- **Add New Item**   Displays a pop-up list of commands, filtered by type. You can select one for quick entry in your script.

- **Find and Find and Replace**   Click the Find button to search through your active scripts for a certain string. If you want to replace it with a different string, use the Find and Replace button.

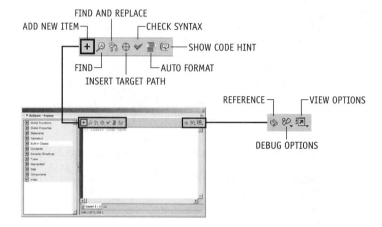

FIGURE 8.2
Menu buttons in the Actions panel.

- **Insert Target Path** Specify a target path for any commands you want to add. The target path defines what movie clip or Timeline an ActionScript command will reference.

- **Check Syntax** Click this button to check the current contents of the Actions panel for script errors. If errors are found, information is displayed in the Output panel.

- **Auto Format** Indent and format your code automatically.

- **Show Code Hint** Displays a list of properties, methods, or events that are available for the ActionScript keyword you're currently entering.

- **Reference** Opens the Reference panel, which contains syntax definitions and usage examples of all Flash commands.

Breakpoints are explained in Chapter 25, "Troubleshooting."

- **Debug Options** This button displays a pop-up menu (see Figure 8.3) for adding or removing a single breakpoint or for removing all breakpoints from your script window.

FIGURE 8.3
The pop-up menu for Debug Options.

- **View Options** This button displays a pop-up menu (see Figure 8.4) that lets you view Escape key shortcuts for commands in the Actions toolbox, view line numbers in the Actions panel, and turn Word Wrap on and off.

FIGURE 8.4

The pop-up Options menu.

Clicking in the top-right corner of the Actions panel, just below the × button, displays the menu shown in Figure 8.5.

FIGURE 8.5

The pop-up menu for all menu commands in the Actions panel.

This menu has all the commands discussed earlier as well as the following:

- **Import Script** Enables you to copy the contents of an .as file (an ActionScript file) into the current script window.

- **Export Script** Export the current Actions panel into a file.

- **Pin Script** Pins the current script in the Actions panel, which enables you to lock multiple code views in your Actions panel. (For example, if you wanted to keep two frames worth of code handy, you could "pin" one or both of them.)

- **Print** Print the contents of the current Actions panel.

- **Auto Format Options** View Auto Format preferences, which determines how your ActionScript is formatted in the Actions panel.

- **Preferences** View your settings in the Preferences dialog box.

- **Help** View the Help panel.

- **Maximize Panel** Maximize the Actions panel.

- **Close Panel** Close the Actions panel.

Actions Panel Features

The following sections describe how to use the Actions panel and take advantage of its features, such as syntax highlighting and code hinting, to improve your workflow in Flash.

Syntax Highlighting

Syntax is the set of rules that determines how a programming language—in this case, ActionScript—should be formatted. Proper syntax is important for correctly functioning scripts, as errors in your syntax cause your scripts to break.

To help you make sure your scripts are properly formatted, Flash offers *syntax highlighting*. This color coding helps you quickly see your code's overall structure and is also a helpful debugging tool. With syntax highlighting, improperly formatted commands and functions aren't color-coded. In the example shown in Figure 8.6, the correctly formatted function is displayed in color-coded text; the incorrectly formatted function is displayed in black text.

FIGURE 8.6

Example of syntax highlighting.

```
// the following function is properly formatted
function setName(firstName, lastName) {
    var firstName = firstName;
    var lastName = lastName;
    var msg = "Name has been set!";

    trace(msg);
}

// this function is not
funcion setPhone(areaCode, num) {
    vaa areaCode = areaCode;
    vaa number = num;
}
```

To customize the color coding to suit your preference, you need to change settings in the Preferences dialog box. You can open it by choosing Edit, Preferences from the main menu or by choosing Preferences from the pop-up menu at the upper right of the Actions panel. Then simply change the settings in the Syntax Coloring section of the ActionScript tab (see Figure 8.7).

Code Hinting

Another useful feature of the Actions panel is code hinting (see Figure 8.8). When you enter commands that Flash recognizes (frame actions such as stop() and gotoAndPlay()), Flash displays a list of properties, events, or parameters relevant to the command you're entering, which is a great time-saver. You can also display code hints at any time by clicking the Show Code Hint button.

FIGURE 8.7
Selecting colors for syntax highlighting in the Preferences dialog box.

FIGURE 8.8
Code hinting in Flash MX 2004.

Actions Toolbox

The Actions toolbox, in the left pane of the Actions panel, gives you an easy way to add new commands to your script (see Figure 8.9). Simply double-click a command, or click and drag a command over to the Actions panel. The new code is inserted at the current cursor location.

Commands that aren't available in the Flash Player version you're exporting for are highlighted in yellow in the Actions toolbox. For example, if you're exporting for Flash Player 6 compatibility, all Flash Player 7 features are highlighted in yellow in the Actions toolbox. You set the version of the Flash Player you're exporting to on a file-by-file basis by accessing the Publish Settings dialog box. (Choose File, Publish Settings from the menu or press **Ctrl+Shift+F12**, and then select the Flash tab.)

FIGURE 8.9
Selecting a command in the Actions toolbox.

Script Navigator

The Script Navigator, a new feature in Flash 2004, is located below the Actions toolbox. It displays a tree listing of elements in your Flash movie that contain ActionScript code. At the top of the Script Navigator is your current selection. Below that is a listing of all scenes in your movie. Every frame containing ActionScript is represented in this list. Below that list is a list of movie clips and buttons containing ActionScript. When you click any item in the Script Navigator, the Actions panel displays the contents of that item. The Script Navigator is useful in helping you keep track of the structure of the ActionScript in your movie.

Spellchecker

New to Flash 2004 is a spellchecker that can be used with code elements and text elements on the stage. To run a spellcheck on your current movie, choose Text, Check Spelling from the main menu (see Figure 8.10).

FIGURE 8.10
The Check Spelling dialog box.

Options in the Check Spelling dialog box are explained in more detail in Chapter 13, "Text."

To configure your spellcheck options, choose Text, Spelling Setup from the main menu (see Figure 8.11). You can also click the Setup button in the Check Spelling dialog box.

FIGURE 8.11
The Spelling Setup dialog box.

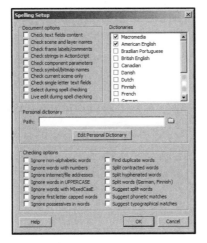

BASIC ACTIONSCRIPT

Flash recognizes two types of code: *embedded code*, which is code written in your Flash movie, and *external code*, which is written outside your Flash movie and loaded when you publish your movie. First, you'll learn about embedded code. Embedded code can go in two places in Flash: on specific frames of the timeline and on instances of movie clips and buttons on the stage.

To place code on a frame, select a keyframe on the Timeline, and enter code in the Actions panel. For example, you might choose to halt playback of your movie on a certain frame by using the stop() command.

To place code on an instance of a movie clip or button, select it with the mouse, and then enter the code in the Actions panel. Note that code placed on a movie clip must be contained in an event handler. (Event handlers are explained later in this chapter, in the sections "The on Event Handler" and "Frame-Based Handlers in Single-Frame Movie Clips.")

Two Essential Commands

When you're programming in Flash, you'll use two commands all the time. The first is the command to indicate a *comment*, which is a line of text used as a note in your code. Comments aren't included when you export your movie, so they exist only inside the authoring environment. Comments are commonly used to leave notes to yourself or to other developers who might be working on your code. You can include usage instructions, information about errors you've fixed, or an explanation of what specific variables do.

A comment has two slashes followed by text, as shown here:

```
// comment goes here
```

A comment can consist of any text you want. These three examples are all valid comments:

```
// hello

// Equation is x = 3 + 4 + 2

// August 25, 2003:
// Bug fixed.
```

If you want to avoid putting double slashes in front of every line for a long comment, you can use this format, which uses /* to denote the beginning of your multiline comment and */ to denote the end of it:

```
/*
    Comment
    Comment
*/
```

Comments are also used for commenting out code. If you want to run your program without a specific line or chunk of code—to test what will happen, for example—you comment out that line of code. In the following example, only the first function, functionOne(), would be called:

```
functionOne();
// functionTwo();
```

The other essential command is the trace() function, which has the following syntax:

```
trace(message);
```

The trace() function displays the contents of *message* in the Output panel. It's extremely useful for functional programming and for debugging your scripts and applications. *message* can consist of any type of data in Flash. You can specify strings (such as "Hello"), variables, or objects. As well, you can put nearly any other line of ActionScript code into a trace() function. For example, you can place mathematical equations in a trace() statement:

```
trace(4 + 5);
```

You can set variable or object properties in a trace() statement:

```
trace(x = 30);
```

```
trace(my_mc._x = 40);
```

You can also reference functions that return values:

```
trace(myfunction());
```

The trace() command is crucial to ensuring successful debugging of your software. You should use it whenever you want to check whether a specific section of code is being reached or to determine why a portion of your code is malfunctioning. For example, the following code tells you which condition in an if statement has been met:

```
if (4 > 5) {
    trace("4 is greater than 5");
} else {
    trace("4 is not greater than 5");
}
```

The following code traces when a function is called:

```
function myFunction() {
    trace("myFunction has been called");
    // other code would go here.
}
```

If the Output panel is closed, trace() opens it. If you close the Output panel and issue a trace() command, it reopens the panel. Note that the Output panel appears only inside the authoring environment, not in the Flash Player.

Always remember to add a line terminator (;) to the end of each line of ActionScript code in your movie. This character tells Flash where the end of the line is. A terminated line of code looks like this:

```
code;
```

Using External Files

In addition to editing your code in the Actions panel, you can create external .as files to hold your code, and load them into your Flash movie. An .as file is a simple text file, so it's easy to create. You create the file, add your code, and then save it. Importing code is useful for creating modular, easy-to-update Flash movies. If you have a lot of code in your movie, it's easier to edit and maintain it in ActionScript files as well as to reuse it in multiple projects.

To import an .as file for use in a movie, use the #include command, which has the following syntax:

```
#include "filename.as"
```

You can include as many as files as you like by adding multiple #include commands. You can also add an #include command inside an .as file. For example, suppose you had a function contained in an ActionScript file and you wanted to use it in your Flash movie. The ActionScript file might look like this:

```
// file: myFile.as
function tester() {
    trace("this function is externally loaded");
}

// code in your Flash movie
#include "myFile.as"
tester();
```

After the script is loaded, it functions as though it were embedded.

Usability Tip

The #include command, being outside the standard flow of code execution, doesn't require a semicolon to end the code line. In fact, adding a semicolon causes the #include statement to break, resulting in a "Malformed #include directive" error.

YOUR FIRST ACTIONS

Now that you have an idea of what ActionScript is, it's time to learn how to use it. If you've read the previous chapters, you already know how to use Flash and how to create and animate graphics. Now you need to know how to navigate through those graphics and animations. The first ActionScript commands you'll learn in the following sections are for controlling your movie's playback.

Frame Actions

Actions are statements that tell a movie to do something while it's playing. For example, gotoAndPlay() sends the movie playhead to a specific frame or label. The following sections describe the eight basic functions you can use to navigate through your Flash movie. If you simply need to navigate through a movie, these functions form the backbone of your programming efforts.

The *play()* Function

The play() function, shown in the following code, makes a movie begin or resume playback from the current frame:

```
// when a button is pressed...
on (release) {
    // ...make movie play
    play();
}
```

If the movie is already playing, nothing different happens; the movie just continues playing.

The *stop()* Function

The stop() function is used to stop the playback of the current Timeline. It's primarily used to control the playback of movie clips and buttons, as shown in this example:

```
// stop movie playback
stop();
```

If playback has already been stopped, nothing happens.

The *gotoAndPlay()* Function

The gotoAndPlay() function moves the Flash movie's playback head to a specific frame number or frame label and begins playback from that point. If any ActionScript code has been placed on the frame that gotoAndPlay() is targeting, that code runs when the playback head is moved. The following code shows two examples of using gotoAndPlay():

```
// jump to frame 5 and play
gotoAndPlay(5);

// jump to a frame with the label "myFrame" and play
gotoAndPlay("myFrame");
```

The *gotoAndStop()* Function

The gotoAndStop() function moves the Flash movie's playback head to a specific frame number or frame label and stops playback there. If any ActionScript code has been placed on the frame that gotoAndStop() is pointing to, that code runs even though playback has been halted. The following code shows two examples of using gotoAndStop():

```
// jump to frame 5 and stop
gotoAndStop(5);

// jump to a frame with the label "myFrame" and stop
gotoAndStop("myFrame");
```

The *stopAllSounds()* Function

The stopAllSounds() function stops all sounds that are currently playing, as shown here:

```
// stop all active sounds
stopAllSounds();
```

The *nextFrame()* Function

The nextFrame() function moves the Flash movie's playback head to the next frame and stops. Here's an example:

```
// move to the next frame
nextFrame();
```

If you're on the last frame of your Timeline, this function does nothing.

The *nextScene()* Function

The nextScene() function moves the Flash movie's playback head to the first frame of the next scene (if there is one) and stops. If there's no next scene, nothing happens. Here's an example of nextScene():

```
// move to the first frame of the next scene
nextScene();
```

The *prevFrame()* Function

The prevFrame() function, shown in the following code example, moves the Flash movie's playback head to the previous frame of the timeline and stops:

```
// move to the previous frame of the movie.
prevFrame();
```

If the current frame is frame 1 (the first frame), nothing happens.

The *prevScene()* Function

The prevScene() function moves the Flash movie's playback head to the first frame of the previous scene and stops. If there's no previous scene, the playback head moves to the first frame of the current scene. Here's an example of using prevScene():

```
on (release) {
    // move to the first frame of the previous scene
    prevScene();
}
```

Using Frame Actions

With the exception of nextScene() and prevScene(), which affect the root Timeline no matter where the commands are placed, all the functions for frame actions discussed in the previous sections refer directly to the Timeline they're in. That means if you place a play() function on the main Timeline, that's where that command is carried out. Likewise, if you place the play() function in a movie clip on the main Timeline, the command affects only the movie clip Timeline. For example, if you placed the following code on your main Timeline, the playhead would jump to frame 5 of the main Timeline:

```
gotoAndStop(5);
```

If you put the same code in a movie clip on the main Timeline, the movie clip's playhead would jump to frame 5 of the movie clip Timeline.

Because movie clips have their own Timelines that operate independently of any other Timelines, you can control the playback of the main Timeline or the movie clip's Timeline without affecting everything else. For example, if you have a movie clip on the main Timeline with a four-frame Timeline, and you place a stop() function on the main Timeline, the main Timeline stops playing, but the movie clip continues.

If you have multiple frame actions in a frame, the first one you add is the one that's carried out. For example, in the following code, the playback head will jump to frame 4, not 2:

```
gotoAndPlay(4);
gotoAndPlay(2);
```

Also, a stop() command is carried out only if it's the only frame command being issued. For example, in the following code, the stop() command will *not* be carried out:

```
stop();
gotoAndPlay(2);
```

Linking to External URLs

Scope is explained in more detail in Chapter 9, "ActionScript Basics: Data and Statements."

Many times when you're building a Flash movie, you need to link to external content: another Flash movie, an HTML page, or a completely different site. To access external content, you can use the getURL() function, which has the following syntax:

getURL(*"url"*, *"window"*, [*variables*]);

When you use this function, you don't have to worry about scope (where the function is carried out), because the function opens a new window (named *"window"*) displaying the content at *"url"*. You can specify three parameters when using the getURL() function:

- *url*   This is the URL of the content you want to appear, such as http://www.macromedia.com/. Note that to test absolute path references, such as http://www.macromedia.com/, you need an active network connection.

- *window* This parameter, which is optional, defines the window the URL will open in. In addition to whatever unique name you might want to use, the following reserved names are available:

    - "_self" Specifies that the URL will be loaded in the same frame in the same window as the Flash movie.

    - "_blank" Specifies a new, essentially unnamed window for the content to appear in. Using a getURL() command with a "_blank" window results in an unnamed window being opened.

    - "_parent" Specifies the parent of the current frame to display the content in. This reserved name is useful if your Flash movie is operating in a frameset, and you want to take over a larger portion of the frameset, or all of it, with your URL.

    - "_top" Specifies the top-level frame of the current window. For example, if your Flash movie is operating in an HTML frameset and you want your link to take over the entire window, you would specify "_top".

    If you name a window with something other than these reserved names ("myWindow", for example), your URL creates a new window only if the specified window doesn't exist. If it does, the new URL replaces the existing content.

- *variables* This optional parameter is used only if you are sending variables to the page you're loading. If you aren't sending variables, don't set this parameter.

    The two options for this parameter are GET and POST, which determine how variables are sent to the URL. The GET method adds variables to the end of the URL and is ideal when you're sending only a few variables. The POST method, on the other hand, sends variables in a separate HTTP header. POST is the recommended method if you have several variables to send or you want a more secure method of sending variables.

Here are some examples of using the getURL() function:

```
// when the user clicks a button, open the new window
on (release) {
    // use getURL
```

```
        getURL("http://www.flashinto.com/", "_blank");
}

on (release) {
    // open a blank window
    getURL("http://www.mrhogg.com/", "_blank");
}

// open a new window, setting the variable transmission
// type to "POST"
trace("opening new browser window");
getURL("http://www.crashmedia.com/", "_blank", "POST");

// open a new window, setting the variable transmission
// type to "GET"
first_name = "Bob";
last_name = "Smith";
getURL("http://www.myserver.com/loadNames.php", "_blank",
"GET");
```

ADDING BUTTONS WITH ACTIONSCRIPT

Now that you know how to use basic frame actions, it's time to find out how to apply them to buttons. When attaching ActionScript code to a button, you must place it within the context of an event handler for Flash to know how to interpret your commands correctly. An *event handler* performs an action (such as jumping to a new frame or opening a browser window) in response to an event, such as a mouse click or a keypress.

The *on* Event Handler

When you place a button on the stage, you probably want users to interact with it in some way, such as clicking it. To do this, you add an on event handler to the button.

First, place a button on the stage by dragging it from the library to a frame in the Timeline or onto the visual stage. Select the newly created button instance and open the Actions panel. You can assign event handlers in two ways: You can type in the handler manually, or insert the handler by clicking the Add New Item menu button or double-clicking the handler in the Actions toolbox. The basic on event handler looks like this:

```
on () {
}
```

The handler type you select is important, as it affects your button's functionality. The following list describes the valid handler types:

- **on (press)** Activated when a user clicks a button. It's activated only once, no matter how long the button remains pressed.

- **on (release)** Activated when a user clicks a button and then releases it.

- **on (releaseOutside)** Activated when a user clicks a button and moves the cursor off the button before releasing it.

- **on (rollOver)** Activated when a user moves the cursor over a button.

- **on (rollOut)** Activated when a user moves the cursor off a button.

- **on (dragOver)** Activated when a user clicks a button, drags the mouse off the button, and then drags it back over the button without having released the mouse button.

- **on (dragOut)** Activated when a user clicks the mouse button while over the button and drags the mouse off the button. An event handler of this type is activated whether or not the mouse button has been released and can be activated more than once per mouse button click.

- **on (keypress *key*)** Activated by pressing a key on the keyboard. In addition to using any standard key character (such as A, B, or C), you can use any of the following keys: "<Left>", "<Right>", "<Home>", "<End>", "<Insert>", "<Delete>", "<Backspace>", "<Enter>", "<Up>", "<Down>", "<Page Up>", "<Page Down>", "<Tab>", "<Escape>", or "<Space>". For example, the following handler would be called when the user presses the spacebar:

```
on (keypress "<Space>") {
    }
```

For example, say you want a button to be activated when a user clicks it. You can use the press or release handler, but this example uses release:

```
on (release) {
}
```

After selecting the handler type, add the code you want to run. You can place almost any ActionScript inside an on handler, except for other handlers, such as additional on event handlers or onClipEvent handlers. (You'll learn about these handlers in the next section.)

If you want a button that opens a page on your website, you would use the following code:

```
on (release) {
    // open new web page
    getURL("http://www.macromedia.com/");
}
```

Note that with the on event handler, you can use multiple handler types at the same time by separating them with commas, as shown here:

```
on (release, releaseOutside) {
    // stop playback of the current movie
    stop();
}
```

THE ALL-POWERFUL MOVIE CLIP

Listeners, a helpful way to run certain code according to specific events, are explained in Chapter 10, "ActionScript: Functions, Events, and Objects."

The movie clip is, in many ways, the backbone of Flash. By holding a number of handlers, it gives you an easy way to monitor activity in your movie and is a handy representation of your code constructs. In previous Flash versions, movie clips were often used as workarounds for classes, which weren't supported. ActionScript 2.0 now supports classes, but the use of movie clips as a programming aid hasn't lessened in Flash 2004.

Movie clips can be created, named, and referred to programmatically, and each one has its own timeline. You can create empty movie clips by using createEmptyMovieClip() to house script of any type. You can also use movie clips to create listeners for events without using real listeners.

Path References

As you've already learned, Flash has a very organized path structure in place. Code in a movie clip can refer to other movie clips, and other objects can refer to objects within movie clips, but to do so successfully, you must make correct path references. For example, if you had a movie clip named bob on the stage, and you wanted to refer to it from a keyframe on the main Timeline, your code would look like this:

```
bob.play();
```

If you wanted to refer to the main Timeline from within bob, your code would look like one of the following:

```
_parent.play();
```

```
_root.play();
```

The difference between these two approaches is that the first statement makes a *relative path reference*, and the second makes an *absolute path reference*. A relative path reference refers to a Timeline within the context of the current Timeline, such as its parent (using parent) or its child (using the name of the child movie clip). An absolute path reference begins with root and begins from the main Timeline.

Suppose you have a movie clip named mary on the same level as bob, and you want one to make a call to the other. The code would look like this:

```
_parent.mary.play();
```

or

```
_root.mary.play();
```

Figure 8.12 shows the path structure for this example.

FIGURE 8.12
The path structure for the *bob* and *mary* movie clips.

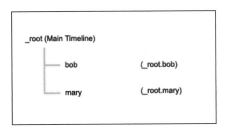

If you had a movie clip called ego inside bob, the path structure would look like Figure 8.13.

FIGURE 8.13
The path structure for bob, mary, and ego.

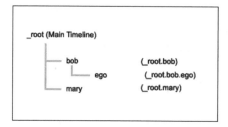

For ego to refer to something on the root level, the code would have to look like one of the following:

```
_parent._parent.play();
```

or

```
_root.play();
```

bob is the parent movie clip of ego, and the root is the parent of both mary and bob. If you wanted mary to refer to bob's ego, it would look like this:

```
_parent.bob.ego.play();
```

Note in the previous code samples that movie clips are separated with dots (periods). ActionScript uses dot syntax, which is a standard notation common to object-oriented programming languages, such as C++, Java, and JavaScript.

One reason to avoid using _root references whenever possible is portability. During the course of a project, often you have to shift locations of movie clips within a file. If a movie clip refers to _root, and you end up modifying the structure (say, by putting everything on the main Timeline into a movie clip that sits on the main Timeline), your _root references won't work. An advantage to using absolute instead of relative path references is that you don't have to keep track of how many levels deep you are at any time; if you know you won't be changing your file structure, that might end up being simpler.

Frame-Based Handlers in Single-Frame Movie Clips

Often you want your script to run continuously for minutes or even hours at a time, but you don't want to have the Player run continuously across hundreds or thousands of frames. A common and helpful trick is using an enterFrame handler to place code that's repeated frequently on a movie clip.

Even on a single-frame movie clip, Flash continually redraws the movie clip's contents. So every time the frame is redrawn, code is carried out, as shown in this example:

1. Create a new movie clip.

2. Click and drag the movie clip from the Library to the stage.

3. Select the movie clip, and open the Actions panel.

4. In the Actions panel, type the following:

```
onClipEvent (enterFrame) {
    trace("I am an enterFrame Handler");
}
```

5. Test your movie (choose Control, Test Movie from the menu or press **Ctrl+Enter**), and you'll see "I am an EnterFrame Handler" displayed repeatedly in the Output panel, as shown in Figure 8.14.

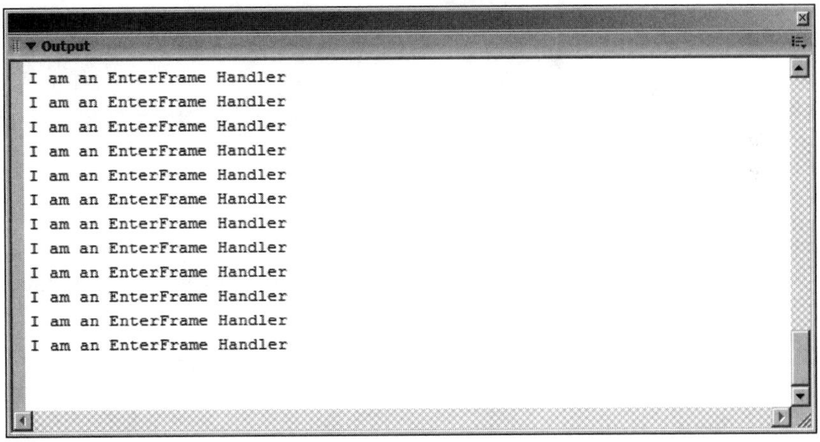

FIGURE 8.14
The Output panel.

Suppose you wanted a clock that continuously displayed the time in a text box onscreen. You could use a movie clip with an enterFrame handler to achieve this, as shown in this example:

```
onClipEvent (enterFrame) {
    myDate = new Date();
    myTextField.text = myDate.getDate();
}
```

Frame Labels

Frame labels are an easy way for Flash designers and developers to delineate content. You can name keyframes (by selecting the keyframe in the timeline and entering a frame name in the Property inspector, as shown in Figure 8.15) and refer to them programmatically with frame actions.

FIGURE 8.15
Naming frames in the Property inspector.

SELECTING A
KEYFRAME

SETTING YOUR
LABEL

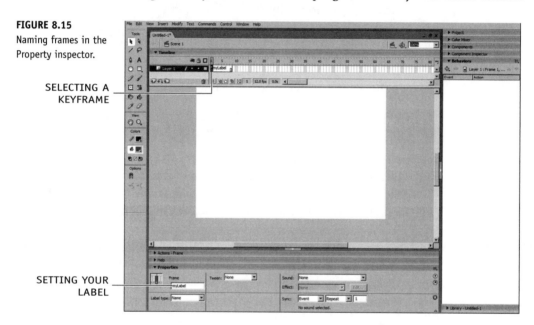

A basic menu system—in which a user clicks a button and is sent to a specific frame—is a good use for frame labels. For example, the following code placed on a button instance jumps the playback head to the frame labeled playAgain:

```
on (release) {
gotoAndPlay("playAgain");
}
```

Chapter Project: Creating Navigation

Now that you've learned some of the basics of ActionScript, try this tutorial to get a better feel for your new skills. If you don't want to follow along with the tutorial, you can jump ahead to Chapter 9.

Still here? Excellent. This tutorial is easy. It consists of a site with four sections linked by a navigation system and includes a `mailto` link and an external web site link.

1. First, you need a blank canvas to work with, so create a new movie.

2. Add 25 new frames to Layer 1, as shown in Figure 8.16.

FIGURE 8.16

Adding new frames.

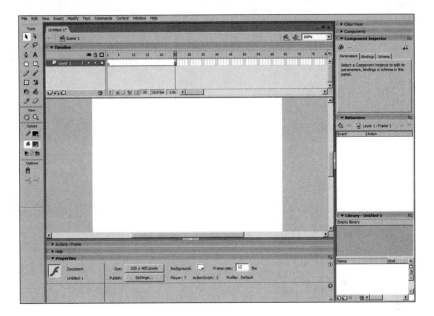

3. Name your layer `Labels`, and make new keyframes every five frames (starting with frame 1 and ending with frame 20). Name these new keyframes `main`, `one`, `two`, `three`, and `four` (see Figure 8.17).

FIGURE 8.17

Adding keyframes.

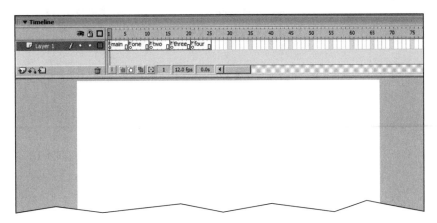

4. Add a new layer and name it button. (This layer should automatically have 25 frames, just like the other layer. If it doesn't, add them before adding your buttons.) Open the Buttons library by choosing Window, Other Panels, Common Libraries, Buttons from the main menu. Add five button instances to your Buttons layer (see Figure 8.18).

FIGURE 8.18
Adding buttons to the stage.

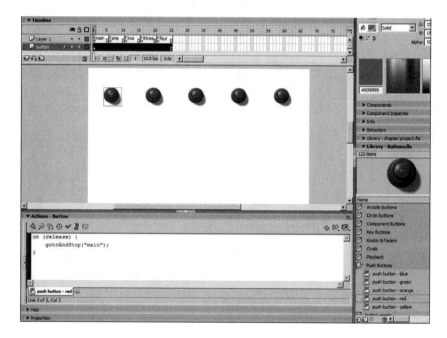

5. Next, you'll add some ActionScript to your first button. Select the button on the stage, and enter the following code in the Actions panel:

```
on (release) {
    gotoAndPlay("main");
}
```

6. Now select each of the remaining buttons and add the same code, substituting a different frame label for each successive button. For example, the first button links to main, but the second should link to one, the third to two, and so on.

7. Create a new layer named Content. (This new layer should be created with 25 frames, to match the other layers. If it isn't, add the frames now.) Add four keyframes corresponding to the keyframes labeled one, two, three, and four. On this layer, in each keyframed section, add some content. The content can be anything you like; simple graphics will suffice, but you can also add text, images, or other movie clips you want to create.

8. In the three keyframe, along with whatever other content you've added, add a link to an external web site. To do that, create a new button and place it somewhere on the stage in the Content layer. Select it, and add the following code in the Actions panel, as shown in Figure 8.19 (*www.mysite.com* can be whatever site you like):

```
on (release) {
        getURL("http://www.mysite.com/");
    }
```

FIGURE 8.19
Adding ActionScript to your button.

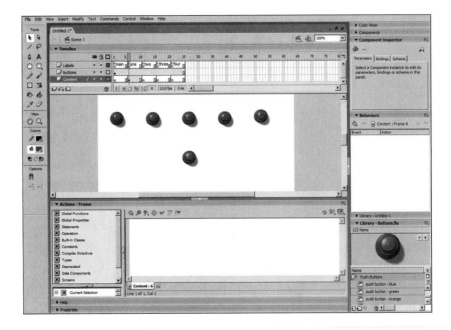

9. Next, add a mailto link to the four keyframe (because everyone needs to know how to drop you a line). To do this, create a new button, and place it somewhere on the stage. Select it, and add the following

code in the Actions panel (of course, *my@address.com* can be what-ever address you like):

```
on (release) {
    getURL(mailto:my@address.com);
}
```

That's it—now test your movie to see it in action. Way to go!

POINTS TO REMEMBER

- ActionScript can be used to control the playback of your movie and to create interactive applications.

- Use the Actions panel's features, such as syntax highlighting and code hinting, to help you add ActionScript quickly and easily.

- ActionScript is embedded (or contained) within a Flash movie, or it's external and referenced within a Flash movie and loaded into it when the movie is published. External code is imported by using the #include command.

- Embedded code is placed on specific frames or instances of movie clips or buttons.

- Event handlers provide a context for your code to ensure that commands are properly interpreted. The on event handler is used with buttons and is activated when users interact with buttons using the mouse.

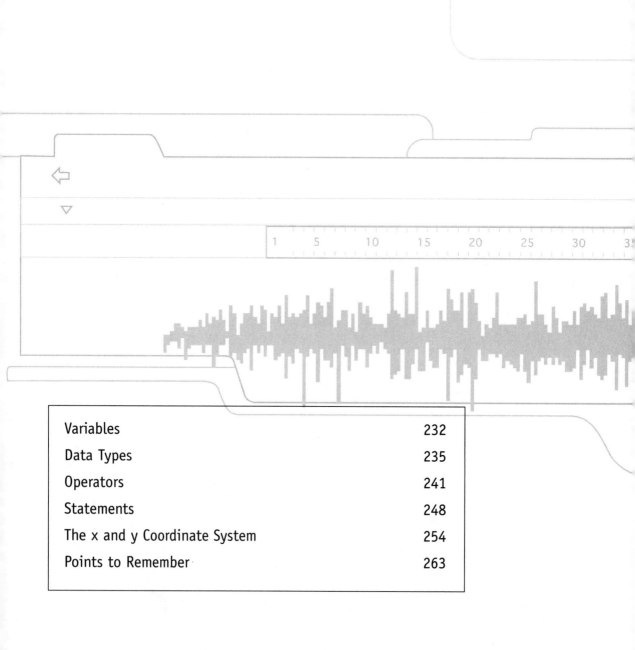

CHAPTER 9

ActionScript Basics: Data and Statements

Now that you've learned some of the basics of ActionScript and how to add it to your Flash movie, you'll build on that knowledge. This chapter introduces you to some additional concepts:

- Variables
- Data types
- Operators
- Expressions and conditional statements
- The x and y coordinate system
- Pinning scripts

In addition to learning these concepts, at the end of this chapter you'll find a short project to help you practice your increasing skills.

VARIABLES

A *variable* is a container for information, and as long as a variable exists, its contents can change. Creating variables and assigning values to them allows you to track a user's progress through your movie, record changing values in your movie, and evaluate conditions within your movie.

Defining a Variable

A variable can hold data of any type and is defined by using var or set:

```
// var syntax
var variableName = initialValue;

// set syntax
set(variableName, variableValue);
```

initialValue is an optional parameter and can be an explicit declaration of a value (hello or 4, for example) or a declaration of type (new Object(), for example). Setting an initial value for your variables—known as *initializing* a variable—is a recommended best practice. You should initialize variables in the first frame of your movie so that you can keep better track of data you're handling throughout your movie.

During the course of your movie, not only can you adjust the value of variables, you can also change their data type. For example, this completely valid piece of code changes the data type from String to Object:

```
// code on frame 1
var myVar = "Hello";     // String type

// code on frame 2
myVar = new Object();     // Object type
```

Note that if you use the var keyword to define a variable that already exists, Flash overwrites the existing variable with a new one, and any previous information contained in that variable is lost.

ActionScript supports automatic data typing, which means that when you define a variable, you don't need to explicitly set its type. In the following example, Flash determines that bob is a string, so it sets your variable data type to String:

```
var myVariable = "bob";
```

Naming a Variable

A valid variable name must adhere to these three rules:

- It must be an identifier that begins with a letter, an underscore, or a dollar sign. Subsequent characters can be letters, numbers, underscores, or dollar signs.

- It can't have the same name as a reserved keyword or a literal, such as null or undefined.

- It must be a unique name within its scope.

Variable Scope

A variable's *scope* is the area in which the variable is known and can be referenced. There are three different types of variables in Flash, each with a different scope.

Local Variables

Local variables are defined within the body of a function and are known only inside that function. To define a local variable, use the var command inside a function body, as shown here:

```
function myFunc() {
    var myVar;
}
```

Local variables are useful as data stores inside methods. In that context, they prevent name collisions, which helps reduce the number of errors in your movie. Name collisions occur when a variable is redefined accidentally. For example, the following code would cause a name collision:

```
var x = 4;
var y = 5;
```

```
function multiplyNumbers() {
    z = x*y;
    trace("z = " + z);
}

function divideNumbers() {
    x = 5;
    y = 6;
    z = x/y;
    trace("z = " + z);
}

multiplyNumbers();
divideNumbers();
```

You initially define x and y as having the values 4 and 5, respectively. The multiplyNumbers() function multiplies x and y and traces the result. This is fine until you call the divideNumbers() function, which alters x and y and then divides them. If you were to call multiplyNumbers() a second time, your result would be different. You could prevent these types of errors by defining x and y, as used by divideNumbers(), as local variables:

```
function divideNumbers() {
    var x = 5;
    var y = 6;
    var z = x/y;
    trace("z = " + z);
}
```

Timeline Variables

Timeline variables are defined in ActionScript and attached to a frame on the main Timeline or within a movie clip timeline. They are accessible within the context of their timeline.

The following is an example of attaching a variable to a timeline. The ActionScript sets the myName variable to the timeline of the my_mc movie clip:

```
my_mc.myName = "Bob Roberts";
```

To define a variable within a movie clip timeline, simply select the keyframe in the timeline where the variable will exist, and enter it there. The following code defines the myName variable after the focus is already on the my_mc timeline:

```
myName = "Bob Roberts";
```

Global Variables

Global variables and functions are accessible from every timeline and every scope unless a local variable is defined with the same name as a global variable. In this case, the local variable is used instead of the global variable for the duration of the method.

Global variables are defined with the _global identifier and referenced as though they were local. For example, the following code defines a global variable and references it:

```
// declare global variable
_global.myFirstName = "bob";

// reference global variable
trace(myFirstName);
```

Deleting a Variable

If you want to remove the variable from system memory, use the delete command:

```
delete variableName;

// example
delete myFirstName;
```

DATA TYPES

A *data type* describes the type of information a variable can contain. There are two kinds of data types: *primitive* (String, Number, and Boolean) and *reference* (MovieClip and Object). A primitive data type means that a variable holds the actual data described; for example, if you define x = 3, x *is* 3. The reference type holds a value that's malleable, so it contains only a reference to the data; for example, x can have a reference to an object with a value of 3, but it is not 3. In addition, there are two special data types, Null and Undefined, which are explained a little later. In Macromedia Flash MX 2004, any built-in object that isn't a primitive data type or a MovieClip data type is of the Object data type.

For a complete listing of methods and properties available to each data type, check your ActionScript Reference Guide, which is available in Flash MX 2004.

Each data type has its own unique *methods*—functions assigned to an object, in this case the data type—and *properties*—values contained inside the data type—that can be referenced and used. The following sections describe the available data types in Flash.

Number

A number in Flash is a double-precision floating-point number. This means that a number can be almost any integer, either negative or positive. The two limits for numeric values are 1.79E+308 (maximum) and 5e–324 (minimum). Here are some examples of numbers:

```
var myOne = 1;

var myTwo = 234.22;

var myThree = 45 + 45;
```

You can adjust the value of numbers by using any of the traditional numeric operators, such as –, +, *, and /. You can also use any of the functions in the Math object to manipulate numbers.

String

The String data type contains a sequence of characters and can represent numbers, letters, or any number of other punctuation and special characters. Strings in Flash are enclosed in single or double quotation marks, as shown in these examples:

```
var myString1 = "Hello!";

var myString2 = 'You are my number 1 neighbor!';

var myString3 = "345";
```

Boolean

The Boolean data type can be true or false. When possible, Flash converts a Boolean's value to 1 or 0. Booleans are useful in logical evaluators, as in the following example, where a trace statement is carried out if a Boolean property is set to true:

```
if (showTrace == true) {
    trace("I am a trace.");
}
```

Object

A Flash object is a container for variables and functions. The variables inside an object are called *properties*, and the functions inside an object are called *methods*. Each property has both a name and a value. Properties of an object can be of any data type, including the Object type, which allows you to reference other objects from within the properties of objects. Placing objects within objects is called *nesting*, which is useful in creating a hierarchical structure for your data. You can refer to properties and methods within an object by using the dot operator. For example, in the following line, house represents the main object. It holds a property containing a reference to an object called rooms, which contains the property numberOfRooms:

```
house.rooms.numberOfRooms
```

You can also refer to functions defined within an object, as in the following example:

```
// create objects
House = new Object();
House.rooms = new Object();

// define number of rooms
house.rooms.numberOfRooms = 4;

// define function
House.rooms.showNumberOfRooms = function() {
Trace("there are " + numberOfRooms + " rooms in this house.");
}
```

```
// execute function
house.rooms.showNumberOfRooms();

// Output
There are 4 rooms in this house.
```

ActionScript contains a number of built-in object types, such as Array, XML, and Math. You can also create your own objects, complete with specific properties and methods to suit your needs. For example, you might create an object to contain a list of users who can log in to your web site, or an object to record high scores in a game you're creating.

MovieClip

The MovieClip data type contains a symbol that can play an animation element. It's the only data type that refers directly to a graphic element. You can create movie clips in the authoring environment (choosing Insert, New Symbol from the menu) or at runtime by using createEmptyMovieClip().

 The createEmptyMovieClip() method is explained in Chapter 10, "ActionScript: Function, Events, and Objects."

Null

The Null data type has only one value: null. Although this means there's no data in a null variable, this variable type is useful in several ways:

- To indicate a variable that hasn't been given a value yet

- To indicate that a variable no longer has a value

- When sent as the return value from a function to inform the caller that no data was sent

- As a placeholder in a list of variables sent to a function

The following code defines the myName variable, giving it an initial value of null:

```
var myName = null;
```

Now that this variable has been defined, you would give it a different value later in your code.

Undefined

The Undefined data type has only one value: undefined. It means that a variable hasn't been assigned a value yet. The following example shows that a newly created variable is first undefined:

```
var bob;
trace("bob is " + bob);
```

The Undefined type is different from the Null type because a Null type variable has a value of null; an undefined variable doesn't have any value.

Assigning Data Types

Flash determines the correct data type for the following language elements:

- Variables
- Parameters passed to a function, method, or class
- Values returned from a function or method
- Objects created as subclasses of classes

Although it isn't necessary to explicitly define a data type when defining variables, it's recommended that you do so, both for code clarity during the programming process and to help in debugging your script. You can explicitly define a data type by using strict data typing, discussed in the following section.

Strict Data Typing

In ActionScript 2.0, you can explicitly state the type of a variable when you create it, which is called *strict data typing*. If you assign a value of the wrong type to a strict-defined variable, you trigger a compiler error. Strict data typing helps ensure that data sent through Flash is always of the correct type. This is the syntax for strict data typing:

```
variable:type
```

```
var myVar:String;    // strict typed string
function sendToBob (name:String, phone:Number) {
}    // strict typed function parameters

var myObj:XML = new XML();    // strict typed object
```

You can also strict-type a variable to be of a custom type, as in the following example that defines Goal as a custom data type:

```
var newGoal:Goal = new Goal();
```

If you attempt to set a variable to a value that the specified data type doesn't support, you get an error. For example, the following code results in a compiler error:

```
var userName:String;
userName = 4;
```

The preceding code generates a "Type Mismatch" error because although you're stating that the userName variable should be of type String, you're attempting to set its value to 4, which is a number, not a string.

 Flash automatically displays code hints for built-in objects that are strictly typed, without the need to add code-hinting suffixes. For example, if you set a variable's data type to Array, every time you type in the name of that variable, you're shown the Array code hints. For more information on code hints, refer to Chapter 8, "Introduction to ActionScript."

ActionScript 1.0 doesn't support strict data typing, and although exporting code with strict data typing to Flash Player might seem to work, the SWF file might not perform as programmed. When using ActionScript 2.0 and exporting for Flash Player 6 (this option is available in Publish Settings), strict data typing isn't enforced—that is, illegal variable settings work without generating an error, allowing mismatched property types to be passed through your program.

Determining Data Types

You can determine the type of data a variable contains by using the typeof() function. You call this function by using the syntax typeof(*variable*). The following example creates a string and traces its data type:

```
var myString;
myString = "I am a string!";
trace(typeof(myString));
```

OPERATORS

An *operator* in Flash calculates a new value from one or more values. As an example, the minus symbol is an operator that performs a subtraction calculation. An *operand* is the values that an operator manipulates. For example, in x = 2 + 4, 2 and 4 are the operands. The following sections explain the many types of operators available for use in Flash.

Numeric Operators

Numeric operators are used to add, subtract, divide, and multiply numbers, along with some other functions. These are the numeric operators in Flash:

- **+** The addition operator.

- **-** The subtraction operator.

- **/** The division operator.

- ***** The multiplication operator.

- **%** The modulo operator returns the remainder of a division of two numbers.

- **++** This increment operator is a shorthand way to add 1 to a given value, as shown in this example:

```
i = 0;
// add 1 to i;
i++;
// will output 1. trace(i);
```

The second line in the preceding example is the same as writing i = i + 1. You can also use the negative increment operator, –, which decreases the value of a variable by 1.

Comparison Operators

Four comparison operators are available for use in Flash. They are used to compare values of two operands and return a Boolean value (true or false). Comparison operators are often used in conditional statements, such as if and while (see "Conditional Statements," later in this chapter, for more on if and while). These are the comparison operators:

- < The less-than operator
- > The greater-than operator
- <= The less-than-or-equal-to operator
- >= The greater-than-or-equal-to operator

Here's an example of using these operators:

```
amSmall = small < big;      // would likely return true

if (scale < 100) {
    // condition 1 : this is fired if scale is less than 100
} else if (scale >= 100) {
// condition 2 : this is fired if scale is equal to or greater
//than 100
}
```

String Operators

The string operator ("") is used to specify a value for a string, as shown in this example:

```
var myName = "Brian";
```

Using an addition operator with strings concatenates (combines) the strings into one string, as shown in this example:

```
var myName = "Brian " + "Hogg";
trace(myName);
// outputs
// Brian Hogg
```

If one operand is a string and the other is a numeric character, the numeric value is converted to a string and concatenated:

```
var myAddress = 5657 + " Bilby";
trace(myAddress);

// outputs
// 5657 Bilby
```

Additionally, comparison operators act differently on strings than on numeric values. The comparison run on strings determines the alphabetic sort of the two operands, as shown in this example:

```
if ("bob" < "jake") {
    trace("bob comes first");
} else {
    trace("jake comes first");
}
```

This code outputs the first `trace` statement, `bob comes first`. If both operands aren't strings, Flash converts both to numbers and compares them.

Equality Operators

There are four operators of this type:

- **== (equality operator)** This operator compares two operands and returns a Boolean value. True is returned if the two operands are equal in value. False is returned if they are not. Strings, numbers, and Boolean values are compared directly, but objects are compared by reference. When you compare by reference, you're comparing the objects that the operands refer to, not the operands themselves. A common mistake is to substitute the equality operator for the assignment operator (which is =). This causes errors because the equality operator returns true or false, but the assignment operator simply sets a value. For example, the following code returns either a true or false, depending on the conditions:

```
if (numberOne == numberTwo) {
    trace("yeah");
}
```

This code returns only `true` because you're telling Flash that `numberOne` is equal to `numberTwo`:

```
if (numberOne = numberTwo) {
    trace("yeah");
}
```

- **=== (strict equality operator)** This operator is much like equality, except that strict equality doesn't perform type conversion (converting to numbers for the comparison) in its comparison.

- **!= (inequality operator)**   This operator is the opposite of the equality operator: It returns a `true` if the two operands aren't the same. For example, the output for the following code would be `no` because it is true that `bob` does not equal `mary`:

```
if (bob != mary) {
    trace("no");
}
```

- **!== (strict inequality operator)**   This operator is like inequality, except that the operator does not perform any type conversion.

Logical Operators

Logical operators compare two Boolean values and return a third Boolean value (such as `yes` or `no`) based on them. Typically, logical operators are used in conditional operators and in `if` and `while` statements. These are the three logical operators:

```
AND     &&

OR      ||

NOT     !
```

Logical `AND` compares the results of two other operators. In this instance, the `&&` returns a true, as shown here:

```
if (10 == 10 && 5 > 4) {
    trace("yes");
} else {
    trace("no");
}
```

Logical `OR` checks to see whether either of the other two operators is true. If so, the `||` operator returns a true, as shown here:

```
if (10 == 11 || 4 == 4) {
    trace("yes");
} else {
    trace("no");
}
```

Logical `NOT` checks to see whether the condition has not been met. In the following example, `gameOver` is set to the value of `true`. The logical operator checks to see whether gameOver is false. Because it isn't, the operator returns a false.

```
gameOver = true;
if (!gameOver) {
    return true;
} else {
return false;
}
```

Conditional Operators

The conditional operator functions in much the same way as the if statement. It uses this syntax:

```
condition ? true outcome : false outcome;
```

For example, in the following line, 4 is greater than 3, so the yes is sent to the Output panel:

```
4 > 3 ? trace("yes") : trace("no");
```

Assignment Operators

Assignment operators set the value of the first operand to the value of the second. There are several different assignment operators:

- **= (assignment operator)** The most common and basic operator, it simply assigns a value, as shown here:

```
var1 = var2;
```

- **+= (addition and assignment operator)** This operator is a shorthand way of adding the value of the second operand to the first operand, as in this example:

```
var1 = 4;
var2 = 5;
var1 += var2;
trace(var1);

// outputs
// 9
```

- **-= (subtraction and assignment operator)** This operator subtracts the value of the second operand from the first, as shown here:

```
var1 = 4;
var2 = 5;
var1 -= var2
trace(var1);
// outputs
// -1;
```

- ***= (multiplication and assignment operator)** This operator multiplies the value of the second operand by the value of the first, like so:

```
var1 = 5;
var1 *= 4;
trace(var1);
// outputs
// 20
```

- **%= (modulo and assignment operator)** This operator divides the two operands, with the value of the first operand being set to the value of a divided remainder of the two numbers, as shown in this example:

```
var1 = 5;
var1 %= 2;
trace(var1);
// outputs
// 1
```

- **/= (divide and assignment operator)** This operator divides the first operand by the second and assigns the first operand the value of the result, as shown here:

```
var1 = 4;
var1 /= 2;
trace(var1);
// outputs
// 2
```

Operator Precedence

You are allowed to use multiple operators in a single statement, as shown here:

```
myVal = 1 + 3 + 4;
result = 2 / 4 + 2;
```

When you do this, note that some operators take precedence over others, meaning that certain operations are performed before others. For example, multiplication is always performed before addition, but items in parentheses take precedence. The result of the following line is 35:

```
myVal = 5 + 10 * 3;
```

Using parentheses, however, as shown in the following line, results in 45:

```
myVal = (5+10) * 3;
```

When multiple operators with the same level of precedence are used in the same statement, the order of execution is determined by their *associativity*, which can be left to right or right to left. Associativity specifies in which direction operators are calculated. Table 9.1 lists operators, their precedence, and their associativity, sorted highest to lowest in order of precedence.

TABLE 9.1 **Operator Order of Precedence and Associativity**

Operator	Precedence	Associativity
+	Unary plus	Right to left
-	Unary minus	Right to left
~	Bitwise one's complement	Right to left
!	Logical NOT	Right to left
++	Post-increment	Left to right
--	Post-decrement	Left to right
++	Pre-increment	Right to left
--	Pre-decrement	Right to left
*	Multiply	Left to right

continues

TABLE 9.1 **Operator Order of Precedence and Associativity**

(continued)

Operator	Precedence	Associativity
/	Divide	Left to right
%	Modulo	Left to right
+	Add	Left to right
-	Subtract	Left to right
<	Less than	Left to right
<=	Less than or equal to	Left to right
>	Greater than	Left to right
>=	Greater than or equal to	Left to right
==	Equal	Left to right
!=	Not equal	Left to right
&&	Logical AND	Left to right
||	Logical OR	Left to right
?:	Conditional	Right to left
=	Assignment	Right to left
*=, /=, %=, +=, -=, &=, |=, ^=, <<=, >>=, >>>=	Compound assignment	Right to left

Source: Flash Help files, Macromedia, Inc., 2003

STATEMENTS

Statements are the lines of ActionScript that tell your movie to do something. The following sections describe the different statements you can use in your ActionScript.

Conditional Statements

Conditional statements are used to create branches in your script, allowing different blocks of code to be carried out depending on different parameters. Typically, comparison and equality operators (==, <, >) are used with conditional statements. The following sections describe the conditional statements in Flash.

The *if* Statement

The if statement carries out the code contained within the statement body (inside the {}) if a condition is met. It uses this syntax:

```
if (condition) {
     // Code to be executed
}

// example
if (myVal == 4) {
     trace("myVal is 4");
}
```

The *else* Statement

The else statement is used with if statements and provides an alternative code block to run if the if condition is not met. Here's an example:

```
if (myVal == 4) {
     trace("myVal is 4");
} else {
     trace("myVal is not 4");
}
```

The *else if* Statement

Similar to the else statement, else if provides an alternative to the if condition with its own condition to be met. The else if statement is useful for testing multiple conditions, as shown in this example:

```
if (myVal == 4) {
     trace("myVal is 4");
} else if (myVal == 5) {
     trace("myVal is 5");
}
```

Loop Statements

Often you need your code to run repeatedly, not just once, based on a condition. To do this, you write a *loop statement*, which iterates through specified commands again and again. Loop statements come in handy in a multitude of situations, such as totaling a series of numbers, checking a group of values, or running a block of code on a number of objects. There are several types of loops, described in the next sections.

The *for* Loop

The most common loop statement is the for loop, which has two variations. The first, the simple for loop, looks like this:

```
for (init; condition; next) {
    // code would go here
}
```

This loop iterates from *init* until the condition is met, incrementing the start variable each time. *init* is the declaration of a variable, and *condition* is the condition at which the for() loop is terminated. *next* is used to adjust the *init* variable each time through the loop. For example, the following code runs the trace statement five times:

```
for (var i = 0; i<5; i++) {
    trace("I am in step " + i + " of the loop");
}
```

The loop goes from the initial value of i as long as the condition is met. After each iteration, the increment is applied to the initial variable (in this case, using the shorthand ++ for adding 1 to a variable). This code produces the following output:

```
I am in step 0 of the loop
I am in step 1 of the loop
I am in step 2 of the loop
I am in step 3 of the loop
I am in step 4 of the loop
```

Increments don't have to start from 1; they can be any number, even negative numbers. The following two examples show different ways to iterate through a for loop.

Starting with greater than 1, as in this example

```
for (var i = 0; i<6; i+=2) {
    trace("I am in step " + i + " of the loop");
}
```

produces the following output:

```
I am in step 0 of the loop
I am in step 2 of the loop
I am in step 4 of the loop
```

And using –1, as shown here

```
for (var i = 5; i>0; i--) {
    trace("I am in step " + i + " of the loop");
}
```

produces the following output:

```
I am in step 5 of the loop
I am in step 4 of the loop
I am in step 3 of the loop
I am in step 2 of the loop
I am in step 1 of the loop
```

The *for...in* Loop

The other variation of the for loop is the for...in loop, which cycles through available properties of an object, array, or string. It has the following syntax:

```
for (variable in object) {
    statements;
}
```

Suppose you had an object, friends, with three properties: _1, _2, and _3. Each property stores the names of your friends, as shown here:

```
friends._1 = "bob";
friends._2 = "mary";
friends._3 = "fred";
```

If you want to loop through this object, you have to use the `for...in` loop because the `for` loop can't access named properties. To trace the name of each friend in sequence, the code would look like this:

```
for (prop in friends) {
    // show the name of the friend
    trace("my friend's name is " + friends[prop]);
}
```

Calling the variable `prop` doesn't indicate anything specific; the variable name can be anything you like. The `for...in` loop simply requires defining the referenced variables as something.

The *while* and *do...while* Loops

Other types of loops include the `while` and `do...while` statements. A `while` statement, shown in the following example, runs all code within the `while` block as long as the specified condition is met:

```
while (condition) {
    // code
}
```

For example, the following code would run five times:

```
i = 0;
while (i < 5) {
    trace("i is now " + i++);
}
```

The `do...while` statement is much the same as `while`, in that it carries out a block of code as long as its condition is met. The syntax for `do...while` is as follows:

```
do {
    // code
} while (condition);
```

The difference between the two is that the `while` statement checks its condition and then carries out the code, and the `do...while` statement carries out the code and *then* checks the condition. It might seem like a subtle difference, but `do...while` is useful if you want to run your code at least once (regardless of what the conditions are) and then break out of it.

The *break* Statement

The break statement is enclosed within a loop statement. It exits the current iteration of the loop, then exits the loop itself, and causes the next line of code to run. For example, the following code causes a for loop to stop running after the second iteration:

```
for (var i=0; i<10; i++) {
    trace("at step " + i);
    if (i == 1) {
        break;
    }
}
```

The *continue* Statement

The continue statement is enclosed within a loop statement and behaves differently depending on what type of loop it's inside:

- In a while loop, continue causes the Flash interpreter to skip the rest of the loop body and jump to the top of the loop, where the condition is retested.

- In a do...while loop, continue causes the Flash interpreter to skip the rest of the loop body and continue the loop by retesting the loop condition.

- In a for loop, continue causes the Flash interpreter to skip the rest of the loop body and jump to the next iteration of the loop.

- In a for...in loop, continue causes the Flash interpreter to skip the rest of the loop body and jump back to the top of the loop, where the next value in the for...in property chain is processed.

The *switch* Statement

The switch statement is similar to the if statement. It checks a condition and carries out statements if that condition is true. This is the syntax:

```
switch (expression) {
    caseClause:
    defaultClause:
}
```

caseClause uses the case keyword, followed by an expression, a colon, and then an amount to be used if the expression matches the `switch` expression using strict equality. *defaultClause* is an optional case that uses the default keyword, a colon, and then a block of code to be run if no case is met. Here's an example of a `switch` statement:

```
switch (myNumber) {
    case 1:
        trace("myNumber is 1");
        break;
    case 2:
        trace("myNumber Is 2");
        break;
    default:
        trace("no case met");
}
```

Calling `switch(1)` results in the following output:

```
myNumber is 1
```

Calling `switch()` results in the following output:

```
no case met
```

Note that in a `switch` statement, a break statement is required to keep Flash from running the code contained in every case *after* the case matching the `switch` expression is performed. For example, the following example traces both one and two:

```
switch (number) {
    case 1:
        trace("one");
    case 2:
        trace("two");
}
```

THE X AND Y COORDINATE SYSTEM

Any object represented visually on the stage is located at a specific point on the stage, represented by x and y coordinates. Although not every object placed on the stage can be referred to programmatically, text fields, buttons, and movie clips can. To refer to the x and y coordinates of an object, you can access its x and y properties, as shown here:

```
instanceName._x;
instanceName._y;
```

instanceName is the name of your movie clip, button, or text field.

If your movie clip, button, or text field is making a reference to itself, you can refer to it in this way:

```
this._x;
this._y;
```

this is a reserved keyword, not unlike _root, that makes a reference to the object in which the command is being made. So if you added the preceding code to a movie clip called my_movie on the main timeline, this would stand for _root.my_movie. In most cases, using this is unnecessary; it's sufficient to omit the path reference altogether, as shown here:

```
_x;
_y;
```

Mouse x and y Coordinates

Although _x and _y apply to objects on the stage, you can also track the mouse's x and y coordinates with the _xmouse and _ymouse properties. For example, if you add the following code to an instance of a movie clip, the movie clip would move to wherever the mouse is:

```
onClipEvent (enterFrame) {
    _x = _root._xmouse;
    _y = _root._ymouse;
}
```

Note that the x and y coordinates are relative. That is, objects on stage have their own internal x-y system. So a nested clip could be located at x0,y0 in its parent clip, but that movie clip could be seated at x45,y237 on the main stage.

The _xmouse and _ymouse properties are also relative. In the preceding code example, you specified _root._xmouse and _root._ymouse because those properties provide a number that's relative to the movie clip on the main stage, not the clip's internal x-y coordinate system.

Converting x and y for Your Movie Clip

Because you'll likely add several different movie clips to your movie, with the clips making references to one another, you'll have to do a lot of translating. You can do it manually by adding up the coordinates of every clip in its hierarchy to find out where an object is. However, that method is error-prone, and you could run into problems with rotated and scaled movie clips. Instead, you can use the `localToGlobal()` and `globalToLocal()` functions, which are helpful in translating references. The `localToGlobal()` function translates relative coordinates to absolute, and `globalToLocal()`translates from absolute to relative. Both functions require creating an object to hold your x/y coordinates.

Suppose that you have a movie clip called dog containing another movie clip named flea. flea is sitting at 45,30 in the dog clip, but the dog clip is sitting at 150,150. You want to find out where flea is on the main stage. First, you would create your object:

```
point = new Object();
```

Then you would assign x and y values to the object:

```
point.x = dog.flea._x;
point.y = dog.flea._y;
```

Then you would translate the coordinates:

```
localToGlobal(point);
```

The `localToGlobal()` function has adjusted the values of x and y from the local movie clip (flea) to the values of its parent (global) movie clip named dog. If you trace the values, you'll see they've changed.

Suppose there is another movie clip called cat on the main stage, and you want to know where cat is from the perspective of the flea movie clip. To do this, you need to translate cat's coordinates from absolute to relative. The first steps you'd take would be the same as `localToGlobal()`, except you run this code from within the flea movie clip:

```
point = new Object();
point.x = _parent._parent.cat._x;
point.y = _parent._parent.cat._y;
```

Then you alter the x and y values:

```
globalToLocal(point);
```

The globalToLocal() function converts the x and y coordinates of the global parent movie clip (cat) to the local coordinates of the local movie clip flea.

Dragging Objects

An easy, visually effective code trick in Flash is the startDrag()/stopDrag() functionality, which allows users to drag a movie clip (which now includes buttons) around the screen. As the function names suggest, you start an object drag by using startDrag() and stop it with stopDrag(). The syntax for startDrag() is as follows:

```
// this is the first startDrag syntax
startDrag(target, lockcenter, left, top, right, bottom);


// this is the second startDrag syntax
target.startDrag(lockcenter, left, top, right, bottom);
```

lockcenter is a Boolean that determines whether the center of the dragged movie clip will snap to the mouse position. *left* is the leftmost boundary of the drag, *top* is the upper boundary, *right* is the rightmost boundary, and *bottom* is the lower boundary. In both syntax examples, *target* is the name of the movie clip to drag. All variables other than *target* are optional.

To stop dragging the object, use this function:

```
stopDrag();
```

If you want to drag a movie clip around the stage when a button is clicked and stop the drag when the button is released, you would place the following code on the button instance you put inside your movie clip:

```
on (press) {
    // start the drag
    startDrag(this);
}
```

Flash allows only one drag operation at a time. Successive startDrag() commands cancel out any previous drag operations.

```
on (release) {
    // stop the drag
    stopDrag();
}
```

This example doesn't constrict the drag of your movie clip in any way. If, however, you want to constrict it to a small square—say, from 0,0 to 50,50—the startDrag() code would look like this:

```
startDrag(this, 0, 0, 50, 50);
```

Script Pinning

A useful feature of the Actions panel is the ability to "pin" multiple code views. Frequently you need to switch between segments of code located in different places. By using pins, you can tack multiple code views into different tabs in the Actions panel, so you can more easily switch between them.

Below the Actions panel is a tab with information about the currently active script (such as the layer/frame or button/movie clip). To the right of this tab is a thumbtack icon. Click this icon to pin your script. Another tab will appear, with your pinned script. You can now click another frame and edit other code without losing an easy reference to the first!

To pin multiple scripts at once, simply repeat the process. To close the pinned script, click the tab of the pinned script, and click the thumbtack icon.

Chapter Project: Creating a Navigation System

So now you know a lot more about how to manipulate data structures with ActionScript, and you also know a bit about the x-y coordinate system that visual elements in Flash adhere to. It's time to apply that newfound knowledge.

This project expands on the project from Chapter 8, "Introduction to ActionScript," but if you didn't do that project, you can start fresh here. The Chapter 8 project created a simple navigation system that allows you to jump between frames by using a row of buttons. This time, you'll add a slider bar that jumps your movie from section to section as you drag it around the screen. Don't worry—this project is easy. Ready?

1. First, open your file from Chapter 8. If you don't have this file, you'll have to do a bit of catch-up work:

   • Create a new movie, and add 25 frames. Insert keyframes every five frames (starting with frame 1 and ending with frame 20). Change the name of the Layer 1 layer to Labels.

   • Name your keyframes main, one, two, three, and four.

   • Make a new layer to hold your content, and add keyframes to match those in the Labels layer. Add a button with a mailto link in the four keyframe and a button with an external link (to a website) in the three keyframe.

2. If you did these steps in Chapter 8, you'll notice that several buttons are missing in the preceding description, but you don't need them for this project. Go ahead and delete them. What you should have now is a movie with five keyframed sections and some content in two of those sections (see Figure 9.1).

FIGURE 9.1

The Chapter 8 project modified for this chapter.

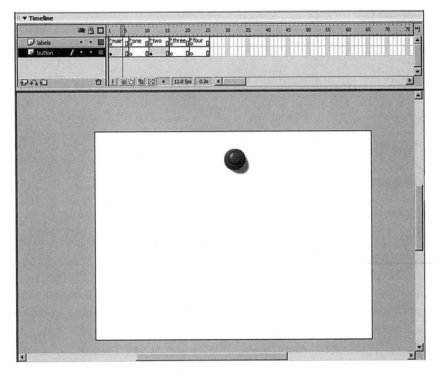

3. Next, you'll add a slider for controlling the movie's current frame. Create a new movie clip. Then create a new button to act as your slider, draw a basic shape for the slider graphic, and place this slider button in your new movie clip.

4. Next, figure out the dimensions of your movie. You can look in the document's property settings for the movie clip dimensions, but if you're using the defaults, that setting is a width of 550 pixels and a height of 400 pixels. You'll use these dimensions to constrain your movie clip's movement.

5. Select the slider button in your movie clip, and add on (press) and on (release) handlers to it. In the press event, add startDrag();, and in the release event, add stopDrag();, as shown in Figure 9.2.

FIGURE 9.2
Adding the drag code.

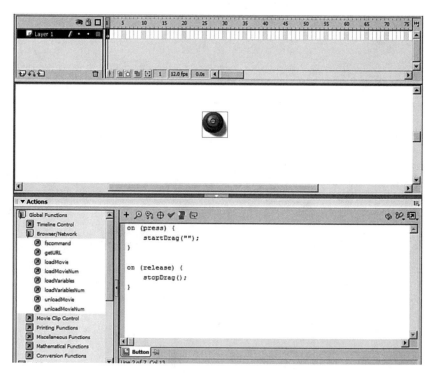

6. In your startDrag() parameters, specify the drag's x-axis constraints based on the width of your movie, and specify the y-axis constraints according to the current _y position (height) of your movie clip, as shown in Figure 9.3.

FIGURE 9.3

Adding constraints to the drag code.

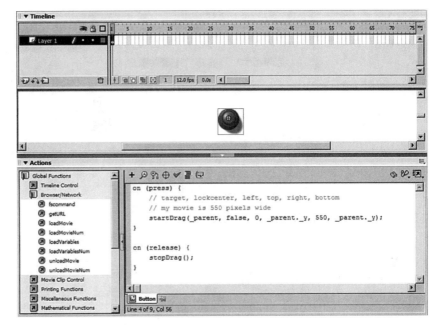

7. Create a new layer in your main timeline, and place your movie clip on it. Name this layer drag.

8. Select your movie clip, and add an onClipEvent handler to it in the Actions panel. The handler type should be enterFrame because you want the movie to run continuously, and the enterFrame handler fires repeatedly as long as the movie is playing. Add the enterFrame type to your handler, as shown in Figure 9.4.

You need to write a handler that checks to see where your movie clip is onscreen and tells the main Timeline to jump to a certain frame based on that position. So you need a series of limits to determine when a frame change occurs, as described in these next steps.

9. Assuming your movie is 550 pixels wide, you want to divide the screen into 110-pixel segments (the main keyframe section and the other four keyframe sections). Therefore, if the _x position of the movie clip is less than 110, the playback head moves to the main keyframe. If it's less than 220, the playback head moves to the one keyframe, and so on.

FIGURE 9.4
The enterFrame
handler type.

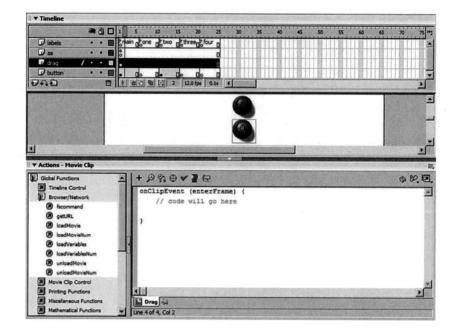

10. Add the `if` conditional statements shown in Figure 9.5 to perform the actions described in step 9. Remember your code must make the parent movie clip's playback head change, not the movie clip itself.

FIGURE 9.5
Your completed
chapter project.

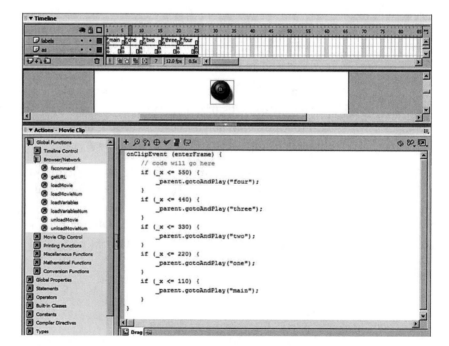

And that's it! If you export your movie, you should be able to drag it across the stage and watch its playhead change. It's a much more interesting way to navigate than just clicking buttons.

POINTS TO REMEMBER

- Variables are used to store information.

- Variables can be of many different data types.

- You can perform a wide variety of operations on variables, such as combining them.

- Using built-in functions such as for and while, you can streamline your programming, saving time and energy.

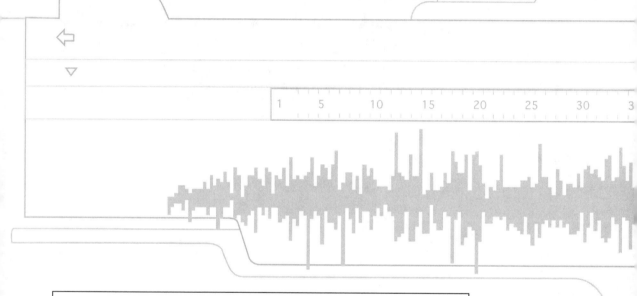

CHAPTER 10

ACTIONSCRIPT: FUNCTIONS, EVENTS, AND OBJECTS

CHAPTER 9, "ACTIONSCRIPT BASICS: DATA AND STATEMENTS," INTRODUCED you to basic programming concepts, such as variables, statements, and operators. In this chapter, you'll learn even more about functions, event handlers, and the wide variety of classes built into Macromedia Flash MX 2004. This chapter covers

- Functions
- Events and event handlers
- Built-in classes
- Dynamic masks
- Dynamic creation and loading of movie clips
- Shared objects
- Depth sorting

You might be wondering why you need to learn about functions, event handlers, and so forth, but you'll use these concepts in a variety of applications, whether you're building a game, an online store, a data form, or a simple questionnaire. After you've learned all these concepts, you can try out the chapter project to help you see them in action.

INTERACTING WITH MOVIES

Much of this chapter involves explaining how to interact with Flash movies and, by extension, onscreen elements. Although the concepts in this chapter are mainly textual—an array doesn't have a visual component, for example—understanding them is integral to learning how to take advantage of the rest of the application environment. Good luck— you'll be coding like a pro in no time!

Functions

A *function* is a block of reusable code. You can pass parameters (also called "arguments") to a function and have it return a value. Functions are useful for saving time and improving the legibility of your code and are immensely helpful for code stability and debugging.

Suppose you're writing a script in Flash, and you need to repeat an action that you've already written, which happens a lot. You could retype that code, but aside from being a waste of time, it's a risky practice, because every time you retype code, you increase the chance of making typos and, therefore, having code that doesn't work. In addition, duplicating code blocks means that if you have to change code down the road, you'll have to apply the changes multiple times, resulting in a maintenance nightmare!

To save time and effort, you can wrap reusable code in a function and then access the code later simply by calling the function. Although the reference to the function might be written several times, the function and its contained code are written only once. Should you need to change your code's functionality—and you will—you need to do it only once and in one place.

Functions are defined as follows:

```
function functionName(param1, param2... paramN) {
    // statements go here
}
```

This is a *named function*. By defining a function this way, you can reference it by using the supplied *functionName* with brackets at the end. For example, say you created a function named addMyNumbers, as shown here:

```
function addMyNumbers(x, y) {
    answer = x + y;
    return x;
}
```

You could refer to it by using this code line:

```
addMyNumbers();
```

Another type of function is an *anonymous function*. Anonymous functions have no function name you can refer to in code, so they must be called by an associated variable, as shown in this example:

```
myFunc = function() {
    trace("this is my function");
}
```

Anonymous functions are frequently used as methods of custom objects. For example, to add a method to an object called myCircle, you might use the following code:

```
myCircle.getArea = function() {
    return area;
}
```

If you had an instance of the myCircle object called circleOne, you would call the getArea function like this:

```
circleOne.getArea();
```

Passing Variables to Functions

Functions allow you to pass variables to them when they're called. Being able to pass variables is useful when you're creating functions that can perform different actions, depending on information supplied to them, and when you're performing calculations based on values that change over the duration of your program. To pass variables to your function, enter them in the parentheses after the function name, as shown here:

```
// call your function
functionName(param1, param2);
```

For your function to receive those variables, they must be declared in the function definition:

```
function functionName(param1, param2) {
}
```

Take a look at the addMyNumbers() function mentioned earlier:

```
function addMyNumbers(x, y) {
    answer = x + y;
    return x;
}
```

This function takes the supplied values x and y and combines them, assigning that value to the variable answer. Then it uses the return keyword to send the value back to the function caller.

Using Arguments

When sending variables to a function, it's possible that the correct number of variables might not be sent, for a variety of reasons—discrepancies in the code sending variables with no value, for example. To avoid errors in your script, use the Arguments class to determine how many arguments have been sent.

The Arguments class is an array of values sent to your function. This class has three accessible properties:

- **Arguments.length**   This property returns the number of variables that have been passed to your function.

- **Arguments.caller**   This property is a reference to the function from which the current function was called.

- **Arguments.callee**   This property refers to the function currently being called. It can be used to create an anonymous function reference for making a *reiterative function call*, which is a function that calls itself. Reiterative function calls are useful when sifting through large amounts of data, for example.

The following code produces an unending series of output traces:

```
function myFunc() {
    trace("calling function");
    arguments.callee();
}
```

Returning Values

After you have sent values to your function, you probably want values returned to you. This is done by using the return command, which is used like this:

```
return value;
```

value can be any variable, object, function, or expression. For example, the following are all valid uses of return:

```
return 1;
```

```
return myName;
```

```
return "hello!";
```

```
return myObject;
```

```
return 4 + 3 + 2 / 5;
```

Note that the return command halts execution of the function or body of code being run, so it should always be the last possible statement in any block of code. Any statements after return are ignored. For example, in the following code, the last line is not carried out:

```
function myFunc(x, y) {
    answer = x + y;
    return answer;
    trace("sent back answer!");
}
```

To take advantage of returned values, you should call the function using the following syntax:

```
variablename = functionName();
```

In this line, *variablename* is set to the function's return value, as shown in this example:

```
function myFunc() {
    return "bob";
}

myVar = myFunc();
trace(myVar);

// outputs
// bob
```

Events and Event Handlers

An *event* is an occurrence that requires a response from your movie. It can be software- or hardware-related. A mouse click, for example, is a *user event* because it occurs as a result of user interaction. An event generated by the Flash Player, such as a movie clip first appearing on the stage, is called a *system event* because the user doesn't generate it directly.

To respond to events, you must use an *event handler*, which is ActionScript code associated with a specific object or event. For example, when a user presses a key, a sound plays, or when an XML file finishes loading, its contents are displayed. ActionScript provides different ways of handling events:

- Event handler methods
- Event listeners
- Button and movie clip event handlers

Button and movie clip handlers were explained in Chapter 8, "Introduction to ActionScript," so this chapter focuses on the first two ways to handle events.

Event Handler Methods

An *event handler method* is a class method that's called when an event occurs on an instance of the class. For example, the `MovieClip` class defines an `onKeyDown` handler that's called whenever the user presses a key. Unlike other class methods, event handlers aren't called directly; the Flash Player calls them when the corresponding event occurs.

Event handler methods are, by default, undefined. That means when an event occurs, its handler is called, but no further response to the event is generated. To have your movie respond to the event, you must define a function (using the `function` statement) and then assign that function to the handler. This function is then called whenever the specific event occurs.

An *event handler* consists of three parts: the object the event applies to, the name of the event handler method, and the function you assign to the handler. The following example highlights the structure of an event handler:

```
object.eventMethod = function() {
// response code here
}
```

For example, suppose you had a movie clip on your stage named my_mc, and you wanted a text field in that clip to display updated date information continuously in a text field named date_field. You would use the onEnterFrame event handler to do this, as shown in the following example:

```
my_mc.onEnterFrame = function() {
    this.date_field.text = new Date();
}
```

Although this functionality is assigned directly to the handler, you can also assign a function reference to an event handler method and define the function afterward, as shown in this example:

```
my_mc.onEnterFrame = my_function;
function my_function() {
    this.date_field.text = new Date();
}
```

Notice that you assign the function reference, not the function's return value, to the onEnterFrame event handler:

```
// Won't work
my_mc.onEnterFrame = my_function();

// will work
my_mc.onEnterFrame = my_function;
```

Some event handlers receive passed parameters that supply information about the event that occurred. For example, the TextField.onSetFocus event handler is called when a text field instance gains keyboard focus. This event handler receives a reference to the text field object that previously had keyboard focus. The following code inserts some text into the text field that just lost keyboard focus:

```
userName_txt.onSetFocus = function(oldFocus_txt) {
    oldFocus_txt.text = "I just lost keyboard focus";
}
```

The following ActionScript classes define event handlers: `Button`, `ContextMenu`, `ContextMenuItem`, `Key`, `LoadVars`, `LocalConnection`, `Mouse`, `MovieClip`, `MovieClipLoader`, `Selection`, `SharedObject`, `Sound`, `Stage`, `TextField`, `XML`, and `XMLSocket`. Of these, `ContextMenu`, `ContextMenuItem`, and `MovieClipLoader` are new to Flash MX 2004. To find out more about these classes and their specific handlers, refer to the ActionScript Reference Guide in Flash.

You can also assign functions to event handlers for objects you create. For example, the following code creates a new movie clip instance, `newclip_mc`, and then assigns a function to the clip's `onPress` event handler:

```
_root.attachMovie("symbolID", "newclip_mc", 10);
newclip_mc.onPress = function () {
    trace("You pressed me");
}
```

Event Listeners

Event listeners allow a listener object to receive events generated by a broadcaster object. The *listener object* is a user-defined object; the *broadcaster object* is a movie clip, a button, or a text field, for example. The broadcaster registers the listener to receive events it generates. For example, you could register a text field object to receive `onSetFocus` notifications, or a movie clip could receive `onKeyDown` notifications generated by the keyboard. You can register multiple listener objects to receive events from a single broadcaster; likewise, you can register a single listener object to receive events from multiple broadcasters. The event listener model is similar to that of event handlers, with two primary differences:

- The object to which you assign the event handler isn't the object itself.

- You call a special method of the broadcaster object, `addListener()`, to register the listener object to receive events.

To use event listeners, you create an object with a property that has the same name as the event the broadcaster object is generating. Next, you assign a function to the listener that responds to the event in some way. Finally, you call `addListener()` on the broadcaster object, passing it the listener name. This is the syntax for using the event listener:

```
listener.event = function() {
    // code
};
broadcaster.addListener(listener);
```

The specified listener can be any object—a movie clip, for example, or a button—or an instance of any ActionScript class. The event name is an event that occurs on the broadcaster; it broadcasts the event to the listener.

To unregister a listener, thus preventing it from receiving events, you call the removeListener() method of the broadcaster, passing it the name of the listener object:

```
broadcaster.removeListener(listener);
```

Event listeners are available to instances of the following ActionScript classes: Key, Mouse, MovieClipLoader, Selection, TextField, and Stage. For a list of event listeners available to these classes, refer to the ActionScript Reference Guide in Flash. In the following example, an event listener is added to the Key class, which traces the code representing the key that has been pressed:

```
listener = new Object();
listener.onKeyDown = function() {
    trace(Key.getCode() + " has been pressed.");
}

Key.addListener(listener);
```

listener is the listener object created to respond to the broadcasted events, Key is the broadcaster object that broadcasts the events to Listener, and Key.getCode() returns the code of the most recently pressed key.

BUILT-IN CLASSES

Although you can create your own classes and objects, Flash 2004 includes a wide variety of useful preprogrammed classes. The following sections describe a number of them and explain how to use them. These classes are covered in this chapter:

- **Array**   Create and manipulate arrays.

- **Date**   Access and store date information.

- **Sound**   Load, play, and manipulate sound files.

- **Color**   Adjust color values of movie clips.

- **Stage**   Get information about the movie's stage.

- **ContextMenu**   Control context menus (the menu you see when you right-click [Windows] or Control-click [Macintosh] anywhere on the stage).

- **PrintJob**   Print multiple pages easily.

- **Error**   Monitor and react to code errors.

The *Array* Object

An *array* is an object useful for storing multiple elements of information. These elements are identified by a unique number, called an *index*. You create a new array by using the array constructor, as shown here:

```
my_array = new Array();
```

You can also create an array by using the *array access operator* shortcut method, as shown here:

```
my_array = [];
```

The numbering of an array's elements is *zero-based*, which means the numbering always starts at 0, with the second element being element 1. In the following example, a new array is created, and four values are assigned to it:

```
authors = new Array();
authors[0] = "Shawn Pucknell";
authors[1] = "Brian Hogg";
authors[2] = "Craig Swann";
```

To refer to any of these elements, refer to their position in the array, as shown:

```
trace(authors[1]);
// outputs
// Brian Hogg
```

Additionally, if you want to create an array and you already know what information will go into it, you can specify that information in the constructor, as shown in the following examples:

```
my_array = new Array(0, 1, 2);
authors = new Array("Shawn Pucknell", "Brian Hogg", "Craig
➥Swann");
```

When you create an array, it has a length property. If you create an empty array, the length is 0. The following example shows how to refer to the length property:

```
my_array.length;
```

A quick way to add a new element to the end of your array is to refer to its length. If your array has three elements (as in the previous authors example), it has a length of 3, even though the highest element is numbered 2. So adding an element in position 3 (the length) results in a new element being added to the end of the array. It looks like this:

```
authors[authors.length] = "Glen Rhodes";
```

Another way is to use the push() method of Array. It functions the same as the previous method but looks like this:

```
authors.push("Glen Rhodes");
```

Note that array elements can be of any data type, including numbers, strings, objects, and even other arrays.

The Array object has many built-in methods and properties, explained in the following sections, to help you manipulate your data.

The *Array.concat()* Method

This method concatenates, or joins, the elements you pass it with the elements in your array and returns a new array. It uses the following syntax:

```
my_array.concat(element1, element2... elementN);
```

For example, if you want to create a new array containing the elements of my_array and the new elements 3, 4, and 5, use the following code:

```
my_array[0] = 0;
my_array[1] = 1;
my_array[2] = 2;
```

```
my_new_array = my_array.concat(3, 4, 5);

trace(my_new_array);
// outputs
// 0, 1, 2, 3, 4, 5
```

The *Array.join()* Method

This method converts all elements in an array into a string, concatenates them, and returns one long string representing your array's contents. It uses the following syntax:

```
my_array.join(separator);
```

separator is an optional string element used as the separator between array elements. The default separator, if this parameter is omitted, is a comma. For example, the following code creates an array and then uses join() to trace the array's concatenation (first with no separator, and then with the separator " || "):

```
authors = new Array("Shawn Pucknell", "Brian Hogg", "Craig
➡Swann");

trace(authors.join());
// outputs
// Shawn Pucknell, Brian Hogg, Craig Swann

trace(authors.join(" || "));
// outputs
// Shawn Pucknell || Brian Hogg || Craig Swann
```

Note that the join() method doesn't alter the data in your array.

The *Array.pop()* Method

This method removes the last element from an array and returns the deleted value. For example, the following code creates a new array, named authors, and then removes the last element:

```
authors = new Array("Shawn Pucknell", "Brian Hogg", "Craig
➡Swann");
wasPopped = authors.pop();
trace(wasPopped);
// outputs
// Craig Swann
```

The *Array.push()* Method

This method adds one or more elements to the end of an array and returns the new length, using the following syntax:

```
my_array.push(element1, element2, ... elementN);
```

For example, this code adds two elements to the authors array and traces the new length:

```
authors = new Array("Shawn Pucknell", "Brian Hogg", "Craig
➥Swann");
didPush = authors.push("Glen Rhodes", "Grant Skinner");
trace(didPush);
// outputs
// 5
```

The *Array.reverse()* Method

This method reverses the order of elements in an array, as shown in this example:

```
authors = new Array("Shawn Pucknell", "Brian Hogg", "Craig
➥Swann");

trace(authors);
// outputs
// Shawn Pucknell, Brian Hogg, Craig Swann

authors.reverse();

trace(authors);
// outputs
// Craig Swann, Brian Hogg, Shawn Pucknell
```

The *Array.shift()* Method

This method removes the first element from your array and returns the deleted value, as shown here:

```
my_array = new Array("dog", "fish", cat");
```

```
shifted = my_array.shift();
trace(shifted);
// outputs
// dog
```

The *Array.slice()* Method

This method extracts an element or a series of elements from your array and returns them in a new array, using the following syntax:

```
my_array.slice(startElement, endElement);
```

startElement is a number representing the first element in your new array, and *endElement* represents the last element in your new array. The following example creates a new array with four elements and slices a new array from it:

```
number_array = new Array("a", "b", "c", "d");
number2_array = numberArray.slice(1, 2);

trace(number2_array.join());
// outputs b, c
```

The *Array.sort()* Method

This method sorts an array, using the following syntax:

```
my_array.sort(compareFunction);
```

compareFunction is an optional reference to a function that's used to determine the sorting order of elements in the array. If you use *compareFunction*, it's passed two variables that correspond to the two elements being compared. When you use *compareFunction*, you must return a value to the sort() function, such as

- -1 if A should come before B in the array

- 0 if A is the same as B

- 1 if B should come before A in the array

In this first example, you see sort() used without *compareFunction*:

```
new_array = new Array("apples", "oranges", "biscuits");
new_array.sort();
trace(new_array);
```

```
// outputs
// apples, biscuits, oranges
```

In the second example, you see *compareFunction* being used:

```
var passwords_array =[
"bob",
"alice",
"larry",
"francine",
"meg"];
function order (name1,name2){
    // Entries to be sorted are in the form name:password
    // Sort using only the name part of the entry as a key
    if (name1 <name2){
        return -1;
    }else if (name1 >name2){
        return 1;
    }else {
        return 0;
    }
}
}
trace (passwords_array.join());
passwords_array.sort(order);
trace ("Sorted:");
trace (passwords_array.join());
```

This code yields the following results:

```
bob, alice, larry, francine, meg
Sorted:
alice, bob, francine, larry, meg
```

The *Array.sortOn()* Method

This method sorts your array based on a specified field within that array. It uses the following syntax:

```
my_array.sortOn(fieldname);
```

If your array elements contain arrays, use a number to specify which element to sort on. In the following examples, the first uses sortOn() to sort an array with elements consisting of arrays, and the second sorts an array with elements consisting of objects:

```
// sortOn used with numbers
var sort_array = new Array();
sort_array[0] = new Array("bob", 1, 2);
sort_array[1] = new Array("mary", 2, 3);
sort_array[2] = new Array("Alfred", 0, 1);
for (var i = 0; i<sort_array.length; i++) {
    trace(sort_array[i]);
}

// outputs
// bob,1,2
// mary,2,3
// Alfred,0,1
```

Because each element of this array contains an array, you can specify which element to perform the sort on by passing the sortOn() method a number representing the index of the element to be sorted by. To sort using the first element, pass 0:

```
sort_array.sortOn(0);
for (var I = 0; i<sort_array.length; i++) {
    trace(sort_array[i]);
}
// outputs
// Alfred,0,1
// bob,1,2
// mary,2,3
```

In the following usage of sortOn(), each element of the array contains an object:

```
// sortOn used with a string
sort_array = new Array();
sort_array[0] = {name:"Bob", city:"Halifax"};
sort_array[1] = {name:"Michael", city:"Oakville"};
sort_array[2] = {name:"Jonathan", city:"Burlington"};

for (var I = 0; i<sort_array.length; i++) {
    trace(sort_array[i].name + " : " + sort_array[i].city);
}
// outputs
// Bob : Halifax
```

```
// Michael : Oakville
// Jonathan : Burlington
```

To perform a sortOn() with an array whose elements contain objects, pass the sortOn() function a string representing the name of the object property to base the sort on. The following code sorts based on the city property of the objects in the array:

```
sort_array.sortOn("city");

for (var I = 0; i<sort_array.length; i++) {
    trace(sort_array[i].name + " : " + sort_array[i].city);
}

// outputs
// Jonathan : Burlington
// Bob : Halifax
// Michael : Oakville
```

The *Array.splice()* Method

This method deletes a range of elements from an array and optionally inserts new elements at the same time. It uses the following syntax:

```
my_array.splice(start, deleteCount [, element1, element2,...
➥elementN);
```

In this syntax, *start* is the number representing the index of the first element to be deleted, *deleteCount* is the number of elements to be deleted, and *element* is an element or group of elements to be inserted into the array at the point specified by *start*. Note that splice() alters an array but doesn't make a new array.

The *Array.unshift()* Method

This method allows you to add a number of new elements to the beginning of your array, and it returns a number representing the new length of your array. unshift() uses the following syntax:

```
my_array.unshift(element1, element2... elementN);
```

For example, to add two new elements to an array with two elements already in place, and then trace the new array length, you would use the following:

```
trace(Authors.unshift("Grant Skinner", "John Cowie"));
```

The *Date* Object

You use the Date object to retrieve date and time information in *UTC* (Universal Time Clock, otherwise known as "Greenwich Mean Time") or the user's system clock. The Date object doesn't contain continually updated date and time information; rather, it contains the date and time information at its creation or the date and time information you supply to it in your script. To create a new Date object, you use the Date() constructor, like this:

```
my_date = new Date();
```

Using this code, Flash inserts the date and time that was correct at the time you created the object (at runtime, in the SWF file). If you want to set the time the Date object contains, you can do so by using the following syntax:

```
my_date = new Date(year, month [, date [, hour [, minute
➥[, second [, millisecond ]]]]])
```

This code can use the following parameters:

- *year*   An integer from 1900 to 1999, if two digits are supplied. To specify a year later than 1999, you must supply all four digits.

- *month*   An integer from 0 (January) to 11 (December).

- *date*   An integer from 1 to 31 that indicates the day of the month. This parameter is optional.

- *hour*   An integer from 0 (midnight) to 23 (11 p.m.).

- *minute*   An integer from 0 to 59. This parameter is optional.

- *second*   An integer from 0 to 59. This parameter is optional.

- *millisecond*   An integer from 0 to 999. This parameter is optional.

The Date object has many predefined methods for extracting all manner of information. For example, the following code creates a new Date object and then extracts and traces the current day of the month, the current hour, and the current year:

```
my_date = new Date();
trace(my_date.getDate() + " : " + my_date.getHours()
➥+ " : " + getYear());
```

For a listing of all of the available Date methods, consult the ActionScript Reference Guide in Flash MX 2004.

The *Math* Object

The Math object contains a wide variety of mathematical functions and constants for you to use. You don't create an instance of the Math object to reference it. Properties and methods of the Math object are *static*, which means you can reference them without having to create an instance of the object.

The Math object, along with its many uses and features, is explained in detail in Chapter 21, "Math for Flashers."

The *Sound* Object

The Sound object is explained in detail in Chapter 15, "Audio."

The Sound object is used to control the playback of audio in Flash. Although you can place sounds anywhere in the Timeline of your movie clip and play them, the Sound object enables you to start and stop audio, load external sounds at runtime, and control the volume, among other features.

The *Color* Object

The Color object lets you set the RGB (red, green, blue) values of a movie clip and retrieve those values after they have been set. You create a new instance of the Color object by using the constructor, as shown here:

```
my_color = new Color(target);
```

target is the name of the movie clip instance you want to color. If you don't include a target, the Color object applies color to the movie clip where the object is being instantiated.

The Color object supports the following methods: Color.setRGB(), Color.getRGB(), Color.setTranform(), and Color.getTransform().

The *Color.setRGB()* Method

This method sets the RGB color value of the Color object using the following syntax:

```
my_color.setRGB(0xRRGGBB);
```

0x tells the ActionScript compiler that the number is a hexadecimal value, and *RR*, *GG*, and *BB* consist of two-digit hexadecimal numbers specifying the offset of each color component (*offset* means the change applied to the given component). Note that setRGB() overrides any previously set setTransform() calls (setTransform() is explained later in this chapter).

Although you can specify, in different cases, the percentage of a color and its offset, it's important to note the difference between the two: *Percentage* represents a change in the percentage of a color that's visible (from –100 to 100). *Offset* represents a change in the color value of a color (from –255 to 255).

The *Color.getRGB()* Method

This method returns the numeric RGB value of the specified Color object, as shown in this example:

```
currentColor = Color.getRGB();
trace(currentColor);
```

To convert the color value to a hexadecimal value, use the toString() method of the Number object, as shown here:

```
currentColor = Color.getRGB();
trace(currentColor.toString(16));
```

The output for the preceding line would be a hexadecimal value, such as #FFFFFF or #060606.

The *Color.setTransform()* Method

This method sets color transformation information for a Color object. The result affects the color of the target object defined when creating your Color object. It uses the following syntax:

```
color.setTransform(transformObject);
```

transformObject is an object that has the following properties: ra, rb, ga, gb, ba, bb, aa, and ab. These properties define percentage and offset values for the red, green, blue, and alpha (transparency) components of a Color object, entered in the format 0xRRGGBBAA. The specific values are defined as follows:

- **ra** The percentage for the red component (–100 to 100).
- **rb** The offset for the red component (–255 to 255).
- **ga** The percentage for the green component (–100 to 100).

- **gb** The offset for the green component (–255 to 255).
- **ba** The percentage for the blue component (–100 to 100).
- **bb** The offset for the blue component (–255 to 255).
- **aa** The percentage for alpha (–100 to 100).
- **ab** The offset for alpha (–255 to 255).

You create a *transformObject* parameter as follows:

```
myColorTransform = new Object();
myColorTransform.ra = 50;
myColorTransform.rb = 244;
myColorTransform.ga = 40;
myColorTransform.gb = 112;
myColorTransform.ba = 12;
myColorTransform.bb = 90;
myColorTransform.aa = 40;
myColorTransform.ab = 70;
```

You can also use the following syntax to create a *transformObject* parameter:

```
myColorTransform = { ra: '50', rb: '244', ga: '40',
➥gb: '112', ba: '12', bb: '90', aa: '40', ab: '70'}
```

For example, to apply a transformation to a Color object, first create a Color object:

```
my_color = new Color(this);
```

Then define the Transform object:

```
Transform = new Object();
Transform.ra
Transform.rb
Transform.ga
Transform.gb
Transform.ba
Transform.bb
Transform.aa
Transform.ab
```

Then apply the transform to the Color object:

```
my_color.setTransform(transform);
```

The *Color.getTransform()* Object

This method returns the transformation value set by
`Color.setTransform()`.

The *Stage* Object

The `Stage` object is a representation of the visual stage of your movie.
Using this object, you can determine the current size of the visible stage,
set scaling options (which control whether the stage scales as the user
scales the SWF, for example), and determine the alignment of visual elements on the stage.

The `Stage` object is unique in that you don't have to define an instance
of it to use it. Although you have to create movie clips and arrays, the
`Stage` object is always there. The `Stage` object has these five properties:

- **Stage.align** If you make your SWF window twice as large as the
  stage, you can determine where the Flash movie will be placed. By
  default, the content is centered both horizontally and vertically.
  Accepted values are T (Top), B (Bottom), L (Left), R (Right), TL (Top
  Left), TR (Top Right), BL (Bottom Left), and BR (Bottom Right).

- **Stage.height** This read-only property tells you the current height,
  in pixels, of the stage.

- **Stage.width** This read-only property tells you the current width, in
  pixels, of the stage.

- **Stage.scaleMode** This property determines the placement of your
  Flash movie on the stage. The accepted values for this property are
  exactFit (scales to fit the stage's exact size and proportions),
  showAll (scales content to fit the stage, maintaining the movie's proportions), noBorder (scales content horizontally), and noScale (content isn't scaled). The default value for this property is showAll.

- **Stage.showMenu** Determines whether the display options in the
  Flash Player are shown when the user right-clicks (Windows) or
  Control-clicks (Macintosh) anywhere on the stage. showMenu is a
  Boolean value: true shows the display options, and false hides
  them. By default, showMenu is set to true.

Additionally, the Stage object has an onResize event handler that you can use to determine when a user scales the movie up or down (such as by scaling the browser window or, if your movie is being viewed in the standalone Flash Player, when the player's dimensions are being changed).

The *XML* Object

The XML object allows you to manipulate data formatted with Extensible Markup Language (XML). You can use it to load data from external sources (such as databases, PHP scripts, or ASP pages) and to send internal data to external sources.

You can find more information about the XML object in Chapter 17, "Accessing External Data."

The *ContextMenu* Object

The ContextMenu object, new to Flash 2004, is used to add and remove user-defined menu items from the context menu, which you can see by right-clicking (Windows) or Control-clicking (Macintosh) the stage during movie playback. You can also use it to display pre-existing menu items (such as Zoom In and Print) and create copies of existing menus.

You can define new context menus on the movie's Timeline or on certain objects in Flash, such as buttons, movie clips, or text fields. To create a new ContextMenu object, first create a new instance of the ContextMenu class:

```
my_menu = new ContextMenu(callbackFunction);
```

callbackFunction is the name of a function that's activated after the user right-clicks or Control-clicks the stage, but before the context menu appears.

Next, you'll likely want to add new items to the context menu. You do this using the ContextMenuItem class, which has the following syntax:

```
new ContextMenuItem (caption, callback, [separatorBefore,]
⇒ [enabled,] [visible]);
```

The following list describes the options you can use:

- *caption*   The text string to be displayed as the new menu item.

- *callback*   The name of the function to be activated after the menu item is selected.

- *separatorBefore*   The optional Boolean value that determines whether a separator bar appears above the new menu option. By default, it's set to `false`.

- *enabled*   The optional Boolean value that determines whether the menu item is active. By default, it's set to `true`.

- *visible*   The optional Boolean value that determines whether the menu item is visible or invisible. By default, this value is set to `true`.

After you have created a new context menu item, add it to the `customItems` array in your `ContextMenu` object. The `customItems` array is created when you create the `ContextMenu` instance.

Last, set your `ContextMenu` instance as a menu of an object on the stage or a menu of the main movie. To do this, use the following syntax:

```
Object.menu = my_menu;
```

The following example creates a new instance of the `ContextMenu` class, creates a series of new `ContextMenuItem` instances and defines handlers for them, assigns the `ContextMenuItems` to the `ContextMenu` object, and then defines the `ContextMenu` instance as a menu for the main Timeline:

```
// create new context menu
my_cm = new ContextMenu();

// write the ContextMenuItem callback handlers
function one() {
    trace("You have selected menu 1");
}

function two() {
    trace("You have selected menu 2");
}
```

```
function three() {
    trace("You have selected menu 3");
}

// create three new ContextMenuItems

cmi1 = new ContextMenuItem("one", one);
cmi2 = new ContextMenuItem("two", two);
cmi3 = new ContextMenuItem("three", three);



// add the ContextMenuItem instances to my_cm
my_cm.customItems.push(cmi1);
my_cm.customItems.push(cmi2);
my_cm.customItems.push(cmi3);

// define the context menu as the menu for the root
// of the movie
_root.menu = my_cm;
```

Instead of defining a function to handle selecting your menu items, you can use the onSelect event handler method contained in ContextMenuItem, as shown here:

```
cmi1.onSelect = function() {
trace("you have selected this option");
}
```

Notice that when you look at the context menu generated with the preceding example, you see all the built-in context items. You can hide them with the hideBuiltInItems() method, using the following syntax:

```
my_cm.hideBuiltInItems();
```

If you want to hide any built-in items individually, you can do so by referencing the builtInItems object, which is located inside your ContextMenu object. It has the following properties, all of which hold Boolean values: save, zoom, quality, play, loop, rewind, forward_back, print, and about.

You can disable any of these options by setting the value to `false`, as in the following example in which both the quality and rewind menu items are disabled:

```
my_cm = new ContextMenu();
my_cm.builtInItems.quality = false;
my_cm.builtInItems.rewind = false;
```

Note that although you can disable most of the built-in items, you can't disable the Settings item, which gives you access to microphone/camera settings, SharedObject settings, and others.

The *PrintJob* Object

New to Flash 2004, the `PrintJob` object allows you to print content from within Flash. It is a much-needed and welcome improvement over the internal printing methods used in Flash MX and previous versions. (Information about using the previous method, which still works, is available in Flash's Help system.)

`PrintJob` lets you set frames of your movie or any movie clip within your movie as printable content and then print that content at any time. `PrintJob` also enables you to render dynamic data (which could be based on a user's feedback during the course of your movie, for example) and add those pages to the printer queue. `PrintJob` is controlled with three methods, described in the following sections.

The *PrintJob.start()* Method

This method opens the Print dialog box and returns a Boolean `true` if the user clicks OK or `false` if the user clicks Cancel or another error occurs. You have to use the `start()` method before being able to add pages to your print job and actually print something.

The *PrintJob.addPage()* Method

You use this method to add content to the print queue after successfully firing `PrintJob.start()`. It has the following syntax:

```
my_printJob.addPage(target [, printArea] [, options]
➥[, frameNumber]);
```

target is a number representing the level you want to print (0 is, for example, the root of the movie) or a string representing the instance name you want to print.

printArea, an optional parameter, is an object that represents the area to be printed (which can refer to an onscreen or offscreen area). The printArea object uses the following format:

{xMin:*topLeft*, xMax:*topRight*, yMin:*bottomLeft*, ➥yMax:*bottomRight*}

topLeft, *topRight*, *bottomLeft*, and *bottomRight* are numbers representing the dimensions of the area you want to print. For example, to print a 50×50 onscreen section, your printArea object would be {xMin:0, xMax:50, yMin:0, yMax:50}. When you use a printArea object, you must include all four numbers, or it won't work.

options, another optional parameter, is an object that specifies whether your new page prints as a vector or a bitmap. It uses the following format: {printAsBitmap:Boolean}. Setting printAsBitmap to true makes the page print as a bitmap; setting it to false makes it print as a vector. By default, all your pages print as vectors.

frameNumber is an optional number for setting which frame of your movie to print. For example, if you had a movie clip with all the frames that could be printed, and the user wanted to print only frame 6, you would set frameNumber to 6. If you don't specify a frameNumber, the current frame of your selected movie clip is printed.

The *PrintJob.send()* Method

This method sends all queued pages (which you have added by using addPage()) to the printer and prints them. The following short example shows how to create a print job, add two frames of a movie clip called my_mc, and print them:

```
// create the new print job object
my_pj = new PrintJob();

// brings up dialog box
if (my_pj.start()) {
    // if user clicks OK, and there are no errors,
    // then the following code runs
```

```
    // add frames 1 through 4 of my_mc
    my_pj.addPage(my_mc, {xMin:0, xMax:50, yMin:0, yMax:50},
➥{printAsBitmap:true}, 1);
    my_pj.addPage(my_mc, null, null, 2);
    my_pj.addPage(my_mc, null, {printAsBitmap:true}, 3);
    my_pj.addPage(my_mc, null, null, 4):

    // send your print job to the printer
    my_pj.send();
}


// now that you're done with your print job,
// you can delete it
delete my_pj;
```

Note that in this example, the print area of frame 1 was set to a 50×50 box, and the content was set to print as a bitmap. In frame 2, the printArea was set to null, and likewise for the optional *options* parameter. For frame 3, the printable area doesn't need to be constrained, but you *do* want to print it as a bitmap.

The *Error* Object

New to Flash 2004 is the Error object, which enables you to track errors that occur within your code. The Error object is useful for debugging and testing your code.

For more information on the Error object, see Chapter 25, "Troubleshooting."

DYNAMIC MASKS

In Chapter 6, "Animation, Effects, and Masking," you learned how to create and animate masked content. This is a powerful capability, but it requires you to manually specify masks during author time. For projects involving canned animation, this method is fine, but what if you don't know what you're masking until the program is running? What if you want the user to specify what's masked at runtime?

How to Use Dynamic Masks

Dynamic masks are just what they sound like: They are masks that are defined programmatically at author time or runtime. To define a dynamic mask, you use the setMask() function, which has the following syntax:

maskedClip.setMask(*maskingClip*);

maskedClip is the movie clip to be masked, and *maskingClip* is the clip that defines the visible area. In the following example, mask_mc is set as the mask for my_mc:

my_mc.setMask(mask_mc);

You can turn off the mask at any time by passing the function a null parameter, as shown here:

my_mc.setMask(null);

All frames in a mask movie clip's timeline are played just like a normal movie clip. Your mask can be positioned and moved programmatically, and it can be scaled and rotated. Dynamic masks make it easy to create complex visual effects. Keep the following guidelines in mind when using setMask():

- You can't set a movie clip to be its own mask.

- The masked area is determined by a movie clip's fill, not by its stroke.

- You can't alter the _alpha (transparency) property of a masked movie clip.

- Device fonts (such as _sans, _serif, and _typewriter) aren't masked.

DYNAMICALLY CREATING AND LOADING MOVIE CLIPS

With Flash, you can generate movie clips on the stage at runtime. This powerful capability enables developers to reuse graphical and programmatic elements easily and create a wide variety of effects.

There are three ways to generate movie clips on the stage: attachMovie(), duplicateMovieClip(), and createEmptyMovieClip(). These methods, along with their advantages and limitations, are discussed in the following sections.

The *attachMovie()* Method

attachMovie() is a useful method because it allows you to take symbols from the Library and place them on the stage at runtime, freeing you from keeping all predefined content on the stage all the time. To make a symbol accessible to attachMovie(), you must define a symbol linkage identifier. You do this when creating a symbol by opening the advanced mode of the Create New Symbol dialog box and clicking the Export for ActionScript check box in the Linkage section (see Figure 10.1).

FIGURE 10.1
Selecting the Export for ActionScript option.

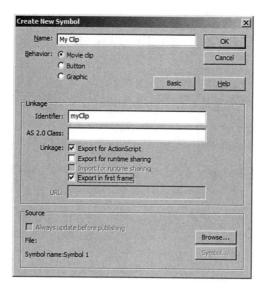

In the Linkage section, enter a name in the Identifier text box. It's the string you'll use when you call attachMovie(). If you select the Export in First Frame check box, your movie clip is added to the list of content loaded before the first frame of your movie begins to load. Therefore, selecting this option adds to the time it takes for any content you might have (such as a preloader) to show up. If you deselect Export in First

Frame, you need to have an instance of your clip placed on the stage at some place in your movie for attachMovie() to work. This is the syntax for attachMovie():

attachMovie(*idName, newName, depth* [, *initObject*]);

idName is the name of the movie clip to be added to the stage, *newName* is the name (including relevant path information) of the new clip, and *depth* is a unique number representing at what level the movie clip will be placed. *initObject*, an optional parameter, refers to an object that contains properties to be assigned to the movie clip when it's added. All properties of *initObject* are copied to the new movie clip.

Movie clips created with attachMovie() can be removed from the stage by using removeMovieClip() and unloadMovie(), as shown in this example:

```
// add clip to the stage.
attachMovie("myClipBase", "myClip", 0);
// remove it from the stage.
myClip.removeMovieClip();
```

The *duplicateMovieClip()* Method

Although the duplicateMovieClip() method is useful for easily creating numerous movie clips on the stage, its main limitation is that it can duplicate only clips that already exist on the stage. This is the syntax for duplicateMovieClip():

my_mc.duplicateMovieClip(*newclipname, depth* [, *initObject*]);

my_mc is the name of the movie clip to be duplicated, *newclipname* is the name (including relevant path information) of the new clip, and *depth* is a unique number representing at what level the movie clip will be placed. The optional *initObject* refers to an object that contains properties to be assigned to the movie clip when it's duplicated. All properties of *initObject* are copied to the new movie clip.

No matter what frame the original movie clip is on at the time of duplication, the duplicated clip begins playback on frame 1.

Movie clips created with duplicateMovieClip() can be removed by using removeMovieClip().

The *createEmptyMovieClip()* Method

This method creates a new, completely empty movie clip on the stage. It's often used with the Drawing application progamming interface (API), but the created movie clips aren't functionally limited in any way. The syntax is as follows:

```
parent_mc.createEmptyMovieClip("instance", depth);
```

instance is the name of the newly created movie clip, and *depth* indicates at what level the new clip will be placed. For example, creating an empty movie clip called new_mc within the parent clip my_mc looks like this:

```
my_mc.createEmptyMovieClip("new_mc", 1);
```

You can remove created movie clips by using removeMovieClip().

Loading External Files

With Flash, you can load SWFs and JPGS into your movie dynamically at runtime. This feature is useful for compartmentalizing content and is a helpful way to limit the time needed to load your movie onto a user's machine. This is the syntax for loading as a function:

```
loadMovie("url",target [, variables])
```

The syntax for loading as a method of the MovieClip object is as follows:

```
my_mc.loadMovie("url" [,variables])
```

url is the absolute or relative reference to the SWF or JPG file to be loaded. *target* is the movie clip or level that the specified URL will be loaded into. *variables* is an optional parameter specifying an HTTP method for sending or loading variables. If no variables are to be sent, omit this parameter. The GET method appends the variables to the end of the URL and is used for a small number of variables. The POST method sends the variables in a separate HTTP header and is used for long strings of variables.

Loaded content overwrites any pre-existing content in the target movie clip or level. For example, the following code line overwrites all content on the root level of a movie:

```
_root.loadMovie("file.swf");
```

When an SWF is loaded into another file, its internal path structure is altered. Before the file is loaded, the movie's base level is _root, but when the file is loaded, the movie's base level becomes whatever level or movie clip the file is loaded into. For example, entering trace(this); in an SWF would, when run by itself, output this:

_level0

When loaded into the movie clip bob, for example, the same SWF would output this:

_level0.bob

This change in path structure can cause considerable trouble if you have multiple absolute path references in your movie clips. Before Flash MX 2004, you had to load your content into a level (such as _level1 or _level2) or make relative path references from within your loaded content. New to Flash MX 2004, however, is the _lockroot property. When set to true, it makes all _root references refer to the loaded movie clip, not to the root of the main movie clip. This property can be set within the loaded clip, as shown here:

```
this._lockroot = true;
```

Or it can be set by the movie clip that's loading it, as shown:

```
onClipEvent (load) {
    this._lockroot = true;
}

this.loadMovie ("file.swf");
```

Although loadMovie() is a helpful tool, it is limited in its ability to monitor the progress of SWFs and JPGs being loaded into your movie; you need to write functions that track the progress of your load by using, among other things, the onEnterFrame handler of a movie clip. MovieClipLoader, a new class written for Flash 2004, does this very thing, however.

The *MovieClipLoader* Class

MovieClipLoader allows for easy access to information about your loading content and includes a number of listener methods to help you coordinate and automate your loading. You create an instance of the `MovieClipLoader` class like this:

```
my_mcl = new MovieClipLoader();
```

To load an external file into a movie clip, use the `loadClip()` method, which has the following syntax:

```
my_mcl.loadClip("url", "target");
```

url is the path reference to your SWF or JPG file. *target* is the movie clip to load the URL into. For example, to use `my_mcl` to load the file `mine.swf` into the movie clip `_root.mineHolder`, your code would look like this:

```
my_mcl.loadClip("mine.swf", "_root.mineHolder");
```

Although it can be said that `loadMovie()` does the same thing as `MovieClipLoader`—both load external SWFs and JPGs— `MovieClipLoader` has a lot more functionality to explore. For instance, `MovieClipLoader` includes the following methods:

- **loadClip()** This method was just described.

- **unloadClip()** This method has the following syntax:

  ```
  my_mcl.unloadClip(target);
  ```

  target is a movie clip that's currently loading content.

- **unloadClip()** This method cancels a download to the target movie clip if the download is already occurring. If it is, `unloadClip()` calls the `onLoadError` handler, sending it the name of the target clip and an error of the type `LoadNeverCompleted`.

- **getProgress()** This method has the following syntax:

  ```
  my_mcl.getProgress(target);
  ```

  It returns an object with these two read-only properties:

  bytesLoaded The current number of downloaded bytes of the movie.

  bytesTotal The total size of the file being downloaded.

As well, MovieClipLoader supports the following listener callback functions:

- **onLoadStart()** This listener callback is called when a download initiated by loadClip()begins. In the following syntax, *target* is always a MovieClip instance regardless of the type of target passed to loadClip():

  ```
  listenerObject.onLoadStart = function (target) {
  }
  ```

- **onLoadProgress()** Flash often calls this listener callback as an alternative to calling movieClipLoaderInstance.getProgress. If users want to run a progress box from a single function, they implement this listener. In the following syntax, *target* is always a MovieClip instance regardless of the type of target passed to loadClip():

  ```
  listenerObject.onLoadProgress = function (target,
  ➥bytesLoaded, bytesTotal) {
  }
  ```

- **onLoadComplete()** This listener callback is called when a download initiated by loadClip() finishes. In the following syntax, *target* is always a MovieClip instance regardless of the type of target passed to loadClip():

  ```
  listenerObject.onLoadComplete = function (target) {
  }
  ```

- **onLoadInit()** This listener callback is called when the download into the target has been completed and the actions on frame 1 have been carried out (but the frame has not been drawn). This callback allows the author to get or set properties on the movie, check the status of components, call functions, or any number of other options. onLoadInit() has the following syntax:

  ```
  listenerObject.onLoadInit = function (target) {
  }
  ```

- **onLoadError()** This listener callback is called when the download initiated by loadClip() fails. Two possible error code strings can be returned. URLNotFound is returned if neither onLoadStart nor onLoadComplete was called. This might occur if the specified file doesn't exist, or if the server is down. LoadNeverCompleted is returned if onLoadStart was called but onLoadComplete was not. This might occur if the server crashes or becomes overloaded. In the following syntax, *target* is always a MovieClip instance regardless of the type of target passed to loadClip():

```
listenerObject.onLoadError = function (target, errorCode) {
}
```

For example, the following code creates listeners for onLoadComplete and onLoadProgress, assigns the listeners to my_mcl (a new movieClipLoader instance), and loads an SWF file into the stan movie clip:

```
// create object
myListener = new Object();
// assign listener functions
myListener.onLoadComplete = function (target) {
    trace("You have finished loading " + target);
}

// assign listener functions
myListener.onLoadProgress = function (target,
➥bytesLoaded, bytesTotal) {
    trace("The progress of the " + target
➥ + " download is " + bytesLoaded + " / " + bytesTotal);
}

// create new MovieClipLoader
my_mcl = new MovieClipLoader();
// add listeners to MovieClipLoader instance
my_mcl.addListener(myListener);

// begin load
my_mcl.load("myfile.swf", "stan");
```

Removing Created Movie Clips

The removeMovieClip() function is used to remove movie clips created by duplicateMovieClip() or attachMovie(). To use it as a function (with *target* representing the name of the movie clip to be loaded), this is the syntax:

```
removeMovieClip(target);
```

To use it as a method of MovieClip, the syntax is as follows:

```
target.removeMovieClip();
```

The unLoadMovie() function removes an attached movie clip from the stage along with any content that has been loaded with loadMovie(). This is the syntax:

```
movieclip.unloadMovie();
```

SHARED OBJECTS

Creating and using remote shared objects is covered in Chapter 18, "Advanced Communications."

Shared objects are similar to cookies, in that they allow you to define information that's stored on the user's machine. However, cookies support saving only simple data; shared objects allow for recording and real-time accessing of any type of Flash data (excluding movie clips).

There are two types of shared objects: local and remote. *Local shared objects* are created and maintained on the user's personal machine. *Remote shared objects* are created on a server, using Flash Communication Server.

If you attempt to access a shared object that doesn't exist, Flash creates it for you.

You create a shared object by using SharedObject.getLocal(). Whatever information you place in the shared object is saved to the user's hard drive, so it's available for access the next time the movie is activated. This is the syntax for creating a local shared object:

```
variable_name = SharedObject.getLocal(shared_Object_name);
```

Setting Your Hard Drive Space

Local shared objects are saved on the user's hard drive. The Flash Player has default settings to determine what size shared objects can grow to. The default is 100KB, but if you attempt to save more than the default, the Player displays the Local Storage dialog box (see Figure 10.2), which allows you to increase the available space or deny the Flash movie's request.

FIGURE 10.2
Request to increase local storage space.

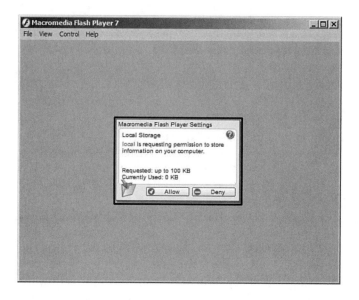

The Local Storage dialog box is 215 × 138 pixels, so a movie using this display needs to be at least that large for the dialog box to be displayed properly.

If the user selects the Allow option, the object is saved and the `SharedObject.onStatus()` method is called, sending the parameter code, which has a value of `SharedObject.Flush.Success`. If the user selects Deny, the object isn't saved, and `SharedObject.onStatus()` is called with the parameter code, which has a value of `SharedObject.Flush.Failed`.

The user can also, without prompting from a Flash movie, specify local storage settings for a domain by right-clicking (Windows) or Control-clicking (Macintosh) as a movie is playing, choosing Settings, and then selecting the Local Storage tab. (The tab has an icon of a file folder on it; see Figure 10.3.)

You adjust the storage setting by sliding the marker along the bar on the left of the dialog box. What happens if you change the Local Storage options?

The size limitation applies only to the Flash Player; there are no such restrictions in the Flash authoring environment.

• If you select Unlimited (by moving the slider all the way to the right), objects are saved locally until all available disk space is used.

• If you select None (by moving the slider all the way to the left), all commands issued for the object return `pending`, and Flash Player asks if more disk space can be allotted to make room for the object.

- If you select an amount, objects are saved locally, and SharedObject.flush() returns true if the object fits within the specified amount of space. If more space is needed, SharedObject.flush() returns pending, and Flash Player asks if more disk space can be allotted to make room for the object.

- If you select a value lower than what's currently being used for local data, Flash Player issues the warning shown in Figure 10.4.

FIGURE 10.3
Specifying settings in the Local Storage dialog box.

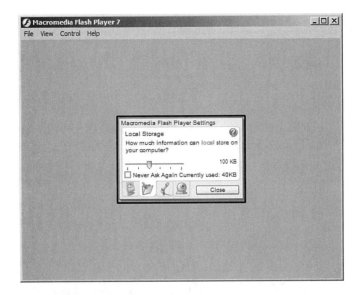

FIGURE 10.4
The warning issued for lowered storage space.

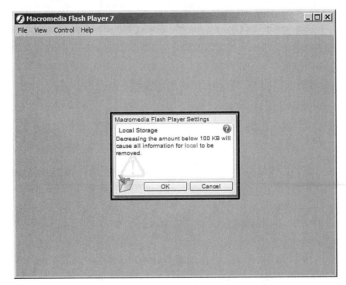

SharedObject Methods and Properties

These are the available SharedObject methods:

- **SharedObject.clear()**   This method purges all data from the shared object and deletes it from the hard drive.

- **SharedObject.flush()**   This method immediately writes a shared object to a file.

- **SharedObject.getLocal()**   This method returns a reference to a local shared object, available only to the current client.

- **SharedObject.getSize()**   This method returns the shared object's current size in bytes.

The SharedObject.data property is a collection of attributes assigned to the shared object's data property. These properties can be any data type and can be stored and shared within the current movie. For example, to add an array to the shared object my_so, use the following code:

```
my_array = new Array();
my_array[0] = "Hi";


my_so.data.my_array = my_array;
```

SharedObject Event Handler

SharedObject has a single event handler, onStatus(), which is called whenever an error, warning, or informational note is posted for a shared object. To respond to this event handler, you must write a function to process it, using the following syntax:

```
SharedObject.onStatus = function() {
    // code here
}
```

In addition to the onStatus() method in SharedObject, Flash provides a "super" function called system.onStatus. Flash processes a function associated with system.onStatus if no specific onStatus function has been defined. This enables you to define a single function to handle all onStatus() handlers for all SharedObjects that don't have unique handlers assigned to them. To define a generic onStatus function, use the following syntax:

```
system.onStatus = function(genericError) {
    // code would go here.
};
```

By default, every information object has a code property containing a
string that describes the result of the onStatus method and a class property containing a string (status, warning, or error). Some information
objects, such as SharedObject, have these additional default properties:

- **SharedObject.Flush.Failed** This property has a class property of
  error. It's sent when a "pending" SharedObject.flush() command
  has failed—the user didn't allot more shared object disk space.

- **SharedObject.Flush.Success** This property has a class property of
  status. It's sent when a "pending" SharedObject.flush() command
  has succeeded—the user allotted more shared object disk space.

DEPTH SORTING

Every movie clip has
its own internal z-
order, which exists
independently of
other timelines.

When you place objects on the stage, they occupy a position in a z-
ordered stack that Flash maintains. This stack determines how objects
overlap within a movie or movie level. Every movie clip has a depth
value, which determines whether the object is drawn above or below
other movie clips in the Timeline.

When you create a movie clip at runtime, using attachMovie(),
duplicateMovieClip(), or createEmptyMovieClip(), you specify a depth
for the new clip. For example, the following code creates an empty
movie clip with a depth of 50 in the z-order space of parent_mc:

```
parent_mc.createEmptyMovieClip("my_mc", 50);
```

If you attached another instance of the same symbol to the timeline of
parent_mc but specified a larger depth value, the new clip would be rendered above the previous clip you created. For example, the following code
attaches two new movie clips to parent_mc. The first clip, named clip_1,
is rendered below clip_2 because it was assigned a lower depth value:

```
container_mc.attachMovie("symbolID", "clip_1", 10);
container_mc.attachMovie("symbolID", "clip_2", 15);
```

Depth values for movie clips can range from -16384 to 1048575. The MovieClip class has several methods for managing movie clip depths: MovieClip.getNextHighestDepth(), MovieClip.getInstanceAtDepth(), MovieClip.getDepth(), and MovieClip.swapDepths().

After you have your movie clip at its depth, changing its depth is often necessary. You can do this by using the swapDepths() method of MovieClip, which has the following syntax:

```
my_mc.swapDepths(depth);
my_mc.swapDepths(target);
```

When you supply a depth (which is always an integer) for swapDepths(), your movie clip occupies that depth. When you supply a target for swapDepths() (such as clip_19), the calling movie clip gets the target's depth, and the target gets the calling clip's depth. To determine the depth of a specified movie clip, use the getDepth() method, which uses the following syntax and returns an integer corresponding to the movie clip's depth:

```
my_mc.getDepth();
```

To determine the name of an instance, if any, at a specified depth, use the getInstanceAtDepth() method, which uses the following syntax:

```
my_mc.getInstanceAtDepth(depth);
```

This method returns a string identifier of a movie clip on this depth. It's helpful for determining whether the depth is available before using attachMovie(), createEmptyMovieClip(), or duplicateMovieClip().

Finally, if you want to create a movie clip that will be above all other currently existing clips, use the getNextHighestDepth() method, which has the following syntax:

```
my_mc.getNextHighestDepth();
```

In the following example, getNextHighestDepth() is used to determine the next available depth in the movie clip my_mc, and a new movie clip, new_clip, is added at that depth by using the createEmptyMovieClip() method:

```
var new_depth = my_mc.getNextHighestDepth();
my_mc.createEmptyMovieClip("new_clip", new_depth);
```

Chapter Project: Using Dynamic Masks

Now that you know all about functions, dynamic masks, and the like, it's time to put that knowledge to use. You won't be building on the project you started in Chapter 8; this time, you'll be starting a completely new project.

For this project, you'll make a movie that attaches a movie clip from the Library, which you'll use as a dynamic mask. You'll also add the ability to control the mask's size and turn it on and off and add a Print button so that you can print the movie.

1. First, create a new movie. Pick whatever dimensions and frame rate you like.

2. Because you'll be using dynamic masks, you need something *to* mask. Make a movie clip, and put a drawing or photo inside it. Then put that movie clip on the stage, and name the instance of the movie clip bg (see Figure 10.5).

FIGURE 10.5
The masked movie clip.

3. Next, you need something to mask the bg movie clip. Make a new movie clip, and assign that clip a linkage identifier, as shown in Figure 10.6. Call it whatever you like, but don't place it on the stage. Instead, draw something inside it. (You can get fancy if you like, but a simple shape will do.)

FIGURE 10.6
The masking movie clip.

4. Next, you need a way of getting that masking clip on the stage. You'll write a function that creates an instance of the movie clip on the stage and makes it mask the bg clip. Create a new layer to hold your function, and write a new buildMask() function (see Figure 10.7). Include an attachMovie() command referencing your movie clip and a setMask() command to turn the clip into a mask.

5. Now that you have a function to create the masked clip, you need a way to call it. Create a new button, and place it on the stage. Select the instance of the button, and add a handler with an action to call the function:

```
on (release) {
buildMask();
}
```

FIGURE 10.7
Adding the
buildMask()
function.

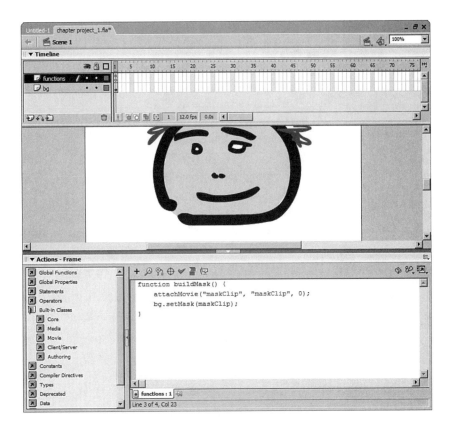

6. If you test your movie now, you probably won't see the masking effect because the masking clip is created at position 0,0. To see the masking effect, you need to add code similar to the following in the masking clip that sets the clip to the mouse's coordinates:

```
onEnterFrame = function() {
    this._x = _root._xmouse;
    this._y = _root._ymouse;
}
```

7. If you test your movie clip now, when you mouse over the content clip, you should see the masked content. Next, you add functionality to flip the mask on and off. Place two buttons on the stage—one to turn the mask off and the other to turn it back on. Although you could just place the setMask() command on each button, in this example, put it into a function. You'll have both buttons call the

same function, passing a parameter to let it know what to do. Here's what it could look like:

```
// function on main timeline
function setMask(which) {
//attach mask movie clip
attachMovie("maskClip", "maskClip", 0);
    if (which == 0) {
        // turn off the mask
        bg.setMask(null);
    } else if (which == 1) {
        // turn on the mask
        // in place of _root.maskClip, enter your movie
        ➡clip name
        bg.setMask(_root.maskClip);
    }
}


// code on button to turn mask on
on (release) {
    setMask(1);
}


// code on button to turn mask off
on (release) {
    setMask(0);
}
```

8. Export your movie now. You should be able to flip the mask on and off.

What if you decide your mask isn't the right size? In Flash, it's possible to resize your mask on the fly. Follow these steps:

9. You need to create two input text fields on the stage. You'll read values from them to set the mask's width and height, so name them something that makes sense to you.

10. Next, add another button to the stage to call the function that sets the mask size:

```
on (release) {
setMaskSize();
}
```

CHAPTER 11

ANIMATION AND DRAWING WITH ACTIONSCRIPT: THE DRAWING API

WHY PROGRAM WHEN YOU CAN USE CLASSIC ANIMATION? FRAME-BASED animation can offer you more control and certainly greater levels of graphical complexity. (You could draw a face, for example, in far less time than it takes to write a program to do the same thing.) However, in many cases, your animation is better when you use scripting.

The Drawing API (application programming interface) is useful in creating simple shapes, for example, and in manipulating those shapes. These shapes can be created in response to an internal event, a user activity, or a system-generated event. Also, the Drawing API enables you to create tools so that users can draw within your movie.

Another use of the Drawing API is in creating masks; you can determine the constraints of a mask yourself, or create a movie that lets users draw their own masks over pre-existing content.

With the Drawing API, you can define shapes of varying complexity, so you can easily use ActionScript to create the entire interface, resulting in a movie that has absolutely no Library items! This is a bit extreme—after all, in many cases it's simply easier to create visual elements manually, in author time—but the Drawing API offers an easy-to-use, compelling alternative.

AN INTRODUCTION TO THE DRAWING API

The Drawing API is a collection of eight methods of the MovieClip class that enable you to add visual content to a movie clip. You can draw lines, curves, and filled shapes. The eight methods are beginFill(), beginGradientFill(), clear(), curveTo(), endFill(), lineStyle(), lineTo(), and moveTo(). With these eight methods, you can draw complex visual elements at runtime and create unique interactive experiences. In short, the Drawing API makes it possible for you do tremendously cool things with Macromedia Flash MX 2004.

Using the Drawing API

For a reminder on using createEmptyMovie-Clip(), see Chapter 10, "ActionScript: Functions, Events, and Objects."

When using the Drawing API, first you should create a movie clip to hold your art. Although you can use any existing movie clip (one that's placed on the stage at author time or created by using attachMovie() or duplicateMovieClip()), using the createEmptyMovieClip() method to create a holder for your drawn content is more convenient.

After creating your movie clip, you'll want to start drawing. Before you actually draw anything on the screen, however, you have to tell Flash what the lines in your drawing will look like by using the lineStyle() method, which has the following syntax:

```
my_mc.lineStyle([thickness[, rgb[, alpha]]])
```

The *thickness* parameter is an integer between 0 and 255 that specifies the thickness, in pixels, of the line to be drawn. Using 0, for example, produces a hairline thickness. If you set a value that's more or less than the allowed range, Flash snaps it back to the default value. For example, if you set *thickness* to 2000, Flash snaps it back to 255.

rgb, an optional parameter, is a hexadecimal color value that determines what color your line will be. For example, 0x000000 is black, and 0xFFFFFF is white. When *rgb* isn't specified, Flash uses black.

alpha, an optional parameter, is an integer between 0 and 100 that specifies the opacity of the line to be drawn. If you set a value that's more or less than the stated range, Flash snaps it back to the default, which is 100% alpha (solid).

After you've set the lineStyle, you can begin drawing your line by using the lineTo() method, which has the following syntax:

```
my_mc.lineTo(x, y)
```

x is an integer representing the horizontal coordinate for where you draw the line, and y is an integer representing the vertical coordinate. Both coordinates are set in relation to your movie clip's current registration point. The following code creates a movie clip and draws a line to the relative 50,50 coordinates:

```
createEmptyMovieClip("lineHolder", 0);
with (lineHolder) {
    lineStyle(1, 0x000000, 100);
    lineTo(50,50);
}
```

When you create a movie clip, by default it's positioned at 0,0, so the preceding code draws a line at the coordinates 50,50. The following example sets a different position for the lineHolder movie clip:

```
createEmptyMovieClip("lineHolder", 0);
lineHolder._x = 20;
lineHolder._y = 35;

with (lineHolder) {
    lineStyle(1, 0x000000, 100);
    lineTo(50,50);
}
```

In this example, the line is drawn from 20,35 to 70,85, not from 0,0 to 50,50. Initially, your movie clip's registration point is 0,0. When you call lineTo(), the registration point is changed to the location specified by the values set in lineTo(). For example, after a call of lineTo(10,10), the registration point changes to 10,10. You can see how this works in the following example:

```
createEmptyMovieClip("lineHolder", 0);
with (lineHolder) {
    lineStyle(1, 0x000000, 100);
    lineTo(50,50);
    lineTo(0, 50);
}
```

The second line doesn't start from the origin of lineHolder and draw the line at 0,50; instead, it starts at 50,50 and draws a straight line. You can manually set the registration point's location without drawing anything on the screen by using the moveTo() method, which has the following syntax:

```
my_mc.moveTo(x, y)
```

The movie clip's registration point is shifted to the coordinates specified by x (an integer representing the horizontal coordinate) and y (an integer representing the vertical coordinate). For example, note the difference between shapes drawn by the following two code snippets:

```
// this example draws two lines, without
// first adjusting the registration point
createEmptyMovieClip("myHolder", 0);
with (myHolder) {
    lineStyle(1, 0x000000, 100);
    lineTo(200, 300);
    lineTo(300, 300);
}

// this example draws two lines, after
// adjusting the registration point
createEmptyMovieClip("myHolder", 0);
with (myHolder) {
    lineStyle(1, 0x000000, 100);
    moveTo(50,50);
    lineTo(200, 300);
    lineTo(300, 300);
}
```

Note in the first example that the drawing began at the top-left corner of the stage. The second example began drawing slightly inward, at 50,50, because the movie clip's registration point was shifted.

Drawing Polygonal Shapes

Next, take lineTo() a bit further and use it to draw a shape. The following code draws a square:

```
createEmptyMovieClip("myHolder", 0);
with (myHolder) {
    lineStyle(1, 0x000000, 100);
```

```
        lineTo(50, 0);
        lineTo(50, 50);
        lineTo(0, 50);
        lineTo(0, 0);
}
```

The following code also draws a square but offsets it 50 pixels (in both x and y) from the movie's initial registration point:

```
createEmptyMovieClip("myHolder", 0);
with (myHolder) {
        lineStyle(1, 0x000000, 100);
        moveTo(50, 50);
        lineTo(100, 50);
        lineTo(100, 100);
        lineTo(50, 100);
        lineTo(50, 50);
}
```

Basically, by adding a series of lineTo() commands, you can create any manner of polygonal shapes with the Drawing API.

Drawing Curves

Control points and anchor points were introduced in Chapter 2, "Overview of the Interface and Tools."

Drawing polygonal shapes seems easy, but what if you want to draw a curved line? In the Drawing API, you use the curveTo() method, which has the following syntax:

```
my_mc.curveTo(controlX, controlY, anchorX, anchorY)
```

controlX and *controlY* are integers specifying the control point's horizontal and vertical position in relation to the parent movie clip's registration point.

anchorX and *anchorY* are integers specifying the next anchor point's horizontal and vertical position in relation to the parent movie clip's registration point.

For example, the following code draws a curve on the screen that looks like Figure 11.1:

```
createEmptyMovieClip ("curveHolder", 1);
with (curveHolder){
        lineStyle (1, 0x000000, 100);
        curveTo(50,0,50,50);
}
```

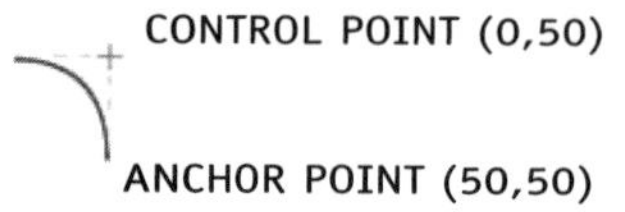

FIGURE 11.1
Drawing a curve with
the Drawing API's
curveTo() method.

CONTROL POINT (0,50)

ANCHOR POINT (50,50)

Take a look at the points labeled in Figure 11.1. The *control point*, which controls the bend of the curve, is similar to the tangent handle in the Pen tool. The *anchor point* is where the curve is drawn *to*; it's basically the same as the *x* and *y* parameters of the lineTo() method.

The curve is defined by the location of the control point. Take the code used to generate the curve in Figure 11.1, and adjust the control point (the first two numbers in the curveTo() method). Try a variety of different settings for the control point, and you'll get a good idea of how to make some nice vector shapes. Just as you can make successive lineTo() calls to create polygonal shapes, you can make successive curveTo() calls. For example, the following code draws an oval:

```
_root.createEmptyMovieClip ("curveHolder", 1);
curveHolder._x = 50;
curveHolder._y = 50;
with (_root.curveHolder){
    lineStyle (1, 0x000000, 100);
    curveTo(25,0, 25, 25);
    curveTo(25,50,0,50);
    curveTo(-25,50,-25,25);
    curveTo(-25,0,0,0);
}
```

To accurately draw curves greater than 45 degrees, you need to manipulate the code a bit more, as explained in "Drawing a Circle," later in this chapter.

Drawing Filled Shapes

What if you want to do more than draw empty shapes—filled shapes, for example? That's where beginFill() and beginGradientFill() come in. Both methods fill the interior area of a drawn shape. The first method, beginFill(), fills a shape with a solid color and uses the following syntax:

```
my_mc.beginFill([rgb[, alpha]])
```

rgb is a hex color value (0x000000 for black and 0xFF0000 for red, for example). If you don't supply this value, no fill is generated. *alpha,* an optional parameter, is an integer between 0 and 100 that specifies the fill's alpha (transparency) value. If you don't provide this value, it defaults to 100 (no transparency). If the value is outside the defined range, Flash snaps the value to the nearest one that's within the range.

The second method, `beginGradientFill()`, fills a shape with a gradient and has the following syntax:

`my_mc.beginGradientFill(`*fillType, colors, alphas, ratios,* `➥`*matrix*`)`

fillType determines the type of gradient and can be set to `linear` or `radial`. *colors* is an array of RGB hex color values that are used to determine the gradient colors.

alphas is an array of alpha values that correspond to the colors in the colors array. Accepted values are 0 to 100. If you enter a value less than 0, Flash uses 0. If you enter a value greater than 100, Flash uses 100. *ratios* is an array of color distribution ratios; accepted values are 0 to 255. This parameter defines the percentage of the width where the color is sampled at 100%.

matrix is a transformation matrix, which is an object with a series of properties that define how the gradient will fill. There are two ways you can define your transformation matrix. The first method defines the position, scaling, and rotation of your matrix, using the properties `matrixType`, `x`, `y`, `w`, `h`, and `r`. They are defined as follows:

- `matrixType` must equal "box", as defined by the following properties. If it doesn't, the gradient won't fill properly.

- `x` is the horizontal position for the upper-left corner of the gradient, set in relation to the parent clip's registration point.

- `y` is the vertical position for the upper-left corner of the gradient, set in relation to the parent clip's registration point.

- `w` is the width of the gradient.

- `h` is the height of the gradient.

- `r` is the rotation of the gradient set in radians.

Here's an example of a gradient created using this method (see Figure 11.2 for the results of this code):

```
createEmptyMovieClip( "grad", 1 );
with ( grad ) {
    colors = [ 0x000000, 0xFFFFFF ];
    alphas = [ 100, 100 ];
    ratios = [ 0, 255 ];
    matrix = { matrixType:"box", x:1, y:1, w:200, h:200, r:2
➥};

    beginGradientFill( "linear", colors, alphas, ratios,
➥matrix );
    moveTo(50,50);
    lineTo(50,200);
    lineTo(200,200);
    lineTo(200,50);
    lineTo(50,50);
    endFill();
}
```

FIGURE 11.2
Drawing a gradient
with the first method.

If a matrixType property exists, it must equal "box" and the remaining parameters are all required. If either condition isn't met, the method call fails.

The second method defines a grid, with each item in the grid defining how the gradient in that section will be filled. The properties in this matrix are a, b, c, d, e, f, g, h, and i. They describe a 3 × 3 matrix of the following form:

a	b	c
d	e	f
g	h	i

In this matrix, a represents the gradient's horizontal scaling, e represents
the vertical scaling, g represents the gradient's horizontal translation (offset, in pixels), and h represents the vertical translation. The following
example uses this second method for a gradient fill (see Figure 11.3 for
the results of this code):

```
createEmptyMovieClip( "grad", 1 );
with ( grad ) {
    colors = [ 0x000000, 0xFFFFFF ];
    alphas = [ 100, 100 ];
    ratios = [ 0, 255 ];
    matrix = { a:100, b:0, c:40, d:0, e:100, f:20, g:100,
    ➥h:250, i:12 };
    beginGradientFill( "linear", colors, alphas, ratios,
    ➥matrix );
    moveTo(50,50);
    lineTo(50,200);
    lineTo(200,200);
    lineTo(200,50);
    lineTo(50,50);
    endFill();
}
```

FIGURE 11.3
Drawing a gradient
with the second
method.

If a matrixType property does not exist, the remaining parameters are all
required. In fact, the function fails if any are missing.

For the fill to begin correctly, both beginFill() and
beginGradientFill() are required before any lineTo() or curveTo()
calls. When you've finished drawing your shape, you have to cap it with
the endFill() method so that Flash knows to stop filling in the interior
space of your shapes. This is the syntax for endFill():

```
my_mc.endFill();
```

To show you what this method looks like, take the code used previously to draw an oval and add a beginFill() to make a blue fill with 60% opacity:

```
_root.createEmptyMovieClip ("curveHolder", 1);
curveHolder._x = 50;
curveHolder._y = 50;
with (_root.curveHolder){
    beginFill(0x333366, 60);
    lineStyle (1, 0x000000, 100);
    curveTo(25,0, 25, 25);
    curveTo(25,50,0,50);
    curveTo(-25,50,-25,25);
    curveTo(-25,0,0,0);
    endFill();
}
```

Alternatively, you might decide to fill the circle with a gradient:

```
_root.createEmptyMovieClip ("curveHolder", 1);
curveHolder._x = 50;
curveHolder._y = 50;
with (_root.curveHolder){
    colors = [ 0xFF0000, 0x0000FF ];
    alphas = [ 100, 100 ];
    ratios = [ 0, 0xFF ];
    matrix = { matrixType:"box", x:100, y:100, w:200, h:200,
    ➥r:2 };
    beginGradientFill( "linear", colors, alphas, ratios,
    ➥matrix );
    lineStyle (1, 0x000000, 100);
    curveTo(25,0, 25, 25);
    curveTo(25,50,0,50);
    curveTo(-25,50,-25,25);
    curveTo(-25,0,0,0);
    endFill();
}
```

All that's left to do now is clear out the movie clip when you're done.

Removing Drawn Content

When you draw new shapes in your movie clip, Flash just piles the vectors onto whatever was already there. If you are drawing in a movie clip created at runtime, Flash adds these new vectors over the existing ones; if you're drawing in a movie clip created at author time, Flash draws these new vectors under that content. So if you draw a circle in frame 1 and a square in frame 2, after the square is drawn, you'll have both shapes in the movie clip. Sometimes this is handy, but if you're trying to animate a changing shape, you'll end up with a large series of overlapping, slightly different shapes. Although this can be a distinctive visual effect, it does have the unfortunate effect of bogging down the Player and causing everything to run more slowly. So when you're done with your art and you want to get rid of it, you use the `clear()` method of `MovieClip`, which has the following syntax:

```
my_mc.clear()
```

This method removes *all* drawn content from your movie clip. However, content you draw manually at author time and drawn content in *other* movie clips aren't affected by `clear()`. If you want to remove just the most recent shape you drew, not every shape in your movie clip in previous frames, you need a workaround, unless the shape you're deleting is actually in a different movie clip. Also, `clear()` resets the `lineStyle` of your movie clip to undefined and uses the default registration point.

To give you an idea of what happens when you don't call the `clear()` method, take a look at the following bit of code. It creates a new movie clip and adds code that draws a new, slightly expanding square every frame. Here's the code, without the `clear()` method:

```
// make new movie clip
createEmptyMovieClip("myClip", 0);

// position movie clip
myClip._x = 50;
myClip._y = 50;

// set initial size of square
myClip.squareSize = 50;
```

```
// define onEnterFrame handler
myClip.onEnterFrame = function() {
    with (this) {
        // define line drawing style
        lineStyle(1, 0x000000, 30);

        // draw square
        lineTo(0, squareSize);
        lineTo(squareSize, squareSize);
        lineTo(squareSize, 0);
        lineTo(0, 0);

        // increment square size
        squareSize+=2;
    }
}
```

Try it out. It looks cool, doesn't it? The only problem is that soon it's going to start slowing the Player down. Now try adding a clear() call near the end:

```
// make new movie clip
createEmptyMovieClip("myClip", 0);

// position movie clip
myClip._x = 50;
myClip._y = 50;

// set initial size of square
myClip.squareSize = 50;

// define onEnterFrame handler
myClip.onEnterFrame = function() {
    with (this) {
// clear previous shapes
clear();

        // define line drawing style
        lineStyle(1, 0x000000, 30);

        // draw square
```

```
lineTo(0, squareSize);
lineTo(squareSize, squareSize);
lineTo(squareSize, 0);
lineTo(0, 0);

// increment square size
squareSize+=2;

    }
}
```

Note that the clear() call is inserted before redrawing the shape; this is important because you're basically flushing out what's come before in the code so that the Player doesn't get bogged down. If you inserted clear() before drawing the square, you wouldn't see a shape at all in the movie.

Although the Drawing API is very powerful, it's made up of just these eight commands you've learned about in the previous sections. Now that you have a good handle on how to draw shapes, it's time to move on to the next section and have some fun.

Guidelines and Tips

There's no mechanism for determining your movie clip's current registration point for drawing. To work around this limitation, you can manually keep track of the registration point. One way to do this is to define a registration point object when creating your movie clip and record the initial x-y point. (By default the registration point is 0,0, so recording the x-y point won't cause any problems.) Then every time you want to draw a shape or set the registration point, you could update the point information in your registration point object and use those values when you call lineTo(), moveTo(), or curveTo(), as shown in this example:

```
// create your movie clip
createEmptyMovieClip("drawHolder", 0);

// create your registration point object
drawHolder.currentPoint = new Object;
```

```
// set initial values
drawHolder.currentPoint.x = 0;
drawHolder.currentPoint.y = 0;
```

currentPoint is your registration point object. Using this system, if you wanted to draw a line at the coordinates 50,50, you would use the following code:

```
with (drawHolder) {
    _currentPoint.x = 50;
    _currentPoint.y = 50;
    lineStyle(1, 0x000000, 100);
    lineTo(_currentPoint.x, _currentPoint.y);
}
```

This way, you can always find the exact position of your registration point.

You might notice that although the preceding code works, it isn't as modular as it could be. You could prototype a function to define and retrieve your movie clip's currentPoint values. The following is a prototype function (*prototyping* enables you to define a method or property once and have it apply to all instances of whatever object you define it for) that defines the currentPoint values:

```
MovieClip.prototype.setPoint = function (x, y) {
    // checks to see if currentPoint exists
    if (!_currentPoint) {
        // it doesn't, create it.
        _currentPoint = new Object();
    }

    _currentPoint.x = x;
    _currentPoint.y = y;
}
```

This function retrieves the _currentPoint values:

```
MovieClip.prototype.getPoint = function(which) {
    // determine which value to retrieve
    if (which == "x") {
        return _currentPoint.x;
```

```
    } else if (which == "y") {
        return _currentPoint.y;
    }
}
```

Notice that you have to send the which value to retrieve a point value. In this example, which must be x or y.

Now revisit this code:

```
// create your movie clip
createEmptyMovieClip("drawHolder", 0);

// create your registration point object
drawHolder.setPoint(0,0);

with (drawHolder) {
    setPoint(50,50);

    lineTo(getPoint("x"), getPoint("y"));
}
```

Notice how much shorter this code is than the first attempt?

Tracking Points

A limitation of the Drawing API is that it doesn't have a way to remember what you've drawn onscreen. When you add something to your movie clip using lineTo() or curveTo(), a vector is added to your movie clip and the registration point is changed, but that's it; no array of drawn lines is retained. If you draw a triangle and want to change its size later, you can't reassign the location of one of the vectors; you have to redraw the whole shape. For example, the following code draws a triangle that looks like Figure 11.4:

```
createEmptyMovieClip("myTriangle", 0);
with (myTriangle) {
    lineStyle(1, 0x000000, 100);
    lineTo(50,50);
    lineTo(50,-50);
    lineTo(0,0);
}
```

However, later you decide that you want the line drawn from 50,50 to 50,–50 to be drawn from 50,50 to 50,–75. You can't access previously drawn vectors, so to adjust the triangle, you have to use clear() to remove the previously drawn content of your movie clip and redraw the entire shape with the following code (which produces the triangle shown in Figure 11.5):

```
with (myTriangle) {
    clear();
    lineStyle(1, 0x000000, 100);
    lineTo(50,50);
    lineTo(50,-75);
    lineTo(0,0);
}
```

What if you want to adjust individual vectors in your drawn shapes and keep track of what you've done? It's simple: Keep track of your points in an array, and use the array elements when drawing shapes. For example, the following code defines an array called myShape and a function called drawMyShape, which takes the contents of myShape and uses it to draw a shape onscreen:

```
// define the array
var myShape = new Array();

// array elements keep track of points
// nested array elements keep track of x/y coordinates
myShape[0] = new Array(20, 0);
myShape[1] = new Array(40, 20);
myShape[2] = new Array(60, 0);
myShape[3] = new Array(45, -30);
```

```
myShape[4] = new Array(120, -7);
myShape[5] = new Array(0, 23);
myShape[6] = new Array(70, 19);
myShape[7] = new Array(0, 0);

// define the function
function drawMyShape () {
    with (myClip) {
        // clear any previous content
        clear();

        lineStyle(1, 0x000000, 100);

        // cycle through myShape elements, draw shape
        for (var i = 0; i<_root.myShape.length; i++) {
            x = _root.myShape[i][0];
            y = _root.myShape[i][1];

            lineTo(x, y);
        }
    }
}


// create movie clip
createEmptyMovieClip("myClip",0);

// draw the shape
drawMyShape();
```

This code generates the shape shown in Figure 11.6.

FIGURE 11.6
Using the array elements in myShape to draw a shape.

If you want to change the shape, just manipulate the array's elements and call the drawMyShape() function again.

Now look at another example. Suppose you're drawing a triangle onscreen; the first and last points are set, but the middle point is determined by the cursor's location. The triangle has a fill, and its transparency (alpha setting) is determined by how far the cursor is from the two preset points.

First, create a new movie clip, and add the shape array to it. Previously the array was defined on the movie's root, but in this code it's added to the drawing object to use a more modular approach:

```
// create the movie clip
createEmptyMovieClip("myTriangle", 0);

// create the array
myTriangle.myShape = new Array();

// first point
myTriangle.myShape[0] = new Array(50, 50);

// last point, to close the shape
myTriangle.myShape[2] = new Array(0, 0);
```

The mouse cursor's position defines the middle point (which will be myShape[1]), so you need to set it dynamically because the mouse is always potentially moving. To do this, create an empty movie clip and add an onEnterFrame handler to it so that every frame readjusts the array's contents:

```
myTriangle.onEnterFrame = function() {
    this.myShape[1] = new Array(_xmouse, _ymouse);
}
```

That's all that's needed for the onEnterFrame handler, but it's not as clean as it could be. Use the following code to write a function called setMyShape that defines the triangle's makeup:

```
myTriangle.setMyShape = function() {
    with (this) {
        myShape[0] = new Array(50, 50);
        myShape[1] = new Array(_xmouse, _ymouse);
        myShape[2] = new Array(0, 0);
    }
}
```

Now, instead of manually defining the array point in the onEnterFrame handler, you can call the setMyShape function:

```
myTriangle.onEnterFrame = function () {
    with (this) {
        setMyShape();
    }
}
```

This function might seem unnecessary, but redefining the first and last myShape elements every frame is useful because if you decide later to change the first and last elements frequently, a function for updating them quickly is already in place.

Before you draw the triangle onscreen, you have to determine the triangle's alpha (transparency) setting by calculating the distance between the first point (50,50) and the mouse position and the last point (0,0) and the mouse position. To perform this calculation, you'll use the determineDist function and pass one parameter to it. This parameter is a numeric value that specifies which myShape element to compare to the mouse position (0 for the first point and 2 for the last point, which corresponds with the myShape array indexes). Here's the code for the determineDist function:

```
myTriangle.determineDist = function (which) {
    with (this) {
        // define variables
        x = myShape[which][0];
        y = myShape[which][1];

        // determine distance along x and y axes
        distX = _xmouse - x;
        distY = _ymouse - y;

        // determine absolute distance
        dist = Math.sqrt( (distX*distX) + (distY*distY) );

        // return distance
        return dist;
    }
}
```

This function returns the distance between the first and last points and
the mouse position. Next is a function to determine the alpha setting. It
calls determineDist twice (once for each comparison location), averages
the two distances, and uses that number to determine the alpha setting:

```
myTriangle.determineAlpha = function() {
    with (this) {
        // determine distances
        dist1 = determineDist(0);
        dist2 = determineDist(2);

        // determine average distance
        avgDistance = (dist1+dist2)/2;

        // if the number is less than 500,
        // the distance will be the alpha.
        if (avgDistance < 500) {
            // return the avgDistance
            return avgDistance/5;
        } else {
            // if the distance is equal to or greater
            // than 500, return 100.
            return 100;
        }
    }
}
```

As you can see, the function returns the determined alpha value because
you call this method of myTriangle when you call beginFill(). All
that's left is writing a function that actually draws the triangle:

```
myTriangle.drawTriangle = function() {
    with (this) {
        // clear any previous content
        clear();

        // set the line style
        lineStyle(1, 0x000000, 100);

        // set the alpha
        beginFill(0x000000, determineAlpha());
```

```
        // draw the shape
        for (var i = 0; i<myShape.length; i++) {
            x = myShape[i][0];
            y = myShape[i][1];

            lineTo(x, y);
        }


        // end the fill
        endFill();
    }
}
```

All the functionality is now in place. The last thing to do, of course, is to call the preceding function so that everything gets drawn. Add the following line to the myTriangle onEnterFrame handler:

```
drawTriangle();
```

Test your movie to see the triangle. The completed code should look like this:

```
// create the movie clip
createEmptyMovieClip("myTriangle", 0);

// create the array
myTriangle.myShape = new Array();

// first point
myTriangle.myShape[0] = new Array(50, 50);

// last point, to close the shape
myTriangle.myShape[2] = new Array(0, 0);

myTriangle.setMyShape = function() {
    with (this) {
        myShape[0] = new Array(50, 50);
        myShape[1] = new Array(_xmouse, _ymouse);
        myShape[2] = new Array(0, 0);
    }
}
```

```
myTriangle.onEnterFrame = function () {
    with (this) {
        setMyShape();
        drawTriangle();
    }
}


myTriangle.determineDist = function (which) {
    with (this) {
        // define variables
        x = myShape[which][0];
        y = myShape[which][1];

        // determine distance along x and y axes
        distX = _xmouse - x;
        distY = _ymouse - y;

        // determine absolute distance
        dist = Math.sqrt( (distX*distX) + (distY*distY) );

        // return distance
        return dist;
    }
}


myTriangle.determineAlpha = function() {
    with (this) {
        // determine distances
        dist1 = determineDist(0);
        dist2 = determineDist(2);

        // determine average distance
        avgDistance = (dist1+dist2)/2;

        // if the number is less than 500,
        // the distance will be the alpha.
        if (avgDistance < 500) {
            // return the avgDistance
```

```
                return avgDistance/5;
        } else {
            // if the distance is equal to or greater
            // than 500, return 100.
            return 100;
        }
    }
}

myTriangle.drawTriangle = function() {
    with (this) {
        // clear anything previous
        clear();

        // set the line style
        lineStyle(1, 0x000000, 100);

        // set the alpha
        beginFill(0x000000, determineAlpha());

        // draw the shape
        for (var i = 0; i<myShape.length; i++) {
            x = myShape[i][0];
            y = myShape[i][1];

            lineTo(x, y);
        }

        // end the fill
        endFill();
    }
}
```

This example is simple, but it shows you how to keep track of what you're drawing and manipulate that data. Try manipulating other elements of the myShape array or adding more elements. Another trick is making the myTriangle movie clip move toward the mouse. You can do this with the following method, seekToMouse, which is called every frame in the onEnterFrame handler:

```
myTriangle.seekToMouse = function() {
    with (this) {
        dX = _root._xmouse - _x;
        dY = _root._ymouse - _y;

        _x += dX/5;
        _y += dY/5;
    }
}
```

The only limitation to what you can do with the Drawing API is what you choose *not* to do with it.

Sample Applications

If you find you're manually redrawing the same shapes over and over, writing a function that automatically draws the shapes for you might be a good idea. The following sections show some prototype MovieClip functions that draw a rectangle, an oval, a triangle, a polygon, and a star.

Drawing a Rectangle

You could write code like the following every time you want to draw a square onscreen:

```
lineStyle(1,0x000000, 100);
lineTo(0,50);
lineTo(50,50);
lineTo(50,0);
lineTo(0,0);
```

However, that could get tiresome. If you're repeating the same code often, why not encapsulate it? The following is a prototyped function called drawRectangle:

```
MovieClip.prototype.drawRectangle = function(ax, ay, bx, by) {
    // draw a square
    lineTo(ax, by);
    lineTo(bx, by);
    lineTo(bx, ay);
    lineTo(ax, ay);
}
```

You need to send the following four parameters to the preceding function:

- ax defines the left x coordinate.

- ay defines the top y coordinate.

- bx is the right x coordinate.

- by is the bottom y coordinate.

You can use this function to define rectangles of any size, and because squares are a type of rectangle, you can use it to draw squares, too. The following function draws a rectangle on the stage, going from the center point of your movie clip to 100,100:

```
createEmptyMovieClip("myRect", 0);

with (myRect) {
    lineStyle(1, 0x000000, 100);
    drawRectangle(0,0,100,100);
}
```

If you want to draw your rectangle with a fill, just place the beginFill() and endFill() calls before and after the drawing takes place, as shown here:

```
createEmptyMovieClip("mySquare", 0);

with (myRect) {
    lineStyle(1, 0x000000, 100);
    beginFill(0x000000, 100);
    drawRectangle(0,0,100,100);
    endFill();
}
```

Drawing a Line

The following function, drawLine, is used to draw a straight line. You pass four variables to drawLine: the x starting position, the y starting position, the x ending position, and the y ending position:

```
MovieClip.prototype.drawLine = function (startX, startY, endX,
➥endY) {
    moveTo(startX, startY);
    lineTo(endX, endY);
}
```

If you want to draw a line from 30,20 to 107,20, for example, use the following code:

```
createEmptyMovieClip("myLine", 0);
myLine.lineStyle(1, 0x0000, 100);
myLine.drawLine(30, 20, 107, 20);
```

Drawing a Circle

Using the curveTo() method of the Drawing API, it's possible to render a circle easily. Although technically you can draw a circle using only four curve segments, this method produces a flattened circle. To make your circle look more like a circle, using at least eight segments is recommended. The following method, drawCircle, uses eight segments to draw a circle. You pass it three variables: the top-left x and y coordinates and the circle's radius:

```
MovieClip.prototype.drawCircle = function(x, y, r) {
    this.moveTo(x+r, y);
    this.curveTo(r+x, 0.4142*r+y, 0.7071*r+x, 0.7071*r+y);
    this.curveTo(0.4142*r+x, r+y, x, r+y);
    this.curveTo(-0.4142*r+x, r+y, -0.7071*r+x, 0.7071*r+y);
    this.curveTo(-r+x, 0.4142*r+y, -r+x, y);
    this.curveTo(-r+x, -0.4142*r+y, -0.7071*r+x, -0.7171*r+y);
    this.curveTo(-0.4142*r+x, -r+y, x, -r+y);
    this.curveTo(0.4142*r+x, -r+y, 0.7071*r+x, -0.7071*r+y);
    this.curveTo(r+x, -0.4142*r+y, r+x, y);
}
```

To use this method to draw a circle with a radius of 55 pixels, starting from the position 0,0, use the following code:

```
createEmptyMovieClip("myCircle", 0);
myCircle.lineStyle(1, 0x0000, 100);
myCircle.drawCircle(0, 0, 55);
```

Drawing an Oval

Circles and ovals are similar, but they have some variations that require a different approach. When drawing an oval, you need to set its size by specifying its height and width, not its radius. The following method draws an oval onscreen. You pass it the oval's starting x and y coordinates and the height and width:

```
MovieClip.prototype.drawOval = function(x, y, w, h) {
    // move to first point in your oval
    this.moveTo(x+w, y);

    // draw the oval
    this.curveTo(w+x, 0.4142*h+y, 0.7071*w+x, 0.7071*h+y);
    this.curveTo(0.4142*w+x, h+y, x, h+y);
    this.curveTo(-0.4142*w+x, h+y, -0.7071*w+x, 0.7071*h+y);
    this.curveTo(-w+x, 0.4142*h+y, -w+x, y);
    this.curveTo(-w+x, -0.4142*h+y, -0.7071*w+x, -0.7071*h+y);
    this.curveTo(-0.4142*w+x, -h+y, x, -h+y);
    this.curveTo(0.4142*w+x, -h+y, 0.7071*w+x, -0.7071*h+y);
    this.curveTo (w+x, -0.4142*h+y, w+x, y);
}
```

To draw an oval that originates at 10,20 and is 50 pixels wide and 85 pixels tall, use the following code:

```
createEmptyMovieClip("myOval", 0);
myOval.lineStyle(1, 0x0000, 100);
myOval.drawOval(10, 20, 50, 85);
```

Drawing a Triangle

The following method draws a triangle. It requires the x and y coordinates of all three points of the triangle:

```
MovieClip.prototype.drawTriangle = function(p1x, p1y,
➥p2x, p2y, p3x, p3y) {
    moveTo(p1x, p1y);
    lineTo(p2x, p2y);
    lineTo(p3x, p3y);
    lineTo(p1x, p1y);
}
```

To draw a triangle located at the points 10,10, 20,20, and 0,20, use the following code:

```
createEmptyMovieClip("myTriangle", 0);
myTriangle.lineStyle(1, 0x0000, 100);
myTriangle.drawTriangle(10, 10, 20, 20, 0, 20);
```

Drawing a Polygon

You can use the following method to draw any number of polygonal shapes. You pass the shape's radius and its number of sides to the method. For example, specifying a radius of 30 and five sides draws a pentagram 30 pixels across, as shown in this example:

```
MovieClip.prototype.drawPolygon = function (r, n) {
    with (this) {
        // set initial registration point
        moveTo(r/2, 0);
        for (var i = 0; i<n+1; i++) {
            // set rotation
            rot = i*360/n;

            // draw long line
            var x = (Math.cos(getRadian(rot)) * r/2);
            var y = (Math.sin(getRadian(rot)) * r/2);
            this.lineTo(x, y);
        }
    }
}
```

This method requires another method, getRadian, which is used to determine the location of the x and y coordinates in the polygon:

```
MovieClip.prototype.getRadian = function (deg) {
    return (Math.PI/180) * deg;
}
```

Drawing a Star

This method draws a star, a slightly more complicated shape, onto the stage. The star is drawn around the center point of your movie clip. You pass the star's radius and its number of points to the method, as shown here:

```
MovieClip.prototype.drawStar = function (r, n) {
    with (this) {
        // set initial registration point
        moveTo(r/2, 0);
        for (var i = 0; i<n; i++) {
            // set rotation
            rot = i*360/n;

            // draw long line
            var x = (Math.cos(getRadian(rot)) * r/2);
            var y = (Math.sin(getRadian(rot)) * r/2);
            this.lineTo(x, y);

            // draw short line
            rot += 360/(n*2);
            var x = (Math.cos(getRadian(rot)) * r/4);
            var y = (Math.sin(getRadian(rot)) * r/4);
            this.lineTo(x, y);

        }
    }
}
```

The Drawing API can also be used with the Math class to create visually complex effects in little time. You'll find some examples in Chapter 21, "Math for Flashers."

And here, again, is the getRadian method:

```
MovieClip.prototype.getRadian = function (deg) {
    return (Math.PI/180) * deg;
}
```

Resources

Advanced drawing methods in Flash MX 2004: www.macromedia.com/devnet/mx/flash/articles/adv_draw_methods.html

Ultrashock: www.ultrashock.com

FlashKit: www.flashkit.com

Actionscript Toolbox: www.actionscript-toolbox.com

POINTS TO REMEMBER

- The Drawing API can be used to draw content in a movie clip.

- Your drawn content can be anything from a line to complicated polygonal shapes.

- Your drawn content can be changed to any color. You can also define alpha and fill properties for your content, as you would if you drew it with any of the Flash MX 2004 drawing tools.

- Using the Drawing API, you can create dynamic animated content and reduce file size.

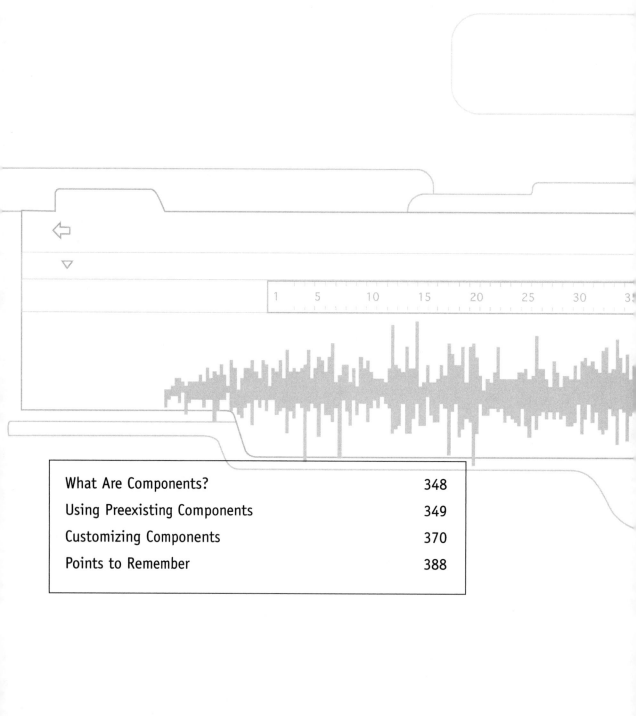

CHAPTER 12

COMPONENTS

COMPONENTS ARE POWERFUL TOOLS TO AID IN YOUR DEVELOPMENT OF RICH Macromedia Flash MX 2004 applications. They are precompiled clips that you can use by simply dropping them onto your stage and setting a few parameters. Components can vastly simplify and speed up your development process by allowing you to reuse existing, stable code repeatedly and easily. This chapter introduces you to the concept of components in Flash MX 2004 and explains how to use them. You'll also learn how to create your own components, which can help you speed up the development of Flash applications.

WHAT ARE COMPONENTS?

Put simply, components are a way to help designers and developers make feature-rich, highly functioning applications quickly. *Components* are movie clips with predefined functionality that enable you to modify their appearance and behaviors. They can be used to provide an incredible range of functionality, from a simple button or scroll bar to a more complicated mechanism, such as a movie preloader that notifies you of the download status. Components are contained in SWC files. These compiled movie clip files can be read into an FLA file and stored in your library.

Most components, such as the List component and the Window component, are visual in nature, but some aren't, such as the XMLConnector component, which simplifies the process of loading and interpreting XML data. These components, although still added to your project in much the same way, have no element that's visible on the stage.

Why would you use predefined functionality when you can create your own? Simply put, speed and ease of use. Because components are highly customizable, developers can easily program them and then hand off their work to the designers to make the components visually appealing.

Say there's a snippet of code you use, over and over, from project to project. This code involves graphical elements and stays more or less the same across multiple projects. Although you could copy and paste this code or retype it every time you want to use it, an easier method is creating a component that performs all the same functions. That way, each time you want to include this functionality, you'd simply drag the component from the Components panel onto the stage, customize a few simple parameters, and go. You'd save time developing your project, and because you're reusing the same code file, you can be confident knowing that it will work the way you intended. Components enable designers to create complex functionality without having to learn ActionScript.

Component Architecture

If you used components in Flash MX, you'll notice that components are built differently and used in a slightly different way in Flash MX 2004. Components are built on the Macromedia Component Version 2 (v2) architecture, which means you can build applications quickly and easily that look and behave in a consistent manner. Here are some new features of the Macromedia Component v2 architecture:

- With the Component Inspector panel, you can modify the parameters of components in both Macromedia Flash MX 2004 and Macromedia Dreamweaver.

- Using themes allows you to customize your components by dragging a new look from the library.

- Using the new listener event model, you can define listener objects to handle events within your components.

- New skin properties let you load new graphical states as needed.

- You can use cascading style sheet (CSS)–based styles to give your applications a consistent look and feel.

- You package components you create as SWC files, which makes it easy to transfer them to other people.

USING PREEXISTING COMPONENTS

Although you can create brand-new components, Flash 2004 comes with a wide variety of components out of the box. The following sections describe each component and show you how to use them.

Flash 2004 comes with the following UI (user interface) components: Button, CheckBox, ComboBox, Label, List, Loader, NumericStepper, PopUpManager, ProgressBar, RadioButton, ScrollPane, TextArea, TextInput, and Window.

Users of Flash MX Professional 2004 have all these components plus Accordion, Alert, DataBinding, DateField, DataGrid, DataHolder, DataSet, DateChooser, Form Class, MediaController, MediaDisplay, MediaPlayback, Menu, RDBMSResolver, WebServiceConnector, XMLConnector, XupdateResolver, Screen Class, and Slide Class.

Components are located in the Components panel, which you can access by choosing File, Window, Development Panels, Components from the menu (keyboard shortcut: Windows **Ctrl+F7**; Macintosh

Command+F7). You can access and modify component properties in the Component Inspector panel by choosing File, Window, Development Panels, Component Inspector from the menu (keyboard shortcut: Windows **Alt+F7**; Macintosh **Option+F7**). To use a component, you simply drag it from the Components panel onto the stage, as shown in Figure 12.1.

FIGURE 12.1
The Components panel.

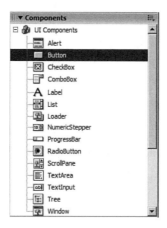

To customize your component's settings, use the Component Inspector panel, shown in Figure 12.2.

FIGURE 12.2
The Component Inspector panel.

Although every component has its own set of unique parameters and properties, most of the UI components share the following four parameters:

- **enabled**   This Boolean value determines whether you can interact with your component.

- **visible**   This Boolean value determines whether your component can be seen on the stage.

- **minHeight** This value is the minimum height, in pixels, of your component.

- **minWidth** This value is the minimum width, in pixels, of your component.

Adding Event Handlers to Components

All Flash 2004 components broadcast events. To interact with your components in any real way, you have to define event handlers that are triggered when an event occurs. You can add event handlers to your components in two ways. In the first method, select the instance of your component and add an on( ) handler. For example, the Button component supports the click event. You could add the following code to your component instance to use this click event:

```
on (click) {
    // response code
    gotoAndPlay(10);
}
```

In addition to the on( ) handler, components have support for event listeners. Event listeners for components operate in much the same way as for other items, such as movie clips, buttons, and the Key object. First you define an object, and then you assign methods to the object that correspond to the events you want to handle, as shown in the following code:

```
newListener = new Object();
newListener.event = function(params) {
    // statements
}
```

Next, you register your new handler as an event listener with your component by using the addEventListener( ) method:

```
component.addEventListener(event, newListener);
```

The Button Component

The Button component, shown in Figure 12.3, is a rectangular button that you can resize and add an icon to. You can make it operate as a regular button or a toggle button. (Toggle buttons, when clicked, stay down until they're clicked again.)

FIGURE 12.3
The Button
component.

These are the Button component's parameters:

- **icon**   This is the name of a movie clip or graphic to be placed inside your button instance. You refer to the movie clip or graphic by the linkage identifier you've given to it.

- **label**   This is the text string that appears on your button.

- **labelPlacement**   This parameter specifies how the label in your button is aligned. It can be set to `left`, `right`, `top`, or `bottom`.

- **selected**   If your button is set to toggle, this parameter forces your button to the On, or selected, state.

- **toggle**   When set to true, your button operates as a toggle. Clicking the button once locks it into the on state, and clicking it a second time locks it in the up state.

These properties can be changed at any time using ActionScript. All you need to do is name the instance of your button and set the properties as you would for any object. The properties are accessed in ActionScript using the same names as in the preceding list. For example, to set the label of a button named my_button to `Click me`, you would use the following code:

```
my_button.label = "Click me";
```

The CheckBox Component

The CheckBox component, shown in Figure 12.4, is a simple check box that can be selected or deselected and can be given a text label.

FIGURE 12.4
The CheckBox
component.

You can modify these parameters for the CheckBox component:

- **label**   The text that appears beside the check box.

- **labelPlacement**   The alignment (`left`, `right`, `top`, or `bottom`) of the label to the check box.

- **selected**   A Boolean value representing the initial state of the check box. If you disable the check box and make it selected (by selecting the appropriate items in the Component Inspector panel at author time), it remains selected, no matter what type of interaction the user attempts.

The CheckBox component has support for the `click` event handler, which is called whenever the user clicks the check box.

The ComboBox Component

The ComboBox is a standard drop-down list (see Figure 12.5), similar to those you've seen on HTML web pages and in dialog boxes. Users can select one item from a list, and, if the ComboBox is editable, the user can enter text in the text box above the list items.

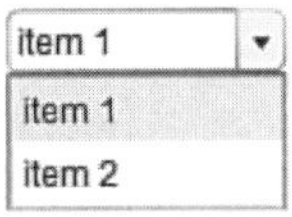

FIGURE 12.5
The ComboBox component.

You can edit these parameters for a ComboBox component:

- **data**   An array that contains data for each element in your ComboBox.

- **editable**   A Boolean value. If true, you can edit the values in the ComboBox.

- **labels**   An array that contains descriptive information about each array element in the `data` property of ComboBox.

- **rowCount**   Determines how many elements can be viewed without needing a scrollbar. The default is five items.

You can also set the following properties at runtime:

- **dropDown**   Returns a reference to the List component that the ComboBox contains. The List component is used to display the elements in your ComboBox when you have the component open.

- **editable**   Returns or changes the editable state.

- **length**   Returns the length of the list.

- **selectedIndex** Returns or applies the selection index, which is the number representing the selected item's position in the ComboBox list. (The first item has an index of 0, the second item has an index of 1, and so on.)

- **selectedItem** Returns an object representing the selected item that contains the label and data as properties. `selectedItem.label` returns the label; `selectedItem.data` returns the data.

The ComboBox component also has a wide variety of methods to manipulate the data in the component:

- **addItem(*label* [,*data*])** Adds a new item to the end of a ComboBox. Can take an object as the argument.

- **addItemAt(*index, label* [,*data*])** Adds a new item at the specified index. Can take an object as the argument.

- **close()** Closes the drop-down list.

- **getItemAt(*index*)** Returns a reference to the item specified by index.

- **open()** Opens the drop-down list.

- **removeAll()** Removes all items.

- **removeItemAt(*index*)** Removes the item at the specified index.

- **replaceItemAt(*index, label* [,*data*])** Replaces the item at the specified index. Can take an object as the argument.

- **setSize(*height, width*)** Used for programmatic resizing. Sets the height and width in pixels.

The ComboBox component supports the following events:

- **change** Whenever the value of a combo box might have changed, the combo box broadcasts an `onChange` event to all registered listeners.

- **close** Whenever the drop-down list of the combo box retracts, the combo box broadcasts a `close` event to all registered listeners.

- **enter** Notifies listeners that text has changed. Applies only when the combo box is editable.

- **itemRollOver** Whenever users roll over items in the combo box list, an `itemRollOver` event is broadcast to all registered listeners.

- **itemRollOut** Whenever the mouse over an item in the combo box pulldown is rolled out, an itemRollOut event is broadcast to all registered listeners.

- **open** Whenever the drop-down list of the combo box opens, the combo box broadcasts an open event to all registered listeners.

- **scroll** Whenever the drop-down list scrolls, the combo box broadcasts a scroll event to all registered listeners.

The Label Component

A Label component is a line of text, as shown in Figure 12.6. It can contain HTML characters and have CSS formatting applied, and you can control the alignment of text in the label. No events are associated with the label, and you can edit the content of a label only during runtime by using ActionScript.

FIGURE 12.6
The Label component.

Label Text

If you create an instance of a label and select it, you can edit the following parameters:

- **text** This is the string of text that appears in your label—for example, bob or This is a Label!

- **html** This is a Boolean value that determines whether HTML content can be rendered in your label. You would set it to true if, for example, you wanted your label to contain a link to a website.

- **autoSize** This property determines whether and how the label resizes to fit the text. These are the valid settings for this property:

  - **none** The label doesn't resize or align to fit the text.

  - **left** The right and bottom sides of the label resize to fit the text, but the left and top do not.

  - **center** The bottom side of the label resizes to fit the text, and the horizontal center of the label stays anchored at its original horizontal center position.

  - **right** The left and bottom sides of the label resize to fit the text, but the top and right sides don't.

Note that although the Label component and the TextField component both have properties named autoSize, the implementation of autoSize in TextField is slightly different.

The List Component

The List component (see Figure 12.7) is a scrollable list of items and can be set to allow for single and multiple selections. Items can be text, graphics, or other components.

When you place an instance of the List component on the stage, you can edit the following parameters in the Component Inspector panel:

- **data** This is an array containing the values of each list item.

- **labels** This is an array containing the labels for each list item. This list is paired with the data parameter.

- **multipleSelection** A Boolean value that determines whether the user can select multiple entries (using Shift to select a continuous range or Ctrl [Macintosh: Command] to select multiple items).

- **rowHeight** Sets the height of each row (list item) in pixels. Note that changing font size does not change the rowHeight value.

In addition to these parameters, the following list describes some other parameters you can set through ActionScript:

- **length** The number of items in the list.

- **rowCount** The number of items visible without a scrollbar.

- **selectedIndex** The index of the selected item in a single-selection list. Although this parameter is a number, if no item is selected, selectedIndex is undefined. If you have multiple items selected, selectedIndex represents the last selected item.

- **selectedIndices** This is an array of indices, representing the index of each item you have selected.

- **selectedItem** A reference to the selected item in a single-selection list. If multiple selection is allowed, this parameter returns a reference to the most recent selection.

- **selectedItems** A reference to a series of item objects in a multiple-selection list. This parameter represents the selected items.

The List component has a number of methods to manipulate the component's contents:

- **addItem(*label* [, *data*])/addItem(*itemObject*)** Adds a new item to the end of the list. *label* is a string for the label of the new item. *data* is optional and is the data for the new item. Alternatively, you can add an object to addItem() with the properties label and data.

- **listName.addItemAt(*index*, *label* [, *data*])/addItemAt(*index*, *itemObject*)** Adds a new item to the list, inserting it at the index specified. Indices greater than the list's length are ignored.

- **getItemAt(*index*)** Retrieves the item at a specific position.

- **removeAll()** Removes all items in the list.

- **removeItemAt(*index*)** Removes the item at a specific position. The item indices for items after the removed items are reset; for example, if item 2 is removed, item 3 becomes item 2.

- **replaceItemAt(*index*, *label* [,*data*])/replaceItemAt(*index*, *itemObject*)** Replaces the contents of the item at the specified index.

- **setPropertiesAt(*index*, *styleObj*)** Sets the properties of the specified item (*index*) to equal the properties specified in *styleObj*. Currently supported properties are icon and backgroundColor.

- **sortItemsBy(*fieldName*, *order*)** This method sorts items in the list alphabetically or numerically (depending on the content), based on *fieldname* and the specified order. If the *fieldName* items contain both strings and integers, integers are listed first. Typically, *fieldName* is either label or data, but advanced users and programmers can specify any primitive data type that suits their needs.

- **sortItems(*compareFunc*)** Sorts the items in the list according to the *compareFunc*, which is a function reference used to compare two items to determine sort order. This functionality is similar to setting the compareFunc of an array sort.

The List component also receives a number of events:

- **change**   Whenever the selection has changed because of direct user interaction, the List component broadcasts a change event to all registered listeners. A change event can be broadcast even when the selection hasn't changed (you can use it to simulate a double-click by having your change handler check to see whether the selection has changed since the last time the change event was called).

- **scroll**   Whenever the list is scrolled, it broadcasts a change event to all registered listeners.

- **itemRollOver**   Whenever users roll over list items, an itemRollOver event is broadcast to all registered listeners.

- **itemRollOut**   Whenever users roll off list items, an itemRollOut event is broadcast to all registered listeners.

The Loader Component

The Loader component loads an SWF or a JPG into itself. It's a simple way to load external content into Flash. You can modify the following parameters for the Loader component:

- **autoLoad**   This Boolean value controls whether the file specified in contentPath is loaded immediately.

- **contentPath**   URL of the SWF or JPG file to be loaded into the Loader component.

- **scaleContent**   This Boolean, when set to true, scales the loaded content to the size of the Loader component. By default, scaleContent is true.

In addition to these parameters, which are visible in the Component Inspector panel, the following parameters can be accessed via ActionScript:

- **bytesLoaded**   This read-only property returns the number of bytes of content that has been loaded.

- **bytesTotal**   This read-only property returns the content's total size in bytes.

- **content**   A reference to the root movie clip of the loaded content.

- **percentLoaded**   This read-only property returns the percentage of the content that has been loaded.

In addition, the Loader component has one method, `load()`, which loads the file specified in `contentPath` into the Loader. The Loader component has the following events associated with it:

- **complete**   This event occurs and is broadcast when the content has finished loading.

- **progress**   This event occurs repeatedly during content loading to indicate how far the loading has progressed.

The NumericStepper Component

The NumericStepper component contains a text field and two buttons (see Figure 12.8). You can adjust the value in the text field, control the maximum and minimum accepted values, and control how much the value changes each time the buttons are clicked. A NumericStepper stepper could be used to select a T-shirt size at an online store, for example.

FIGURE 12.8
The NumericStepper component.

NumericStepper has the following parameters:

- **maximum**   Maximum allowed value.

- **minimum**   Minimum allowed value.

- **stepSize**   The increment that each button click represents. The bottom button represents a negative `stepSize`. For example, if `stepSize` is 1, clicking the top button increases the value by 1, and clicking the bottom button decreases the value by 1.

- **value**   This is the starting value of the instance of the NumericStepper component.

NumericStepper has one event, `change`, that occurs when the value of the NumericStepper is changed.

The PopUpManager Component

The PopUpManager component is a nonvisual component that allows you to create overlapping windows. These windows can contain other content (such as text fields, movie clips, or buttons) and can be modal or nonmodal. A *modal window* does not allow user interaction with other windows while it is open; a *nonmodal window* does. To create a pop-up with the PopUpManager component, you use the createPopUp() method, which has the following syntax:

```
PopUpManager.createPopUp(parent, class, modal
➡ [, initobj, outsideEvents])
```

You can use the following parameters with the createPopUp() method:

- **parent**   The window that hosts the pop-up window.

- **class**   The class of the object you want to create.

- **modal**   This is a Boolean value. If true, the window is modal.

- **initobj**   This optional parameter specifies an object containing properties that the window will use.

- **outsideEvents**   This is a Boolean value. If true, when the user clicks outside the window, an event is generated. It's useful when tracking user activity with a modal window.

createPopUp() returns a reference to the window being created. For example, in the following code, newWindow is a reference to the newly created window:

```
var newWindow = PopUpManager.createPopUp(this, Window, true);
```

The following code creates a modal window when a button is clicked:

```
listener = new Object();
listener.click = function(){
    mx.managers.PopUpManager.createPopUp(_root,
    ➡ mx.containers.Window, true);

}
button.addEventListener("click", listener);
```

To delete a pop-up created with createPopUp(), use the deletePopUp() method of PopUpManager, which has the following syntax:

```
myPopUp.deletePopUp();
```

The ProgressBar Component

The ProgressBar component is used to display the progress of a loading process (see Figure 12.9). Typically, it's used with the Loader component, but the Loader component is not required. The ProgressBar component can be used to display a known (determinate) load or an unknown (indeterminate) load. An example of a known load is XML data or an SWF file, where the file size is known by the server. An unknown load might be a stream, which wouldn't have a determined size. ProgressBar can also be attached to an object (such as an instance of the Loader component) and be automatically updated with the loading progress. You can also specify the progress of a download or some other event.

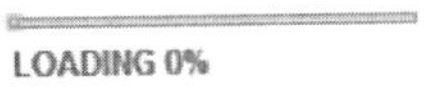

FIGURE 12.9
The ProgressBar component.

LOADING 0%

The ProgressBar component contains the following parameters:

- **conversion** The `getBytesLoaded()` and `getBytesTotal()` methods are divided by this number before the component is displayed. The default is 1. This property is useful if you want the ProgressBar to determine the kilobytes loaded instead of bytes; in this case, the `conversion` parameter would specify dividing by 1,000.

- **direction** This parameter controls in which direction the loading bar grows. Accepted values are `right`, which is the default, and `left`.

- **label** This parameter is the text that indicates the progress of the load. The label uses four placeholders: %1, which represents current bytes loaded; %2, which represents total bytes; %3, which represents the percentage of the movie loaded; and %%, which represents the percentage symbol.

- **labelPlacement** This parameter specifies the label's alignment. It can be set to `left`, `right`, `top`, `bottom`, or `center`.

- **mode** This parameter is the mode in which the ProgressBar operates. Accepted values are `event`, `polled`, or `manual`. The following sections explain these three modes.

- **source** A string representing the instance name that has content loaded into it (for example, `_root.myClip`).

Event Mode

Using ProgressBar in event mode requires a loading element that sends out `progress` and `complete` events. The Loader component sends out these events. To use the ProgressBar to display the progress of a Loader component load, do the following:

1. Drag a ProgressBar component from the Components panel onto the stage.

2. In the Component Inspector panel, name the instance `progressBar`, for example.

3. Select the instance of ProgressBar you've just created. In the Component Inspector panel, find the parameter called "mode" and select Event from the Mode drop-down.

4. Drag a Loader component onto the stage.

5. Name the component instance `loader`.

6. Select the ProgressBar component. In the Property inspector, click the Parameters tab and click the `source` parameter in the left column. In the right column (beside `source`), enter the instance name of your Loader component as the source (the movie clip your content will be loaded into).

7. Select the Loader component. In the Component Inspector, enter the URL of your content in the `contentPath` parameter field to specify the content to load. (See "The Loader Component" earlier in this chapter.)

That's all you have to do. Test it by exporting your movie.

Polled Mode

Using ProgressBar in polled mode requires a Loader component that has both `getBytesLoaded()` and `getBytesTotal()` methods, such as the Sound object. A ProgressBar using polled mode continually checks with the loading object to determine the progress. To use the ProgressBar component to display load progress in polled mode, do the following:

1. Drag a ProgressBar component onto the stage.

2. Name this component instance `progressBar`.

3. Choose polled as the mode for this instance.

4. Enter `my_sound` as the name of your loading object source.

5. Select the first frame in the main Timeline, open the Actions panel, and enter the following code. This code creates a new Sound object and begins loading a sound file:

```
var my_sound:Sound = new Sound();
my_sound.loadSound(url, true);
```

Manual Mode

Using the ProgressBar in manual mode requires you to specify the completed percentage of the load progress. You set the minimum, maximum, and indeterminate properties and use the setProgress() method to display your progress. There's no need to specify the source when using manual mode. To use ProgressBar in manual mode, do the following:

1. Drag a ProgressBar component onto the stage.

2. Name the component instance progressBar.

3. Select manual as the mode for this component.

4. Select the first frame in your Timeline, and open the Actions panel.

5. Enter the following code:

```
for (var:Number i=1; i<total; i++) {
    // insert code
    progressBar.setProgress(i, total);
}
```

The setProgress() method uses the following syntax:

```
pBarInstance.setProgress(completed, total)
```

completed is a number indicating the current progress, and total is a number representing the total file size to be downloaded.

For example, if you want your ProgressBar component to display your progress through the frames of your movie, in each frame you would put the following code:

```
pBarInstance.setProgress(_currentFrame, _totalFrames);
```

In addition, three properties of ProgressBar are relevant to using it in manual mode:

- **minimum** This determines the minimum allowable progress display for your ProgressBar.

- **maximum** This determines the maximum allowable progress display for your ProgressBar.

- **indeterminate** This Boolean value indicates whether the progress bar has a candy-cane striped fill and a loading source of unknown size (true), or a solid fill and a loading source of a known size (false). An indeterminate load doesn't show the specific progress, only that loading is continuing.

The RadioButton Component

The RadioButton component (see Figure 12.10) is a standard item used in forms and dialog boxes to make a choice from a series of options. Multiple RadioButtons can be grouped (a minimum of two instances is required in a group), and selecting one RadioButton in a group deselects all others in that group.

FIGURE 12.10
The RadioButton
component.

⊙ Radio Button

You can edit the following parameters for a RadioButton component:

- **label** This is the text for the button; the default is Radio Button.

- **data** This is the value of the button, such as a string, a number, or an object. Unlike the label parameter, there is no default value for data.

- **groupName** This is the name of the group that the RadioButton belongs to. The default is radioGroup.

- **selected** This parameter specifies whether the button is initially selected (true) or not. When selected, a radio button has a dot in it. The default value is false. Only one radio button per group can be selected at any time; if more than one in a group is defined as selected, only the last one remains selected.

- **labelPlacement** This parameter aligns the button text. Accepted values are left, right (the default), top, or bottom.

As well, RadioButton supports the click event, which is triggered when the user clicks a RadioButton.

If you have multiple RadioButtons on the stage at one time, you'll likely want to group them so that you can specify a range of options relating to a specific topic. To define a group, simply use the `groupName` parameter to assign the RadioButtons appropriately. If you want to bunch six RadioButtons into two groups of three, you could specify the `groupName` parameter of the first three as `radioGroup1`, and the second three as `radioGroup2`. To navigate between radio buttons in the same group, click one of the buttons, and then use the arrow keys.

The ScrollPane Component

The ScrollPane component (see Figure 12.11) is used to display movie clips, SWFs, and JPGs in a scrollable window. The content displayed in a scrollable area can be loaded locally or remotely (over the Internet). A ScrollPane is useful for displaying lengthy content in a small area, such as a map of a city or a large photograph.

FIGURE 12.11
The ScrollPane component.

ScrollPane has the following parameters:

- **contentPath**   This is the content that gets loaded into ScrollPane. It can be a path to a JPEG or SWF file or the linkage identifier of a movie clip symbol in the Library (set to export for ActionScript).

- **hLineScrollSize**   This is the number of pixels the horizontal scrollbar moves each time the user clicks an arrow button. The default is 5.

- **hPageScrollSize**   This is the number of pixels the horizontal scrollbar moves each time the user clicks the track (the bar between the scroll buttons). The default is 20.

- **hScrollPolicy**   This controls the display of horizontal scrollbars. Accepted values are on, off, and auto. When set to auto, the scroll-bars appear and disappear as specified by the ScrollPane.

- **scrollDrag**   This Boolean value determines whether a user can scroll content in a ScrollPane.

- **vLineScrollSize**   This is the number of pixels the vertical scrollbar moves each time the user clicks an arrow button.

- **vPageScrollSize**   This is the number of pixels the vertical scrollbar moves each time the user clicks the track.

- **vScrollPolicy**   This controls the display of vertical scrollbars. Accepted values are on, off, and auto.

You can also edit the content parameter using ActionScript. This parameter is a reference to the content in a ScrollPane.

ScrollPane supports the following methods:

- **getBytesLoaded()**   This method returns the number of bytes of the ScrollPane component that have been loaded.

- **getBytesTotal()**   This method returns the total file size of the ScrollPane content.

- **refreshPane()**   This method refreshes the ScrollPane content.

ScrollPane supports the following events:

- **complete**   This event is broadcast when the content finishes loading.

- **progress**   This event is broadcast while loading is underway.

- **scroll**   This event is broadcast when the user clicks the scrollbars.

The TextArea Component

The TextArea component (see Figure 12.12) is a wrapper for a text field. If the content of a TextArea component exceeds the visible area, scrollbars appear. The text in a TextArea component can be formatted with HTML or be password-protected text—that is, ******* is used to mask the actual content. Styles can also be applied to the text.

FIGURE 12.12
The TextArea
component.

The following TextArea parameters can be edited at author time:

- **editable**   If this Boolean value is true, the contents of TextArea can be modified.

- **html**   If this Boolean value is true, the contents are rendered as HTML.

- **password**   If this Boolean value is true, all characters in the TextArea are rendered as asterisks.

- **text**   The text to be displayed in the TextArea component.

- **maxChars**   The maximum allowed length of text. Default is null, which means there's no limit.

- **restrict**   This is a list of characters that are allowed in the TextArea. For example, if you wanted to allow only the characters *a*, *b*, and *c*, restrict would equal a,b,c.

The following properties can be accessed at runtime:

- **length**   This read-only property specifies the number of characters in your TextArea.

- **wordWrap**   This Boolean value determines whether the text in your TextArea wraps to the next line.

The TextArea component supports the change event, which is broadcast when the contents of TextArea change.

The TextInput Component

The TextInput component (see Figure 12.13) contains a single-line text field where a user can enter text. Like TextArea, text can be formatted as HTML or password-protected text and can have styles applied.

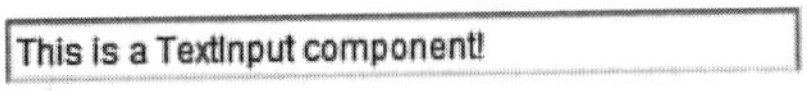

FIGURE 12.13
The TextInput component.

| This is a TextInput component! |

The following list describes some parameters you can set for a TextInput component:

- **editable**   If this Boolean value is true, the contents of TextInput can be modified.

- **password**   If this Boolean value is true, all characters in TextInput are rendered as asterisks.

- **text**   The text in the TextInput component.

- **maxChars**   Maximum allowed length of text. The default is null, which means there's no limit.

- **restrict**   This is a list of characters that are allowed in the TextInput component.

The TextInput component has no methods but supports two events:

- **change**   This event is broadcast when the text of a TextInput changes. Note that because this event is broadcast *after* the change has occurred, you can't use it to prevent changes.

- **enter**   This event is broadcast when focus is on the TextInput component and the user presses the Enter key.

The Window Component

The Window component (see Figure 12.14) is a generic window with borders, a title bar, and a close button (optional). A Window component can be modal or nonmodal (as with the PopUpManager component) and can be dragged around the screen by clicking and dragging the title bar.

FIGURE 12.14
The Window
component.

The Window
component can't be
resized by clicking
and dragging the
borders.

The following parameters are accessible in the Component Inspector panel:

- **closeButton**   If this Boolean value is true, a button appears in the upper-right corner of the title bar. When clicked, it broadcasts a click event with the property of target. The value of target is a reference to the movie clip to be closed. To close the window, you must define an event handler to remove it.

- **contentPath** This parameter determines what will be loaded into your Window component. It can be a linkage identifier or a URL reference to an external SWF or JPEG file.

- **title** This is the text that appears in the title bar of the window.

Additionally, the following properties are accessible during runtime:

- **content** This is a reference to the loaded content of the window.

- **titleStyleSheet** This sets the style sheet to use for text in the Window component's title bar.

Window supports two methods:

- **createPopUp()** This method (defined in "The PopupManager Component," earlier in this chapter) creates a new instance of Window on the stage. It uses the following syntax:

  ```
  PopUpManager.createPopUp(parent, class, modal, initobj,
  outsideEvents)
  ```

- **deletePopUp()** This method is used to delete an instance of Window created by using `PopUpManager.createPopUp()`. It has the following syntax:

  ```
  windowInstanceName.deletePopUp();
  ```

  If your pop-up has a close button (if `closeButton` is set to `true`), you can use the `click` event broadcast by clicking the close button and call the `deletePopUp()` method to remove the window.

The Window component also has support for the following events:

- **click** This event is called when the close button is released.

- **mouseDownOutside** This event is broadcast when the user clicks the mouse button outside the modal window area. Used rarely, but it can be used to close the pop-up window if the user tries to interact with something outside the window.

- **load** This event is broadcast when the window is created.

- **unload** This event is broadcast when the window is removed from the stage.

Component File Size

Users of Flash MX might notice that the components in Flash MX 2004 have much larger file sizes. An SWF file with only an instance of the Button component, for example, is 27KB. Likewise, an SWF file with just the ComboBox component is twice that size—54KB. This increase in file size is caused by the significant amount of ActionScript powering every component that ships with Flash. The architecture itself is extremely large.

Although increased file size might seem like a drawback to using components, each component uses much of the same code. Therefore, after you've loaded one component, the second component, which uses much the same code as the first, won't take up as much additional room.

This code sharing means that although an SWF with a Button component is 27KB and one with a Button and a ComboBox is 54KB, an SWF file with a Button, a ComboBox, and a CheckBox is only 55KB. With the new v2 component architecture, the more components you use in a movie, the smaller the individual impact on size for each component.

CUSTOMIZING COMPONENTS

In addition to setting properties for your components, in Flash 2004 you can customize the appearance of your components in a variety of ways, as described in the following sections.

Using Skins

Skins are the symbols (graphic and movie clip) a component uses for its appearance. While most skins contain graphical information, some contain only ActionScript, which is used to define the appearance of a component using the Drawing API.

Because v2 components are compiled clips, you can't see any of their assets in the Library. FLA files that are installed with Flash contain every component skin, however. These FLA files, essentially large collections of skins, are called *themes*. Each theme has a unique appearance and behavior, but they all share the same symbol names and linkage identifiers. This lets you edit the graphics in a theme and drag the theme onto the stage in a file to alter its appearance. Skins are located in the Themes folder of the theme's FLA file. Flash MX 2004 comes with one theme called Halo (see Figure 12.15). The Halo theme file is located in the `First Run\ComponentFLA` folder, in your Flash MX 2004 installation folder.

FIGURE 12.15
The Halo theme in Flash MX 2004.

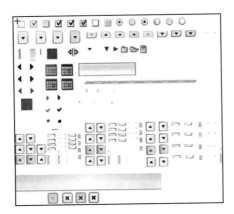

Each component consists of a multitude of skins. In the ScrollBar component, for example, the down arrow is made up of three skins: ScrollDownArrowUp, ScrollDownArrowDisabled, and ScrollDownArrowDown. Some components share skins. For example, components that use scrollbars, such as ComboBox and ScrollPane, use skins from the ScrollBar Skins folder. To alter a component's appearance, you can edit and create skins.

To skin a component, you can do either of the following:

- You can replace all the skins in a file with an entirely new set by applying a theme. This method, which doesn't require any ActionScript, is recommended for beginners.

- Use different skins for multiple instances of the same component in your file.

Editing Skins

If you want to use one skin for one instance of a component and a different skin for another instance, open a Theme FLA file and create a new skin symbol. You'll need to edit this new skin. To do this, follow these steps:

1. Open the Theme FLA file you want to use as a template. (Theme FLAs are located in the folder where you installed Flash 2004, in the

en\First Run\ComponentFLA folder.) You'll find the following files: HaloTheme.fla, which contains elements for the Halo theme; StandardComponents.fla, which has elements for various components; and SampleTheme.fla, which contains theme elements intended to be customized. Open SampleTheme.fla for this example, and save it with a new name.

2. Select the skin you want to edit from the Themes\MMDefault\ <ComponentName> Assets folder. Open Themes\MMDefault\ RadioButton Assets\States for this example, and select RadioFalseUp.

3. Right-click the skin, choose Duplicate, and give the symbol a unique name (MyRadioFalseUp, for example).

4. Click the Advanced button in the Symbol Properties dialog box (opened by right-clicking the symbol and selecting Properties), and select the Export for ActionScript option.

5. Edit the new skin (double-click the symbol in the library).

6. Modify or replace the movie clip. When you do this, be sure to maintain the registration point. Keep the upper-left corner of all edited symbols at 0,0 so that they're displayed correctly.

After you've edited your skin, you need to apply it to your component. There are two ways you can do this, depending on how you add components: You can use the createClassObject() method to dynamically create the component instances, or you can manually place component instances on the stage. You must test your movie to see the changes. The first way is applying an edited skin to a dynamically created component, as shown in these steps:

1. Create a new Flash file, and save it.

2. Drag your component (in this example, the RadioButton component) from the Components panel to the stage, and delete it. This adds the symbol to the document's library, but because you've deleted it from the stage, it's not visible in the document.

3. Drag your customized symbol (in this example, MyRadioFalseUp) from the edited theme file onto the stage, and delete it.

4. In the Actions panel, enter the following code:

```
import mx.controls.RadioButton
createClassObject(RadioButton, "myRadio", 0,
{falseUpIcon:"MyRadioFalseUp"});
```

5. Test your movie to see the results.

The second method is applying an edited skin to a component on the stage, as shown in these steps:

1. Create a new Flash file, and save it.

2. Drag to the stage any components you want to use in your file, including the component whose skin you edited—in this example, RadioButton.

3. Drag the symbols you edited in your customized theme file to the stage of your FLA file, and delete them.

4. Select your component on the stage and open the Actions panel.

5. Attach the following code to the RadioButton instance:

```
onClipEvent(initialize){
falseUpIcon = "MyRadioFalseUp";
}
```

6. Test your movie to see the results.

Using Styles

Many default components allow assigning *style elements*, which are used to control the appearance of elements of your component. You can set style elements to control the size, color, and appearance of fonts used by components and specify what color a disabled component uses, for example. You can define styles during author time or runtime. Styles are useful for quickly customizing aspects of components to fit your needs. You set a style element by using the component's setStyle() method, which has the following syntax:

componentInstance.setStyle(*propertyName, value*);

propertyName is a string representing the name of the style property to set. *value* is the new value of the style property.

For example, to set the `borderStyle` of a Window component called `my_window` to none, you would use the following code:

`my_window.setStyle("borderStyle", "none");`

The following list shows common style elements supported by Flash MX 2004 components:

- **themeColor**   This is the background of a component. Accepted values are `haloGreen`, `haloBlue`, and `haloOrange`.

- **color**   The text color of a component label.

- **disabledColor**   The text color if the component is disabled.

- **fontFamily**   The font family used for the text.

- **fontSize**   The point size of the font.

- **fontStyle**   The font style, which can be `normal` or `italic`.

- **fontWeight**   The font weight, which can be `normal` or `bold`.

The following lists show which components support style elements and describe the style elements specific to those components:

Button

- The Button component supports only the common style elements listed previously.

CheckBox

In addition to the common style elements listed previously, the Checkbox component supports this style element:

- **textDecoration**   The font decoration, which can be `none` or `underline`.

ComboBox

The ComboBox component supports the following styles in addition to the common styles:

- **textDecoration**   The font decoration, which can be `none` or `underline`.

- **openDuration**   The number of milliseconds it takes to completely open the drop-down list. The default is `250`.

- **openEasing**   A reference to the tweening function that controls how the drop-down list opens. The default value is sine in/out.

NumericStepper

The NumericStepper component supports the following styles in addition to the common styles:

- **textDecoration**   The font decoration, which can be none or underline.

- **textAlign**   The horizontal alignment of text in the NumericStepper text field, which can be left, right, or center.

ProgressBar

- **textDecoration**   The font decoration, which can be none or underline.

RadioButton

- The RadioButton component supports only the common style elements listed previously.

ScrollPane

- The ScrollPane component itself doesn't support styles, but the scrollbars it contains do support the themeColor style, described previously.

Window

- The Window component supports only the borderStyle style, which defines the window's border style. Accepted values are none, inset, outset, and solid.

Using Themes

A theme is a collection of styles and skins. In Flash MX 2004 and Flash MX Professional 2004, the default skin is called Halo (HaloTheme.fla), which was previously shown in Figure 12.15. Theme files in Flash MX 2004 are located in First Run\ComponentFLA (on Windows) and First Run/ComponentFLA (on Macintosh).

You can create new themes and use them to control the look of components in your movie. You might want to create a new theme to match the movie you're adding them to.

The new component architecture uses skins to determine the appearance of components in Flash MX 2004. Each component loads specific skin information, such as which movie clips are loaded for each element of the component. For example, the RadioButton component uses a symbol with the linkage identifier `RadioFalseUp` to determine the Up state of a deselected radio button.

You can also define a new set of styles for a theme, using ActionScript to create a global style sheet that all components adhere to. See the "Using Styles" section earlier in this chapter for more information.

To apply a new theme to a file, open your theme FLA as an external library. Drag the Theme folder from this library into the file's library. Here is the process in greater detail:

1. Open or create a file that uses any of the new components. Save it with a unique name.

2. Open the theme FLA that you want to apply to your file by choosing File, Import, Open External Library. If you haven't yet created a new theme, use the Sample theme, located in the `Flash 2004\en\First Run\ComponentFLA` folder.

You won't see the new themes until you test your movie.

3. Select Flash UI Components 2, Themes, MMDefault in the theme FLA's Library panel. Drag the `Assets` folder of components used in your file into the library of your file. Don't worry—the skins in the `Themes` folder are automatically assigned to the components in your file.

If you don't want to use an existing theme, you can modify one to create a new theme. You do this by modifying the various skins within themes. Note that some skins are a fixed size. This means you can adjust the size of the skins, and components automatically resize to match. Other skins are a fixed size, and others are made up of a number of elements; for these skins, some elements don't resize, and others can stretch.

Some skins, such as ButtonSkin and RectBorder, use the ActionScript Drawing API to render their graphical appearance. ActionScript is more efficient with simple shapes than traditional drawing methods. If you're editing any ActionScript-drawn theme elements, you can adjust the

ActionScript code in those skins to suit your needs. Perform the procedure for creating a new skin, repeating it for each element in your theme file that you want to alter. When you've finished, apply the theme to your movie using the process described previously.

Downloading and Installing Additional Components

If you find that none of the existing components suits your needs and you don't have the time to build your own, you can go to the Macromedia Exchange site (`www.macromedia.com/cfusion/exchange/index.cfm`) and choose from a growing list of components to download and install.

After you've selected and downloaded your new components, you'll need to install them for use in Flash. Installing new components is very simple. First, place the SWC or FLA file containing the component in the Configuration folder. If you use a Macintosh, the folder is `Hard Drive: Applications:Macromedia Flash MX 2004:First Run: Components:`. If you use a Windows machine, the folder is `\Program Files\Macromedia\ Flash MX 2004\language\First Run\Components`.

If Flash isn't running when you copy the SWC or FLA file into the appropriate folder, simply start it now. If it's already running, click Reload from the pop-up menu in the Component Inspector panel. That's it! You should now be able to see your newly installed component.

Creating Custom Components

Many helpful components are included with Flash 2004, and you can find great components available for download at the Macromedia site. But what if you want to make your own? What if what you're looking for doesn't exist?

Well, you're in luck. You can create new components! First, you need to create an SWC file or a compiled SWF. To do this, right-click a movie clip in your movie and choose Convert to Compiled Clip to create a compiled SWF, or choose Export SWC File to create an SWC file (see Figure 12.16).

FIGURE 12.16
Viewing the Symbol
context menu.

A compiled clip is a symbol that functions as a component, but it's contained only within the FLA file that creates it. If you convert to a compiled clip, it's automatically brought into your current document in the library. The name of your clip will be the name of your original movie clip plus SWF, so Symbol 1, for example, becomes Symbol 1 SWF, and the type of symbol is listed as Compiled Clip under the Kind column in the library.

If you export as an SWC file, you're prompted to select a save location for your new file. This creates a component file. After you've created an SWC file, you need to quit Flash and manually import your SWC file by putting it into the First Run\Components\ folder. After the SWC file is in place, start Flash. Your component appears in the Components panel.

To see how this works, create a movie clip named TestClip, and draw a shape inside it. In the Library, right-click the movie clip and choose Convert to Compiled Clip. Now, right-click the movie clip again, and choose Export SWC File. A component with only a shape certainly won't do very much, but it's a quick way of showing you how to make components.

Note that when you place an instance of your component on the stage or use a compiled clip, Flash renders the movie clips in real time. This means if your component contains an enterFrame handler that runs all the time, it will run in the authoring environment, complete with any changes to the content of the component, trace() actions, and the like. Being able to see your movie clips in real time is a handy tool, as it allows you to view changes in your component without having to export your movie. For example, say you created a movie clip with an onEnterFrame handler that performed the following action:

```
trace(new Date());
```

If you exported this movie clip as an SWC file and imported it into Flash, when you place an instance of your new component on the stage, it continually adds new date information to the Output panel.

Configuring Your Component

It's all well and good that you can export your component, but you'll probably want to be able to change its settings in the authoring environment or during runtime by using ActionScript. You can do this easily in the Component Definition dialog box. To open the Component Definition dialog box (see Figure 12.17), simply right-click a movie clip in the Library and choose Component Definition.

FIGURE 12.17
The Component Definition dialog box.

In the Parameters section at the top, you can add parameters to your components that can be modified in the Component Inspector panel. To add a parameter, click the button with the plus symbol. To delete a parameter, select it and click the button with the minus symbol. If you want to change the order of the parameters, select the parameter you want to move, and then click the up and down arrows at the upper right.

When you add a parameter to your component, you need to enter several pieces of information:

- **Name**   This is the name that's visible in the Component Inspector panel.

- **Variable**   This is the name of the variable that ActionScript references in the component.

- **Value**   The value of the parameter.

- **Type**   This is a drop-down list of available parameter types. Depending on your selection, you have different options when attempting to change the parameter's value. For example, if the type is Boolean, clicking the Value heading opens a True/False drop-down list. Selecting a Color type displays a color palette. These are the available types:

  - **Default**   You can type any text for a value that you want.

  - **Array**   Clicking the button with a magnifying glass icon next to the Value field opens the Values dialog box, where you can enter a series of new values.

  - **Object**   Opens a Value dialog box, where you can enter a series of properties (shown as Name/Value pairs).

  - **List**   Similar to Array, a Value dialog box opens.

  - **String**   Type in a string value.

  - **Number**   Type in a number.

  - **Boolean**   A True/False drop-down list is shown.

  - **Font Name**   A list of fonts available for use on your system.

  - **Color**   Opens a color palette. Selecting a color records it in hexa-decimal (#FFFFFF) format.

  - **Web Service URL**   Opens a Values dialog box, where you can enter a URL or a number of URLs that define the location of Web Service operations. This option is used in Flash MX Professional 2004.

  - **Web Service Operation**   Opens a Values dialog box, where you can enter information about the WebServiceOperation you're con-necting to. This option is used in Flash MX Professional 2004.

  - **Collection Item**   Opens a Values dialog box, where you can add information about which DataSet collection to use. The DataSet component is used in Flash MX Professional 2004.

- **Collection**   Opens a Values dialog box, where you can add information about which DataSet collection to use. The DataSet component is used in Flash MX Professional 2004.

You can also set the following parameters:

- **AS 2.0 Class**   Specify the class to be associated with an instance of your component. If you've written a class for your component, this is where you would associate it.

- **Custom UI**   Click the Set button to change your custom user interface settings.

- **Live Preview**   Click the Set button to change your live preview settings. Live Preview (which allows Flash to automatically update component content in real time on the stage) is enabled by default and can be disabled.

- **Description**   Enter a description for your component. You can click the Set button to indicate whether the description is plain text or a help item (in which case you select an element from the Help panel to represent the description). You can also choose to have no description.

Also, directly below the word *Description* is a button that when clicked displays a list of icons you can select to represent your component in the Component Inspector panel and the Library.

In the Options section, you can select the following:

- **Parameters Are Locked in Instances**   Selecting this check box means users cannot edit parameters.

- **Display in Components panel**   Selecting this check box means you can enter ToolTip text for your component. This is the text that's shown when the user rolls over your component icon or name in the Component Inspector panel.

Chapter Project: Creating a Clock Component

Now that you know what components are and how to create your own, it's time to put this knowledge to the test. In this project, you'll make a new clock component that you can reuse or share with other Flash developers. This component is simple so that you or your end users can modify it later, if needed.

1. First, open a new document, create a movie clip, and call it My Clock. Create two layers in this movie clip called Actions and Text (see Figure 12.18).

FIGURE 12.18
Adding layers.

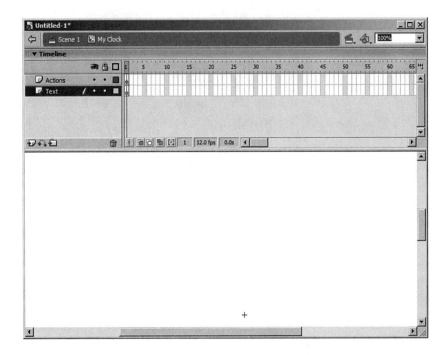

2. In the Text layer, add a dynamic text field, and give it the instance name theTime. Click the Character button to open the Character Options dialog box. Figure 12.19 shows a range of characters selected. Select the No Characters radio button to make sure no characters are embedded.

3. This clock needs to show the time continually, so you'll add an onEnterFrame handler to the component. Select the first frame of the Actions layer, and add an onEnterFrame handler (see Figure 12.20).

4. Every time the onEnterFrame handler is called, a new Date object needs to be created to populate the text field. Use the following code to create a Date object and extract some information from it:

```
onEnterFrame = function() {
    // create new Date object
    currentDate = new Date();
    // get hour information from currentDate
```

```
        currentHour = currentDate.getHours();
        // get minutes information from currentDate
        currentMinutes = currentDate.getMinutes();
        // get seconds information from currentDate
        currentSeconds = currentDate.getSeconds();
    }
```

FIGURE 12.19

Checking settings in the Character Options dialog box.

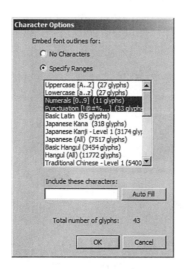

FIGURE 12.20

Adding an onEnterFrame handler.

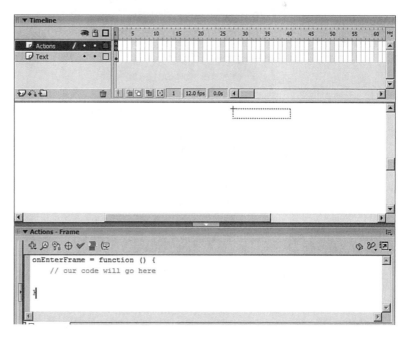

Although this code has variables containing the separated hours/minutes/seconds information, it isn't formatted nicely, and it isn't being drawn onscreen. First you'll tackle the formatting.

5. The getHours() method returns a number representing the hour, but it does so according to military time (0 to 23 hours). You want the clock to show AM/PM information. So you need to add the following code within the function you created in step 4 (add it just before the final close bracket) to adjust the formatting if the current time is in the afternoon:

```
// check to see if it's in the afternoon
if (currentHour > 11) {
    // yes, it is afternoon
    Suffix = "PM";
    currentHour -= 12;
} else {
    // it is still the morning
    suffix = "AM";
}
```

6. A new variable, suffix, has been added to hold the AM/PM data. Notice that if the current time is in the morning, currentHour doesn't need to be adjusted. Next, add the code to draw the current time information onscreen. The completed code looks like this:

```
onEnterFrame = function() {
    // create new Date object
    currentDate = new Date();
    // get hour information from currentDate
    currentHour = currentDate.getHours();
    // get minutes information from currentDate
    currentMinutes = currentDate.getMinutes();
    // get seconds information from currentDate
    currentSeconds = currentDate.getSeconds();

    // check to see if it's in the afternoon
    if (currentHour > 11) {
        // yes, it is after noon.
        Suffix = "PM";
        currentHour -= 12;
```

```
    } else {
        // it is still the morning
        suffix = "AM";
    }

    // draw time to the screen
    theTime.text = currentHour + ":" + currentMinutes + ":"
+ currentSeconds + " " + suffix;
    }
```

7. To make sure everything's working, place an instance of your movie clip on the stage, and test it (keyboard shortcut: **Ctrl+Enter**). You should see the current time displayed.

Next, you'll create a new TextFormat object to customize the clock's appearance. You can use the TextFormat object to specify font, color, and size information.

8. In frame 1 of the Actions layer, define a new TextFormat object, called myFormat. Add this code before the onEnterFrame handler:

```
myFormat = new TextFormat();
```

9. Next you'll set the properties of the TextFormat object to update the clock's appearance, but first you have to make sure the text field can assume the properties of myFormat. To do this, insert the setTextFormat() function *after* you draw the time onscreen in the onEnterFrame handler. The code looks like this:

```
// set the format of the text field
theTime.setTextFormat(myFormat);
```

Now whatever changes you make to myFormat will be applied to the text field.

10. Next, decide what parameters you want the user to be able to modify in the component. For this project, select Size, Color, and Font. Open the Component Definition dialog box and add these three new parameters to the component (see Figure 12.21). Under the Type column, the Size parameter (named newSize) will be a Number type, the Color parameter (named newColor) will be a Color type, and the Font parameter (named newFont) will be a Font Name type.

FIGURE 12.21
Adding parameters in
the Component
Definition dialog box.

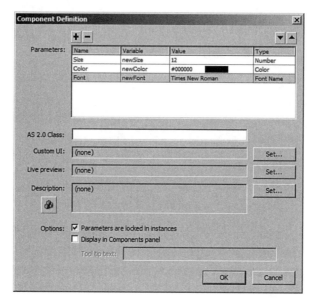

The only thing left to do is make the script inside the component react
to the variables, and then you can export the component. Notice in
Figure 12.21 that the variables are named based on the parameters:
newSize, newColor, and newFont. You'll use these names to refer to the
parameters inside the clock.

11. Inside the onEnterFrame handler above the line containing
    theTime.setTextFormat(myFormat), insert the following code to
    assign the properties of myFormat:

```
// set size of font in clock
myFormat.size = newSize;
// set color of font in clock
myFormat.color = newColor;
// set Font in clock
myFormat.font = newFont;
```

Your final code should look like this:

```
myFormat = new TextFormat();

onEnterFrame = function() {
    // create new Date object
    currentDate = new Date();
    // get hour information from currentDate
```

```
currentHour = currentDate.getHours();
// get minutes information from currentDate
currentMinutes = currentDate.getMinutes();
// get seconds information from currentDate
currentSeconds = currentDate.getSeconds();

// check to see if it's in the afternoon
if (currentHour > 11) {
    // yes, it is afternoon
    suffix = "PM";
    currentHour -= 12;
} else {
    // it is still the morning
    suffix = "AM";
}
// draw time to the screen
theTime.text = currentHour + ":" + currentMinutes + ":" +
➥currentSeconds + " " + suffix;

// set size of font in clock
myFormat.size = newSize;
// set color of font in clock
myFormat.color = newColor;
// set Font in clock
myFormat.font = newFont;

// set the format of the text field
theTime.setTextFormat(myFormat);
}
```

Code-wise, that's it! Next, export your new movie clip as an SWC file, and save the file in the appropriate folder: If you use a Macintosh, the folder is `Hard Drive:Applications:Flash 2004:First Run: Components:` If you use a Windows machine, the folder is `\Program Files\Macromedia\Flash 2004\language\First Run\Components`. After saving the file, click Reload in the Components panel drop-down list. In some circumstances you might be required to restart Flash to see your new component. Also, it's a good idea to save your new component in a folder within the Components folder to better organize your components. After your component has been added to the Components panel, try it out by dragging it onto the stage.

A word about the fonts used in this component:

The text field in the component doesn't have any characters embedded, because if you embed fonts in your text field (which anti-aliases fonts and guarantees that users see the proper font, regardless of which fonts are installed on their systems) and set the font using TextFormat, you have to have a text field somewhere in your movie with that font embedded. That text field doesn't have to contain any text; in fact, the text field doesn't even have to be inside the component. However, the proper characters have to be embedded in a text field somewhere.

Points to Remember

- Components allow you to quickly add complex interactivity to your Flash movies.

- Flash MX 2004 and Flash MX Professional 2004 both feature the new v2 component architecture, which includes a new event model, themes, skins, and a CSS-style properties interface.

- Existing components can be customized quickly and easily by using skins and themes.

- Using Flash MX 2004, it's easy to create and distribute your own custom components.

- Many of the components that ship with Flash MX 2004 and Flash MX Professional 2004 are compatible with Flash Player 6 r65 and later.

PART III
ELEMENTS

CHAPTER 13

TEXT

IN THIS CHAPTER, YOU'LL LEARN HOW TO TAKE FULL ADVANTAGE OF TEXT IN Macromedia Flash MX 2004. In earlier chapters you learned how to add text fields to your Flash movie; now you'll see how to control, edit, and even create them with ActionScript. This chapter covers the following topics:

- How to modify text with ActionScript
- Changing the attributes of a text field with ActionScript
- Using HTML in a text field
- Creating and using the TextFormat class
- Creating and loading cascading style sheets in Flash MX 2004
- The Strings panel
- Small font support in Flash
- Using the Spell Checker
- Using the Find and Replace panel

MODIFYING TEXT FIELDS WITH ACTIONSCRIPT

You can modify the contents of text fields in several ways; however, to do this, the text field must be of the right type. The three types are Static, which must be populated in the author environment and can't be edited by ActionScript or the user; Dynamic, which can be edited during author time and with ActionScript, but not by the user; and Input, which can be modified during author time, by ActionScript, and by the user. Input text fields are used when you need a user to enter information, such as a username or password. You can edit the contents of a text field at *runtime* only if the text field type is set to Dynamic or Input. For static text fields, you can alter the contents only in the Strings panel. (For more information, see "The Strings Panel" later in this chapter.)

The most common way to edit the contents of a dynamic or input text field using ActionScript is to modify its text property. To do this, you must give the text field instance a name (as shown in Figure 13.1). You can also give your text field a variable name (in the Var text box shown in Figure 13.1), the method used in Flash 5 and earlier. Although this variable-naming method functions in Flash MX 2004, it isn't recommended because you can't control other properties of your text field or apply any style sheet settings.

FIGURE 13.1
The two ways of naming your text field in the Property inspector.

To modify the text in a text field, use the following syntax:

```
text_field.text = "text";
```

To modify the value of a text field if it's named as a variable, use this syntax:

```
text_field = "text";
```

HTML IN TEXT

In Flash, you can place HTML-formatted text inside a text field. To do this, you need to enable HTML text in a text field by setting the `html` property of a `text_field` object to true, as shown here:

```
text_field.html = true;
```

To assign HTML content to a text field, modify the `htmlText` property. Flash MX 2004 supports the HTML tags described in the following sections.

The Anchor Tag (*<a>*)

The `<a>` tag creates a hyperlink, which supports the following attributes:

- **href**   Specifies the URL to load in the browser; this URL can be absolute or relative.

- **target**   Specifies the name of the window that loads the page.

The following tag creates the link `Flash MX 2004 Demystified`, which opens `www.flashdemystified.com` in a new browser window:

```
<a href="http://www.flashdemystified.com/" target="_blank">
➥Flash MX 2004 Demystified</a>
```

As well, you can define `a:link`, `a:hover`, and `a:active` styles for anchor tags by using style sheets, which are explained later in this chapter in "Cascading Style Sheet Support."

The Bold Tag (*<b>*)

The `<b>` tag renders text as bold, as long as a bold typeface exists for the font displaying your text. Here's an example of using the `<b>` tag:

```
<b>This is bold text.</b>
```

The Break Tag (*
*)

The <br> tag adds a line break to a text field, as shown in this example:

```
First line of text<br>Second line of text<br>
```

The Font Tag (*<font>*)

The <font> tag is used to determine the appearance of text enclosed by the tag. It supports the following attributes:

- **color**   Hexadecimal color values (such as #FFFFFF and #000000) are the only values supported by this tag. The following line, for example, creates red text:

  ```
  <font color="#FF0000">This is red text!</font>
  ```

- **face**   This specifies the name of the font to use. If the specified font isn't on the user's machine or isn't embedded in the SWF file, the Flash Player chooses a substitute font. You can also specify a list of comma-separated font names. If you specify a list of fonts, Flash Player chooses the first available one. Here's an example of using the face attribute:

  ```
  <font face="Times, Times New Roman">This text is in either
  ➥Times or Times New Roman.</font>
  ```

- **size**   Specifies the size of the font, in pixels, as shown in the following example. In addition to absolute sizes, you can use relative point sizes (such as +2 or –4).

  ```
  <font size="24" color="#0000FF">This is green, 24-point
  text</font>
  ```

The Italic Tag (*<i>*)

The <i> tag displays the tagged text in italics. An italic typeface must be available for the font used.

```
That is very <i>interesting</i>.
```

The preceding code would render as follows:

That is very *interesting*.

The List Item Tag (*<li>*)

The <li> tag places a bullet in front of the text it encloses.

```
Pet list:
<li>Cats</li>
<li>Dogs</li>
<li>Marmosets</li>
```

The preceding code would render as follows:

Pet list:

- Cats

- Dogs

- Marmosets

The Paragraph Tag (*<p>*)

The <p> tag creates a new paragraph. It supports the following attributes:

- **align**   Specifies alignment of text within the paragraph; valid values are left, right, and center.

- **class**   Specifies a CSS style class, defined by an instance of the TextField.StyleSheet class, which controls the appearance of the text in the paragraph. (For more information, see "Cascading Style Sheet Support" later in this chapter.)

The following tag example uses the align attribute to align text in the center of a text field:

```
textField.htmlText = "<p align='center'>This text appears in
➡ the middle of this text field</p>";
```

The following example defines a new text style class and uses the class attribute to assign it to a <p> tag:

```
var myStyleSheet = new TextField.StyleSheet();
this.createTextField("test", 10,0,0,300,100);
test.styleSheet = myStyleSheet;
```

```
test.htmlText = "<p class='body'>This is some body-styled
➥text.</p>.";) tags>)>) tag (HTML);sample scripts>) tag
(HTML;attributes of>
```

The Span Tag (*<span>*)

The <span> tag is available only for use with CSS text styles. (For more information, see "Cascading Style Sheet Support," later in this chapter.) It supports the following attribute:

- **class** Specifies a CSS style class defined by an instance of the TextField.StyleSheet class.

The Text Format Tag (*<textformat>*)

The <textformat> tag lets you use a subset of the paragraph formatting properties of the TextFormat class in HTML text fields. This subset includes line leading, indentation, tab stops, and margins. You can combine <textformat> tags with the built-in HTML tags. This tag has the following attributes:

- **blockindent** This specifies the block indentation, in points; corresponds to TextFormat.blockIndent.

- **indent** This specifies the indentation of text from the left margin to the first character in the paragraph; corresponds to TextFormat.indent.

- **leading** This specifies the amount of leading (vertical space) in points between lines; corresponds to TextFormat.leading.

- **leftmargin** This specifies the left margin of the paragraph, in points; corresponds to TextFormat.leftMargin.

- **rightmargin** This specifies the right margin of the paragraph in points; corresponds to TextFormat.rightMargin.

- **tabStops** This specifies custom tab stops. TabStops is an array of non-negative integers (for example, [5, 10, 15]); it corresponds to TextFormat.tabStops.

The Underline Tag (*<u>*)

The <u> tag underlines the tagged text, as shown in this example:

```
This text is <u>underlined</u>
```

The preceding code would render as follows:

This text is <u>underlined</u>.

The Image Tag (*<img>*)

Flash MX 2004 provides support for adding inline images to your HTML field (provided those images aren't progressive JPEGs, which the Flash Player doesn't support). The <img> tag supports the following attributes:

- **src**   This specifies the URL of the JPEG or SWF file to load or the linkage identifier for a movie clip in your library. This attribute is required. Note that externally loaded files aren't displayed until they're fully downloaded.

- **id**   This specifies the name of the movie clip instance (created by Flash Player) that contains the embedded JPEG, movie clip, or SWF. It's used if you're controlling content via ActionScript.

- **width**   This is the width of the displayed image in pixels.

- **height**   This is the height of the displayed image in pixels.

- **align**   This specifies the horizontal alignment of the image in the text field. Accepted values are left and right. If no value is specified, the alignment is left.

- **hspace**   This specifies how much horizontal space surrounds the image. The default value is 8.

- **vspace**   This specifies how much vertical space surrounds the image. The default value is 8.

Other Attributes

In addition to `text` and `htmlText`, the `TextField` class has the following properties that can be set:

`TextField.autoSize`   This property determines how a text field is resized to fit its contents:

- If the value is `none`, the text field doesn't resize or align to match the text.

- If the value is `left` and the text field line type is set to `multiline`, the text field expands or contracts its right and bottom sides to fit the text.

- If the value is `left` and the text field line type is set to `multiline no wrap`, the text field expands or contracts only its right side to fit the text.

- If the value is `center`, the text field autosizes, but the horizontal center of the text field stays anchored at the text field's original horizontal center position. The bottom and right sides still expand or contract to fit the text.

- If the value is `right`, the left and bottom sides expand or contract, with the top and right sides remaining in their original positions.

`TextField.background`   This is a Boolean that determines whether the text field has a background.

`TextField.backgroundColor`   If the background property is true, this parameter sets the color of the background, such as 0xFFFFFF.

`TextField.border`   This Boolean value determines whether a border is drawn around the text field.

`TextField.borderColor`   If the border property is true, this parameter determines the color of the border, such as 0xFFFFFF.

`TextField.embedFonts`   If this Boolean value is set to true, this text field includes font outlines for all characters.

`TextField.html`   This Boolean value determines whether the text field renders HTML content.

TextField.htmlText   If the html property is true, htmlText specifies the HTML content to display.

TextField.menu   This is a reference to the context menu of the text field. For information about setting context menus, see Chapter 10, "ActionScript: Functions, Events, and Objects."

TextField.mouseWheelEnabled   If this Boolean value is set to true, the text field recognizes mouse wheel actions, which are used to scroll the contents of the text field.

TextField.multiline   This Boolean value determines whether the text field is a multi- or single-line text field.

TextField.password   This Boolean value determines whether the text field is a password text field. If true, the text in the text field is rendered using only asterisks (*).

TextField.restrict   This is the allowed set of characters you can enter into the text field. If this property is null or undefined, you can enter any character. Although you can enter a series of characters separated by spaces, you can also specify ranges of characters.

The following example allows the use of uppercase letters as well as the numbers 0, 1, 3, and 4:

```
my_text.restrict = "A-Z 0 1 3 4";
```

To specify a character to exclude, place the ^ character in front of it, as in the following examples:

```
my_text.restrict = "^x";
```

```
my_text.restrict = "A-Z ^T";
```

The first example allows all characters except the lowercase *x*, and the second allows all uppercase letters except the uppercase *T*.

You can use a backslash to enter a ^ or – verbatim (if you want to allow using the ^ or – characters specifically, for example). The accepted backslash sequences are \-, \^, and \\. The backslash must be an actual character in the string, so when specified in ActionScript, a double backslash must be used. For example, the following code includes only the dash (–) and caret (^):

```
my_txt.restrict = "\\-\\^";
```

You can also use the \u escape sequence to make restrict strings. For example, the following code includes only the characters from ASCII 32 (space) to ASCII 126 (tilde):

```
my_txt.restrict = "\u0020-\u007E";
```

TextField.selectable This Boolean value determines whether characters in the text field can be selected. If you're using an input text field, this value is always true.

TextField.hscroll This indicates the current horizontal scrolling position. To scroll your text horizontally, you adjust the hscroll property of a text field. If hscroll is 0, the text isn't horizontally scrolled.

TextField.scroll This defines the vertical scrolling position of text in a text field. To scroll your text vertically, you adjust the scroll property of a text field.

TextField.tabIndex This number allows you to define a custom tabbing order for elements on the stage. Tabbing is defined in ascending order. For example, if you have two text fields with tabIndex defined, and their values are 1 and 2, the text field with the index of 1 takes priority. By default, tabIndex is undefined. If there's no defined tabIndex on the stage, Flash automatically determines the tabbing order for the stage.

The tab ordering defined by the tabIndex property is *flat*, which means that hierarchical relationships of objects in your SWF file are ignored. Objects in your SWF with defined tabIndex values are placed in a tab order. If you have two or more objects with the same tabIndex value, the one that goes first is undefined. As a rule, you should try to avoid assigning the same tabIndex value to multiple objects.

TextField.tabEnabled This specifies whether the text field is included in automatic tab ordering. By default, this value is undefined (which is the same as setting a value of true).

TextField.text This is the text in the text field.

TextField.textColor This is the color of text in a text field, indicated in hexadecimal format. For example, a valid value would be 0xFFCC33.

TextField.textHeight This is the height of the text.

`TextField.textWidth`   This is the width of the text.

`TextField.type`   This specifies the type of the text field. Accepted values are as follows:

- `dynamic`, which specifies a dynamic text field. Dynamic text fields can't be edited by the user.

- `input`, which specifies an input text field.

`TextField.variable`   This is the name of the variable associated with the text field. Using this property isn't recommended, but it can be used for compatibility with the Flash 5 coding style.

`TextField.wordwrap`   This is a Boolean value that indicates whether a text field has word wrap.

The following are read-only properties of `TextField`:

- **`TextField.maxhscroll`**   This returns the maximum value of the `hscroll` property.

- **`TextField.maxscroll`**   This returns the maximum value of the `scroll` property.

- **`TextField.length`**   This returns the number of characters in the text field.

`TextField` has the following built-in methods:

- **`TextField.getFontList()`**   This method returns a list of fonts available for use on the current system. Note that this list represents fonts available to the user at runtime, not those available to the author at author time.

- **`TextField.getDepth()`**   This method returns the depth of the text field.

- **`TextField.getNewTextFormat()`**   This method returns a reference to the `TextFormat` object associated with the display of new text.

- **`TextField.getTextFormat()`**   This method returns a reference to the `TextFormat` object associated with the display of existing text.

- **`TextField.replaceSel(*text*)`**   This method replaces any selected text in a text field with the text parameter sent to the method. This text is inserted using the current default character format and default paragraph format at the position of the current selection. Note that even if your text field is set to display HTML text, HTML-formatted content loaded with this method is displayed as regular text.

For example, if the text in a text field is The dog is brown, and the user selects the word dog, the following code changes the text to The cat is brown:

```
my_text.replaceSel("cat");
```

The following are events generated by TextField:

- **TextField.onChanged**   This is called when the contents of the text field are changed.

- **TextField.onKillFocus**   This is called when the text field loses focus.

- **TextField.onScroller**   This is called when one of the text field scroll properties changes, such as maxscroll, as new content is added to an input text field.

- **TextField.onSetFocus**   This is called when the text field receives focus.

Of these four events, onChanged and onScroller can be added as listeners to the TextField. For example, the following code adds an onChanged listener to the my_txt text field:

```
newListener = new Object();
newListener.onChanged = function() {
trace("text has been changed");
}

my_txt.addListener(newListener);
```

You can remove a dynamically created text field from the stage by using removeTextField(). For example, the following code creates a text field named my_tf and then removes it:

```
createTextField("my_tf", 0, 0, 0, 10, 10);
my_tf.removeTextField();
```

As you can see, you can control text fields in Flash in a wide variety of ways. The TextField class has become very powerful in Flash MX 2004.

SCROLLING TEXT

A common effect with a text field is scrolling its contents. This is usually done with a scrollbar, but often you need to automatically scroll the contents of a text field by snapping to a specific position (to highlight a specific passage, for example) or by scrolling the entire field. You can control the scroll values of your text field with the TextField.scroll and TextField.hscroll properties.

You set the scroll and hscroll properties of a text field to adjust its visual scroll. The scroll property controls the vertical scroll, and the hscroll property controls the horizontal scroll. Take a look at the following examples:

```
onClipEvent (enterFrame) {
    // scroll down
    my_text.scroll++;
}
```

and

```
onClipEvent (enterFrame) {
    // scroll right
    my_text.hscroll++;
}
```

The first example scrolls the contents of the my_text text field one line at a time, and the second scrolls the contents to the right. Both scroll examples appear to stop after they reach the limits of the text field, but the preceding code would continue trying to adjust the scroll, even if it no longer appears. It would be useful to check against the maximum allowable scroll for the my_text text field, which is determined by the contents of the text field using the following read-only properties:

```
TextField.maxscroll
TextField.maxhscroll
```

As you might expect, maxscroll indicates the maximum allowable vertical scroll value, and maxhscroll indicates the maximum allowable horizontal scroll value. Although both properties are variable, the minimum scroll for a text field is always 0.

Take a look at the following scrolling examples, which now check to see whether adjusting the scroll is allowed:

```
onClipEvent (enterFrame) {
    // scroll down if possible
    if (my_text.scroll < my_text.maxscroll) {
        my_text.scroll++;
    }
}
```

and

```
onClipEvent (enterFrame) {
    // scroll right if possible
    if (my_text.hscroll < my_text.maxhscroll) {
        my_text.hscroll++;
    }
}
```

See the difference? Now when the maximum scroll values are reached, the script stops trying to adjust them.

CREATING DYNAMIC TEXT FIELDS

Using the createTextField method (which is a method of the MovieClip class), you can create a new TextField object on the stage at runtime. This operates similarly to createEmptyMovieClip, in that you specify a name and depth for the new text field. However, when creating a new text field, there are other options to set, including height, width, and whether the text field scales based on its contents. This is the syntax for createTextField():

my_mc.createTextField(*instanceName, depth, x, y, width, height*)

instanceName is the name of the new text field. *depth* is the depth that the text field sits at. *x* is the x coordinate of your text field, and *y* is the y coordinate of your text field. *width* is the _width value of the text field, and *height* is the _height value of the text field.

For example, the following code creates a text field called first_name and fills it with the text bob:

```
createTextField("first_name", 1, 50, 50, 150, 10);
first_name.text = "bob";
```

When you create a new text field, it contains the following properties you can modify:

```
type = "dynamic"
border = false
background = false
password = false
multiline = false
html = false
embedFonts = false
variable = null
maxChars = null
```

Also, it's sent a default TextFormat object, which has the following settings:

```
font = "Times New Roman"
size = 12
textColor = 0x000000
bold = false
italic = false
underline = false
url = ""
target = ""
align = "left"
leftMargin = 0
rightMargin = 0
indent = 0
leading = 0
bullet = false
tabStops = [] (empty array)
```

For more information on creating and using the TextFormat class, see "The TextFormat Class" later in this chapter.

Note that you can set the properties of a dynamically created text field in the same way you do for a text field created at author time. For example, the following code creates an input password text field called new_password:

```
createTextField("new_password", 0, 0, 0, 100, 20);
```

```
new_password.type = "input";
new_password.password = true;
```

After you have created a text field, you can assign it a TextFormat object (explained in "The TextFormat Class" later in this chapter).

An inconsistency in the way text fields created at author time and runtime handle embedded fonts is that although you can specify that fonts in a new text field are embedded (text_field.embedFonts = true), these fonts don't show up unless they exist somewhere else in the movie. This isn't a concern if you place a text field on the stage and embed all characters. For example, if the following code is all that exists in a movie, nothing would be visible:

```
createTextField("my_text", 0, 0, 0, 100, 20);
```

```
my_text.text = "Hi!";
my_text.embedFonts = true;
```

If the movie contains a dynamic or input text field with the default Times New Roman font embedded, however, you would see the word Hi!.

THE *SELECTION* OBJECT

With the Selection object, you can control the selection of specific characters in your text field. You can replace text, delete it, or insert it. You select characters in your text field by clicking and dragging over them. Selected text is displayed with a reversed color scheme, as shown in Figure 13.2.

In Flash 2004 you can access the Selection class (which has existed since Flash 5). The Selection class lets you set and control the text field in which the insertion point is located—that is, the field that has focus. When you set a text selection, you define a *selection-span index*, which is an array containing indexes of the first and last position of your selection. Selection-span indexes are zero-based.

FIGURE 13.2
Selected text is displayed here with white characters on a black background.

There is no constructor function for the Selection class because there can be only one currently focused field at a time. This class lets you control the selected content. It's used independently of specific text fields; Selection is used as an object on top of text fields.

Selection allows you to monitor when a user selects text characters onscreen with the keyboard or the mouse. In addition, the Selection object enables you to replace or remove content that has been selected. For example, you might build an application that allows users to select text and then replace it with a number of predefined text elements. The following sections explain the methods available to the Selection object.

The *Selection.getBeginIndex()* Method

This returns the index at the beginning of the selected text span. The value is –1 if there is no index or no currently selected text field. For example, if you have the string Hello in a text field and you select the characters ello, the beginIndex value would be 1.

The *Selection.getCaretIndex()* Method

The *caret* is the insertion point represented by the cursor, and this method returns the caret position in the current selection span. This value is –1 if there's no caret position or no selection span.

The *Selection.getEndIndex()* Method

This returns the index at the end of the text selection span. This value is –1 if there's no index or no currently selected field. For example, if you have a string Hello in a text field and you select the characters ello, the endIndex value would be 4.

The *Selection.getFocus()* Method

This returns the name of the variable for the selected text field. Its value is null if no text field is selected.

The *Selection.setFocus(instanceName)* Method

This sets the focus to the text field specified in the parameter instanceName. For example, to set the focus to a text field named my_text, you would use the following code:

```
Selection.setFocus("my_text");
```

The *Selection.setSelection(start, end)* Method

This sets the beginning and ending indexes of the selection span in the text field that currently has focus. For example, if the text field my_text contains the text I am the best! and you want to select the word best, you would use the following code:

```
Selection.setSelection(9, 12);
```

If, after you've set the selection span, you want to replace it with different text, you can use the TextField method TextField.replaceSel. The following code would select the first three characters of the selected text field and replace those characters with the text xxx:

```
// get reference to text field with focus
focus_field = Selection.getFocus();

// set selection
Selection.setSelection(0, 2);

// replace selected text
focus_field.replaceSel("xxx");
```

As well, Selection supports the listener onSetFocus, which is triggered whenever a text field receives focus. When triggered, onSetFocus receives two parameters: oldFocus and newFocus. oldFocus is the name of the text field that was previously selected, and newFocus is the name of the text field that's currently selected. For example, to specify a function to be called when a user sets the focus to any text field, you might use the following code:

```
Selection.onSetFocus = function (oldFocus, newFocus) {
    trace("Focus was on " + oldFocus);
    trace("Focus is now on " + newFocus);
}
```

THE *TEXTFORMAT* CLASS

You can use the ActionScript TextFormat class to set the formatting properties of a text field. The TextFormat class contains character and paragraph formatting information. Character formatting information describes the appearance of individual characters: font name, point size, color, and an associated URL. Paragraph formatting information describes the appearance of a paragraph: left margin, right margin, indentation of the first line, and left, right, or center alignment.

If you want to use the TextFormat class, first create a TextFormat object and set its parameters. Then you apply the TextFormat object to a text field by using the TextField.setTextFormat() or TextField.setNewTextFormat() methods, described later in this chapter.

Creating a *TextFormat* Object

You create a new TextFormat object using the following syntax:

```
new TextFormat([font, [size, [color, [bold, [italic,
⇒[underline, [url, [target, [align, [leftMargin, [rightMargin,
⇒ [indent, [leading]]]]]]]]]]]]])
```

All these parameters are optional:

- **font**   This is the font name specified as a string.

- **size**   This integer indicates the point size.

- **color**   This is the text color in hexadecimal format.

- **bold**   This Boolean value indicates whether text is boldface.

- **italic**   This Boolean value indicates whether text is italicized.

- **underline**   This Boolean value indicates whether text is underlined.

- **url**   This is the URL to which the text in the TextFormat object links. If this parameter is undefined (or defined as an empty string), the text doesn't link to anything.

- **target**   This is the target window where the hyperlink is displayed. If no target window is specified, the text is displayed in the default target window, _self. If url has been set to an empty string or null, this property has no effect.

- **align**   This is the alignment of the paragraph. Accepted values are left, right, and center.

- **leftMargin**   This is the left margin of the paragraph specified in points.

- **rightMargin**   This is the right margin of the paragraph specified in points.

- **indent**   This integer specifies how far the first character in the paragraph is indented from the left margin.

- **leading**   This numeric value sets the amount of leading (vertical space) between lines.

You can change any of these properties at any time. For example, to set the font of a TextFormat object to Arial, you would use the following code:

```
my_fmt.font = "Arial";
```

In addition, the TextFormat class includes one method: TextFormat. getTextExtent(*text* [, *width*]). In this method, *text* is a string. The *width* parameter, which is optional, determines at what width text should wrap. If this parameter is supplied, Flash simulates word wrapping in its calculations. (Otherwise, text extents are calculated without word wrapping.)

TextFormat.getTextExtent() is used to determine what size a specified piece of text would occupy onscreen, given the formatting settings of the TextFormat object. It returns an object containing text measurement information for the text parameter specified in the getTextExtent() call. The object has the following properties (all values are in pixels):

- **ascent** This is the distance above the baseline for the text. The baseline is located at the origin of the text field plus the ascent measurement.

- **descent** This is the distance below the baseline for the text.

- **width** This is the width of the specified text.

- **height** This is the height of the specified text.

- **textFieldWidth** This is the width required for a text field to display the specified text. Text fields have a 2-pixel-wide gutter around them. This means textFieldWidth is equal to width +4 (2 for the left and right sides of the field).

- **textFieldHeight** This is the height required for a text field to display the specified text.

If you want to determine how large a text field needs to be to fit all your text, use the getTextExtent() method of TextFormat and refer to the textFieldWidth and textFieldHeight values specifically.

After you have defined your TextFormat object and specified the settings, you apply it to an existing text field. You can use two methods to do this, which are described in the following sections.

The *TextField.setTextFormat()* Method

This method has three different syntaxes you can use. In each one, the *textFormat* parameter represents a TextFormat object. Use the following format if you're applying the properties of the *textFormat* parameter to all text in the text field:

my_txt.setTextFormat (*textFormat*)

To apply the properties of *textFormat* to the character at the position specified by *index*, use this syntax format:

my_txt.setTextFormat (*index*, *textFormat*)

index is a number representing of the index of the text character to be replaced.

Use the following syntax format if you want to apply the properties of *textFormat* to the text starting at *beginIndex* and ending at *endIndex*:

my_txt.setTextFormat (*beginIndex*, *endIndex*, *textFormat*) *beginIndex* is a number representing the position of the first text character to format. *endIndex* is a number representing the position of the last text character to format.

To set the `textFormat` parameter for text defined at author time, follow these steps:

1. Create a new Flash movie.

2. Place a dynamic text field on the stage, and initialize it with the text value This is text.

3. Enter an instance name for this text field, such as my_text.

4. Create a new layer, insert a new keyframe, select the keyframe, and enter the following code:

    ```
    my_fmt = new TextFormat();
    my_fmt.size = 20;
    my_fmt.font = "Arial";

    my_text.setTextFormat(my_fmt);
    ```

When you test this movie, you'll see the following text:

This is text.

`TextField.setTextFormat()` specifies the formatting options for text already present in the text field.

The *TextField.setNewTextFormat()* Method

To specify the formatting for text that the user enters (in an input text field) or that's specified with ActionScript, you must use the `TextField.setNewTextFormat()` method, which has the following syntax:

my_text.setNewTextFormat(*textFormat*);

This method specifies a format for all text entered by the user or added to a text field using ActionScript. To set the format for new text, follow these steps:

1. Create a new Flash movie.

2. Place a dynamic text field on the stage, and populate it with the text `This is text.`

3. Enter an instance name for this text field, such as `my_text`.

4. Create a new layer, add a keyframe, select the keyframe, and enter the following code:

```
my_fmt = new TextFormat();
my_fmt.size = 20;
my_fmt.font = "Arial";

my_text.setTextFormat(my_fmt);

// new text format
my_fmt_two = new TextFormat();
my_fmt_two.size = 12;
my_fmt_two.font = "Verdana";

my_text.setNewTextFormat(my_fmt_two);

my_text.text += ", and this is more text!";
```

If you test this movie, you'll see the following text:

This is text, and this is more text!

THE STRINGS PANEL

The Strings panel, new to Flash MX 2004, makes it easy to create and update multilingual content. You can define content for text fields that span multiple languages and have Flash automatically determine when the content should be shown in a certain language, based on the settings of the user's system. This is an incredibly powerful feature, as it allows you to create your Flash movie once, yet have it localized for several different languages. To open the Strings panel (see Figure 13.3), choose Window, Other Panels, Strings from the menu (keyboard shortcut: Windows **Ctrl+F11**; Macintosh **Command+F11**).

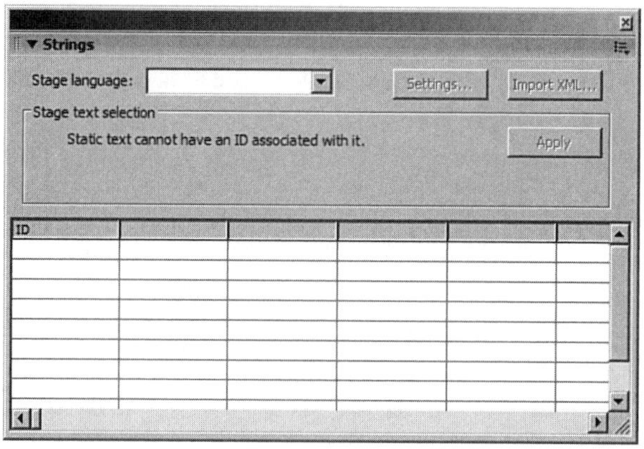

FIGURE 13.3
The Strings panel.

Before you create multilingual content for your Flash movie, you have to specify the languages to be used. To do this, click the Settings button to open the Settings dialog box (see Figure 13.4).

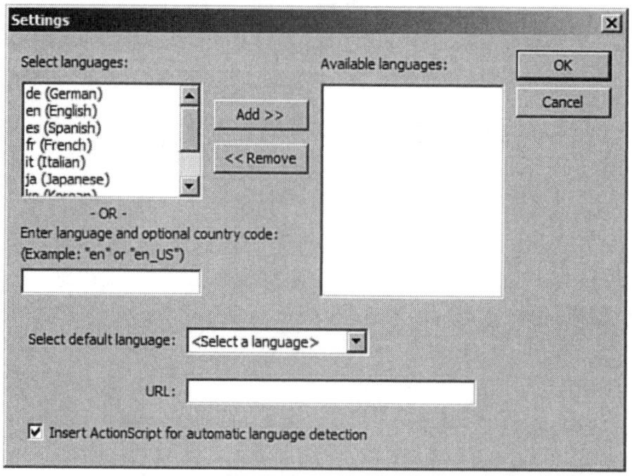

FIGURE 13.4
The Settings
dialog box.

1. Click any language listed in the Select Languages list box, and click Add to add it to the list of languages used in your movie. You can also manually enter a language/country code in the text box below the Select Languages list box. To remove a language, select it in the Available Languages list box, and click Remove.

2. Select the default language in the Select Default Language drop-down list.

3. In the URL text box, specify the location for any existing XML files that contain your localized multilingual content.

4. Select the Insert ActionScript for Automatic Language Detection check box to have Flash automatically determine which language set to show when your movie is loaded.

Now that you have the languages determined, you have to add text fields to your stage and connect them to the Strings panel. To keep things simple, the following examples involve a movie with localized English and French content.

The Strings panel has three columns: ID, en, and fr. ID represents the IDs you associate with text elements on the stage. The en column shows what content will look like if the system language is English, and the fr column shows what the French content will be.

Now that you have the languages selected, it's time to add some text elements to the stage. Create a dynamic or input text field, and select the text field. Notice that in the Stage Text Selection section of the Strings panel, the String text box displays the contents of your text field. In the ID text box above it, enter a label to identify the text field on the stage, and click Apply or press Enter. Note that specifying an ID is not the same as giving a text field an instance or variable name. A text field can have both an ID and an instance name; it won't affect the functionality of the Strings panel.

Now add two more text fields to the stage, and give them unique IDs. Duplicate IDs cause errors in localized content. After you have applied IDs to the text fields, they show up in the bottom half of the Strings panel (see Figure 13.5.)

FIGURE 13.5
Three defined IDs.

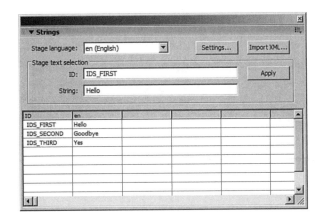

Note that Flash adds the prefix IDS_ to the ID name you supplied. When you select a text field on the stage, the information in the Stage Text Selection section of the Strings panel is updated.

Now that you have the languages defined and the text fields created and linked to the Strings panel, it's time to add multilingual content. You can do this two ways:

- Manually entering content via the Strings panel

- Importing XML documents

To manually enter multilingual content with the Strings panel, double-click the cell representing the language associated with the text field you want to set, and enter the content (see Figure 13.6).

FIGURE 13.6

Manually entering multilingual content.

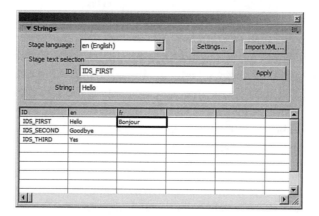

You can see what the stage will look like using different languages by changing the currently selected stage language in the Stage Language drop-down list (see Figure 13.7).

FIGURE 13.7

Setting a stage language.

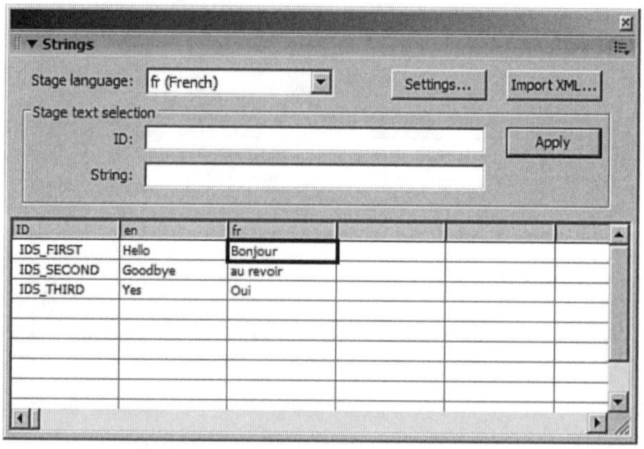

When you link text fields to specific content, Flash automatically generates an XML file for each language your movie uses. These XML files are built according to the XML Localization Interchange File Format (LIFF), which is a specification for an extensible format that allows any software provider to produce a single interchange format. You can find more information on this format at www.oasis-open.org/committees/xliff/.

These files, which are created when you publish your movie, are located in a series of directories local to your SWF file. These directories are named for the two-letter language abbreviation they represent. (For example, if you have French content, when you publish your movie, Flash generates an fr directory.) These directories contain only one file each, which is the localized content for this language.

These files make it easy to modify multilingual content without having to make any modifications to the Flash movie. A sample XML LIFF file looks like this:

```
<?xml version="1.0" encoding="UTF-8"?>

<!DOCTYPE xliff PUBLIC "-//XLIFF//DTD XLIFF//EN"

"http://www.oasis-open.org/committees/xliff/documents/
➥xliff.dtd" ><xliff version="1.0" xml:lang="fr">

<file datatype="plaintext" original="thingo.swf" source-
➥language="EN">
    <header></header>
    <body>
      <trans-unit id="001" resname="IDS_FIRST">
        <source>Bonjour</source>
      </trans-unit>
      <trans-unit id="002" resname="IDS_SECOND">
        <source>au revoir</source>
      </trans-unit>
      <trans-unit id="003" resname="IDS_THIRD">
        <source>Oui</source>
      </trans-unit>
    </body>
  </file>

</xliff>
```

As you can see in the preceding code sample, Flash generates a series of <trans-unit> tags that represent the text fields linked on your movie's stage. The <trans-unit> tag with the resname attribute of IDS_FIRST contains a source tag that represents the actual content of the text field. You would change this value to update your movie's content.

If you have already generated your localized content with a different Flash file or an external file, you can still use it with the Strings panel. To import an XML file for use with the Strings panel, following these steps:

1. Click the Import XML button in the Strings panel.

2. In the Language of File drop-down list, select the language the XML file contains.

3. In the File Open dialog box, navigate to the XML file you intend to use, and click Open.

SMALL FONT SUPPORT

Another new feature in Flash MX 2004 is improved support for small fonts. This feature is especially helpful if the content you're developing is intended for the small screens of mobile devices. The Alias Text feature allows you to force the display of aliased text (text that has not been smoothed) in a text field. This feature isn't activated through code; rather, it's activated by clicking the Alias Text button in the Property inspector (see Figure 13.8).

FIGURE 13.8
The Alias Text button.

To give you an example of what the Alias Text feature does to small text, take a look at the text line shown in Figure 13.9.

FIGURE 13.9
Small text before using the Alias Text feature.

Yet more tebhrut.

This is 9-point Times New Roman, without the Alias Text feature. It's readable, but only barely. Now look at the same text after clicking the Alias Text button (see Figure 13.10).

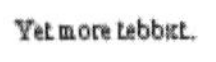

FIGURE 13.10
Small text after using the Alias Text feature.

Yet more rabbit.

It's much more legible, don't you think? This feature is activated on a per-text field basis.

CASCADING STYLE SHEET SUPPORT

Flash MX 2004 now supports cascading style sheets (CSS), which is a simple, standardized mechanism for defining visual attributes (such as color, size, and font) of text. CSS is used frequently in HTML web sites all over the web. In Flash, you can implement CSS in your movie in two ways:

- You can create a new StyleSheet object and apply it to your text elements.

- You can load an external CSS file into your movie, and apply the styles to your text elements.

If you're familiar with using CSS in HTML documents, you've probably used it to define the location of elements on a web page. CSS support in Flash is limited, however, in that it allows you to define only visual attributes of the text, not any positioning information. Table 13.1 lists the CSS properties supported in Flash.

TABLE 13.1 ## Supported CSS Properties

In CSS	In ActionScript	Description
font-size	fontSize	Font size
font-weight	fontWeight	Accepted values are normal and bold
font-style	fontStyle	Accepted values are normal and italic

continues

TABLE 13.1 **Supported CSS Properties** *continued*

In CSS	In ActionScript	Description
font-family	fontFamily	A comma-separated list of fonts to use. The first available font in the list is used. Generic font names are converted to the appropriate device font. The following generic font names are converted: mono to _typewriter, sans-serif to _sans, and serif to _serif.
margin-left	marginLeft	The left margin value
margin-right	marginRight	The right margin value
text-indent	textIndent	Text indentation
color	color	Text color, which must be in hexadecimal format
display	display	Accepted values are inline, block, and none
text-align	textAlign	Accepted values are left, center, and right
text-decoration	textDecoration	Accepted values are none and underline

Creating a New Text Style

You can create new text styles with ActionScript by using the setStyle() method of the TextField.StyleSheet class. This method takes two parameters: the name of the style and an object that defines that style's properties. For example, the following code creates a StyleSheet object named styles that defines two styles:

```
var styles = new TextField.StyleSheet();
styles.setStyle("bodyText",
  {fontFamily: 'Arial,Helvetica,sans-serif',
  fontSize: '12px'}
);
styles.setStyle("headline",
  {fontFamily: 'Arial,Helvetica,sans-serif',
  fontSize: '24px'}
);
```

Loading an External CSS File

In addition to creating your own StyleSheet objects, you can load external CSS files into a StyleSheet object. The styles defined in the CSS file are added to the StyleSheet object. To load an external CSS file, you use the load() method of the TextField.StyleSheet class. To determine when the CSS file has finished loading, use the StyleSheet object's onLoad callback handler. In the following example, you create and load an external CSS file and use the TextField.StyleSheet.getStyleNames() method to retrieve the names of the loaded styles. To load an external style sheet, follow these steps:

1. In your preferred text or XML editor (Dreamweaver MX 2004, for example), create a new file.

2. Add the following style definitions to the file:

```
// Filename: styles.css
bodyText {
font-family: Arial,Helvetica,sans-serif;
font-size: 12px;
}

headline {
font-family: Arial,Helvetica,sans-serif;
font-size: 24px;
}
```

3. Save the CSS file as styles.css.

4. In Flash, create a new FLA document.

5. In the Timeline, select Layer 1.

6. Open the Actions panel, and add the following code:

```
var css_styles = new TextField.StyleSheet();
css_styles.load("styles.css");
css_styles.onLoad = function(ok) {
if(ok) {
// display style names
trace(this.getStyleNames());
} else {
trace("Error loading CSS file.");
}
}
```

7. Save the file to the same folder that contains `styles.css`.

8. Test the movie.

You should see the names of the two styles displayed in the Output panel:

body

headLine

If you see `Error loading CSS file` displayed in the Output panel, make sure the FLA and the CSS file are in the same folder and that you typed the name of the CSS file correctly.

SPELL CHECKER

New to Flash MX 2004 is a full-featured spell checker. You can use it to check for spelling errors in the following places:

- ActionScript strings

- Text fields

- Scene and layer names

- Frame labels and comments

- Symbol names

You activate the spell checker by choosing Text, Check Spelling from the main menu. If an error is found, the Check Spelling dialog box opens (see Figure 13.11).

FIGURE 13.11
The Check Spelling dialog box.

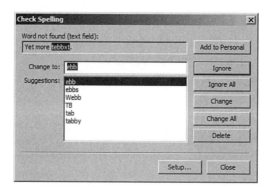

In this dialog box you can fix the spelling of the word, tell Flash to ignore certain terms in your search, or add any new words flagged as "errors" to your personal dictionary. Adding flagged words is helpful if, for example, you're working on a project that has a product name that doesn't appear in your dictionary, and you want to avoid having to continually skip over it when spell-checking.

To specify the settings of the spell checker, open the Spelling Setup dialog box (see Figure 13.12) by choosing Text, Spelling Setup from the menu or by clicking the Setup button in the Check Spelling dialog box.

FIGURE 13.12

The Spelling Setup dialog box.

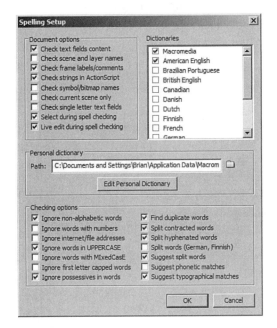

In the Spelling Setup dialog box, you can specify what terms are checked, which dictionaries to compare against, and the location of your personal dictionary file. For example, by default the spell checker checks for spelling in the content of text fields in your FLA, in frame labels and comments, and strings in your ActionScript code.

THE FIND AND REPLACE PANEL

New to Flash MX 2004 is the Find and Replace panel, which you can use to search for specific content and, if you want, replace it with other content. In addition to the usual text search and replace, you can use the Find and Replace panel to search for fonts, colors, symbols, sounds, video, and bitmap images.

To open the Find and Replace panel (see Figure 13.13), choose Edit, Find and Replace from the menu (keyboard shortcut: Window **Ctrl+F**; Macintosh **Command+F**). By default, it's a free-floating panel, but you can dock it like any other panel.

FIGURE 13.13
The Find and Replace panel.

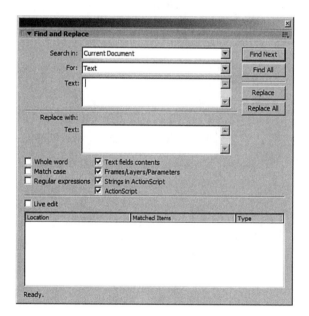

The first option you see is the Search In drop-down list, where you can specify whether to search the entire document or just the current scene in your FLA file. Below that is the For drop-down list, where you select the type of information you want to search for. Below that is a host of type-specific search parameters. Selecting the Regular Expressions check box means that the search is conducted within ActionScript expressions in your movie. At the bottom is a window that shows the matches of your search results. The Type column in this window shows the media type of the matched object (movie, graphic, text field, and so forth). Click the Live Edit check box to modify the results of your search from within the Find and Replace panel.

Replacing Text

When you open the Find and Replace panel the first time, the For drop-down list is set to Text, by default. The options here are standard find-and-replace features: Enter what you want to look for in the Text field, and enter what you want to replace the search text with in the Replace With field (see Figure 13.14).

FIGURE 13.14
Replacing text.

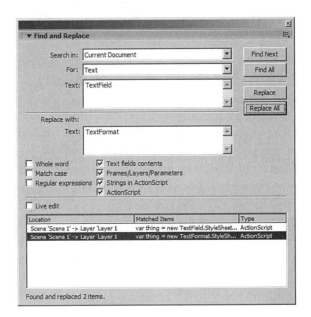

Clicking Find Next locates the first instance of the text in your movie (as determined by the options you select, such as whether to search in text fields, ActionScript, or strings in ActionScript). Clicking Find All shows the location of every instance of the text. Clicking Replace replaces the first instance of the found text with the text in the Replace With field.

Replacing Fonts

The Find and Replace panel allows you to search for specific fonts (see Figure 13.15) and replace them with other fonts.

FIGURE 13.15
Replacing fonts.

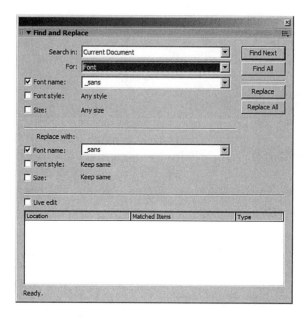

You are shown a list of available system fonts to search from. You can also narrow your search to specific font styles (such as plain, bold, and italic) and sizes (even a range of sizes). To narrow your search, click the Font Style and Size check boxes, and set the style and size parameters. If you want to replace a specific font with a different font and a different size, you can specify a replacement size by selecting the font style and size in the Replace With section of the panel. If you like, you can deselect the Font Name check box and search for type that matches specific font sizes or styles. For example, if your movie contains text in 24-point Arial, you could search and replace it automatically with 20-point Verdana.

Replacing Colors

You can search for specific colors (see Figure 13.16) used in your movies and replace them with other colors. You can specify search locations, allowing you to search for colors used in text, fills, or strokes.

FIGURE 13.16
Replacing colors.

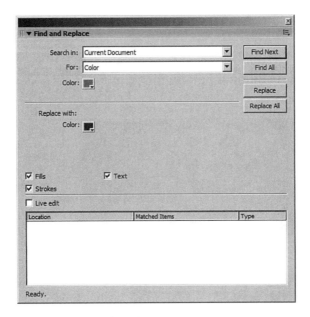

Replacing Symbols, Sounds, Videos, and Bitmaps

You can also search and replace symbols, sounds, videos, and bitmaps (see Figure 13.17). Using this feature, you can search for specific instances of symbols, sounds, videos, or bitmaps and replace them with other items in the Library. This feature is a real timesaver if, for example, you use the same sound file several times in your movie and you need to replace every instance with a newer sound.

To search and replace a symbol, sound, video, or bitmap, select the type of object in the For drop-down list, and then select the symbol you want to replace in the Name text box. Select the item you want to use as a replacement in the Replace Name text box, and click Find, Find All, Replace, or Replace All.

FIGURE 13.17

Replacing a symbol.

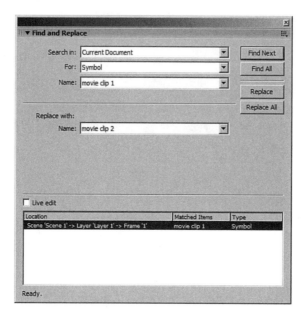

Resources

Cascading Style Sheets: www.w3.org/Style/CSS/

XML Localization Interchange File Format:
www.oasis-open.org/committees/xliff/

POINTS TO REMEMBER

- Flash MX 2004 supports the use of HTML in text fields, including new support for the <img> tag.

- Using ActionScript, you can dynamically create new text fields at runtime and control their formatting.

- The Selection object lets you track what text the user has selected and control it.

- Using the TextFormat class, you can define reusable formatting for your text and apply it at any time.

- Flash MX 2004 now supports loading CSS files and creating StyleSheet objects that support a wide variety of CSS properties.

- Using the Find and Replace panel, you can access and modify a range of information in your movie quickly and easily.

- Flash MX 2004 has improved support for small fonts.

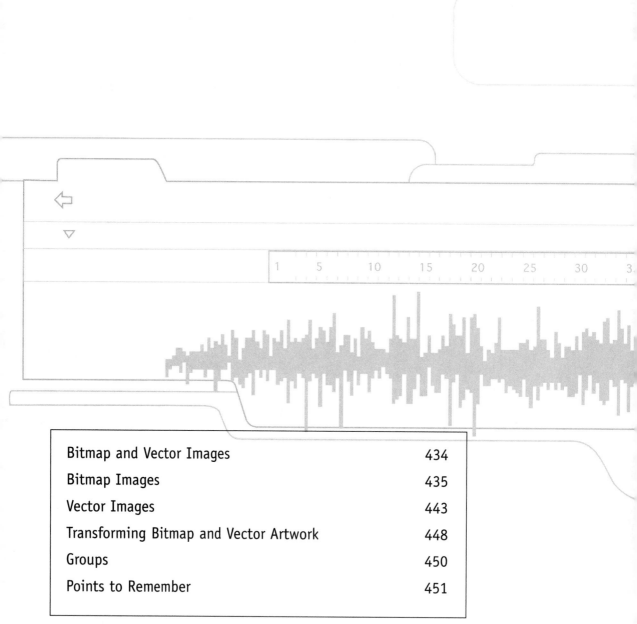

CHAPTER 14

IMAGES

THE VISUALS IN YOUR FLASH MOVIE ARE ESSENTIAL TO YOUR PROJECT'S effectiveness. Sure, you can have great sound and skillful code, but with boring, ineffective, or inappropriate graphics, your application will fall short of meeting users' expectations. With Flash, you can import a wide variety of digital image formats, which certainly makes it easy to create visually appealing work. This chapter explores the two groups of graphics, bitmap and vector, and discusses their strengths and weaknesses as well as some interesting things you can do with them.

BITMAP AND VECTOR IMAGES

All artwork imported or created in Flash can be placed in one of two categories: bitmap or vector. These image types were introduced in Chapter 5, "Importing," but let's start with a review of their definitions.

Bitmap images (also known as "raster images"), such as JPGs, GIFs, and PSDs, are made up of a grid of tiny dots called *pixels*. Each pixel of an image is assigned a color. Bitmap images can be visually richer and have more of a visual impact than vector images but are generally larger in file size than vector artwork and aren't suitable for scaling. In other words, if you enlarge a bitmap image, its quality starts to deteriorate.

Vector images are made up of points, lines, and fills, so they are usually smaller in file size than bitmap images. Also, vector images can be scaled up or down without any loss in quality. Any drawing in Flash, for example, is a vector image. Examples of vector formats include EPS, Illustrator, and shape drawings done in Flash with the drawing tools.

When to Use Bitmap or Vector

Deciding whether to use a bitmap or vector image depends on many factors. Here are a few guidelines and exceptions to help you make that decision:

- Images such as faces, landscapes, or other photographic images with gradients are usually best suited to the bitmap format.

- Images with solid shapes and lines, such as a simple company logo or a line drawing, are usually better as vector artwork.

- For a different effect or artistic style, converting bitmaps to vector using Flash (discussed later in this chapter under "Using Trace Bitmap") sometimes gives you interesting results.

- Complex vector artwork is processor-intensive, especially if you're moving it onscreen. Converting it to a bitmap image can sometimes be more effective.

- Using both image types together can produce attractive results. Having a bitmap image with crisp vector artwork layered on top can be quite effective.

When in doubt, experiment by testing your image in both formats to see the differences. You might be surprised by the results visually and in terms of performance.

BITMAP IMAGES

All available image formats are discussed in detail in Chapter 5.

The three main types of images you work with in Flash are JPGs, GIFs, and PNGs. The following sections give you an idea of these formats' intended uses and differences.

GIF

GIFs work well for a wide variety of images, but the format supports a maximum of 256 colors in its palette, so it isn't recommended for images with a broad range of colors, such as photographs or images with complex gradations in color—skin tones, sunsets, or water, for example. Figure 14.1 shows a photograph saved as a GIF.

FIGURE 14.1
An example of a bitmap image in GIF format, showing banding and pixelation.

The photograph looks fairly good, but you can see some color banding in the background and pixelation in the facial area.

JPG

JPG files can have smaller file sizes than GIF files and offer more color support. The downside is that they use lossy encoding, which means that as you increase the compression, you also increase artifacts in the image, which in turn reduces the image quality. With lossy encoding, you permanently lose image quality because of the compression. Figure 14.2 shows the previous GIF image saved as a JPG at 100% quality.

FIGURE 14.2
Saving an image as a JPG at maximum quality.

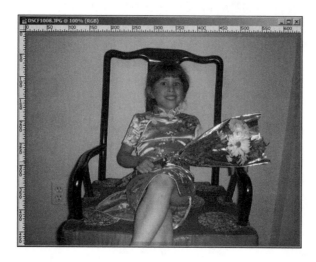

This photo looks great, don't you think? Unfortunately, as a 1600×1200 image, it's almost 550KB. Figure 14.3 shows the same image at 0% quality.

FIGURE 14.3
Saving the same image at minimum quality.

The file is now only 51KB, but the quality has gone way down. You can see artifacts all over the image, and it's very blurry.

PNG

The PNG format is technically superior to GIF and JPG because it supports alpha channels and a higher number of colors.Despite that, however, it isn't nearly as ubiquitous as GIFs and JPGs. That's unfortunate, because not only do PNGs handle photographic imagery and technical, art-based imagery, they also use lossless encoding, so there are no image artifacts.

PNG-24 also supports multiple levels of transparency; GIF supports only a single level of transparency, and JPG supports none. With PNGs, you can create an image with partially or completely transparent elements; in short, whatever the image looks like in your image authoring environment, that's what it will look like in Flash. Figure 14.4 shows the previous image as a PNG file.

FIGURE 14.4
The same image saved in the PNG format.

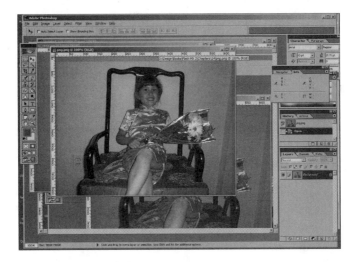

The image is more than 900KB, but the quality is the highest, and it offers the most versatility for your use, as it's retained all the color information without any loss of quality.

When using images in Flash, don't pick one format over another haphazardly; if you're using a drawn graphic, select GIF. If you're using a photo, choose JPG. If you need complicated transparency effects or a very high-quality image, use a PNG file.

Compression in Flash

As you have learned, you can compress bitmap artwork before importing it into Flash. For example, when saving a JPG image from an image program such as Macromedia Fireworks, you can set the compression anywhere between 1% and 100%. With PNG images, you can choose from 8-, 24-, or 32-bit, and with GIF images, you can select the number of colors (up to 256).

However, because Flash has the built-in capability to apply compression to any imported images, it's usually best to import the highest quality image you can. You can then adjust the compression from directly within Flash. To do this, open the Bitmap Properties dialog box by right-clicking the image in the Library and selecting Properties (see Figure 14.5).

FIGURE 14.5
Adjusting compression in the Bitmap Properties dialog box.

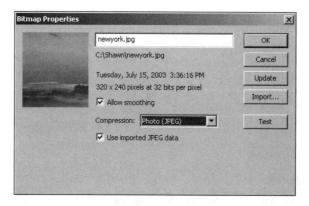

The Photo (JPEG) Compression Setting

In the Bitmap Properties dialog box of a JPG image, the compression is set to Photo (JPEG). By default, the Use Imported JPEG Data check box is selected, and the compression is set to the percentage the image was originally saved at. If you clear the Use Imported JPEG Data check box, you can enter a quality setting between 0 and 100, with 100 being the highest quality. Remember: If the image was created at 80%, setting it at 90% does *not* improve the quality. As well, if you import a JPEG with 80% compression and set the compression in Flash to 80%, you're actually compressing the image twice—its compression setting would then equal about 60%.

As a rule of thumb, between 40% and 70% is usually acceptable compression. You can also select Lossless (PNG/GIF) from the Compression list box, but for JPG images, this setting results in a very large file size, so it's not recommended.

The Lossless (PNG/GIF) Compression Setting

With a GIF or a PNG image, the compression is set to Lossless (PNG/GIF). There are no settings for this option (other than smoothing, which is discussed later in this chapter), but you can still select the Photo (JPEG) compression setting and apply JPEG compression to those images.

Instead of selecting Use Imported JPEG Data, however, select the Use Document Default Quality option. This option sets the JPEG compression to whatever the document default setting is in the publish settings. This enables you to use one setting for many or even all images in a project. As a general rule, setting compression for each bitmap in your project is recommended.

See Chapter 23, "Publishing," for more information on global settings.

Testing Compression Settings

You can quickly test your compression changes by clicking the Test button, which shows you the compressed file size at the bottom of the Bitmap Properties dialog box (see Figure 14.6).

FIGURE 14.6
A JPEG image with compression set to 50%.

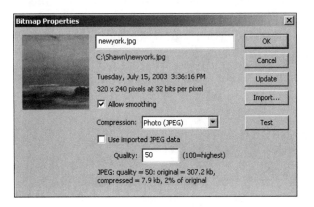

The preview image in the top-left corner of the Bitmap Properties dialog box updates to show you what the compressed image will actually look like. You can also right-click the image and zoom in and out to check the quality for artifacts and banding, as shown in Figure 14.7. This allows you to play with the setting for each image. You can also adjust the quality to low, medium, or high, but keep in mind this is only the preview quality setting, not the image quality or the document setting. You can read more on the Quality setting in Chapter 23. The ideal is a balance between an acceptable file size and an acceptable image, which depends on the project needs and the image itself.

FIGURE 14.7
The preview menu in the Bitmap Properties dialog box.

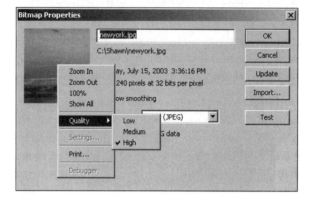

The Allow Smoothing Option

The Allow Smoothing check box controls whether anti-aliasing is turned on or off; when you select this check box, anti-aliasing is enabled for your image. Figure 14.8 compares two images with Allow Smoothing turned on and off. Deciding whether to enable this option depends on the image. Again, clicking Test allows you to preview it in the Bitmap Properties dialog box. This option normally doesn't affect file size, so it's purely a visual decision.

FIGURE 14.8
A magnified example of turning smoothing on and off.

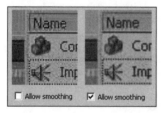

Importing Compressed Images

To ensure maximum image quality, you should import the highest quality image possible, which enables you to set the image quality in Flash.

Editing a Bitmap

Sometimes after importing a bitmap image into your movie, you need to edit it. You might find that you need to resize the image or crop it or alter it in some way. You can change your bitmap in any of the following ways:

- You can edit your bitmap outside Flash and reimport the updated image. To do this, edit your image in another application (such as Adobe Photoshop or Macromedia Fireworks), save it (overwriting the original image you imported into Flash), right-click (Macintosh: Control-click) the image in the Library, and choose Update from the pop-up menu. A slightly shorter method is right-clicking (Macintosh: Control-clicking) the image in the Library and selecting Edit With to choose the program you want to use for editing.

- You can break apart your bitmap by choosing Modify, Break Apart from the menu or by right-clicking (Macintosh: Control-clicking) the bitmap on the stage and selecting Break Apart. *Breaking apart* turns your bitmap into an editable square and enables you to delete portions of it, using the Selection tool (and pressing Delete) or using the Eraser or Magic Wand tool. You can make small selections and reuse portions of your bitmap, but even if you take only one pixel from an 800×600 image and use that, Flash exports the entire image when you publish your movie, so this method is *not* recommended.

- You can use the Trace Bitmap command (described later in this chapter in "Using Trace Bitmap") to convert your bitmap into a vector image.

Loading Images Using ActionScript

In addition to importing images into the Flash authoring environment, you can load JPG images into Flash at runtime, which enables you to create photo albums and slide shows without needing to have all your images stored in your Flash movie. Loading images at runtime helps cut down on your movie's initial load time—the user has to load only the movie itself, not the accompanying images, before playback starts—and frees you from needing to know how many images you're loading into your environment. It also enables you to change an image in your project without having to open the Flash movie and export it again. To load images into your movie, use loadMovie() or loadMovieNum(). To use loadMovie() as a function, use the following syntax:

loadMovie("*url*", *target* [, *method*]);

The difference between GET and POST is explained in Chapter 10, "ActionScript: Functions, Events, and Objects."

url is a string representing the location of your file. *target* is the movie clip to load the file into. *method* is an optional parameter, which can be GET or POST, that determines how any variables you're attaching to the end of the URL are sent. Here's an example of using loadMovie():

loadMovie("my_picture.jpg", my_mc);

To use loadMovie() as a method of the MovieClip object, use the following syntax:

my_mc.loadMovie("*url*" [, *method*]);

url is a string representing the location of your file. Again, *method* is an optional parameter (GET or POST) that determines how any variables you're attaching to the end of the URL are sent. For example, to load a file into a movie clip named my_clip, you would use the following code:

my_clip.loadMovie("my_picture.jpg");

To use loadMovieNum(), use the following syntax:

loadMovieNum("*url*", *level* [, *method*]);

url is a string representing the location of your file. *level* is a number representing the level (for example, 0 is the root) into which you're loading the file. The optional *method* parameter is used for the same purpose as with loadMovie(). For example, to load an image into level 1 of your movie, you might use the following code:

loadMovieNum("my_picture.jpg", 1);

When used with the XML class, loadMovie() enables you to create slideshow applications that let you maintain external lists of images to load. You can update this list without having to alter your SWF. It's an incredibly powerful feature to have at your disposal.

For more information on XML, see Chapter 17, "Accessing External Data."

It's also possible to load an image into HTML-formatted text in a text field using the <img> tag. For more information, see the "HTML in Text" section of Chapter 13, "Text."

When you place an image in your movie and export it, it gets compressed according to the settings you choose, whether individually or in the publish settings. When you load a JPG into your movie using loadMovie() or loadMovieNum(), no compression takes place. As a result, a JPG that's shifted, rotated, or scaled onscreen can start to look jagged and rough. You won't have the same problem with bitmaps loaded at runtime.

VECTOR IMAGES

Vector artwork comes in a few different formats. You can create it directly in Flash with the drawing tools or import it as EPS, PDF, or Illustrator files. After importing vector artwork into Flash, you can modify it directly, unlike bitmap images. You can add, delete, and modify any lines, points, fills, and gradients the vector image is composed of.

Optimizing Vector Artwork

Generally, vector files are smaller than bitmap files, so why would you need to optimize vector artwork? With more complex vector artwork, the file size can increase, and there's usually room to optimize the file to make it smaller. The other important reason to optimize is playback speed. Depending on your artwork, moving a lot of lines, fills, points, and gradients around the screen can be processor-intensive, thus slowing down playback, especially on older computers. This is where optimizing comes into play. As with everything, you need to balance the look you want with file size and playback speed.

The following list describes the three commands available under the Modify, Shape menu choice to help you optimize your vector artwork. Keep in mind that you can reuse these commands until you get the result you want.

- **Smooth**   The Smooth command reduces the number of irregular points and curves in your artwork, aiming to smooth it out. As you can see in Figure 14.9, you can reuse this command until you get the desired effect.

FIGURE 14.9
The Smooth command in action.

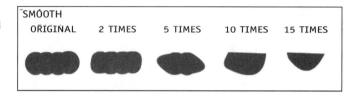

- **Straighten** This command also reduces the number of irregular points and curves in your artwork, but with more angular results (see Figure 14.10).

FIGURE 14.10
An example of using the Straighten command.

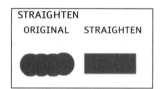

- **Optimize** This command optimizes the curves in your artwork. It's similar to using the Smooth command several times. Use the Smoothing slider control to adjust the smoothing level. Select the Use Multiple Passes check box to further increase the smoothing (see Figure 14.11). This option also enhances optimization by running the command multiple times.

FIGURE 14.11
The Optimize Curves dialog box.

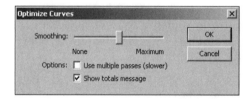

If you select the Show Totals Message check box, you'll see a message box after the optimizing is finished (see Figure 14.12), which displays the number of curves before and after optimizing and indicates the amount of reduction as a % value.

FIGURE 14.12
The message box showing optimization results.

Modifying Vector Artwork

You learned a few ways of modifying vector artwork, such as with the Free Transform, Pen, and Selection tools, in Chapter 2, "Overview of the Interface and Tools." These tools are great for modifying your vector artwork, whether it's moving a point or line or changing or adding a curve in your drawing. The following list explains a few additional methods for modifying your vector artwork. All the following commands can be found under the Modify, Shape menu (see Figure 14.13):

FIGURE 14.13
Options under the Modify, Shape menu.

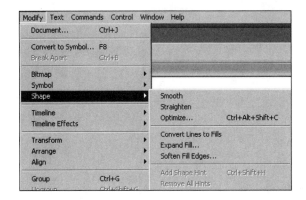

- **Convert Lines to Fills**   This command does exactly that—converts any selected lines to fills. With this command, you can apply different fills, including gradients, which you can't do with lines. Fills also offer more manipulation possibilities than lines and are slightly less processor-intensive, meaning you can further optimize your artwork.

- **Expand Fill**   You can expand or contract (inset) a selected fill with this command and set the distance of the expansion or contraction in pixels (see Figure 14.14).

FIGURE 14.14
The Expand Fill dialog box.

- **Soften Fill Edges**   This command is the closest thing Flash has to a blur effect. Flash accomplishes this softening by creating copies of the selected fill and adjusting the alpha (transparency) level on each subsequent copy. Use the Soften Fill Edges dialog box (see Figure 14.15) to select the distance of each copy in pixels and the number of copies (steps). You can also choose the direction for this operation—expand or contract (inset).

FIGURE 14.15
The Soften Fill Edges dialog box.

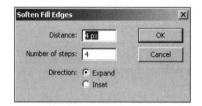

Figure 14.16 shows a magnification of a solid black circle with the Soften Fill Edges command applied. I used a distance of 5 pixels and specified 5 steps, set to Expand.

FIGURE 14.16
A magnified example of the Soften Fill Edges command.

The Soften Fill Edges command works by adjusting the alpha level of shapes or symbols. Movement onscreen can be processor-intensive for older machines, so use it with care.

Using Trace Bitmap

At times you need to convert a bitmap image to vector artwork when you're trying to achieve a certain look or style. Maybe you're testing to see whether a vector version would result in a smaller file size, or you might think the artwork is better suited to vector, but you have only a bitmap version. To do this, you could trace over the image with Flash tools or use another program, such as Adobe Streamline. You can also have Flash do it for you with the Trace Bitmap command. Simply select any bitmap image on the stage, and choose Modify, Bitmap, Trace Bitmap from the menu. Use the Trace Bitmap dialog box (see Figure 14.17) to select and enter values determining how you want your bitmap image traced.

FIGURE 14.17
The Trace Bitmap
dialog box.

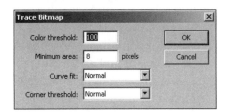

To achieve the look you want with this command, you'll probably need to try out different settings. It's best to try the default settings first and see the result; then you can adjust settings and check the difference. When using this command, keep in mind that converting to vector doesn't always guarantee a smaller file size. Complex vector artwork with a lot of points, lines, curves, and fills can sometimes be larger in file size than bitmap images. As well, complex vector artwork can be processor-intensive if you're moving it onscreen, making animation next to impossible. Experimenting with different settings is the best way to determine whether vector is the way to go. These are the options available in the Trace Bitmap dialog box:

- **Color Threshold** The Color Threshold value can be between 0 and 500, with a default of 100. This value sets the threshold Flash uses to determine how many colors are in your vector artwork, with 0 being the most colors and 500 the least.

- **Minimum Area** This value sets the size of the area that the Color Threshold uses to determine colors. The range is between 1 and 1,000. A smaller number gives you more precise color results. The default setting is 8.

- **Curve Fit** This setting controls the Minimum Area size in the vector artwork and determines how smoothly the lines are drawn. Choose from Curve Fit, Pixels, Very Tight, Normal, Smooth, and Very Smooth.

- **Corner Threshold** This setting controls how corners are handled in your vector artwork. Choose from Many Corners, Normal, and Few Corners.

When you're experimenting with settings for the Trace Bitmap command, remember that complex artwork can take a while to process.

Figure 14.18 shows three images. The original on the left is a JPG image. The center image was produced by using the Trace Bitmap command, with the Color Threshold set to 100 and the other settings at their defaults (Minimum Area of 8, Curve Fit set to Normal, and Corner Threshold set to Normal). The third image, on the right, was created by using a Color Threshold setting of 500 and leaving the other settings at their defaults. As you can see, sometimes you achieve the most interesting results with the simplest changes.

FIGURE 14.18
Examples of experimenting with Trace Bitmap settings.

ORIGINAL JPG
IMAGE

VECTOR IMAGE
WITH COLOR
THRESHOLD
OF 100

VECTOR IMAGE
WITH COLOR
THRESHOLD
OF 500

TRANSFORMING BITMAP AND VECTOR ARTWORK

You can use the Free Transform tool to manipulate bitmap or vector objects as well as symbols. You can also use the commands available under the Modify, Transform menu choice (see Figure 14.19).

Many of the commands described in the following list can also be performed with the Free Transform tool:

- **Free Transform** This command is the same as clicking the Free Transform tool on the toolbar.

- **Distort** This command enables you to pull any corner or midline point and move it around freely. Try it out—the results are interesting.

- **Envelope** This command gives you control of the Subselection tool. It's similar to the Distort command but gives you more points to choose from. You can bend and stretch your shape a number of different ways for some cool results.

- **Scale**   This command enables you to scale your object in the same way as holding down the Shift key and selecting a corner.

- **Rotate and Skew**   This command turns corner points into rotating points and line points into skewable points.

- **Rotate 90 CW**   This command rotates the object 90 degrees clockwise.

- **Rotate 90 CCW**   This command rotates the object 90 degrees counterclockwise.

- **Flip Vertical**   This command flips your object vertically.

- **Flip Horizontal**   This command flips your object horizontally.

FIGURE 14.19
Commands available under the Modify, Transform menu choice.

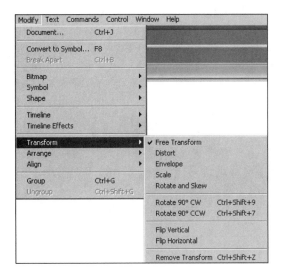

Flash remembers any modification made using these commands on a symbol or a bitmap. You can, at any time, select Modify, Remove Transform from the menu (keyboard shortcut: **Ctrl+Shift+Z**), and your symbol is transformed back to its original state before skewing, resizing, rotating, or distorting. Unfortunately, this doesn't work on vector artwork. After you've deselected a vector object, the transformation is not reversible with Remove Transform, but you can always use the Undo command (keyboard shortcut: **Ctrl+Z**).

GROUPS

As with other popular graphics programs, Flash supports *grouping*, which enables you to select a number of items of any kind and group them. Grouping makes it easier to move several items at once and perform actions (such as transforming) on all items in a group simultaneously. Grouping is especially useful for organizing nonanimated, static artwork.

Creating a Group

To group items, simply select the items you want to group using the Selection tool, and then choose Modify, Group from the menu (keyboard shortcut: **Ctrl+G**). A group is treated as an object, and a blue keyline is displayed around the group. In Figure 14.20, I've selected a bitmap image, some text, and some vector artwork and grouped them all.

FIGURE 14.20
A group containing different objects, including a bitmap image, text, and some shapes.

A group acts somewhat similarly to a movie clip containing items. To edit group items, double-click the group on the stage. You're then in Edit Group mode, as shown in Figure 14.21.

FIGURE 14.21
The icon indicates you're in Edit Group mode.

In Figure 14.22, notice that the only properties available for a group are height, width, and x/y position.

FIGURE 14.22
Group properties.

Using Symbols Versus Groups

For more information on symbols, see Chapter 3, "The Library, Symbols, and the Timeline."

Keep in mind that symbols are much more powerful than groups. You can't name groups, assign a color to them, or control them with ActionScript. As well, groups don't have their own independent timeline, as symbols do. Technically, you *can* perform tweening with groups, but using symbols is the recommended method.

Ungrouping

To ungroup a group, select the group, and then choose Modify, Ungroup from the menu (keyboard shortcut: **Ctrl+Shift+G**), or use Modify, Break Apart (Windows: **Ctrl+B**; Macintosh: **Command+B**).

POINTS TO REMEMBER

- The decision to use vector or bitmap isn't always an easy one. Experimenting with both is sometimes necessary.

- The PNG format is usually the best format for bitmap images.

- Always try to import the highest quality (the least compressed) bitmaps available. You can compress bitmapped images from within Flash.

- Loading bitmaps with ActionScript cuts down on the initial file size of your movie and allows you to change bitmaps without opening the Flash movie and exporting an SWF again.

- The Trace Bitmap command can be useful for giving bitmap images a different look and style.

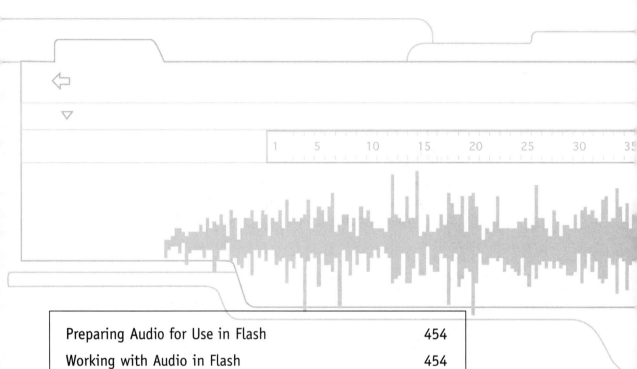

CHAPTER 15

AUDIO

SOUND IS OFTEN THE LAST COMPONENT THAT'S CONSIDERED IN AN INTERACTIVE project. For example, all too often you see a last-minute impulsive decision to throw in an infinite techno loop without offering a Stop or Turn Off button for the user. Developers and designers often don't put enough thought into the intelligent and appropriate use of sound. Of course, sometimes no sound at all is appropriate; however, even subtle navigational "click" sounds help communicate successful interaction to users.

Unlike visuals, which are limited to about a 180-degree range of sight, sound can be sensed from a full 360 degrees. As a medium, sound can communicate without requiring much energy or focus, unlike images that require direct visual contact.

PREPARING AUDIO FOR USE IN FLASH

If you prefer to export your compressed sounds from a third-party sound application, Flash has options for using the quality of the original sound file.

When gathering, creating, and preparing your audio for integration into Macromedia Flash MX 2004, the most important step is ensuring that you use the highest quality sample possible. Although you might be using sound applications to crop, edit, and apply effects, keeping your sounds at a top quality of 44.1KHz (stereo quality) is essential.

A sound file is no different from an image file, in that both are just digital representations. If you compress either type of file, you can't get back the quality you originally had. Because Flash has its own audio export options, you should compress your audio only one time.

Flash MX 2004 accepts the most common audio formats: WAV files, AIFF (Macintosh), and, of course, MP3. Before importing audio into Flash MX 2004, you can save time by editing and cropping the audio file into the exact audio pieces you want. Although Flash MX 2004 does include an audio editor, it's quite rudimentary and doesn't perform more fine-tuned editing. If you have access to an audio editor, do all your sound cropping with it to get the file as small as possible. Flash MX 2004 does not have prebuilt audio effects such as reverb or delay, either, so you should apply any sort of audio enhancements, such as reverb, chorus, or delay, before importing the audio file.

WORKING WITH AUDIO IN FLASH

There are several different ways in which audio can be used with and integrated into Flash. You can apply sounds directly to button frames and states, you can drop audio onto timeline frames, you can stream external and internal sounds that are synchronized with the Timeline, and you can create event-based sound interactions by using the Sound object in ActionScript.

If you're looking for a quick and easy way to add sound to buttons, have simple background music, or include audio with no controls, you can perform these tasks quite simply by dragging audio files from the Library.

Adding Sounds to Buttons via Frames

If you're familiar with using buttons from previous Flash versions, you should recognize the button Timeline shown in Figure 15.1.

FIGURE 15.1
Timeline of a button.

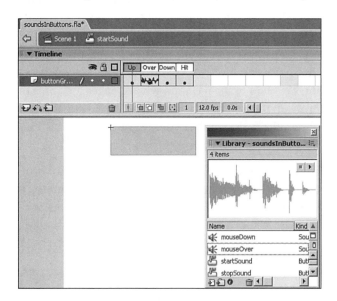

After you have imported a sound into the Library, you can simply drag it from the Library onto the frame corresponding to the mouse state you want. You can see in Figure 15.1 that the waveform of the mouseOver sound is visually displayed in the Timeline frame. You can also add sounds to other frames in the button to complete the navigational sounds.

Chapter 5, "Importing," explains some of the options available when importing audio into Flash. Feel free to review this chapter again for a refresher on the importing process.

Adding Sounds to the Timeline: Linear Scoring

One of the most common ways to incorporate sound for linear or narrative pieces, whether they be animations, product demos, or e-learning applications, is through *timeline scoring*. This is a great way to put together a linear piece, because you have an excellent visual display of where sounds start and stop to help you arrange your sound and music. Even more important, with timeline composing you can take advantage of Flash's streaming property, which synchronizes your animations with your sound design.

For almost all storytelling, motion graphics, and animation work done with Flash, synching visuals with the audio is essential. Much like other video formats, such as QuickTime, the process of displaying graphics and playing audio relies on dropping visual frames to create a cohesive experience. It's easier to process information when audio is continuous and there's a loss in visuals than when images are constant but there are drops in the audio. For this reason, when streaming sounds, audio is always the first priority. If necessary, the Timeline can skip ahead to keep up with the audio, thus ensuring proper synching of visuals and audio.

Sound is a much more pleasing and effective form of information delivery if you skip visual frames to keep up with audio that does not skip, hiccup, or buffer. This is precisely what Flash does when you place sounds on the Timeline and set them to streaming. Figure 15.2 shows a snapshot of a Timeline used to compose the audio in the animation that's playing.

FIGURE 15.2
Timeline composing: In this timeline, the streaming sound on the bottom layer is used in an animation sequence.

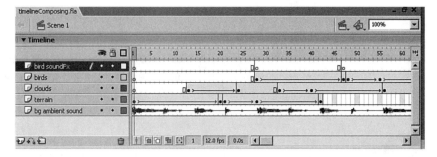

You can see that just as animated elements have their own layers, so do their accompanying sounds. This layer structure gives you an easy visual way to organize, structure, and design your sound and animations. To place sounds on the Timeline, you simply select the frame where you want to add it, insert a keyframe, and drag the sound from the Library to the stage. Next, click the frame in the Timeline and make some modifications in the Property inspector (see Figure 15.3).

FIGURE 15.3
Properties for frame-based sound.

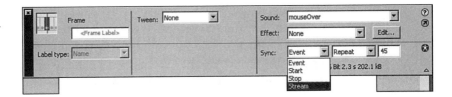

Here you can see that you can use a number of different properties to affect the way sound is produced. If you select the frame in the Timeline where the sound starts, you can view the properties for that sound. The bg music sound file from the Library was selected from the Sound drop-down list, and in the Sync drop-down list, the sound was changed from the default Event setting to Stream. This selection ensures that the accompanying visuals will flow and move at the same tempo and pace as the audio, which is essential for audio-visual synchronization.

Notice in Figure 15.3 that there are two other properties next to the Sync options. Use the drop-down list to the right to select Repeat or Loop. Use the text box to the right to specify how many times you want to play the sound (if you select Repeat). Selecting Loop means you want to have the sound loop continuously.

To find out what the Edit button does, continue reading.

Editing Sounds in Flash

When you click the Edit button in the Property inspector, the Edit Envelope dialog box, shown in Figure 15.4, opens.

FIGURE 15.4
Editing sound properties for the bg music loop.

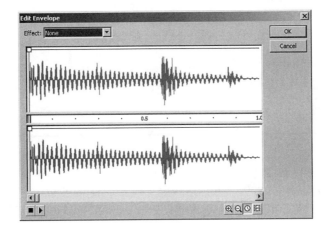

This interface gives you control over the envelopes used for sound volume and pan. It's the only place where you can access sounds using *envelopes*, which enable you to create node points. Node points act as a sort of "keyframe" for shifting a sound's volume or pan properties. To create a node point, you click the envelope where you want to create the node and then adjust volume and pan properties. Envelopes are the perfect visual metaphor for the way sounds behave.

Notice that two separate channels are visible. They represent the left and right channels of a stereo sound, so you can control the volume and pan of each channel separately. For example, by turning the volume down on one channel, in essence you're panning that sound in the direction of the channel that still has volume. *Pan* refers to the left/right stereo range a sound can be played in. Panning to the left represents a sound moving from the center to the left. If you imagine it with headphones, panning refers to the left and right outputs. This is a powerful way to move sound in space and create more realistic soundtracks for elements that are moving from left to right or right to left onscreen.

Flash's prebuilt effects make it easier to modify sound properties. Figure 15.5 shows selecting the Fade In effect to automatically create a gradual volume increase at the beginning of the sound file.

FIGURE 15.5
Selecting one of Flash's prebuilt effects.

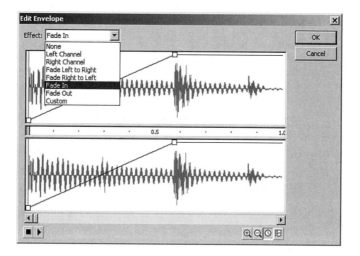

You can use any of these preset effects and then customize the node points on your own. You can create and manipulate as many as eight node points for each sound, which gives you some flexibility in fading sounds in and out. Flash's prebuilt effects give you the opportunity to focus on more interesting sound editing.

Although you can certainly do a professional-level job of applying sounds directly to buttons and Timeline frames, the true power of interactive sound with Flash comes from the Sound object, discussed in the remainder of this chapter. Using the Sound object is quick and easy and adds an element of fun to your project development.

INTERACTIVE AUDIO

If you don't have any available sound files or loops, feel free to download the sample music files from this book's companion web site at www. flashdemystified. com.

Without the Sound object, you'd be stuck in a linear landscape, and when you want to create an interactive application, linear often falls short. By incorporating the Sound object, which just means giving a sound a unique name and identifier, you can control audio with a number of different elements, such as dynamic input, mouse positions, mouse clicks, objects colliding, number of simultaneous visitors—the ideas are endless. You can use several parameters to control, manipulate, and move sound around the user's environment. You can obtain data for these parameters from key presses, mouse position, or data that loads dynamically, such as the date and time or stock information. There's no limit to what you can use to control sound.

With this degree of control over sound, effects, and music, you can programmatically create sophisticated environments that respond to other objects as well as the user. So take a look at the process of taking a sound already in the Library and turning it into a Sound object.

In this example, the same bg music sound used to illustrate timeline composing is used to explain how to work with the Sound object. When you import a sound into the Library, first you need to give it a linkage identifier. Right-click (Macintosh: Command-click) the sound in the Library, and choose Linkage to open the Linkage Properties dialog box, shown in Figure 15.6.

Setting the Export for ActionScript option makes the Sound object available for use in ActionScript code. Select the Export for ActionScript check box, and enter a name for this sound in the Identifier text box. Make sure you use a name that's relevant for the sound you're using, especially if you're using multiple sounds in your movie. In this example, the name drums has been entered as the identifier for the sound.

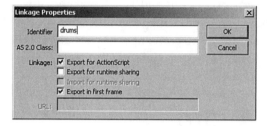

Creating a *Sound* Object

Now that you've assigned an identifier to the sound in the Library, you're ready to create the Sound object with ActionScript. It takes only a few steps to create a Sound object and get it to start playing. Take a look at the following code for setting up the Sound object:

```
drums = new Sound();
drums.attachSound("drums");
drums.start();
```

If you enter that code and test your movie (keyboard shortcut: **Ctrl+Enter**), you should hear the sound start and then stop when it's finished. Now take another look at this code to get a better grasp of what just happened. The following line creates a new instance of a Sound object and an identifier called drums:

```
drums = new Sound();
```

You need to add this code line for every sound whose properties (such as volume and pan) you want to control. The second line is where you use the identifier you gave the sound in the Linkage Properties dialog box:

```
drums.attachSound("drums");
```

This code literally attaches the sound with the identifier drums to the newly formed Sound object. Last, you start the sound by calling the Sound object's start() method:

```
drums.start();
```

This line is actually a simplified form of the start() method. Two parameters can be used to control the sound playback. The actual syntax is as follows:

```
drums.start([SecondOffset, loop]);
```

The first parameter, *SecondOffset*, is a value used to determine where you want to start from in the sound. This value is in seconds, so for more accuracy, you need to use milliseconds. (For example, 2.500 milliseconds is equal to 2.5 seconds.) If you use a value other than 0 for this parameter, after the sound has reached the end, it starts over and loops again from the same offset position specified in the original parameter.

The second parameter, *loop*, is the number of times you want the sound to repeat. It's equivalent to the parameter used in the Timeline composing example. Setting this parameter in ActionScript, however, means you can change this value dynamically if you like.

To stop the sound, attach the following code to a button, a frame, or an event:

```
drums.stop();
```

Before you get into adjusting a sound's volume and pan, it's important to understand the constructor for the Sound object a bit more clearly so that you can use and control more than one sound separately.

Using Multiple *Sound* Objects

When you're planning to use multiple sounds, it's important to place each sound inside its own movie clip so that you can control the sounds separately. If you don't assign specific references to the Sound object when it's created, any changes to volume or pan affect other Sound objects as well. To assign specific references, you simply need to alter the preceding code so that it's embedded inside a MovieClip object, as shown here:

```
_root.createEmptyMovieClip("drums", 100);
drums.loop = new Sound(this);
drums.loop.attachSound("drums");
drums.start(0,999);
```

This code creates a Sound object called loop inside the newly created movie clip, drums. In the second line, including the this reference means you're referencing the drums movie clip. You now have a reference to a Sound object that can be controlled independently of all other sounds.

Because you need to create movie clips to act as containers for each Sound object, creating one movie clip that can be used to automatically create Sound objects is handy. In the following pages, you'll create a simple movie clip component for creating and controlling sounds easily.

Create a new movie clip on the stage, and give it the name soundObject. Right-click the movie clip to edit it. Inside this new soundObject movie clip, place the following code on the first frame of the Timeline:

```
loop = new Sound(this);
loop.attachSound(this._name);
loop.start(0,999);
```

Now you have the same thing as the previous example, in which you created an empty movie clip through code, with the exception that the attached sound is set to the movie clip's instance name. This makes it easy to quickly get control over sounds. Now you can just create instances of this one soundObject movie clip and give it different instance names in the Property inspector to change the reference to the sound linked in the Library.

Now that you have a self-contained movie clip that you can use as a prototype for all sounds, you can add start and stop buttons inside this movie clip so that you can turn the sound on and off. Inside the newly created movie clip, create two buttons—one for starting the sound and one for stopping it. In this example, the buttons have been labeled and given the instance names playBTN and stopBTN, and the following code has been added to the frame action:

```
playBTN.onPress = function(){
    loop.stop();
    loop.start(0,999);
}

stopBTN.onPress = function(){
    loop.stop();
}
```

Notice that a stop() command was also added in the playBTN code. It's been added in case the sound is already playing and the user clicks the Play button; the stop() command ensures that the sounds aren't doubled up and overlapping. Try testing the movie with this code to make sure these buttons trigger the sound to start and stop.

Now that you have an easy way to get Sound objects initialized and running in your movie, take a look at controlling sound properties in the next section.

Controlling Volume of Sounds

If you want to modify a sound's volume, there are only two methods you can use: getVolume() or setVolume(). By default, all sounds are set to a maximum value of 100. To change or affect the volume for the previous drums example, you would use the following code:

```
drums.loop.setVolume(50);
```

This line of code sets the volume of the specific sound drums.loop to a level of 50—cutting the volume in half from the preset value of 100. Continuing with the self-contained Sound object movie clip, you can create two more buttons, + and -, to increase and decrease volume. After creating these buttons and giving them instance names of addVolume and reduceVolume, you can use the following code to let the user increase the sound's volume:

```
addVolume.onPress = function(){
loop.setVolume(getVolume() +5);
}
```

Just like that, you're dynamically increasing the volume based on the sound's current volume. The volume range for playback is between 0 and 100, so you should add an if statement, as shown in the following code, that checks to see whether you're at the maximum value, thus ensuring that you never go over 100:

```
addVolume.onPress = function(){

if (loop.getVolume <100){
loop.setVolume(getVolume() +5);
}

}
```

If you try to increase the volume when the sound is already at 100, you bypass the if statement, and nothing happens. It's even more important to place similar code on the reduceVolume button. When Flash receives negative numbers as pan values, it doesn't register the value's negative aspect and treats the number as a positive. For this reason, you should add a measure to prevent negative values from being used when reducing volume, as shown in this example:

```
reduceVolume.onPress = function(){

if (loop.getVolume >0){
loop.setVolume(getVolume() -5);
}


}
```

This one little if statement is registered and runs only if the sound's volume still stands above 0. If not, no action is performed.

These code examples have illustrated basic volume control over an imported sound that was turned into a Sound object. It's really as easy as it looks. There are only two primary methods or properties that you can control in a Sound object that directly affect its sound: volume and pan. Now that you've seen an example with volume, turn your attention to one of the most powerful aspects of interactive audio: panning.

CONTROLLING PAN VIA ACTIONSCRIPT

Pan, one of the most important properties when dealing with sound, allows full movement of audio in a stereo landscape. The use of pan is what makes the sound "move"—or seem to. Panning is altering or shifting the balance of a Sound object between the left and right channels.

You can affect both volume and pan through direct editing of the sound. However, this method of achieving sound movement is limited. When editing a sound in the Sound Editor, you lose the ability to control the same sound dynamically—through code. A better way to change volume or pan is directly through the methods and properties of the Sound object.

Just as you have getVolume() and setVolume() for changing volume, you have a similar pair of methods for changing the location of sound in your stereo framing: getPan() and setPan(). The people at Macromedia were certainly on their toes when they labeled these methods to control sound!

Not many developers think about panning sound when they're putting together interactive projects. Often, just controlling multiple sounds is considered serious audio work in a project. However, taking some extra time to play with panning your Sound objects can take your audio effects as well as your entire interactive application to another level.

Games are an excellent example of successfully producing sound in Flash. Gaming is synonymous with sound and music, and games are filled with background audio, narration, sound effects, musical transitions, and more. Often multiple sounds are played and fired off simultaneously in games, and pan is used extensively to get the most out of layering sounds, giving each sound its own "place" in the stereo field.

Just as a visual designer has a canvas or stage to work on, so does an audio engineer or designer. Although sound involves working in a larger environment than visual images do, you can still "visualize" your sound design. When panning sounds, you can place a sound anywhere between the extremes of the left channel (–100) and the right channel (+100). The scope of the stereo range looks somewhat like this:

```
LEFT - 100 ]---------[ CENTER (0) ]------------[ RIGHT +100
```

You can place audio anywhere in this range. By default, sounds are set to 0 and placed in the center, so why would you need to change this? One of the first uses that comes to mind is following a character or an object in a 2D or 3D game. Say you have a shooting game in which you shoot arrows at a flying dragon. Several sounds could be involved: the background environment, theme music, the dragon flapping its wings and breathing fire, shooting the arrow, hitting a target with the arrow, and so on. To simulate the sound of the dragon "moving" with the actual dragon on stage, you could tie the dragon's location to the setPan() method of the Sound object.

Instead of a dragon, take a look at an example of tying the sound directly into the cursor's position. As the mouse is moved left to right, the Sound object follows. Place this code on a main Timeline frame:

```
this.onMouseMove = function(){
drums.loop.setPan((Math.round(_root._xmouse/2.5)-100));
};
```

That's all there is to it. If you added this code to the previous code examples and tested the movie, you should notice the sound following as you move the mouse left to right. All this functionality is a result of this one code line inside an onMouseMove function:

```
drums.loop.setPan((Math.round(_root._xmouse/2.5)-100));
```

Note that this particular line of code assumes a stage width of 500. Because pan gives you a range of –100 to +100 to place your sounds, you need to transfer the possible values to be interpreted for pan to between 0 and 200 so that you can subtract 100 to get to your range of –100 to +100. In other words, if the user's cursor is at the extreme left, or 0, you need to turn this value into –100 by subtracting 100, which is equivalent to panning the sound all the way to the left sound channel. If the cursor is all the way to the right, which equals a value of 200, you subtract 100 to get an end value of +100, which is equivalent to panning the sound all the way to the right sound channel.

You're now starting to see how powerful audio can be with little additional code. The preceding example of shifting the pan is really only one line of code, and now you have sound directly tied into an object. This same code could easily be modified and worked into the _x and _y values of a movie clip so that both volume and pan are affected by the position on stage.

You can track and control a number of other things with the Sound object, and you'll get a closer look at them in the following section as you explore another native sound feature in Flash—dynamically loading sound via MP3s.

LOADING AND PLAYING EXTERNAL MP3 FILES

One of the easiest features to use when working with audio with Flash is accessing MP3 files dynamically without the added nuisance of having to import and modify them inside the Flash environment.

The capability to load external audio files has existed since Flash MX, and not much has changed on the authoring side to affect this feature. Flash can access an external MP3 file in two ways: externally streamed or preloaded into memory.

Streaming an MP3

The most basic way to load an MP3 is to stream it into the Flash Player. As soon as the MP3 has buffered enough to begin playing, it starts. It's the most instantaneous way to begin hearing an external audio source with Flash; however, it comes with a price. First, examine the code used to load an MP3 file from the web. Place this code in a Timeline frame inside a new document:

```
myMP3 = new Sound();
myMP3.loadSound("http://www.crashmedia.com/music/Trogdor.mp3,
➥true");
```

That's it. That code alone will start playing the sound when you test the movie. It's an easy way to control audio, but there are a few catches. The biggest downfall to streaming an MP3 file is that unlike a regular Sound object, you can't access the entire sound file whenever you want, meaning you can't start and stop in different parts of the MP3 file. To understand this, take a look at the .position and .duration properties of a Sound object.

If you create three dynamic text fields on the stage and give them the instance names position, duration, and percent, you can add some code to illustrate what happens when you stream in an MP3 file. Below the original code that was entered, enter the following function:

```
this.onEnterFrame = function(){
position.text = myMP3.position;
duration.text = myMP3.duration;
percent.text = (myMP3.position / myMP3.duration )*100;
}
```

This onEnterFrame function constantly grabs the position and duration values and displays them in the dynamic text fields that were created and calculates the percentage of the MP3 that has loaded.

When this code runs, you can see that the duration value, which is the entire length of the MP3, is constantly increasing. This is because, unfortunately, Flash cannot access the entire length of the file until it has been completely downloaded—and therein lies the rub for maintaining strict control over playback. If you were to stop this sound through the regular means—myMP3.stop();—it would stop the sound, but when you wanted to start it again, you would have to start over at the beginning. When loading an MP3 file that's set to streaming==true, you lose all options to start the sound anywhere except from the beginning.

Loading an External MP3 as a *Sound* Object

Loading external MP3s as streaming becomes a problem if you want to use a longer piece as narration or a voiceover for linear visual content. If you want to use an external MP3 for your audio, yet keep the ability to start and stop anywhere inside the sound, you need to load it as a complete Sound object, as shown here:

```
myMP3=new Sound();
myMP3.loadSound("http://www.crashmedia.com/music/Trogdor.mp3",
➥false);
myMP3.onLoad = function(){
myMP3.start(0,1);
}
```

When you set the streaming parameter in the loadSound() call to false, you need to add an extra handler function that runs when the sound is completely loaded. This is convenient because it saves you from having to build your own preloader, although you certainly can. When the sound is loaded in its entirety, the onLoad() function is called, and whatever code is placed inside this function runs. This example merely starts the sound, but you can use this same function to trigger other events.

For instance, if you wanted to create a visual buffer progress bar for a streaming MP3, you could simply create a new progressBar movie clip at the width you want for 100% and then add the following code into the onEnterFrame function created earlier. The last line is what you're interested in for the progress bar. You can see that the _xscale of the progressBar movie clip scales to the percentage of the MP3 loaded.

When the MP3 is completely loaded at 100%, the `progressBar` movie clip will be the length it was created at.

```
this.onEnterFrame = function(){
position.text = myMP3.position;
duration.text = myMP3.duration;
percent.text = (myMP3.position / myMP3.duration )*100;
progressBar.xscale = (myMP3.position/myMP3.duration )*100;

}
```

This `progressBar` movie clip that's created then grows along the `_xscale` as the percentage of the streaming MP3 being listened to increases.

MP3 Player Deconstruction

To get a better idea of how to incorporate loading into an online MP3 player, take a look at the `Ch15_MP3Player.fla` file available on the book's website. The following code is used to simply play MP3s entered as a URL in an input text box. You can enter this code in a new file, which creates buttons.

The first piece of code is a default value for the Input text box on the stage. An existing online MP3 has been used for this example:

```
currentSong =
"http://www.flashdemystified.com/mp3s/
➥liquid_morphine_maalstroom.mp3";
//********************* LOAD NEW MP3
```

Take a look at the first function, `loadMP3()`, which is used mainly as an initializer:

```
loadMP3 = function()
{
stopAllSounds();
tracker. progressBar._xscale = 0;
startStreaming();
}
```

When this function is called, all sounds that are currently playing stop, `progressBar`'s `_xscale` is set to 0, and then the `startStreaming()` function, which you'll create in a moment, is called. The purpose of the `progressBar` movie clip is to display the amount of music played from the loaded MP3 file.

The following function is where the important stuff happens. The new Sound object is created, the MP3 is loaded via `loadSound()`, and something new and exciting happens—the `onSoundComplete()` method is introduced.

```
startStreaming = function()
{
mp3 = new Sound();
mp3.loadSound(currentSong, true);
mp3.onSoundComplete = function()
{
delete mp3;
tracker. progressBar._xscale = 0;
}
}
```

The first two lines of the preceding code create the Sound object and perform a `loadSound()` operation. `currentSong` is used as the value of the MP3 file instead of the URL that was shown earlier. This is because you're dynamically grabbing this value from the Input text box on stage. When a new URL is added and the Load button is clicked, the value of the string entered in the Input text box is used as the source for the streaming MP3.

The `onSoundComplete()` method is explained in "Using the `onSoundComplete()` Method" later in this chapter, but for now, it's a function that acts as an event handler. The event it's handling is the completion of the sound file embedded in the Sound object. When this sound is completed, this function is called and anything residing inside is triggered. In this example, the `mp3` Sound object is being deleted to ensure that no unnecessary RAM is being used by the system, and the `progressBar` movie clip is reset to 0 `_xscale`.

Finally, everything kicks off when the `startStreaming()` function is called. The default MP3 begins to load and starts playing when enough of the file has been buffered for playback. The following code shows the button actions used to start, stop, and load the MP3 files:

```
//************************ ACTIONS ON BUTTONS
loadBtn.onPress= function()
{
loadMP3();
}

playBtn.onPress= function()
{
stopAllSounds();
startStreaming();
}

stopBtn.onPress= function()
{
stopAllSounds();
}

stop();
```

Now that MP3 files are playing in Flash, the next thing to consider are ID3 tags, which are tags associated with MP3 files that provide information such as song name, album name, and artist. This useful information can be extracted very easily by using a little bit of code, as explained in the following section.

Using ID3 Tags

If you're an avid music collector or an MP3 enthusiast, you're probably familiar with ID3 tags. You might not know exactly what ID3 is, but every time you look at your MP3 player and read the song title or check to see who the artist is, you're accessing ID3 information. ID3 tags are used to store information about a piece of music, from the artist to the composer to comments and beats per minute (BPM).

In the past few years, the number of tags has increased because people want to classify and organize music with more detail. Flash Player version 6.40 and later supported reading MP3 files that used ID3 v1.0 and 1.1 tags. The tags that were supported in those versions were as follows:

```
Sound.id3.comment
Sound.id3.album
```

```
Sound.id3.genre
Sound.id3.songname
Sound.id3.artist
Sound.id3.track
Sound.id3.year
```

This information was handy when you wanted to highlight certain music or artists or access other information. Although these tags handled the core information, much more information can be included now with Flash Player 7 and later, which supports ID3 v2.4 tags. These tags are a significant improvement. Now you have a much wider variety of ID3 tags to choose from. This new format offers many new options, such as BPM, Lyricist, Length, Lead Performers, and so on. With all this new information, MP3 files can be like mini databases full of valuable song information. Table 15.1 lists supported ID3 properties you can access.

TABLE 15.1   **ID3 Properties**

ID3 Property	Description
COMM	Comment
ISRC	International standard recording code
TALB	Album, movie, or show title
TBPM	Beats per minute
TCOM	Composer
TCON	Content type
TCOP	Copyright message
TDAT	Date
TDLY	Playlist delay
TENC	Encoded by
TEXT	Lyricist/text writer
TFLT	File type
TIME	Time
TIT1	Content group description
TIT2	Title, song name, or content description
TIT3	Subtitle or description refinement
TKEY	Initial key

ID3 Property	Description
TLAN	Languages
TLEN	Length
TMED	Media type
TOAL	Original album, movie, or show title
TOFN	Original filename
TOLY	Original lyricists/text writers
TOPE	Original artists and performers
TORY	Original release year
TOWN	File owner or licensee
TPE1	Lead performers or soloists
TPE2	Band, orchestra, or accompaniment
TPE3	Conductor or performer refinement
TPE4	Interpreted, remixed, or otherwise modified by
TPOS	Part of a set
TPUB	Publisher
TRCK	Track number or position in set
TRDA	Recording dates
TRSN	Internet radio station name
TRSO	Internet radio station owner
TSIZ	Size
TSSE	Software/hardware and settings used for encoding
TYER	Year
WXXX	URL link frame

As you can see, you can access much more data through ID3 than you could in Flash MX. Additional tags are available in some audio applications that can also be read through Flash.

Reading ID3 Tags

Now that you know what you can access, how do you go about it? You can directly access any of the properties listed in Table 15.1 by referencing the myMP3.id3 object. For instance, if you want to access the composer for an MP3 song, use the following code to access the TCOM property:

```
myMP3.id3.TCOM
```

To display this information on stage, you could use the following code:

```
ArtistName.text = "Artist" + myMP3.id3.TCOM;
```

Information such as song name and artist are important pieces of data when you want to display information about a piece of music or build an MP3 player. In Flash MX, you could obtain ID3 information only by accessing the end of the MP3 file, so you couldn't stream an MP3 into Flash and display song information. The only workaround was preloading the entire MP3 song, which isn't very practical when you're using several megabytes of bandwidth.

With Flash Player 7 and the new ID3 v2.4, however, you can gather all this information at the beginning of the file and access that information within a streaming environment. To do this, you use the onID3 handler, discussed in the following section.

Using the *onID3* Handler

The onID3 handler is called every time Flash receives new ID3 data when loading an MP3 file. Both ID3 1.0 and ID3 2.0 tags are supported, so this handler is called twice because ID3 1.0 tags are located at the end of the MP3 file and ID3 2.0 tags are at the beginning.

Before you can access any ID3 information, however, you must load the MP3 file:

```
myMP3.loadSound("sample.mp3", false);
myMP3.onLoad = function(){
     this.start(0,1);
}
```

Make sure to replace *sample.mp3* with the name of an MP3 file located in the same directory as the Flash file you're working with.

If you're curious about what types of data you might have in an MP3 file, you can run the following piece of code that cycles through all the properties in the ID3 set and traces them to the Output panel. The following for loop is located inside the onID3 handler, so it's called only when the ID3 data has been received. After receiving the data, the loop goes through the existing properties and returns the values:

```
myMP3.onID3 = function(){
  for( var prop in myMP3.id3 ){
    trace( prop + " / "+ myMP3.id3[prop] );
  }
}
```

Make sure you pay attention to letter case when working with ID3 tag code. The onID3 handler uses the uppercase ID. However, when you're accessing the actual ID3 properties, you must reference them with the lowercase id3, as shown in the preceding code.

If you have worked with ID3 tags before, the output might surprise you. Much of the information is pulled from an Internet database when you create MP3 files from your CD collection. Often this information contains interesting notes in the comments section, for instance, with information about the actual track. You can, of course, customize MP3 tags in standard MP3 applications and create the content you want for your Flash project inside MP3 tags to make it self-contained.

You've learned the core principles of using sound. Although there aren't many options for controlling audio—primarily just volume and pan—you can still learn to use these simple properties skillfully and use input information creatively to affect audio output.

Before you try the chapter project, which covers dynamically synchronizing site navigation to an audio structure, read the following section for a better understanding of the new onSoundComplete() method.

USING THE *ONSOUNDCOMPLETE()* METHOD

When onSoundComplete() was added as a new method to the Sound object in Flash MX, it opened up a number of new possibilities to consider when integrating audio. As mentioned, onSoundComplete() is an event handler, which means it's event-based and is called when that event occurs. In this instance, the event is the completion of a Sound object playing. When a sound has reached its end point (or its .duration property), the onSoundComplete() method is called if it has been assigned. Take a peek at the following code example to get a better understanding of how this method works:

```
createEmptyMovieClip("drums", 100);
drums.loop = new Sound(drums);
drums.loop.attachSound("drums");
drums.loop.start(0,1);
```

This code isn't new—it's the standard way to create Sound objects and attach audio from the Library. Notice that an empty movie clip in which to place the Sound object was created first to ensure maximum independent control over the sound's volume and pan properties.

This code causes the drums sound from the Library to start and play just one time, as specified in the start() method. By adding the following onSoundComplete() method, you can control what happens when that sound finishes:

```
drums.loop.onSoundComplete = function(){
    trace ("sound is complete");
    this.start(0,1);
}
```

This code adds a trace() statement to inform you that the sound is in fact complete and lets you know that onSoundComplete() was called. Next, the code simply starts the same sound by referencing this and plays it once. This onSoundComplete() method is referenced *every* time the sound is finished until the function is nullified, modified, or deleted.

In essence, you have the basic components of a sequencer. However, if you tested this code, you'd notice a tiny gap in the loop restarting, which is the one downside to onSoundComplete(). This method isn't perfect for millisecond-precise audio timing, but it's useful for structuring more intricate audio pieces.

Although this small "glitch" in onSoundComplete() doesn't make accurate sequencing possible in Flash, you can still compose some beefier audio tracks. Instead of having just a single loop on a web site, you can use onSoundComplete() to mix up the audio. Take a look at the following code to see how it would create dynamic background audio:

```
CreateEmptyMovieClip("drums1", 100);
drums.loop = new Sound(drums1);
drums.loop.attachSound("drums");
drums.loop.start(0,4);
```

You have the same initial code as before, except it's used differently. For example, the sound loops four times instead of just once. This example also has four different loops of drums in the Library with linkage IDs of drums1, drums2, drums3, and drums4.

Having these sounds available in the Library means you can swap them in dynamically through the onSoundComplete() call. Take a look at the new function:

```
drums.loop.onSoundComplete = function(){
    trace ("sound is complete");
randomDrum = random(4)+1;
this.attachSound(["drums"+randomDrum]);
    this.start(0,4);
}
```

With the addition of the following two lines, you have made the background audio to the site completely dynamic—after every four loops of a previous sound, a new sound is randomly chosen and played:

```
randomDrum = random(4)+1;
this.attachSound(["drums"+randomDrum]);
```

Because it's random, you never get the same mix of sounds twice. Although this example might seem very simple and straightforward, it illustrates the principle used to create powerfully integrated audio applications.

Chapter Project: Building Navigational Audio

As mentioned previously, audio is often overlooked in interactive projects. The remainder of this chapter explains a sample project that uses audio in a new and powerful way—integrating navigation with audio. The sample site's audio alters as the user clicks sections and navigates through the site. As a user enters a new section, the music and sound are updated to reflect this decision, which creates a seamless experience between content and audio. The audio transition is handled gently, slowly dissolving or cross-fading between one sound and another.

You can download the Ch15_AudioNav.fla file from this book's web site.

The days of endlessly playing techno loops are over! It's time to start thinking of new, tasteful ways of integrating music and audio into online projects. This project gives you an opportunity to extend what you've discovered about the Sound object in this chapter and modify it to create a navigational system that's strongly tied to audio content.

The premise is simple. You have five different interactive sections, each with an accompanying sound that correlates with that section. As a user clicks through the different sections, the sound slowly fades in and out to the matching navigational sections. So the first thing you need to do is assign two variables to represent the section you're leaving (the "old" section) and the section you're entering (the "new" section):

```
var oldSection;
var newSection;
```

These variables are manipulated on the buttons relating to the sections. Like the previous examples, you need to create and initialize your Sound objects. In the following code, you're creating a prototype of the MovieClip object to easily extend this functionality across all movie clips.

```
//define the sound object associated with MovieClip
MovieClip.prototype.initializeSound = function()
{
    this.loop=new Sound(this);
    this.loop.attachSound(this._name);
    this.loop.setVolume(0);
    this.loop.start(0,9999);

}
```

You can see that this code is very similar to what's been shown previously in this chapter, with the exception of the prototype, which enables you to use initializeSound to attach sounds dynamically to movie clips based on their name. This is why the reference to the clip's name is used in the attachSound syntax. This setup makes it easy to add new sounds: Simply add the clip to the stage and give it a name corresponding to a sound that's been linked in the Library.

Essentially, this code example does nothing more than shift volumes between sounds. Five sounds have the same beats per minute (BPM), so they play in sync. Having the same BPM for these sounds isn't completely necessary, but your transitions will be smoother if they do have the same BPM.

Before you dig further into this code, you need to understand exactly what's being accomplished. When the Flash file is executed, the initialize code shown previously runs, and all movie clips that are initialized have an attached sound from the library. The premise is that all sounds will play at the same time so that they're all synchronized. However, they'll be playing at volume 0, so they will be inaudible. When a user clicks a section, the volume for its associated sound fades in, and the volume for the sound associated with the previous section fades out. This creates a cross-fade between pieces of music when a user navigates through the site, creating a rich audio experience.

Fading Sounds

The following code is used to fade sound volume. As you can see, it's also a prototype, but this time of the Sound object. This prototype makes it very easy to fade an existing sound. Notice that this function also accepts several parameters—fadeTarget, fadeSpeed, and mc—to give you more control over fading. The fadeTarget parameter sends a target volume to fade to, and fadeSpeed alters how quickly the fade happens. Take a look at the following code:

```
//Fade prototype function

Sound.prototype.fade=function(fadeTarget,fadeSpeed,mc)
{

    //if fade() is running, clear it
    clearInterval(this.intID);
    this.currentVolume=this.getVolume();
    //call dofade() every 100 milliseconds
    this.intID=setInterval(function(thisObj){
            thisObj.doFade();
```

```
}, 100,this);

//define fade function
    this.doFade=function()
    {

        if(this.currentVolume>fadeTarget)
        {//fade out
            this.currentVolume-=_root.fadeSpeed;
            this.setVolume(this.currentVolume);
            if(this.currentVolume<=fadeTarget)
            {//fade complete
                this.onFadeComplete();
                clearInterval(this.intID);
            }
        }
         else if(this.currentVolume<=fadeTarget)
{//fadein
            this.currentVolume+=_root.fadeSpeed;
            this.setVolume(this.currentVolume);
            if(this.currentVolume>=fadeTarget)
            {//fadein complete
                this.onFadeComplete();
                clearInterval(this.intID);
            }
        }

        navigation[mc].volume=this.currentVolume;

    //end doFade() function
    }
```

The prototype sets an interval for performing the actual fade. It's performed every 100ms, or 10 times per second, which is more than adequate for creating a smooth volume transition. Of course, you can change this value to whatever period of time you'd like.

The doFade function, which is run as the interval, is where all the magic happens. The if...else statement checks to see whether the new fadeTarget is lower or higher than the current volume and then adjusts the fade accordingly. When the sound volume meets the fadeTarget that was initially set, the interval is cleared.

```
this.onFadeComplete=function()
{
        this.currentVolume=fadeTarget;
         this.setVolume(this.currentVolume);


}
//end fade prototype function
}
```

Now that you've seen the core code responsible for fading the sound, the user interaction is all that's left to explore. If you double-click inside the navigation movie clip on the stage, you can see five movie clips called section1, section2, and so forth. Each movie clip represents a sound in the Library with the same linkage name. The buttons inside these movie clips contain the following code:

```
on (press)
{
    _root.changeSection(_name);
}
```

In the following code, the changeSection() function is called, and the name of the movie clip is passed to it. The purpose of this function is to handle the current section—the one the user clicked. As you can see in the following code, the section that was previously newSection is transferred to oldSection, and newSection is given the argument in the function call (which is the name of the movie clip). For example, section2 might have been passed as a parameter.

```
changeSection=function(arg)
{
oldSection=newSection;
newSection=arg;
crossfade(newSection,oldSection);

}
```

After the new hierarchy of sections is established, the crossFade() function is called, sending new values for oldSection and newSection as parameters. This final function is ultimately responsible for performing the volume cross-fade. Take a quick look at this function:

```
crossfade=function(newSec,oldSec)
{
    navigation[newSec].loop.fade(100,newSec);
    navigation[oldSec].loop.fade(0,oldSec);

}
```

You can see why establishing fade properties earlier was a good idea. In the preceding code, you merely set new volumes for the old and new sections. oldSection is given a volume value of 0, and newSection is given a new volume level of 100. This is how the cross-fade operates. As soon as the user clicks a new section, the old section's sound begins fading to 0 and the new sound fades up to 100, completing the cross-fade.

This piece of code isn't technically challenging, but the power it lends to site development is significant. With this code for creating a cross-fade, you're no longer limited to playing one sound loop endlessly during a site visit. You can create music that changes and shifts dynamically to create a better user experience. Try using this trick for your next project and see how much more interesting it is for your users!

Resources

Here are some great resources to check out when you're searching for music that's put together in easy-to-use packages:

www.platinumloops.com

www.flashkit.com

POINTS TO REMEMBER

- Decide whether it is important to run your sounds as event or streaming. Streaming allows pure synching to visuals but results in loss of individual control over the audio.

- If narration is important, streaming is an excellent option, as it allows you to place actions in the narration timeline to accurately trigger and control actions in the main movie.

- Always try to compress audio just once. If you are using MP3 files, make sure you select the default quality in the Sound Properties dialog box to ensure that you don't get double compression.

- Try to use small, reusable pieces of audio to reduce bandwidth footprint.

- When working with MP3 files, you can access a wide variety of ID3 tags to store and access information about these files.

- Keep in mind that onSoundComplete is useful for creative sound sequencing, but it's not millisecond-accurate enough to do advanced audio sequencing.

- Pan is the most underused audio property in Flash. Try using it for interesting effects, such as tying sound to the location of an object on stage to create more realistic interactive environments.

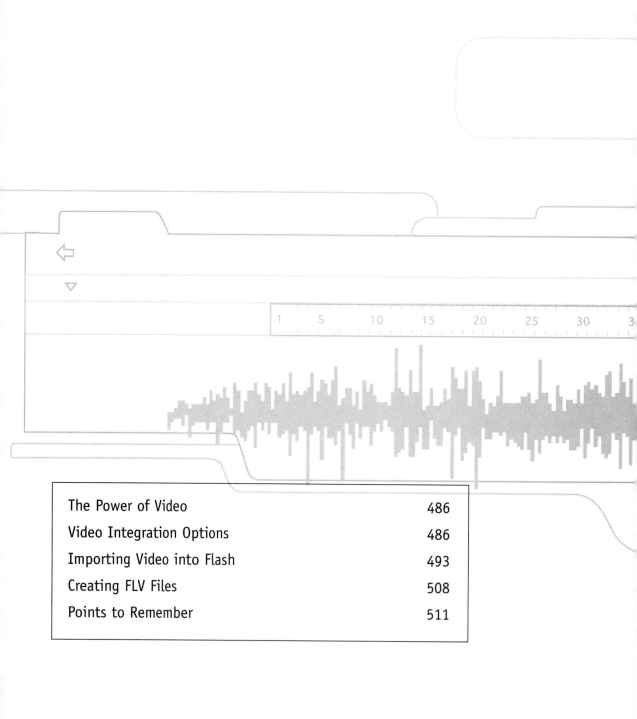

CHAPTER 16

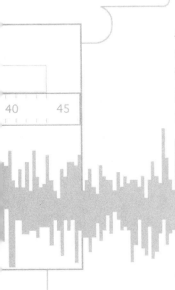

VIDEO

As you witnessed in Chapter 15, "Audio," the power of well-structured audio content can truly make an impact on your interactive projects. Video is another multimedia tool that can be used with Macromedia Flash MX 2004 to expand the possibilities of both online and offline new-media applications.

Video was introduced in Flash MX. Since that time, it has been widely adopted by Flash users around the world to create engaging and interactive presentations. With Flash MX 2004, video-handling capabilities have increased significantly. Being able to quickly and easily edit, modify, and import video with Flash MX 2004 will surely win people over and open doors for further experimentation. This chapter covers the following topics:

- Importing video via the Video Import Wizard

- Editing video

- Optimizing video for web playback

- SWF versus FLV video formats

The Flash MX 2004 Professional version offers capabilities for handling video as well as specific streaming media components. Because these components aren't available in the standard Flash MX 2004 release, you'll see how video playback can be controlled through a simple interface.

The Power of Video

Video, which is a sequential set of images often synced with audio, is just as powerful as audio in conveying emotion and can be used effectively in an instructional manner.

Often, video is the best way to show how something works, to demonstrate a product, or to teach a concept. A video product demonstration, if done well, can be as effective as an in-person demonstration. In the e-learning market, video is fast becoming one of the most popular distribution methods for educational information. Today's video compression capabilities have enabled the transmission of "talking-head" video, even with narrow-band connections.

There are also huge opportunities to use video in exciting and extremely interactive ways with Flash. The concept of nonlinear is welcomed with open arms in the interactive environment. No longer do videos need to be represented as rectangular boxes containing the video. With Flash, video can be masked and controlled dynamically and used as single elements in a larger presentation. Instead of the traditional linear approach of viewing video from start to finish, with Flash MX 2004 you can create compelling interactive video integration that takes users beyond the traditional means of viewing video and allows them to experience video in new and exciting ways.

Understanding what's possible is certainly a first step, but first take a closer look at the different ways in which you can use video with Flash.

Video Integration Options

There are a number of different methods for delivering video when using Flash:

- Embedded video using SWF files
- Progressive FLV (Flash video file format) delivery
- Streaming FLV delivery

Note that streaming FLV delivery is reserved for use in the Flash Communication Server framework. This method takes advantage of the server architecture to deliver streams that scale the quality based on the user's connection, thus offering the highest quality stream possible based on the current bandwidth connection.

Embedded SWF Video

The oldest method of incorporating video in Flash is embedding it into a Flash movie (an SWF file). This is accomplished by importing the video into Flash, placing it on the main timeline, and publishing it as an SWF file. This approach is similar to the way streaming sounds are imported and delivered via Flash.

This method of producing video with Flash is very visual; as with audio, you can see the individual video frames represented in the timeline frames. This approach is useful if you're interested in syncing other visual elements on the stage with the displayed video. Interactive overlays and crisp vector type treatments can easily be added.

Take a look at Figure 16.1 to see the timeline of the video layer and the other elements added on subsequent layers. These additional elements seem to be part of the actual video, yet they are actually extra elements to support the video frames.

FIGURE 16.1

Timeline with video frames and supporting text.

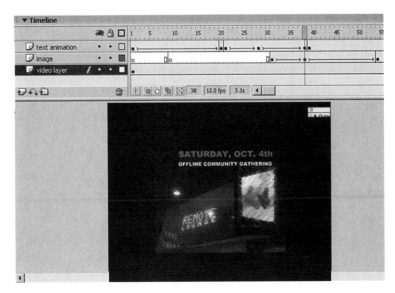

Although this method is a great way to overlay and add media elements to existing video, there are a number of limitations when using embedded video in SWF files:

- **File size issues** When using SWF files and video, you might run into problems with the files being too large for the Flash Player to handle correctly. The Flash Player reserves a lot of memory when using extremely large SWF files embedded with video; therefore, large high-quality movie files could cause the Player to crash.

- **Memory limitations** Extremely large files that use a lot of disk space must fit into the memory the Flash Player has available to play back and perform correctly. Memory limitations can be of particular concern to Macintosh users, as Macs allocate memory much differently than PC machines.

- **Audio sync** With large video files, there's also a tendency for drift between the audio and video to occur. That means the audio-video synchronization, over time, can begin to fall out of sync. Quite often the audio begins to slowly drift out of step with the visuals, which makes viewing awkward. As soon as the audio from a talking head, for example, begins to lose synchronization with mouth and face movements, the viewing experience becomes jarring and attention is focused on the loss of sync, not the content being presented.

- **Download all frames to play** Because the entire SWF file is run through memory, downloading all the frames is necessary before the movie can begin playing. This is perhaps the biggest disadvantage to using this method. Users generally prefer to have video playing immediately; however, sometimes further timeline syncing and extra interactivity is needed, which can only be accomplished by embedding video within a Flash movie. The price, therefore, is preloading the entire clip.

Progressive FLV Delivery

New to Flash 2004 through the introduction of Flash Player 7 is a completely new way to handle video delivery. This new technique, called *progressive downloading,* allows an ActionScript call from an existing SWF file to load external FLV files (Flash video files) for playback of video content.

Before the addition of this new FLV progressive format, they could be used with Flash only if Flash Communication Server was running. Originally, this proprietary video format was designed to run on the Communication Server framework; however, with this release of Flash MX 2004, this technology has been modified to work with standard HTTP streaming, not just Flash Communication streaming. This opens a whole new world of video possibilities for Flash developers who don't have the advantage of using Flash Communication Server.

The "progressive download" process means just what you might expect. It progressively downloads the video content, easing the pressure on the Flash Player and the host machine. This new approach has some advantages over the previous method of embedding SWF files:

- **Perfect sync, unlimited length, and memory issues are resolved** Because the file is downloaded progressively, memory is constantly being released for subsequent frames later in the file. As video runs through the Flash Player, the memory it uses is released to make room for more current video information. This eliminates one of the biggest problems of using SWF files—the memory limitation of the Flash Player and host machine. Also, because memory is freed up, the size of an FLV file can be practically unlimited.

- **Quick playback** Unlike videos that use embedded SWF files, using progressive FLV files allows almost instantaneous playback of video. Because you don't need to download all the embedded frames, FLV files begin playing as soon as the first segment has been downloaded and cached to the user's local disk. After only a very short buffer time, the video begins playing as the rest of the file downloads in the background. This method is analogous to using the streaming method for audio playback, which has the advantage of delivering high-impact media content quickly to the audience.

- **Frame rate independence** As you might know from using loaded movies, any movie loaded into Flash adapts and runs at the parent movie's frame rate. However, when you're using multiple content SWF files, often this isn't the behavior you want. An advantage of delivering video via the progressive FLV format is that it's completely frame rate-independent. An FLV file plays back at the frame rate you create it at, regardless of the frame rate the _root or other SWF files run at. Frame rate independence ensures that playback and performance are consistent across platforms and machines.

Comparing Embedded SWF and External FLV Files

Before you start learning about importing and incorporating video in Flash, take a look at the following sections, which compare the two methods of incorporating video to help you decide which one would work best for your Flash project.

Encoding

For embedded SWF files, video and audio are encoded via the Sorenson Spark codec. Macromedia has adopted this format and included it as the default compression method in Flash. Compression settings are discussed in "Compressing Video" later in the chapter.

With external FLV files, video and audio are also encoded with the Sorenson Spark codec if you're importing your video into Flash and then outputting to an FLV file. However, a QuickTime to FLV Exporter is included with Flash MX Professional 2004, which gives you more options, better control, and a more robust compression codec.

The Sorenson Spark codec, optimized to perform within the Flash framework, is one of the most widely used compression formats and delivers incredible video while leaving a small bandwidth footprint. When importing and encoding video files in Flash, this is the compression algorithm that's used. As mentioned, the Flash Professional version also comes with export options for standard video applications, such as Premiere and Final Cut.

File Size

Embedded SWF files contain audio and video as well as any user interface (UI) elements. Including all these elements increases file size; however, video clips can be created as separate SWF files and loaded sequentially to avoid the long buffer time required to download the entire video clip. Longer videos embedded as separate smaller SWF files can simulate a progressive download by downloading the first clip and then downloading second and subsequent clips in the background while the first clip is playing. This requires creating a loading queue for the different video clips, but it's effective if you're using longer pieces of video.

Because FLV files are created separately from the UI elements in the SWF file, the overall file size is smaller. This is, however, of little consequence, as the nature of progressive downloading makes it feasible to have extremely large files because they don't need to be completely loaded and cached before playback.

Timeline Access

Using embedded SWF files is similar to using streaming sound, so all frames in the movie are visible. This feature makes it easy to add more information to the video. For instance, if you want to add an interactive element in particular frames of a video—such as creating a hotspot that links to other content or a URL, or placing buttons on certain elements in the timeline—an embedded SWF file is required.

FLV files do not allow access to the Timeline or offer a linear visual output for adding interactivity. The video is loaded and played back during runtime. Individual video frames aren't visible on the Flash stage, so adding interactivity successfully is almost impossible.

Publishing

The pitfall to embedding SWF video into the same movie as your interface and layout is the extra time required to test or publish your movie. Every time you test or publish from the Flash environment, the video is also republished, which requires additional time and processing by Flash. Although this method might be necessary if you're testing elements that interact directly with the video, such as dynamic hotspot buttons or visual overlays, it eats up time when publishing.

FLV files are referenced only during runtime and do not require republishing. The advantage of using FLV files is that after they're published or exported, they're available instantly to Flash because they are loaded dynamically. This makes working with FLV video much quicker than using embedded SWF files.

Using progressive FLV files also gives you a level of extraction because the video content is separate from the Flash movie interface and navigation structure. Any change to the video requires swapping only FLV files; no changes need to be made to SWF files. So after building the design and interface, you don't need to touch it again. Simply swapping, switching, or adding FLV files updates the video content.

Frame Rate

When using the embedded SWF file method, any SWF files that are loaded and any movie clips residing inside an SWF file must adhere to the frame rate of the _root movie. This can cause problems if you need to run your main application at a slower or faster frame rate than the video you want to include. This method causes inconsistent playback if you use variable frame rates.

An advantage of the progressive method is that FLV files are self-contained and run at an separate frame rate from all other timeline frame rates that the Flash movie currently includes. This offers more flexibility for including video in Flash applications that can be built at different frame rates than the original video file.

Access via ActionScript

Controlling video via ActionScript in embedded SWF files involves controlling the actual timeline. Such properties as _currentframe and _totalframes can be accessed to display position and show duration as well as to create scrubbing features. A number of Behaviors are now available with Flash 2004 to simplify control over video.

The FLV format was first introduced through the Flash Communication Server, so several methods and objects have been created specifically for controlling video in this format. Primarily, the NetConnection and NetStream objects can be used to connect, load, play, and seek through external FLV files. These objects are explained in more detail in "Playing FLV Files" later in the chapter.

Usage

The ideal type of video used with the SWF file format is shorter video clips that generally run less than a minute and are smaller in dimensions, such as the standard 320×240 resolution. If you need to add interactivity, such as linkable hotspots, with your video, or you want to sync motion or text over video, embedded video is the only real choice you have for smooth integration. Just remember that the entire video must download before playing.

Using progressive FLV files is by far the most effective method if you plan to use large or extremely high-quality video and don't require any direct interactivity (such as hotspots). Video clips as large as 720×480 can be progressively downloaded and support frame rates up to 30fps. The biggest advantage of this method is that long pieces of video don't need to be fully downloaded; they just need to be buffered slightly to begin playback. Progressive downloading allows for near-instantaneous video playback, which is the ultimate video experience you can deliver over the web.

This is similar to MP3 streaming, discussed in Chapter 15. The processor can easily handle large high-quality files with streaming audio or video, which also result in smoother playback for long pieces of video.

IMPORTING VIDEO INTO FLASH

Now that you've reviewed some of the key differentiating factors between SWF and FLV delivery, it's time to step through the processes of importing video into Flash and exporting FLV content.

Flash's video import methods have been dramatically enhanced since Flash MX. Editing, resizing, adjusting color, and other interesting options are all available when you're importing a video file into Flash 2004. You import video files in much the same way you import images or sound. After you choose File, Import from the menu (keyboard shortcut: **Ctrl+R**) and select the video file, the Video Import Wizard starts.

Flash allows importing a number of different video types. If QuickTime 4 is installed on Windows or Macintosh, the following files are supported:

.avi	Audio Video Interleaved
.dv	Digital Video
.mpg, .mpeg	Motion Picture Experts Group
.mov	QuickTime Movie
.flv	Flash Video

If a Windows system has DirectX 7 or later installed, supported video file types include the following:

.avi	Audio Video Interleaved
.mpg, .mpeg	Motion Picture Experts Group
.wmv, .asf	Windows Media Files
.flv	Flash Video

If you're importing a QuickTime file, you'll see the options shown in Figure 16.2. The purpose of this window is to choose whether you want to import the movie file directly into Flash or have it remain a reference to the external video file.

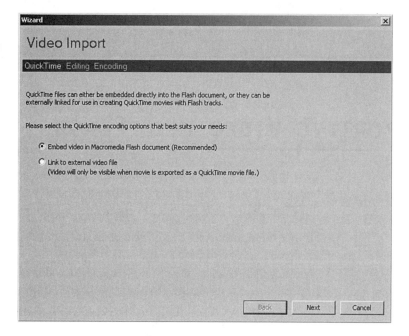

Why would you want to link to an external file, however? Many design and animation houses use Flash drawing and animation tools in their projects. If you're using Flash to add a level of interactivity or animations with text and graphics, you would simply export the Flash file later as a QuickTime movie. If you're planning to export your Flash work to QuickTime, use it as an external file. Instead of having to import the file directly, Flash can reference the original movie file and embed it at final output to QuickTime. Particularly if you're using several different movie files or large files, using a reference makes it easier to make changes to this source file than having to embed it separately each time. Referencing files is a good option when dealing with large files meant for final broadcast output to QuickTime.

For now, however, select the option for embedding the video in the Flash document and set this option as your default preference by clicking the check box at the bottom left.

Importing Video Subclips

Next, you see the following two options, which are new to Flash MX 2004 (see Figure 16.3):

- Import the entire video

- Edit the video first

FIGURE 16.3
New options in the Video Import Wizard.

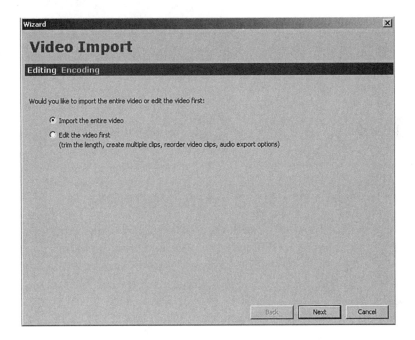

Although the default selection is importing the entire video, take a look at this new option of editing your video first. Selecting the Edit the Video First option opens the window shown in Figure 16.4.

This editing window is certainly quite different from what was available in Flash MX. A mini application has been added in the Video Import Wizard to handle basic video editing. It's particularly useful if you need to crop or edit a video and need to do it quickly without having to open a third-party video application. With this new interface, you can create any number of subclips from the original video content.

FIGURE 16.4
The editing window in the Video Import Wizard.

SCRUBBER BAR

Selecting a Clip Region

To create a subclip, first you need to create a clip region. Use the small draggable in and out points under the small timeline (called the *scrubber bar*). In Figure 16.5, you can see that the in and out points have been moved to select a small region of the original video clip.

FIGURE 16.5
Selecting a small subclip.

IN AND OUT POINTS

When you alter the in and out points, you can click Preview Clip to watch the selected region. As you drag the in and out points, the preview window updates the video with the current position. When you're happy with the clip, click the Create Clip button, and the clip is added in the window to the left as clip1, as shown in Figure 16.6.

FIGURE 16.6

Creating a subclip in the Video Import Wizard.

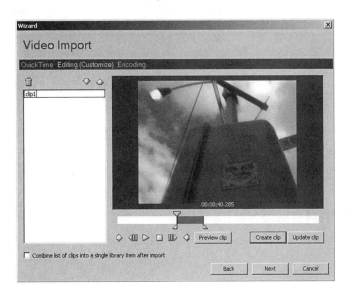

By default, the new subclip has the same name as the original file, but you can simply click the highlighted name and enter another name. Then repeat this process if you need to create more subclips.

In Figure 16.7, another subclip has been created and named clip2. You can continue to make subclips until you have sliced the video into the number of segments you need. If you have modified the original source video file, you can click the Update Clip button to reload it in Flash.

The Video Import Wizard has a handy option at the bottom left of this editing window. If you select this check box, Flash splices all the subclips into one video object in your Library. Although this option can be useful, for now leave this check box cleared and see what happens when you bring the clips in separately. Click Next to go to the encoding window of the Video Import Wizard.

FIGURE 16.7
Creating another
subclip.

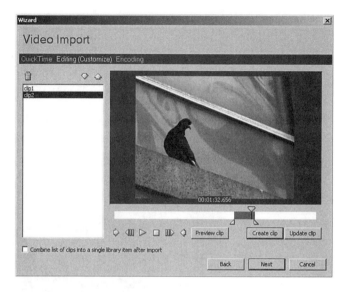

FIGURE 16.7
Creating another
subclip.

Compressing Video

Now you're in the second stage of the importing process, where you have a number of options for compressing video files for online delivery. First, look at the Compression Profile list box at the top of Figure 16.8. You'll see a number of default options to select from.

FIGURE 16.8
Default compression
options in the
encoding window.

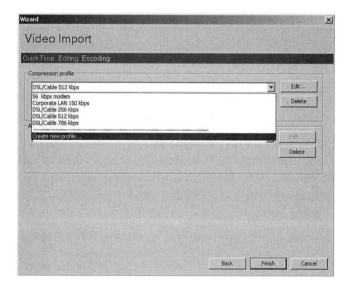

These are the default options for connection speeds:

- 56Kbps modem

- Corporate LAN 150Kbps

- DSL/Cable 256Kbps

- DSL/Cable 512Kbps

These choices offer a wide range in delivery options, from a 56K modem to broadband cable. You can also override these defaults and create your own compression profile by selecting the Create New Profile option shown in Figure 16.8. Selecting this option opens the customizing window, shown in Figure 16.9, which offers very specific control over video quality.

FIGURE 16.9
Creating a custom compression profile.

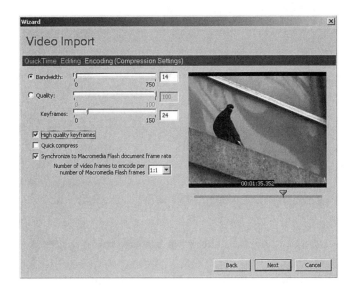

This window has sliders for adjusting the quality of the video. You can adjust the bandwidth you want the video to adhere to, or you can make your selection more visually clear by using the Quality slider. In Figure 16.9, the quality is set to 100. In Figure 16.10, the Quality value has been lowered and the resulting preview image is considerably compressed.

Using the Quality slider to adjust the video is a visual, responsive method. You can see the video preview update instantly so that you know what the final video file will look like when compressed at those settings.

FIGURE 16.10
Lowering the quality
of the video clip.

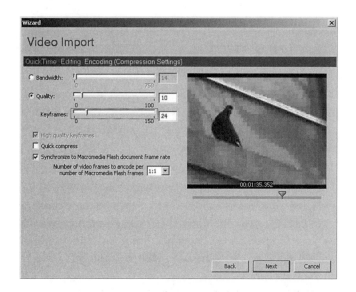

The Keyframes slider is used to set the number of keyframes you want to advance or seek through the video, particularly if you plan to export an FLV file in the end. Flash looks for the number of keyframes in this setting when you try to advance video through some sort of interface. Accessing frames in an FLV file that's loaded externally is slightly different from an imported video in an SWF file. The SWF file has timeline frames, but the FLV file uses keyframes set here for advancing or moving through the video clip. The more keyframes you set here, the more accurately you (or your users) can advance to specific points in the video.

You can select the check box at the bottom to synchronize the video frame rate to the frame rate of the current Flash movie. This setting can be an important aspect of importing your video. If you're running your Flash movie at 12 frames per second (fps), the video file is at 30fps, and you import the video at a 1:1 ratio, your Flash movie file plays at 12fps, yet the video file contains more than twice that number of frames per second. As a result, the video plays back slower than its original setting of 30fps. Synchronizing to the Macromedia document frame rate allows you to account for any discrepancies in frame rate settings. To avoid any problems, set your Flash movie's frame rate to that of the video. If you're looking for ways to further reduce the overall file size, you can modify these settings to cut down the number of frames used in Flash. This decreases the total number of frames in the video and, therefore, reduces the overall size and bandwidth.

Accessing Advanced Settings

When you're happy with the video's quality setting, click Next to open the window shown in Figure 16.11.

FIGURE 16.11
Saving the encoding options.

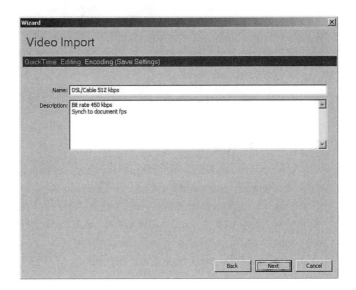

This window displays an overview of the settings you have chosen. Assuming that everything is consistent here, clicking Next saves this setting in the compression profiles and brings you back to the main encoding window shown earlier in Figure 16.8. Below the compression profiles is the Advanced Settings drop-down list. Select Create New Profile from this drop-down list and click Next to go to the window shown in Figure 16.12, where you have several options for fine-tuning your video.

This window offers options for adjusting your video's colors and dimensions. You're most likely familiar with some of these imaging options, such as brightness and contrast; however, the following sections step through them quickly to give you an idea of what you can adjust in this window.

FIGURE 16.12
Advanced settings in the Video Import Wizard.

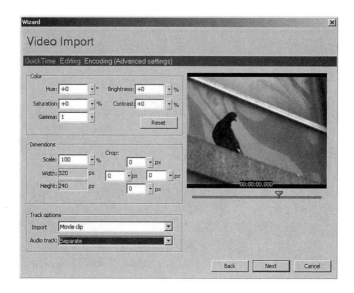

Adjusting Hue

The first option in the Color section is Hue (see Figure 16.13), used to shift the image's color balance. In essence, you can tint the video image to a color different from its original value. This option is also handy if you're working with poor-quality video or the color balance in the original wasn't what you wanted. Adjusting these settings offers a wide range of control over the file's final color output.

FIGURE 16.13
A positive Hue value of +160 tints the image blue.

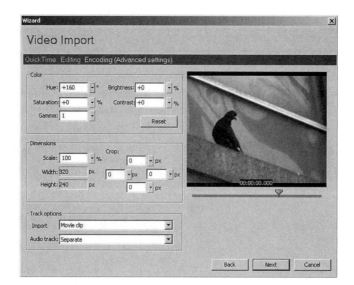

Adjusting Saturation

Use the Saturation slider (see Figure 16.14) to increase (saturate) or decrease (desaturate) the brightness of the image's colors. Positive values raise the saturation; negative values lower it. Lowering the setting to –100 desaturates the image until it's grayscale.

FIGURE 16.14
Taking the Saturation value down to –100 turns the video image black and white (grayscale).

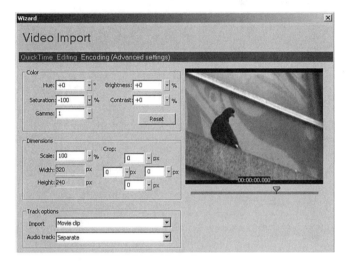

Adjusting Gamma

The Gamma setting adjusts the overall tone of the image. In Figure 16.15, the Gamma setting has been lowered until the entire image is darkened. It looks as though the image has a black overlay.

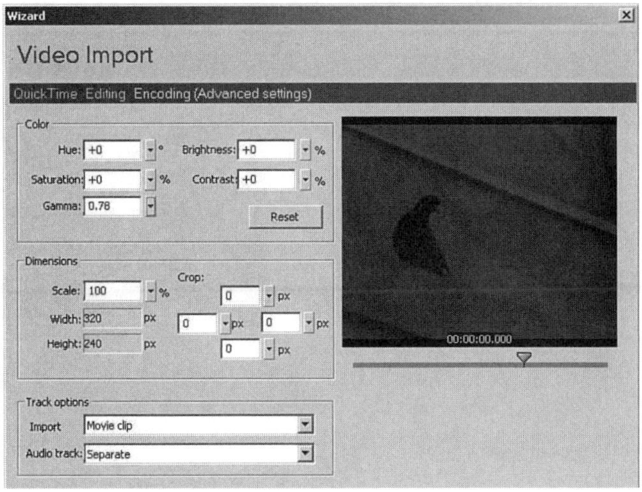

FIGURE 16.15
Adjust the Gamma setting to adjust the video's color and contrast.

Adjusting Brightness

The Brightness setting does what you'd expect—brightens or darkens the image (see Figure 16.16). This feature is similar to the Brightness option in Flash that allows you to brighten (or darken) a movie clip object.

FIGURE 16.16
The video image is made brighter with a Brightness value of +58.

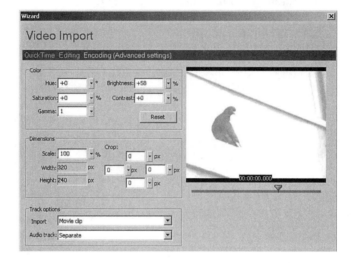

Adjusting Contrast

As expected, the Contrast slider adjusts the image contrast. Increasing this value makes portions of the image stand out more (see Figure 16.17); decreasing it blends color values to reduce contrast.

FIGURE 16.17
Increasing the Contrast value to +100.

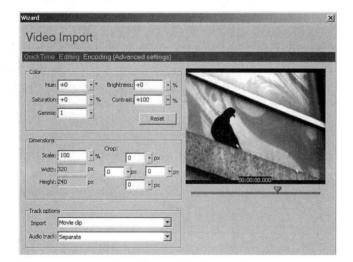

Cropping Your Video

The Dimensions section has controls for changing your video's dimension and for cropping your video. On the left is the Scale slider for sizing the overall video. You can reduce the percentage if you want to import the video at a smaller size than the original to save file size and make downloads faster for your users.

However, there is another interesting option here—cropping the video. Say you have a video in the letterbox format. Although this format makes it possible to see the video in its full-screen version, it results in black bands at the top and bottom of the screen. You could use the cropping controls to select only the portion of the video you want to import and eliminate the black bands. You can also use cropping to eliminate areas of the video so that you can emphasize a main character or other focal point in the frame, for example. You can see in Figure 16.18 that as you modify the left, right, top, and bottom crop values, a framed box with white lines forms over the video preview, so you can see exactly what areas will be included in the final import.

FIGURE 16.18
Using the Dimension values to crop an area of the video, indicated by the white lines.

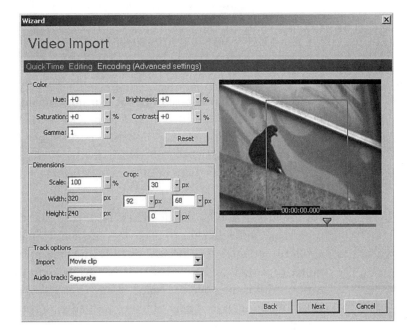

Additional Import Options

Before importing this newly modified video into your Library, there are a number of final options you can choose to specify how the video makes it into the Library. At the bottom of the Advanced Settings window (refer back to Figure 16.18) in the Track Options section, you'll notice some additional options for importing your edited video.

You can choose to import the video directly onto the timeline in Flash or as a Library item. This choice depends on what you intend to do with the video in your final project. If you're working on a simple linear narration piece with little interaction, going directly into Flash should be adequate. However, if you're interested in doing more dynamic things with the video, have multiple video clips, or want to add dynamic transitions or elements through ActionScript, it's best to import the video to the Library where you can easily customize it and convert it into video and movie clip objects that can be dynamically controlled via code.

Two drop-down lists in the Track Options section affect the way the video is finally imported. The Import list box has three options: Current Timeline, Movie Clip, and Graphic Symbol. How you want to integrate the video affects the choice you make here. You'll probably rarely choose the Graphic Symbol option because with a graphic symbol, you have no way of using ActionScript to interact with the video.

The options you'll use most often are Current Timeline and Movie Clip. If you're exporting the video in SWF format to be loaded in by another Flash file, Current Timeline is probably your best bet. If you want to do some interesting things with the video, the Movie Clip option is the quickest and easiest way to place the video inside a self-contained, self-named movie clip.

For instance, if you have a video mixer/editor application that allows users to cut and edit clips to make their own video piece in Flash, this application demands some serious code integration. In this case, using movie clips that can be easily and dynamically controlled via ActionScript is the obvious choice. However, if you're simply embedding video or adding it for linear timeline animation, importing the video directly into the main timeline in Flash is often the best and easiest method to start with.

In the Audio Track drop-down list are the Separate, Integrated, and None options. If you select Separate, audio and video are imported as separate elements into the Library. This option gives you the most flexibility in working with audio and video separately. If you just want to have the video self-contained, choosing Integrated is your best bet. It incorporates the audio element into the embedded video.

After making all your choices and clicking Finish, the video is imported into the Library. Figure 16.19 shows two clips that were imported. The Audio Track option was set to Separate.

FIGURE 16.19
Two clips have been imported into the Library, with the audio track imported separately.

As you can see, Flash does an excellent and exceptionally organized job of importing multimedia assets. There are now individual movie clips for each video file and a separate audio track that can be added to the timelines or further modified.

By simply dragging the movie clip onto the timeline, you can instantly see the video play when you get to the frame where the movie clip is placed. You can control the video in the same way you would control a movie clip animation. You can use ActionScript methods such as stop(), play(), _currentframe, and _totalframe to navigate through the video. For this reason, importing video into movie clips makes it extremely easy to build a simple interface for controlling the video because it's treated just like a movie clip.

CREATING FLV FILES

So far this chapter has concentrated on importing video into Flash and publishing it as an SWF file. However, there are a number of advantages to publishing video as FLV files, such as progressive downloads and the ability to use larger files and longer video clips.

Creating an FLV file is easy. If you don't have any third-party software, such as Sorenson Squeeze, you can create FLV files directly in Flash. To do this, first import the video you want to use with the methods explained previously in this chapter. After the video is in the Library, you can export it as an FLV file. Right-click the video in the Library, and choose Properties (see Figure 16.20).

FIGURE 16.20
Right-clicking a video in the Library displays this menu.

In the Embedded Video Properties dialog box that opens (see Figure 16.21), simply click the Export button to export the movie as an FLV file, and save the file to the directory you want.

FIGURE 16.21
The Embedded Video Properties dialog box.

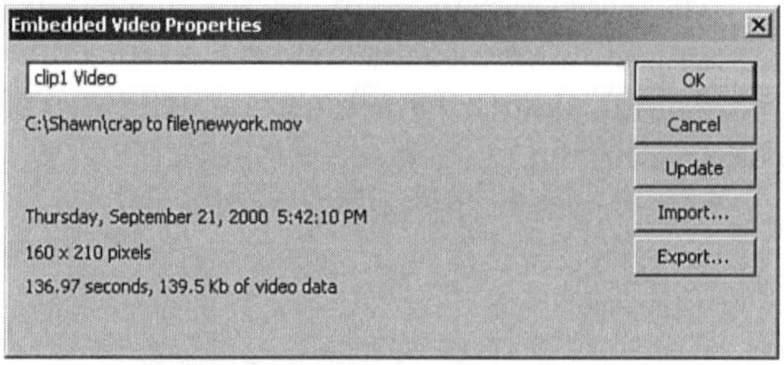

Playing FLV Files

Now that you have an FLV file, how do you play it? The process is much different from what you've seen so far. The FLV format, created with the introduction of Flash Communication Server, was developed to offer true streaming via Flash Communication Server. This same format is now available to use for progressive downloads through local or HTTP connections.

FLV files are loaded just as other SWF, MP3, or JPEG files are. You must make sure you place your files in a location you can easily access. For the following examples, the FLV file that's loaded must be in the same place where the FLA and SWF files reside. If not, you simply need to adjust the path to the file.

To access and play FLV files, you need to use the NetConnection object, which was also introduced with Flash Communication Server. All video streams (called NetStreams) run through this object. Think of it this way: The NetConnection object is like the cable coming into your television. Any video you want to receive comes through a stream *inside* the NetConnection object.

If you don't have an FLV file to use, you can download the sampleFLV.flv file from this book's companion web site at www.flashdemystified.com. Open a new document in Flash. In the Library panel (choose Window, Library from the menu), select New Video to create a new video object in the Library (see Figure 16.22). You access this Library options menu by clicking the arrow at the top-right corner of the Library panel.

FIGURE 16.22
Creating a new video object in the Library.

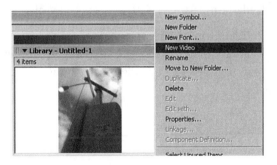

Next, drag this new video object onto the stage and give it an instance name. For this example, use myVid. Now you can add the code needed to play the FLV.

Select the first frame in the timeline and make sure the Actions panel is open. Add the following code to create the NetConnection and NetStream objects, which play the video in the myVid Video object:

```
_root.myNC = new NetConnection();
_root.myNC.connect(null);
root.myStream = new NetStream(root.myNC);
root.myVid.attachVideo (_root.myStream);
_root.myStream.play("myVideo.FLV");
```

As you can see, setting up a connection to stream the video clip with is fairly straightforward. After creating a new NetConnection instance, connecting the NetConnection to create a local streaming connection is a good practice. This same code is used when connecting via the Flash Communication Server. It's also important to reference the NetConnection that's made when you create the NetStream (see the third line in the preceding code). After you have established the NetConnection and NetStream objects, all that's required is attaching the Video object to the stream and playing it.

That's all there is to it! Although the NetConnection method can seem daunting, it's just a matter of *first* establishing a NetConnection object, then creating a NetStream object (with the argument equal to the NetConnection), attaching the stream to the Video object you created, and then playing the FLV file. This example assumes that you have saved your Flash file in the same location as your FLV file.

To pause a video, you can use the pause() method of the NetStream object. This method acts as a toggle, allowing you to repeatedly start and stop a video file. To pause the video in the previous example, use the following code:

```
_root.myStream.pause();
```

This code line halts the video from playing. Using the same code then plays the same file from where it was paused. This inherent toggle nature makes it easy to use. If you had a movie clip on stage with the instance name Pause, you could add pause/play functionality with just the following code:

```
Pause.onPress = function(){
_root.myStream.pause();
}
```

You can see how easy it is to incorporate external files in Flash. If you're interested in more advanced capabilities, such as building preloaders based on the buffer of the video instead of bytes loaded, as you would with an external SWF file, it's worth exploring the NetStream object.

Resources

Wildform Flix (www.wildform.com/flix): This is another third-party supplier of video to Flash formats. Its software includes some additional effects that can be applied.

FlashAnts (www.flashants.com): The SWF2Video application allows Flash developers to create video files from SWF files, including embedded movie clips and capturing dynamic ActionScript code.

Flash/QuickTime discussion group (http://groups.yahoo.com/group/flashquicktime/): An online discussion forum covering issues related to integrating Flash and QuickTime.

Sorenson Squeeze (www.sorenson.com/application_custom/en/store/catalog.php#mxwf): Using the same core engine that Flash video import does, Squeeze is a standalone package offering more options and powerful compression features for creating SWF and FLV files.

POINTS TO REMEMBER

- Video clips can be imported into Flash as embedded files if they are MOV, AVI, MPEG, and other video formats (depending on your platform and system). Use SWF files if you want to control your video files through ActionScript as you do with movie clips.

- You can also use the Behaviors included with Flash MX 2004 that allow you to easily add functionality for controlling imported embedded video files.

- Choose FLV files if you're using large, long, or high-quality video clips. The progressive playing of FLV files allows for better handling of high-quality video. You can play back external FLV files during runtime by using the NetConnection and `NetStream` ActionScript objects.

- Try to avoid compressing video files more than once. It's best to use the highest quality video you can and do the compression once through Flash. For ultimate control, you might want to consider third-party options, such as Sorenson Squeeze, to generate video outputs to SWF and FLV formats.

- To save time, you can capitalize on the new importing features of Flash MX 2004 to import multiple subclips from just one original source clip. This can help you create interactive features and makes importing quick and easy.

- Importing QuickTime video clips as linked files doesn't make the video file part of the Flash file. It's used only as a reference to the actual file; you must export your Flash file as QuickTime to view the compiled result.

PART IV
EXTENDING FLASH

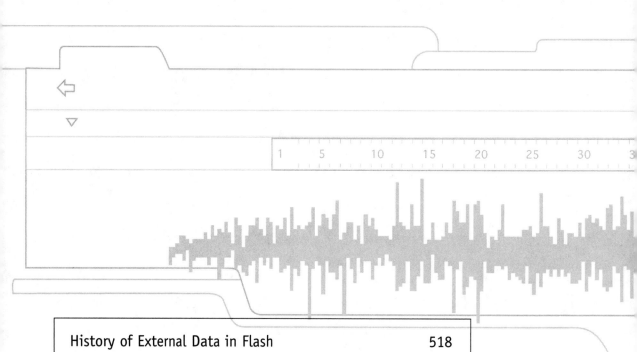

CHAPTER 17

ACCESSING EXTERNAL DATA

NOW THAT YOU KNOW HOW TO WRITE ACTIONSCRIPT AND HOW TO MANIPULATE data inside your movie, you've probably noticed that it's limiting to use only the data you supply at author time or data supplied by the user at runtime. Therefore, to get around that limitation, you need to be able to access external data in Flash. Luckily, there are numerous ways to bring external data into Flash. In this chapter you'll look at some of the ways to bring external data into your Flash file and how to use this data after you've brought it in.

History of External Data in Flash

Although Macromedia Flash MX 2004 is far from the first version of Flash to support loading outside data, it does offer the most robust set of features for doing so.

It wasn't until Flash 4 that developers were able to load *external data*— data not directly entered by the author or user. In Flash 4, developers could load URL-encoded data entered in <embed> and <object> tags in the HTML page housing a movie. Additionally, Flash 4 had the loadVariables() and loadVariablesNum() functions, which load URL-encoded variable information from a remote source, such as an Active Server Pages (ASP) page or a PHP or CGI script.

In Flash 5, Macromedia introduced the XML object, which enabled users to create, load, and manipulate data within Flash. This object was an immensely powerful tool and opened possibilities for developers to create dynamic, data-rich applications. Also, with the XMLSocket object, developers could establish persistent connections between the user and a server, bypassing the limitations of stateless HTTP connections. HTTP connections, such as loading a web page, require the "client" to ask the server for information. Doing so frequently, as with many Flash 4 chat applications, caused a drain on the server that a socketed connection doesn't.

In Flash MX, Macromedia introduced the LoadVars object, which is similar to the loadVariables() and loadVariablesNum() functions, except this object had a variety of methods for tracking and responding to the process of acquiring external data. Flash MX also introduced Flash Remoting. When teamed with ColdFusion MX, for example, Flash Remoting allowed for a direct connection between a Flash movie and a ColdFusion data source component. With an established connection to a ColdFusion component, methods can be called on the component to return data from a data source.

After Flash MX was released, Flash Communication Server MX was introduced, which makes it possible to have a seamless, real-time communication between a Flash movie, an ActionScript-based server-side environment, and hundreds of other Flash movies on other users' machines.

INTRODUCTION TO ACTIONSCRIPT CLASSES

As mentioned, there are many different ways to load data into a Flash movie:

- `loadVariables()` and `loadVariablesNum()` functions
- LoadVars class
- XML class
- XMLSocket class

The following sections examine these methods in more detail.

The *loadVariables()* and *loadVariablesNum()* Functions

These two functions are used to load the contents of an external file (such as a text file or a dynamically generated CGI script) and to convert URL-encoded data in that file into variables that Flash can read.

These functions perform largely the same task, but with `loadVariables()`, you can load data into a specific movie clip (such as _root.myClip), and with `loadVariablesNum()`, you can target data to a level (such as _level0). The syntax for `loadVariables()` is as follows:

```
loadVariables ("url" , "target" [, variables])
```

In this syntax, *url* is a string representing the URL containing the data to be loaded, such as "mydata.txt" or "http://www.myserver.com/mydata.php". *target* is the path and name of the movie clip into which variables are loaded—for example, "_root" or "_root.myClip". *variables* is an optional argument that specifies the HTTP method for sending variables, if there are any. The parameter must be GET or POST. The GET method adds variables to the end of the URL and is used for small numbers of variables. The POST method sends the variables in a separate HTTP header and is used for long strings of variables.

For example, if you want to load the variables located in `mydata.txt` into a movie clip named `dataStor` off the main Timeline, you would use the following code:

```
loadVariables("mydata.txt", "_root.dataStor");
```

Likewise, if you were sending variables as part of this string (if, say, a server-side script returned different data, depending on the information passed to it), you would include the optional variables. For example, if you want to load data from "http://www.myserver.com/data.php", after passing that script certain variables, you could use this code:

```
loadVariables("http://www.myserver.com/data.php?name=bob&age=30",
➥ "_root.dataStor", "GET");
```

For loadVariables() to work, data must be in the MIME format application/x-www-form-urlencoded. URL-encoded data looks like data you pass to a web server in the http string. Variables are separated by the & character. An example of URL-encoded data is name=bob%20smith&address=215%20Picadilly%20Rd. This standard format is supported by CGI scripts. Using this format, you can load multiple variables. Note, too, that the movie and the variables being loaded must reside within the same subdomain. For example, if you're loading "http://www.myserver.com/data.php", the SWF making the loadVariables() call must also reside somewhere on http://www.myserver.com.

In addition to using loadVariables() as a function, you can use it as a method of the MovieClip object with the following syntax:

```
movieClipInstance.loadVariables("url" [, variables]);
```

In this implementation, you don't need to specify *target* as one of the parameters because you're calling that method within the target. This is the syntax for loadVariablesNum():

```
loadVariablesNum ("url" ,level [, variables])
```

url is a string representing the URL containing the data to be loaded, such as "mydata.txt" or "http://www.myserver.com/mydata.php". *level* is an integer specifying in what level variables are loaded. For example, a level of 0 means that variables are loaded into the root (main timeline) of your movie. *variables* is an optional argument specifying the HTTP method (GET or POST) for sending variables, if there are any.

For example, to load variables stored in mydata.txt into the root (_level0) of your movie, use the following code:

```
loadVariablesNum("mydata.txt", 0);
```

A serious drawback of both functions is that you don't receive a notification when the variables you requested have been loaded. In some cases, this doesn't matter, but if you want to know when the variables you asked for have been received, you need to use the LoadVars class, discussed in the following section.

The *LoadVars* Class

LoadVars operates much the same way as the XML class (covered in "Extensible Markup Language (XML)" later in this chapter): It uses the load(), send(), and sendAndLoad() methods to communicate with a server. However, the XML class transfers an XML Document Object Model (DOM) tree, whereas LoadVars transfers ActionScript name and value pairs.

To use a LoadVars object, you must create a new instance of the LoadVars class, as shown here:

```
var my_lv = new LoadVars();
```

After you have instantiated your LoadVars object, you can load data from an external source, send data to an external source, and receive notification that your data has finished loading. The LoadVars class has the following properties:

- **contentType** This property indicates the data's MIME type. application/x-www-form-urlencoded is a common type.

- **loaded** This property is a binary value that indicates whether a load() or sendAndLoad() call has been completed.

The LoadVars class has the methods described in the following sections.

The *load()* Method

This method, which downloads variables from a specified URL, has the following syntax:

```
load(url)
```

For example, the following code would instruct a LoadVars instance named my_lv to begin loading "http://www.myserver.com/data.php":

```
my_lv.load("http://www.myserver.com/data.php");
```

The *send()* Method

This method posts variables from a LoadVars object to a URL and uses the following syntax:

```
send(url, method)
```

url is the URL to post the variables to, and *method* is the HTTP method (GET or POST) for transmitting the variables. For example, the following code creates an instance of LoadVars, adds two variables, and then transmits that data to the URL http://www.myserver.com/receiveData.php:

```
// create new instance of LoadVars
var my_lv = new LoadVars();


// add variables to my_lv
my_lv.name = "Bob";
my_lv.occupation = "Super model";


// transmit variables
my_lv.send("http://www.myserver.com/receiveData.php", "GET");
```

The *sendAndLoad()* Method

Using the load() and sendAndLoad() methods results in the onLoad event handler being called, but send() doesn't return any data. To send data to a script *and* have data returned, use sendAndLoad():

```
sendAndLoad("url", targetObject [, method]);
```

url is the URL that variables are posted to, and *targetObject* is the LoadVars object that receives any downloaded variables. The optional parameter *method* specifies the HTTP variable type (GET or POST). If no method is specified, the variables are transmitted via POST. This method posts variables in the LoadVars object to the specified URL and places any response sent from the server into the specified *targetObject*. For example, if you want to send a variable to a script on a server (http://www.myserver.com/receiveData.php) and load the variables resulting from this call, use the following code:

```
// create new LoadVars
my_lv  = new LoadVars();


// add variable
```

```
my_lv.nameToLookUp = "bob";

// send and load
my_lv.sendAndLoad("http://www.myserver.com/receiveData.php",
➡my_lv);
```

The *toString()* Method

This method returns a URL-encoded string containing all the variables within your instance of LoadVars. The following code creates a new LoadVars instance, assigns three variables, and then outputs them to a string:

```
// create new LoadVars
my_lv = new LoadVars();

// assign variables
my_lv.name = "Bob";
my_lv.age = 33;
my_lv.address = "215 Siccamore Rd.";
// output to string
my_lv_string = my_lv.toString();
trace(my_lv_string);
```

This code displays the following in the Output panel:

```
address=215%20Siccamore%20Rd%2E&age=33&name=Bob
```

The *getBytesLoaded()* Method

This method returns the number of bytes loaded by the load() or sendAndLoad() call. It's useful in determining how much of your data has been loaded, as in the case of a preloader. This is the syntax:

```
my_lv.getBytesLoaded();
```

The *getBytesTotal()* Method

This method returns the total size, in bytes, of the data being downloaded by a load() or sendAndLoad() call. When used with getBytesLoaded(), it enables you to determine the percentage of data downloaded. For example, the following code uses getBytesTotal() and getBytesLoaded() to determine how far you've progressed with your data download:

```
// placed on the main timeline of your movie
my_lv = new LoadVars();
my_lv.load("http://www.myserver.com/loadData.php");

// placed on the main timeline of your movie
onEnterFrame = function() {
    // determine percentage
    percentLoaded = ( my_lv.getBytesLoaded() /
    ➡my_lv.getBytesTotal() ) * 100;
    // output status
    trace(percentLoaded);
}
```

The *addRequestHeader()* Method

This method is used to add or change the HTTP request headers sent with POST actions, such as Content-Type. There are two ways to use it. The first way is to pass the headerName along with the headerValue, as shown here:

```
my_lv.addRequestHeader(headerName, headerValue)
```

For example, the following code sets the Content-Type of a LoadVars instance named my_vars to x-www-urlencoded:

```
my_lv.addRequestHeader("Content-Type", "x-www-urlencoded");
```

The second way is to pass several headers at once by using the following syntax:

```
my_lv.addRequestHeader(["headerName_1", "headerValue_1" ...
➡"headerName_n", "headerValue_n"])
```

In this example, you pass a series of headerName and headerValue values to the method. The following code sets the Content-Type and X-ClientAppVersion values for my_lv:

```
var headers = ["Content-Type", "x-www-urlencoded",
➡"X-ClientAppVersion", "2.0"];
my_lv.addRequestHeader(headers);
```

Note that the following standard HTTP headers cannot be added or changed with the addRequestHeader() method: Accept-Ranges, Age,

Allow, Allowed, Connection, Content-Length, Content-Location, Content-Range, ETag, Host, Last-Modified, Locations, Max-Forwards, Proxy-Authenticate, Proxy-Authorization, Public, Range, Retry-After, Server, TE, Trailer, Transfer-Encoding, Upgrade, URI, Vary, Via, Warning, and WWW-Authenticate. Other headers, such as Content-Type or X-ClientAppVersion, or any custom headers can be added or changed.

LoadVars uses the onLoad event handler, which is invoked whenever a load() or sendAndLoad() call has completed. You define a function for this handler in the following manner:

```
my_lv.onLoad = function() {
    // code here
}
```

EXTENSIBLE MARKUP LANGUAGE (XML)

XML is a markup language containing structured information that's recorded in documents. These documents also contain markers indicating the structural arrangement of that documentation.

As with an HTML file, you use tags when creating an XML file to mark up (specify) a body of text. In HTML, you use predefined tags to indicate how text should appear in a web browser; the <u> tag makes text underlined, for example. In XML, you define tags that identify what *type* a piece of data is—for example, <address>215 Cherry Brook Lane</address> identifies the data as address information. XML separates the structure of the information from the way it's displayed, so an XML document can be reused in multiple environments.

Every XML tag is called a *node* or an *element*. Each node has a type (1, which indicates an XML element, or 3, which indicates a text node), and elements can also have attributes. A node attribute is a value named and defined within the tag. For example, in <user new=true>, new is an attribute of the <user> tag. A node nested inside a parent node is called a *child node*.

XML information is usually contained within .xml files, although server-side scripts, such as PHP or ASP, can generate XML data that Flash can read. In the following example, <person> is the parent node, and <name> is the child, which contains a value:

```
<person>
    <name>Bob Roberts</name>
</person>
```

In this slightly more complicated example, <person> is the parent node, and <name> is the child node, with two attributes, type and value:

```
<person>
    <name type="first_name" value="Bob" />
    <name type="last_name" value="Roberts" />
</person>
```

This code might look familiar if you have experience coding in HTML, which is a subset of XML. As such, they share several visual and structural elements. Where they differ, however, is that the HTML specification is rigid, whereas XML is intended to allow you to define the structure of any type of data you want to record or manipulate.

Although some basics of XML are explained in the following sections, this chapter is not intended as an in-depth primer of the XML specification. If you're interested in more information, check the URLs listed at the end of this chapter in the "Resources" sidebar. For the purposes of this chapter, the following sections explain the basics of creating XML as well as the specifics of the Flash 2004 XML class, which enables you to import, manipulate, and send XML data to and from a variety of sources.

Creating an *XML* Object

Before you can load, send, or manipulate any XML data in Flash, you need to create an instance of the XML object using the constructor, as shown here:

```
var my_xml = new XML();
```

You can send an optional parameter, *source*, to the constructor. This parameter is a text string to be converted into XML formatted data. For example, the following line of text appears to be XML, but Flash doesn't understand how to access it this way:

```
var my_text = "<xml><tag name='my_tag' /></xml>";
```

To convert this line into XML, specify it as the optional *source* parameter used when creating an instance of the XML class, as shown here:

```
var my_xml = new XML(my_text);
```

Loading XML Data

After you have created your XML object, you can add XML information to it or load in XML information from an external source. Adding your own information is described in "Modifying XML Data," later in this chapter. To load external data, you can use one of the two methods of the XML class: load() or sendAndLoad().This is the syntax for the load() method:

```
xmlInstance.load(url)
```

url is the relative or absolute URL containing the XML data. The XML data can be contained in an XML file or in any type of dynamic file format (such as PHP or ASP, which are described in "Dynamic Data Sources" later in this chapter).

So if you want to load the contents of http://www.myserver.com/myXML.xml into the my_xml object created in the previous section, you would use the following code:

```
my_xml.load("http://www.myserver.com/myXML.xml");
```

You can also use the sendAndLoad() method to load data into an XML object. In addition, as the method name suggests, you use sendAndLoad() to send XML data and load any resulting data into an XML object. This is the syntax for sendAndLoad():

```
xmlInstance.sendAndLoad(url,targetXMLObject);
```

url is the relative or absolute URL that the XML data is initially sent to, and *targetXMLObject* is the name of the XML object that the server's response is loaded into.

For example, suppose you had a second XML object, my_other_xml, and you wanted to send its contents to a script at http://www.myserver.com/receiveXML.php. This script would take the sent data and return an XML object containing information about the transfer (whether the data was received or whether an error occurred). If you want the server's response loaded into your my_xml object, you would use the following code:

```
my_other_xml.sendAndLoad("http://www.myserver.com/
➥receiveXML.php", my_xml);
```

Whether you're using `load()` or `sendAndLoad()`, when you ask the server for data, you want to know if you've gotten it. You can find out by defining an event handler—in this case, a *callback function*—for your XML object.

The first callback function you can use is `onLoad`, which returns a Boolean (true or false) indicating whether the `load()` or `sendAndLoad()` call was successful. You need to define a callback function to interpret the completion of the data loading because `onLoad` is undefined by default. You can define it in the following ways:

```
function my_onLoad(success) {
    // code to respond to load
    if (success == true) {
        trace("successfully downloaded xml");
    } else {
        trace("error downloading xml");
    }
}
my_xml.onLoad = my_onLoad;
```

or

```
my_xml.onLoad = function (success) {
     // code to respond to load
    if (success == true) {
        trace("successfully downloaded xml");
    } else {
        trace("error downloading xml");
    }
}
```

The other callback function is `onData`. It's similar to the `onLoad` callback, except that `onData` returns the information the server downloaded; `onLoad`, on the other hand, returns the status of the download when it's called to determine the successful or unsuccessful completion of a `load()` or `sendAndLoad()` method. By default, `onData` calls `onLoad`. This is what `onData` looks like by default:

```
XML.prototype.onData = function (src) {
  if (src == undefined) {
    this.onLoad(false);
  } else {
    this.parseXML(src);
    this.loaded = true;
    this.onLoad(true);
  }
}
```

You can override onData, but if you do, onLoad isn't called unless you specifically call it within your version of onData.

After your data is loaded, you want to be able to read and manipulate it. Before you learn how to do that, however, you need to learn about sending data in XML in the next section.

Sending XML Data

If you want to send XML data in your Flash movie to an external script, you can do so by using two XML methods: send() and sendAndLoad(). The sendAndLoad() method was explained in the previous section, "Loading XML Data." The send() method is used to transmit the contents of an XML object to a server. It uses the following syntax:

xmlInstance.send(*url* [,*window*])

url is the relative or absolute URL where you're sending the XML data, and *window* is the optional parameter that specifies the window for displaying any data the server returns. You can use any of the following to specify which window:

- **_self**   Specifies the current frame in the current window.

- **_blank**   Specifies a new window.

- **_parent**   Specifies the parent of the current frame.

- **_top**   Specifies the top-level frame in the current window.

If no window is indicated, it's the same as specifying _self.

If you had an XML object called my_xml, and you wanted to send its contents to a script on your server, your code would look like this:

my_xml.send("http://www.myserver.com/receiveXML.php");

Now that you know how to send and load XML data, continue reading to learn how to modify it.

Modifying XML Data

As mentioned, you can nest XML nodes (tags), with nested nodes being the children of the parent nodes containing them. This relationship is similar to the parent-child relationship in ActionScript. There are two ways to access data in XML: read and modify existing data, or add new data to an XML object. The next section explains adding new data to an XML object.

Creating Elements

Suppose you have a script on your server that receives a block of XML data, reads the information from it, and saves it to a database. You also have a form that users of your site can fill out. You would like to send information from the form to this script so that their information can be saved.

The movie on your site has three text fields for the user to fill out: name, email, and comments. After filling out these three fields, the user clicks a Submit button. When this button is clicked, you want to send the data to a script on your server, where the data is saved. To do this, first you need to create an XML object and populate it with data from your text fields, as shown here:

```
// create XML object
my_xml = new XML();

// add name field
my_name = my_xml.createElement("NAME");

// assign it the value of inputName
my_name.attributes.value = inputName.text;

// update the NAME element
my_xml.appendChild(my_name);
```

```
// add email field
my_email = my_xml.createElement("EMAIL");

// assign it the value of inputEmail
my_email.attributes.value = inputEmail.text;

// update the EMAIL element
my_xml.appendChild(my_email);


// add COMMENTS element
my_comments = my_xml.createElement("COMMENTS");

// add a text node
my_comments_text = my_xml.createTextNode("COMMENTS");

// update the COMMENTS element
my_comments.appendChild(my_comments_text);

// assign the text node the value of COMMENTS
my_comments_text.nodeValue = comments.text;

// update the COMMENTS element again
my_xml.appendChild(my_comments);
```

The code first creates a new XML object called my_xml. Then the XML method createElement() creates a new element and gives it a name. Then attributes for the newly created element are set. Next, you use the XML method appendChild() to update the element in the XML object. The appendChild() method has the following syntax:

```
xml.appendChild(child);
```

child is the child element to be updated or added. If you perform an appendChild() on an XML element that's outside the current XML object, the child element is copied into the XML object. If it exists in the calling XML object, the child is updated. If you don't use appendChild(), your element won't be present in your XML object.

This process—creating the element, setting attributes, and using appendChild()—is repeated for the EMAIL element.When you create the COMMENTS element, however, the process is a little different. Take a look at the section of the code that defines the COMMENTS element:

```
// add COMMENTS element
my_comments = my_xml.createElement("COMMENTS");

// add a text node
my_comments_text = my_xml.createTextNode("COMMENTS");

// update the COMMENTS element
my_comments.appendChild(my_comments_text);

// assign the text node the value of COMMENTS
my_comments_text.nodeValue = comments.text;

// update the COMMENTS element again
my_xml.appendChild(my_comments);
```

First, this code creates a new element called COMMENTS and then creates a new text node, also called COMMENTS. Next, the value of the new text node is set to match the contents of the TextField named comments. The nodeValue property is set instead of using attributes because an attribute is a piece of identifying data contained inside a tag; the node's value is what's contained between the element's opening and closing tags. For example, if an element has no node value (which is to say no child), it looks like this:

```
<element val="123" />
```

The /> denotes the end of the tag. This element has an attribute, val, but no nodeValue. Now take a look at this element:

```
<element val="123">
Node Value Text
</element>
```

This element has a node value, which is the text Node Value Text. A node value doesn't have to be text, however. It can be another element or a series of elements, as shown here:

```
<element val="123">
    <sub val="234" />
    <sub val="345">
        <subsub val="456" />
```

```
    </sub>
</element>
```

In this code, ELEMENT has a nodeValue that consists of two child nodes, one of which has its own child nodes. So when you set the value of COMMENTS, you set the nodeValue as shown here because you're saving a block of text, not just a descriptor or two:

```
// add COMMENTS element
my_comments = my_xml.createElement("COMMENTS");

// add a text node
my_comments_text = my_xml.createTextNode("COMMENTS");

// update the COMMENTS element
my_comments.appendChild(my_comments_text);

// assign the text node the value of COMMENTS
my_comments_text.nodeValue = comments.text;

// update the COMMENTS element again
my_xml.appendChild(my_comments);
```

After that, the value of the COMMENTS element is updated to contain the COMMENTS text node. Therefore, when you update the value of my_xml, you're actually including an element with its own element. Sample XML generated from the preceding code would look like this:

```
<NAME val="Bob" />
<EMAIL val="mailto:email@bob.com" />
<COMMENTS>
    I love this place!
</COMMENTS>
```

Another useful method is removeNode(), which removes an element from an XML object. To remove a node, you must refer to it in the context of the childNodes array. childNodes is an array that represents child nodes of any given tag. For example, take a look at the following XML structure:

```
<parent>
    <good_child />
    <bad_child />
</parent>
```

The PARENT element has a childNodes array. In this array, element 0 is the GOOD_CHILD element, and element 1 is the BAD_CHILD element. To refer to these elements in code, first you need to make a reference to the PARENT element. Because PARENT is the first element in this XML structure, it's the firstChild. You use firstChild to refer to the very first child element. Similarly, you use lastChild to refer to the last child element. So if the XML object is named new_xml, you would refer to PARENT as shown here:

```
new_xml.firstChild;
```

To refer to BAD_CHILD, you would use the following code:

```
new_xml.firstChild.childNodes[1];
```

To delete the BAD_CHILD element (because nobody likes a bad child), you would use the following code:

```
new_xml.firstChild.childNodes[1].removeNode();
```

There—no more BAD_CHILD. XML also has a hasChildNodes() method, which enables you to check for any child nodes of a specific node or element. For example, the following statement would return true because PARENT has two child nodes:

```
does_have_children = new_xml.firstChild.hasChildNodes();
trace(does_have_children);
```

Back to the previous example: Now that the XML has been created, you want to send it off and be notified that it's been saved. To do this, you define an XML object to handle the reply and send the information with sendAndLoad(). The finished code would look like this:

```
function sendMyXMLData() {
    // create XML object
    my_xml = new XML();

    // add name field
    my_name = my_xml.createElement("NAME");

    // assign it the value of inputName
    my_name.attributes.value = inputName.text;
```

```
// update the NAME element
my_xml.appendChild(my_name);

// add email field
my_email = my_xml.createElement("EMAIL");

// assign it the value of inputEmail
my_email.attributes.value = inputEmail.text;

// update the EMAIL element
my_xml.appendChild(my_email);

// add COMMENTS element
my_comments = my_xml.createElement("COMMENTS");

// add a text node
my_comments_text = my_xml.createTextNode("COMMENTS");

// update the COMMENTS element
my_comments.appendChild(my_comments_text);

// assign the text node the value of COMMENTS
my_comments_text.nodeValue = comments.text;

// update the COMMENTS element again
my_xml.appendChild(my_comments);

// create reply XML object
var replyXML = new XML();
replyXML.ignoreWhite = true;
replyXML.onLoad = replyFunction;

// send the XML object to the server
my_xml.sendAndLoad("http://www.server.com/receive.php",
➥replyXML);

// reply handler
// this calls in the replyXML.onLoad handler
```

```
function replyFunction (response) {
    // response handler


    }
}
```

That's a quick look at creating XML content. The next section explains what to put in the replyFunction.

Reading XML Data

In the previous example, you sent an XML object to a script on the server, and any reply you got was sent to the reply handler called replyFunction. Suppose this is the response you get:

```
<response>
    <status value="good">
    <note>
    Your submission has been accepted. Thanks!
    </note>
</response>
```

Depending on the outcome of the transmission, the STATUS element might be good or bad. The nodeValue of the NOTE element would change, too, depending on the STATUS element.

How do you handle this data? First, you need to make sure the XML structure is correct (that is, check to see whether you've been sent both STATUS and NOTE elements). Then you examine the value of STATUS and display the nodeValue of NOTE.

Before you get started, however, you need to know about an important property of the XML object: ignoreWhite. When an XML object is sent to you, sometimes lines of empty text are included because of extra line breaks, for example. When Flash reads XML data, by default it doesn't ignore empty whitespace. In fact, Flash records the whitespace as part of the XML data. For example, the following pieces of XML are different:

```
<response>
    <status value="good">
    <note>
    Your submission has been accepted. Thanks!
    </note>
</response>
```

```
<response>
    <status value="good">

    <note>
    Your submission has been accepted. Thanks!
    </note>
</response>
```

The first RESPONSE element has only two child nodes, but the second has three because Flash reads the empty line break. To prevent this, set the ignoreWhite property to true after you create your new XML object:

```
my_xml = new XML();
my_xml.ignoreWhite = true;
```

This property will save you a lot of time and frustration. Now, back to the example. Here is the function that's called when onLoad is called in the replyXML object:

```
function replyFunction (success) {
}
```

If you've received the data (success equals true), you check to see whether the STATUS tag exists:

```
function replyFunction (success) {
    if (success == true) {
        // data has been received!
        // make reference to RESPONSE
        my_response = this.firstChild;

        // see if RESPONSE has child nodes
        if (my_response.hasChildNodes()) {
            // the first child should be STATUS
            if (my_response.childNodes
            [0].nodeName.toUpperCase()
            ➥== "STATUS") {
                // status exists
            }
        }
    }
}
```

Notice that a couple of things were added in that last if statement. nodeName is a property that returns the name of the specified node. In this case, if the structure returned to you is correct, the name of the first child of the RESPONSE element is STATUS. To make sure there are no sentence case errors, the string method toUpperCase() is used to convert status to STATUS. This method also corrects any errors such as Status or sTatus, for example.

Now that you know the STATUS element exists, you need to react to its value. In this example, if the STATUS is good, you jump to a frame named success_good; if the STATUS is bad, you jump to a frame named success_bad, as shown here:

```
if (my_response.childNodes[0].nodeName.toUpperCase() ==
➥"STATUS") {
    // STATUS exists
    my_status_element = my_response.childNodes[0];

    // check value of STATUS
    if (my_status_element.attributes.value == "good") {
        gotoAndPlay("success_good");
    } else if (my_status_element.attributes.value == "bad") {
        gotoAndPlay("success_bad");
    }

}
```

Now, if the success is equal to bad, you'll jump to the appropriate frame. Imagine that you have a text field called outcome in both frames. Regardless of the value of STATUS, you want to display the contents of the NOTE element in this text field. To do this, you add the following code after the previous if statement:

```
if (my_response.childNodes[1].nodeName.toUpperCase() == "NOTE")
{
    // this element is NOTE
    my_note = my_response.childNodes[1];

    // display the contents of this in the text field
    outcome.text = my_note.nodeValue;

}
```

That's it. Not too hard, right? But wait—what if the response from the server is something like this:

```
<response>
    <phrase value="A rolling stone..." />
    <phrase value="A bird in the hand..." />
    <phrase value="Let there be light!" />
</response>
```

Instead of two different elements within RESPONSE, you have the same type of element repeated three times. What if there are four PHRASE tags next time? Or 12? How do you read them all? You find out the length of the childNodes array.

First, to handle the received XML content, you take the value of each PHRASE element and add it to a text field called wisdom. So you need to loop through the XML document one time for each PHRASE element. Make a reference to the child nodes of the RESPONSE element (which are the three PHRASE elements in the preceding example):

```
if (my_xml.firstChild.hasChildNodes()) {
    my_responses = my_xml.firstChild.childNodes;
}
```

Next, to find out how many PHRASE elements you have, use the length property:

```
if (my_xml.firstChild.hasChildNodes()) {
    my_responses = my_xml.firstChild.childNodes;
    // determine number of PHRASE elements
    number_phrases = my_responses.length;
        trace("There are " + number_phrases + " phrases.");
}
```

Now that you know the number of PHRASE elements, you need to loop through them. First, check to make sure they are the right data type by using the XML property nodeType. If the element is a regular XML element, nodeType equals 1. If it is a text node, nodeType equals 3. If the PHRASE element has a nodeType of 1, you add the value attribute to the wisdom text field, as shown here:

```
if (my_xml.firstChild.hasChildNodes()) {
    my_responses = my_xml.firstChild.childNodes;
    // determine number of PHRASE elements
```

```
number_phrases = my_responses.length;
 trace("There are " + number_phrases + " phrases.");
 // empty the wisdom text field
 wisdom.text = "";
 for (var i = 0; i<number_phrases; i++) {
     // set current PHRASE
     current_phrase = my_responses[i];
     // check node type
     if (current_phrase.nodeType == 1) {
         // node type is correct
         // add PHRASE to outcome text field
         wisdom.text += current_phrase.attributes.value;
     }
 }
}
```

If you test this code now, you'd see the wisdom text field fill up and display the following:

```
A rolling stone...
A bird in the hand...
Let there be light!
```

XML isn't so hard to deal with, is it? There are a few additional XML methods and properties, but in most cases, you don't have to use them. To see a full list of the methods and properties of the XML class, refer to the ActionScript Reference Guide in Flash 2004.

 Flash Remoting is a way to allow your Flash movie to connect directly to server-side components, such as those developed with ColdFusion MX. It is a powerful, easy way to make data-rich applications. If you use Remoting, you can write ColdFusion scripts using ActionScript. For more specifics, see Chapter 18, "Advanced Communication."

External File Formats

Still a little confused about how certain file formats work? The following sections cover some common format types, the code elements (classes, functions, and so forth) you use them with, and some best-practice tips on how to use them.

URL-Encoded Name-Value Pairs

As mentioned, Flash can translate name-value pairs into Flash variables. A *name-value pair* is exactly whate it sounds like: the name of a variable and its value. Here's a simple name-value pair:

```
name=bob
```

In Flash, you can place these name-value pairs in text files or add them to the end of the <EMBED> and <OBJECT> tags in HTML files. (See the following section, "Using FlashVars in HTML," for examples.) Suppose you have three variables, as shown here:

```
name="Bob Roberts";
age=30;
gender="Male";
```

You could place these variables as URL-encoded name-value pairs in a text file, like this:

```
name=Bob%20Roberts
&age=30
&gender=Male
```

Or you could add them after the file specification in your <EMBED> or <OBJECT> tag:

```
src="file.swf?name=Bob%20Roberts&age=30&gender=Male"
```

Note that this is a deprecated way of adding variables to your Flash movie. It's recommended that you add them using FlashVars, as explained in the following section.

Using *FlashVars* in HTML

When placed within the <EMBED> or <OBJECT> tag, the FlashVars property can be used to import variables into the root level of your movie. These variables are loaded *before* the first frame of the SWF is played. FlashVars is a string composed of a set of name-value combinations, with each one separated by an ampersand (&). You can escape special and nonprintable characters with a % followed by a two-digit hexadecimal value. To add a single blank space, use the + sign.

Browsers support string sizes up to 64KB (65,535 bytes). To work in all browsers, FlashVars must be set in both the <OBJECT> and <EMBED> tags. This is what FlashVars looks like in the <OBJECT> tag:

```
<PARAM NAME=FlashVars
➥VALUE="book=Flash+Demystified&author1=Brian%20Hogg
➥&author2=Shawn%20Pucknell&author3=Craig%20Swann">
```

In the <EMBED> tag, FlashVars looks like this:

```
<EMBED src="file.swf"
➥FlashVars="book=Flash+Demystified&author1=
➥Brian%20Hogg&author2=Shawn%20Pucknell&author3=Craig%20Swann">
➥</EMBED>
```

Encoding for this string is the same as the page containing it. Internet Explorer is responsible for providing UTF-16–compliant strings on a Windows platform. Likewise, Netscape provides a UTF-8–encoded string to the player.

As mentioned, XML is a language specification designed to enable you to create and organize structured data of any type. It is extremely useful, powerful, and easy to write. Because it is supported by so many different programming languages, it's also very portable.

For more detailed information on XML usage, read the "Extensible Markup Language (XML)" section earlier in this chapter, and check the ActionScript Reference Guide in the Flash 2004 Help panel.

DYNAMIC DATA SOURCES

Although external data often consists of static files, such as configuration files, that sit on the server alongside your SWF, frequently you need dynamic data, too. A *dynamic data source* creates data that's generated immediately before you access it. PHP, ASP, and ColdFusion scripts are all examples of dynamic data sources. The content in dynamic data sources varies according to information passed to those scripts when they are accessed (for example, file.php?var=20) or information that the script accesses (such as a database).

Dynamic data sources are valuable because they enable you to transcend the data you have at the time you create your application. You can create rich, flexible applications that generate varying responses to unique user requests.

You can use several formats to create Flash-readable dynamic content. As long as the script generates data of a type that Flash can read (XML or URL-encoded data, for example), it doesn't matter what type of script it is. Of the different kinds of data sources that Flash can connect to, there are two classifications to consider: whether the data source is stateless or socketed.

A *stateless connection* exists solely for the duration of your request for information from the server. For example, HTTP requests are stateless: Your browser contacts a server, makes a brief connection to receive HTML data, and then the connection is broken. The server might have a record of your previous connections, but the server does not realize that, over the course of multiple requests, the same person is generating those requests.

A stateless connection is like phoning a person, asking him a single question, and then hanging up. This is the most common method of data transfer on the Internet, as it requires far fewer resources than socketed connections; the server needs to be aware of your connection only while the connection is made. After your request is fulfilled, the server can direct those resources elsewhere.

A *socketed connection,* on the other hand, is a continued connection between server and client—analogous to phoning someone, asking a single question, and remaining on the line until you think of another question. Socketed connections are handy if you want to push data to a client (sending data without getting a request for it first, much as television pushes programming to viewers). However, socketed communications take up far more resources and bandwidth than stateless connections do. The server must devote resources to responding to client requests and maintaining its connection to the client.

Socketed connections are frequently used in chat applications and online games (multiuser games, for example), when clients need to make repeated, nearly continuous requests of the server and other connected clients. If your application doesn't require a continuous connection with the server (as in a game that needs to connect to the server only to transmit and download high scores), using a socketed connection is overkill.

Stateless Data Sources

The following sections describe different types of stateless data sources. These types are only a few of the variety that's available, but this discussion should give you a feel for the different types of sources you can connect to in Flash. In addition, users of Flash MX Professional have access to the WebServices component, which allows for a connection to almost any type of Web Services Description Language (WSDL) data source. You can find more information on using the WebServices component in the Flash MX Professional 2004 Help files.

PHP

PHP, which stands for *PHP Hypertext Processor* (seriously), is an HTML-embedded scripting language. Much of its syntax is borrowed from C, Java, and Perl, with a few unique PHP-specific features thrown in, written with the intention of allowing web developers to write dynamically generated pages quickly.

To perform properly, PHP script files, which have the extension .php, need the PHP server application. PHP makes it possible to develop applications quickly and has a clean way of connecting to data sources, such as mySQL, SQL, and Access databases.

PHP mixes elements of PHP script with HTML code. Script in .php files is wrapped in the code markers <? and ?>. For example, the following simple PHP page would output the phrase "Flash Demystified" five times:

```
<? php ?>
<html>
<head>
    <title>test</title>
</head>
<body>
<?
for ($i = 0; $i<5; $i++) {
?>
Flash Demystified<br>
<?
}
?>
</body>
</html>
```

To learn more about PHP, check out www.php.net/. You'll find online documentation and links to download PHP 5, the most recent version of the PHP server.

As you can see, PHP's syntax is similar to ActionScript. It is, as well, a robust yet easy-to-learn language. With PHP, you can write scripts that provide data that's readable by `loadVariables()`, `loadVariablesNum()`, the `LoadVars` class, and the `XML` class.

ASP

To learn more about ASP, check out http://msdn. miscrosoft.com/asp for documentation and tutorials on ASP and information on how to obtain and install Internet Information Services.

Microsoft Active Server Pages (ASP) is the server-side environment in Microsoft Internet Information Services. It enables you to run ActiveX script and ActiveX server components. You can use ASP to connect to databases or just to produce dynamic content. ASP files have the extension `.asp`. Script in these files is wrapped in the code markers `<%` and `%>`. For example, the following simple ASP page would output the phrase "Flash Demystified" five times:

```
<%@ LANGUAGE="VBScript" %>
<html>
<head>
      <title>test</title>
</head>
<body>
<%
myVar = "Flash Demystified"
for i=1 to 10
<response.write myVar & "<br>"
next
%>
</body>
</html>
```

Using ASP, you can write scripts that provide data readable by `loadVariables()`, `loadVariablesNum()`, the `LoadVars` class, and the `XML` class.

.NET

For detailed information on .NET, including language references and sample applications, visit http:// www.microsoft.com/ net/.

.NET is a programming framework that's intended to facilitate developing rich, powerful web applications. .NET, which is used with a wide variety of languages, is enhanced with many built-in controls, the capability to use different languages, and the use of compiled code rather than interpreted code for faster execution.

ColdFusion

Macromedia ColdFusion MX is the rapid server-scripting environment for creating Rich Internet Applications (RIA). ColdFusion MX combines easy-to-use scripting with effortless connectivity to enterprise data and powerful built-in search and charting features. It enables developers to easily build and deploy dynamic websites, content publishing systems, self-service applications, e-commerce sites, and more.

ColdFusion Markup Language (CFML) is the tag-based server-scripting language that ColdFusion uses. Its syntax is similar to HTML and XML, so if you know how to code a text web page, you can pick up ColdFusion easily. ColdFusion script files use the .cfm file extension. The following simple ColdFusion script file queries a database and displays the result:

```
<cfquery name="myQuery" datasource="myDataSource">
    SELECT * FROM myTable
</cfquery>
<html>
<head>
    <title>My page</title>
</head>
<body>
<table border=0>
<tr>
<td colspan="2>My Results</td>
</tr>
<cfoutput name="myQuery">
    <tr>
        <td>#name#</td>
        <td>#address#</td>
    </tr>
</cfoutput>
</table>
</body>
</html>
```

You can get more information about ColdFusion and CFML from Macromedia's web site at http:// www.macromedia.com /software/ coldfusion/.

As you can see, the syntax is similar to HTML. Using ColdFusion, you can write scripts that provide data readable by loadVariables(), loadVariablesNum(), the LoadVars class, and the XML class.

Socketed Data Sources

Flash MX 2004 can connect to socketed data sources by using the XMLSocket class and the NetConnection class, which connects to Flash Communication Server. These classes enable you to create persistent connections with a server, allowing for a wide variety of exciting applications.

The *XMLSocket* Class

XMLSocket is a native ActionScript class that enables you to create a continuous connection to another computer at a specified IP address. XMLSocket is useful in creating multiuser applications, such as chat rooms and online multiplayer games. XMLSocket is typically used to connect to a Java-based server application, such as Colin Moock's Unity Server (available at http://www.moock.org/unity/).

You can find more detailed information about the usage of XMLSocket, including a listing of available methods and properties, in the ActionScript Reference Guide in the Flash 2004 Help files.

Flash Communication Server

Flash Communication Server is an application server, developed by Macromedia, that enables you to connect Flash movies to a server in real time and quickly develop robust, feature-rich, multiuser applications. You can use Flash Communication Server to connect to other data sources and share information with connected servers.

Programming with Flash Communication Server involves using server-side ActionScript files, which are saved as .asc files on your server, as well as ActionScript (.as) files, which can be loaded into .asc files. Server-side ActionScript uses the same language as regular ActionScript but adheres more closely to the ECMA language specification.

Flash Communication Server is explored in more detail in Chapter 18, "Advanced Communication."

With Flash Communication Server, you can build applications quickly, as you don't have to learn any new languages to build server-side components. This is unlike XMLSocket, which requires learning additional programming languages and environments, such as Java, to build the back-end functionality.

JavaScript and Flash

The FSCommand function is explained in more detail in Chapter 23, "Publishing."

The FSCommand function enables you to communicate between a Flash movie and its host environment. Typically, this communication takes place with the standalone player as you set scaling options or enable or disable the display of your movie in full-screen mode.

FSCommand offers more than simple commands such as allowscale and fullscreen. It also allows a movie to communicate with a browser; in other words, movies can send JavaScript commands to browsers, and browsers can send JavaScript commands to movies. This communication is useful if, for example, you wanted to use a function defined in JavaScript to open a pop-up window. You could send the URL and the window's height and width to JavaScript and then open the correct URL in the correctly sized window. Additionally, you could pop up an alert box; when the user clicks its button, it would send a play command to a Flash movie.

Flash Player 4 and later support Flash JavaScript methods and FSCommand in Netscape 6.2 and later. For Netscape 6.2 and later, setting the <EMBED> parameter swLiveConnect to true isn't necessary, but doing so has no adverse effects. Flash sets this value automatically depending on your publishing settings. (For more information, see Chapter 23, "Publishing.")

When you send an FSCommand to a standalone player, you're restricted to a few commands. If you send an FSCommand to a browser, however, you can send any type of command you'd like. You pass two arguments, *command* and *arguments*, as shown here:

```
fscommand(command, arguments)
```

These arguments can be strings or expressions. They are used in a JavaScript function that's written to handle the fscommand() function.

fscommand() calls a function called *moviename*_DoFSCommand, which you define yourself. *moviename* is the name of the Flash Player, which you set as NAME in the <EMBED> tag or ID in the <OBJECT> tag. For example, if you named the movie my_movie in the code for <EMBED> or <OBJECT>, the function that fscommand() calls would be my_movie_DoFSCommand.

To interpret the message sent to the browser, you must write the *moviename*_DoFSCommand function. For example, the following code checks the passed *command* string; if it's cowboy, the code displays the text yee-haw in a JavaScript alert box:

```
my_movie_DoFSCommand(command, args) {
    if (command == "cowboy") {
        alert("yee-haw");
    }
}
```

Additionally, if Internet Explorer is your target browser, you can attach an event handler in a <SCRIPT> tag in the page's HTML code, as shown here:

```
<Script Language = "JavaScript" event="FSCommand (command,
➥args)" for= "theMovie">
...
</Script>
```

Although the Publish settings in Flash by default don't define the name of your movie in the HTML code, if you select the Flash with FSCommand template in the HTML Publish Settings dialog box (see Figure 17.1), those settings are made in the HTML code.

FIGURE 17.1
Selecting the Flash with FSCommand template.

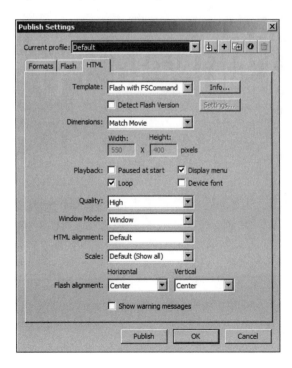

Resources

XML

XML.org: http://www.xml.org/

PHP

PHP Hypertext Preprocessor: http://www.php.net/

ASP

Active Server Pages Development Center:
http://msdn.microsoft.com/asp

.NET

Microsoft .NET: http://www.microsoft.com/net/

ASP.NET Web: http://www.asp.net/

ColdFusion

ColdFusion MX: http://www.macromedia.com/software/coldfusion/

ColdFusion Development Center:
http://www.macromedia.com/devnet/mx/coldfusion/

Flash Communication Server

Flash Communication Server MX:
http://www.macromedia.com/software/flashcom/

Flash Communication Server Development Center:
http://www.macromedia.com/devnet/mx/flashcom/

POINTS TO REMEMBER

- Flash can import data in different formats, such as XML and URL-encoded name-value pairs.

- Flash can access this data from any file type (such as PHP, ASP, or ColdFusion files).

- External data sources enable you to create updatable, dynamic Flash movies.

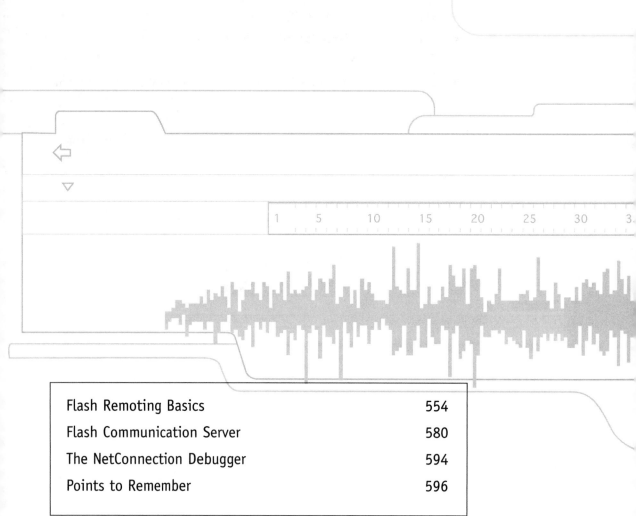

CHAPTER 18

ADVANCED COMMUNICATION

THIS CHAPTER EXPLORES TWO POWERFUL METHODS OF ESTABLISHING COMMUNICATIONS between a server environment and your Flash movie. You'll learn what these tools can do and how to use them to your best advantage. First, you'll learn about Flash Remoting and its capabilities for providing network communications between Flash applications and remote services. Then you'll learn about Flash Communication Server 1.5, a standalone server that provides support for robust real-time applications. You'll also take a look at the NetConnection Debugger, a powerful tool for tracking and troubleshooting communications between Flash and your target server environment.

FLASH REMOTING BASICS

This section is not intended to be a comprehensive documentation of the capabilities of Flash Remoting or Macromedia ColdFusion, the preferred server environment. It's meant to provide an overview of Remoting and its capabilities and to allow you to experiment by creating a simple application with it. For more detailed information, please consult the ColdFusion MX documentation (for information on setting up databases and data sources and using ColdFusion Markup Language) and the Flash Remoting MX documentation.

Macromedia Flash Remoting MX is an application server gateway that provides a network communications channel between Flash applications and remote services. Compared to other techniques for connecting Flash applications to external data providers, which include HTTP functions such as getURL() and loadVariables() and XML functions such as XMLSocket(), Flash Remoting MX offers the following advantages:

- **Ease of use**   Flash Remoting MX automatically performs data type conversion from remote services code, such as Java, ColdFusion Markup Language (CFML), and C#, to ActionScript and back again. In addition, Flash Remoting MX automatically performs logging, debugging, and security integration.

- **Performance**   Flash Remoting MX serializes messages between Flash applications and remote services. It does this using the Action Message Format (AMF), a binary format based on the Simple Object Access Protocol (SOAP) format.

- **Extensibility**   Flash Remoting MX is built to integrate with existing, established application design patterns and best practices. This speeds the creation of well-designed Flash applications.

On the server, Flash Remoting MX runs as a servlet in Java application servers, an assembly in .NET servers, and a native service in ColdFusion MX. Depending on the platform, Flash Remoting MX on the server contains a series of filters for error handling, logging, and security authentication and automatically maps service function requests to the appropriate server technology.

You use NetServices ActionScript functions to connect to application server technologies and web services. In addition, the NetDebug and

DataGlue ActionScript functions help debug Flash applications and display record sets in Flash components that come with Flash MX Professional 2004.

The Speed of Remoting

To demonstrate the features of Flash Remoting, ColdFusion is used as the server-side environment. Although Flash Remoting can connect to other server-side development platforms, such as the .NET and Java server environments, for these platforms you should use Flash MX Professional 2004. This Flash edition contains the WebServices component, which is a powerful, streamlined mechanism for connecting to all types of server environments.

The main benefit of connecting to data sources through Flash Remoting is speed. The following code, written in CFML, defines a component object with one method, qGetData, and returns all fields from the MyTable table:

```
<CFCOMPONENT>
    <CFFUNCTION NAME="qGetData" access="remote">
        <CFQUERY NAME="qGetData" Datasource="MyDSN">
        SELECT * FROM MyTable
        </CFQUERY>
        <CFRETURN qGetData>
    </CFFUNCTION>
</CFCOMPONENT>
```

Using Flash Remoting, this data can be transmitted as is to Flash, where your movie can interpret the record set. To provide the same data using XML, your code would look like this:

```
<data>
    <record id="1">
        <firstName>Brian</firstName>
        <lastName>Hogg</lastName>
        <email>brian@mrhogg.com</email>
    </record>
    <record id="2">
        <firstName>Shawn</firstName>
        <lastName>Pucknell</lastName>
```

```
        <email>pucknell@flashinto.com</email>
    </record>
</data>
```

To create this XML packet, you'd also need to write a script to generate the XML. It's certainly possible, but look how much longer the script to generate the XML is than the ColdFusion Component:

```
<CFSCRIPT>
  function CreateXMLNode(ID,FirstName,LastName,Email)
  {node="<Record ID='#ID#'>";

node=node&"<FirstName>"&xmlformat(FirstName)&"</FirstName>";
    node=node&"<LastName>"&xmlformat(LastName)&"</LastName>";
    node=node&"<WebSite>"&xmlformat(Email)&"</WebSite>";
    node=node&"</Record>";
    return node;
    }
</CFSCRIPT>

<CFQUERY NAME="getData" Datasource="App.MyDSN">
    SELECT * FROM MyTable
</CFQUERY>

<!--- Loop to generate the XML Node Tree --->
<CFLOOP Query="getData">
  <CFSCRIPT>
    MyXML=MyXMLDoc&CreateXMLNode(#ID#,'#FirstName#',
    ➥'#LastName#','#Email#);
  </CFSCRIPT>
</CFLOOP>

<!--- Create the XML document -->
<CFOUTPUT><myXML>#myXML#</myXML></CFOUTPUT>
```

You can see how much time ColdFusion can trim from your database development work. This allows you to spend more time developing data-aware Flash applications and less time worrying about server-side logic.

What You Need To Get Started

To take advantage of Flash Remoting, you need more than just Flash MX 2004. You need the following components:

*   The Flash Remoting MX Installer, which is available for download at www.macromedia.com/software/flashremoting/.

*   ColdFusion MX or a ColdFusion data source to connect to. You can download ColdFusion MX from www.macromedia.com/software/coldfusion.

*   If you're connecting to a remote ColdFusion data source, you need an active Internet connection.

Flash can use different types of files for accessing ColdFusion data, such as ColdFusion Component files and server-side ActionScript files. These file types and others are discussed in the following sections.

ColdFusion Component Files

ColdFusion Component (CFC) files are made up of CFML tags, which are basically functions. They are programmed to send data back to the caller, which in this case is the Remoting server. A simple component might look like this:

```
<CFCOMPONENT>
    <CFFUNCTION NAME="qGetData" access="remote">
      <CFQUERY NAME="qGetData" Datasource="App.MyDSN">
       SELECT * FROM MyTable
      </CFQUERY>
     <CFRETURN qGetData>
    </CFFUNCTION>
</CFCOMPONENT>
```

There are several benefits to using CFC files with Flash Remoting:

*   CFCs allow you to leverage your existing knowledge of ColdFusion.

*   CFCs are written with CFML, an easy-to-learn markup language.

*   CFCs can be accessed by other CFML files.

In addition to ColdFusion Components, Flash Remoting can be used to access ColdFusion pages (.cfm files) and web services.

Server-side ActionScript Files

A server-side ActionScript file (an ASR file) is composed of ActionScript code. An ASR file can contain multiple functions, which are called by using the getService() method of NetServices (explained in "Communication with ColdFusion" later in this chapter). ColdFusion MX supports many native ActionScript objects and methods and includes support for the CF object. This object is native to the ColdFusion implementation of ActionScript and contains two methods: CF.http and CF.query.

You use CF.http to retrieve information from a remote HTTP server. You can call CF.http, passing positional or named arguments. If you specify named arguments, this is the syntax for CF.http:

```
CF.http
    ({
        method:get/post,
        url:url,
        username:username,
        password:password,
        resolveurl:yes/no,
        params:params,
        path:path,
        file:filename
    });
```

If you specify positional arguments, this is the syntax:

```
CF.http(method, url);
CF.http(method, url, params, username, password);
```

The following parameters can be used:

- *method* can be get or post. If it's get, ColdFusion downloads a file (binary or text) or creates a query based on the contents of a text file. If it's post, ColdFusion sends information to the server page (specified in url) or CGI program to be processed. If you use post, *params* is required.

- *username*, which is optional, is used to authenticate the connection request, if required by the server.

- *password*, which is optional, is used to authenticate the connection request, if required by the server.

- *resolveurl*, which is optional, can be yes or no. If it's not specified, the value is no. If the value is yes, the page reference that's returned in the Filecontent property has its internal links fully resolved (including port number) so that everything remains intact.

- *params* is required only during post operations. It's an array of objects that have the following properties: name, type, and value.

- *path*, which is optional, defines the path in which to store files. If you specify this parameter, the *file* parameter is required.

- *file*, which is optional, is the name of the file being accessed. If *path* is specified, *file* is required.

CF.query performs a query against the ColdFusion data source, using the following syntax:

```
CF.query
  ({
    datasource:"data source name",
    sql:"SQL stmts",
    username:"username",
    password:"password",
    maxrows:number,
    timeout:milliseconds
  })
```

The following parameters can be used:

- *datasource* is the name of the data source the query retrieves data from.

- *sql* is the SQL statement to be performed.

- *username*, an optional parameter, overrides the username specified in the data source setup.

- *password*, an optional parameter, overrides the password specified in the data source.

- *maxrows*, an optional parameter, determines the maximum number of rows to return in the record set.

- *timeout*, an optional parameter, determines the maximum number of seconds for the query to run before returning an error stating that the query has timed out.

For example, if you want to request all entries from the my_table table in the my_ds data source, you would use the following code:

```
CF.query
  ({
    datasource:"my_ds",
    sql:"SELECT * from my_table",
  })
```

The results of a CF.query call are a RecordSet ActionScript class, which you can manipulate by using any of the following Recordset methods:

```
RecordSet.getColumnnames
RecordSet.getLength
RecordSet.getItemAt
RecordSet.getItemID
RecordSet.sortItemsBy
RecordSet.getNumberAvailable
RecordSet.filter
RecordSet.sort
```

In the following example, a query is issued, but the resulting record set is sorted before being returned:

```
function getAllSorted() {
myQuery = CF.query
  ({
    datasource:"my_ds",
    sql:"SELECT * from my_table",
  });
myQuery.sort();
return myQuery;
}
```

Although ASR files are accessible only by Flash Remoting, it's beneficial to consider them when developing applications that use remoting, because they enable you to code server-side components without needing to learn ColdFusion. This can be a tremendous timesaver.

Other File Types

With Flash MX 2004 Professional, you can connect to a wide variety of other web services, such as Java 2 Enterprise Edition (J2EE), the .NET version of Active Server Pages (ASP.NET), and Simple Object Access

Protocol (SOAP). Flash MX Professional 2004 comes with the WebServices component, which makes it easy to connect your Flash movie to these web service sources. For more information on connecting to these services, consult the Flash documentation on the WebServices component or the book *Macromedia Flash MX Professional 2004 Application Development: Training from the Source* (see the "Resources" sidebar at the end of this chapter for more information).

Communication with ColdFusion

Now that you've seen the different options for connecting a ColdFusion data source to Flash, you can take a look at configuring Flash to send requests to the server and handling responses to those requests.

First, you need to add the `NetServices.as` file with an `#include` statement. This file contains a definition of the `NetServices` object, which facilitates communication between your movie and other sources:

```
#include "NetServices.as"
```

Next, you need to set the URL of the default gateway you'll be using. It's the IP address of the machine you're connecting to. You can use one of the following formats for default gateway URLs:

```
http://127.0.0.1/flashservices/gateway
```

or

```
http://servername/flashservices/gateway
```

You might need to change the gateway reference based on the web server's port number where you're running the ColdFusion server.

Note that the `flashservices/gateway` path reference is not a real folder on the web server; rather, it's a logical mapping for the Flash Remoting service in ColdFusion MX. After the flashservices/gateway is mapped, your services are referenced in their actual folders under the `wwwroot` folder. Dot notation delineates folders under the `wwwroot` folder and defines a path to the ColdFusion component. For example, for Flash Remoting to access a ColdFusion component called `my_comp.cfc` on the server located at `/webroot/my_app/`, the Flash Remoting service refers to it like this:

```
http://127.0.0.1:8500/flashservices/gateway/my_app.my_comp.cfc
```

This is the syntax for setting the default gateway URL (*url* represents the URL):

```
NetServices.setDefaultGatewayUrl(url);
```

After you have set the gateway URL, you need to create a connection to it. You do this using the createGatewayConnection() method of NetServices, which uses the following syntax:

```
NetServices.createGatewayConnection(url);
```

url is an optional parameter. If included, it establishes a connection to the specified URL, if possible. If this parameter is omitted, a connection is established with the URL specified as the default gateway URL.

After you've established a connection to the server, you can access a specific CFC or ASR file and carry out a function in that file. You do this with the getService() method of NetConnection, which has the following syntax:

```
connection.getService(service, defaultResponder);
```

service is a string that identifies the fully qualified Remoting service name. It contains the name of the folder where the service file is located along with the name of the file itself, separated by a period. For example, if you want to connect to a file located at the path C:\CFusionMX\wwwroot\service\file.cfc, *service* would be service.file. You don't need to specify a file type, such as CFC, for your service.

defaultResponder is the object that receives the results of Flash Remoting service methods. For example, the following code creates a connection to the local ColdFusion server and makes a connection to the file service in the service folder:

```
#include "NetServices.as"

NetServices.setDefaultGatewayURL(http://127.0.0.1/flashservices
➥/gateway);
my_connection = NetServices.createGatewayConnection();
my_service = my_connection.getService("service.file", this);
```

After you've opened the connection and created a reference to the service, you can access methods in your Remoting script. The format for doing so is the same as calling any method for any other object you might interact with; you call it using dot syntax, and you can send the method variables. For example, if a method is defined in the `service.file` named `tester`, you would call it with the following code:

```
my_service.tester();
```

Getting Information Back

When you call a function in your service, you receive one of two notifications from the server. A Result notification is sent back if the method was called successfully. It contains any recordset information you might have requested. A Status notification is sent back if an error occurred during your method call. A Status callback notification is generated, for example, if your code has a syntax error, if a requested parameter wasn't sent to the method, or if your database query has an error. Result and Status notifications can be defined in two ways. The first way is to define a callback object to handle returned data, like so:

```
service = getService("", new CallBack());

function CallBack() {
    this.onResult = function(info) {
        trace("result");
    }

    this.onStatus = function(info) {
        trace("Status");
    }
}
```

The second way is to define functions based on the function name you send. For example, if you call the `getData` function from the `myService` service, you would define the following functions to handle the returned data:

```
function getData_Result (info) {
    trace("result");
}

function getData_Status (info) {
    trace("status");
}
```

Receiving Data from the Server

Aside from returning full recordsets to Flash from a ColdFusion source, you can also return data in a number of other formats. Table 18.1 lists the data types in ColdFusion and how they appear to Flash.

TABLE 18.1 ## ColdFusion Data Types in Flash

Data Type in ColdFusion	Data Type in Flash
Boolean	Boolean
String	String
Date	Date
Array	Array
Struct	Associative (named) Array
Query object	Recordset
Query object (Flash.pagesize variable set)	Paged Recordset
XML	XML

The *RecordSet* Object

The RecordSet object enables you to manipulate recordsets returned from Flash Remoting or to create client-side recordsets. A *recordset* is a list of records, with methods for fetching, accessing, and manipulating the list of records in various ways.

Recordsets created on an application server usually consist of database query results. Each record in a RecordSet object is represented by a type-less ActionScript object. In a RecordSet object, individual records are identified by an index number. The index starts at zero. When the recordset is sorted or a record is added to or deleted from the recordset, the index changes.

Each field of the record is represented by a field in the object. For a RecordSet object that originated from an application server, the field names are the same as the names of the fields defined by the server-side recordset. For local RecordSet objects, the field names are defined in the original call to the new RecordSet() function.

Remote recordsets are created by the services that send them to Flash. For example, when requesting a recordset from ColdFusion, the ColdFusion

Component or ASR file creates the recordset. You can create a local RecordSet object, however, by using the following constructor:

```
new RecordSet(columnNames);
```

columnNames is an array of strings, with each string containing a name of one of the recordset columns.

The RecordSet object has many methods, described in the following paragraphs.

RecordSet.addItem()   This method adds a new record to your RecordSet. You pass the RecordSet an object with properties corresponding to the fields in your RecordSet. It uses the following syntax:

```
my_recordSet.addItem(record);
```

For example, to add a record to a RecordSet with the fields ID, name, and email, you would use the following code:

```
var itemToAdd = {id:1, name:"Brian Hogg",
➥email:brian@mrhogg.com};
my_recordSet.addItem(itemToAdd);
```

Errors can occur during the following conditions:

* The *record* parameter isn't an object.

* The *record* parameter has unknown or missing fields.

* The RecordSet is associated with an application server and hasn't been fully retrieved.

The record causing the error can still be added to the RecordSet in the first two conditions, but if you attempt to add a record to a partial RecordSet, the addItem() method fails, and the following error is generated:

```
Operation not allowed on partial RecordSet objects.
```

RecordSet.addItemAt()   This method allows you to specify an index for inserting a new record. It has the following syntax:

```
my_recordSet.addItemAt(index, record);
```

For example, to add a record to element 12 of your RecordSet, you would use the following code:

```
var itemToAdd = {name:"Brian Hogg", email:brian@mrhogg.com};
my_recordSet.addItemAt(12, itemToAdd);
```

Errors occur if any of the following conditions are met:

- The index is out of range.

- The *record* parameter is not an object.

- The *record* parameter has unknown or missing fields.

- The RecordSet object is associated with an application server and is not fully populated yet.

Depending on the error condition, the outcome differs, as shown in Table 18.2.

TABLE 18.2 *RecordSet* **Error Conditions**

Error Condition	What Happens	Error Message
index is less than zero.	The RecordSet object is not changed.	No error message
index is greater than the length of the RecordSet object.	The RecordSet object length is extended, and the record is added to the RecordSet object.	No error message
The *record* parameter is not an object.	The record is added to the RecordSet object.	No error message
The *record* parameter contains missing or unknown fields.	The record is added to the RecordSet object.	No error message
The RecordSet object is associated with an application server and is not yet fully populated.	No change is made to the RecordSet object, and an error message is reported to the Flash Output panel and Debugger console.	Operation not allowed on partial RecordSet objects.

RecordSet.addView() This method defines an object that receives notification of updates when the RecordSet object changes. The object must contain a modelChanged function, which takes one parameter, and an event descriptor object. Table 18.3 describes event descriptor messages.

TABLE 18.3 *RecordSet.addView* Messages

Message	Description
{event:"addRows", firstRow:*x*, lastRow:*y*}	Rows *x* through *y* have been added.
{event:"allRows"}	All records have arrived from the server. In other words, the RecordSet object is now fully populated.
{event:"deleteRows", firstRow:*x*, lastRow:*y*}	Rows *x* through *y* have been deleted.
{event:"fetchrows", firstRow:*x*, lastRow:*y*}	Rows *x* through *y* have been requested from the server but have not arrived yet.
{event:"sort"}	The recordset has been sorted.
{event:"updateAll"}	The RecordSet object has changed in some way, such as a new view being added.
{event:"updateRows", firstRow:*x*, lastRow:*y*}	Rows *x* through *y* have changed in some way.

For example, the following code defines a local RecordSet, defines an object to receive update notification, and adds two new records to the recordset:

```
#include "NetServices.as"

function modelChanged(info) {
    trace(info.event);
}

var productList = new RecordSet(["Name","Price","Color"]);

// whenever productList changes, call this.modelChanged().
productList.addView(this);

// modify the RecordSet object, and see if "modelChanged" gets
called
productList.addItem({Name: "milk", Price: 3.50, Color:
➡"0xffffff"});
productList.addItem({Name: "eggs", Price: 1.75, Color:
➡"0xffffff"});
```

Recordset.filter()   This method is used to filter the contents of a RecordSet object based on criteria you supply. It uses the following syntax:

RecordSet.filter(*filterFunction, context*)

- *filterFunction*   A function that takes one or two parameters and returns true or false. The first parameter is a single record from the RecordSet object. The second parameter, which is optional, is a value that the function uses to determine whether to include the record in the result. The function must return true if the record should be included in the resulting RecordSet object.

- *context*   A value supplied by the caller. This value is the second parameter to *filterFunction* and is used to determine whether the current record will be present in the filtered record set.

This method creates a new RecordSet object by calling the filterFunction function one time for every record in the RecordSet object. The filterFunction evaluates each record based on the provided *context* and returns true or false. Records that return true are added to the new, filtered RecordSet.

If you attempt to filter a RecordSet that isn't fully populated, only the currently available records are filtered. When filtering a RecordSet, it's important to note that the filtered RecordSet object doesn't inherit the original RecordSet object's list of views or have any association with a server-side RecordSet object. The following example demonstrates how to filter a RecordSet object:

```
#include "NetServices.as"
var allLocations =new RecordSet(["city","province"]);
allLocations.addItem({city: "Halifax", province:: "NS"});
allallLocations.addItem({city: "Dartmouth", province: "NS"});
allallLocations.addItem({city: "Toronto", province: "ON"});
allallLocations.addItem({city: "Oakville", province: "ON"});
function locationFilter(aRecord, reqProvince) {
    return (aRecord.province == reqProvince);
}
myListBox.setDataProvider(allocations.filter(locationFilter,
➥"ON");
```

RecordSet.getColumnNames() This method returns an array of strings representing the names of the columns in your RecordSet. Its syntax is as follows:

```
my_recordSet.getColumnNames();
```

The following example gets the column names of the my_recordSet RecordSet and displays them in text fields on the stage:

```
var titles = my_recordSet.getColumnNames();

firstTitle.text = titles[0];
secondTitle.text = titles[1];
```

RecordSet.getItemAt() This method returns the record at the specified *index* parameter. It uses the following syntax:

```
my_recordSet.getItemAt(index);
```

An error occurs if you supply an index that's out of range. For example, if you have two records in your recordset, and you attempt to use getItemAt(12), you generate this error:

```
RecordSet warning 104: getItemAt(index) index out of range
```

This error call returns null. For example, the following code adds and then retrieves a record from a recordset:

```
# include "NetServices.as"
var locationList = new RecordSet(["city","province"]);
locationList.addItem({city:"Toronto", province:"ON"});
var record = locationList.getItemAt(0);
```

RecordSet.getLength() This method returns the number of records in the specified recordset. This is the syntax:

```
my_recordSet.getLength();
```

RecordSet.getNumberAvailable() This method returns the number of records available for access in your RecordSet. Although it always equals the getLength() value in a local RecordSet, when downloading information from a database, this method shows the current number of records that have been downloaded. The following example uses the getNumberAvailable() method:

```
#include "NetServices.as"
function reportDownloadStatus(aRecordSet) {
```

```
        trace(aRecordSet.getNumberAvailable()+ "of " +
aRecordSet.getLength() + "records have been downloaded.");
}
```

RecordSet.isFullyPopulated()   This method determines whether all data to be returned from a server has actually been returned. It uses the following syntax:

```
my_recordSet.isFullyPopulated();
```

This method returns true if the recordset has been completely downloaded and false if it hasn't. A RecordSet object must be fully populated before you can use these data editing and manipulation methods: addItem, addItemAt, replaceItemAt, setField, removeItem, removeAll, filter, and sort. This method works the same way as the RecordSet.isLocal() method (discussed next).

RecordSet.isLocal()   This method determines whether the recordset is local or remote. It uses the following syntax:

```
my_recordSet.isLocal();
```

This method returns true if the recordset is local and false if it isn't.

RecordSet.removeAll()   This method removes all records from your recordset. It uses the following syntax:

```
my_recordSet.removeAll();
```

RecordSet.removeItemAt()   This method removes the record at the specified index. It uses the following syntax:

```
my_recordSet.removeItemAt(index);
```

This method fails if the index is out of range, or if the recordset is remote and hasn't been fully retrieved from the server yet.

RecordSet.replaceItemAt()   This method replaces the record at the specified index with the supplied record. It uses the following syntax:

```
my_recordSet.replaceItemAt(index, record);
```

This method generates an error if any of the following conditions exist:

- The index is out of range.

- The *record* parameter is not an object.

- The *record* parameter has unknown or missing fields.

- The RecordSet object isn't fully populated yet.

Table 18.4 shows how replaceItemAt() responds to different errors.

TABLE 18.4   *RecordSet.replaceItemAt* **Errors**

Error Condition	What Happens	Error Message
The RecordSet object is not fully populated.	No change is made to the RecordSet object, and an error message is sent to the Flash Output panel and Debugger console.	Operation not allowed on partial RecordSet objects
index out of range.	The RecordSet object is not changed.	No error message
Unknown field name.	The RecordSet object is not changed.	No error message

The following code is an example of using replaceItemAt():

```
#include "NetServices.as"
var locationList =new RecordSet(["city","province"]);
var locationToAdd = {city:"Toronto",province:"ON"};
locationList.addItem(itemToAdd);
myListBox.setDataProvider(locationList);
var newItem ={city:"Oakville", province:"ON"};
locationList.replaceItemAt(0,newItem);
```

RecordSet.setDeliveryMode()   Sets the delivery mode of a RecordSet associated with an application server. It uses the following syntax:

```
my_recordSet.setDeliveryMode(mode, pagesize, lookahead amount);
```

You can use the following parameters with this method:

- *mode* is a string representing the delivery mode. Values can be ondemand (the default), fetchall, or page.

- *pagesize* is an optional parameter. In page mode, it specifies the page size. In fetchall mode, it sets how many records to fetch in each server request. The default value is 25.

- *lookahead* is an optional value. In page mode, it sets the number of pages to prefetch (how many pages ahead of the current page it will request). The default is 0 (fetches only the required page).

At any time, a RecordSet object associated with an application server operates in a particular data-delivery mode. The new mode setting takes effect immediately, except that pending application server requests are allowed to finish. You can change mode settings and delivery mode parameters.

Until you call RecordSet.setDeliveryMode() for a RecordSet object, it operates in ondemand mode. When using fetchall mode, you can supply a pagesize parameter. The entire recordset is fetched from the application server in a series of requests, and each request fetches only the number of records specified in the pagesize parameter.

Note that this function has no effect after the recordset has been fully loaded.

When using page mode, you can supply the pagesize and preFetchPages parameters. In page mode, when you request a record using the getItemAt() method, the RecordSet object ensures that the number of pages specified by numPrefetch (after the page containing the requested record) is already available in the client or requested from the server. If numPrefetch is zero, only the current page containing the requested record is fetched.

RecordSet.setField()   This method replaces one field of a record with a new value. It uses the following syntax:

```
my_RecordSet.setField(index, fieldName, value);
```

The following parameters can be used with this method:

- *index* is a number representing the index of the record to be adjusted.

- *fieldName* is the name of the field to be adjusted.

- *value* is the new value for that field.

The following code shows an example of using setField():

```
var names = new RecordSet(["first_name", "last_name"]);
var itemToAdd = {first_name:"Brian", last_name:"Hogg"};
names.addItem(itemToAdd);
names.setField(0, "first_name", "Brian");
```

RecordSet.sort()   This method sorts the records in a recordset. It uses the following syntax:

RecordSet.sort(*compareFunction*)

compareFunction is a function that determines the sorting order. Given the arguments A and B, the comparison returns a value as follows:

• -1 if A appears before B in the sorted sequence

• 0 if A = B

• 1 if A appears after B in the sorted sequence

The following example shows an example of using sort() without specifying a *compareFunction*:

my_recordSet.sort();

This example specifies a *compareFunction*:

```
function determineOrder(aRecord, bRecord) {
        var aKey = aRecord.city + aRecord.province;
        var bKey = bRecord.city + bRecord.province
        if (aKey < bKey)
        {
            return -1;
        }
        else if (aKey > bKey)
        {
            return 1;
        }
        else
        {
            return 0;
        }
}
locationList.sort(determineOrder);
```

RecordSet.sortItemsBy()   This method sorts the records in a recordset according to the field and sort direction supplied to it. This is the syntax for this method:

my_recordSet.sortItemsBy(*field, direction*);

field is the name of the field, and *direction* is an optional parameter specifying the sort direction. DESC means descending sorting. Any other value is interpreted as ascending sorting (the default). To sort your RecordSet in descending order by the contents of the field province, you would use the following code:

```
my_recordSet.sortItemsBy("province", "DESC");
```

Packaging ActionScript Data for Return to the Server

When you send data to ColdFusion, its data type remains the same when ColdFusion accesses it. Likewise, data can be transmitted from ColdFusion to your Flash movie and be interpreted as its correct data type. There are exceptions, however; for a listing of data types as they appear in Flash and ColdFusion, refer to Table 18.1 earlier in this chapter.

ColdFusion MX defines a scope called Flash that you use to access parameters passed from Flash applications and return values to Flash applications. The Flash scope has the following predefined variables you can use to pass information:

- **Flash.Params** An array containing the parameters passed from the Flash application to the ColdFusion page. If you don't pass any parameters, Flash.Params still exists, but it's empty. For example, if you send ColdFusion two parameters, the first is referenced as Flash.Params[0] and the second is referenced as Flash.Params[1].

- **Flash.Result** The result the ColdFusion page returns to the Flash application. Because of ActionScript's automatic type conversion, you should not return a Boolean literal to Flash. Instead, return 1 to indicate true and 0 to indicate false.

- **Flash.Pagesize** The number of records in each increment of a recordset that a ColdFusion page returns to Flash.

Data Types in Flash Remoting

When you transmit data from ColdFusion to Flash or from Flash to ColdFusion, data type conversion is performed. Table 18.5 lists Flash data types and their corresponding data types in ColdFusion.

TABLE 18.5 ## Flash Data Types in ColdFusion

Data Type in Flash	Data Type in ColdFusion
Null	Null (not defined)
Boolean	Boolean
Number	Number
String	String
Date	Date
Array (numeric indexes)	Array
Associative Array (named indexes)	Struct
RecordSet	Can't be sent to server; can be sent only from ColdFusion to Flash
Object	Struct
Object of type	FlashGateway.IO.ASObject

Chapter Project: Flash Remoting Example

This example requires you to have Flash MX Remoting, Flash MX 2004, and ColdFusion MX installed.

To help you understand the basics of using Flash MX Remoting with ColdFusion, this example explains how to create a simple application—an address book—that uses Flash Remoting and ColdFusion. Because this example has been kept simple, the address book allows you to display only existing entries.

Setting Up the Data Source

First, you need to create an address book database to access. Add your database to ColdFusion, and create a new table. For the purposes of this example, the data source is called new_source, and the table is referred to as address_book. Your new table should have the following fields: id, first_name, last_name, email, and phone_number.

You'll be directly modifying all the fields except id. The id field should be an index field and should auto-increment. For information on creating index fields, consult the documentation of whatever environment (such as mySQL) you use for creating your database. After you've built the database, add a few new entries for testing.

The Server Scripts (in CFC/ASR)

Only Flash will access the server-side functionality for this application, so the server-side functionality is written using an ASR file. ASR files make it possible to create functionality quickly, without necessarily having to learn CFML. You can take advantage of the ActionScript knowledge you already have. For this application, server-side functionality consists of retrieving all address book entries.

The retrieve function, shown in the following lines, returns a record set containing information about all address book entries:

```
function getAllEntries() {
    sqlStatement = "SELECT * FROM address_book";
    retData = CF.query("new_source", sqlStatement);

    return retData;
}
```

This function is stored in a file named `addressBook.asr`, which is placed in the `\\CFusionMX\wwwroot\address\` folder.

Building the Front End

Now that you have the database and the script that accesses it, you need to create a new Flash movie and connect it to the source, following these steps:

1. First, create a new movie with these four layers: `buttons`, `functions`, `as`, and `text`.

2. To include the `netservices.as` file, place this code on the first frame of the `as` layer:

   `#include "NetServices.as"`

3. Next, set your default gateway using the `defaultGatewayURL` defined earlier in this chapter. If you're connecting to ColdFusion on the same machine where you're developing Flash, you can use the server address 127.0.0.1. The ColdFusion built-in web server listens by default on port 8500. Use this port number if you're going to connect using the built-in web server. Add the following line to your code:

   `NetServices.setDefaultGatewayUrl(http://127.0.0.1:8500/`
   `↪flashservices/gateway);`

4. Now create a gateway connection using this line of code:

   `myConnection = NetServices.createGatewayConnection();`

5. Next, you need to build the interface for your address book. Add a ComboBox component to the `text` layer, and name it `user_list`.

6. Add four text fields named `first_name`, `last_name`, `email`, and `telephone` to the same layer.

Figure 18.1. shows an example of the layout at this point.

FIGURE 18.1

The basic layout of the movie for your address book application.

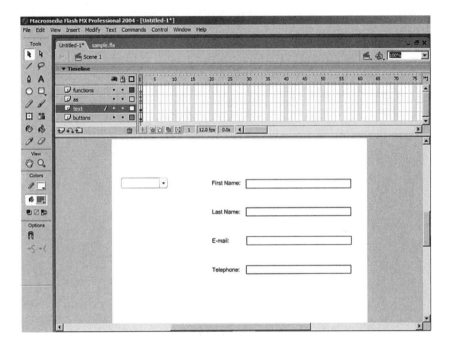

7. Now that you've laid out the section of the movie that displays address book records, it's time to add code to it. First, you need to define a function to call data from the Flash Remoting service. Add this code to the `functions` layer:

```
function getRecords() {
    // creating a reference to the service
    retrieveService = myConnection.getService(
    ➥"address.addressBook", this);
```

```
        // call the function
        retrieveService.getAllEntries();
}
```

8. Define the callback functions:

```
function getAllEntries_Result(result) {
        // this function has been called if
        // data has been sent back
        // first, save the result from the server in myAddresses
        myAddresses = result;

        // next, call the function to display the results
        populateEntryList();
}

function getAllEntries_Status(info) {
        // this function is called if an error has occurred
        trace("An error has occurred!");
        trace(info.code);
}
```

9. When you receive the recordset from the server, you call the populateEntryList() function. Define that function next:

```
function populateEntryList() {
        // how many addresses are there?
        numEntries = myAddresses.getLength();

        // clear out the user_list combo box
        user_list.removeAll();

        // this for loop takes each item from the database
        // result (saved as myAddresses) and adds the item id
        // and nameto user_list
        for (var i = 0; i<numEntries; i++) {
                currentEntry = myAddresses.getItemAt(i);
```

```
            combinedName = currentEntry["first_name"]
        ➥ + " " + currentEntry["last_name"];

            user_list.addItem(combinedName, currentEntry["id"]);

}
```

When called, this function adds new items in the ComboBox component onscreen, with a label matching the name of the person in the address book and a value matching the value of the record's ID. This function is used later to select which entry you want to view in its entirety.

10. Add a keyframe in the as layer of the second frame of your movie, and call the getRecords() function:

```
getRecords();
```

11. Next, you need to define the on (change) handler for the user_list ComboBox. It needs to call the showEntry function, which displays the contents of the selected entry onscreen. Select the user_list ComboBox and enter the following code:

```
on (change) {
    id = this.selectedItem.data;
    _parent.showEntry(id);
}
```

You've probably noticed that even though the ComboBox now calls the showEntry function, it hasn't been defined yet. This is what it should look like:

```
function showEntry(id) {
    numEntries = addresses.getLength();
    for (var I = 0; i<numEntries; i++) {
        // see if this is the correct entry
        if (addresses[i]["id"] == id) {
            // If it is, populate the text fields onscreen
            currentEntry = addresses.getEntry(i);
            first_name.text = currentEntry["first_name"];
            last_name.text = currentEntry["last_name"];
```

```
            email.text = currentEntry["email"];
            telephone.text = currentEntry["telephone"];



        }


    }
}
```

That's about it. Publish your movie and test it. Although this application is very simple, it should give you an idea of how to get started developing applications that take advantage of Flash MX Remoting.

FLASH COMMUNICATION SERVER

As with the coverage of Flash Remoting, this section is intended to give you an overview of Flash Communication Server and some possible uses for it. Flash Communication Server 1.5 (FCS) is a standalone server that provides support for robust real-time applications. You can use it to send and receive video and audio, as well as other types of data, and to call remote functions on the server and the client (SWF files that connect to the server). FCS uses Real-Time Messaging Protocol (RTMP), a Macromedia messaging format, to connect client SWF files to the FCS architecture.

You can download a developer edition of FCS from www.macromedia.com/software/flashcom/ to install on your server. The developer edition of Flash Communication Server MX 1.5 allows five simultaneous connections, or 256KB of traffic (whichever comes first). This developer edition has no time limitations and contains the full feature set, so you can spend all the time you need learning how to use it and developing your own killer applications. In addition to the server, you need to install Flash Remoting MX on your local machine and download the FCS components from Macromedia.

Creating New Applications

Now that you've downloaded FCS, how do you create new applications? The answer to that can be very simple or incredibly complex. First, look at the simple answer.

By default, applications are stored in the `\\Program Files\Macromedia\ Flash Communication Server MX\applications` folder. If you look at this folder, you'll see a number of sample folders representing applications you can access. To create the simplest application, you can create a new folder, and name it anything you like. There—you just created an application. It's as easy as that. Then if you create a new Flash movie, you can connect to the application. If you named your new folder `test_app`, for example, the following code in a Flash movie allows you to connect to it:

```
#include "NetServices.as"
nc = new NetConnection();
nc.connect("rtmp://127.0.0.1/test_app");
```

Of course, this application doesn't actually do anything, but that's beside the point. It's an application, and it works. There are many easy applications you can create that use no server-side coding at all. A number of the components available from the Macromedia Exchange at `www.macromedia.com/cfusion/exchange/index.cfm` (such as the whiteboard and chat components) allow you to create applications that don't require any server-side programming. However, what if you do need to add code on the server? The following section explains how to add server-side ActionScript files for this purpose. Continue reading to find out how to create more complex Flash Communication Server applications.

Server-Side ActionScript Files

Flash Remoting uses server-side ActionScript (SSA) files with the `.asr` extension, but Flash Communication Server uses files with the extension `.asc`. Specifically, it uses the `main.asc` file, which is saved in your application folder and can contain all your ActionScript. If you prefer to place your code in separate files, you can use the `load` function to load external files:

```
load(filename);
```

This provides the same functionality that the `#include` directive does in Flash MX 2004.

What else can you do with SSA? SSA is largely the same as client-side ActionScript. It fully conforms to the ECMAScript specification, it supports case-sensitive variables, and it supports many of the same objects that Flash does, with some exceptions. No timeline exists on the server side, so there are no path references (no _root or _parent), and you can't use the `getTimer()` method. Likewise, XML does not exist on the server.

You can take advantage of the following server-specific objects in Flash:

- **Application**   This object is a reference to the application being run. You can use a number of methods in this powerful object. For example, the following code saved in your `main.asc` file notifies all connected clients when someone disconnects from the application:

```
application.onDisconnect = function(client) {
    nClients = application.clients.length;

    for (var I = 0; i<nClients; i++) {
        application.clients[i].send("userLeft",
client.userName);
    }
}
```

  The `Application` object supports a number of events, such as `onDisconnect`, which is triggered when a user leaves the application, as well as `onStartApp`, `onStopApp`, `onConnect`, and others.

- **Client**   This object is a reference to a specific connected client. It allows you to track information about a connected client, such as the IP address. You can add new methods to this object (as well as to the `Application` object), as you would in Flash MX 2004, to extend the server's functionality. You send messages to connected clients via the `Client` object by using the `send()` method:

```
client.send("functionToCall", paramsToSend);
```

  This method lets you call functions and methods in the client's SWF file from the server at any time and enables you to send almost any type of information. You can use it to send text information, any kind of data stored on the server, or information of other types, such as the position of avatars onscreen or new high scores.

Remote Shared Objects

Server-side ActionScript also enables you to use remote shared objects. In Chapter 10, "ActionScript: Function, Events, and Objects," you learned that there are two types of shared objects: local and remote. Chapter 10 covered the local type, and in this section, you learn about remote shared objects.

A *remote shared object* (RSO) is largely the same as a local shared object, except that it's stored on the server, and multiple users can connect to it at the same time, updating and receiving updates for the object. An RSO can be temporary, or it can persist on the server; if you're using an RSO to save configuration data or other information that won't change, having it stored on the server is useful.

Connecting to Remote Shared Objects

You connect to a shared object with the getRemote() method of the SharedObject class:

```
my_so = SharedObject.getRemote(name, remotePath[,
➥persistenceOption]);
```

```
my_so.connect();
```

Note that you won't be able to connect to an RSO until you've successfully connected to an FCS application. The following code connects to the local FCS application called my_app, and when the connection is established, connects to the RSO:

```
#include "NetServices.as"
```

```
my_nc = new NetConnection();
my_nc.connect("rtmp://127.0.0.1/my_app");
```

```
my_nc.onStatus = function (sInfo) {
if (sInfo.code == "NetConnection.Connect.Success") {
    trace("Connection to Application Established");
    my_so = SharedObject.getRemote("myVar", my_nc.uri, true);
} else {
    trace("Unable to Establish Connection");
}
```

After you've connected to the RSO, Flash Communication Server sends updates to the RSO for all users subscribed to it. When this happens, you'll likely want to know about it. To be notified of updates to your shared object, you define an onSync handler in your shared object. The following code sends "I have been changed" to the Output panel whenever an update to a shared object is received:

```
my_so = SharedObject.getRemote("myVar", my_nc.uri, true);

my_so.onSync = function(changed) {
    trace("I have been changed");
}
```

The onSync method of the RSO is useful for a variety of reasons; it's an easy way to perform updates on your SWF file, based on updates to the RSOs you're subscribed to. For example, if you have an RSO containing a list of high scores for a game, you might want to update your display of these scores in your SWF file. Using the onSync method of SharedObject would let you do this.

Monitoring Applications

Don't worry about being able to keep track of happenings on the server; FCS comes with an Administration Console, shown in Figure 18.2, that contains product documentation, information on sample applications, and a host of tools for monitoring the server's status and the status of any applications.

From the Administration Console, you can also access the Communication App Inspector (see Figure 18.3) to view the status of specific applications and the real-time application output. It's similar to viewing the Output panel in Flash MX 2004.

You can find more information about using the Administration Console and the Communication App Inspector in the Flash Communication Server MX documentation.

FIGURE 18.2
The FCS
Administration
Console.

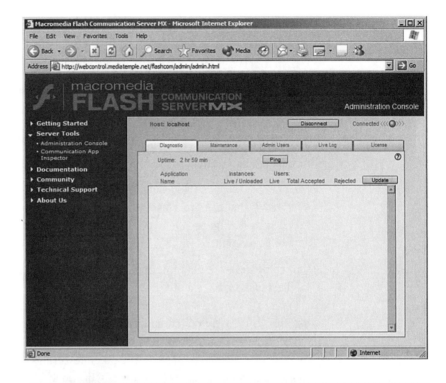

FIGURE 18.3
The Communication
App Inspector.

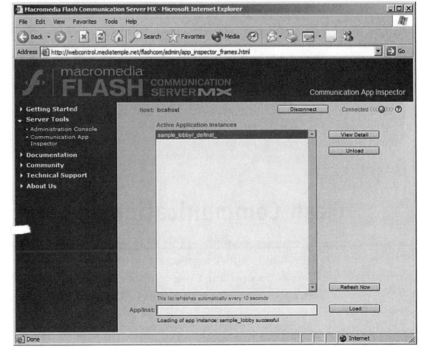

Compensating for Lag in Flash Communication Server

When you begin to develop applications for Flash Communication Server, probably the main factor to remember is that you're developing multiplayer applications. This statement might seem obvious, but it reminds you, as the developer, to change the way you look at solving problems or building applications.

For example, suppose you build an Asteroids-style game in Flash. You have a ship that can fire a laser to destroy asteroids. You have a hitTest function to determine when your laser intersects with the asteroid. Not very difficult, right?

Now consider developing this application in FCS. Multiple users might be in the same space, shooting at the same asteroid. Each client has to maintain its own view of the application's current state, but the server has the "true" view of the application. You need to consider what will happen in these situations because given the difference in users' connections and processor speeds, it's possible to have two users with a completely conflicting view of the application. To use the Asteroids example, a user connecting with a slow computer might see an asteroid that has already been destroyed, or might take a shot and hit that asteroid before he received a signal telling him the asteroid has been destroyed.

There are many different ways to compensate for the lag generated by network communication latency and the difference in users' computer speeds. When you're developing multiuser applications, it's essential to keep these solutions in mind.

Flash Communication Server Example

The simple example in this section is intended to show you how easy it is to build a quick application with Flash Communication Server MX. This example doesn't use components, but if you'd like to see several excellent samples using components, open the FLA files in the Flash

Communication Server Sample Application folders. This sample application allows users to connect to an FCS and control the position of a graphic representing them onscreen; this type of graphic is called an *avatar*. To build it, you need to create the application in Flash Communication Server. Then create a new folder called `avatar` in your applications folder, and create a `main.asc` file inside it.

Creating a Server-side Script

First, you need to create the server-side script. Define a function to accept new connections, and place it in the `main.asc` file:

```
application.onConnect = function(newClient, avatarName) {
    // accept new user connection
    application.acceptConnection(newClient);
    newClient.avatar = avatarName
    clientJoined(newClient);
}
```

The preceding function takes the avatar name passed by the FLA file (you'll add this part soon) and sets it as a property of the new client. Also, you have to explicitly accept the new connection for FCS to be able to communicate with the client. You do this by using the `acceptConnection` method of the `Application` object. In the last line of the preceding method, the `clientJoined` function, shown in the following code, is called:

```
function clientJoined (client) {
    trace("new client has joined");
    for (var i = 0; i<application.clients.length; i++) {
        thisClient = application.clients[i];
        // if this is not the client that has just joined,
        // inform the client of the one new user
        if (thisClient != client) {
            thisClient.call("addBall", null, client.avatar);
        } else if (thisClient == client) {
            // if this is the client that has just joined,
            // tell him about every connected user
            for (var j = 0; j<application.clients.length;
            ➥j++) {
```

```
                              currentClient = application.clients[j];
                              client.call("addBall", null,
                              ➥currentClient.avatar);
                          }
                      }
                  }
              }
```

This `clientJoined` function cycles through all connected clients (including the one that just connected) and triggers the `addBall` function on the client, sending the username that the new user has selected. When the script comes across the new client, it sends one `addBall` call for each connected client. This lets every user see every connected person, regardless of when they connected to the application. The client-side aspects will be created shortly. The `addBall` function adds a movie clip representing the new user to the client's stage.

Next, you need to define functionality to handle what happens when a user disconnects:

```
application.onDisconnect = function (client) {
    // user has left
    clientLeft(client);
}
```

In this case, you call the `clientLeft()` function, which sends a message to all connected clients, telling them that a user has left:

```
function clientLeft(client) {
    for (var i = 0; i<application.clients.length; i++) {
        thisClient = application.clients[i];
        thisClient.call("removeBall", null, client.avatar);
    }
}
```

The `clientLeft()` function cycles through all clients and triggers the `removeBall` function, which removes the movie clip representing the departed user.

That's it for the server-side component of the application. Next you need to build the FLA file so that your users can connect to your application.

Creating an FLA File

For the purposes of this example, you can use whatever stage size and frame rate you like. These are the key components of your FLA file:

- A login screen

- A movie clip with a linkage ID

- ActionScript to connect to the application

Your movie should have four layers: labels, functions, as, and bg.

In the labels layer, add a keyframe labeled yes on frame 2 and a keyframe labeled no on frame 7.

In the first frame of the bg layer, add a text field named username and a button with the label connect that calls the following doConnect() function:

```
on (click) {
    parent.doConnect();
}
```

Your file should look something like Figure 18.4.

FIGURE 18.4
Connecting to Flash
Communication
Server.

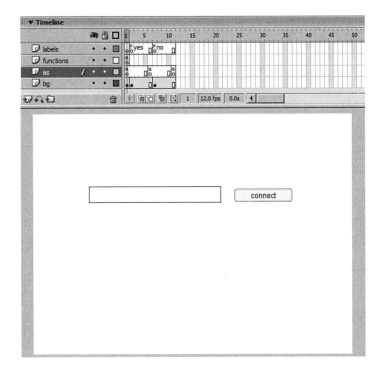

In Figure 18.4, notice that the bg layer has keyframes to correspond to the yes and no labels. When you add the code to connect to your FCS application, the movie jumps to the yes keyframe if the connection is successful and to the no keyframe if it isn't. Although it isn't required, adding some text or another kind of visual indicator is a good way to let the user know whether the connection has been successful.

Creating an Avatar

This application uses avatars to visually represent the users who are connected to it, so create a new movie clip that's drawn when a user connects. Fill it with whatever graphics you like, and give this clip a linkage ID of avatar.

When the user connects to the application, the clip is told to create a new instance of avatar onscreen. Each user is given control of an avatar. The movie clip is placed wherever users click on the stage, and that position is transmitted to all connected users. To do this, you'll use remote shared objects and an onMouseDown event handler. Insert the following code in your avatar movie clip:

```
my_so = SharedObject.getRemote(avatar, _parent.my_nc.uri,
➥true);

my_so.onSync = function() {
    x = my_so.data.x;
    y = my_so.data.y;
}

my_so.connect(_parent.my_nc);
```

This code creates a reference to a shared object on the server and defines how to handle updates to it. Each avatar clip connects to its own RSO and positions itself independently of the other clips.

Last, you connect to the RSO to receive updates. (It might seem pointless to connect to the server to get information about the position of *your* movie clip, but this code is used for all users, so it's usually controlling the position of clips under the control of other users.)

Next, you define the onMouseDown handler:

```
this.onMouseDown = function() {
    // first, make sure to update the correct shared object
    if (avatar == _root.my_username) {
        // below, define the x and y properties
        // based on the position of the mouse
        my_so.data.x = _root._xmouse;
        my_so.data.y = _root._ymouse;
    }
}
```

As you can see, when you click the mouse (using onMouseDown, the mouse button press is registered everywhere on the screen), your movie checks to see whether it's the movie clip that belongs to you. If it is, the movie sends an update to the positional information stored in the my_so shared object.

Adding ActionScript

Now that you've created the FLA file and the avatar movie clip, it's time to add more code. First, add the following code for connecting to the server to the first frame of the as layer:

```
my_nc = new NetConnection();
```

This line creates a new NetConnection object. When you attempt to connect to it, the server responds by sending a callback that triggers the onStatus method of NetConnection. You define it like this:

```
my_nc.onStatus = function(info) {
    if (info.code == "NetConnection.Connect.Success") {
        gotoAndPlay("yes");
    } else {
        gotoAndPlay("no");
    }
}
```

onStatus takes one parameter, supplied by the server. It's an object that provides a property called code, which tells you whether the connection is successful. If the connection is successful, the value for the code property is NetConnection.Connect.Success. If the SWF file is unable to connect to the server, the value for the code property is NetConnection. Connect.Failed. Last, if the SWF file contacts the server but can't create a continuous connection (because of a script error in your application or because acceptConnection isn't called on the server), the code property is set to NetConnection.Connect.Rejected.

As mentioned, it's always a good idea to group any variables you need to define at the beginning of your movie, and place them in a function. The init() function is defined in the "Adding Functions" section later in this chapter.

The application on the FCS server can trigger methods of your NetConnection object. Therefore, you need to define a method to perform whatever operations are needed or refer to an external (outside the NetConnection object) method to perform your operations. In this case, because of the application's simplicity, the functionality is contained in the NetConnection object, as shown here:

```
my_nc.addBall = function (info) {
    newName = "avatar_"+info;
    obj = attachMovie("avatar", newName, nextDepth);
    obj.avatar = info;
    nextDepth++;
}
```

This code creates a new instance of the avatar movie clip and assigns the info parameter (sent from the server in the clientJoined function, defined in "Creating a Server-Side Script" earlier in this chapter) to the new movie clip as the value avatar. The avatar uses this parameter to determine whether to update the shared object it's connected to.

Next is the removeBall method, which is sent to users when any other user disconnects from the application:

```
my_nc.removeBall = function (info) {
    trace("remove ball");
    removeMovieClip(_root["avatar_"+info]);
}
```

This method takes the passed info parameter (which is the username specified by that user) and deletes the movie clip.

Now call the init() function (defined in the next section, "Adding Functions"), which instantiates any variables needed in the application:

```
init();
```

Last, to avoid jumping forward unnecessarily, insert a stop() command in this frame:

```
stop();
```

After your code has been added, frame 1 of the as layer should look like this:

```
my_nc = new NetConnection();


my_nc.onStatus = function(info) {
    if (info.code == "NetConnection.Connect.Success") {
        gotoAndPlay("yes");
    } else {
        gotoAndPlay("no");
    }

}


my_nc.addBall = function (info) {
    newName = "avatar_"+info;
    obj = attachMovie("avatar", newName, nextDepth);
    obj.avatar = info;

    nextDepth++;
}
my_nc.removeBall = function (info) {
    trace("remove ball");
    removeMovieClip(_root["avatar_"+info]);
}
init();
stop();
```

Adding Functions

The next step is defining the doConnect() function, which is called by the button in frame 1:

```
function doConnect() {
    trace("attempting connection");
```

```
        my_username = username.text;
        my_nc.connect("rtmp:/avatar", username.text);
}
```

As you can see, this function sends the value of the username text field to the FCS server when it tries to connect. When this connection attempt succeeds or fails, the onStatus() method is called, and the user is taken to the yes or no keyframe.

If you're connecting to a remote FCS server, you use the syntax rtmp://server/app to define where the connection attempt is made. If you're connecting to a local server, you can use the shorthand rtmp:/app.

Last, define the init() function, which is called as shown here:

```
function init() {
        nextDepth = 0;
}
```

In this case, there's only one variable to define, but calling it like this is still a good idea. The nextDepth variable is used to determine at what depth new avatars are created. After creating the new avatar, the addBall method of my_nc increments the value of nextDepth by 1.

That's it! Put all that code together, test your movie, and see it go. You can enhance this simple application in a variety of ways, such as displaying the name of the newly connected user on his avatar, allowing constant avatar movement, or enabling keyboard interaction. Play around with it, and see what you can accomplish. When you get the hang of Flash Communication Server MX, you'll find it's an incredibly powerful tool.

THE NETCONNECTION DEBUGGER

The NetConnection Debugger, shown in Figure 18.5, is a debugging panel for viewing server output from Flash Communication Server applications and the Flash Remoting service. It's installed automatically when you install Flash Remoting MX and FCS.

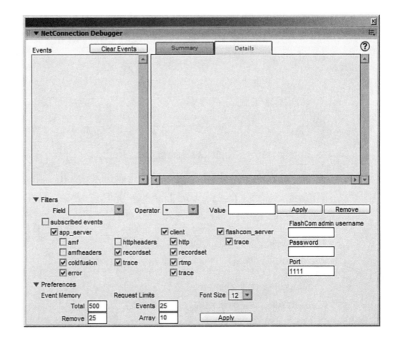

To use the NetConnection Debugger for your applications, you have to include the following line of ActionScript in your movie:

`#include "NetDebug.as"`

If you simply test a movie that connects to an FCS application, you won't see any Debugger output. To connect to your FCS source, you need to supply the administrator name and password and the port reserved for administrative connections (the default is 1111). If you enter this information in the appropriate fields, Flash connects the NetConnection Debugger to FCS when your application runs.

After connecting successfully to the FCS application, you can start receiving all the system and application output the server generates. You can view this information in the Events section of the NetConnection Debugger. If you click an event in the Events section, you can view summary information or specific details by selecting the corresponding tab on the right.

When you connect to the NetConnection Debugger, you connect to the output for the server, not just a specific application, so you might be inundated by the number of events and trace statements being generated. To better handle this influx, you can specify which information to display

TIP

For detailed information about using the NetConnection Debugger, see the help files for Flash Communication Server MX or Flash Remoting MX.

in the debugger (such as ColdFusion information, Flash Communication Server traces, and the like) and apply filters to the specific data that's displayed.

Resources

Flash Remoting MX: www.macromedia.com/software/flashremoting/

ColdFusion MX 6.1: www.macromedia.com/software/coldfusion/

Macromedia Flash MX Professional 2004 Application Development: Training from the Source, Jeanette Stallons (Macromedia Press, November 2003, ISBN: 0321238346).

Macromedia Flash Communication Server: www.macromedia.com/software/flashcom/

Macromedia Exchange: www.macromedia.com/cfusion/exchange/index.cfm

POINTS TO REMEMBER

- Flash Remoting MX enables you to connect to a wide number of external data sources, such as ColdFusion, Java application servers, and .NET environments.

- Flash Remoting MX is fast and extensible.

- The RecordSet object allows you to manipulate recordset information in Flash with no loss of data.

- Flash Communication Server MX is a server environment for creating dynamic multiuser applications.

- Flash Communication Server MX uses server-side ActionScript, which is similar to client-side ActionScript, allowing developers to begin coding immediately.

- With Flash Communication Server MX, you can quickly and easily create multiuser applications without needing to learn entirely new languages and syntaxes.

PART V
NEXT STEPS

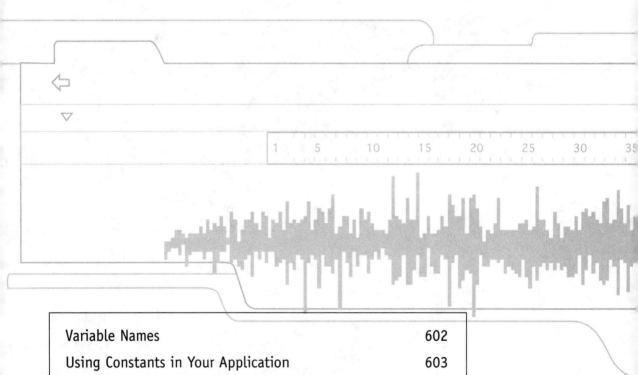

CHAPTER 19

WRITING CODE THAT ROCKS: ACTIONSCRIPT BEST PRACTICES

THIS CHAPTER COVERS SEVERAL CODE STANDARDS—THE "BEST PRACTICES" for programming in Macromedia Flash MX 2004. What follows aren't rules, but rather guidelines to help you, as a programmer, make better content in Flash more quickly.

40   45

VARIABLE NAMES

Although you can, technically, name variables almost whatever you want, naming them descriptively and applying naming rules consistently are generally good ideas. You might be the only programmer working on an application, but you'll likely have to revisit your code at some point or hand it off to another developer. Consequently, it's a good idea to name your variables clearly and consistently; their names should be consistent with how they will be used or the values they'll contain. Flash doesn't enforce a strict variable-naming scheme; it allows you to choose your own scheme, more or less. However, after picking a scheme, it's recommended that you stick to it. You should be able to recognize the use of the variable simply by its name. For example, although `username` is a good, descriptive name, `uN`, even if it contains exactly the same information, is not.

For your own consistency and consistency with other programmers, you should begin function and variable names with lowercase letters. Objects and object constructors should be capitalized. When defining classes with ActionScript 2.0, for example, you *must* capitalize the names.

As mentioned in Chapter 8, "Introduction to ActionScript," variable names can consist only of letters, numbers, and underscores. You can't begin a variable name with a number, nor can you include a space or any extended character (such as !, ?, or @, with the exception of $, which can be used in the definition of a variable) in your variable names. You can begin a variable with an underscore, but by convention, Flash built-in properties begin with an underscore, so limit your use of beginning variable names with an underscore to avoid confusion.

The following are examples of illegally named variables:

```
var 5dime:Number = 1;     // variable begins with a number
```

```
var five/dime:Boolean = false // variable contains
➡nonalphanumeric character
```

```
var five and dime:Boolean = true // variable contains a space
```

These are legally named variables:

```
var five_and_dime:Boolean = true;
```

```
var fiveAndDime:Boolean = true;
```

```
var five10:Boolean = 0;
```

Also, you can't use a reserved keyword as a variable name. A *reserved keyword* is any word that ActionScript itself uses. For example, var is a reserved keyword because it's used to define a variable. The following examples are all illegal variable names because they use common reserved keywords:

```
var = "me";
if = "something";
MovieClip = "myMovieClip";
```

ActionScript is now fully ECMAScript-compliant, so you can find a list of reserved keywords by looking at the ECMA specification, which can be found at **www.ecma-international.org/publications/files/ecma-st/Ecma-262.pdf**.

USING CONSTANTS IN YOUR APPLICATION

Flash doesn't enforce the use of constant variables, but if you are going to define constants within your application, you should do so consistently. For example, a good rule to follow is to name constants with all uppercase letters, as shown here:

```
MAXLIMIT = 10;
```

```
MAINURL = http://www.myserver.com/
```

CODE HINTING

The ActionScript editor provides code hinting, which means that methods and properties related to the object you're referencing can be displayed in the Actions panel. To take advantage of this code hinting, you have to add a suffix to the name of your object or variable. Table 19.1 lists object types that code hinting is enabled for and the suffixes required for code hinting.

TABLE 19.1 **Code Hinting Suffixes**

Object Type	Suffix String	Example
String	_str	myString_str
Array	_array	myArray_array
MovieClip	_mc	myMovieClip_mc
TextField	_txt	myTextField_txt
Date	_date	myDate_date
Sound	_sound	mySound_sound
XML	_xml	myXML_xml
Color	_color	myColor_color

You should also extend your naming scheme to your SWF files—for example, name your movie my_movie.swf, not mM.swf.

In addition to code-hinting support, naming your variables and objects with these suffixes makes your naming scheme much easier to read and understand.

In addition to using the suffixes, code hinting is provided automatically when you use strict typing to define your variables. For example, the following method defines an XML variable:

```
var xmlBase:XML = new XML();
```

When you type xmlBase in the Actions panel, you'll see a listing of XML-specific properties and methods. This is a useful tool to have at your disposal, and it doesn't require you to adhere to the older, Flash MX style of code hinting.

COMMENTING CODE

When you are programming, consistently and clearly commenting your code is recommended not only as an aid for other programmers who might see your code, but also for you, so that you'll know what your code was intended for if you look at it later. Comments can be used to describe a function or an individual line of code, to explain what specific variables are used for, and to specify what variables should be passed to functions or methods. Here is an example of a comment for a variable:

```
var myName:String = "Brian";     // name of character onscreen
```

And here is an example of using a comment to explain the purpose of a function:

```
function getName():String {
    // this function returns the variable myName
    // to whatever called it.

    return myName;
}
```

If you have a function that has varying parameters passed to it, you might want to comment it like this:

```
function getName(which:Number):String {
    // this function returns a username from nameList_array
    // which is the index of the nameList_array entry to return
    return nameList_array[which];
}
```

If your comments will be long, you can use block comments:

```
/*
    When the application starts, the following functions are
    called, which determine the initial application variables.
*/
```

Comments are also useful as notes when developing your application. For example, if something works, but not as efficiently as you'd like, you might want to comment it:

```
// :HACK: This works, barely. Optimize the code.
```

Or, if there is a bug, you might comment it like this:

```
// :BUG: The function isn't returning the right data!
```

Alternatively, you might be defining where your code will go before you've written it. In that case, you might want to add placeholders where you plan to add new functionality or complete your functionality:

```
/*
    :TODO: Right now, this function is sending back dummy
    data. Have to make it return the right data, depending
    on the information sent to it.
*/
```

VARIABLE SCOPE

Macromedia Flash Player 7 uses a *scope chain*, which is a list of ActionScript objects. To resolve an identifier, ActionScript looks for it in the last element in the scope chain and then proceeds backward if it can't be located. Without the scope chain, Flash would be unable to determine how to properly use ActionScript elements in your code.

Typically, a scope chain consists of the following items:

- Global object
- Enclosing `MovieClip` object
- Local variables

When you use the `with` method, you temporarily add an object to the end of the scope chain. This object is removed after the action is finished running.

When you define a method using the `function()` statement, the current scope chain is duplicated and stored in the method object. When that method is called, the scope chain switches to the method object's scope chain, and a new local variables object is added to the end of the chain. The following code is an example of defining a method outside the movie clip:

```
my_mc.myMethod = function() {
    // code
}
```

The scope chain of the method in this example doesn't involve the `my_mc` `MovieClip` object; rather, it involves whatever holds the preceding code. For example, if this code is added to a frame on the main timeline, the scope chain would involve the main timeline. In this case, you need to use the `this` keyword inside the method body to reference elements of the movie clip.

To define a variable as being local, use the `var` keyword when defining your variable. Take a look at the following code:

```
function myFunction() {
    var myVar:Number = 4;
    trace(myVar);
}

trace(myVar);
```

The preceding code would output this:

```
4
undefined
```

Because a local variable exists only for the object, function, or level in which it is defined, not any other part of your script or movie, local variables are useful in ensuring that variables aren't accidentally overwritten when your program runs.

Relative Addressing

You should specify the scope for all variables, except function parameters and local variables. When at all possible, they should be scoped in relation to their current path. Also, the excessive use of _root, as in the following example, is discouraged:

```
// code in a movie clip on the root
if (_root.myName == "Bob Roberts") {
    _root.myDisplayName.text = _root.myName;
    _root.setUserPreferences(_root.myName);
}
```

Code heavy with absolute references isn't as portable as code with relative references, as shown in this example:

```
// code in a movie clip on the root
obj = _parent;
if (obj.myName == "Bob Roberts") {
    _obj.myDisplayName.text = _obj.myName;
    _obj.setUserPreferences(obj.myName);
}
```

If you do need to make references to the main timeline, create an alias to represent your _root. The following code defines a global variable to use in place of _root:

```
_global.myRoot = this;
```

You would reference this global variable in a script as shown in this example:

```
trace(myRoot.myVar);
```

The benefit of using global variables is that you can make what seem to be _root references, but if you need to change what the code references, you can change it once and have the changes reflected immediately everywhere in your application.

_global Versus _root

Although _global and _root are similar, there are differences in implementing these two properties. _root is different for every loaded movie, whereas _global applies to all movies within the player. You also can set the _lockroot property (defined in Chapter 9, "ActionScript Basics: Data and Statements") in Flash 2004, which specifies what _root refers to in a loaded SWF. When set to true, _root in a loaded SWF refers to the main timeline of the loaded SWF. When it's set to false, it refers to the main timeline of the entire movie.

GENERAL GUIDELINES

The general guidelines in the following sections will help you create robust, easily modified applications.

Define All Your Variables at Once

Your application will likely involve many variables, and it can get difficult to keep track not just of their values, but also of their names and intended uses. It's recommended that you define all your variables (excluding those defined locally inside functions) as close to the beginning of your movie as possible. You might want to create a layer to contain all your variables or have a specific .as (ActionScript) file to include them.

For example, if you create a Variables layer, you might want to organize the ActionScript code block into different categories of variables, as shown here:

```
// User Defined Variables
...
// Application Controlled Variables
...
// Constants
```

Localize Your Code (with Preloader Exception)

If at all possible, placing your code on the first frame of your movie is recommended. That might prove difficult in certain circumstances, but the fewer places you write your code, the fewer opportunities you have to misplace your code and the fewer places you have to check when debugging. Localizing your code not only saves you time, but also makes the time you spend developing your application much more pleasant.

An exception to placing all your code on the first frame is when you have a preloader in your movie. In that case, place your ActionScript on the first frame *after* the preloader. For example, if your preloader occupies the first three frames of your movie, add your code to frame four.

Don't Set Movie Clip or Button Code on Instances

Although you can select a movie clip or button instance on the stage and attach code to it (by selecting the instance and typing in the Actions panel), this practice is discouraged in the development of medium to large applications. Attached code looks like this:

```
on (release) {
    // code
}
```

or

```
onClipEvent (enterFrame) {
    // code
}
```

This is tricky because you're placing the code in several different locations, making it easier to lose track of much of your ActionScript. As well, if you delete a movie clip or button that has code on the instance, you might lose that code. Instead, to aid in centralizing your code, it's recommended that you define your handlers, for example, outside the instances that will use them in a centralized location. This means you need to use the this keyword to specify the targets of your actions, but it saves you a lot of time when you need to search through your code to debug it or make enhancements. The following example is the recommended method of defining event handlers in medium to large applications:

```
// movieclip handler
my_mc.onEnterFrame = function() {
    // code
}

// button handlers
my_button.onRelease = function() {
    // code
}
```

If you anticipate having a large number of processes running simultaneously, you should be aware that the demands on the system will increase rapidly. When you need to have a large number of repeating events running, you could try using the setInterval() function, which can be used to define repeating actions without requiring as many of the user's system resources.

Externalizing Code

If your application contains a lot of ActionScript, containing as much of your functionality as possible in external .as files is a good idea. You could create numerous layers and write all your script within your application, but large amounts of code quickly become hard to manage, and it's possible to misplace functions you need to finish or fix.

All .as files are text files. You load them into an FLA file when your movie is compiled and include them in that FLA file with the #include directive, which uses the following syntax:

```
#include "filename.as"
```

The #include directive runs before any script, so if you reference variables in the .as file that are defined in your FLA file, you might run into problems. To avoid this, try to externalize code that doesn't get called right away.

It's a good idea to save similar functions in the same .as file to keep better track of your application. For example, if you're building a game in which the user controls a rocket ship, you might cluster all functions related to the control and operation of the rocket ship into the same file. Remember, too, to save your .as files with easy-to-understand filenames. For example, if an .as file is composed of functions used to govern character movement in a game you're building, you might save it as character_movement.as instead of an obscure name such as cM.as.

Using Frames as Delimiters of Application States

A helpful visual and programmatic aid is using frames to represent application states. For example, if you're building an asteroids-style game, you might divide the functionality of your movie into four sections: intro, playing, gameOver, and highScores. If you define four keyframes and name them accordingly, when you want to start playing your game, you could tell the movie to jump to the playing frame. All ActionScript for starting your game could be referenced on that frame (by a function call, not by locating the code itself on the frame). When the game is over, you can have the movie jump to the gameOver frame. This allows you to remove any game content from the timeline without having to use code, as you could jump to a frame that doesn't have the content on the timeline.

If you're using Flash MX 2004 Professional, the Forms feature can be used quite effectively to achieve the same results.

Initialization of Code

When an application begins, it usually needs to have a variety of variables and properties set and have certain data loaded. You can make this happen on the first frame of your movie, as in the following example:

```
// Frame 1
myScore = 0;
myName = "Bob";
myShipColor = 0xFFFFFF;
```

However, using this method isn't recommended. If you need to jump back to frame one for any reason, you'll be redefining your initial application state, whether you want to or not. Instead, you should create an initialization function containing all the information you need to set at the start of your movie. For example, you could change the previous code to use an initialization function, as shown here:

```
function init() {
    myScore = 0;
    myName= "Bob";
    myShipColor = 0xFFFFFF;
}
```

You can simply define the initial state of your application by calling the init() function. Not only that, but if you need to reset conditions at any point while your application is running, you can do so by calling init().

Prototyping Objects

When you're creating custom objects in Flash, instead of defining methods and properties for each instance of the object you create, you should define methods and properties in the prototype of your object. Using prototyped functions saves programming time and system memory because they exist in system memory only once, regardless of how many copies of your object you create. The following method of creating objects is discouraged:

```
MyNewObject = new Object();

MyNewObject.myName = "";

MyNewObject.myMethod = function() {
    // code
}

MyNewObject.getName = function() {
    return myName;
}
```

This is the recommended practice for creating objects:

```
MyNewObject = new Object();
```

```
MyNewObject.prototype.myName = "";

MyNewObject.prototype.myMethod = function() {
    // code
}

MyNewObject.prototype.getName = function() {
    return myName;
}
```

Object Inheritance

When using classes in Flash 2004, defining a prototype chain for your custom classes and objects is the recommended practice. A prototype chain using Flash MX–style inheritance looks like this:

```
function Car() {

}

function Van() {
}

Van.prototype = new Car();
```

Inheritance using classes looks like this:

```
class Car {

}

class Van extends Car {

}
```

For more information on classes, see Chapter 20, "OOP for Flashers."

In both examples, methods and properties defined in Car are available in Van, as Van inherits from Car. The first example, using functions, is a workaround. The class structure, new to Flash MX 2004, is a more standardized implementation of inheritance, and using this newer method is recommended. In addition, as you can see, it's quicker to define classes and class inheritance using class.

When using classes in Flash 2004, developers can define a new class contained in an `.as` file. Using classes, you define methods and properties in much the same way as prototyped functions, although using strict typing is recommended when defining new classes.

File Size of Flash MX 2004 Elements

When developing applications in Flash MX 2004, keep in mind the different sizes that ActionScript objects take up. An empty SWF might use only 30 bytes, but that size increases drastically when you start to add elements to your movie. The following list contains file sizes of some elements in Flash MX 2004:

String (7 characters long): 28 bytes

Number: 22 bytes

Object (created using `newObject()`): 35 bytes

Empty movie clip (created using `emptyMovieClip()`): 51 bytes

A new function (`x = function() {}`): 20 bytes

Text field (7 characters long, using Arial font): 73 bytes

As you can see, these elements don't add very much on their own to the size of an SWF file, but for every line of code you add to your functions or objects, and every text field you add to your timeline, the file size increases. It's important to be aware of the size of various elements in Flash.

As well, you'll probably use components in Flash. Because of the vast amount of code stored in the components that ship with Flash, the size of your movie jumps noticeably when you add a component. This impact is lessened, however, as you add more components because each component uses many of the same classes and functionality the others do. For more information on file size concerns with components, refer to Chapter 12, "Components."

Optimizing Code

No matter what application you're trying to build or what problem you're trying to solve with your script, there's always more than one way to do it. Sometimes you have to partially or completely rewrite your code, but if your code runs more efficiently as a result, rewriting is a good thing.

When developing applications, your first concern should be functionality. Does your application work the way it should? After you achieve that goal, however, you'll want to start thinking about how efficiently you've achieved your functionality and how fast your application runs.

For example, suppose you're building a trivia game in which users can answer questions in whatever sequence they like. As users progress through the game, you want to record the choices they have made. You could do this by adding to an array every time a choice is made and recording the question and answer. The code for the array might look like this:

```
// this section is used to define the questions
// define array
questions = new Array();

/*
    this is what the array might look like after the questions
    have been answered. The first element is a reference to
    the question number, and the second is the answer given
    (0 for false, 1 for true).

    questions[0] = [5, 0];
    questions[1] = [1, 1];
    questions[2] = [3, 1];
    questions[3] = [0, 1];
    questions[4] = [4, 0];
    questions[5] = 2, 1];
*/

// this function would be called by a user when answering a
// question presented to him or her
function answerQuestion (question, answer) {
    questions[questions.length] = [question, answer];
}
```

```
/*
     this function would be used after the questions have been
     answered, and might be used to determine the user's score.
*/

function getAnswer(question) {
     // cycle through questions
     for (var i = 0; i<questions.length; i++) {
          // check to see if this is the right question
          if (questions[i][0] == question) {
               // it is the right question, so send the answer.
               return questions[i][1];
          }
     }
}
```

This code has a definition of an array, the functionality to add an answer to the questions array, and the functionality to retrieve the questions. However, having to root through the entire array every time you want to extract an answer is inefficient. A better way is directly referencing the value of the array, without having to check whether the array element contains the correct value. Take another look at this code after optimizing it for efficiency:

```
// define array
questions = new Array();

/*
     this is what the array might look like after the questions
     have been answered. The first element is a reference to
     the question number, and the second is the answer given
     (0 for false, 1 for true).
     questions[0] = 0;
     questions[1] = 1;
     questions[2] = 1;
     questions[3] = 1;
     questions[4] = 0;
     questions[5] = 1;
*/
```

```
// this function would be called by the user, when
// answering a question presented to him or her.
function answerQuestion (question, answer) {
    questions[question] = [answer];
}

/*
    This function would be used to determine the answer given
    to a specific question. It would be used in determining
    the user's score.
*/
function getAnswer(question) {
    return questions[question];
}
```

The questions are entered into the array differently this time. Instead of adding a new element to the end of the array with both the question and answer, the question ID determines its position in the array. For example, in the first code example, the first element in the array might correspond to question 1 or question 5; in this second code example, the first element in the array always corresponds to the first question. This makes it possible to ask for the value of a question without making sure it's in the right place. Although the speed benefits of this second method aren't glaringly obvious when you have an array of only five or six elements, if you have hundreds of questions a user could answer, the savings in processor time do become obvious.

When developing applications, keep in mind that there's always more than one way to approach and solve a problem. The first time you build something, it probably won't be as efficient as it can be.

Chapter Project: Creating Something from Nothing

Flash MX 2004 allows you to minimize the number of library items in your movie at both author time and runtime. With the `createEmptyMovieClip()` method, you can create an entirely new empty movie clip on the stage and load external files into it.

This project takes you through the process of creating a simple Flash movie consisting of five navigational buttons that when clicked display different content in a text field onscreen. As well, colors change to represent the section you're in. This project is a useful exercise because it gives you an idea of what you can do without needing graphical elements of any kind. It makes changes of visual or textual content very easy and helps reduce the file size of your application.

1. First, create a new Flash movie and add four layers: Prototypes, Variables, Functions, and AS.

2. Draw five rectangular buttons for your menu. Add the drawRectangle() function you learned about in Chapter 11, "Animation and Drawing with ActionScript: The Drawing API," to the Prototype layer, using the following code:

```
// drawing a square
MovieClip.prototype.drawRectangle = function(ax, ay, bx, by) {
    with (this) {
        // draw a square
        lineTo(ax, by);
        lineTo(bx, by);
        lineTo(bx, ay);
        lineTo(ax, ay);
    }
}
```

3. Because your buttons will be dynamic, you need to assign functionality to them. The following prototyped functions tell your new movie clips to redraw themselves when the mouse rolls over and off them and when the user clicks and releases the button:

```
MovieClip.prototype.drawUp = function() {
    // this method draws the Up state of the button
    with (this) {
        // clear previous drawn elements
        clear();
        // set the line and fill style for your button
        lineStyle(1, 0x666666, 100);
        beginFill(0xFFFFFF, 100);
```

```
        // draw the button Up state using drawRectangle
        drawRectangle(0,0,70,20);
    }
}

MovieClip.prototype.drawOver = function() {
    with (this) {
        clear();
        lineStyle(1, 0x666666, 100);
        beginFill(0x000000, 10);
        drawRectangle(0,0,70,20);
    }
}

MovieClip.prototype.drawDown = function() {
    with (this) {
        clear();
        lineStyle(1, 0x666666, 100);
        beginFill(0xFFCC33, 100);
        drawRectangle(0,0,70,20);
    }
}
```

The color values for these buttons are hard-coded into the functions, which works fine for this example. For a real-world application, however, you would likely want to assign each button a color scheme and have the prototyped functions refer to the values stored in each object.

4. Next, add the following code to the Variables layer, which holds all your content-related variables, your TextFormat object, and nextButton, the variable used to create your buttons:

```
// counter
nextButton = 0;

// button labels
buttonLabels = new Array();
buttonLabels = ["One", "Two", "Three", "Four", "Five"];
```

```
// text format
textSettings = new TextFormat()
textSettings.font = "Arial";
textSettings.size = "10";

// content
contentSections = new Array();
contentSections[0] = "<font face='Arial' size='10'>
➥This is content section one. \n \n Content will go
➥here.</font>";
contentSections[1] = "<font face='Arial' size='10'>
➥This is content section two. \n \n Content will go
➥here.</font>";
contentSections[2] = "<font face='Arial' size='10'>
➥This is content section three. \n \n Content will go
➥here.</font>";
contentSections[3] = "<font face='Arial' size='10'>
➥This is content section four. \n \n Content will go
➥here.</font>";
contentSections[4] = "<font face='Arial' size='10'>
➥This is content section five. \n \n Click
➥<a href='http://www.macromedia.com/'><b>
➥<font color='#FFCC33'>Here</font></b></a> to go to
➥macromedia.com.</font>";

// background color
bgColor = new Array();
bgColor.push([0x000000, 10]);
bgColor.push([0xFF0000, 20]);
bgColor.push([0x00ff00, 30]);
bgColor.push([0xffffcc, 30]);
bgColor.push([0x00cc00, 20]);
```

The contentSections array holds the content to be displayed in your content movie clip, and bgColor is used to determine the different colors of the movie clip.

5. Next, add the function for creating your buttons to the Functions layer:

```
function makeButton() {
    // create button clip
```

```
createEmptyMovieClip("button"+nextButton, nextButton);

// shorthand
obj = this["button"+nextButton];

// used to display content to the screen
obj.contentReference = nextButton;

// position first button
obj._x = 10+(nextButton*70);
obj._y = 10;

// assign button handlers
obj.onRollOver = function() {
    this.drawOver();
}

obj.onRollOut = function() {
    this.drawUp();
}

obj.onPress = function() {
    this.drawDown();
}

obj.onRelease = function() {
    drawContent(this.contentReference);
    this.drawOver();
}

obj.onReleaseOutside = function () {
    this.drawUp();
}

// draw button
obj.drawUp();

// create text element
obj.createTextField("myText", 0, 5, 5, 60, 20);
```

```
        // set format
        obj.myText.setNewTextFormat(textSettings);

        // set label
        obj.myText.text = buttonLabels[nextButton];

        // increment next button
        nextButton++;
    }
```

After creating the movie clip, you define all the button states, refer-ring to the prototyped functions. Also, you create a text field and set the TextFormat object (defined in the Variables layer).

6. You might have noticed that the defined onRelease function calls the drawContent function. Before you get to that, you need to add the function to build the content area:

```
function makeContent() {
    // create content holder
    createEmptyMovieClip("content_mc", 10);

    // position content holder
    content_mc._x = 10;
    content_mc._y = 40;

    // draw background
    content_mc.lineStyle(0, 0, 0);
    content_mc.beginFill(0x000000, 10);
    content_mc.drawRectangle(0, 0, 350, 350);
    content_mc.endFill();

    // add text
    content_mc.createTextField("content", 0, 5, 5, 340, 340);
    content_mc.content.multiline = true;
    content_mc.content.html = true;
    }
```

This code builds a movie clip, draws a background, and adds a new text field to hold the content specified by users' button clicks.

7. Now add the function to populate the content text field with the appropriate text, and redraw the background elements:

```
function drawContent (which) {
    // populate the text field.
    content_mc.content.htmlText = contentSections[which];
    // draw the background elements.
    content_mc.clear();
    content_mc.lineStyle(0, 0, 0);
    content_mc.beginFill(bgColor[which][0],
bgColor[which][1]);
    content_mc.drawRectangle(0, 0, 350, 350);
    content_mc.endFill();
}
```

8. All that's left is to call the functions that draw everything. Add the following code to the AS layer:

```
// make nav bar row
for (var i = 0; i<5; i++) {
    makeButton();
}

// make content holder
makeContent();
```

That's it. Export your movie, and check it out. A fully functioning menu with nothing on your stage and nothing in your library—pretty cool, huh?

POINTS TO REMEMBER

- Clean code is the key to efficiency and optimization of your applications.

- Try to use relative references in your code, instead of absolute references.

- Using classes, you can create structured inheritance chains, allowing you to reuse code and cut down on errors or redundant code.

- You can use Flash MX 2004 to create entire applications that exist only as ActionScript.

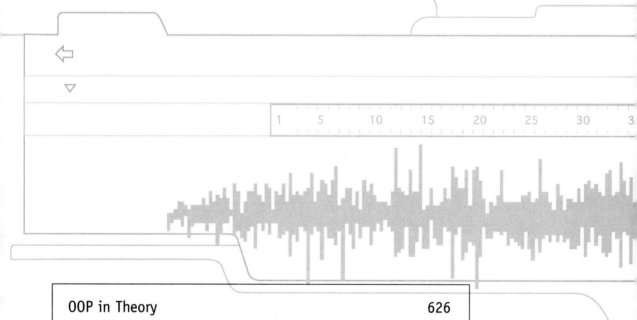

CHAPTER 20

OOP for Flashers

HAVING GOTTEN THIS FAR, YOU'RE PROBABLY IN THE MOOD TO JUMP INTO THE Flash integrated development environment (IDE) and start coding some web-based business applications, and I certainly won't discourage you. Play around, experiment, and get familiar with the environment, the syntax of the language, and the keywords. Before you start on any serious project (read: something you might make money doing), however, it's in your best interests to read this chapter thoroughly and learn a bit about object-oriented programming (OOP) techniques. Properly applied, OOP saves you time, money, and hassle, without too much work up front.

Object-oriented programming is a topic that can (and does) easily fill books, but this chapter should get you pointed in the right direction and prime you for more in-depth reading on the subject. This chapter teaches you about the basic principles of OOP, its benefits, and how to apply object-oriented principles in ActionScript 2.0.

As you proceed, you'll apply what you learn to creating a simple project in which a user can control a UFO's movement with the keyboard (and that's about all you really need for world domination).

OOP IN THEORY

For ActionScript 1.0 Developers

I wish I could give ActionScript 1.0 OOP veterans a concise list of changes in ActionScript 2.0 and turn you loose, but it isn't that simple because much has changed. The core OOP principles have remained the same, but the syntax used to apply them has changed. At the very least, I suggest scanning through this chapter and paying particular attention to the code samples. If you aren't quite an OOP veteran, I recommend reading the whole chapter.

Object-oriented programming (OOP) is a methodology for planning and coding programs in which tasks are broken up and assigned to a number of self-contained "objects." An *object* is a programming construct composed of data (in the form of properties) and related functions (called methods) used to manipulate, modify, and access that data, as shown in Figure 20.1. These properties and methods are referred to as *members* of an object, and members that can be accessed by other objects are cumulatively called the *interface* for that object.

FIGURE 20.1
An object with methods and properties. The outer ring of methods (the ones that are publicly accessible) are the interface for the object.

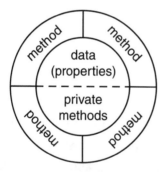

As in real life, the interactions between objects dictate the program's flow and functionality. For example, a FlashGeek object could interact with a Computer object to edit a FlashBookChapter object (see Figure 20.2). Completing the task is possible only through the interactions and relationships of these objects.

As you plan objects and interactions for any application, you should keep three major concepts in mind when dealing with OOP: encapsulation, polymorphism, and abstraction.

FIGURE 20.2
The arrows indicate object interactions.

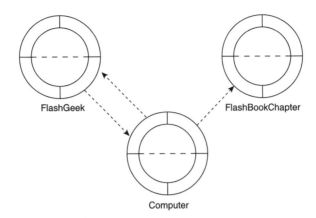

FlashGeek   FlashBookChapter

Computer

Encapsulation

In OOP, *encapsulation* refers to the need to make every object self-contained and to restrict external access to each object to a defined interface.

My computer is a great real-world example of encapsulation. As I sit here typing this chapter, the computer is carrying out millions of processes and dealing with reams of data. I, as a separate object, am unaware of these processes. Sure, I know my computer is doing stuff, but I don't know or care about the details. Similarly, my computer doesn't know or care about the details of how I'm thinking up these brilliant examples I'm writing. All my computer and I are worried about is our mutual interface—the keyboard and the screen.

In code, encapsulation is typically enforced by limiting the communication between objects to a documented set of methods, known as the *interface* (see Figure 20.3). Directly affecting the properties of another object is strongly discouraged in OOP. By accessing properties directly, you're eliminating your ability to change how the object handles changes to its data and the structure of that data. Implicit get and set methods (covered later in this chapter in "Making Properties Act Like Methods: Implicit *get* and *set*") enable you to create methods that can be accessed like properties, without the associated problems of accessing properties directly.

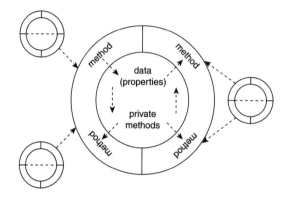

Polymorphism

A useful side effect of encapsulation is *polymorphism*. Because objects couldn't care less about the internal workings of other objects, you can easily replace an object with any other object that presents the same interface. Because both objects present exactly the same set of public methods, any objects that interact with one object already know how to interact with the other. This allows you to easily swap polymorphic classes with one another in an application, without having to modify any other part of the program.

To continue my example, if I were running Word on my PowerBook and it was replaced with WordPerfect or TextPad, I wouldn't care. (Okay, I'd be ticked off, but stay with me here.) My interface would remain basically the same—I'd still be typing on a keyboard and watching the output on a screen. The differences in how the two word processing applications function internally wouldn't have any bearing on the interaction.

Abstraction

Abstraction involves taking a complex model and simplifying it to the point that it contains only those members (properties and methods) that are absolutely necessary in the context of the system.

For instance, when modeling a user in a system, you could include extraneous details, such as hair color and shoe size. By simplifying the complex concept of a user to just the necessary properties, such as name, password, and email address, you can create smaller, more easily understood objects. Figure 20.4 shows an example of abstraction in action.

FIGURE 20.4
Using abstraction to reduce a flower to its essential components. Despite the lack of detail, it still clearly represents a flower.

BENEFITS OF OOP

Before going into technical detail about how to do object-oriented programming, you need to understand *why* you would want to do it in the first place. OOP has three major benefits: planning, modularity, and division of labor.

Planning

With object-oriented programming, you can divide a complex task into a number of small tasks. Instead of trying to plan and design the functionality of an entire application, you can focus on the functionality of a single element of that application, such as a menu (or even a menu item), and then consider the interactions or relationships that element will have with other objects in the system.

In real life, tasks are defined based on interactions with objects: "The MAN reads the BOOK." A similar set of definitions is used for computer tasks: "Open the FILE MENU, and select the QUIT MENU ITEM." This approach closely parallels that of object-oriented programming, which makes planning projects much simpler.

An established process called *object-oriented analysis and design* (*OOAD*) helps organize, document, and focus your development efforts for object-oriented programs. Figure 20.5 shows an example of the OOAD process, using Unified Modeling Language (UML) diagrams. OOAD is quite an in-depth process (and beyond the scope of this chapter), but it's worth spending some time to learn. Do a Google search for OOAD or UML, or pick up a good book on the topic if you'd like to learn more.

FIGURE 20.5
OOAD: A UML class diagram generated with the easy-to-use gModeler.com modeling application for Flash.

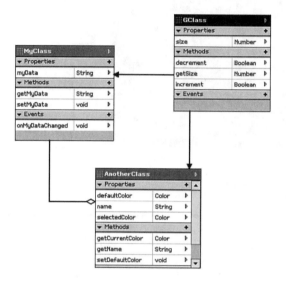

Modularity

The code in OOP is divided into self-contained, functional objects. These objects are easy to isolate and test, making debugging and quality control much easier. Similarly, maintaining and expanding a project developed with OOP is much easier because you have to work with only the objects involved in the update.

Objects can be reused easily in different projects. As you build a library of stable, reliable code, this reuse vastly decreases development time on projects and makes it easy to share code within the Flash community—which benefits everyone!

Division of Labor

Because OOP projects are divided into self-contained, well-documented pieces (this is where OOAD is useful), dividing tasks among members of your coding team is easy. Similarly, because the relationships between objects are well defined during the planning phase, communication between team members is much simpler. Team members have to discuss only the interactions between objects and their defined interfaces, not the internal workings of each object.

OOP IN PRACTICE: CLASSES

Classes form the core of object-oriented programming. You're already familiar with many of the classes built into Flash MX 2004, such as `Array`, `Math`, and `MovieClip`, but you can also create your own.

A class acts as a definition (or template) for a new object. Like a cookie cutter, it prescribes an object's initial shape by defining its data (called properties) and the functions that operate on that data (called methods). Just like a cookie, you can add sprinkles and icing (that is, new data) to new objects, but the initial shape remains virtually the same.

Creating a new (hint, hint) object using a class is easy; in fact, you've done it before in this book. As you've probably already guessed, you use the `new` keyword. For example, if you want to create a new object based on the built-in `Array` class, you would use the following code:

```
var myArray:Array = new Array();
// let's add some sprinkles :)
myArray.push("chocolate");
```

This code creates a new object of the `Array` class, usually referred to as an *instance* of the `Array` class. This new instance has access to all the methods that are part of the `Array` class, and you used one of them—the `push()` method—to sprinkle in some data specific to that instance. Similarly, this instance has access to all the properties defined for the class, but those properties can change to hold data specific to the instance. In this example, if you were to trace `myArray.length`, it would return a value of 1. Now that you have a reasonably good idea of what a class is, take a look at how to create one of your own.

Defining Your First Class

In ActionScript 1.0, classes were little more than customized functions. In ActionScript 2.0, Macromedia added a `class` keyword and an entire methodology for defining and creating classes. The syntax for the `class` keyword is very simple:

```
class MyClassName {
    // everything between the braces is part of the class
}
```

Actually implementing that syntax is a little trickier. In Flash MX 2004, each class must be defined in a separate `.as` (ActionScript) file, located in a recognized classpath (see the following list). Further, this `.as` file must have exactly the same name as the class it contains.

By default, Flash MX 2004 has two classpaths: the path of the directory containing the current document and the global Classes folder installed with Flash, as shown in this list:

You can also define classpaths that are specific to FLA files in the publish settings for the FLA. This process is described in Chapter 23, "Publishing."

- **Windows 2000 or XP**   C:\Documents and Settings\<user>\Local Settings\Application Data\Macromedia\Flash 2004\<language>\ Configuration\

- **Windows 98**   C:\Windows\Application Data\Macromedia\Flash 2004\<language>\Configuration\

- **Mac OS X**   Hard Drive/Users/Library/Application Support/ Macromedia/Flash 2004/<language>/Configuration/

To demonstrate how class definitions work, you can begin building your UFO by defining a `SpaceShip` class that the UFO is instantiated from (that is, based on).

Open Flash, and select the option to create a new ActionScript File. Type the following code into the main window, and save it to your project folder with the name `SpaceShip.as`. Don't forget that ActionScript 2.0 is case sensitive!

You should always name classes beginning with a capital letter. It helps distinguish them from variables, which start with lowercase letters.

```
class SpaceShip {
    // boy I'm excited!
}
```

Finis! You've created your first class. It doesn't actually do anything yet, but it's a fully formed class. Note the use of braces as a way of setting boundaries for the class definition. Now you can start adding members (properties and methods) to the class, as described in the next section.

Adding Properties to a Class

Compile-time constants are values that are available before your code runs. They include string literals, such as "dog", and numbers, such as 152.7.

Adding properties to a class is easy. Simply define a variable inside the braces of a `class` statement, and it's added to that class. You can also initialize variables with values, but the catch is that the value must be a *compile-time constant*.

For the `SpaceShip` object, you'll add four numeric properties that track velocity and location on both the x- and y-axes. You'll also initialize variables with the value of 0:

```
class SpaceShip {
    // define properties
    var velocityX:Number = 0;
    var velocityY:Number = 0;
    var _x:Number = 0; // x location
    var _y:Number = 0; // y location
}
```

Note that in ActionScript 2.0, all members of a class must be defined before runtime, with the exception of dynamic classes (which are covered in "Dynamic Classes," later in this chapter).

Adding Methods to a Class

Your class contains data now, but you need to create methods you can use to manipulate and access that data. In strict object-oriented programming, it's considered a good practice to allow access to data only through methods, never by direct access to properties. In most situations, abiding by this rule is a good idea because it enforces encapsulation.

Consider this rule in the context of a construction site. As foreman, you wouldn't physically pick up every worker, carry him to the right location, and then physically manipulate his limbs to do the job (this could get *you* physically manipulated). Instead, you would issue concise instructions to workers and leave the details up to them. They know their job best, so let them do it.

Adding methods to a class is just like adding properties. Simply define functions within the `class` statement, and they become methods of the class. Methods behave exactly like functions; they just have a different

In ActionScript 2.0, the scope in a method defaults to this, so you don't have to refer to properties of the class prefixed by this., as you do in ActionScript 1.0.

scope (the place they look for variables). To get data, methods always look inside the object they belong to first.

For now, you'll add methods for increasing the x and y velocity of your spaceship and a toString() method to display the status of the spaceship. Whenever an object is converted to a String type (when you trace it, for instance), its toString() method is automatically called.

```
class SpaceShip {
    // define properties:
    var velocityX:Number = 0;
    var velocityY:Number = 0;
    var _x:Number = 0; // x location
    var _y:Number = 0; // y location

    // define methods:
    function thrustX():Void {
        // increment the x velocity:
        velocityX++;
    }
    function thrustY():Void {
        // increment the y velocity:
        velocityY++;
    }
    function toString():String {
        var foo:String;
        foo = "velocityX: "+velocityX;
        foo += " velocityY: "+velocityY;
        foo += " locationX: "+_x;
        foo += " locationY: "+_y;
        return foo;
    }
}
```

The Constructor

For every class, you can define a special function called the *constructor*. This function takes values passed to it as parameters during the instantiation of a new object and uses them to "personalize" the new instance.

To define a constructor, add a method in the class statement with exactly the same name as the class. For your SpaceShip class, you'll add a constructor that lets you set an initial location for your SpaceShip. Then you'll test the whole thing in the next section.

```
class SpaceShip {
    // define properties:
    var velocityX:Number = 0;
    var velocityY:Number = 0;
    var _x:Number = 0; // x location
    var _y:Number = 0; // y location

    // define the constructor:
    function SpaceShip(x:Number,y:Number) {
        _x = x;
        _y = y;
    }

    // define methods:
    function thrustX():Void {
        velocityX++;
    }
    function thrustY():Void {
        velocityY++;
    }
    function toString():String {
        var foo:String;
        foo = "velocityX: "+velocityX;
        foo += " velocityY: "+velocityY;
        foo += " locationX: "+_x;
        foo += " locationY: "+_y;
        return foo;
    }
}
```

So now, when you create a new SpaceShip, you should be able to specify initial x and y locations by passing them as parameters in the new statement.

Instantiating Instances

So how do you take your lovely SpaceShip class and create instances of it? You already know you need to use the new keyword, but first you need a place to put some more code.

Save the changes to the ActionScript document you have been working on, and then create a new Flash Document (FLA). Select the first keyframe in the new timeline, enter the following code, and then save the file as ufo.fla in the same directory you saved the ActionScript document.

```
var ufo:SpaceShip = new SpaceShip(100,50);
trace(ufo);
```

If you run this script by choosing Control, Test Movie from the main menu, the Output panel should display the text shown in Figure 20.6.

FIGURE 20.6

The results of your test are displayed in the Output panel.

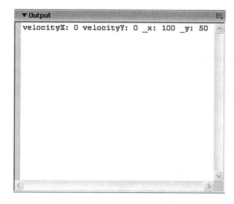

```
velocityX: 0  velocityY: 0  _x: 100  _y: 50
```

Take a look at what's happening:

1. When you compile the ufo.fla file (that is, create an SWF), Flash sees the reference to the SpaceShip class and searches its classpaths for a file named SpaceShip.as. When it finds the one you created, it includes the class definition in the SWF.

2. At runtime (that is, when the SWF is playing), the code you just wrote creates a new variable on the root timeline named ufo, casting it as type SpaceShip, and then makes it equal to a new instance of the SpaceShip class included in step 1.

3. As the ufo instance of SpaceShip is created, the constructor runs and assigns the values you passed to it to the new instance's location property.

4. When you trace the value of ufo, Flash automatically calls the toString() method of the SpaceShip class, which returns the string you saw in the Output panel.

Note that although every instance of a class shares the same methods, each instance's data is independent. You can do a simple test to prove this. Create two SpaceShip instances (ufo and mfalcon), each with different locations, and then output their status, as shown in this example:

```
var ufo:SpaceShip = new SpaceShip(100,50);
var mfalcon:SpaceShip = new SpaceShip(15,60);
mfalcon.thrustX();
trace("ufo: " +ufo);
trace("mfalcon: "+mfalcon);
```

When you run this script, your output should look something like Figure 20.7.

FIGURE 20.7

Output from the two trace statements. Notice that each instance has its own set of properties.

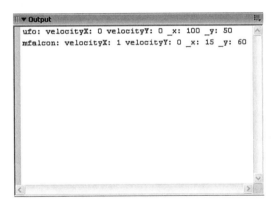

```
ufo: velocityX: 0 velocityY: 0 _x: 100 _y: 50
mfalcon: velocityX: 1 velocityY: 0 _x: 15 _y: 60
```

You can see that each instance has retained its own set of data. You can also see that when you called the thrustX method of the mfalcon instance, it affected only that object's _x property. Now that you can create instances of the SpaceShip class, it's time to start work on giving your UFO an onscreen presence and controlling it with the keyboard.

Binding a Class to a Movie Clip

So far you have been working purely with data, which can get boring, so take a look at how you give your class an onscreen presence. First, you need to create the graphics for your UFO. Open the ufo.fla file you created earlier, and create a new MovieClip symbol in your library named ufo. Draw a simple UFO graphic in the symbol, and make sure it's centered on the clip's origin (see the example in Figure 20.8).

FIGURE 20.8
A work of pure art.

Return to the main timeline of ufo.fla, and add a single copy of the ufo clip from the Library onto the stage, giving it an instance name of ufo_mc in the Property inspector. Next, change the code on the first frame of the main Timeline to the following:

```
ufo_mc.thrustX();
trace(ufo_mc.toString());
```

Now you just have to bind the SpaceShip class to the ufo clip. To do this, right-click (Control-click in Macintosh) the ufo clip in the Library and select Properties to open the Symbol Properties dialog box (see Figure 20.9). In the Linkage section, select the Export for ActionScript check box, and then set its identifier to ufo and its AS 2.0 class to SpaceShip, which associates the clip with the SpaceShip class you defined earlier.

Click OK, and test the movie. You should see your UFO graphics where you placed them and the familiar status line in your Output panel.

By associating the ufo clip with the SpaceShip class, you made every ufo clip instance into an instance of the SpaceShip class. This gives every ufo clip (including the one you named ufo_mc) access to members of the SpaceShip class. Unfortunately, it also broke its association with the built-in MovieClip class and its members (such as lineTo() and getDepth()). You'll need those members when you start making your UFO move, so you had better look at how to reintroduce them in the next section.

FIGURE 20.9
The properties for the
UFO movie clip.

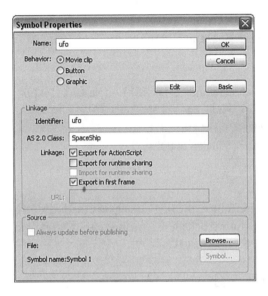

INHERITANCE: THE *EXTENDS* KEYWORD

Inheritance, an extremely powerful concept, can simplify and reduce the amount of code you have to write and make reuse and expansion much easier. Inheritance enables you to base a new class (called a *subclass*) on another class (called the *superclass*), inheriting all its members. This process is chainable, meaning you can have a class inherit from a second class, which in turn inherits from a third class.

Inheritance works much like biological taxonomy: You might define a base Animal class, and then have a Mammal class inherit from it but add in a hair property. You might then have a Dog class that inherits from the Mammal class but adds a bark method.

You can represent this process in code fairly simply with the extends keyword, which is used to designate that the class being defined is inheriting from the class specified after the extends statement. It looks like this:

```
class Animal {
    var mitochondria:Boolean = true;
}
```

```
class Mammal extends Animal {
    var hair:Boolean = true;
}


// Dog is a subclass of Mammal - Mammal is Dog's superclass
class Dog extends Mammal {
    function bark():Void {
        trace("BARK LOUD");
    }
}
```

Through inheritance, the Dog class gains the `hair` property that `Mammal` defines and the `mitochondria` property that `Mammal` inherited from `Animal` (see Figure 20.10).

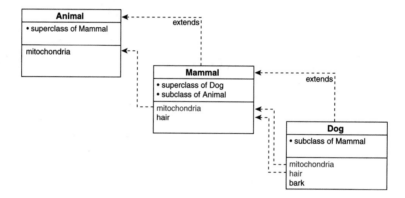

This is all very handy, but suppose you want to define a `QuietDog` class that inherits all the members from `Dog` but doesn't bark loud? In this situation, you can use *member overwriting*—that is, you can redefine the function you inherited in the subclass, as shown in this example:

```
class QuietDog extends Dog {
    // overwrite Dog's bark
    function bark():Void {
        trace("DOESN'T BARK LOUD");
    }
}
```

If you call the bark method of a `QuietDog`, it would output `DOESN'T BARK LOUD`. Another handy keyword, called `super`, could make this code even neater. super gives you access to the superclass and its methods, which enables you to modify QuietDog as shown (see Figure 20.11 for a diagram of this process):

```
class QuietDog extends Dog {
    // overwrite Dog's bark:
    function bark():Void {
        trace("DOESN'T");
        // call Dog's bark method
        super.bark();
    }
}
```

This time, if you call the bark method for QuietDog, it outputs DOESN'T and then calls its superclass's bark() method, which outputs BARK LOUD. Not the most practical application, perhaps, but it gives you an idea of what's possible.

FIGURE 20.11
Member overwriting with quiet dogs.

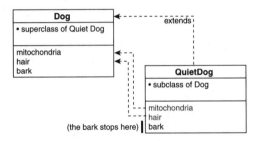

Applying Inheritance to the UFO

Now try applying this inheritance rigmarole to your UFO. You want the SpaceShip class to inherit the built-in MovieClip class's members, so all you have to do is add extends MovieClip to the first line of your class declaration. Open your SpaceShip.as file, and change the first line to this:

```
class SpaceShip extends MovieClip {
```

This line does two things for you:

- It gives the SpaceShip class access to all the MovieClip class's methods and events, a couple of which you'll be using shortly.

- It gives you access to the MovieClip class's properties.

That second point is important because MovieClip already has _x and _y properties defined, so you can remove your redundant declarations for these properties by deleting the following two lines from the SpaceShip class:

```
var _x:Number = 0; // x location
var _y:Number = 0; // y location
```

Your UFO is ready to do something fun—and that means it's time to learn about events.

EVENTS WITH OBJECTS

Think back to the construction worker example earlier in this chapter. Just as you wouldn't walk workers through every step of their tasks, you also wouldn't watch over their shoulders to see whether they have finished a task. Instead, you would ask them to let you know when they're finished.

In programming, the process of constantly checking on the status of an object is called *polling*, and it's considered a bad practice because of the huge waste of resources it entails. Asking an object to report back when a certain condition is met is what events are all about. You can find more information on events in Chapter 10, "ActionScript: Functions, Events, and Objects," but it's important to recognize that together events and methods form the entire basis for object interaction in OOP.

A number of built-in classes use events, and you'll take advantage of two of them so that you can move and control your UFO.

Adding Keyboard Interactions to the UFO

First, you want to take advantage of the Key class's events so that you can be notified when the user presses a key on the keyboard. To do this, you'll subscribe the SpaceShip class as a listener to the Key object. This process is relatively easy; just add the following line to the SpaceShip constructor:

```
Key.addListener(this);
```

Next, you have to add a method in the SpaceShip class to handle the onKeyDown event that the Key class generates. For now, to make sure everything is working, you'll just use trace() to make the method display a KEY PRESSED message when it's triggered. Add the following method to your class:

```
function onKeyDown():Void {
    trace("KEY PRESSED");
}
```

Save your changes to the SpaceShip.as file, and then open your ufo.fla file and test the movie. You should see the same unmoving UFO and the same status output. However, if you press a key on your keyboard now, you should see KEY PRESSED in the Output panel. If not, don't worry too much; you'll be taking a look at all the code in just a second.

Now that you're trapping the Key class's events successfully, you can do something with those events. While you're at it, you might want to get rid of some unused code in the constructor. Remove the toString() method (you won't be using it any more) and improve on the thrust methods. Jump back to the SpaceShip.as file, and modify it to look like this:

```
class SpaceShip {
    // define properties:
    var velocityX:Number = 0;
    var velocityY:Number = 0;

    // define the constructor:
    function SpaceShip():Void {
        Key.addListener(this);
    }

    // define methods:
    function onKeyDown():Void {
        // get the keyCode for the last key that was pressed:
        var keyCode:Number = Key.getCode();
        // carry out the appropriate action, depending
        // on what key was pressed:
        switch (keyCode) {
            case Key.LEFT:
                thrustX(-1);
```

```
                              break;
                      case Key.RIGHT:
                          thrustX(1);
                          break;
                      case Key.UP:
                          thrustY(-1);
                          break;
                      case Key.DOWN:
                          thrustY(1);
                          break;
                  }
              }
              function thrustX(direction:Number):Void {
                  velocityX += direction;
              }
              function thrustY(direction:Number):Void {
                  velocityY += direction;
              }
          }
```

For more information
on switch and break
statements, see
Chapter 9,
"ActionScript Basics:
Data and
Statements."

When you press an arrow key now, the x or y velocity is increased or
decreased, depending on which key was pressed. All you have to do is
make the UFO actually move, and to do that, you'll use an event handler
you inherited from the MovieClip class: onEnterFrame.

Making the UFO Move (Finally!)

If you modify the location of the UFO slightly every frame based on
its velocity, you can achieve animated motion. By tapping into the
onEnterFrame event you inherited from MovieClip, you can do just that
because the event is triggered once per frame. It's easy to do, too—just
add a method called onEnterFrame to the SpaceShip class and have it do
the dirty work:

```
function onEnterFrame():Void {
    // apply some friction for nicer motion:
    velocityX *= 0.92;
    velocityY *= 0.92;
```

```
// move me:
_x += velocityX;
_y += velocityY;
}
```

Save your SpaceShip.as file again, go back to the ufo.fla file, delete all the script on the first frame, and test the movie. You should be able to fly the UFO around the screen by using the arrow keys. If not, the full code for the chapter project is at the end of the chapter. Compare it and make sure you don't have any typos (and remember case sensitivity). You can also download a finished version of the project from this book's companion website at www.flashdemystified.com.

MORE OOP GOODIES

Now you know all the basics of object-oriented programming in ActionScript 2.0. You can create and work with classes and instances. You know how to add members (properties and methods) and can control interactions between classes. Indeed, you're an OOP god or goddess (or at least a minor deity).

Take some time to play with these concepts a bit, and when you feel comfortable with them, read on to learn some more advanced techniques.

Class Members: The *static* Keyword

By default, variables created inside a class statement become associated with each instance of that class as properties. However, by prefixing a member declaration with the static keyword, you can designate that member as a *class member*. Class members are associated with the class, not its instances, and can be referenced directly through the class name.

For more information on the Math object, see Chapter 21, "Math for Flashers."

This method is used frequently in classes that don't lend themselves to creating multiple instances, such as the Math object. Rather than create an instance of the Math class to access its methods and properties, you simply access its class members directly, as shown here:

```
Math.PI;
Math.sin();
```

Class members can also be used to track aggregate data about class instances. For instance, you could create a counter in a class to keep track of how many instances of that class have been created:

```
// Doughnut class declaration in Doughnut.as :
class Doughnut {
    // declare a static class member to act as a counter:
    static var nDoughnuts:Number = 0;

    // constructor method:
    function Doughnut() {
        nDoughnuts++;
        trace(nDoughnuts+" have been instantiated");
    }
}


    // code in an FLA:
var bostonCream:Doughnut = new Doughnut();
var sprinkled:Doughnut = new Doughnut();
var doubleDipped:Doughnut = new Doughnut();
```

Controlling Access to Members: The *private* Keyword

By default, all the members you declare in a class statement are public and can be accessed by any other class or script. Preventing direct access to instance properties is often a good idea to enforce encapsulation. You might also want to prevent access to a method, such as an internal helper method, for instance.

In ActionScript 2.0, you can protect members from access by other classes by prefixing the member declaration with the private keyword, like so:

```
// TestClass declaration in TestClass.as
class TestClass {
    private var myPrivateProperty:String = "fun stuff";
    private function myPrivateMethod():String {
        return myPrivateProperty;
    }
```

```
function myPublicMethod():String {
    return myPrivateMethod();
}
}

// code in an FLA
var myTestClass:TestClass = new TestClass();
trace(myTestClass.myPrivateProperty);  // compiler error
trace(myTestClass.myPrivateMethod());  // compiler error
trace(myTestClass.myPublicMethod());   // traces "fun stuff"
```

In the preceding example, the first two `trace` attempts generate compiler errors (shown in Figure 20.12) because they try to access private members of TestClass. The third `trace` would succeed, however, because it's accessing a public method. The public method has permission to access private methods in its own class.

FIGURE 20.12
Compiler errors in the Output panel.

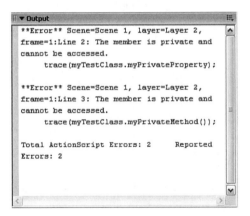

Note that member protection is enforced only at compile time, not at runtime. Therefore, member protection is handy for enforcing integrity when developing in a team environment, but it's not a security measure, by any means.

Making Properties Act Like Methods: Implicit *get* and *set*

As mentioned, you need to limit all data access to methods to enforce encapsulation, but sometimes it's much easier to work with properties than methods. Wouldn't it be nice if you could gain the encapsulation and scalability advantages of working with methods but retain the ease of working with properties?

Thanks to implicit get and set methods, you can! Much like the addProperty command in Flash MX, get and set methods enable you to create pseudo-properties that trigger functions when their values are accessed or manipulated. To use them, all you have to do is create a matching pair of functions incorporating the get and set keywords, as shown in this example:

```
class Product {
    private var priceInCents:Number;

    // define implicit get/set methods for the price property
    function set price(amount:Number):Void {
        priceInCents = Math.floor(amount*100);
    }
    function get price():Number {
        return priceInCents/100;
    }
}
```

This code defines a Product class with a price property. When a script assigns a value to the price property, as in the following line, the set function multiplies the value by 100 and stores the resulting integer in a private property (priceInCents):

```
myProduct.price = 129.31;
```

When the price property is retrieved, as shown in the following line, the get function runs and returns the stored integer divided by 100:

```
var myPrice:Number = myProduct.price;
```

The get method must not take any parameters, whereas the set method must take only one (the value assigned to the pseudo-property). The value the get method returns is the value assigned to the pseudo-property when it's accessed.

Dynamic Classes

With most class instances in ActionScript 2.0, attempting to add or access members that don't exist results in a compiler error because all members must be defined in the class definition. Take a look at this code example:

```
// TestClass declaration in TestClass.as
class TestClass {
    var myProperty:Number;
}

// code in an FLA:
myTest:TestClass = new TestClass();
myTest.myProperty = 7; // succeeds because myProperty exists
myTest.myOtherProperty = "popsicle"; // compiler error
```

In this example, the myOtherProperty member isn't defined in the class statement, so attempting to access it in the instance of TestClass generates a compiler error. As with private members, this is enforced only at compile time.

By preceding a class definition with the dynamic keyword, as shown in the following code, you permit adding and accessing instance members that aren't defined in the class:

```
// TestClass declaration in TestClass.as
dynamic class TestClass {
    var myProperty:Number;
}
// code in an FLA:
myTest:TestClass = new TestClass();
myTest.myProperty = 7; // succeeds because myProperty exists
myTest.myOtherProperty = "popsicle"; // succeeds - dynamic class
```

In this second example, assigning a value to myOtherProperty doesn't generate a compiler error because accessing undefined variables is allowed for instances of a dynamic class.

Enforcing Polymorphism: Using Interfaces

You've learned that a class's interface is composed of its publicly accessible members—that is, the members and properties that are made accessible to other classes and scripts. You have also learned about the concept of polymorphism, creating different classes with the same interface so that they can be easily interchanged.

In this section, you learn to use the `interface` keyword to define an interface that can be implemented across numerous classes. The `interface` keyword is used in much the same manner as `class`, but instead of defining properties and functional methods, you define abstract methods that must be implemented by classes using this interface. The following code uses the `interface` keyword to define two abstract methods that must be present in any class implementing the `DataManager` interface:

```
interface DataManager {
    // define abstract methods:
    function getData(url:String):Number;
    function putData(url:String,data:String):Number;
}
```

Note that the abstract methods don't actually do anything. They merely define the name, parameters, and return type for the methods.

To use the interface in a class, you use the `implements` keyword in the class definition, like so:

```
class DatabaseManager implements DataManager (
    function getData(url:String):Number {
        return 1;
    }
    function putData(url:String,data:String):Number {
        return 0;
    }
}
```

When you implement an interface in a class, you must include every method that was defined in the interface.

Organizing Your Classes: Using Packages

As you build more complex projects and expand your library of reusable classes, you'll start running into organization issues. With *packages*, you can separate your classes into a hierarchical structure on your hard drive and in your code. Packages are simply containers that allow you to organize your classes. You can place related classes together in a package and access them by using dot syntax. Packages are easy to set up; all you have to do is create directories in your classpaths.

To clarify, take a look at an example. If I create a new class for drawing rectangles called Rectangle, naturally it's defined in a file called Rectangle.as in one of my classpaths. I want to place it in my personal package, gskinner, in a nested package called draw. To do this, I simply create a directory named gskinner in my classpath, create a directory named draw in it, and place the Rectangle.as class file in it. I could then access the Rectangle class by using dot syntax, as shown here:

```
var MyRectangle:gskinner.draw.Rectangle = new
➥gskinner.draw.Rectangle()
```

Figure 20.13 shows the resulting directory structure.

FIGURE 20.13
Directory structure for the sample package.

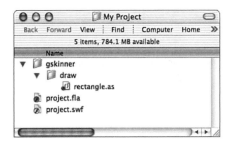

FINAL CODE FOR THE UFO PROJECT

ufo.fla should not have any code in it. It should have only a single instance of the ufo movie clip, named ufo_mc, on the stage. The ufo movie clip in the Library should have the properties shown in Figure 20.14.

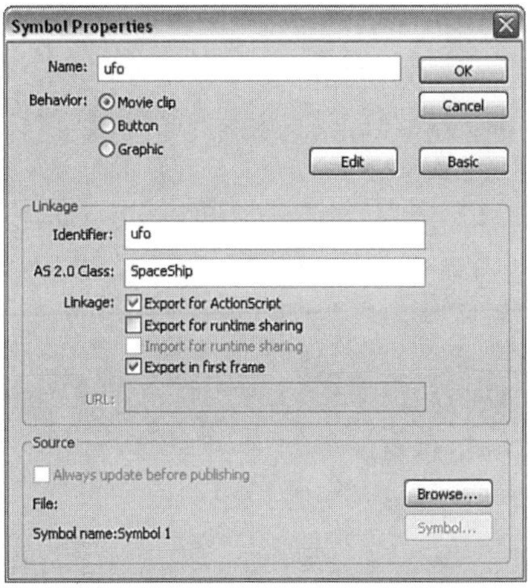

FIGURE 20.14
The Symbol Properties dialog box for the ufo movie clip.

The SpaceShip.as file should be located in the same directory as
ufo.fla and contain the following code:

```
class SpaceShip {
    // define properties:
    var velocityX:Number = 0;
    var velocityY:Number = 0;

    // define the constructor:
    function SpaceShip():Void {
        Key.addListener(this);
    }

    // define methods:
    function onKeyDown():Void {
        // get the keyCode for the last key that was pressed:
        var keyCode:Number = Key.getCode();
        // carry out the appropriate action, depending
        // on what key was pressed:
        switch (keyCode) {
            case Key.LEFT:
                thrustX(-1);
                break;
            case Key.RIGHT:
                thrustX(1);
                break;
            case Key.UP:
                thrustY(-1);
                break;
            case Key.DOWN:
                thrustY(1);
                break;
        }
    }
    function thrustX(direction:Number):Void {
        velocityX += direction;
    }
    function thrustY(direction:Number):Void {
        velocityY += direction;
    }
```

```
function onEnterFrame():Void {
    // apply some friction for nicer motion:
    velocityX *= 0.92;
    velocityY *= 0.92;

    // move me:
    _x += velocityX;
    _y += velocityY;
}
}
```

Resources

While you're waiting for more in-depth books on object-oriented programming for ActionScript 2.0 to hit the shelves, take a look at any Java books you have access to. Because ActionScript 2.0 is based on ECMAScript 4, it closely resembles Java in many respects, and these books can provide an invaluable resource until more Flash-specific resources are available.

General OOP information:

Extropia Introduction to OOP:
www.extropia.com/tutorials/java/oop.html

Object FAQ: www.objectfaq.com/oofaq2/

Sun OOP concepts:
http://java.sun.com/docs/books/tutorial/java/concepts/

Netscape ECMAScript 4 proposal:
www.mozilla.org/js/language/es4/ index.html

General OOAD web sites:

gModeler UML tool: http://gmodeler.com/

OOAD Road Map:
www.gvu.gatech.edu/edtech/BOOST/designmap.html

Sites to watch for relevant information:

Grant Skinner's Blog: www.gskinner.com/blog/

Peter Hall's Blog: www.peterjoel.com/blog/

Dave Yang's Blog: www.swfoo.com/

FullAsAGoog (blog aggregator): www.fullasagoog.com/

Ultrashock: www.ultrashock.com/

POINTS TO REMEMBER

- Objects are self-contained and consist of data (properties) and functions that act on that data (methods). The interaction between objects defines an application's flow and functionality.

- Together, properties and methods are referred to as members. Publicly accessible members are called the interface.

- Interaction between objects occurs in two ways: calling methods and passing events.

- Classes act as templates for new objects. Objects based on a class are called class instances.

- The three primary guiding concepts in object-oriented programming are encapsulation (making objects self-contained), abstraction (simplifying objects to their necessary members), and polymorphism (building objects that share a common interface).

- Coding in an object-oriented fashion conveys many benefits, including ease of planning, reuse of code, scalability, and a more effective division of labor.

- You can bind a class directly to a movie clip by setting the ActionScript 2.0 class in the movie clip's properties dialog box.

- The extends keyword lets you inherit class members in a hierarchical manner. This simplifies code and makes reuse and expansion simpler.

- The interface and implements keywords can help you enforce polymorphism in your code.

- Implicit get and set methods enable you to present an interface with property-like access, but without jeopardizing encapsulation.

- The static keyword lets you define class properties that will be shared across all instances of that class.

- Features such as strong typing, private members, and dynamic classes can help you write clean code with less debugging, but they are only compiler-time features. This means they can be easily bypassed and should not be relied on too heavily.

CHAPTER 21

MATH FOR FLASHERS

THE ACTIONSCRIPT PROGRAMMING LANGUAGE IS THOROUGH IN ITS COVERAGE of mathematics. In fact, as in many other object-oriented languages, ActionScript has an entire Math object for programmers to make good artistic use of.

How can math be artistic? In the traditional sense, math is all numbers and operators (such as + and −) and tends to lack artistry. However, in Macromedia Flash MX 2004, a visual layer is added. Because of Flash's nature as a visual web medium, most of the math you create is expressed in a visual fashion, which adds an artistic element to it.

Whether you're talking about single-screen mathematically based renderings or entirely scripted motions, the math that drives them is straightforward and made up of the same general principles. This chapter is just a primer. The best way to learn is to read and play around with the concepts. Feel free to change the code in this chapter to see what will happen. Only by doing this can you learn not to regurgitate math, but to use it and even be artistic with it.

PHYSICS AND MATH: HOW MUCH IS NEEDED?

When approaching math and physics in Flash, non-programmers tend to look at it as black magic. They see all this mathematically driven motion and know that it would take hours to design and animate what they see programmers doing in five minutes. Conversely, most programmers look at a beautifully drawn and animated cartoon character and know they couldn't code that in a million years. So where, logically, are math and physics best used in the ActionScript world?

- Web sites with lots of moving elements, where the positioning of these elements isn't necessarily known at design time. For example, if you have a box that flies onscreen when a user selects a certain menu option, all this "flying" is best left to simple physics and motion math.

- Extremely interactive elements, with simply too many things going on to keep track of with difficult hand-drawn motion and animation.

- Flash games in which all action is based on math and physics. These games tend to be the Flash creations that rely most on math and physics, as they're often trying to mimic real life.

These are just a few of the possible examples. The best way to determine your math needs is to look at your requirements: If you have a Flash site with four or five static pages, you probably won't need to use much math. However, if you have elements transitioning from one position onscreen to another, you'll probably want to get into the easing and equations. Drawing keyframe animations of an object moving from point a to point b is easy, but what if you want to move something to point c, d, e, or z at runtime? In other words, what if you want the object to move to a position the *user* decides? Animating for that ahead of time is difficult; it's a job for math.

You might also want to move an object in a different path than just a straight line. Perhaps the object should follow a curved arc and then bounce past its target before finally coming to rest. To create this action, you need math, especially for the curve and bounce concepts.

What if a character is supposed to fall from the top of the screen, bounce randomly on the ground, head off toward a wall, bounce off that wall and keep going, and so on? The word *randomly* in that description rules out keyframe animation, not to mention the sheer amount of animation required to create that action by hand.

So how much math is needed? It depends on the project. This chapter should give you enough of a basis to get an idea of what can be done, and you can go from there to creatively apply these concepts to your own work.

THE BASICS OF TRIGONOMETRY

You might not find this section title very exciting, but trigonometry isn't as bad as most people think. It's complex, yes, but for Flash, you're concerned with only a small aspect of it: sine and cosine. The sine and cosine functions can give you some interesting results for creating motion. You're probably familiar with the basic sine wave, shown in Figure 21.1.

FIGURE 21.1
A sine wave.

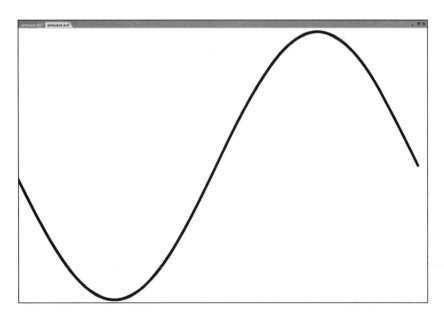

You've seen this wave on oscilloscopes and in science shows; you can also see it reflected in the motion of waves in the ocean, ripples in a pond, and even the way a roller coaster track falls and rises. It represents a physically perfect reversal of motion: from down to up and back down again.

The cosine wave is exactly the same, except it starts in a slightly different position, as shown in Figure 21.2.

FIGURE 21.2
A cosine wave.

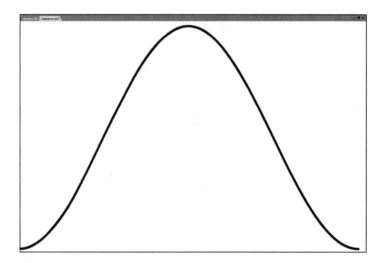

By the way, in both figures, you're looking at one complete cycle of the wave. Waves do, in fact, tend to go on for longer than one cycle, so you can repeat the wave over and over again, as in Figure 21.3.

FIGURE 21.3
The wave goes on forever.

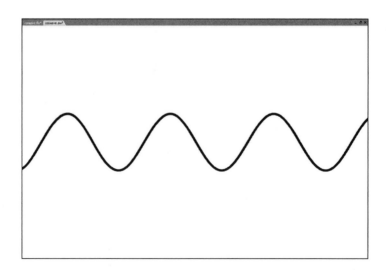

Whether you make the wave tall and skinny or short and wide, it's important to understand that it's still a basic sine or cosine wave.

To draw these waves, you use the sine and cosine functions. In math class, you called them functions, and guess what? In ActionScript, they're also functions. In math class, if you want a sine value of 40 degrees, you use this:

SIN 40

As in programming, you can look at that line and say that SIN is the function and 40 is the parameter. Nothing new there. A number between –1 and +1 is returned. Depending on the number you pass to SIN, you get a different number *back* (between –1 and +1) from SIN.

What does this mean? These numbers aren't random; their practical application comes when you feed in parameters in some sort of sequence. So SIN 40, SIN 41, SIN 42, SIN 43, and so on return numbers that are nearly the same: 0.643, 0.660, 0.669, and 0.682. Notice those numbers are less than 1.

The trick is this: Although you increment the number you pass into SIN, the number passed *back from* SIN doesn't just increment. It goes up until it slows down and reaches 1, and then it begins to go in a negative direction, speeding up and then slowing down as it approaches –1. The whole thing repeats and repeats. So as you pass higher and higher numbers into SIN, you get the same repeating up-and-down pattern passed back.

Visually, you can say that as you increment x along the screen and use x as the parameter (SIN x), the result goes up and down from –1 to 1 to –1 to 1, and so on. If you take this result and multiply it by a number, such as 80, you turn the results into –80 to 80 to –80 to 80. If you use x as the parameter and the result as the y (vertical) location, voilà—you'll have a nice smooth wave onscreen.

Now that you've looked at math 101 notation, take a look at ActionScript notation. It's not that different:

a = Math.sin(b);

The a represents the number passed back from the computation of SIN b. You're not looking at angles yet, but usually you pass an angle into the Math.sin or Math.cos function. In ActionScript, however, you don't pass an angle in degrees (0 to 359), the way you're used to. The Math.sin and Math.cos functions expect their angles to be measured in a different way: in radians, as explained in the next section.

Degrees Versus Radians

Converting from degrees to radians is simple; it's somewhat similar to converting from miles to kilometers or pounds to kilograms. This is the conversion formula:

```
1 degree = 0.01745329252 radians
```

That's not an easy number to remember, especially when you realize that one full circle of 360 degrees is actually equal to 6.283185 radians. That's right: One full circle isn't an even number of radians. Most people expect that a full circle will have an even number of degrees and an even number of radians, but why would it? Just because something weighs an even 100 pounds doesn't mean it weighs an even number of kilograms. However, there's an easy way to remember these numbers:

```
180 degrees = 3.14159265 radians
```

The number 3.14159265 is the mathematical constant pi (pronounced "pie"). There are exactly pi radians in half a circle (180 degrees). A full circle is 2×180 degrees, which means it has 2×pi radians, as shown in this line:

```
1 degree = Pi / 180
```

In ActionScript, you can get the constant pi by using the `Math.PI` property. So if you have a number in degrees, you can convert it to radians like so:

```
radiansPerDeg = Math.PI / 180;
radians = degrees * radiansPerDeg;
```

By computing the number of radians in one degree, you can then calculate the number of radians in *any* degree angle simply by precomputing the number `radiansPerDeg`. Conversely, you can convert radians to degrees like so:

```
degrees = radians / radiansPerDeg;
```

Using *Math.sin*

For this first simple use of `Math.sin`, you'll make a boat bob up and down in place. Or think of it as a spaceship, helicopter, or hummingbird hovering; it's all the same motion. Here's the formula in ActionScript:

```
this._y += Math.sin(this.angle+=0.1) * scale;
```

This one line of code causes the _y value of this to change steadily with each frame because this.angle+=0.1 causes the this.angle variable to constantly increment by 0.1. As this increments, the value of Math.sin(this.angle) goes from +1 to –1 over time, which causes this._y to increase and decrease over time. When you do this to a movie clip, it moves up and down. The scale variable allows you to adjust the size of the bobbing motion; a value of 0 would cause no motion, and anything higher than about 50 is huge motion. Here's that code in context:

```
ball.angle = 0;
var scale:Number = 2;
ball.onEnterFrame = function()
{
    this._y += Math.sin(this.angle+=0.1) * scale;
}
```

Note that when running this code, you must have a movie clip on the stage with the instance name ball. Then this code is placed on the main Timeline at frame 1. The motion function is attached to the onEnterFrame function of the ball movie clip, which means this code runs every single frame, at the frame rate specified in your movie settings. The preceding code also sets the initial value of the angle property to 0 and sets the scale property to 2.

Don't confuse the angle variable for the standard movie clip _rotation property; they're not related. angle is simply a variable that's been created to increment the value being fed to Math.sin. It's called *angle* because that's what's typically used with Math.sin, but you could also use a name such as counter or stepper.

You can download files for this chapter's examples from the book's companion web site at www. flashdemystified. com.

Make sure you've created a movie clip on the stage and given it the instance name ball. Then run this movie by choosing Control, Test Movie from the menu (keyboard shortcut: **Ctrl+Enter**), and watch the movie clip begin to bob up and down gently. You can find this example in bobber.fla on this book's companion website.

You can attach this useful piece of code to the onEnterFrame function of just about any movie clip, as long as angle is initialized to 0 and scale is set before creating the onEnterFrame function (as in the sample code).

Radial and Rectangular Motion

One of the key concepts in creating smooth, rounded motion is using radial versus rectangular coordinates. In Flash, you're naturally accustomed to working in rectangular coordinates, which are, simply put, coordinates based on x and y (and sometimes z, but that's for another chapter). With a rectangular coordinate system, you can draw a rectangle between the origin point (both x and y are equal to 0, notated simply as 0,0) and any other point (x,y) onscreen.

Think about an automobile's motion. Does it move in such a way that its position can freely and arbitrarily be adjusted at any time? No, its position depends on its heading and speed. You couldn't just place a car in a parking lot and watch it move around arbitrarily without turning or accelerating.

Figure 21.4 shows a car moving in a rectangular world. Figure 21.5 shows how a car really moves—in a radial world.

FIGURE 21.4
Incorrect motion for a car.

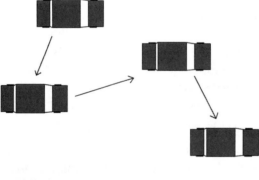

FIGURE 21.5
Correct radial motion for a car.

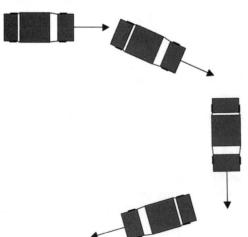

Technically, the car's position can ultimately be expressed in terms of an x and y position; however, its *motion* can't be expressed that way at first. Its motion must be expressed in terms of direction (angle) and speed (velocity).

Onscreen, when you move a movie clip, you can think of its rate of movement in terms of changes in x position and y position. These two position modifiers are typically called dx and dy. So if you have a movie clip at the position (x, y), its next position will be (x + dx, y + dy). Take a look at this code:

```
myMovieClip._x = 10;
myMovieClip._y = 10;

myMovieClip.dx = 5;
myMovieClip.dy = 0;

myMovieClip.onEnterFrame = function()
{
  this._x += this.dx;
  this._y += this.dy;
}
```

This code causes the myMovieClip movie clip to move horizontally by 5 pixels (the dx value) and vertically by 0 pixels (the dy value) every frame. What will this motion look like when you run the movie clip? The movie clip will simply move horizontally across the screen, with no change in the vertical (dy) position. If you modify the code so that dy is 5 and dx is 0, the movie clip moves *down* by 5 pixels every frame, instead of to the right.

Now that you're thinking in terms of movie clips and a stage, if you want the car to move based on angle and velocity, you must find a way of converting angle and velocity into dx and dy so that its motion can be reflected realistically onscreen. How do you do this? Take a look at a few simple equations from math class:

```
dx = COS angle * velocity
dy = SIN angle * velocity
```

In other words, if you have an angle and a velocity, you can compute both the x position change (dx) and the y position change (dy) by using the cosine and sine functions. Here's what it would look like in code:

```
this.dx = Math.cos(this.ang) * this.vel;
this.dy = Math.sin(this.ang) * this.vel;

this._x += this.dx;
this._y += this.dy;
```

This code is still doing the same old this._x += this.dx and this._y += this.dy; however, this time you're actually *calculating* dx and dy rather than hard-coding these values to specific numbers. This means you're setting values for the ang and vel variables. Fully functioning code would look like this:

```
myMovieClip._x = 10;
myMovieClip._y = 10;

myMovieClip.vel = 5;
myMovieClip.ang = 0;

var radiansPerDeg:Number = Math.PI / 180;

myMovieClip.onEnterFrame = function()
{
  this.dx = Math.cos(this.ang) * this.vel;
  this.dy = Math.sin(this.ang) * this.vel;

  this._rotation = this.ang / radiansPerDeg;

  this._x += this.dx;
  this._y += this.dy;
}
```

There are many similarities between this code and the previous motion example. This time, you're presetting the value for the vel variable to 5 and the ang variable to 0. Also notice that you're creating the radiansPerDeg variable, as you did earlier. It's used to convert your ang variable, which is in radians, into degrees so that you can apply this rotation to the movie clip's _rotation property. You want the movie clip to rotate and follow the path of its angle and velocity. Notice the new line added to the onEnterFrame function:

```
this._rotation = this.ang / radiansPerDeg;
```

Now the movie clip aligns itself to its apparent direction of motion. If you run the preceding code as is, the movie clip moves to the right at exactly 5 pixels per frame. In other words, its dx is 5 and its dy is 0, as shown in this formula:

```
dx = COS angle * velocity
dy = SIN angle * velocity
```

The angle is 0 and velocity is 5. Using a calculator, you discover that COS 0 is 1 and SIN 0 is 0, so you can look at it like this:

```
dx = 1 * velocity
dy = 0 * velocity
```

When velocity is 5, you get these results:

```
dx = 1 * 5
dy = 0 * 5
```

In other words, dx = 5 and dy = 0. That's exactly what you had hard-coded earlier, but this method works much better. Now say that your angle is 1 instead of 0, as shown here:

```
dx = COS 1 * velocity
dy = SIN 1 * velocity
```

Using a calculator, you can find out that COS 1 is 0.540302 and SIN 1 is 0.841471, so this is the formula:

```
dx = 0.540302 * velocity
dy = 0.841471 * velocity
```

Remember that SIN and COS always return a number between –1 and 1, so when you take these results and multiply by velocity (5), you always get a number less than 5. In other words, the following code

```
dx = 0.540302 * 5
dy = 0.841471 * 5
```

ultimately produces these results:

```
dx = 2.702
dy = 4.207
```

To move at an angle of 1 (that's one radian, not one degree) and a velocity of 5, you need to change the x position by 2.702 and the y position by 4.207 every frame. When you change the code so that myMovieClip.ang = 0; becomes myMovieClip.ang = 1; and run the movie, you'll see just that happening: moving right by 2.702 pixels and down by 4.207 pixels every frame.

What if you want the car to speed up? Easy! Just increase the velocity (because that's what speeding up is), and the numbers scale accordingly. Take a look back a few lines at the math:

```
dx = 0.540302 * 5
dy = 0.841471 * 5
```

Remember, these numbers are rounded for this book. In actuality, the dy value would be more like 8.41470984807897, but that's more detail than you need, especially when talking about pixels.

Say that instead of 5, you want a velocity of 10, as shown here:

```
dx = 0.540302 * 10
dy = 0.841471 * 10
```

Then the dx and dy values become the following, which is correct:

```
dx = 5.403
dy = 8.415
```

It's easy to see that as you increase the velocity (which is essentially just a multiplier of the sine/cosine result), the overall dx and dy increase, so your movie clip moves exactly the equivalent distance of 10 pixels every frame.

If you're inclined to prove this, you can quickly do a Pythagorean equation on dx and dy to determine the distance moved; it's the square root of (dx * dx + dy * dy). Using the previous numbers, it produces 10, which is the velocity.

Now try changing the angle every frame by placing the following code at the bottom of the onEnterFrame function, below this._y += this.dy:

```
this.ang += 0.05;
```

The expected result? The movie clip will move in a circle, and that's exactly what happens when you test the movie. You can find the final working version of this example in the radialmotion.fla file on this book's web site.

Interactive Acceleration and Deceleration

A useful extension of the car example is making it interactive. In radial motion, users have simple expectations of controls: They expect to be able to turn left or right, and they expect to be able to speed up and slow down. To accomplish this, I've changed the movie clip to a mouse (the rodent, not the computer peripheral device) and added some key detection code:

```
if (Key.isDown(Key.UP)) this.vel += 0.5;
if (Key.isDown(Key.DOWN)) this.vel -= 0.5;

if (Key.isDown(Key.RIGHT)) this.ang += 0.1;
if (Key.isDown(Key.LEFT)) this.ang -= 0.1;
```

In this simple code, you're modifying the ang and vel variables based on the conditions of certain keys. Press the up key, and the velocity increases by 0.5 (acceleration); press the down key, and the velocity decreases by 0.5 (deceleration). The entire code looks like this:

```
myMovieClip._x = 10; // Set the initial position of the movie clip
myMovieClip._y = 10;

myMovieClip.vel = 0; // Set the initial velocity and angle to 0
myMovieClip.ang = 0;

var radiansPerDeg:Number = Math.PI / 180; // conversion factor

myMovieClip.onEnterFrame = function()
{
  this.dx = Math.cos(this.ang) * this.vel; // Set dx and dy speed
  this.dy = Math.sin(this.ang) * this.vel; // from angle and velocity

// Set the movie clip _rotation based on ang, converted to degrees
  this._rotation = this.ang / radiansPerDeg;
```

```
    this._x += this.dx; // Move according to dx and dy
    this._y += this.dy;

// Check keypresses
    if (Key.isDown(Key.UP)) this.vel += 0.5;  // Speed up
    if (Key.isDown(Key.DOWN)) this.vel -= 0.5; // Slow down

    if (Key.isDown(Key.RIGHT)) this.ang += 0.1; // Turn right
    if (Key.isDown(Key.LEFT)) this.ang -= 0.1; // Turn left
}
```

You can find this code in the interactiveradialmotion.fla file on this book's web site. Run it, and have fun controlling the little mouse and watching him run around the screen. Don't accelerate too much, however, or he'll fly off the screen and become impossible to find!

MOTION

Creating ActionScript-coded motion is straightforward. Everything to do with motion revolves around the simple concept of *inertia*, or acceleration and deceleration. You had a brief look at using the keyboard to control the velocity of a mouse onscreen. Now you'll see how to extend that concept to create realistic motion systems.

What is motion? Motion is the *change in position* of an object *over time*. That's all there is to it. The trick is how you accomplish it. Animating motion by hand is a fairly straightforward venture: Create a movie clip on a keyframe, go to another frame in the timeline, create another keyframe, move the movie clip to a new position, set the frame properties to motion tweening, and you're done.

However, you're not interested in hand animation right now. Everything you'll look at in this example can be done on one frame only with code. The variables dx and dy are used to specify how far an object moves along the x and y axes, frame by frame. As a reminder, this is the basic motion code for a movie clip:

```
myMovieClip.onEnterFrame = function()
{
  this._x += this.dx;
  this._y += this.dy;
}
```

This code moves myMovieClip each frame along the _x position by the amount specified by dx and along the the _y position by the amount specified by dy. That alone is worth its weight in gold, but eventually a movie clip exits the screen, never to be seen again, unless you put in a system to stop the movie clip at the edge of the screen and bounce or wrap to the other side of the screen.

Take a look at creating this motion with one axis for now. Assume that your screen is 640×480 in size. First, you want to stop the movie clip when it reaches the right edge of the screen. Here's the code to do that:

```
if (this._x > 639)
{
  this.dx = 0;
  this._x = 639;
}
```

This code checks to see if the movie clip's _x position has passed 639, the far right edge. If it has, the code sets the movie clip's horizontal velocity (dx) to 0, effectively stopping its horizontal motion. As one final step, this code brings the movie clip back to 639, in case it had over-stepped the edge.

If you're checking the position of the movie clip, how can it have moved *past* the wall? Look at it like this: If dx is 2 (moving right at 2 pixels per frame) and the movie clip got to position 638, its next position would put it at 640 (638 + 2 = 640). When this happens, the if condition is true (because 640 is greater than 639), so you halt the movie clip's motion. However, the movie clip has technically moved past the "wall" (the far right edge of the screen). That's not really possible, so you must move it back into the "real" space at 639. If you don't, the condition repeatedly evaluates as true because the movie clip's x position is always 640.

How about the left edge of the screen? Same basic code:

```
if (this._x < 0)
{
  this.dx = 0;
  this._x = 0;
}
```

If the movie clip has surpassed the left edge (x < 0), you halt its horizontal motion and move it back into valid screen space. In this case, `this.dx` must be a negative number for the motion to be in a leftward direction.

Reflection and Bounce

In the previous example, the movie clip hit the edge of the screen and then abruptly stopped. If you think of this movie clip as a physical object and the edge of the screen as a wall, that's not very realistic motion. Physical objects tend to *reflect* or bounce off surfaces because their kinetic (motion) energy has to go somewhere. Usually this energy goes back into the object in the opposite direction.

Imagine throwing a ball at a wall and watching it in slow motion. The ball deforms and squashes as it hits the wall because its energy has to go somewhere, and the wall doesn't accept that energy (the wall doesn't deform at all). Eventually, the ball's elasticity causes its energy to go back in on itself; the ball's entire motion is reversed, and it begins to travel back in the opposite direction from which it came. This exact same principle applies to any solid body hitting any other solid body. We have Newton's third law to thank for this: For every action there is an equal and opposite reaction. Because the wall doesn't budge, the ball must retain almost all its energy and bounce in the *opposite* direction, with *equal* speed.

So how do you change the direction of motion? The direction is determined by the number's sign; a negative number means motion to the left, and positive means to the right. All you have to do is reverse the number's sign, and the movie clip starts moving in the opposite direction. It's a slight modification of the previous code, like so:

```
if (this._x > 639)
{
  this.dx *= -1;
  this._x = 639;
}
```

Notice that instead of setting `this.dx` to 0, you're simply multiplying it by –1, which causes its direction to reverse. If it were moving at 5 pixels per frame to the right and `this.dx` were 5, multiplying it by –1 would change `this.dx` to –5. After that, the movie clip begins moving in the opposite direction. The same thing is true for the left edge of the screen:

```
if (this._x < 0)
{
  this.dx *= -1;
  this._x = 0;
}
```

Note that this code causes the movie clip to bounce absolutely 100% off each edge; no momentum is lost. In reality, the wall absorbs some kinetic energy from the bounce. Otherwise, you would have discovered perpetual motion. So instead of using `this.dx *= -1;`, you could use `this.dx *= -0.5;`.

You're still reversing the sign, but you're also halving the value of `this.dx`. Therefore, if `this.dx` is 6, multiplying it by –0.5 would make it –3; the movie clip would begin moving left, but at a slower speed. This result illustrates *elasticity*. Experimenting with different values is a good idea to help you see what looks most realistic. For example, a rubber ball on a steel wall probably reflects with a value around –0.99. However, an apple bouncing off a felt-covered wooden wall probably reflects at around –0.2.

Gravity

You haven't looked at the y-axis yet because, for the most part, it's the same thing as the x-axis. However, in real life, the y-axis (up and down) tends to have one more factor influencing it: gravity. If your screen is 640×480, the bottom of the screen is at 479. You'll treat this value as your "floor." Here's the bounce code for hitting the floor:

```
if (this._y > 479)
{
  this.dy *= -1;
  this._y = 479;
}
```

This code causes a perfect reversal of vertical velocity, but as you can see, it's similar to the horizontal x code in the previous example. Of course, you could also have the movie clip reflect off the "ceiling," like so:

```
if (this._y < 0)
{
  this.dy *= -1;
  this._y = 0;
}
```

What's the magic of gravity? Gravity is simply an influence on velocity over time. In other words, the velocity changes each frame. It's not the reversal you've already seen; it's actually *adding* a certain number to `this.dy` every frame. The code is very short:

```
this.dy += 1;
```

What's this code doing? Say that the movie clip has a dy value of –6, so it's moving *up* 6 pixels each frame. However, when you run the gravity code, dy will change to –5, so it won't move up as far. In the next frame, dy will be –4, then –3, then –2, and finally –1. It moves up less and less with each frame.

This action is what happens when an object is thrown into the air. So what happens next? In the next frame, the movie clip's dy will be 0, so it will be motionless for a frame. This is the top of the motion. When you add 1 yet again, dy becomes 1 and the movie clip starts moving down. Then dy changes to 2, 3, 4, 5, and so on, moving down faster and faster.

What happens when the movie clip hits the floor? If its dy reaches 10 by the time it hits the floor, dy suddenly becomes –10, and the movie clip rockets upward. However, the gravity that's been added to the code slows the movie clip down, and you have a bouncing ball. Boing, boing.

The value 1 might not be the number you want, however. Gravity varies its realism based on this number. Perhaps something like the following would look more realistic:

```
this.dy += 0.2;
```

It takes some playing and tweaking to get it right. Again, experiment and have fun.

Putting It Together

Now that you've learned the basic principles, try putting them together in a working movie by following these steps:

1. First, in a new movie, create a circle on the stage with a width and height of 30 pixels.

2. Select the circle and convert it to a movie clip, making sure the registration point is the center of the circle. Give it the instance name myMovieClip.

3. On frame 1 of the movie, enter the following code:

```
myMovieClip.dx = 15;
myMovieClip.dy = 45;

myMovieClip.onEnterFrame = function()
{
  this._x += this.dx; // Move according to dx and dy
  this._y += this.dy;

  this.dy += 1; // Increase dy - gravity

  if (this._x > 639)
  {
    this.dx *= -1; // Hit Right Wall
    this._x = 639;
  }

  if (this._x < 0)
  {
    this.dx *= -1; // Hit Left Wall
    this._x = 0;
  }

  if (this._y > 479)
  {
    this.dy *= -.7; // Hit Ground
    this._y = 479;
  }

}
```

Run this movie, and watch as the ball bounces around the screen. You're starting with an initial dx of 15, so the ball is moving to the right, and an initial dy of 45, so the ball looks as though it's being thrown downward quite hard. You've used a floor bounce of –0.7 so that the ball's motion slowly decays with each bounce; however, the walls are fully reflecting.

Notice that you're not detecting any ceiling collision. In this case, you want the ball to bounce upward freely, even if it goes offscreen for a while. The effect is a ball bouncing in a big well with walls and a floor but no ceiling.

Wind

Wind is essentially just gravity, except in a horizontal direction. For example, you use the following code for gravity:

```
this.dy += 1;
```

To create a wind flow to the right, however, you use this:

```
this.dx += 1;
```

To create a wind flow to the left, you use this:

```
this.dx += -1;
```

You can adjust the value to increase or decrease wind strength, just as you do with gravity. Try values of 1, .5, or .2, for example, and see what works best for the effect you're trying to create.

MATHEMATICALLY GENERATED IMAGES

In this final example, you see how to use sine and cosine to create some interesting images with the Drawing API. First, look at the basic sine wave:

```
_root.createEmptyMovieClip("graph", 1);
graph._y = 200;
graph._x = 75;
```

```
graph.lineStyle(3, 0);

for (i = 0; i < Math.PI * 4; i += 0.01)
{
  x = i * 50;
  y = Math.sin(i) * 150;
  graph.moveTo(x, y);
  graph.lineTo(x + 1, y);
}
```

This code draws a sine wave that looks like Figure 21.6.

FIGURE 21.6
The ActionScript-generated sine wave.

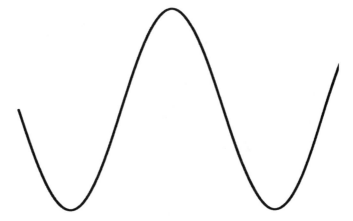

Making a small modification to the code (indicated in bold in the following lines) produces a circle:

```
_root.createEmptyMovieClip("graph", 1);
graph._y = 200;
graph._x = 275;

graph.lineStyle(3, 0);

for (i = 0; i < Math.PI * 2; i += 0.01)
{
  x = Math.cos(i) * 150;
  y = Math.sin(i) * 150;
  graph.moveTo(x, y);
  graph.lineTo(x + 1, y);
}
```

From there, you can build and create many different circle-inspired images. For example, changing the value of x with the code in the following lines produces the butterfly shown in Figure 21.7:

```
for (i = 0; i < Math.PI * 4; i += 0.01) change 2 to 4
{
    x = Math.cos(i / 2) * 150;
```

FIGURE 21.7
The ActionScript-generated butterfly.

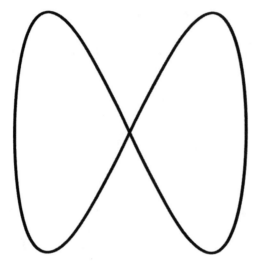

Changing the code to the following produces the image shown in Figure 21.8.

```
for (i = 0; i < Math.PI * 16; i += 0.1)
{
    x = Math.cos(i / 2) * 150;
    y = Math.sin(i / 3) * 150;
    graph.moveTo(x, y);
    graph.lineTo(x + 1, y);
}
```

Notice that the lines in Figure 21.8 look dotted, rather than solid? This is because the drawing code uses a combination of moveTo() and lineTo(). The Drawing API is essentially moving the "pen" to (x, y), and then drawing a very small, one-pixel-long line to (x + 1, y). The dot itself looks larger than one pixel, however, because the lineStyle code sets the Drawing API to draw a 3-point-thick line.

FIGURE 21.8
Creative mathematically generated images.

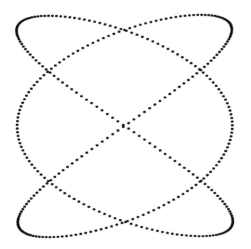

Looks like a drawing done with a spirograph, doesn't it? Try all sorts of different values inside Math.cos and Math.sin to see what you can get. For example, the following code creates the fish shown in Figure 21.9:

```
x = Math.cos(i / 1.5) * 150;
y = Math.sin(i) * 70;
```

FIGURE 21.9
Fishius mathematica.

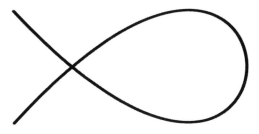

Resources

For further understanding of trigonometry:
www.math.com/tables/algebra/functions/trig/functions.html

Physics of ball games:
http://library.thinkquest.org/C0115986/index.html

Spirograph: www.wordsmith.org/~anu/java/spirograph.html

Newton's Laws of Physics:
www.glenbrook.k12.il.us/gbssci/phys/Class/newtlaws/
newtltoc.html

POINTS TO REMEMBER

- Using math in a Flash project greatly increases your projects' versatility and adds to the uniqueness and interactivity of visitors' experience.

- Trigonometry is used to create smooth motion effects, such as gentle bobbing, and to properly simulate motion along a user-controlled path that involves velocity and angle of rotation.

- Using simple physics with x and y velocity, along with Flash's built-in MovieClip object, simulations of advanced physics are easy. Adding motion such as gravity and bounce needs only a few lines of code.

- The Drawing API, along with simple trigonometric functions, can be used to create original and artistic mathematical images. By modifying a few small parameters, you can create entirely different images.

CHAPTER 22

3D IN FLASH

WHEN MOST PEOPLE THINK ABOUT 3D IN FLASH, THEY USUALLY ENVISION A 3D animation created with prerendered 3D graphics or a spinning cube created with ActionScript. Another common way to describe 3D in Flash is to say, "There will never be a 3D shooter game made in Flash that's like Quake." This is true, but that doesn't mean you should stop at a spinning cube.

Macromedia Flash MX 2004 does not have any new features specifically for creating 3D effects, although third-party extensions for 3D are available for purchase. However, Flash MX 2004 offers a lot of potential with the use of prerendered 3D graphics or ActionScript. This chapter focuses mainly on using prerendered 3D effects and core 3D programming concepts. Flash MX 2004 does offer a lot in terms of object-oriented programming and data structures that are great for organizing your 3D effects, but this chapter focuses on the raw code that you can customize as you like and leaves the structure up to you.

You can create 3D effects in Flash in two main ways: with prerendered 3D graphics or by using ActionScript. This chapter is organized accordingly into two major sections. The section on using prerendered 3D graphics helps you discover the potential for using Flash to manipulate and present prerendered 3D models and animation. The ActionScript section breaks down 3D programming into core concepts and teaches you how to apply these concepts to several types of projects.

FLASH AND 3D: ADVANTAGES AND LIMITATIONS

The advantages of creating 3D effects in Flash include Flash's inherent advantages, such as the universal web penetration of the Flash Player, a small file size, the ability to add interactivity, and an easy-to-use development environment. In Flash, you can also use ActionScript to create any kind of 3D movement of a movie clip that you want, including camera movement. By manipulating prerendered 3D animations, you can also re-create 3D animations at very small file sizes.

In spite of these advantages, Flash does have some major limitations when it comes to creating 3D effects. The first is graphics. Flash has no 3D graphics engine, so you don't have texture mapping and, therefore, you can't dynamically create detailed 3D landscapes or models. You can position movie clips onscreen according to their positions in 3D space, which enables you to create 3D placement and movement of flat graphics. You can also use prerendered 3D graphics and animations or use the Drawing API to draw simple shapes between 3D points.

The second limitation is speed. Flash chokes if it tries to handle 3D calculations and draw many objects at the same time. Depending on the types of graphics and the code's efficiency, Flash can handle about 20 to 100 movie clips when using 3D programming to position movie clips. Planning to have Flash handle around 30 movie clips at one time usually works best. This is a limitation, but it can be solved by writing code so that Flash doesn't have to calculate objects that are not in view.

Most 3D motion requires that you use code, which excludes many designers and explains why 3D in Flash hasn't gone much past spinning cubes. If you have some familiarity with programmatic motion, any motion created with code in 2D can easily be extended to 3D. So the obstacle isn't creating 3D motion—it's creating programmatic motion. You'll see how this works in the section on translation transformations later in this chapter.

Decisions for 3D

When you have a project with the potential for using 3D, you need to make two decisions. First, you need to decide if 3D is necessary. 3D should be used to help you convey your message, not just used for show. More often than not, 3D has the tendency to disorient the user, so you have to make sure you can justify its use.

Second, you need to decide whether Flash is the tool you want to use for the project, considering its graphics and speed limitations. Often you can take advantage of these limitations by applying a creative solution, which is usually a combination of prerendered graphics and 3D programming. To effectively apply these solutions, you have to learn what's possible.

PRERENDERED 3D GRAPHICS

Prerendered 3D graphics for Flash can be divided into two categories: vector and bitmap. Vector graphics have the advantages of smaller file sizes and more possibilities for manipulation. However, Flash can handle bitmap images more quickly to produce more detailed 3D models. When using bitmap images, be aware of images that include alpha (transparency) channels because they can decrease the speed of the movie.

There are many effects you can create by importing and manipulating prerendered 3D graphics in Flash. The following sections focus on splitting up elements of prerendered models and animations and making them interactive.

Swift 3D Importer

Before moving on to specific examples, take a quick look at one of the best tools for preparing a 3D vector animation that you can manipulate in Flash: the SWFT format, which is the format for the Swift 3D importer (see Figure 22.1).

When you import a SWFT file directly into a movie clip, Flash places your animation's registration point in the center of the stage rather than in the upper-left corner, as it typically does when you import a standard

SWF file. This feature gives you better control over the placement of your 3D animation.

Note that to import SWFT files, you'll need to install the Swift 3D importer. For instructions on installing this importer, check the Flash Help files under "importers" or the Macromedia site at www.macromedia.com.

Another advantage of the SWFT format is SmartLayers. This feature automatically splits your animation into separate layers in Flash, depending on factors such as color, outline, shadow, highlights, reflections, transparency, and moving objects. Having separate layers makes it easier to split elements of your 3D vector animation in preparation for manipulating it.

FIGURE 22.1
The Swift 3D importer includes SWFT format files and SmartLayers.

Manipulating Prerendered 3D Models

For more information on masking and animation, refer to Chapter 6, "Animation, Effects, and Masking."

To manipulate a prerendered vector model, one of your first steps is separating the vector graphic into individual parts. This step is as simple as selecting an area of the prerendered model in Flash. After selecting an area, you can change its color or turn it into a movie clip, for example. Converting a graphic area to a movie clip allows you do things such as dynamically add color to it, mask a graphic with it, or even animate fragments of it to create an explosion effect.

Splitting Up Scene Elements

In a 3D animation, often some elements don't change at all throughout the animation, so it doesn't make sense to render them more than once. To reduce file size, animating only what's necessary is a good rule of thumb. If you have these type of static elements in your 3D animation, you need to render only one frame of the static element and use it as a

You can download the project files for this chapter from the book's accompanying website at www.flashdemystified.com.

foreground or background in Flash. Then you render the animation of the elements that *do* move and combine them with the static foreground or background.

Your first project (`Project01_cityScene.fla`) is a simple vector animation of a rectangle moving in front of a static city scene. If you open the Flash file shown in Figure 22.2, you'll notice that the static city scene is on its own layer and has only one keyframe. The SWF file for this animation is only 1.5KB. This was accomplished by importing a SWFT file of the animation that uses SmartLayers to automatically separate moving objects and static objects into different layers in Flash. You can download another file of the same animation (`Project01_citySceneBackgroundNotSeparated.swf`), but the file size is 13.5KB because the city scene background wasn't separated into its own layer and is rendered in every frame. This proves the point that Flash is an excellent medium for delivering light 3D animations over the web and opens the door for manipulating elements of your animation in Flash.

FIGURE 22.2
In this city scene, only the blue rectangle at the lower left is animated.

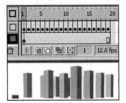

Interactive Prerendered Frames

Manipulating prerendered animation is a lot of fun when you add a little interactivity. You can, for example, render a rotation of a 3D model spinning 360 degrees and then use the `gotoAndStop()` method to tell your model which frame to display. An easy way to do this is to render a 360-frame animation, thus having one frame for each angle or every degree that your model faces as it spins. Then use `gotoAndStop()` to tell the 3D model to go to the angle you want to display and stop there.

If you don't need to display every angle, you don't have to render 360 frames. For example, if you want to display an image every 10 degrees, you need to render only a 36-frame animation. In the project file `Project02_rotatingModel.fla`, a slider is used to call the `gotoAndStop()` method for the movie clip containing the model (see Figure 22.3), but you could just as easily use another method to control the angle, such as using the `_xmouse` property to supply a number between 1 and 360.

**10 degree angle increments
36 frames**

Interactive Prerendered Animation

The previous project used a simple gotoAndStop() method to determine
which frame of the animation to display. You can also use gotoAndPlay()
to determine which prerendered animation to play, which makes it
possible for the user to trigger different animations. Check project file
Project03_animatedPlanes.fla, which uses buttons to call gotoAndPlay()
to trigger different transition animations for a 3D menu prototype (see
Figure 22.4).

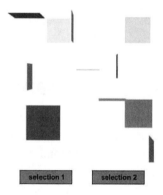

REAL TIME: BASICS OF 3D PROGRAMMING

3D programming is much easier to grasp when you look at it in terms of
transformations, which are like building blocks you can reuse and
rearrange to view your 3D data. Creating 3D with code is like a form of
data visualization, and to visualize data, you need to "transform" it. You
start with 3D coordinates in space and then transform those points to

produce 2D screen coordinates. By learning all the major ways to transform your data, you'll be set to display your 3D data on a 2D screen any way you like.

Transformations

The transformations you'll learn in this chapter are screen, projection, scale (changing the distance from the origin), translation (moving points in a certain direction), and rotation (see Figure 22.5). These transformations are all you need to create 3D effects. The most important transformations are screen and projection because they transform your 3D points into 2D screen coordinates by "projecting" them onto 2D projection planes and converting them to screen coordinates so that you can plot them. In some projects, these transformations are the only ones you'll need. In other projects, you might want to manipulate data a little before projecting it to the screen by running it through some more transformations, such as scaling, translating, or rotating.

FIGURE 22.5
Types of transformations.

Left-handed Coordinate System

Before learning more about transformations, you need to determine how you'll define data in your 3D world. The 3D dimensions are x, y, and z, and you position them by using the *left-handed coordinate system*. As shown in Figure 22.6, this system is similar to a Cartesian coordinate system, but with a positive z-axis extending into the distance to represent the dimension of depth. The x-axis extends right and left of the origin, with positive x representing the axis to the right of the origin. The y-axis extends above and below the origin, with positive y representing the axis above the origin. The z axis extends in front of and behind the origin, with positive z representing the axis in front of the origin.

For 3D virtual spaces, the left-handed coordinate system is easy to remember because many people are familiar with the Cartesian coordinate system, and the axes are positive when they extend to the right, up, and forward. Conversely, the axes are negative when extending to the left, down, or backward. This coordinate system resembles the real world, in which elevation increases upward and decreases downward from sea level. Also, you tend to associate moving forward with a positive direction and moving backward with a negative direction.

FIGURE 22.6
The left-handed coordinate system is like a Cartesian coordinate system with a positive z-axis extending into the screen.

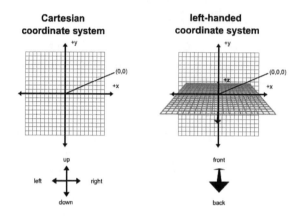

Transformation Matrix Notation

Matrix math is beyond the scope of this chapter, but the concept of combining transformation matrices to apply to a point or vector can still be applied without all the matrix math. If you want to create data structures and 3D classes, I recommend studying matrix math and how it applies to 3D.

Essentially, the code for each transformation in this chapter is the same as the result of the matrix multiplied by the point. The math is already done for you. All you need to do is figure out which transformations you want to apply to a point and in what order to apply them. Matrix notation is used in this chapter to describe which transformations you're applying to a point. The shorthand for a transformation matrix in this chapter is the capital letter T followed by a description of the type of transformation, like so:

$T_{type\ of\ transformation}$

Transformations change a point or vector in a certain way through matrix multiplication. Matrix multiplication is different from regular multiplication, but the code for each transformation includes the results of matrix multiplication. Essentially, this is the shorthand for showing that a transformation is applied to a point:

$p\ *\ T_{type\ of\ transformation}$

If you apply more than one transformation to a point through matrix multiplication, it looks like this:

$$p * T_{type\ of\ transformation}\ T_{type\ of\ transformation}\ T_{type\ of\ transformation}$$

Order Does Matter

Transformations are applied from left to right. For example, in the series of transformations p * T1 T2 T3, T1 is applied first and T3 is applied last. Projection and screen transformations are always applied last, but they are covered first in this chapter because they are always used in any 3D project. The reason for this is that projection transformations are like painting your viewing plane with what you want to see in your view. The screen transformation just adjusts it for Flash.

In Figure 22.7, you can see that if the order in which you apply identical transformations to a point is different, the resulting point will be different. The top example applies translation and then rotation, and the resulting point is in the lower-left corner. In the bottom example, rotation is applied first and then translation, and the resulting point is in the lower-right corner.

FIGURE 22.7
Applying the same transformations in a different order can give you completely different results.

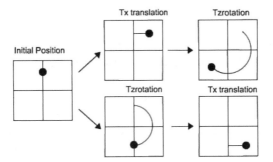

Misconceptions About 3D

Most people stay away from 3D because they think it involves trigonometry or because 3D code can look confusing. However, trigonometry is necessary only for rotation transformations and isometric projections. Because 3D effects are created in terms of transformations, you can see that the code is very modular, like building blocks, so you can pick and choose how you want to visualize your 3D data/world. You can start by learning the transformations that don't use trigonometry, and after you know what's possible, you'll have the incentive to learn the rotation transformation, which uses trigonometry to rotate objects. So focus on learning orthographic and perspective projections first when you get to the section "Projection Transformations" later in this chapter. The following sections fill in the details of how to implement each transformation and offer a basic example of each one, so you can test each transformation yourself.

Screen Transformations

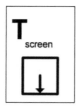

The screen transformation transforms coordinates from a projection plane that represents your viewing area into Flash movie clip properties, such as _x, _y, _xscale, and _yscale. Here's the matrix notation for this transformation:

$p * T_{screen}$

Essentially, this transformation converts projection plane coordinates into Flash movie clip coordinates. You should place the movie clips that represent your 3D points inside a view movie clip instead of on the main Timeline. Embedding 3D movie clips inside a view movie clip has two advantages. It separates depth handling from movie clips and graphics outside your view, and it saves you from continuously having to shift your movie clips to the center of the screen.

To represent a projection plane on a computer screen, the projection plane's center needs to be in the center of the viewing area. In a view movie clip, the origin is 0,0 and the movie clip can be placed anywhere on the main Timeline. The main Timeline's origin of 0,0 is at the upper-left corner, however, so if you didn't use a view movie clip, you would have to shift the origin and all other points down and to the left so that everything in the movie clip is visible.

Next, you need to flip the y-axis. In the left-handed coordinate system you're using to define your 3D points, the y-axis is positive as it moves upward from the origin. However, the _y property in Flash is negative to represent upward movement from the origin. To force movie clips in Flash to appear the same way they would on your projection plane, you need to flip the y-axis by setting _y in Flash equal to the negative of the projection plane's y point, as shown here (see Figure 22.8):

```
_y= -sy;
```

FIGURE 22.8
Screen transformation: converting to screen coordinates.

To perform a screen transformation on a movie clip embedded inside a view movie clip, sx and sy represent the x and y coordinates on the projection plane, as shown here:

```
mc._x = sx;
mc._y = -sy;
```

All the 3D programming projects in this chapter have screen transformations set up in this way, using a view movie clip. Take a moment to look at the project file for the screen transformation, Project04_screenTransformation.fla, to make sure you understand what it involves.

For example, as shown in Figure 22.9, if you were to plot the point that had sx = 50 and sy = 50, it should appear in the upper-right corner of the screen. However, if you were to set _x to 50 and _y to 50, the point would appear in the lower right because _y increases as you go down the screen. To correct this, you do a screen transformation that sets _y to the opposite of sx, thus flipping the point from the lower left to the upper left, where it should be.

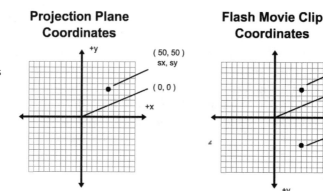

FIGURE 22.9
Converting from projection plane coordinates to Flash movie clip coordinates with the screen transformation.

Projection Transformations

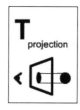

Projection transformations convert a point's 3D coordinates to coordinates on a 2D projection plane, according to the type of projection. Here's the matrix notation for this transformation:

$p * T_{projection}$

The 3D data points are converted into points on the 2D projection plane by drawing lines from the points in 3D space to the projection plane. The projection transformation can be divided into two major types: parallel projection and perspective projection. Figure 22.10 compares these two types of projection transformations.

In a parallel projection, parallel lines are drawn through the points. Where they intersect with the projection plane represents the projected points' position on the projection plane. In a perspective projection, lines are drawn through all points to a single viewpoint. Where they intersect with the projection plane represents the projected points' position on the projection plane. These lines all converge at the viewpoint, much like the way your eyes detect objects in the real world. The lines drawn for these projections resemble rays of light reflected off the points into the viewer's viewpoint.

FIGURE 22.10
Parallel projection
(top) versus perspec-
tive projection
(bottom).

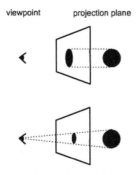

Parallel Projection

Although there are many types of parallel projections, the most commonly used ones in Flash are orthographic and isometric, covered in the
following sections.

Orthographic Projection

This is the matrix notation for an orthographic projection:

$$p * T_{\text{orthographic projection}}$$

Ortho refers to right angles, so in an orthographic projection, the lines
drawn from the object to the projection plane are perpendicular to the
projection plane. This transformation is also known as a *map view*, and
that's probably what you'll use it for when viewing 3D points. If you use
3D modeling software, you're probably already familiar with orthographic
views, such as front, top, and right. Figure 22.11 illustrates orthographic
projections.

FIGURE 22.11
Orthographic
projections.

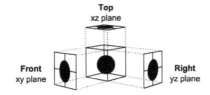

Points are projected perpendicular to the xy plane (the front view):

```
sx = x;
sy = y;
```

Points are projected perpendicular to the xz plane (the top view):

```
sx = x;
sy = z;
```

Points are projected perpendicular to the yz plane (the right view):

```
sx = z;
sy = y;
```

In the project file Project05_orthographicProjectionTop.fla, three points are created and displayed by using an orthographic projection for a top-down view. In the following code, movie clips are attached to the view movie clip with an initialization object that gives the movie clips initial values for x, y, and z. At the same time, they are also placed in the mcList array so that they can easily be referenced later. Then you call the projection function for each movie clip, using a for loop.

```
//create mcList movie clip
mcList = [];

mcList[0] = view.attachMovie("ball", "ball0", 0, {x:100, y:0,
➥z:-100});
mcList[1] = view.attachMovie("ball", "ball1", 1, {x:100, y:0,
➥z:0});
mcList[2] = view.attachMovie("ball", "ball2", 2, {x:100, y:0,
➥z:100});

//apply projection for each movie clip in list
for (var i in mcList) {
    orthographicProjectionTop(mcList[i]);
}
```

You can take a look at the other two project files for the front and right orthographic projections of the same 3D points: Project05_orthographicProjectionFront.fla and Project05_orthographicProjectionRight.fla.

Figure 22.12 shows three movie clips plotted according to their 3D coordinates using top-down orthographic projection. This kind of projection converts z coordinates into y screen coordinates so that positive values of z appear above the origin and negative values of z appear below the origin.

FIGURE 22.12
The same three points plotted from the front, top, and right using the orthographic transformation.

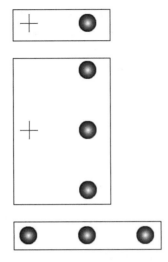

Isometric Projection

This is the matrix notation for an isometric projection:

$$p * T_{isometric\ projection}$$

Iso means equal, so *isometric* means of equal measure. This refers to all the axes being drawn at an equal length. Also, the angle between all the projected axes is equal at 120 degrees. This makes it easy to draw 3D because you can represent all three dimensions at the same time without having to do any additional calculations of length because of foreshortening. An isometric view is essentially one type of parallel projection that has two additional rotation transformations applied. As you can see in the following transformations and in Figure 22.13, points are first rotated in the 45 degrees around the z-axis and then 30 degrees around the x-axis.

$$p * T_{isometric\ projection} = p * T_{z\text{-rotation}(45\ degrees)} *$$

$$T_{x\text{-rotation}(30\ degrees)}$$

FIGURE 22.13
Transformations for an isometric projection.

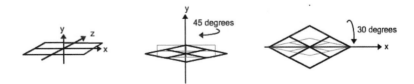

The following code demonstrates how to implement an isometric projection. Because rotation transformations haven't been covered yet, the code might look intimidating. However, if you look closer, it's composed of only two rotation transformations.

```
//isometric projection
function isometricProjection(mc){
    //y-axis rotation of 45 degrees
    var tx = mc.z*sin45 + mc.x*cos45;
    var ty = mc.y;
    var tz = mc.z*cos45 - mc.x*sin45;

    //x-axis rotation of 30 degrees
    var nx = tx;
    var ny = ty*cos30 - tz*sin30;
    var nz = ty*sin30 + tz*cos30;

    //projection from front onto projection plane
    var sx = nx;
    var sy = ny;

    //screen transformation
    mc._x = sx;
    mc._y = -sy;
}
```

Figure 22.14 shows the result of the project file Project06_isometricProjection.fla. Nine movie clips were laid out in a grid pattern on the xz plane, and an isometric projection transformation was applied to all of them. As a result, they were rotated 45 degrees on the y-axis and then 30 degrees on the x-axis.

FIGURE 22.14
An isometric projection.

It's easier to see what's going on if you create some square tiles—in this case, 100×100 pixels. You can see this on the left in Figure 22.15. These squares are rotated 45 degrees and scaled by half to match the isometric projection, as shown on the right in Figure 22.15. Using the Transform panel is a convenient way to accurately scale and rotate your tiles.

FIGURE 22.15
Creating tiles.

After you replace the sphere graphic with the tiles (you can see this done in the Project06_isometricProjectionTiles.fla file) and publish your movie, you'll get the results shown in Figure 22.16.

FIGURE 22.16
An isometric
projection with
tiles.

Perspective Projection

This transformation, illustrated in Figure 22.17, transforms 3D coordinates into screen coordinates by applying a perspective ratio. This is the matrix notation:

$$p * T_{\text{perspective projection}}$$

FIGURE 22.17
Perspective
projection.

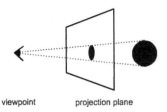

viewpoint   projection plane

Perspective means that the farther away an object is, the smaller it looks (decreased scale) and the closer it is to the vanishing point (or center of the view). In code, perspective would be described this way:

```
perspective = focal distance / z
```

Perspective is a ratio. *Focal distance* is the distance from the viewpoint to the projection plane, and *z* is the distance from the viewpoint to the point. It can be interpreted as the relative z distance or vector from the viewpoint.

When an object is at the viewing plane, it has the same z as the focal distance; therefore, perspective becomes 1. If the object is twice as far from the viewpoint as the focal distance, perspective is .5 and, therefore, half the distance—in other words, half the x offset from the center and half the y offset from the center. If an object is four times as far from the viewpoint as the focal distance, perspective is .25. In Figure 22.18, notice the z value and the corresponding perspective value of each movie clip. The distance from the viewpoint to the projection plane in the figure is 600. So if an object's distance from the projection plane is also 600, its perspective would be 1. If the distance is 1,200, its perspective is .5. Notice that perspective affects not only the scale, but also the x and y position in relation to the vanishing point.

FIGURE 22.18
Calculating
perspective.

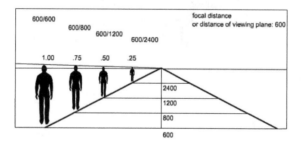

As you can see in the following code, perspective is applied by multiplying perspective by an object's x and y position in 3D space and also by 100, which is the object's normal scale:

```
sx = x*perspective;
sy = y*perspective;
_xscale = _yscale = 100*perspective;
```

Perspective looks like this inside a function with the screen transformation:

```
function perspectiveProjection(mc){
    //perspective transformation
    //find perspective
    var perspective = focalDistance/mc.z;

    //project onto projection plane with perspective
    var sx = perspective*mc.x;
    var sy = perspective*mc.y;
    var scale = perspective*100;
    var depth = 100000-mc.z;


    //screen transformation
    mc._x = sx;
    mc._y = -sy;
    mc._xscale = mc._yscale = scale;
    mc.swapDepths(depth);
}
```

Adding Z Sorting

The swapDepths() method is covered in Chapter 10, "ActionScript: Functions, Events, and Objects."

Movie clips that appear farther away (meaning they have a higher z value) need to appear behind an object that's closer to the viewpoint (meaning the object has a lower z value). Use the swapDepths() method to dynamically change the stacking order of movie clips. Normally, movie clips with a higher depth parameter are stacked on top of movie clips with a lower depth parameter.

To stack a movie clip according to its depth, you use view.mc.swapDepths (100000-z). This way the opposite happens: Movie clips with a higher z value are stacked below movie clips with a lower z value.

Figure 22.19 shows the SWF file (on the left) created from the Project07_perspectiveProjection_withoutSwapDepths.fla file. It demonstrates how important overlapping is as a cue for indicating depth. Calling swapDepths() easily fixes this problem, as you can see in Figure 22.19 on the right and in the Project07_perspectiveProjection.fla file.

FIGURE 22.19
Using swapDepths() with the object's z position arranges the stacking order according to the depth.

To position movie clips according to their 3D coordinates, you use this matrix notation (illustrated in Figure 22.20):

$$p * T_{\text{perspective projection}} * T_{\text{screen}}$$

FIGURE 22.20
Implementing a perspective projection.

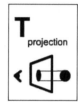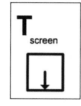

For more information on using the Drawing API, see Chapter 11, "Animation and Drawing with ActionScript: The Drawing API."

Drawing an object in 3D is almost as simple as drawing it in 2D. The only trick is using a perspective projection to figure out which points to connect. After connecting those points, you have 2D screen points; this process is exactly the same as connecting points with the Drawing API in 2D. You can then draw any wireframe structure you like. These are the basic steps:

1. Place the points using perspective projection.

2. Draw lines between points using their _x and _y values and the Drawing API.

Figure 22.21 is a screenshot of the SWF file produced from Project07_perspectiveProjectionDraw.fla. A line drawn with the Drawing API connects the screen coordinates of two movie clips that were positioned with the perspective projection.

FIGURE 22.21
Draw between screen coordinates with the Drawing API.

Scale Transformations

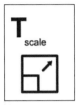

The scale transformation increases or decreases the position of points from the origin. Here's the matrix notation for this transformation:

$p * T_{scale}$

You can transform the size of your world by multiplying points by a scalar value. Essentially, the code looks like this:

```
x *= scalar;
y *= scalar;
z *= scalar;
```

scalar is a variable representing the amount for scaling your other values. A scale transformation is useful for changing the local coordinates of a 3D model's points, for scaling your 3D world, or for scaling an orthographic view. Here is an example (illustrated in Figure 22.22) of how you would apply this transformation with an orthographic view to create a small-scale top-down map view of your 3D world:

$p * T_{scale} * T_{orthographic\ projection} * T_{screen}$

FIGURE 22.22
Implementing a scale with an orthographic projection.

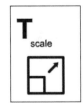 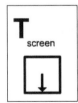

The following code contains the three transformations shown in Figure 22.22: scale, projection, and screen. In addition to scaling the position, a scale transformation is also being applied to the movie clip.

```
//orthographic projection from the top with scaling
//transformation, top-down map view with scale
function orthographicProjectionTop(mc){
    //scaling transformation
    var nx = mc.x*scale;
    var ny = mc.y*scale;
    var nz = mc.z*scale;

//orthographic projection from top onto projection plane
    var sx = nx;
    var sy = nz;

    //screen transformation
    mc._x =  sx;
    mc._y = -sy;
    //scale movie clip
    mc._xscale = mc._yscale = 100*scale;
}
```

In Figure 22.23 at the left, you can see that the points have been scaled to 50% of their original position and size (see project file Project08_scaling_50percent.fla). On the right, the scaling is 25% (see project file Project08_scaling_25percent.fla).

FIGURE 22.23
Scaling an ortho-
graphic projection
from the top at 25%
and 50%.

Translation Transformations

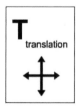

A translation transformation changes the position of points by moving or shifting them in the x, y, or z direction. Here's the matrix notation for this transformation:

$\mathrm{p} \;*\; \mathsf{T_{translation}}$

The code for moving or shifting points in the x, y, or z direction looks like this:

```
x += xIncrement;
y += yIncrement;
z += zIncrement;
```

Increment is a variable value representing the amount to add to the x, y, or z position. A good rule of thumb for creating movement in 3D is to do it in 2D first. Basically, 3D movement is 2D movement with another dimension. This is the matrix notation for using a translation transformation and then a perspective projection (illustrated in Figure 22.24):

$\mathrm{p} \;*\; \mathsf{T_{translation}} \;*\; \mathsf{T_{perspective\ projection}} \;*\; \mathsf{T_{screen}}$

FIGURE 22.24
Implementing the translation transformation with perspective.

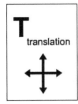
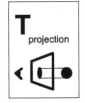
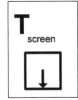

Converting 2D Movement to 3D Movement

The following sections describe four examples of using a translation transformation followed by a perspective projection. To keep it simple, these examples don't list the specific code used for each transformation; if you're interested in learning how to apply additional motion to your 3D objects, consult the project files mentioned for each example, and compare the results of your published files against the figures in the following sections.

Example 1: Moving in the X and Z Direction with Arrow Keys

As shown in the project file `Project09_translationArrowKeys.fla`, you can add to and subtract from the x and z position of an object by using the arrow keys. The changes in 3D position update the screen position and scale, allowing you to move the object around in 3D space.

Figure 22.25 shows what this project file looks like when published. Although you can't see the actual motion in this figure, of course, the arrow keys control the middle movie clip.

FIGURE 22.25
2D to 3D: Translating in the x and z direction with arrow keys.

Example 2: Using the Ease to Method

As shown in the project file `Project10_translationEaseTo.fla`, a pair of cursors are continually set to ease to a target z value in 3D space. Each object's `onPress` event reassigns a new target z value for the cursors so that when you click an object, the cursor moves toward it.

In Figure 22.26, you can see the cursors have moved to the middle movie clip because that is the current target.

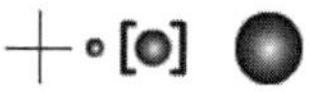

FIGURE 22.26
2D to 3D: Easing to a target z value.

Example 3: Bounce

The project file `Project11_translationBounce.fla` demonstrates a sphere moving on the xz plane in the x and z direction by a given amount every frame. The sphere is also constrained inside boundaries so that when it attempts to cross them, the sphere's velocity is reversed, thus appearing to bounce off an imaginary wall. Figure 22.27 shows how the project file has been set up with four movie clips representing the corners of the boundaries and a fifth movie clip that bounces between them.

For an example of bounce in 2D, see Chapter 21, "Math for Flashers."

FIGURE 22.27
2D to 3D: Bouncing in x and z.

Example 4: Drive

This example is similar to Example 1, but it uses radial motion. In other words, the object controlled with arrow keys rotates and moves forward and backward in relation to the direction it's facing, instead of just in the x and z direction. Figure 22.28 is a screenshot of the published `Project12_translationDriveArrowKeys.fla` project file. To see a noticeable difference from Example 1, you need to test this project file yourself.

FIGURE 22.28
2D to 3D: Driving in x
and z.

FIGURE 22.28
2D to 3D: Driving in x
and z.

You can also add a graphic and drive it around. Take a look at project file `Project12_translationDriveArrowKeys_Car.fla`; you can see a simple prerendered model of a car used instead of the silver ball in Figure 22.29.

FIGURE 22.29
Using drive with a
prerendered car
model.

Rotation Transformations

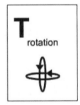

A rotation transformation changes the position of points by rotating around the origin on the x-, y-, or z-axis. Here's the matrix notation for this transformation:

$p * T_{rotation}$

The code for rotating points around an axis looks like this:

```
Rx
X = x;
Y = y*cos – z*sin;
Z  = y*sin + z*cos;


Ry
X  = z*sin + x*cos;
Y = y;
Z  = z*cos - x*sin;
```

```
Rz
X = x*cos - y*sin;
Y = x*sin + y*cos;
Z = z;
```

Rotation in the x-, y-, and z-axes is illustrated in Figure 22.30.

FIGURE 22.30
Rotation around the
x-, y-, and z-axes.

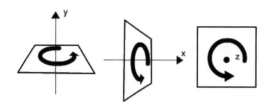

The following sections describe examples of using the rotation transformation.

Example 1: Rotation Around an Axis with Arrow Keys

This first example uses the right and left arrow keys to increase and decrease the angle of y-rotation and then calls a function that performs these three transformations (illustrated in Figure 22.31):

$$p * T_{y\text{-}rotation} * T_{perspective\ projection} * T_{screen}$$

FIGURE 22.31
Implementing the
rotation transforma-
tion with perspective.

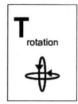

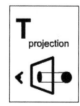

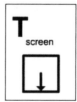

Figure 22.32 is a screenshot of the SWF file produced from project file `Project13_rotationYaxisArrowKeys.fla`, in which three movie clips rotate around the viewpoint on the y-axis. You can also find examples of rotating around the x- and z-axes in project files `Project13_rotationXaxisArrowKeys.fla` and `Project13_rotationZaxisArrowKeys.fla`.

FIGURE 22.32

Rotation trans-

formation.

Example 2: Rotation Transformation Pushed Out with Translation

The example in project file Project14_rotationYaxisArrowKeys
PushedOut.fla also performs a y-rotation transformation, as the previous
example does. The main difference is that after the points are rotated, they
are pushed away from the viewpoint in the z direction with a translation
transformation. Therefore, the points don't rotate around the viewer; rather,
they spin around a point located in front of the viewer. Figure 22.33 shows
how all the points are visible in front of the viewer in this example.

FIGURE 22.33

Local rotation around
an object's y-axis.

Example 3: Y-axis and X-axis Rotation Transformation with Arrow Keys

The example in project file
Project14_rotationYXaxisArrowKeysPushedOut.fla is the same as
Example 2, except that an additional x-rotation transformation is added
so that you can change the angle of rotation of the movie clips around
the x-axis with the up and down arrow keys. Figure 22.34 shows the
movie clips slightly tilted, indicating x-rotation.

FIGURE 22.34

Local rotation around
an object's x and y
axes.

POINTS TO REMEMBER

- The transformations described in this chapter are the building blocks for creating 3D in Flash.

- First, decide whether 3D is necessary for your project, and then decide whether the techniques for creating 3D effects in Flash are sufficient.

- Move only what's necessary. Separate moving objects from the background to improve performance and decrease file size.

- A projection transformation takes a point in 3D space and finds the corresponding 2D point on the projection plane.

- Approach 3D programming in terms of transformations.

- Make a prototype of your project and all its motion in 2D before converting it to 3D.

PART VI
FINISHING

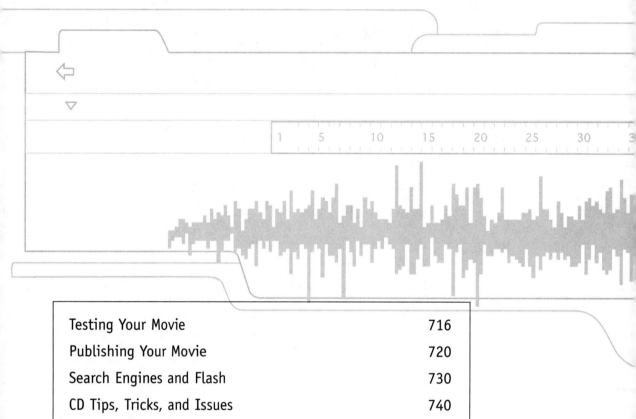

CHAPTER 23

PUBLISHING

PUBLISHING IS, IN MANY WAYS, THE MOST IMPORTANT PART OF THE FLASH development process. Without it, you can't share your content with the world. Whether you are making a Flash movie for a website, creating a CD-ROM, or producing a Flash movie for a pocket device, publishing is the final step in your project.

This chapter covers the following topics:

- How to publish your SWF file
- How to check the bandwidth profiler
- How to select which version of Flash you'll use
- How to use the standalone Flash player
- How to make standalone projector files
- How to export non-Flash files

TESTING YOUR MOVIE

As you've learned, there are two ways to test your movie: playing it in the Timeline in the authoring environment, and using the Test Movie command. The following sections describe these approaches.

Playing the Movie in the Authoring Environment

To play your movie in the authoring environment, you can use the commands under the Control menu to play, rewind, and go to the end as well as move the playhead one frame forward or backward. You can also use the Controller toolbar (choose Window, Toolbars from the menu), which gives you VCR-like control of your movie (see Figure 23.1).

FIGURE 23.1
The Controller
toolbar.

You can also use keyboard shortcuts to control your movie, which are listed under the Control menu in the application menu:

Step Forward One Frame: , (comma)

Step Backward One Frame: . (period)

Play: Enter

Rewind: **Ctrl+Alt+R** (Macintosh: **Command+Option+R**)

Playing your movie in the authoring environment to preview your work has certain limitations. It shows you only the most basic ActionScript and simple buttons, and it doesn't show you actions or animation within a movie clip. In addition, you don't get an accurate indication of the frame rate your movie plays at. You can control certain actions of this previewing method, however, by using the bottom six items in the Control menu (see Figure 23.2):

• **Loop Playback**   Your movie loops back to the beginning after it's finished and plays again.

- **Play All Scenes**   By default, Flash plays only the current scene. Selecting this option plays all your scenes.

- **Enable Simple Frame Actions**   Allows simple frame actions, such as Goto, Play, and Stop, to function while previewing your work in the authoring environment.

- **Enable Simple Buttons**   Allows you to preview all button states (Up, Over, Down, and Hit) when you interact with a button using your mouse in the authoring environment.

- **Enable Live Preview**   Allows any components used in your movie to be previewed in the authoring environment.

- **Mute Sounds**   Mutes all sounds during playback in the authoring environment.

For more information on live previews, see Chapter 12, "Components."

FIGURE 23.2
Options in the Control menu.

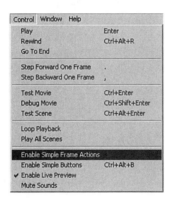

Using the Test Movie Command

The Test Movie method (choose Control, Test Movie from the main menu) gives you a much more accurate test of your movie than is possible by previewing it in the authoring environment, as it actually creates an SWF file and shows it to you in the test movie window. Flash uses the current settings in the Publish Settings dialog box (see "Publishing Your Movie," later in this chapter, for more information on this dialog box) to render this SWF file. To use this method, you can use the keyboard shortcut **Ctrl+Enter** (Macintosh: **Command+Enter**), or you can choose Control, Test Movie from the menu. If needed, you can test only the current scene by choosing Control, Test Scene from the menu (keyboard shortcut: **Ctrl+Alt+Enter**; Macintosh: **Command+Option+Enter**). The following sections explain additional options you have when using the Test Movie method.

You can open any SWF file to test by using the File menu. Opening an SWF file in Flash opens it in a test movie window. You can also import an SWF file, as discussed in Chapter 5, "Importing."

Options in the Test Movie View Menu

In the test movie environment, your menu options change to give you more options while testing your movie. Using the View menu (see Figure 23.3), you can zoom in and out, control your movie's magnification level, simulate download at different connection speeds, and set the quality to low, medium, or high. Remember that adjusting these settings doesn't change your finished rendered project; it simply changes your current view in Flash.

FIGURE 23.3
View menu options.

Options in the Test Movie Control Menu

The test movie window also includes a Control menu that's different from the Control menu in the authoring environment (see Figure 23.4). This menu allows you to play, rewind, and step forward and backward frame by frame.

By default, Flash movies are set to loop, but you can deselect the Loop option on the View menu while viewing your test movie. Again, anything you adjust here doesn't affect your finished project.

FIGURE 23.4
Control menu options in the test movie environment.

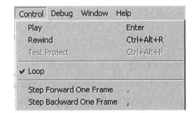

Bandwidth Profiler

One of the more interesting features available in the View menu is the Bandwidth Profiler, which enables you to see your movie's bandwidth, frame by frame. This is an excellent way to see how your movie will load for your users. To toggle the Bandwidth Profiler on and off, use the View menu (keyboard shortcut: **Ctrl+B**).

The Bandwidth Profiler is divided into two panes. The left pane shows information about the movie, such as dimensions and frame rate; indicates the download setting (which is the simulated download speed selected with the View, Download Settings menu choice); and displays the state (current frame and bytes on that frame). The right pane shows the bandwidth required for each frame in your movie. You can select a frame by selecting a bar in this graph. In Figure 23.5, you can see that the first frame of the movie is 16KB, the second frame is just under 4KB, and so on.

FIGURE 23.5
The Bandwidth Profiler in Streaming Graph view.

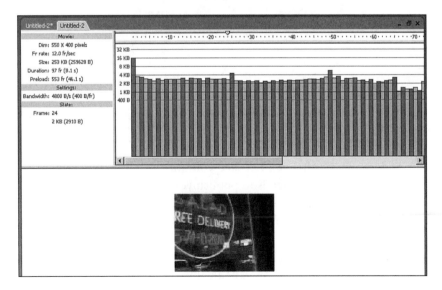

Two views are available for the Bandwidth Profiler. The default view is Streaming Graph, which displays alternating light gray and dark gray blocks that represent each frame of your movie. The height of the bar indicates its byte size. The second view, Frame by Frame Graph, helps you see which frames contribute to streaming delays. If any frame bar extends above the red line in the graph, the playhead stops there until that frame is loaded.

The test movie environment includes debugging features. For details on debugging your movie, see Chapter 25, "Troubleshooting."

Simulate Download

Selecting the Simulate Download option in the View menu enables you to preview your movie in a simulated download state, thereby showing the movie as though it were being downloaded onto a computer. These settings are adjustable, so you can select a preset setting, such as a 56K or T1 connection, or define your own settings with the Customize option (see Figure 23.6).

FIGURE 23.6
Available settings in the Simulate Download option.

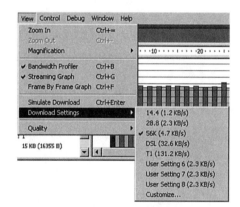

PUBLISHING YOUR MOVIE

After you've tested your movie and it's working the way you'd like, the next step is to publish your movie. To do this, open the Publish Settings dialog box by choosing File, Publish Settings (keyboard shortcut: **Ctrl+Shift+F12**). In this dialog box, you can select and customize the formats for publishing your Flash movie (see Figure 23.7). Eight formats are available. The most common are SWF and HTML; next are three image formats (GIF, JPEG, and PNG), two projector formats (Windows and Macintosh), and the QuickTime format. Any selected formats are created when you click the Publish button.

FIGURE 23.7
The Formats tab of
the Publish Settings
dialog box.

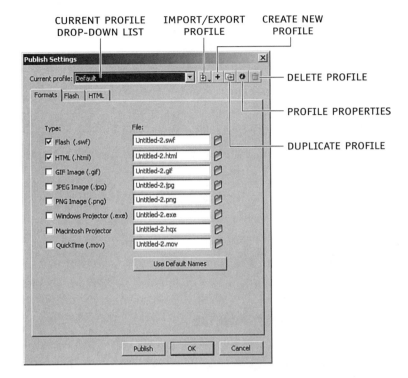

Use the Formats tab to select a publishing format and specify a filename
and location. Click the Use Default Names button to configure all formats to use the default filename, the default folder (the same folder as
the original FLA file), and the default extension for that format. After
you select a format under the Type list, a new tab is added to the Publish
Settings dialog box, which allows you to adjust settings for that specific
format.

Setting Up Profiles

At the top of the Publish Settings dialog box is the Current Profile drop-
down list, along with a few buttons to the right. This area is used to set
up profiles for formats. You can adjust settings for the format you want
to publish and then save that setting as a profile, giving it a unique
name. This allows you to load the profile again in another Flash movie
where you want to use the same publish settings.

Here's an explanation of the options in the profile area of the Publish Settings dialog box:

- **Profile drop-down list**   Select any saved profile from this list.

- **Import/Export Profile**   Here you can save your profiles to be exported to other computers or load profiles saved from other users or computers. Files are in .xml format.

- **Create New Profile**   After creating a profile, you can save it with a unique name.

- **Duplicate Profile**   Allows you to duplicate the current profile and give it a new name.

- **Profile Properties**   Displays the profile name, so you can edit it if needed.

- **Delete Profile**   Deletes the currently selected profile.

The Flash Format

When you select the Flash format, a Flash tab is added where you can customize the settings of the exported SWF file (see Figure 23.8).

FIGURE 23.8
Publish Settings:
The Flash tab.

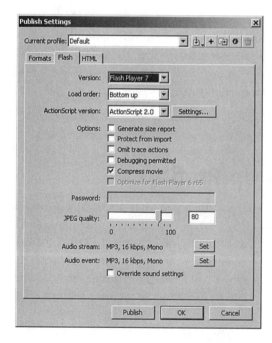

Generally, an SWF file is created for web-based access in a browser, but there's another way to view SWF files. The standalone Flash Player is an application that allows you to run SWF files outside a browser. It's installed on your computer when you install Flash and is also available for download from Macromedia's site. For more information on the Flash Player, see Chapter 27, "The Flash Player."

The following settings are available in the Flash tab:

- **Version** Select the Flash Player version for the movie from this drop-down list. Whichever version you choose, remember that anyone with a lower version probably won't be able to view your movie properly, yet anyone with the same or higher version will be able to view your movie properly. Note that you receive an alert if you attempt to publish a movie containing content (such as ActionScript 2.0 code) in a version of Flash that doesn't support it. Macromedia has a breakdown of the different versions and their market penetration levels at www.macromedia.com.

- **Load Order** Select Bottom Up or Top Down from this list box to specify the load order, which controls how Flash loads the layers on an SWF file's first frame. The default is Bottom Up.

- **ActionScript Version** Sets the code version to ActionScript 1.0 or ActionScript 2.0. If you select ActionScript 2.0 and are creating classes, you can click the Settings button to set the relative classpath to class files that differ from the default directory path in the Preferences dialog box.

- **Generate Size Report** Generates a report as a text document that lists each frame's file size and each item in your Flash movie with its file size. Excellent for helping you optimize your movie.

- **Protect from Import** This option prevents others from importing your movie into an FLA file. If you select this option, you can also password-protect your file by adding an entry to the Password text box.

For more information on trace() statements and the Flash Debugger, see Chapter 25.

- **Omit Trace Actions** Forces Flash to ignore any trace() statements in your movie. When selected, trace() statements are *not* displayed in the Output panel.

- **Debugging Permitted** Activates the Debugger and allows remote debugging. If selected, you can also assign a password.

- **Compress Movie**   Compresses the SWF file to help reduce file size and download time. This option, enabled by default, applies only to Flash Player 6 or later. This compression is for text and ActionScript, not objects such as audio, video, bitmaps, or vector artwork.

- **Optimize for Flash Player 6 r65**   When exporting a file for Flash Player 6, this option improves performance by allowing use of the ActionScript register allocation. Users must have Flash player 6 r65 or later to view the file.

All Flash players have a version number and a build number. Flash Player version 6 r65 refers to build r65 of Flash Player 6, and it contains certain functionality that previous versions of the Flash 6 player don't have. Build r65 uses the ActionScript register allocation to improve performance and supports the new v2 component architecture, so it supports most of the Flash MX 2004 components.

- **Password**   Enter a password in this text box when you're using the Protect from Import or Debugging Permitted options.

For more information on JPEG quality, see Chapter 14, "Images."

- **JPEG Quality**   Sets the compression rate for all bitmap images in your movie that don't have a specific compression rate. A lower number generates smaller file sizes but lowers the quality; a higher number increases file size but also increases quality. Generally, a setting between 40 and 60 is acceptable for most images, but experiment with different settings and check the quality and the file size. Setting the compression for each image individually is usually recommended.

For more information on these audio settings, see Chapter 15, "Audio."

- **Audio Stream and Audio Event**   These options set the sample rate and compression for all streaming sounds or event sounds in your movie. As with the JPEG Quality setting, these settings apply only to audio that doesn't have sample rates and compression already set.

- **Override Sound Settings**   Select this check box to force settings you've entered here to override any settings you might have already given to audio in your movie. This option is a quick way to create a highly compressed or extremely high-quality version of your movie, as it allows you to easily override any sound settings you've given individual audio files in your movie, but in general, setting the compression of your audio pieces individually is best.

The HTML Format

When you select the HTML format, the HTML tab is created in the Publish Settings dialog box (see Figure 23.9), which allows you to adjust settings for the HTML that's created when you click the Publish button.

FIGURE 23.9
Publish Settings: The HTML tab.

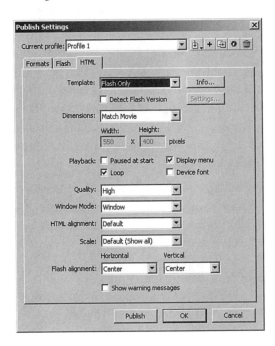

These settings are available in the HTML tab:

- **Template**   Select a template for specific HTML requirements from this drop-down list or create your own customized template. These are the available templates:

  - **Flash for Pocket PC 2003**   Display your Flash in HTML with Pocket PC–specific settings, suitable for Pocket Internet Explorer (IE) and for desktop IE and Netscape browsers.

  - **Flash HTTPS**   Displays your Flash movie in HTML and directs users to an HTTPS server to download the Flash Player if they don't have it on their systems.

  - **Flash Only**   Basic HTML to display your Flash movie.

  - **Flash with AICC Tracking**   HTML that includes support for Aviation Industry CBT Committee (AICC) tracking, used with Macromedia learning components.

- **Flash with FSCommand**   HTML that includes support for FSCommands and JavaScript. FSCommands are covered in-depth later in this chapter.

- **Flash with Named Anchors**   HTML that includes scripts and HTML anchors to enable bookmarking. Applies only to Player 6 and later.

- **Flash with SCORM Tracking**   Advanced Distributed Learning (ADL) publishing templates for standard quiz templates and the FS Shareable Content Object Reference Model (SCORM) sample file. SCORM is a suite of technical standards for web-based learning. Includes JavaScript to find and initialize an ADL API object and the FS command glue for using Learning Management System (LMS) functions.

- **Image Map**   Publishes a bitmap with a client-side image map. You need to select an image format (GIF, JPEG, or PNG), too, to use this setting. Any keyframe containing buttons with attached getURL() actions can be made into an image map. Insert #map as the keyframe of your movie to be used for the image map. To specify the graphic for an image map, label the frame containing the graphic #static for a GIF or PNG. To specify a JPEG, set the playhead to the frame containing the graphic in your movie *before* opening the Publish Settings dialog box.

- **QuickTime**   Publishes HTML with embedded code for a QuickTime movie. This setting creates the HTML that holds a QuickTime movie, but you need to select QuickTime in the Formats tab to use this template to create a QuickTime file.

- **Detect Flash Version**   Select this check box to have your HTML detect a specific version of Flash. The Flash version is taken from the setting you make in the Flash tab. Click the Settings button to see the options in Figure 23.10. You can select major or minor revisions (which apply to specific versions of the Flash Player—use this setting if your SWF requires a very specific version of a Flash player). You can also specify three HTML files: the detection page itself, the content page, and the alternate file. The alternate file is used for those who don't have the specified version of Flash. This page usually contains information on how to upgrade the user's Flash plug-in.

FIGURE 23.10
Version detection
settings.

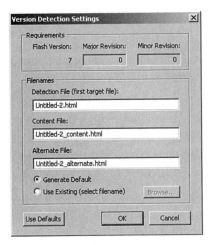

- **Dimensions** Specifies the dimensions of your Flash file in HTML. You can select the Match Movie option, or you can set the width and height in pixels or as a percentage of the browser window. This setting does not change the size of your Flash movie; it controls the viewable area in which your movie is displayed.

- **Paused at Start** Pauses your Flash movie at the start of playback. Requires a play() command to start the movie.

- **Loop** This option, which is enabled by default, causes your Flash file to loop indefinitely. If you deselect it, Flash stops at the end of the movie.

- **Display Menu** Indicates whether the user can access the context menu by right-clicking the Flash movie. This option, enabled by default, allows the user to zoom in and out, to stop and play the movie, and to control the quality setting.

- **Device Font** Available only on Windows machines, this option replaces fonts not installed on the player's system with anti-aliased system fonts.

- **Quality** The options in this section are used to set the quality of your movie and determine the balance between processing time and graphic quality:

  - **Low** Sets the quality to low, turning off all anti-aliasing. Useful for improving playback on slower processors.

  - **Auto Low** Sets the quality to low, but your movie automatically switches to high if the processor can handle the playback.

- **Auto High** Sets the quality to high, but the movie automatically switches to low if the processor can't handle the playback.

- **Medium** Sets the quality to medium, which uses medium anti-aliasing for vector graphics (using a 4-pixel square, a medium anti-alias setting), but not for bitmap images.

- **High** Sets the quality to high, which applies high anti-aliasing to all vector graphics (using a 16-pixel square, a high anti-alias setting). It also smoothes all bitmaps, unless they're in a tween. This setting is the default in Flash.

- **Best** Same as the High setting, but smoothes all bitmap images, including ones used in bitmap tweens. This setting is very processor-intensive.

- **Window Mode** Modifies how Flash content appears in relation to HTML content on the same page. Select from Window, Opaque Windowless, and Transparent Windowless mode, which are different HTML window settings:

  - **Window** Sets the background of Flash content to opaque and uses the HTML background color. Does not embed any window-related attributes in the <object> or <embed> tags. Window is the standard and default setting.

  - **Opaque Windowless** Sets the background color of Flash content to opaque, covering anything underneath the Flash content. This option allows HTML content to be displayed on top of Flash content.

  - **Transparent Windowless** Sets the background of Flash content to transparent, which allows HTML content to be displayed on top of and behind Flash content. Keep in mind that windowless mode is supported in Mac 10.1.5 using IE 5.1 or Windows machines using IE 5.0, 5.5, or 6.0. Both Mac and Windows also support windowless mode in Netscape 7.0 and later, Opera 6.0 and later, Mozilla 1.0 and later, AOL, and CompuServe.

- **HTML Alignment** Sets the horizontal and vertical alignment of your Flash movie within the browser window. Default centers content in the browser window and crops it to fit if necessary. Left, Right, Top, and Bottom align content along an edge of the browser window and crop the remaining sides to fit.

- **Scale** Works with the Dimensions setting to set the size of your Flash movie. The following options are available:

- **Default (Show All)**   Sets the entire Flash movie in the area defined in the Dimensions setting and does not change the original movie's ratio. If the Dimensions settings have a different ratio from the Flash movie, the movie is sized to have a border in the extra height or width areas (similar to the black stripes you see in video letterbox formats).

- **No Border**   Similar to the default setting, it preserves the ratio of the original Flash movie but crops the movie to remove any borders.

- **Exact Fit**   Stretches or shrinks the Flash movie to fit the Dimensions settings. Vertical or horizontal scaling (which can result in distortion) is possible, depending on your dimensions.

- **No Scale**   This option locks your Flash movie at the dimensions set in the Document Properties dialog box.

- **Flash Alignment**   This setting controls the horizontal and vertical alignment of the Flash movie within the player window created by the Dimensions setting. The default is Center for both horizontal and vertical.

- **Show Warning Messages**   Specifies whether to show you warning messages during the publishing process. Default is on and is recommended.

If you're familiar with HTML and want to edit HTML templates yourself, you can do so with an HTML editor. This can be useful if you want to customize code in HTML templates. The HTML templates are stored on your machine in these locations:

Windows 2000 and XP HTML files:

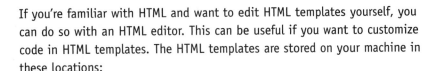

```
<boot drive>:\Documents and Settings\<user>\Local Settings\
➥Application Data\Macromedia\Flash MX 2004\<language>\
➥Configuration\HTML
```

Windows 98 HTML files:

```
<boot drive>:\Program Files\Macromedia\Flash MX 2004\
➥<language>\First Run\HTML
```

Macintosh OS X, 10.1.5, 10.2.6, and later:

```
<Macintosh hard drive>/Applications/Macromedia Flash MX 2004/
➥First Run/HTML
```

SEARCH ENGINES AND FLASH

You've published your SWF and your HTML, and everything is working well. However, your site isn't being listed on major search engines. Why? Because search engines usually can't access text in a Flash movie. Without this information, search engines have no way of cataloging and listing your site or its content. There are a few ways to handle this, however:

- **Publish an HTML and a Flash version of your site.** This allows search engines to easily access your content and enables users who don't have the Flash Player to access your site.

- **Create synopsis pages.** You can create an HTML synopsis page that describes the content. This allows search engines to easily index your site's content.

- **Use <META> tags.** The HTML page storing your Flash content can contain <META> tags, which allow you to fill in basic information about your site's content. Some search engines read these <META> tags as they index sites for their listings.

    Many <META> tags are available, but the two relevant ones here are description and keywords. Here is an example of them in use:

    ```
    <HEAD>
    <TITLE>All About Macromedia Flash</TITLE>
    <META name= "description" content= "Everything you wanted
    ➡to know about Macromedia Flash.">

    <META name= "keywords" content= "Flash, web, internet,
    ➡Macromedia, rich media, new media">
    </HEAD>
    ```

    You can find more information about <META> tags at http://searchenginewatch.com/webmasters/article.php/2167931.

- **Customize HTML publishing templates.** If you're familiar with HTML, you can modify HTML template variables to create a text report. The $MT template variable causes Flash to insert all text from the current Flash movie as a comment in the HTML code. This method is useful for indexing a movie's content and making it visible to search engines.

- **Use the Macromedia Flash Search Engine SDK.** The Macromedia Flash Search Engine SDK provides a set of objects and source code designed to convert a Flash file's text and links into HTML for indexing. This SDK is designed for search engine application engineering teams and for intermediate and advanced Flash developers. For more information, visit `www.macromedia.com/software/Flash/download/search_engine/`.

The Image Formats

Flash also supports publishing different image formats. Although most developers don't often need these formats, they can sometimes be useful in certain situations, such as creating a static page for users who don't have the Flash Player. Selecting any of these image formats creates a corresponding tab in the Publish Settings dialog box, allowing you to customize the settings for that format.

Generally, exporting images with the Export Image command (File, Export, Export Image) is preferable because you have more control over the images. (This command is discussed later in this chapter in "Exporting Non-Flash Formats.")

GIF Image Format

This format allows you to export an animated or static GIF graphic of your Flash movie. Selecting this format adds a GIF tab to the Publish Settings dialog box (see Figure 23.11).

The following settings are available in the GIF tab:

- **Dimensions** Match Movie, the default, sets the height and width to match your original Flash movie. You can also deselect Match Movie and enter your own height and width settings.

- **Static** Exports the first frame of your Flash movie as a GIF image. If you'd prefer another frame, add `#static` as a frame label to the frame you want. A better method for exporting a GIF static image is using the File, Export menu command. (See "Exporting Non-Flash Formats" later in this chapter.)

FIGURE 23.11
Publish Settings: The
GIF tab.

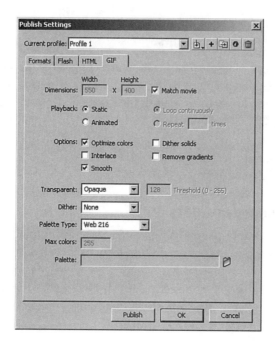

- **Animated**   Exports your entire Flash movie as an animated GIF file. If you need only a portion of your Flash movie exported, use the frame labels #first and #last to designate the frames you want exported.

- **Loop Continuously**   Sets your animated GIF to loop indefinitely.

- **Repeat *x* Times**   Sets the number of times the animated GIF loops.

- **Optimize Colors**   Removes any colors not used in the Flash movie when using a palette type other than adaptive. Can save a lot on file size.

- **Interlace**   Creates an interlaced GIF image, which means the image's resolution sharpens incrementally as it downloads. This method can reduce download time.

- **Smooth**   Anti-aliases your artwork, including text. Test with and without this option to see the results. Not recommended for transparent GIFs because halos can result.

- **Dither Solids**   Allows dithering of solid colors. This option creates a two-color pattern to mimic a color that's not available in the color palette, so it's useful for colors that might not be found in the available color palette.

- **Remove Gradients**   GIF images are not suited for gradients, so this setting allows you to remove all gradients and replace them with a solid color in your GIF. The solid color is determined by the first color in the gradient, so it's best to test this option to check the results.

- **Transparent**   Use this list box to select one of these transparency settings for your movie:

  - **Opaque**   Creates a solid background of the selected color as the background color in the Flash file.

  - **Transparent**   Creates a transparent background.

- **Alpha/Threshold**   Controls which alpha level in your Flash movie is treated as transparent in your GIF file. A level of 128 is equivalent to 50% alpha.

- **Dither**   In dithering, two colors are used in a pattern to emulate another color. This option affects file size, so make sure you compare the results for quality as well as file size when selecting a dithering option. These are the available options:

  - **None**   No dithering is applied.

  - **Ordered**   Applies medium dithering, resulting in a slight increase in file size.

  - **Diffusion**   Applies high-level dithering. Usually produces slightly better results than ordered dithering, but also results in a larger file size.

- **Palette Type**   Use this list box to select one of the following palettes:

  - **Web 216**   Uses the 216-color web palette.

  - **Adaptive**   Flash creates a custom palette for your GIF file. This usually produces better visual results, but also can result in larger file sizes. Also, the image might not be displayed correctly on older 8-bit machines.

  - **Web Snap Adaptive**   Flash creates a custom palette, using any 216 web colors it can, and converts any colors outside these 216 colors to web-safe colors.

  - **Custom**   Allows you to create a custom palette, which is in the `.act` file format.

- **Max Colors**   Allows you to specify how many colors are in the palette. Used only with Adaptive and Web Snap Adaptive palettes.

- **Palette**   Allows you to use a custom palette. Browse to the location where your custom palette will be stored (if you select the Custom option in the Palette Type drop-down list).

JPEG Image Format

You can select this format to export a JPEG image from your Flash movie, but using the Export Image command is recommended because it gives you better control of the image. With the JPEG format selected, Flash creates a JPEG tab in the Publish Settings dialog box (see Figure 23.12) and exports the first frame of your movie as a JPEG file. You can also include a #static frame label in your movie, which tells Flash to export that frame instead of the movie's first frame.

FIGURE 23.12
Publish Settings: The JPEG tab.

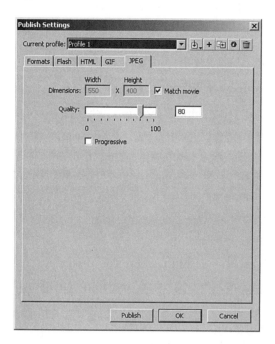

These settings are available in the JPEG tab:

- **Dimensions**   Sets the dimensions of the JPEG image. With Match Movie selected, the image has the same dimensions as your Flash movie. Deselecting this option means you can set your own width and height.

- **Quality**   Set the quality of the JPEG image. The higher the number, the better the quality, but the file size increases.

- **Progressive**   Allows the JPEG to be progressively downloaded in stages in the browser; similar to the Interlace option for a GIF image.

PNG Image Format

Selecting this format exports a PNG image when publishing your movie and creates a PNG tab in the Publish Settings dialog box (see Figure 23.13). Using the Export Image command is recommended, however, for better control of PNG images.

FIGURE 23.13
Publish Settings: The PNG tab.

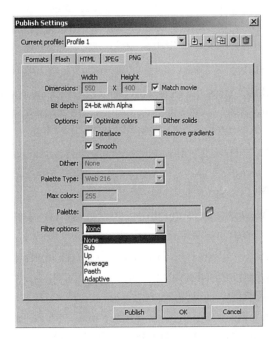

The following image settings are available in the PNG tab:

- **Dimensions**   Sets the height and width of the PNG image. The default setting is Match Movie.

- **Bit Depth**   Allows you to set the bit depth and, therefore, the number of colors in the PNG image:

  - **8-bit**   256 colors maximum. No alpha is available at this setting, but you can adjust the dither and palette type. Smallest file size, but lower image quality.

- **24-bit** Thousands of colors. Larger file size than 8-bit, but much better image quality.

- **24-bit with Alpha** Same as 24-bit, but includes an alpha channel. The image's background is rendered as an alpha channel.

- **Options** The settings in this section work the same as they do with a GIF image, as described previously.

- **Dither, Palette Type, Max Colors, Palette** These settings work the same as they do with a GIF image, as described previously. Available only for 8-bit PNGs.

- **Filter Options** Select the type of compression sampling used for your PNG image. Try some of the following options, and check the resulting image and its file size:

  - **None** No filter. Larger file size. Not recommended.

  - **Sub** Uses the difference between each pixel and the value of the pixel beside it to determine the color. Images with similar horizontal colors work best with this filter.

  - **Up** Uses the difference between each pixel and the value of the pixel above it to determine the color. Images with similar vertical colors work best with this filter.

  - **Average** Uses the difference between the left and above pixel to determine the color.

  - **Paeth** A specific formula, Paeth (yes, that's the correct spelling) uses the neighboring left, above, and upper-left pixels to determine color.

  - **Adaptive** Analyzes the entire image and creates a unique color table. The most accurate of the filters, but results in the largest file sizes.

The Projector Formats

Selecting a projector format creates a standalone file, or projector, in Windows or Macintosh format, which is ideal for distributing your Flash movie on a CD. Because it's a standalone executable file, you don't need the Flash Player, or even a browser, to use a projector file. For Windows, Flash creates an .exe file that runs on any Windows machine. For Macintosh, Flash creates a projector that runs on Mac OS X. Note that

You can also use FSCommands to pass messages to Macromedia Director, Visual Basic, Visual C++, and other programs that host ActiveX controls. As well, FSCommands enable you to communicate between a Flash movie and its host environment, as discussed in Chapter 17.

creating a Macintosh projector on a PC results in a compressed .hqx file, which requires a decompression program such as Stuffit, available from www.aladdinsys.com.

Projector files are larger than SWF files. Creating a Windows projector adds approximately 960KB to the file size. Creating a Macintosh projector (on a Macintosh machine) adds roughly 1MB to the file size; creating a Macintosh projector on a Windows machine adds about 1.4MB.

FSCommands and Projectors

FSCommands can be used to communicate between a Flash movie and its host environment, as you learned in Chapter 17, "Accessing External Data." FSCommands can also be used to add functionality to an SWF file exported as a projector (as well as an SWF being played in the standalone Flash Player). This section discusses the FSCommands specific to projectors and SWF files being played in the standalone Flash Player. FSCommands are added to your Flash movie by using the Actions panel.

This is the syntax for using an FSCommand:

```
fscommand(command, parameters)
```

Table 23.1 describes the available FSCommands.

TABLE 23.1

FSCommands Used with Projectors and SWF Movies Playing in the Flash Player

Command	Parameters	Description
quit	No parameters	Closes the projector.
fullscreen	True or false	Toggles full-screen or regular view.
allowscale	True or false	Specifies whether scaling is allowed. When set to false, the SWF does not change size. When set to true, the SWF file is forced to scale to 100% of the Player's size (in other words, the same size as the Player).
showmenu	True or false	True enables the set of context menu items. False disables all context menu items except About Flash Player.
trapallkeys	True or false	True sends all key events to the onClipEvent handler in the Flash Player.
exec	Path to application	Runs an application from within the projector.

The QuickTime Format

Use this format to export a QuickTime movie of your Flash movie (see Figure 23.14). Flash publishes a QuickTime movie in the version that's installed on your machine. QuickTime 6 and later supports all interactive features of Flash 5. For the interactivity to perform properly in QuickTime 6 format, the ActionScript must be Flash 5 compatible, and you must select Flash 5 from the Version list box in the Flash tab of the Publish Settings dialog box. If your Flash document contains a QuickTime movie, Flash creates two tracks in the published QuickTime movie: a QuickTime video track and a Flash track. Tracks, which are specific to QuickTime, are played on top of each other in QuickTime, so you can have a video playing on the bottom track while your Flash movie and ActionScript run on the top track.

FIGURE 23.14
Publish settings: The QuickTime Tab

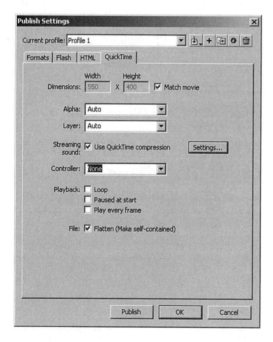

The following settings are available in the QuickTime tab:

- **Dimensions**   Sets the height and width of the QuickTime file. The default setting is Match Movie.

- **Alpha**   This setting controls how the background of your Flash movie is handled. You have the following options:

- **Auto**   Sets the Flash track to transparent if it is on top of any other tracks, but opaque if it is the bottom or the only track in the SWF file.

- **Alpha-Transparent**   Creates a transparent background for the SWF file.

- **Copy**   Makes the Flash track opaque and masks all content in the tracks behind the Flash track.

- **Layer**   Controls where the Flash track plays in the stacking order of the QuickTime movie. You can choose from these options:

  - **Auto**   Places the Flash track in front of other tracks if Flash objects are in front of video objects in your Flash movie, and behind all other tracks if Flash objects are not in front.

  - **Top**   Places the Flash track at the top of all other tracks.

  - **Bottom**   Places the Flash track at the bottom of the other tracks.

- **Streaming Sound**   Sets all sound to be a streaming audio track in QuickTime. Recompresses the audio using QuickTime audio settings. You can change these settings by clicking the Settings button.

- **Controller**   Sets the type of controller for your QuickTime movie. You have the following options:

  - **None**   No controller.

  - **Standard**   Uses the standard QuickTime controller.

  - **QuickTime VR**   Uses the QuickTime VR controller for playing back QuickTime VR files (panorama or object files).

- **Playback**   You can set the following options for playback of your movie:

  - **Loop**   Loops your movie indefinitely.

  - **Paused at Start**   Pauses the movie at the beginning. User must click the Play button to begin the movie.

  - **Play Every Frame**   Plays back every frame of your movie, but drops audio frames if the processor cannot keep up.

- **File**   Selecting the Flatten check box combines the Flash and imported video content into a single QuickTime movie. Deselecting this option makes the QuickTime movie refer to imported files externally; keep in mind that this setting causes problems if the external files are missing.

CD Tips, Tricks, and Issues

As you've seen, Flash is not just for the web. Another popular place for Flash content is on CD-ROMs. By creating a projector file from your Flash content, putting content on a CD and distributing it are very easy. The following sections offer some tips, tricks, and issues related to preparing content for CD-ROMs.

Target Processor

It's best to determine a target machine for projects being published to a CD. You need to test your project on different processors to see check the playback results. Pick a target machine with the lowest possible processor speed your project can run on, and test throughout your development to ensure that it runs acceptably on that machine.

File Size

Depending on the size of your finished Flash movie, dividing your movie into smaller segments for loading and unloading can be effective. This method improves playback on slower machines and sometimes makes it easier to work with files during authoring.

Hybrid CDs

When creating a CD, you should create one that both Macintosh and Windows users can read. To create a hybrid CD, you need the right software, and you must burn the CD from a Macintosh computer, as you cannot create a hybrid CD on a PC. Toast 6 Titanium (www.roxio.com), a popular software tool, offers a full set of features.

Auto-Start CDs

To create an auto-start CD on a Windows machine, you need to create a small text file called autorun.inf. Windows looks for this file when a CD is loaded and runs it first. The text inside this file should look like this:

```
[autorun]
open=yourfile.exe
```

yourfile.exe is the file to run (also called the "target file"). If it is an
`.exe` file, Windows will run it. If it's an HTML file, such as
`open=index.html`, it's launched in the default browser on that machine.
Make sure the target file and the `autorun.inf` file are both on the root
level of your CD.

To create an auto-starting Macintosh CD, you need to use Toast 6
Titanium or another similar software package.

Many users have disabled auto-start on their machines to guard against
viruses. Always include a readme.txt file with instructions on how to launch
your CD-ROM.

Testing CDs

A CD-ROM must be thoroughly tested on as many machines as possible
to ensure it works the way you intended. Test it on several operating systems and with different configurations, especially on lower-end machines.

Distributing and Licensing CDs

When you've created a projector and want to distribute it, Macromedia's
royalty-free licensing policy means you can distribute applications (such
as a Flash projector) free. However, you must include a "Made with
Macromedia" logo on your product's packaging or include a splash or
credits screen, and register your product with Macromedia. You can find
more information at www.macromedia.com/support/programs/mwm/.

EXPORTING NON-FLASH FORMATS

Even though Flash was designed to create SWF files, you can also export
other formats, including images, video, and audio. The following sections describe the export formats available in Flash.

The Export Image Option

Choosing File, Export, Export Image from the menu enables you to export many different image formats, both bitmap and vector (see Figure 23.15). When using the Export Image option, keep in mind that Flash exports *only* a still of the current frame in the selected format. You can easily move the playhead to select which image you want exported.

FIGURE 23.15
The Export Image menu.

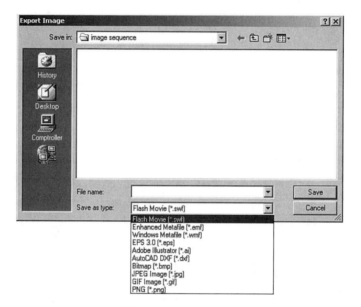

The settings available when exporting Flash, JPEG, GIF, and PNG images using the Export menu are the same ones discussed earlier in this chapter under "Publishing Your Movie." However, you'll find one more setting, Include, which has these options:

- **Minimum Image Area** This option exports only the artwork currently on stage, not necessarily the entire frame, so it could change the image dimensions. If you have only a small object on stage, the dimensions are set to export only that object, not the entire stage or frame.

- **Full Document Size** Exports the image and sets the dimensions to be the same as the document—that is, the entire frame.

The Export Movie Option

Use the File, Export, Export Movie menu option to export a range of different movie and image sequence formats (see Figure 23.16). Although these non-Flash formats are useful for specific needs, generally their file sizes are much larger than SWF files. The settings for these movies are the same as those discussed earlier under "Publishing Your Movie."

FIGURE 23.16
The Export Movie dialog box.

POINTS TO REMEMBER

- Test, and test often.

- Play your movie in the authoring environment for a quick visual test of your movie. Use the Test Movie method for a more accurate test.

- Use the bandwidth profiler in the Test Movie View menu to see how your movie plays over an Internet connection.

- You can customize and create your own publish settings and save them by using the profile settings in the Publish Settings dialog box.

- Creating a projector allows others to view your content without needing a browser or the Flash Player plug-in.

CHAPTER 24

DEVELOPING FOR POCKET DEVICES

YOU HAVE JUST FINISHED DEVELOPING A FULL-OUT FLASH APPLICATION. YOU have made sure to structure your code properly, you have made sure it's efficient, and you have made sure it works on all popular browsers. It's now ready to go! Or is it? Have you put any thought into whether your application will be viewed on something other than a personal computer? Possibly a pocket device? Is your application a good fit for a pocket or mobile device? These questions are ones you should consider (if you haven't already), but have no fear. If your application is built with Macromedia Flash MX 2004, you're probably closer than you think. This chapter shows you how to get your application displayed and working on a Pocket PC.

In this chapter, you learn what you need to take into consideration when developing for Pocket PCs. From a Flash development point of view, there are no special technical considerations for Pocket PCs. This chapter, therefore, approaches the subject from a conceptual standpoint and explains some best practices for planning, designing, and deploying Flash applications for Pocket PCs.

BACKGROUND ON DEVELOPING FOR POCKET PCS

Over the past several years, Macromedia has made the Flash Software Development Kit (SDK) available to software and hardware manufacturers, with the goal of having the Flash plug-in available for use on different types of devices. Currently, a wide variety of manufacturers, including those who produce phones, TVs, gaming consoles, and PDAs, integrate the Flash player into their product line. Because of this recent surge in manufacturers integrating Flash into their products, the days of assuming that your application will be available only for desktop computers is over. It's time to start talking about the variety of ways in which the public will be viewing your application.

Although many different types of devices support Flash, this chapter focuses on the most common and widely adopted device: the Pocket PC. There's currently a worldwide user base of about 10 million people. What does this mean to Flash developers? Of this current user base, there's a potential audience of about 7 million users who have the capability to view Flash-based applications on Pocket PCs. When you put it this way, Flash developers have a whole new market for which to develop applications. Before you get into developing for Pocket PCs, however, take a close look at Pocket PC devices.

What Is Pocket PC?

If you're new to the world of pocket devices, you might be wondering what a Pocket PC is. To put it simply, it's the Microsoft version of a personal digital assistant (PDA) and refers to both the hardware and software. Experts predict that the current number of 10 million devices in use worldwide will likely grow within the next year or two. As you can see, there's a huge audience of potential users who could be interested in viewing your application on a Pocket PC.

Pocket PC comes in two main models: Pocket PC and Pocket PC Phone Edition. Each device is similar in operating system and software specifications. Pocket PC Phone Edition, however, has all the features of Pocket PC with the added feature of phone capabilities.

There are two types of operating systems for Pocket PC: Pocket PC 2002 and the new release of Windows Mobile 2003. Many devices currently on the market include Pocket PC 2002; however, new devices are being shipped with Windows Mobile 2003. From a development point of view, developing for Pocket PC 2002 and Windows Mobile 2003 are seamless, as both versions run the Flash 6 Player.

The recent Windows Mobile 2003 release has a series of new software enhancements. These enhancements include improved Wi-Fi support, enhanced Bluetooth support, and software updates. For more information, visit www.microsoft.com/windowsmobile/.

Pocket PC also has different versions: an edition for home and office and an enterprise edition. The main differences in these two versions are hardware specifications and types of connectivity. Among different model numbers, you'll also find variations in processor speeds and RAM capacity. Generally, processor speeds range from 200MHz to 400MHz, and RAM ranges from 32 to 128 SDRAM and up to 48MB of Flash ROM. Most of the newer Pocket PC models can be upgraded as well.

An important feature of Pocket PCs is that known hardware and software standards exist for these devices. From a development point of view, having a known standard for development is an advantage. Microsoft is strict on Pocket PC specifications to prevent compatibility issues with hardware and software for developers. As a developer, knowing that every web application you develop will be viewed on a computer system with a known hardware and software specification eliminates some guesswork and makes development that much easier.

Microsoft also has a listing of Pocket PC devices per region that's useful if you know what region in the world will be interacting with your application. You can visit the Microsoft web site at www.microsoft.com/mobile/pocketpc/learnmore/hardware/default.asp for more details.

Connected and Unconnected Applications

Of the many different Pocket PC models, some have the capability to access a network wirelessly and some do not. When developing applications for Pocket PCs, remember that users have different ways of accessing content, depending on the model they're using. The following sections review the types of connectivity available to Pocket PCs.

Personal Area Networks

In a personal area network (PAN), devices can work together to share information and services. In the Pocket PC world, this is accomplished by using Bluetooth and infrared (IR) beaming. Bluetooth, a wireless technology developed by Ericsson, Nokia, Intel, and Toshiba, specifies how mobile phones, computers, and PDAs interconnect (see Figure 24.1). Data transfer rates up to 2.4 GHz are possible using Bluetooth. IR beaming can also be used when transferring files to and from Pocket PCs. This type of data transfer, shown in Figure 24.2, uses a set of protocols for infrared exchange of data between two devices in close proximity. Throughput is generally about 4Mbps.

FIGURE 24.1
The Bluetooth connection window.

FIGURE 24.2
The IR beaming connection window.

Wireless Local Area Networks

With wireless local area networks (WLANs), you can connect to a network or the Internet via a wireless Ethernet card. In the Pocket PC world, this is accomplished with a built-in wireless Ethernet or by adding an expansion pack with a CompactFlash (CF) wireless card. 802.11 Wi-Fi is the industry-standard WLAN. 802.11 currently has three standards: 801.11a (5GHz), 802.11B (2.4GHz), and 802.11g (5GHz at a closer distance than 802.11a). Browsing content via a WLAN is sometimes interrupted by latency, but generally, connection speeds are quite good.

Wireless Wide Area Networks

Wireless wide area networks (WWANs) enable users with external wireless cards to pay for a wireless Internet service and have access pretty much anywhere at any time, although location can affect access to a degree. Connection speeds vary, too, depending on your location and wireless provider, but connection speeds generally range from 2 to 34Mbps. Wireless cards are usually around $400, and monthly access fees are from $40 to $60. As costs come down and cards become cheaper, more devices will be capable of always-on connections.

There are several business reasons for having a WWAN connection to a device such as a Pocket PC. WWAN connections allow an office and a virtual employee to instantly become connected. They can allow sales personnel to have instant access to documentation sitting in an office infrastructure or even allow field engineers to instantly send back reports to a computer database with up-to-date information.

How Does Connectivity Affect Development?

Now that you understand the different types of connections, it's time to see how connectivity affects developing for pocket devices. Knowing whether the device that's viewing your application can connect to the Internet affects your decision of what functions to include.

For example, you can expand an application's functionality based on whether a Pocket PC is online. Say you've developed a Pocket PC application that's a Flash-based trip organizer for planning itineraries. Your application could enable users to store maps, locations, phone numbers, and a daily planner for use as a reference tool when on the road. On long road trips or trips that involve visiting a new city every day, users might want to know what the weather will be like. Of course, weather forecasts would be difficult to include in a static application. You could assume that users have wireless adapters for accessing weather information on the Internet, but these adapters might not work in every location; users might be in areas where wireless connectivity is an issue. You could, however, write all the application logic to dynamically pull weather information from a portal web site and send it to your application. You could have this function loaded dynamically only when the application knows the device is connected to the Internet. With the Flash 6 Player for Pocket PC, developers can access Pocket PC system resources by writing ActionScript commands.

Figure 24.3 shows the types of Pocket PC resources that can be pulled from the device. Developers can take advantage of some useful system resources when creating applications. In this figure, notice the resource called `system.capabilities.ramAvailable`. By knowing the amount of RAM that's available on a Pocket PC, you can customize the application based on the device's specifications. For example, you can write some code to see how much RAM is available on the device. If your application is RAM-intensive, you can provide an optimized version of the application to devices that can handle it and a less-RAM-intensive application to devices that have less available RAM. Another useful resource is `system.capabilities.network`. This resource lets the viewer see whether the device is attached to a network. This information is good to know, depending on whether the application needs to send live data to and from the device. By writing some conditional logic for your application, you could check to see whether the device is connected to a network and then customize the application accordingly.

When determining whether the application you're developing should reside locally on a Pocket PC or on a web server, consider whether real-time information is required for your application to function. When real-time information *is* required, as in multiplayer games, e-learning, and access to a company intranet, your application should run on a Pocket PC that's connected to the Internet. If your application doesn't require real-time information (as with single-player games, maps, and so forth), you can get away with storing the application locally on a Pocket PC. For instance, if you're traveling across the country and want to build a Flash application that stores digital maps of each state, you could get away with developing an application that doesn't need to be connected to the Internet.

FIGURE 24.3
Viewing system resources.

DEVELOPING FLASH FOR POCKET PCs

The Flash 6 Player for Pocket PC is a fully functional version of the popular Flash Player that has been optimized specifically for Pocket PCs. Developing and exporting applications to Pocket PCs is easier now with the Flash 6 Player. Flash developers can now take advantage of the features and benefits of Pocket PCs. This player is available for download at www.macromedia.com/software/Flashplayer/pocketpc/.

An advantage of developing Flash for Pocket PCs is the small footprint of the user plug-in required to play the application. When developing Flash applications for traditional media (personal computers and browsers), you can offer rich content with a plug-in that's roughly 1,030KB, which keeps download time to a minimum for users, if they don't already have the plug-in installed on their systems. With the Flash 6 Player for Pocket PC, this small footprint is even more crucial because of the limited storage space on pocket devices. The current Flash 6 plug-in is 471KB and acts much like an ActiveX plug-in after it's installed.

Why Develop for Pocket PCs?

There are many different reasons to develop for Pocket PCs, and they all depend on what you use Flash for. Do you develop Flash as a hobby?

Are you learning Flash in school? Do you focus your time in Flash to work on personal projects? Do you use Flash to develop applications for clients? In a nutshell, if you're interested in having a portable version of your Flash application, developing for Pocket PCs is a good option for you. If you're building an application in Flash, migrating it to the Pocket PC world is easier than you might think.

Several development tools are available to help you. They are built right into the Flash authoring environment. You can create a Pocket PC canvas using existing templates. New to Flash 2004 are a series of 22 templates for developing Flash content for pocket devices; six of these new templates are specifically for Pocket PC. These templates include the option to render text full screen and determine when the soft input panel is open.

This is a great place to start, so open Flash now and take a look at how this tool works.

Creating a Pocket PC Work Area with the Flash Authoring Environment

1. Choose File, New from the main menu.

2. This dialog box has two tabs to choose from: General and Templates. Click Templates.

3. In the list of options under Category, click Mobile Devices (see Figure 24.4).

FIGURE 24.4
Template options for pocket devices.

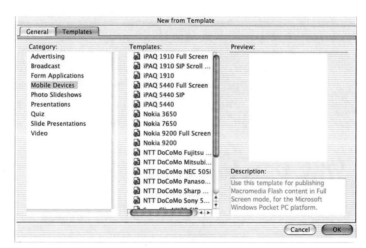

4. You have 22 different device templates to choose from. Select IPAQ 5440 and click OK. The authoring environment changes to the Pocket PC publishing template (see Figure 24.5).

FIGURE 24.5
The Pocket PC IPAQ 5440 template.

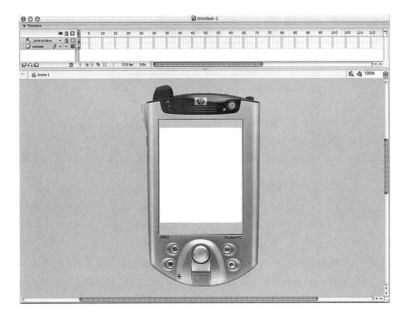

5. Take a look at the canvas size you'll be working with. Choose Modify, Document from the main menu (or simply view the document dimensions in the Property inspector). Notice that the canvas size is 240 (width) by 268 (height).

The canvas you have to work with is small, but that's part of the wonderful world of developing for pocket devices. More information on this topic is covered in the next section. Flash templates provide a graphic of mobile device interfaces, such as the IPAQ 5440, on the Device guide layer so that you have a visual context as you work—very helpful when designing on a small canvas.

6. Using the Text tool, select the content layer and create the text Hello World on the stage.

7. Change the font to Arial and font size to 20, and then edit the text to Pocket PC Hello World on the stage.

8. Next, choose Control, Test Movie from the main menu (keyboard shortcut: **Ctrl+Enter**). You'll see a real-life representation of the canvas area you need to work with for your application to be viewable on a Pocket PC (see Figure 24.6).

FIGURE 24.6
Your first Pocket PC "Hello World."

You have just created your first Flash movie optimized for Pocket PCs. As you can see, there's not a lot of room to work with when the template size is this small, so screen real estate is a crucial usability issue for Pocket PCs.

Usability Issues with Pocket PCs

One of the most challenging aspects of developing for any device is the effect of limited screen real estate on usability. Usability is key when designing anything that humans interact with and goes far beyond mere functionality. People interact with objects based on circumstances and past experiences that are out of the developer's control. For example, when you enter an office building and want to go to the 15th floor, you take the elevator. When interacting with an elevator, you know that the button for the elevator is next to the door and that the arrow button pointing up triggers the elevator to open the door, allowing you to enter and choose a destination. You do all this without thinking about it; it's just common sense. You don't need a how-to manual hanging beside each elevator button. You simply know how to interact with an elevator based on your past experiences.

This example might sound oversimplified, but it illustrates the native instinct of humans to interact with objects based on comfort and common sense. When designing any application, you need to take this usability factor into account to design an application that functions the way users expect. In the Pocket PC world, this is even more of a challenge.

When users are interacting with a device, they could be in the middle of doing anything, anywhere. For example, many people buy mobile devices to have information when they're on the go. For people who travel often or salespeople who are out of the office often, having a device that can keep you connected with people around you is a valuable resource. Pocket devices are used in many different settings, too—while stuck in traffic, on an airplane, in a sales meeting, and so on. In these situations, users don't have the time to determine how the application works and how to retrieve information. They need to instantly understand how the application works, get what they need quickly, and get out as fast as possible. In other words, users rely on their own common sense when searching for and finding information on pocket devices.

As a developer, you need to think about these scenarios when developing for pocket devices. You can't assume that the user will be looking at a computer monitor and sitting down in a relatively controlled environment when interacting with your application. The following sections outline how you can design for an application's usability factor based on a user's level of common sense—in other words, design applications to be as usable and easy to figure out as possible.

Screen Resolution and Text Input

When developing applications for Pocket PCs, you need to consider screen resolution. As a rule of thumb, a canvas created at 240×240 centers the application within the window without needing to scroll. Figure 24.7 shows an application displayed in the Internet Explorer window on a Pocket PC.

After selecting the correct screen resolution for a pocket device, you need to consider navigation in Pocket PCs to determine how users will be viewing and interacting with your application. The main method of interaction with a Pocket PC is with a stylus, which is used for tasks such as making notes, clicking URLs, and typing text in a word processing application or an HTML form. Typing on a Pocket PC is not the same as typing on a computer keyboard, however. With Pocket PCs, you can use character recognition software that converts handwriting to text (see

Figure 24.8). Another input method is using the onscreen keyboard to enter text (see Figure 24.9). From an interface point of view, you need to realize that users might be entering text in multiple ways and provide an interface that accommodates different means of text input.

FIGURE 24.7
A simple interface displayed on a Pocket PC. Note that scrolling isn't necessary to see the entire window.

FIGURE 24.8
The Letter Recognizer for text input in Pocket PCs.

FIGURE 24.9
The onscreen keyboard for Pocket PCs.

Whatever input method users choose, displaying the character recognition interface or the onscreen keyboard consumes screen real estate. Therefore, you need to think about factors such as button placement. If the application interface had a critical button in the lower part of the window, the text entry area in Pocket PCs would hide this button, causing a huge usability problem. Remember that something that looks cool might not be usable for people interacting with your device.

Macromedia Flash 6 for Pocket PC Content Development Kit

An excellent resource for designers and developers is the Macromedia Flash 6 for Pocket PC Content Development Kit. This free resource, available for download at www.macromedia.com/devnet/devices/development_kits.html, is a suite of resources aimed at designers and developers. It includes best practices, documentation, and sample applications. The kit is divided into the following sections:

- **Macromedia Flash MX Content Development Kit for Pocket PC 2002**   This section covers tips, techniques, and sample code for developing Flash content for Pocket PCs.

- **Macromedia Flash MX Interface Development Kit for Pocket PC 2002**   This section covers tips, techniques, and sample code for developing user interfaces (UIs) for the Pocket PC 2002 platform. The resources in this section can help you work around usability issues with Pocket PCs.

- **Components**   This section includes prebuilt movie clips that simplify handling common tasks or user interface elements.

Because of the screen real-estate issue with Pocket PCs, you must be careful with interface components. Macromedia has created some simple drag-and-drop components optimized for Pocket PCs that enable you to develop applications quickly and easily. The Flash UI components are CheckBox, ComboBox, ListBox, RadioButton, and ScrollBar. You can use these components to build highly interactive and fast applications for Pocket PCs. This development kit offers great resources for people with all different levels of experience to develop Pocket PC applications.

Tips and Tricks

The following sections cover some best practices for developing Pocket PC applications.

Follow a Process Workflow

Developing applications for Pocket PCs doesn't mean you don't need to follow standard development processes. Although there are some differences when developing for Pocket PCs, remember that it's still Flash and it's still a web production. Using a process workflow that works for you and following standard production practices still apply when developing for Pocket PCs.

Alias Text Support

Because devices have small display areas, developers are forced to use small but legible font sizes when presenting content onscreen. Often, this results in a font that's blurry and difficult to read. Developers now have the option to render text by using the Alias Text button (see Figure 24.10).

FIGURE 24.10
Use the Alias Text button to render text.

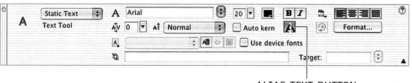

ALIAS TEXT BUTTON

With this option, mobile developers can render text with small font sizes. It makes small text more readable by aligning text outlines along pixel boundaries. Although the Flash 7 Player allows aliasing for static, dynamic, and input text, Pocket PC still uses the Flash 6 Player, so aliasing is supported only for static text.

Optimize Your Application for Pocket PCs

Flash is Flash, whether you view it on a PC or a pocket device. Technically, you can have your PC-optimized Flash site displayed on a Pocket PC, so why worry about formatting specifically for Pocket PCs? In this section, you'll take a look at a sample videoconferencing application that has been developed in Flash. In this demonstration, you'll see an application that has been optimized for both PCs and pocket devices so that you can understand the decisions to be made for useful display and functionality in each medium. Figure 24.11 shows the application viewed on a PC.

FIGURE 24.11
A sample Flash site viewed on a PC.

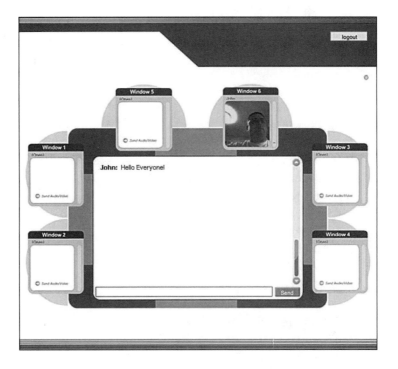

Before continuing, you need to know that you can determine whether a user accessing your web application is viewing it on a PC or a device. Having this information ahead of time is crucial so that you can add code directing viewers to different versions of the same application, depending on what medium they're using to view the application. On your application's physical server (the computer that holds your web files) is a service for rendering web content. If your web server is in the Windows world, the service is Internet Information Services (IIS); in the Linux world, it's Apache. These services are constantly running on your web server. When a user browses to your application, a file (or multiple files) is called and your web server goes to work. In simple terms, your web server gets the request that a file has been called, looks at the file type to see what it is, and returns the file's content to the browser.

When a web server receives a request, it checks to see what type of browser is requesting the file. All web servers have a directory containing details on the types of browsers available on the market. This information is stored in a file residing on your web server. In Windows, this file, called browsercap.ini, sits in the Inetsrv folder. Included in this folder are details for Pocket Internet Explorer (Pocket IE). The web server checks these details to determine what to do with the content. The following code is an example of Pocket IE's description in the Windows browsercap.ini file:

```
; Pocket IE
[Microsoft Pocket Internet Explorer/0.6]
browser=PIE
Version=1.0
majorver=1
minorver=0
frames=FALSE
tables=TRUE
cookies=FALSE
backgroundsounds=TRUE
vbscript=FALSE
javascript=FALSE
javaapplets=FALSE
ActiveXControls=FALSE
Win16=False
beta=False
AK=False
SK=False
AOL=False
platform=WinCE
```

Now that you know how a web server recognizes content and browsers hitting your application, you need to know how to present a customized Flash application based on whether a PC or device is requesting the file. To do this, you can use a middleware scripting language and write some conditional logic to see what browser is hitting the application and then direct the viewer to the correct application. The following code is an example of how you can do this in ColdFusion:

```
<!---Get the user agent from the request sent by the browser. ->

<cfset DeviceType="#CGI.http_USER_AGENT#">
<cfset isPocketPC = false>
```

```
<!---check to see if the string contains PocketPC ->

<cfif (find("PPC", #DeviceType# GT 0)>
<cfset isPocketPC = true>
</cfif>

<cfif isPocketPC>
    <cflocation url="success.html">
<cfalse>
You are not connected to a Pocket PC device!
```

Next, you need to think about how you can use this conditional logic in an application. The following discussion explains why it's necessary to optimize an application for Pocket PC and how to do it. The example uses a videoconferencing application built in Flash that needs to be usable on both PCs and Pocket PCs. Figure 24.12 shows the same application you saw in Figure 24.11, but now it's running on a Pocket PC connected to the Internet.

FIGURE 24.12
The same video-conferencing application, optimized for Pocket PC.

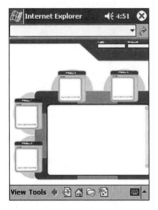

This application functions on a Pocket PC, but it fails in the area of usability. First, to see the entire application, you need to get out your stylus and adjust the IE scrollbar horizontally and vertically, which can be frustrating for users. Second, the information that's most viewable in the application is probably the least important information to the viewer. There's no way to easily log in and log out of the application. Also, the application is off-center and only a portion of the video screens can be seen. The viewer can't fully use the chat component, either.

When you develop an application for a Pocket PC device, chances are that users have a specific need for using the application. In the example shown in Figure 24.11, the Pocket PC user is logging in to a videoconferencing application. The user might have a wireless WAN card and be logging into a meeting virtually, or could be on an internal network—say, on a film set, communicating with the production crew via a video-conference.

Because of an operating system limitation with Pocket PC, it's not possible to encode video streams through the Flash Player, so there's no point to including the video component because it would take up valuable screen real estate and be confusing to users if they assumed video streaming was possible. You can, however, have a low-bandwidth audio stream sent to the application. In this example, because of screen real estate and bandwidth, streaming video of just the conference organizer (the director or crew manager, for example) would optimize the application for Pocket PC. Because typing can be cumbersome on a Pocket PC and text input areas take up valuable screen real estate, you can take that component out. How would the Pocket PC user interact with the conference, then? With Pocket PCs, you can stream out audio through the Flash Player, so adding an audio conference component to the application enables the user to talk to people in the conference. Basically, you're creating a cool walkie-talkie! Figure 24.13 shows the same application optimized for Pocket PCs.

FIGURE 24.13
Optimizing the user interface for Pocket PCs.

The Future of Pocket PC Development

You can build powerful applications for Pocket PCs by using Flash. Pocket PC development is still, however, a new frontier in many aspects. As Pocket PC use becomes more widespread, more developers will begin creating Flash-based content for Pocket PCs, and the Flash Player could be installed in pocket devices as a built-in component, which means users wouldn't have to go to the Internet and download the plug-in to use Flash content.

To help Pocket PC development become more popular, consider sharing your applications with the development community. Many sites showcase Pocket PC applications. An excellent resource is Macromedia Devnet, located at www.macromedia.com/devnet/devices/. If you're developing Pocket PC applications, make sure to let the development community know about it!

POINTS TO REMEMBER

- Usability is the number-one challenge when developing applications for Pocket PC.

- Make sure to spend time creating a usable interface.

- People want to spend time experiencing your application, not trying to figure it out.

- While developing your application, test often, especially on the targeted device if you know what it is beforehand.

- Have others who aren't familiar with your application test its usability.

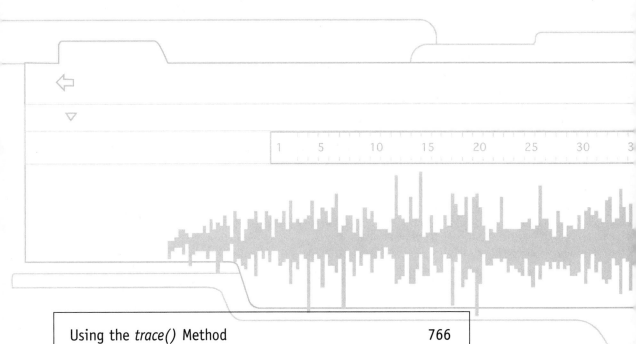

CHAPTER 25

TROUBLESHOOTING

SO YOU'VE DESIGNED AND PROGRAMMED YOUR FLASH APPLICATION. IT WORKS much the way you intended, except that every so often, something doesn't work as expected. If something untoward is happening in your application, chances are you have a bug.

A bug, in programming terms, is an error. If you find a bug in your application, you need to squash it just like you'd squash a bug you find in your kitchen. In this chapter, you learn some recommended methods for troubleshooting your application:

- Using the trace() method

- Using the Error class and try..catch..finally statements

- Using the Flash Debugger

Using the *trace()* Method

As you learned earlier in this book, the trace() method displays information in the Output panel during runtime (within the authoring environment). It uses the following syntax:

```
trace(message);
```

message is the statement to display in the Output panel. You can use any type of information for this parameter: a text string, a number, an expression, an object, or a property of an object.

To combine multiple statements into a single trace() command, use the + operator, as shown here:

```
trace("Username is " + username);
```

If the username variable is equal to bob, this line would display the following in the Output panel:

```
Username is bob
```

The trace() method is frequently used to highlight specific information at runtime. For example, suppose you have an application that positions a movie clip on the stage based on a number calculated by the position of other objects onscreen. For some reason the movie clip to be positioned always winds up off the screen. You could use trace() to view the position of the movie clip or the result of the calculated position of other objects. Say you're using the following code, which is giving you errors:

```
// determine the average x position of 3 movie clips
var avgPosX = (clip1._x + clip2._x - clip3._x)/3;

// determine the average y position of 3 movie clips
var avgPosY = (clip1._y + clip2._y + clip3._y)/3;

// set the position of myClip
myClip._x = avgPosX;
myClip._y = avgPosY;
```

You could trace the averaged values into this code, as shown here:

```
// determine the average x position of three movie clips
var avgPosX = (clip1._x + clip2._x - clip3._x)/3;

// determine the average y position of three movie clips
var avgPosY = (clip1._y + clip2._y + clip3._y)/3;

// set the position of myClip
myClip._x = avgPosX;
myClip._y = avgPosY;
trace("x average = " + avgPosX);
trace("y average = " + avgPosY);
```

If you test your movie with these traces added, in the Output panel, you would see the average of the object positions and, therefore, the position you're setting the myClip movie clip to. If you use the following code:

```
clip1 is at x 23, y 120,
clip2 is at x 100, y 140,
clip3 is at x 300, y 160,
```

You would expect the this code to yield the following results:

```
X average = 141
Y average = 140
```

However, this is the actual output:

```
X average = -59
Y average = 140
```

How could this be? Has mathematics folded in on itself? The x values aren't being averaged correctly. Take another look at this line of code to see if you can spot the error:

```
// determine the average x position of 3 movie clips
var avgPosX = (clip1._x + clip2._x - clip3._x)/3;
```

The problem is that the code adds clip1._x and clip2._x and then *subtracts* clip3._x. No wonder myClip is being placed incorrectly. Correct the code as shown here:

```
// determine the average x position of 3 movie clips
var avgPosX = (clip1._x + clip2._x + clip3._x)/3;
```

If you test the movie again, it should work perfectly, without any bugs.

> A word about the Output panel: If your script generates any errors during run-time (such as a with() statement targeting a nonexistent movie clip), or if script formatting errors are generated during compile time, these messages are displayed in the Output panel, in much the same way a trace() method is.

Using the *Error* Class and *try...catch...finally* Statements

Another handy way to troubleshoot your application is to use the new Error class with the try {} function. The Error class contains information about errors that occur in your script. You create an instance of Error manually, typically within a try {} code block, which is then "thrown" to a catch {} or a finally {} code block. The Error class contains two properties:

- **message**   The description of the error

- **name**   The name of the Error object

Additionally, the Error class contains one method, toString(), which produces a text string representing information contained in the Error object.

A typical usage of Error involves checking values or a condition in your movie and creating a new error message if the values don't match what your program requires. For example, suppose you have a function that displays the properties of an object representing a TextArea component. This function does so only if an object has been passed to it, so before blindly displaying the contents of your object, you check the type of the parameter passed to this function:

```
function dispProperties(obj) {
    if (typeof obj != "object") {
        // obj is not an object. generate an error object
        throw new Error("Incorrect data type!");
    } else {
        // code to display object properties
    }
}
```

As you can see, the code checks the condition and, if necessary, generates a new `Error` object (specifying the message in the constructor) and throws it to a `catch {}` code block. You might notice, however, that there's no `catch {}` block, but it will be added soon. First, however, you have to call the `dispProperties()` function from within a `try {}` code block so that if an error is produced, there's something to catch it:

```
try {
    dispProperties("hello");
}
```

All this code does is call the function. You still need to add something to catch the generated error:

```
try {
    dispProperties("hello");
} catch (newError) {
    trace(newError.message);
}
```

If an error is generated, the code traces the `Error` object's message to the Output panel. A benefit of using the `Error` class is that it gives you a quick, convenient way to be aware of the state of your code. It shows you exactly where errors are originating.

In addition to catching errors, you can use the `finally` condition of `try...catch...finally`. The `finally {}` code block is placed after the `catch` (or after the `try` if no `catch` is specified) and is carried out regardless of whether an error is found. The `finally` block is guaranteed to run and can contain code for cleanup processing or for releasing resources that are no longer needed, such as remote connections. In the previous example, suppose you want to trace the fact that the condition was tested, no matter what the outcome of the test is. You would modify the code like this:

```
try {
    dispProperties("hello");
} catch (newError) {
    trace(newError.message);
} finally {
    trace("Checking typeof in dispProperties");
}
```

When used wisely, this method is a powerful way to troubleshoot your applications. It enables you to test for specific error conditions and trap those errors in a structured, organized way.

Don't forget a simple check you can do at any time on your ActionScript: The Check Syntax method (keyboard shortcut: **Ctrl+T**) verifies whether ActionScript code is accurate.

Another important aspect of creating content in Flash is making sure that externally loaded files load and play properly over networks. Flash MX 2004 lets you simulate downloads at different speeds, which allows you to test for any potential errors or conflicts when loading external content or your main SWF file. For more information on this subject, refer to Chapter 23, "Publishing."

THE FLASH DEBUGGER

Aside from using trace() and the Error class to troubleshoot your applications, you can use the Debugger, shown in Figure 25.1. The Debugger is a panel that shows a continuously updated hierarchical list of all movie clips currently loaded in the Flash Player. You can use the Debugger to display and modify variable and property values while your movie is playing.

FIGURE 25.1
The Flash Debugger.

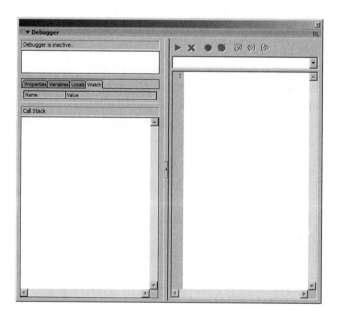

You can use the Debugger to troubleshoot both local (on your machine) and remote (at another location, either over a network or over the Internet) Flash movies, as explained in the following sections.

Locally Debugging a Movie

To debug a file locally, open the `.fla` file in Flash, and choose Control, Debug Movie from the menu (keyboard shortcut: **Ctrl+Shift+Enter**). Testing your movie in Debug mode opens the Debugger window on top of your content, as shown in Figure 25.2.

FIGURE 25.2
Viewing the output in the Debugger window.

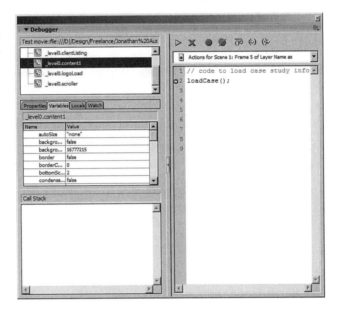

Notice in Figure 25.2 that the movie has been paused. To begin playback, you click the Play button (the green arrow button). A detailed explanation of how to use the Debugger is included in the section "Viewing Information in the Debugger," later in this chapter.

Remotely Debugging a Movie

You can debug a remote Flash movie by using the standalone, ActiveX, or plug-in versions of Flash Player. You must enable debugging when you export your Flash movie. If you don't, you won't be able to remotely debug your movie.

When you export your movie, you can set a password so that only selected people can debug your movie. This is a very good idea if you have any valuable trade secrets or you want to keep the specifics of your movie's structure private.

When you export, publish, or test a movie, Flash creates an SWD file containing debug information. To debug remotely, you must place the SWD file in the same folder as the SWF file on the server.

You can remotely debug only movies that have been created with the version of Flash you're using. For example, if you're using Flash MX 2004, you can remotely debug only movies that were published for Flash Player 7.

Enable Remote Debugging

To enable remote debugging for your Flash movie (which must be done for each movie you want to debug), simply do the following:

1. Choose File, Publish Settings from the menu.

2. In the Publishing Settings dialog box, select the Flash tab. In the Options section, select the Debugging Permitted check box (see Figure 25.3).

FIGURE 25.3
Enabling remote debugging.

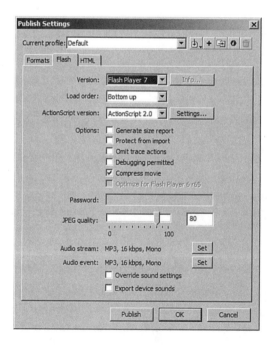

3. When you select Debugging Permitted, the Password text box is enabled. This is where you enter the password for debugging. If you don't need a password, you can leave this field blank.

4. Close the Publish Settings dialog box, and select one of the following menu commands:

   Control, Debug Movie

   File, Export Movie

   File, Publish Settings, Publish

Flash creates a debugging file with the file extension .swd and saves it alongside the SWF file. The SWD file contains information that allows you to use breakpoints and step-through code.

To enable remote debugging, you must place the generated SWD file in the same directory on the server as the SWF file. If you don't, you can still debug, but the Debugger ignores breakpoints, and you won't be able to step through your code.

Finally, open the Debugger panel in Flash. Click the button at the upper right of the panel, and select Enable Remote Debugging from the menu.

Activate the Debugger from a Remote Location

Now that your SWF file is configured for debugging and Flash is ready to remotely debug, you have to activate the Debugger from your remote location. To do this, first make sure Flash is running. Next, open the SWF in a browser (or standalone player) from its remote location. For example, if your movie myfile.swf is on the www.myserver.com server, you need to open www.myserver.com/myfile.swf. After opening the SWF file, the Remote Debug dialog box should open (see Figure 25.4).

FIGURE 25.4
The Remote Debug dialog box.

If the Remote Debug dialog box *doesn't* appear, it means the SWD file couldn't be found. Never fear—you can still debug your movie, although with a more limited feature set. To do this, right-click (Windows) or Control-click (Macintosh) somewhere on the movie, and select Debugger from the list of options (see Figure 25.5).

FIGURE 25.5
Manually activating the Remote Debugger.

When the Remote Debug dialog box opens, you're asked where the Flash 2004 authoring tool is running. Your options are Localhost and Other Machine. Select Localhost if the Debugger and the Flash authoring application are on the same computer; if they're not, select Other Machine. Enter the IP address of the computer running the Flash authoring application.

Next, click OK, and Flash attempts to make a connection between the SWF file and Flash. When this connection is established, a password prompt appears, where you enter the debugging password you set. If you didn't set a password, click OK to launch the Debugger.

Viewing Information in the Debugger

When the Debugger starts, information about the movie is displayed. The following sections describe the information available in the Debugger.

The Variables Tab

The Variables tab, shown in Figure 25.6, displays the names and values of any global and Timeline variables in your movie. You can edit these variables, and any changes you make are reflected immediately in your movie. This tab is useful if you want to test programmed functionality, such as a proximity detection script. To display a variable in the Variables tab, click the movie clip in the display list (the hierarchical list at the top left) containing the variable, and then click the Variables tab.

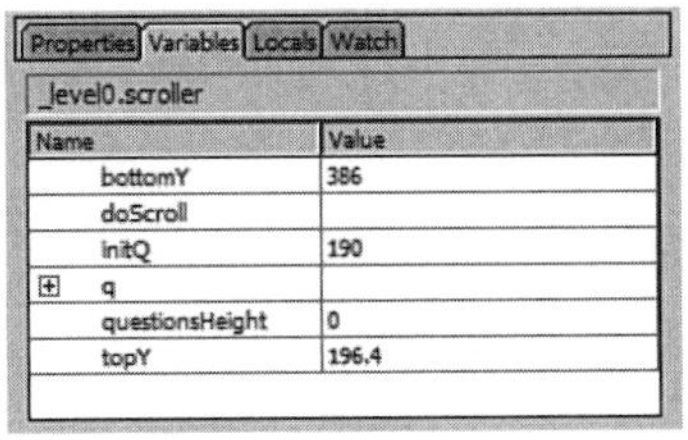

FIGURE 25.6
The Variables tab.

Properties	Variables	Locals	Watch

_level0.scroller

Name	Value
bottomY	386
doScroll	
initQ	190
⊞ q	
questionsHeight	0
topY	196.4

At the top of the display list is a movie clip named _global. Click it to view global variables and properties.

You'll see all variables within the scope of the selected movie clip. If the movie clip being viewed is removed from the Timeline, it's also removed from the display list, and the corresponding variables are removed, too.

To edit a variable, double-click the variable's value, and enter a new value. Note that when you enter a new value for a variable, it can't be an expression. For example, entering bob or 50 is valid, but you can't enter y * 3. The value can be a string, a number, or a Boolean value, but you can't enter object or array values.

The Locals Tab

The Locals tab in the Debugger displays the names and values of local variables that are available when the movie has stopped at a breakpoint or anywhere else within a user-defined function. In other words, if you halt playback of your movie while a function is being carried out, any variables local to that function are displayed in the Locals tab.

The Properties Tab

Select the Properties tab (see Figure 25.7) to view all properties of a movie clip on the stage. The properties shown in the Debugger can be edited, which means you can enter a new value in the Debugger and see how it affects the movie as it's running. If a property is read-only, however, you can't change it. To change a property in the Debugger, follow these steps:

1. First, select a movie clip from the display list.

2. Click the Properties tab to see a current list of properties for the movie clip.

3. To edit a value, double-click it and enter your new value.

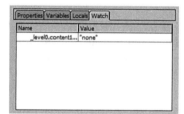

The same restrictions for variable values you can enter in the Variables tab apply to what you can enter in the Properties tab.

The Watch Tab

With a large number of variables and objects active at any given time, it's hard to keep track of everything in the Debugger, and making sense of the variables you need to keep track of can be difficult. To this end, the Debugger has a Watch tab (see Figure 25.8), where you can earmark specific variables in a sort of Favorites list.

You can add only variables to the Watch tab, not properties or functions. If you add a local variable to the Watch tab, it's displayed only if the Debugger has halted playback in the section of code where the local variable resides. Also, if you add a variable name the Debugger can't identify, the value is shown as undefined.

There are two ways to add variables to the Watch tab:

- In the Variables or Locals tab, right-click (Macintosh: Control-click) a variable, and choose Watch. A blue dot appears beside the variable to indicate that it's been added to the Watch tab.

- In the Watch tab, right-click (Windows) or Control-click (Macintosh) anywhere in the white area, and choose Add. A new entry is added under the Name column. Double-click this entry, and type in the new variable to monitor. Press Enter, and the Debugger enters this variable's changed value under the Value column.

If you no longer need to monitor a variable in the Watch tab, you can remove it by right-clicking (Macintosh: Control-clicking) and choosing Remove.

Using Breakpoints

A *breakpoint* enables you to stop your movie at a specific line of ActionScript to test possible trouble spots in your code. For example, if you've written a set of if...else statements and can't determine which code block is running, you can add a breakpoint before the statements and step through them one by one in the Debugger. For internal scripts, you can set breakpoints in the Actions panel or in the Debugger. For external scripts, you must use the Debugger.

You can enter breakpoints in two different places: in the Actions panel at author time and in the Debugger at runtime. Breakpoints set in the Actions panel are saved with the Flash document (the FLA file). Breakpoints set in the Debugger aren't saved in the FLA file and are valid only for the current debugging session. To set or remove a breakpoint in the Actions panel, follow these steps:

1. Click in the left margin, beside the line of code you want to add a breakpoint to. Clicking an existing breakpoint removes it.

2. Click the Debug Options button at the top of the Actions panel.

3. With the cursor on the line of code where you want to add or remove a breakpoint, right-click (Macintosh: Control-click), and choose Set Breakpoint, Remove Breakpoint, or Remove All Breakpoints.

4. With the cursor on the line of code where you're adding or removing a breakpoint, press **Ctrl+Shift+B** (Windows) or **Command+Shift+B** (Macintosh).

Clicking in the left margin of the Actions panel to set a breakpoint is new to Flash MX 2004. In Flash MX, clicking the left margin selects that line of code. To do this in Flash MX 2004, hold down the Ctrl (Windows) or Command (Macintosh) key and click the margin.

To set or remove breakpoints in the Debugger, follow these steps:

1. Click in the left margin. A red dot indicates the breakpoint.

2. Click the Toggle Breakpoint or Remove All Breakpoints button at the top of the Debugger's Script pane.

3. Right-click (Macintosh: Control-click) the corresponding line of code, and choose Breakpoint, Remove Breakpoint, or Remove All Breakpoints.

4. Press **Ctrl+Shift+B** (Windows) or **Command+Shift+B** (Macintosh).

After the Flash Player has stopped at a breakpoint, you can step over, step into, or step out of that line of code. If you have set a breakpoint at a comment or an empty line in the Actions panel, the Flash Player ignores the breakpoint and continues playing.

Stepping Through Your Code

If you have tested a movie in Debug mode, you'll notice that the movie is paused at first. If breakpoints have been set (through the Actions panel), you click Continue, and your ActionScript keeps running until it reaches a breakpoint. For example, suppose a breakpoint is set inside a movie clip on the line myFunc();. When you debug your movie, the breakpoint is reached, and the Flash Player pauses. You can then step in to bring the Debugger to the first line of myFunc() wherever it's defined in the document.

If you haven't set breakpoints in the Actions panel, you can use the Jump menu, shown in Figure 25.9, in the Debugger to select any script in the movie. After selecting a script, you can add breakpoints to it and then click the Continue button to resume running your code.

As you step through lines of code, the values of variables and properties change in the Variables, Locals, Properties, and Watch tabs. A breakpoint icon (see Figure 25.9) along the left side of the Debugger's Script pane indicates the line at which the Debugger stopped. You can control the debugging process by using the buttons at the top, above the Jump menu.

These are the buttons you can use:

- **Step In** Advances the Debugger (the breakpoint icon indicates the currently selected line of code) into a function. Step In works only for user-defined functions. In the following code example, if you place a breakpoint at line 7 and click Step In, the Debugger advances to line 2. A subsequent click of Step In advances you to line 3. Clicking Step In for lines that don't have user-defined functions advances the Debugger over a line of code. For example, if you stop at line 2 and click Step In, the Debugger advances to line 3:

```
1 function myFunction() {
2 x = 0;
3 y = 0;
4 }
5
6 mover = 1;
7 myFunction();
8 mover = 0;
```

- **Step Out**   Advances the Debugger out of a function. This button works only if you're currently stopped in a user-defined function; it moves the breakpoint icon to the line after the one where that function was called. If you click Step Out at a line that isn't within a user-defined function, it's the same as clicking Continue. For example, if you stop at line 6 and click Step Out, the Player continues running the script until it encounters a breakpoint.

- **Step Over**   Advances the Debugger over a line of code. This button moves the breakpoint icon to the next line in the script and ignores any user-defined functions. In the preceding example, if you stop at line 7 and click Step Over, you go directly to line 8, and myFunction() is ignored.

- **Continue**   Leaves the line where the Player is stopped and continues playing until reaching a breakpoint.

- **Stop Debugging**   Makes the Debugger inactive but continues to play the movie in Flash Player.

FIGURE 25.9
The Debugger Jump menu.

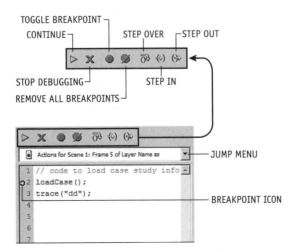

POINTS TO REMEMBER

- You can use trace( ) to display information in the Output panel.

- The new Error class enables you to troubleshoot code in a highly efficient, structured way.

- Using the Flash Debugger, you can track the state of your applications at runtime and track all the variables and properties being used.

- The Flash Debugger can be used for local and remote files.

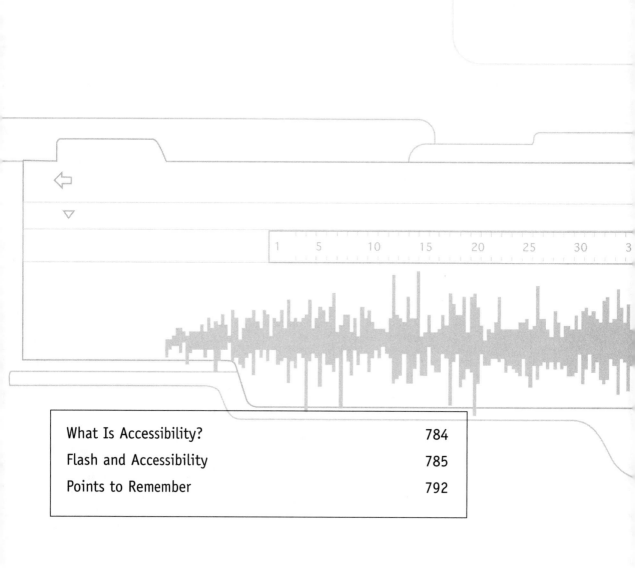

1 5 10 15 20 25 30 3

CHAPTER 26

ACCESSIBILITY

ACCESSIBILITY. IT SEEMS WE'RE HEARING MORE ABOUT IT THESE DAYS, AND for good reason. As technology continues to progress, barriers for people with disabilities are slowly being removed. Ever since eyeglasses were invented, opportunities for people with vision disabilities have increased dramatically. With wheelchairs, ramps, elevators, and other devices, people with mobility disabilities are able to move around and go places that weren't accessible to them previously. When it comes to the web, visitors with vision, motor, or auditory disabilities face certain barriers and challenges; incorporating accessibility features into your applications can improve these users' experiences.

Accessibility in digital content continues to make strides, with more information and tools available to users with special needs. This chapter explores accessibility as it relates to Flash and shows how developers can improve accessibility to their web applications and make a difference in overcoming some of the barriers faced by people with disabilities.

WHAT IS ACCESSIBILITY?

Accessibility involves two key issues: how users with disabilities can access information, and how developers and designers can create content that is more accessible to those with disabilities. Disabilities can be categorized as *visual, hearing, cognitive,* and *motor* impairments. After determining what areas in your application might cause a problem in these categories, you need to take two more steps: Identify what assistive technologies and tools would help people with disabilities use your application, and remove obstacles to your application's content or incorporate content that can be accessed with assistive technologies and tools.

Accessibility is important for the following reasons:

- **It's the right thing to do**   The benefits of making your applications accessible to users with disabilities are huge—assisting them in gaining independence, giving them access to information and services, offering a broader range of employment opportunities, and increasing communication opportunities. It just make sense to consider accessibility guidelines in Flash development.

- **It's good business**   If I owned a store, I would want as many customers as possible to be able to visit. That means I'd want a door wide enough for wheelchair access, my elevators to have Braille writing and verbal cues, my stairs to have a ramp for wheelchairs, and so forth. By *not* having access for people with disabilities, you're cutting off potential customers—or, if you're developing web applications, potential site visitors. This is simply bad business, because you're limiting your audience, which equates to lost revenue.

- **It's the law**   Canada, the United States, and European countries are introducing national accessibility requirements that will make certain accessibility features on the web mandatory. It has already started in the United States with Section 508, which has set web page standards for federal agencies and state and local governments. By starting early and progressing in stages, you can avoid a complete overhaul of your site when new laws are passed in your country.

 The World Wide Web Consortium (W3C) is developing accessibility standards that consist of 14 guidelines, each with three checkpoints for developers. You can find more information at www.w3.org/TR/WCAG/.

508 Explained

Section 508 of the U.S. Rehabilitation Act mandated that all U.S. federal agencies make their websites accessible by June 21, 2001. Even though accessibility policies vary between countries, Section 508 was based on the W3C priority checkpoints, which were adopted from the standards based on the W3C's Web Content Accessibility Guidelines (WCAG). Most countries have used the WCAG as a basis for their own standards.

Section 508 prohibits federal agencies from buying, developing, maintaining, or using electronic and information technology that is inaccessible to people with disabilities. Even though this section applies only to U.S. federal agencies, many countries, organizations, and major companies are using it as a guideline for minimum accessibility standards.

FLASH AND ACCESSIBILITY

The Macromedia Flash Player 6 was the first rich media player to make content available to screen readers. With the Accessibility panel in Flash (available since Flash MX), developers can create accessible rich media content even more easily. In Flash, you can supply descriptions for text, text fields, movie clips, and buttons, and you can provide keyboard shortcuts for input text fields or buttons.

The Accessibility Panel

The Accessibility panel in Flash (see Figure 26.1) allows you to specify text equivalents and descriptions for elements in Flash movies. You can access this panel by choosing Window, Other Panels, Accessibility from the main menu or by using the keyboard shortcut **Alt+F2** (Macintosh: **Option+F2**).

With the Accessibility panel open, select a movie clip, button, text, or text field, and fill in the appropriate information (name and description) in the panel. You can also add a keyboard shortcut for that object, but the Accessibility panel doesn't add the shortcut code for you; you must still program the action for that keyboard shortcut by using ActionScript or Behaviors.

FIGURE 26.1
The Accessibility
panel with an object
selected.

With an object selected as accessible, the names and descriptions you supply are identified and read out loud by a screen reader if the user has one installed and operational on his or her computer. The Make Child Objects Accessible option, which is available only for `MovieClip` objects, instructs the Flash Player to pass child object information to the screen reader. This option is selected by default; deselecting it effectively hides any content in the movie clip from the screen reader, which is useful for hiding extraneous objects.

With the Accessibility panel open, selecting the stage shows one more option, Auto Label (see Figure 26.2). This option, which is selected by default, causes Flash to auto label buttons or input text fields in your document, as discussed in the following section.

FIGURE 26.2
The Accessibility
panel with the stage
selected.

Auto Labeling

As shown in Figure 26.2, selecting the stage adds the Auto Label option to the Accessibility panel. Often, you have a button name or a text label near a button or text field. Flash, by default, assumes that the text object is the label for the button or text field. This capability of automatically assigning labels for specific objects, referred to as *auto labeling*, is enabled by default.

You can turn auto labeling off by deselecting it in the Accessibility panel when the stage is selected. You can also name any specific button or text field in the Accessibility panel, which causes the automatic label's text string to be read as a regular text object for that object. You can also convert the text object to dynamic text in the Property inspector, and then deselect the Make Object Accessible check box in the Accessibility panel for that text object.

Screen Readers

Screen readers are software programs that deliver graphics and text as speech to the user. For a user who is visually impaired and doesn't need a monitor, a screen reader is used to "speak" everything shown onscreen. In essence, a screen reader converts a graphical user interface into an audio interface.

The Flash Player communicates content to a screen reader's software; in turn, the screen reader generates spoken audio from the content it reads. The following items are automatically defined as accessible in all Flash movies, without the developer needing to configure anything:

- Text
- Input text fields
- Buttons
- Movie clips
- Entire movies

Keep in mind that screen readers are primarily intended to help with navigation, including items requiring user input, so they rely heavily on objects such as text, buttons, and input fields. Static and dynamic text objects are automatically named to reflect their content (that is, any text in text fields), so they don't need names assigned to them in the Accessibility panel.

If a screen reader encounters an object that's not named, it says something generic, such as "button," depending on the screen reader software and its settings. As you can imagine, this is incredibly confusing for users with disabilities, because knowing that something is a "button" doesn't help them unless they know what that button's action is. Imagine a vending machine without any labels or pictures! Therefore, you should concentrate on labeling buttons and input text fields, which are the objects users with screen readers rely on most often.

In addition, keep the following tips in mind for screen readers:

- In some situations, you might not want an object labeled. Some animations, for example, don't need labeling if you already have text on the stage that states what the animation is. For example, an animation of an opening envelope for an email link probably doesn't need a label. Some accessible objects contained inside movie clips don't require labeling.

- If you have already labeled a button, movie clip, or text field using the Property inspector, you don't need to name it using the Accessibility panel because a screen reader picks up the name from the label.

Microsoft Active Accessibility (MSAA)

MSAA, developed by Microsoft, is a standard that provides a highly descriptive and standardized way for applications and screen readers to communicate. It serves as a bridge between the Flash Player and screen readers, such as Window-Eyes. Adopting MSAA standards makes it easier for other vendors of screen readers and assistive technologies to integrate support for the Flash Player. You can find more information on MSAA standards at www.microsoft.com/enable.

Text in Screen Readers

Static text blocks do not have instance names. Their contents are automatically made available to screen readers by default. If you need to make them otherwise accessible, such as requiring a label that's different from the text itself, convert them to dynamic text fields.

Animations and Graphics

Screen readers can't read graphics or animations, so keep this in mind when building Flash movies. To help remedy this limitation, use the Accessibility panel to add names or descriptions to objects that users with disabilities need to have named, such as icons, gestural animations, informational animations, and so forth. For example, an animation of the earth revolving around the sun could be labeled "earth rotation," and you could add a description such as "An animation showing the earth's yearly rotation around the sun."

Tab Indexing Order

The *tab order* is the order in which objects receive input focus when the user presses the Tab key. The *reading order* is the order in which a screen reader reads information about the objects. Both the tab order and the reading order are determined by the tab indexing order on the current frame. By default, the Flash Player uses a left-to-right and top-to-bottom tab indexing order.

Users with mobility disabilities might be limited to using only the Enter and Tab keys to navigate your site. You can set the Tab key to cycle through all available buttons and set the Enter key to be equivalent to a mouse click. Screen readers rely on this tab indexing order to determine the order in which they read the objects on the current frame, but you must create a tab index for every accessible object, not just the objects that can receive focus. For example, dynamic text must have tab indexes even though a user can't tab to dynamic text. If you don't create a tab index for every accessible object, the screen reader uses the default order: left to right and top to bottom.

You can control the tab order in a Flash movie by using ActionScript. To specify a tab order, you assign an order number to the `tabIndex` property, as discussed in the next section, "Accessibility ActionScript."

Because you can't assign an instance name to a static text object, it cannot be included in the `tabIndex` property values. Therefore, a single static text object on the frame causes the reading order to revert to the default.

Accessibility ActionScript

Using the `Accessibility` class, developers can direct communications between objects in Flash files and screen readers. Methods in this class can be used without creating an instance of the class. The following list is an overview of methods used with the `Accessibility` class:

- **System.capabilities.hasAccessibility** This property is a Boolean value that indicates whether the user's assistive device supports communication between the Flash Player and accessibility aids, such as screen readers. The default value is false.

- **Accessibility.isActive()** This method indicates whether a screen reader program is currently active. Use this method when you want your movie to behave differently in the presence of a screen reader. This method is best used when the Flash Player needs to make a decision about accessibility, instead of using it at the beginning of a movie. If you do need to use it at the beginning, introduce a short delay of one to two seconds to give Flash content enough time to contact the Flash Player.

- **tabIndex** To specify a tab order, assign an order number to the tabIndex property. If you don't specify a tab order for an accessible object in a frame, the Flash Player ignores all your custom tab order assignments. Therefore, providing a complete tab order for all accessible objects is recommended. Additionally, all objects assigned to a tab order, except frames, require an instance name that's specified in the Property Inspector. Here are some examples of using tabIndex:

  _this.myOption1.btn.tabIndex=1

  _this.myOption2.btn.tabIndex=2

- **Accessibility.updateProperties()** Use this method to inform screen reader users of Flash content changes. Calling this method causes Flash Player 7 to re-examine all accessibility properties and update property descriptions. This code line goes at the beginning of your Flash movie.

- **_accProps** Use this property to set accessibility properties for the entire document or for specific objects. To set this property globally, use _accProps. To set it for specific objects, use *Instancename*._accProps.

Table 26.1 lists the available accessibility properties and describes where you can use them.

TABLE 26.1 ## Applying Accessibility Properties

Property	Type	Equivalent Selection in Accessibility Panel	What It Can Be Applied To
.silent	Boolean	Make Movie Accessible/ Make Object Accessible (inverse logic*)	Buttons, movie clips, dynamic text, input text
.forceSimple	Boolean	Make Child Objects Accessible (inverse logic*)	Entire document, movie clips
.name	String	Name	Entire document, buttons, movie clips, dynamic text, input text
.description	String	Description	Entire document, buttons, movie clips, dynamic text, input text
.shortcut	String	Shortcut	Buttons, movie clips, input text
.tabIndex	Numeric	N/A	Screens, buttons, movie clips, compiled movie clips, dynamic text, input text, timeline frames

*Inverse logic means that the values are 0 = on and 1 = off, instead of the traditionally used values, which are 0 = off and 1 = on.

For more information on tab indexing, refer to the ActionScript dictionary in Flash under the following entries: Button.tabIndex, MovieClip.tabIndex, TextField.tabIndex, MovieClip.tabChildren, MovieClip.tabEnabled, and TextField.tabEnabled.

Resources

Macromedia's accessibility section:

www.macromedia.com/macromedia/accessibility/

W3C Web Content Accessibility Guidelines 1.0: www.w3.org/TR/WCAG/

Section 508 of the U.S. Rehabilitation Act: www.section508.gov/

W3C checkpoints: www.w3.org/WAI/Resources/#ch

Federal IT Accessibility Initiative: www.cmpinc.net/section508/

MSAA home page: www.microsoft.com/enable

POINTS TO REMEMBER

- Accessibility involves two key issues: how users with disabilities can access information, and how developers and designers can create content that's more accessible to those users.

- Accessibility is important because it's the right thing to do, it's good business, and it's already the law in some countries and organizations.

- Keep the Accessibility panel open as you're working. This allows you to name objects as you work, saving you time later.

- Keep in mind that screen readers are primarily intended to help with navigation, using items such as text, buttons, and input fields. Imagine a voice reading the objects in the order you've set them, as that is what a screen reader does. When working with the tab index order of objects, imagine being able to use only the Tab and Enter key to navigate your site.

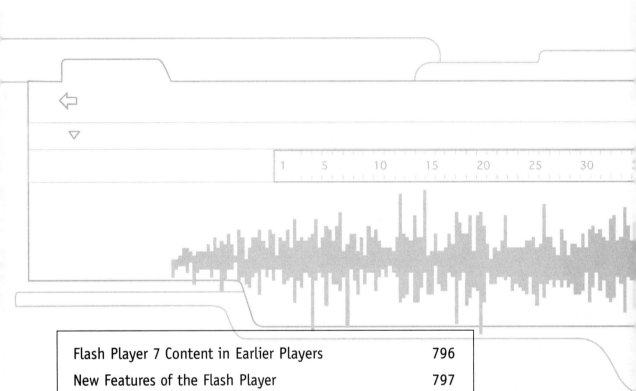

CHAPTER 27

THE FLASH PLAYER

ANOTHER VERSION OF FLASH, ANOTHER VERSION OF THE FLASH PLAYER. Although it's always tremendous to see what new features have been added to Flash—and this release is no exception—the thrill is tempered by the realization that not everyone will have the latest version right away. Luckily, however, downloads of the new Flash Player 7 have been increasing. It's possible that by the time you read this, enough people will have Flash Player 7 to convince your client to use it on your next project.

FLASH PLAYER 7 CONTENT IN EARLIER PLAYERS

If a user attempts to view a Flash movie built for Flash Player 7 in an earlier version of Flash, there's a good chance the movie won't play or function correctly. As a general rule, the Flash Player successfully carries out code that existed in the version of ActionScript supported by the Player, and nothing beyond it. For example, if your movie loads XML data from a server and has a customized context menu, both features are functional when using Flash Player 7, but only the XML code would be carried out in Flash Player 6 because Flash Player 6 doesn't support the context menu.

Also, although frame actions such as stop() and play() work in most versions of the Flash Player (versions 2 and up), this code won't always run properly. Look at the following code:

```
var my_pj:PrintJob = new PrintJob();

if (my_pj.start()) {
    my_pj.addPage(this);
    my_pj.send();

    gotoAndPlay("printing_complete");
}
stop();
```

In Flash Player 7, all this code will run because Flash Player 7 has support for the PrintJob class. The Print dialog box is displayed, and if the user clicks Print, content is added to the print queue and the playhead jumps to printing_complete. Of you're viewing this in earlier versions of the Player, not only does the print functionality not work, but the gotoAndPlay() command doesn't work because it's contained in code (the if statement using PrintJob as its argument) that earlier versions of the Player don't recognize.

Earlier Content in Flash Player 7

The latest Flash Player is designed for the utmost compatibility with content built for earlier versions of the Flash Player. As such, you can be confident that any content you have built in earlier versions of Flash can still be viewed correctly in Flash Player 7.

New Features of the Flash Player

The following sections describe some key new features of Flash Player 7.

ActionScript Features

Several new ActionScript enhancements, discussed in the next sections, are supported by Flash Player 7.

Array Sorting API Enhancements

The `Array` class has been updated, and the `Array.sortOn` application programming interface (API) has been expanded. (You can find full information about this in Chapter 10, "ActionScript: Functions, Events, and Objects.") The new `sortOn()` method allows you to specify one field to sort by—for example, `sortOn("firstname")`—or multiple fields, such as `sortOn(["firstname", "lastname"])`. If you're sorting by one field, the field is a string. If you're sorting by multiple fields, you send the method an array of strings. The sort is based on the first field, and if two elements in this field have the same value, the sort is based on the value of the next fields.

As well, `Array.sort` and `Array.sortOn` can now take an additional parameter, which is a combination of the following:

- **Array.DESCENDING**   Instead of sorting the array from lowest to highest value, you sort the array from highest to lowest.

- **Array.CASEINSENSITIVE**   Sorting isn't case sensitive.

- **Array.NUMERIC**   Use numeric sorting instead of a string comparison if the two elements being compared are numbers. If they aren't numbers, a string comparison is used (which can be case insensitive if that flag is specified).

- **Array.UNIQUESORT**   If two objects (using `sortOn()`) or two array elements (using `sort()`) are identical, an error code (0) is returned instead of the sorted array.

- **Array.RETURNINDEXEDARRAY**   Instead of returning a sorted array, an integer index array that is the result of the sort is returned. If you sort the following array without this option

  ["a", "d", "c", "b"]

you get the following result:

["a", "b", "c", "d"]

If you use this option, the original array is unchanged and this array is returned:

[1, 4, 3, 2]

This option allows multiple different sorts to be performed on a single array without having to replicate the entire array or re-sort it repeatedly.

These options can be passed into the sort and sortOn APIs by combining them into one value. For example, Array.sort (Array.NUMERIC | Array.DESCENDING) combines the numeric and descending sort options, as shown in the following example:

```
var my_array = ["apples", "oranges", "grapefruits", "pears"];
trace(my_array.join());
my_array.sort(Array.NUMERIC | Array.DESCENDING);
trace(my_array.join());
```

The preceding code generates the following output:

```
apples,oranges,grapefruits,pears
pears,oranges,grapefruits,apples
```

For more information on context menu customization, see Chapter 10, "ActionScript: Functions, Events, and Objects."

Context Menu Customization

With this feature, you can customize the appearance of the context menu. In Flash 2004, you can add new context menu items and assign custom actions to them. As well, you can selectively hide the default context menu items at runtime.

ECMA-262 Strict Mode Compliance

Flash Player 7 now supports full ECMA-262 strict mode compliance. This means, among other things, support for case sensitivity, strict data typing, and data casting.

Case Sensitivity

All Flash content is now strictly case sensitive. Case sensitivity is not enforced, however, on movies exported using Flash Player 6 or earlier. Variables, function names, objects, and classes are all case sensitive. The following items are not:

- Built-in string property values (such as the `_quality` property, which determines the quality at which a movie plays)

- URL handling/parsing

- Flash label names

Strict Data Typing

ActionScript 2.0, which is supported by Flash Player 7, lets you explicitly declare the type of a variable when you create it, which is called *strict data typing*. This helps you prevent script errors, as type mismatches (defining a variable as a certain type, and then assigning it a value of a different type) cause compile-time errors. To assign a variable a strict data type, you define the variable by using the `var` keyword. Remember that when creating a variable with the `var` keyword, you're creating a local variable, one that exists only in the function or level that created it. Strict data typing is shown in the following example:

```
// strict typing of variable or object
var x:Number = 12;
var anniversary:Date = new Date();


// strict typing of parameters
function myFunction(name:String, age:Number){
}
```

As well as defining variable types and parameter types, strict data typing enables you to define what data type a function must return. In the following code, this is accomplished with the use of `:Number` to define the type of data the `calcSquare()` function must return:

```
// strict typing of parameter and return value
function calcSquare(x:Number):Number {
  var squaredVal = x*x;
  return squaredVal;
}
```

In the preceding code, `x:Number` means that for the code to function properly, you must send the `calcSquare()` function a numeric value.

You can define data types as any of the classes built into Flash, such as `Date`, `Function`, or `Number`, as well as any custom classes or objects you create. Using strict typing helps ensure that you don't accidentally assign an incorrect type of value to an object. Flash checks for typing mismatch errors at compile time. For example, suppose you type the following code, which sets the data type of a variable to be a custom class:

```
// Employee.as
class Employee {
  var status:Boolean;
}
```

```
// in your script
var employeeBobRoberts:Employee = new Employee();
employeeBobRoberts.status = "hired";
```

When Flash compiles this script, a "Type mismatch" error is generated.

Strict typing is not supported in content exported for Flash Player 6 or earlier or for Flash Player 7 content exported with ActionScript 1.0.

Data Casting

Using ActionScript 2.0, you can cast one data type to another. Casting lets you assert that an object is of a certain type, so that when compile time type-checking occurs, the compiler treats the object as having a set of properties that its initial type doesn't contain. This is useful, for example, when iterating over an array of objects that might be of differing types. This is the casting syntax:

type(item)

The compiler behaves as though the object type is of the type item. Casting is basically a function call that returns null if the casting fails and returns type if the casting succeeds. The following example shows a typical usage of data casting:

```
// Auto.as
class Auto {}
// Car.as
class Car extends Auto {
    function trunk() {
        trace("Cars have trunks");
    };
}
// Truck.as
class Truck extends Auto {
```

```
    function bed() {};
}
// in your FLA
var chevy:Car = new Car();
var ford:Truck = new Truck(chevy);
ford.trunk();
```

In this example, calling the trunk function doesn't do anything, as the function doesn't do anything, but it doesn't cause an error because the ford object has been cast as the object type chevy, which is Car. Although you wouldn't know if an error had been generated, you could perform a check to see if the casting succeeded. In this way, you could generate type mismatch errors, both at runtime and compile time.

Note that you can't override primitive data types, such as Boolean, Date, and Number, with a cast operator of the same name.

Exception Handling

Flash MX 2004 adds support for new exception- and error-handling methods. Aside from the new Error class, there is now support for throw, try, and catch statements, which enable you to add powerful error-checking and debugging functionality in your applications. These additions are a tremendous boon to developers, helping speed the development process of applications. For complete information on using error handling and throw, try, and catch statements, see Chapter 25, "Troubleshooting."

Hyperlink Context Menu Support

New to Flash Player 7, if a user right-clicks on an HTML link in a text field, the context menu contains a Link Menu item, which is made up of the following:

- Open

- Open in New Window (when viewed in a browser)

- Copy Link

These options behave as they do when right-clicking on a link in a browser: Open behaves as though the user had clicked on a link, Open in New Window opens the link in a new window, and Copy Link copies the link URL to the clipboard.

As well, if a user clicks on a link while holding down the New Window key, the link opens in a new window. The New Window keys are as follows:

- Windows ActiveX: Shift

- Windows Netscape: Ctrl

- Mac Netscape: Command

You don't have to tell Flash to enable these options. They are enabled automatically by the Player in the browser environment.

Mouse Wheel Support

Windows Flash Player 7 players have support for vertically scrolling text boxes with a mouse wheel for all Flash movies (not just version 7). You can turn scrolling off on an individual text field by setting the new `TextField.mouseWheelEnabled` property to false (the default is true).

In addition, a new Mouse listener event has been added: `Mouse.onMouseWheel([int delta])`. This listener works only for movies that are version 7 and higher. This functionality is explained in Chapter 10, "ActionScript: Functions, Events, and Objects."

Movie Clip Depth Management

Depth management is explained in depth in Chapter 10, "ActionScript: Functions, Events, and Objects."

Flash Player 7 now includes advanced depth management functionality that complements the `swapDepths()` method, which was present in Flash Player 5. This new functionality includes the following methods:

- **`MovieClip.getDepth()`**   Returns the depth of a specified object.

- **`MovieClip.getInstanceAtDepth()`**—Returns the instance name of a movie clip at a specified depth.

- **`MovieClip.getNextHighestDepth()`**   Returns the next highest available depth value.

MovieClipLoader (Preloader) API

New with Flash Player 7 is the MovieClipLoader API, which gives you easy-to-use, structured control of loading SWF and JPG content in your movie. This API is a dramatic leap over the old methods of loading new content and provides a variety of event listeners, so you have more knowledge of and control over the load process. This feature is described in Chapter 10.

PrintJob API

Printing from within Flash has been drastically improved with the new PrintJob API. It allows you to create a print queue and add any number of frames of any movie clip in your movie—including dynamic content—and requires a user to accept only one print job at a time. In previous versions of Flash, it was not uncommon for users to have to okay multiple print jobs. This feature is explained in detail in Chapter 10.

Text Enhancements

Flash Player 7 includes support for many text improvements and features:

- **Text flow around images**   New to Flash Player 7 is support for inline images in a text field. You can now add HTML content to dynamic text fields that include images. The images can be external files (JPEGs or SWFs) or movie clips contained in the Library.

- **Text metrics**   Flash Player 7 includes enhanced support for determining the extent of your text fields and for tracking the metrics of your text. This is done by using the improved TextField.getTextExtent() method, which is useful in creating and lining up complex text and image layouts in Flash.

- **Text style sheets**   Flash Player 7 now supports the use of cascading style sheets (CSS), much as browsers do. They are used to define and add style information, such as fonts, color, and spacing, to web documents. You can associate HTML-enabled text fields with a StyleSheet object defined in Flash, or you can load an external CSS file and apply it to your text field, ensuring consistency between your Flash and HTML content.

These features are explained in detail in Chapter 13, "Text."

Virtual Root

The behavior of _root in ActionScript is not consistent. It changes when an SWF is loaded into a movie clip. When operating on its own, _root refers to the movie's main Timeline. When loaded into a movie clip, _root refers to the main Timeline of the movie that has loaded it.

Flash Player 7 allows developers to specify that _root remain consistent no matter where a movie is run or loaded. This is done with the _lockroot property, which is a Boolean value you use to determine whether _root is consistent or varies. It can be set in a movie (for example, file.swf setting its own lockroot property) and for a movie that's loaded (main.swf can set the lockroot property of file.swf when it loads it).

The specific use of _lockroot is detailed in Chapter 10.

Security Features

The following sections give you an overview of some of the new security features supported by Flash Player 7.

Exact Domain Matching

Flash Player 7 content operates under stricter security rules than Flash Player 6 content. Flash Player 6 content is allowed to perform cross-movie scripting between movies that are subdomain-related; for example, a movie from www.myserver.com is allowed to script a second movie loaded from store.myserver.com. In Flash Player 7, cross-movie script-ing is permitted only between movies originating from the same domain. Any other cross-movie scripting works only after calling System.security.allowDomain to permit access. The following example shows how you would use System.security.allowDomain to permit access to www.myserver.com and store.myserver.com:

```
System.security.allowDomain("www.myserver.com".
↪"store.myserver.com");
```

The exact domain match requirement also applies to the use of runtime shared libraries. If the loading or loaded movie in a shared library rela-tionship is version 7, symbol importing works only if both movies come from the same domain.

In addition, exact domain matching applies to all methods of loading non-SWF data: XML.load(), XML.sendAndLoad(), LoadVars.load(), LoadVars. sendAndLoad(), loadVariables(), loadVariablesNum(), XMLSocket.connect(), and Flash Remoting (NetServices.createGatewayConnection). For these methods, unlike cross-movie scripting and runtime shared libraries, an exact domain match is required regardless of the version of the movie making the request.

This change, which affects all content regardless of the version of Flash it was produced for, means that existing content can fail in Flash Player 7 because of the new restrictions. Users will see a small dialog box prompting them to allow or deny the cross-domain access. This dialog box appears only for version 6 and earlier content to prevent existing content from breaking. Version 7 content must abide by the new exact-domain rules.

Cross-Domain Policy Files

New to Flash Player 7 are *policy files*, which let you allow access from certain domains that might try to access content on a remote server or to specify that all domains have access. To allow Flash to access your domain from other domains, you must create a policy file, which is an XML file called `crossdomain.xml`, and place it on the root of your server. For example, a cross-domain policy file at `myserver.com` would have the path `http://www.myserver.com/crossdomain.xml`.

When the Flash Player makes a cross-domain request for data, it looks for the presence of a policy file. If the file is found, data access is permitted based on the rules that the file dictates. The policy file format is defined as follows:

```
<!- Cross-domain policy file for http://www.myserver.com/ ->
< cross-domain-policy>
    <allow-access-from domain="www.myfriend.com" />
    <allow-access-from domain="*.friend.com" />
    <allow-access-from domain="127.6.35.406" />
</cross-domain-policy>
```

The following policy file would enable access from anywhere:

```
<cross-domain-policy>
    <allow-access-from domain="*" />
</cross-domain-policy>
```

This feature affects these data-loading calls:

```
XML.load(), XML.sendAndLoad()

LoadVars.load(), LoadVars.sendAndLoad(),loadVariables(),
loadVariablesNum()

XMLSocket.connect()
```

NetConnection.call() (If NetConnection is used to connect to a Flash Communication Server application, cross-domain security concerns don't apply. However, they do apply if you are using NetConnection to stream an FLV file from a non–Flash Communication Server source.)

Importing a shared library, initiated by symbol usage

Cross-domain loading of SWFs and JPEGs using loadMovie() isn't affected by this feature. To script cross-domain loaded movies, use the existing method System.security.allowDomain.

 Flash Player 7's new security rules require SWF files and data to be in the same domain, as subdomain data requests are no longer allowed by default. If no policy file exists, any subdomain data requests result in the Flash Player Setting dialog box being displayed, asking the user to accept or deny the request. This dialog box isn't the best experience for users, but you can use policy files to make sure it never appears.

Media Features

New media features supported by Flash Player 7 are covered in the following sections.

ID3 v2 Support

Flash Player 7 adds v2 support of MP3 ID3 information. ID3 information contains data such as the name of the MP3, its duration, and the name of the artist, among others. Unlike the v1 support in Flash Player 6, v2 support allows information to be read before the entire MP3 file has been downloaded. As well, v2 support adds enhanced features, such as freestyle text tags you can use to create fully featured MP3 players. This feature is explained in detail in Chapter 15, "Audio." You can also find a description of supported ID3 tags in the Flash MX 2004 help files, under Sound.id3.

Loading FLV over HTTP

Flash Player 7 supports displaying FLV (Flash video) files without the need for Flash Communication Server. Both HTTP and local file playback are supported. The FLV file is controlled through the NetStream object, which allows you to play, pause, and seek the FLV file. This feature is described in Chapter 16, "Video."

User Interface Features

The next sections give you a look at some new capabilities of Flash Player 7. They aren't necessarily controlled through code (although the runtime shared library improvements certainly are), but they contribute nicely to the quality of users' Flash experiences.

Player Auto-Updating

Flash Player 7 includes support for auto-updating. That means the Player automatically checks to see if updates are available for download from macromedia.com. If so, you're prompted to download them. You can specify how often the Player checks for an update by going to www.macromedia.com/support/flashplayer/help/settings/global_notification.html and selecting an update interval. Valid choices are every 7, 14, 30, or 60 days.

For more information on shared libraries, see Chapter 3, "The Library, Symbols, and the Timeline."

Runtime Shared Library Improvements

With Flash Player 7, you can use a shared library that contains its own shared library. In addition to being a Flash Player 7 feature, this functionality exists in later versions of Flash Player 6 (build r65 and later).

Performance Features

In Flash Player 7, performance in all areas—text, ActionScript, video, audio, and graphics rendering—has greatly increased. Not only does content created for Flash Player 7 perform, on average, 2 to 10 times faster than comparable Flash Player 6 content, existing Flash Player 6 content runs much faster when viewed with the version 7 player.

These performance enhancements extend to both PC and Macintosh versions of the Player. Some specific improvements include the following:

- **ActionScript** Array and String manipulations, as well as Math calculations, are much faster. You'll notice a boost when exporting Flash Player 6 content as Player 7 content, even if there have been no changes to the code. You can find more information on new ActionScript elements in Part II, "ActionScript," and Part V, "Next Steps."

- **Rendering** The visual performance of the Flash Player has been greatly improved.

- **Text**   Memory optimizations in Flash Player 7 mean that large text fields run faster, without the slowdown that was sometimes noticeable in Flash Player 6.

- **Video**   Video display color depth is now 24-bit (up from 18-bit). This is most noticeable in dark gradients, which in previous Player versions were patchy and displayed only large blocks of color. Dark gradients are now smoother, with a more even gradation of colors. Video performance has also dramatically improved in Flash Player 7, which is now 15% to 70% faster than Flash Player 6. These speed increases are most noticeable in lower-end machines, so they should be able to keep up with your video's playback speed more easily.

Distributing the Flash Player

Although you can download the Flash Player free from Macromedia's web site, if you want to include a copy of the Player in an intranet or on a CD-ROM, there are guidelines you must follow.

For information on the Macromedia Flash and Shockwave Players Distribution Program, which governs distribution of the Player, go to www.macromedia.com/support/shockwave/info/licensing/.

Resources

Flash Player global notification settings: www.macromedia.com/support/flashplayer/help/settings/global_notification.html

Macromedia Flash and Shockwave Players Distribution Program: www.macromedia.com/support/shockwave/info/licensing/

POINTS TO REMEMBER

- Flash Player 7 supports many new features in security, ActionScript enhancements, performance, and a wide range of other areas.

- Flash Player 7 allows you to view content created in previous Flash versions.

- Flash Player 7 is significantly faster than earlier Player versions, running 2 to 10 times faster than Flash Player 6.

- To enable cross-domain access with Flash Player 7, you must create policy files and store them on your server.

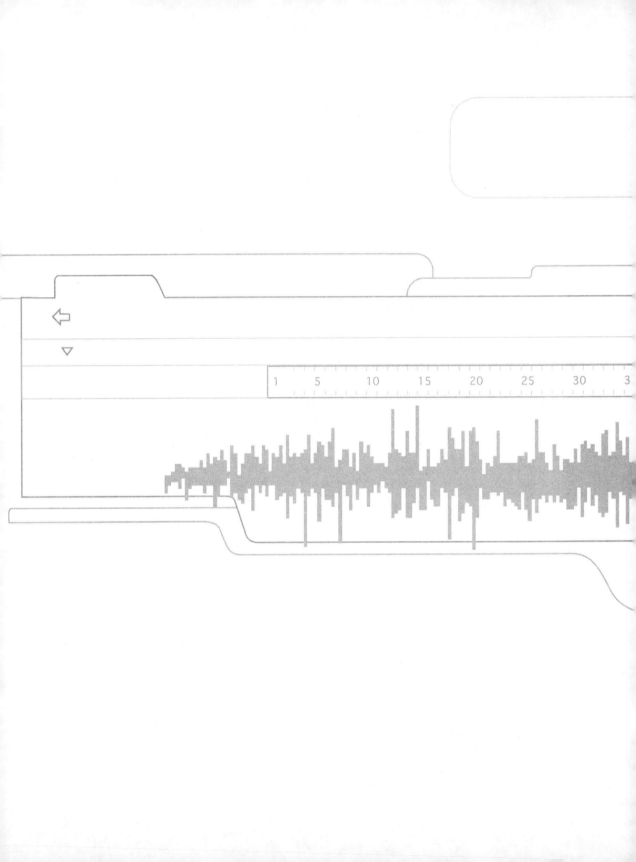

INDEX

Symbols

matrix notation of, 697
square tiles, rotating, to show process, 699
trigonometry, as used in, 691

J

Java
  ActionScript 2.0, as closely resembling, 653
  conversion to ActionScript, as performed by Flash Remoting MX, 554
  Java-based servers, as used with XMLSocket class, 547
Java application servers, 554-555
JavaScript
  displaying, as History panel view option, 120
  and Flash
    as used in Flash with SCORM Tracking template, 726
    using FSCommand function to work with, 548-549, 726
Java 2 Enterprise Edition (J2EE), 560
JPEG files (.jpg extension)
  as bitmap images, 127-128, 434-435
  compression level on, as adjustable, 128-129
  compression rate, setting, when publishing, 724
  Loader component, as used with, 358
  loading, using ActionScript, 441-442
  loading dynamically into movie clips, 192-193, 296
  lossy compression, use of, as affecting quality, 436-437
  non-support of transparency by, 437
  Photo (JPEG) Compression Setting, 438-439
  publishing, 720, 734-735
Jump menu (Flash Debugger), 778-779

K

Key class, 273, 642-644
keyframe animation, using math-based coding instead of, 658-659
keyframes
  adding, tutorial on, 225
  adding sound to, 456-457
  animating objects with, as problematic, 151
  blank (empty) keyframes, working with, 66, 67, 69
  converting frames to, 65-66, 69
  converting layers to, 132

converting pages to, 132
making into image maps, 726
naming, using frame labels, 224, 726
setting number of, to advance through video when importing, 500
as used in shape tweening tutorial (bouncing ball animation), 160-162
Key object, 351
keywords, individual
  case (as used in switch statements), 254
  class, 631-632
  default (as used in switch statements), 254
  dynamic (to allow access to undefined members), 649
  extends (to designate inheritance), 639-640
  get and set (to make methods act as properties), 648
  implements (to use interfaces in classes), 650
  interface (to implement interfaces across numerous classes), 650
  new (to create objects), 631, 636
  private (to control access to members), 646-647
  reserved keywords, 603
  set (to define variables), 232
  static (to designate class members, 645
  super (to access superclasses), 640-641
  this (path reference), 255, 609-610
  var (to define variables), 232, 603
keywords, reserved, 603

L

Label component, 355-356
labeling, to facilitate accessibility, 786-789
labels, frame. *See* frame labels
languages, support for. *See also* Strings panel
  globalization features, 19
  multilanguage files, creating, 19
  Strings panel, as providing, 415-416
  Unicode, support for, 19
Lasso tool, 47-48
  Magic Wand option, 47-48, 441
layer context menu, 71-73
Layer Properties dialog box, 73-74, 166-167
layers
  adding, 70, 226
  animation layer, as used in motion guide tutorial, 158-160
  as components of Timeline, 62
  context menu, commands in, 71-73
  converting to keyframes, 132
  creating, 227